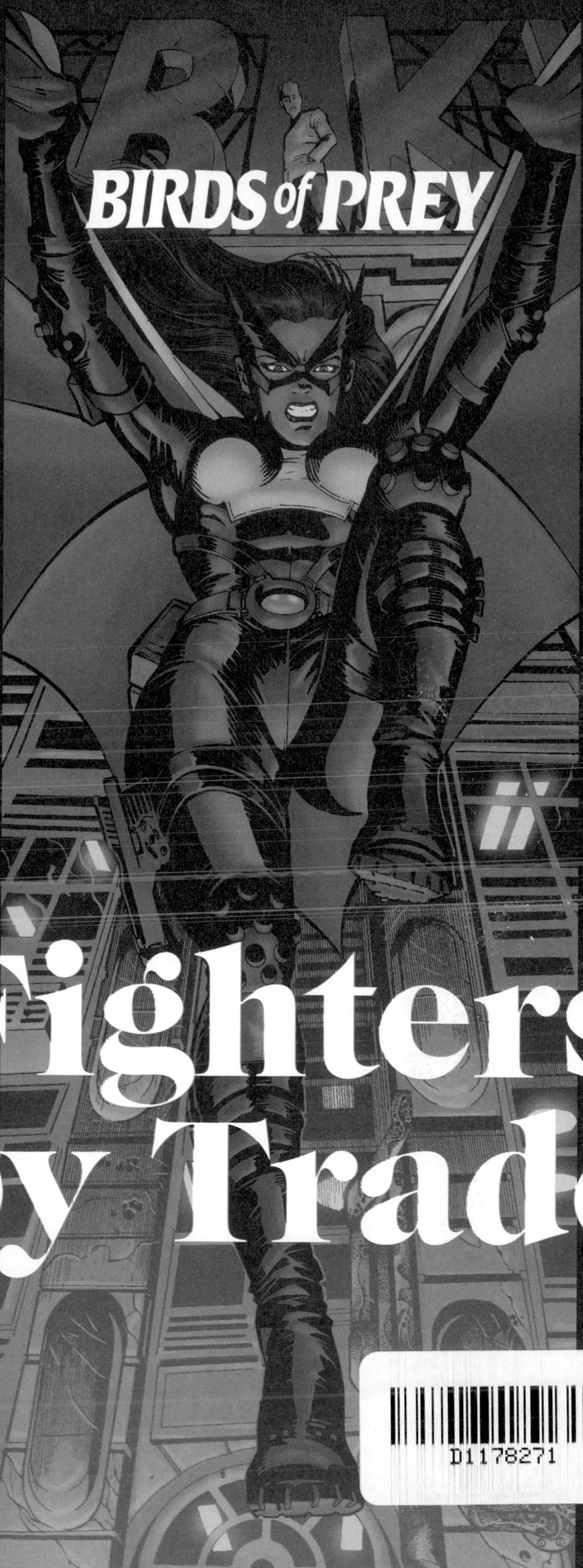

BIRDS of PREY

Fighters by Trade

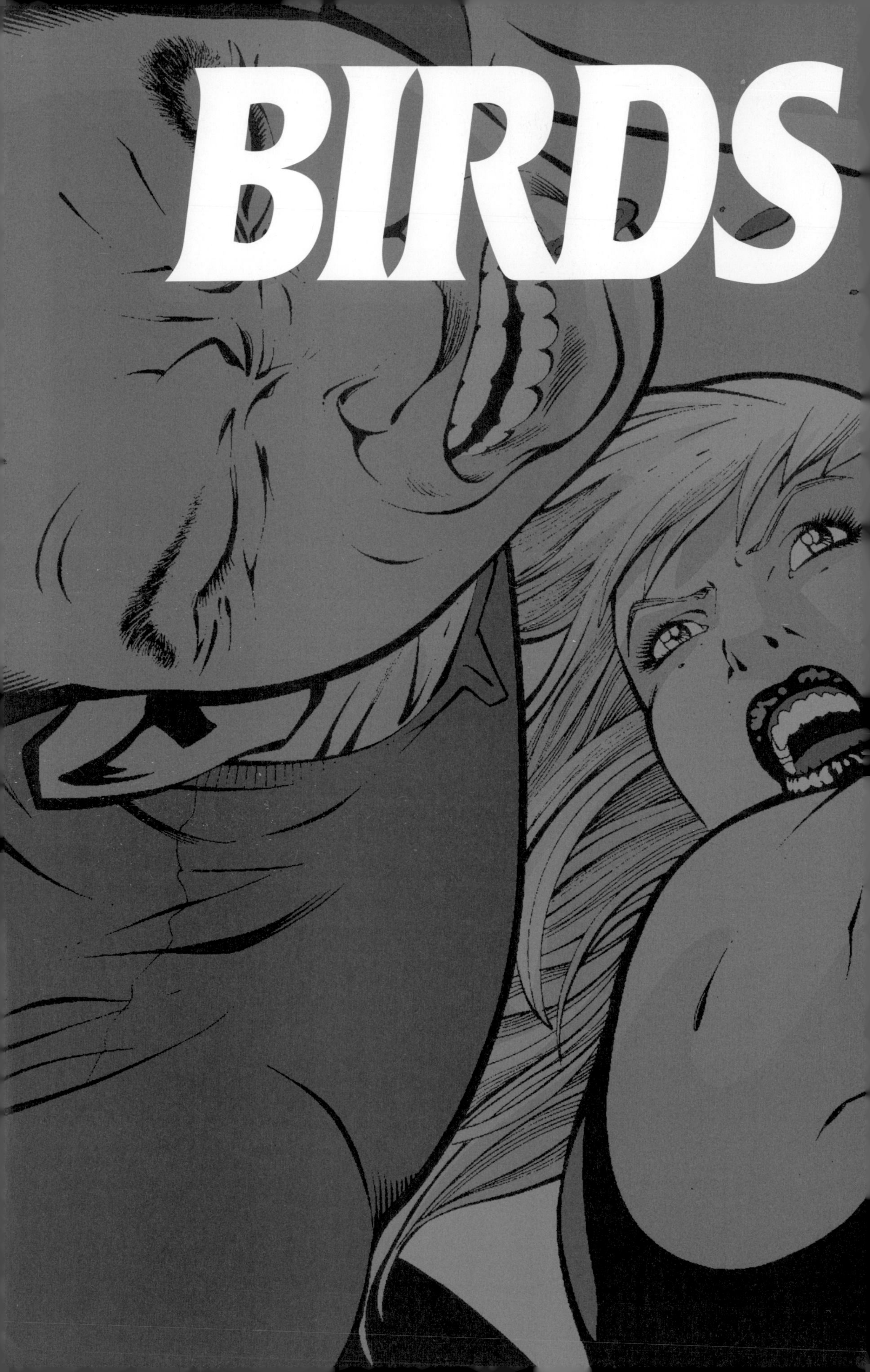
BIRDS

of PREY

Fighters by Trade

GAIL SIMONE
JIM ALEXANDER
writers

JOE BENNETT
EDDY BARROWS
PAULO SIQUEIRA
ADRIANA MELO
ADAM DeKRAKER
DAVID LOPEZ
BRUCE TIMM
BRAD WALKER
pencillers

JACK JADSON
ROBIN RIGGS
FERNANDO BLANCO
WILL CONRAD
BRUCE TIMM
JIMMY PALMIOTTI
inkers

HI-FI
colorist

JARED K. FLETCHER
ROB LEIGH
letterers

ADRIANA MELO and **WILL CONRAD**
collection cover artists

SUPERMAN created by
JERRY SIEGEL and JOE SHUSTER
By special arrangement with
the JERRY SIEGEL family

Birds of Prey: Fighters by Trade

Published by DC Comics. Compilation and all new material Copyright © 2021 DC Comics. All Rights Reserved. Originally published in single magazine form in *Birds of Prey* 81-91. Copyright © 2005, 2006 DC Comics. All Rights Reserved. All characters, their distinctive likenesses, and related elements featured in this publication are trademarks of DC Comics. The stories, characters, and incidents featured in this publication are entirely fictional. DC Comics does not read or accept unsolicited submissions of ideas, stories, or artwork. DC – a WarnerMedia Company.

DC Comics, 2900 West Alameda Ave., Burbank, CA 91505
Printed by LSC Communications, Owensville, MO, USA. 8/13/21. First Printing.
ISBN: 978-1-77950-802-7

Library of Congress Cataloging-in-Publication Data is available.

PEFC Certified
This product is from sustainably managed forests and controlled sources
PEFC/29-31-337   www.pefc.org

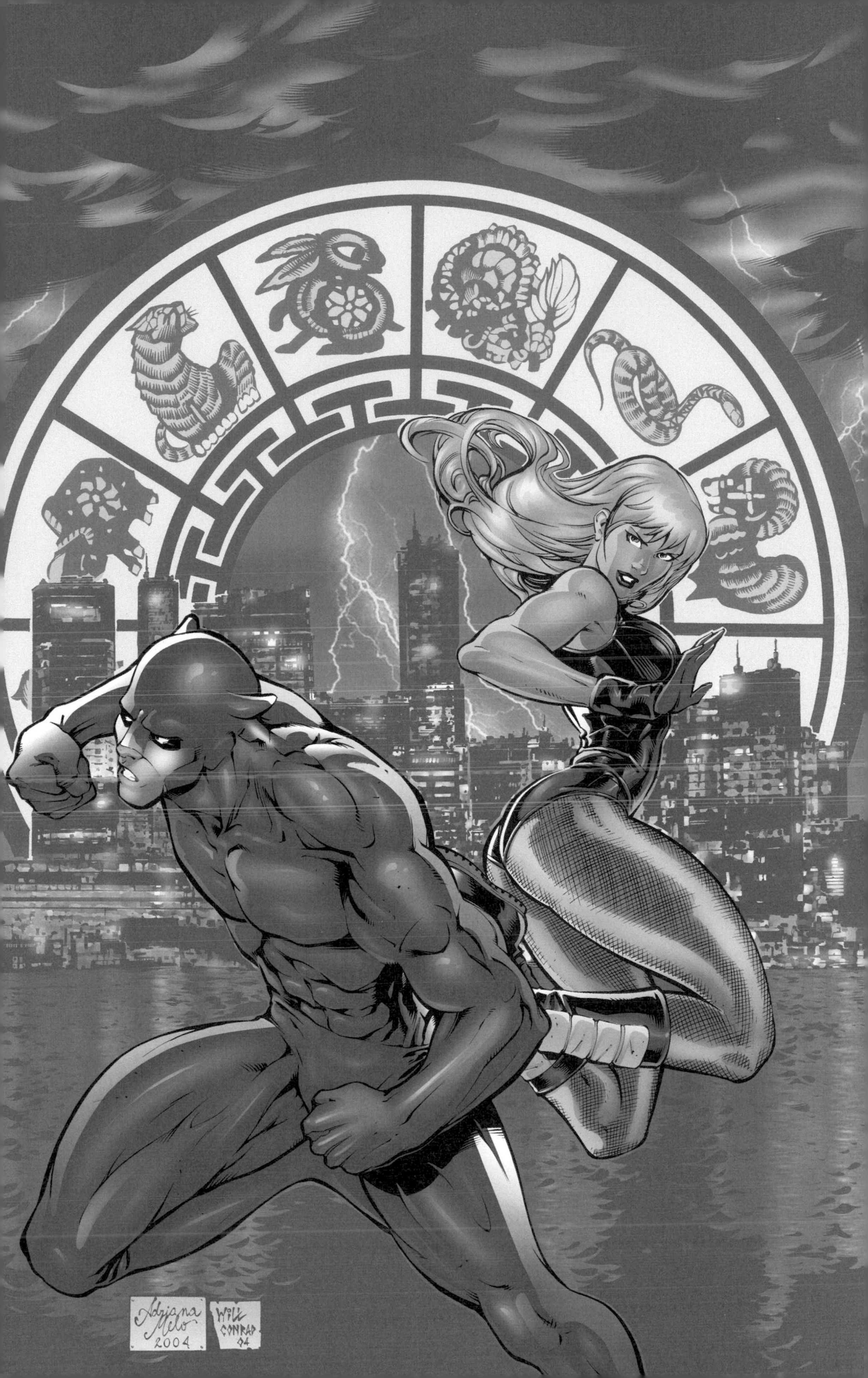
Adriana Melo 2004
Will Conrad 04

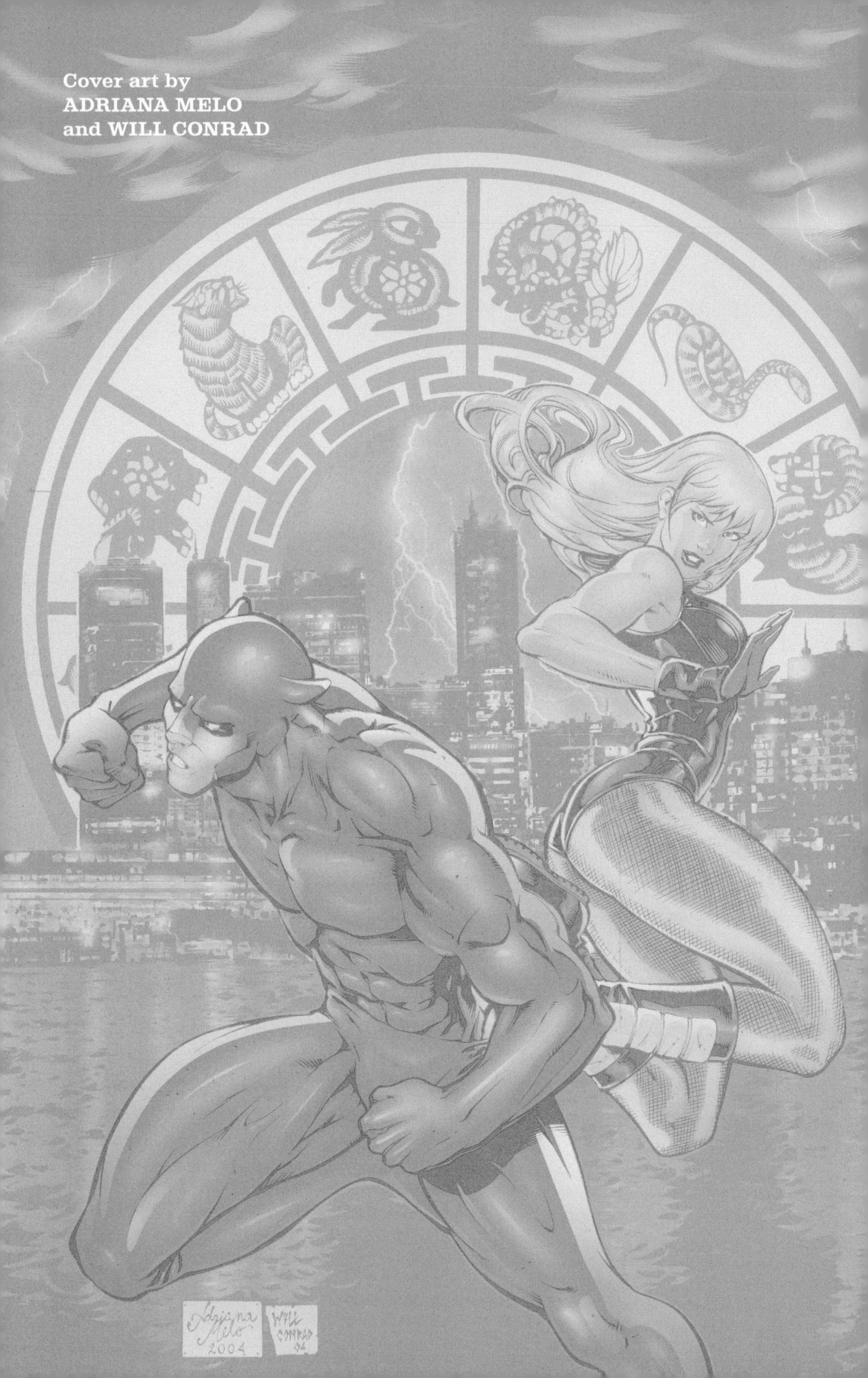
Adriana Melo 2004
Will Conrad 04

Cover art by
ADRIANA MELO
and WILL CONRAD

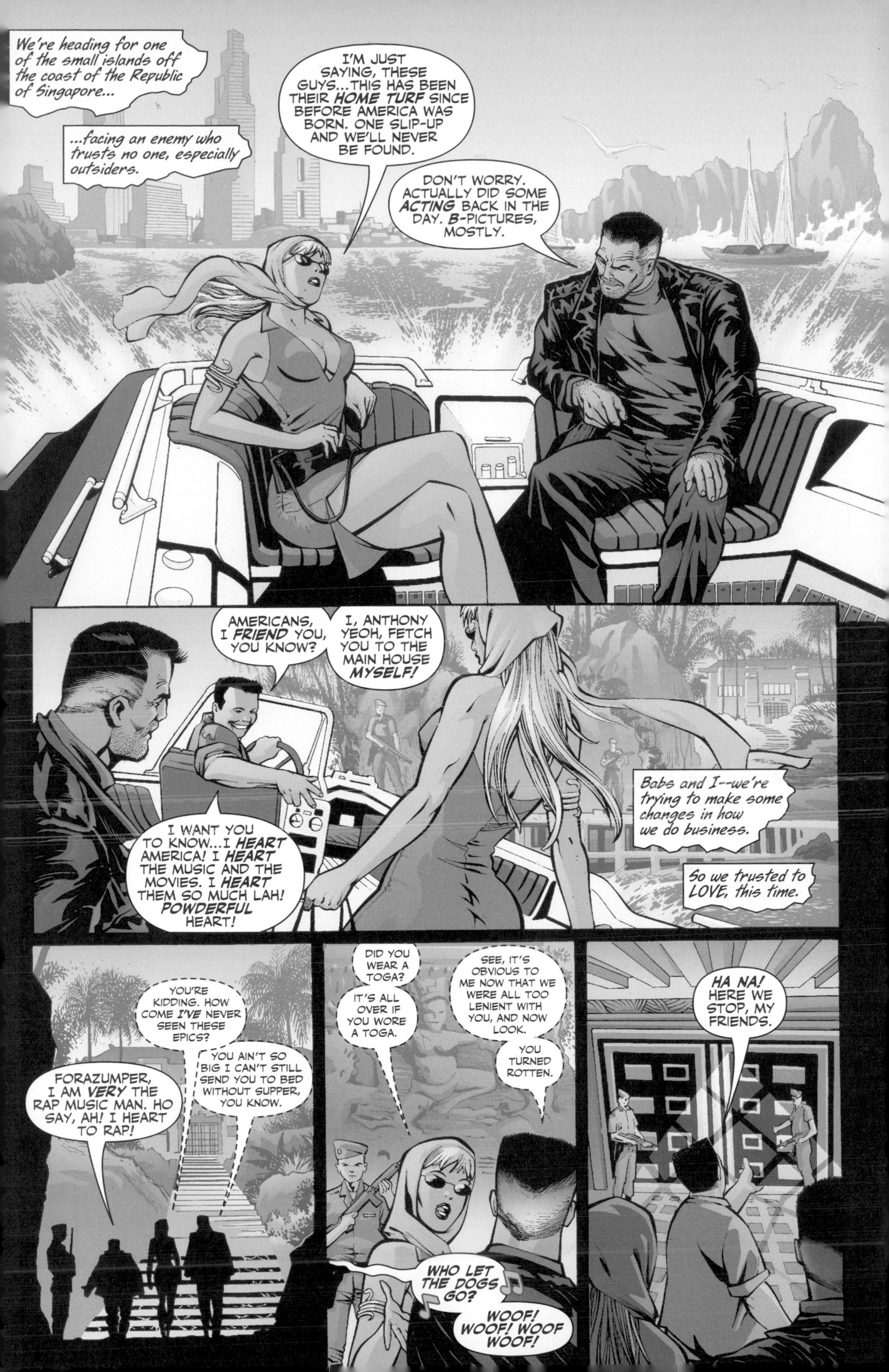
We're heading for one of the small islands off the coast of the Republic of Singapore...
...facing an enemy who trusts no one, especially outsiders.
I'M JUST SAYING, THESE GUYS...THIS HAS BEEN THEIR HOME TURF SINCE BEFORE AMERICA WAS BORN. ONE SLIP-UP AND WE'LL NEVER BE FOUND.
DON'T WORRY. ACTUALLY DID SOME ACTING BACK IN THE DAY. B-PICTURES, MOSTLY.
AMERICANS, I FRIEND YOU, YOU KNOW?
I, ANTHONY YEOH, FETCH YOU TO THE MAIN HOUSE MYSELF!
I WANT YOU TO KNOW...I HEART AMERICA! I HEART THE MUSIC AND THE MOVIES. I HEART THEM SO MUCH LAH! POWDERFUL HEART!
Babs and I--we're trying to make some changes in how we do business.
So we trusted to LOVE, this time.
YOU'RE KIDDING. HOW COME I'VE NEVER SEEN THESE EPICS?
YOU AIN'T SO BIG I CAN'T STILL SEND YOU TO BED WITHOUT SUPPER, YOU KNOW.
FORAZUMPER, I AM VERY THE RAP MUSIC MAN. HO SAY, AH! I HEART TO RAP!
DID YOU WEAR A TOGA?
IT'S ALL OVER IF YOU WORE A TOGA.
SEE, IT'S OBVIOUS TO ME NOW THAT WE WERE ALL TOO LENIENT WITH YOU, AND NOW LOOK.
YOU TURNED ROTTEN.
WHO LET THE DOGS GO?
WOOF! WOOF! WOOF WOOF!
HA NA! HERE WE STOP, MY FRIENDS.

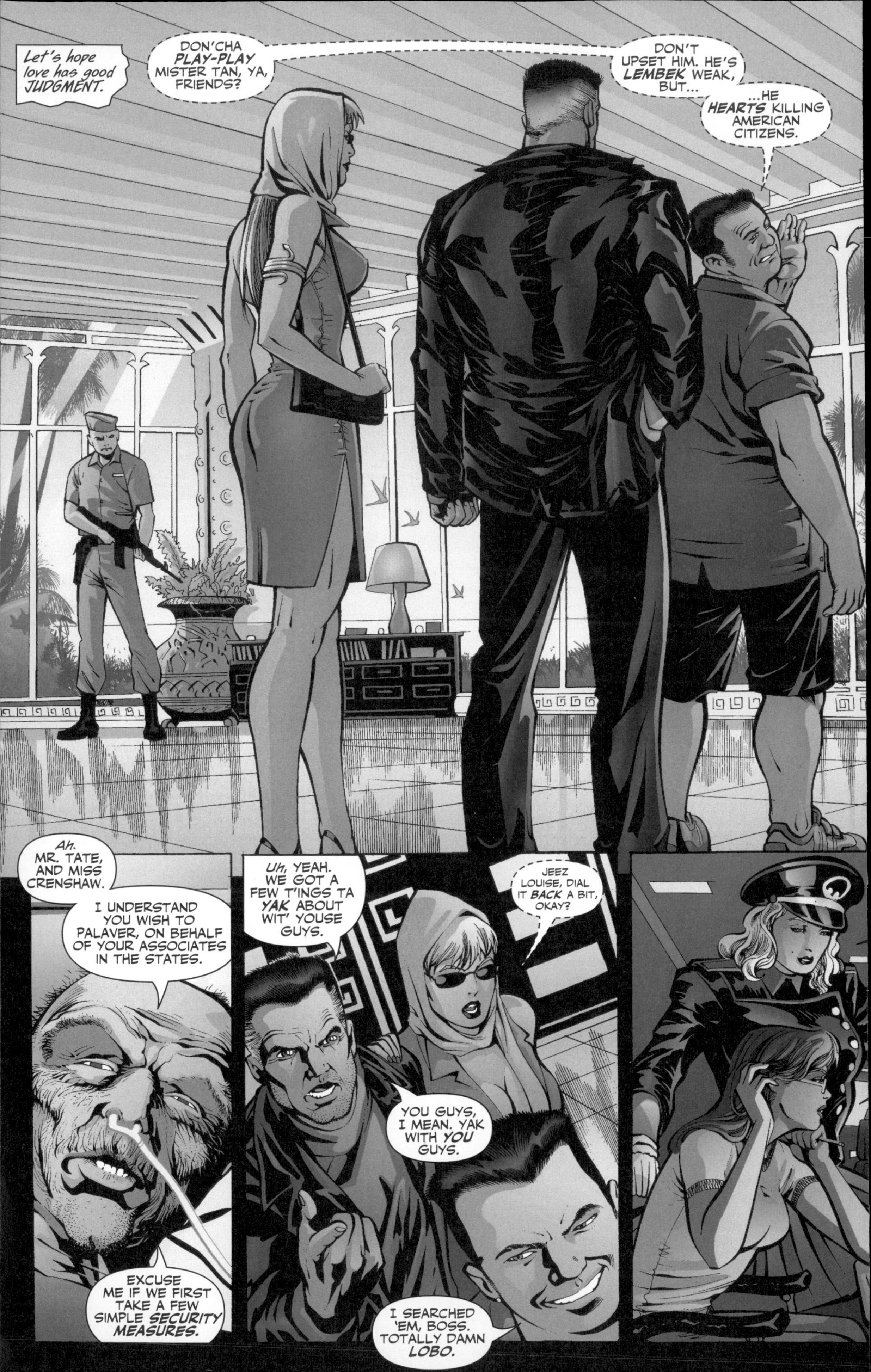
Let's hope love has good JUDGMENT.
DON'CHA PLAY-PLAY MISTER TAN, YA, FRIENDS?
DON'T UPSET HIM. HE'S LEMBEK WEAK, BUT...
...HE HEARTS KILLING AMERICAN CITIZENS.
Ah. MR. TATE, AND MISS CRENSHAW.
I UNDERSTAND YOU WISH TO PALAVER, ON BEHALF OF YOUR ASSOCIATES IN THE STATES.
EXCUSE ME IF WE FIRST TAKE A FEW SIMPLE SECURITY MEASURES.
Uh, YEAH. WE GOT A FEW T'INGS TA YAK ABOUT WIT' YOUSE GUYS.
JEEZ LOUISE, DIAL IT BACK A BIT, OKAY?
YOU GUYS, I MEAN. YAK WITH YOU GUYS.
I SEARCHED 'EM, BOSS. TOTALLY DAMN LOBO.

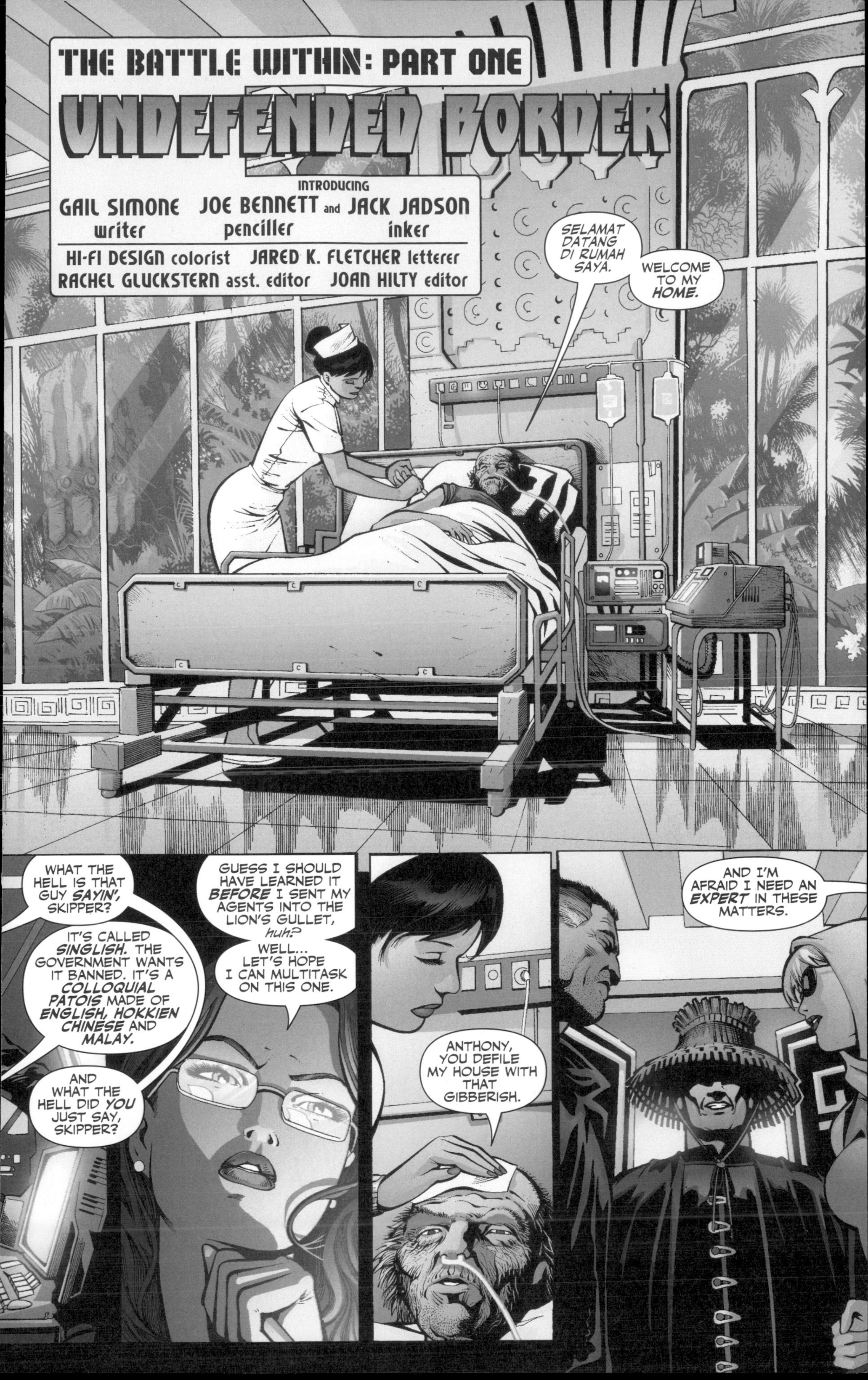
THE BATTLE WITHIN: PART ONE
UNDEFENDED BORDER
INTRODUCING
GAIL SIMONE writer JOE BENNETT penciller and JACK JADSON inker
HI-FI DESIGN colorist JARED K. FLETCHER letterer
RACHEL GLUCKSTERN asst. editor JOAN HILTY editor
SELAMAT DATANG DI RUMAH SAYA.
WELCOME TO MY HOME.
WHAT THE HELL IS THAT GUY SAYIN', SKIPPER?
IT'S CALLED SINGLISH. THE GOVERNMENT WANTS IT BANNED. IT'S A COLLOQUIAL PATOIS MADE OF ENGLISH, HOKKIEN CHINESE AND MALAY.
AND WHAT THE HELL DID YOU JUST SAY, SKIPPER?
GUESS I SHOULD HAVE LEARNED IT BEFORE I SENT MY AGENTS INTO THE LION'S GULLET, huh?
WELL... LET'S HOPE I CAN MULTITASK ON THIS ONE.
ANTHONY, YOU DEFILE MY HOUSE WITH THAT GIBBERISH.
AND I'M AFRAID I NEED AN EXPERT IN THESE MATTERS.

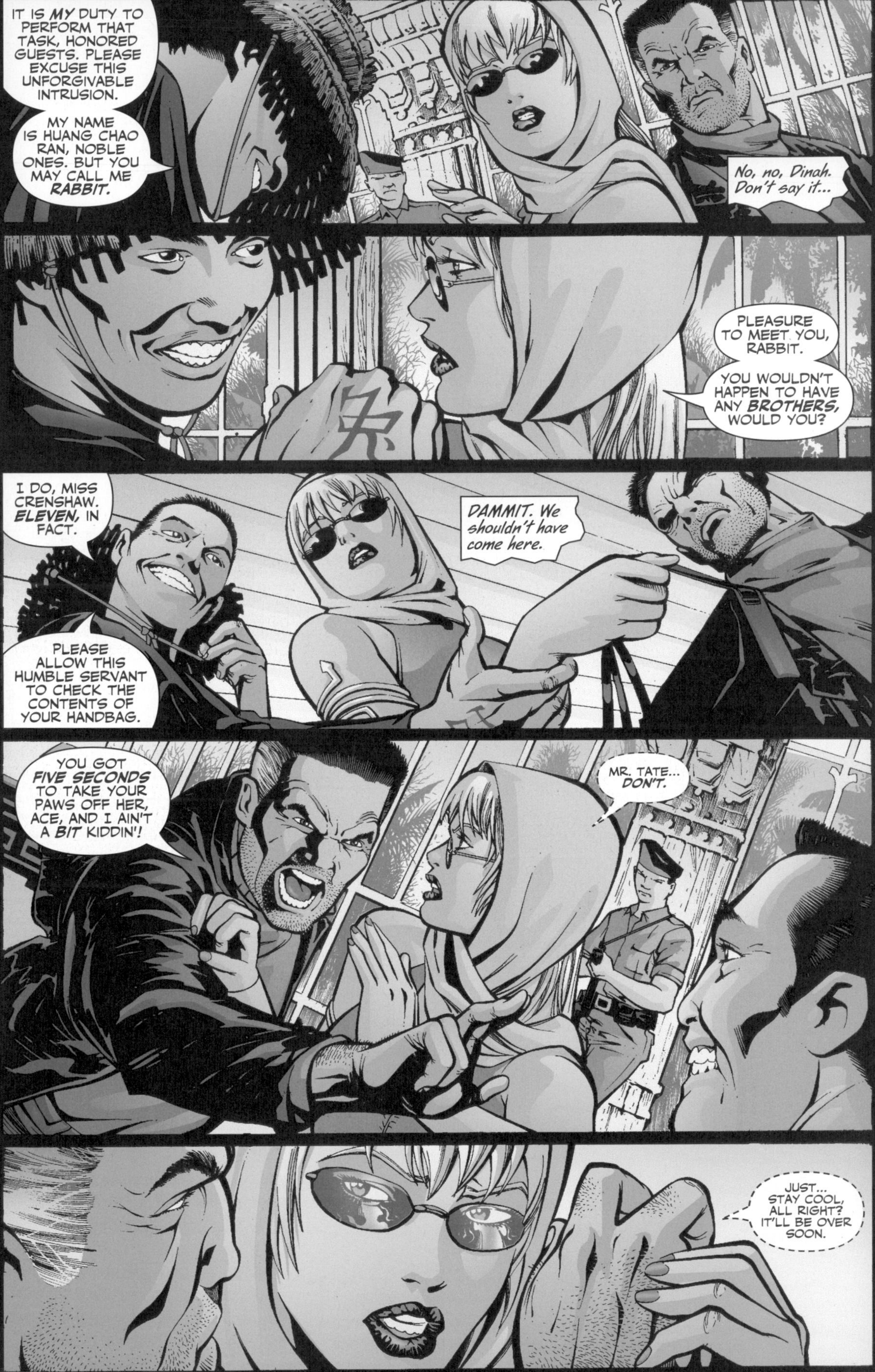
IT IS MY DUTY TO PERFORM THAT TASK, HONORED GUESTS. PLEASE EXCUSE THIS UNFORGIVABLE INTRUSION.
MY NAME IS HUANG CHAO RAN, NOBLE ONES. BUT YOU MAY CALL ME RABBIT.
No, no, Dinah. Don't say it...
PLEASURE TO MEET YOU, RABBIT.
YOU WOULDN'T HAPPEN TO HAVE ANY BROTHERS, WOULD YOU?
I DO, MISS CRENSHAW. ELEVEN, IN FACT.
DAMMIT. We shouldn't have come here.
PLEASE ALLOW THIS HUMBLE SERVANT TO CHECK THE CONTENTS OF YOUR HANDBAG.
YOU GOT FIVE SECONDS TO TAKE YOUR PAWS OFF HER, ACE, AND I AIN'T A BIT KIDDIN'!
MR. TATE... DON'T.
JUST... STAY COOL, ALL RIGHT? IT'LL BE OVER SOON.

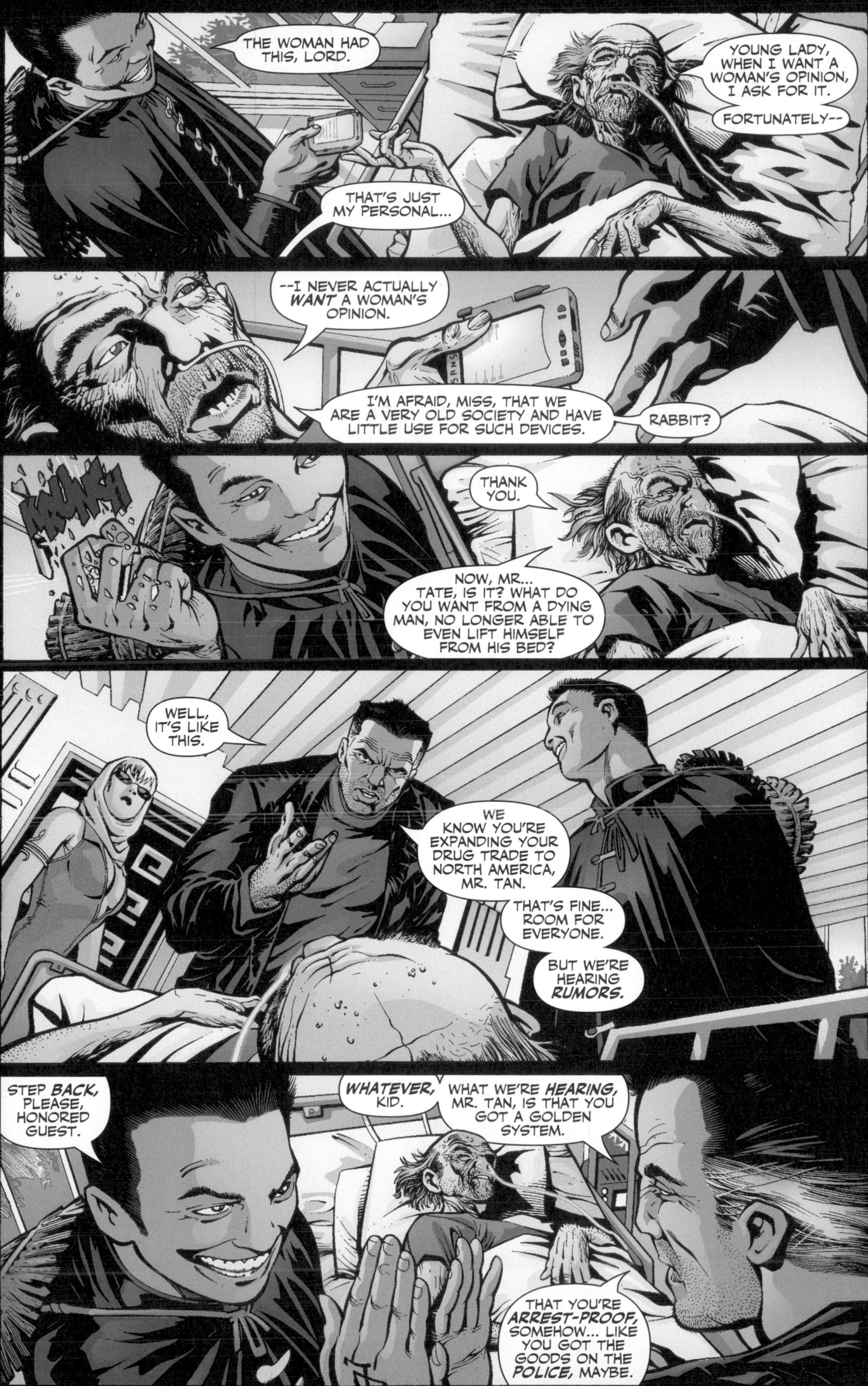
THE WOMAN HAD THIS, LORD.
YOUNG LADY, WHEN I WANT A WOMAN'S OPINION, I ASK FOR IT.
FORTUNATELY--
THAT'S JUST MY PERSONAL...
--I NEVER ACTUALLY *WANT* A WOMAN'S OPINION.
I'M AFRAID, MISS, THAT WE ARE A VERY OLD SOCIETY AND HAVE LITTLE USE FOR SUCH DEVICES.
RABBIT?
KRUNCH
THANK YOU.
NOW, MR... TATE, IS IT? WHAT DO YOU WANT FROM A DYING MAN, NO LONGER ABLE TO EVEN LIFT HIMSELF FROM HIS BED?
WELL, IT'S LIKE THIS.
WE KNOW YOU'RE EXPANDING YOUR DRUG TRADE TO NORTH AMERICA, MR. TAN.
THAT'S FINE... ROOM FOR EVERYONE.
BUT WE'RE HEARING *RUMORS.*
STEP *BACK,* PLEASE, HONORED GUEST.
WHATEVER, KID.
WHAT WE'RE *HEARING,* MR. TAN, IS THAT YOU GOT A GOLDEN SYSTEM.
THAT YOU'RE *ARREST-PROOF,* SOMEHOW... LIKE YOU GOT THE GOODS ON THE *POLICE,* MAYBE.

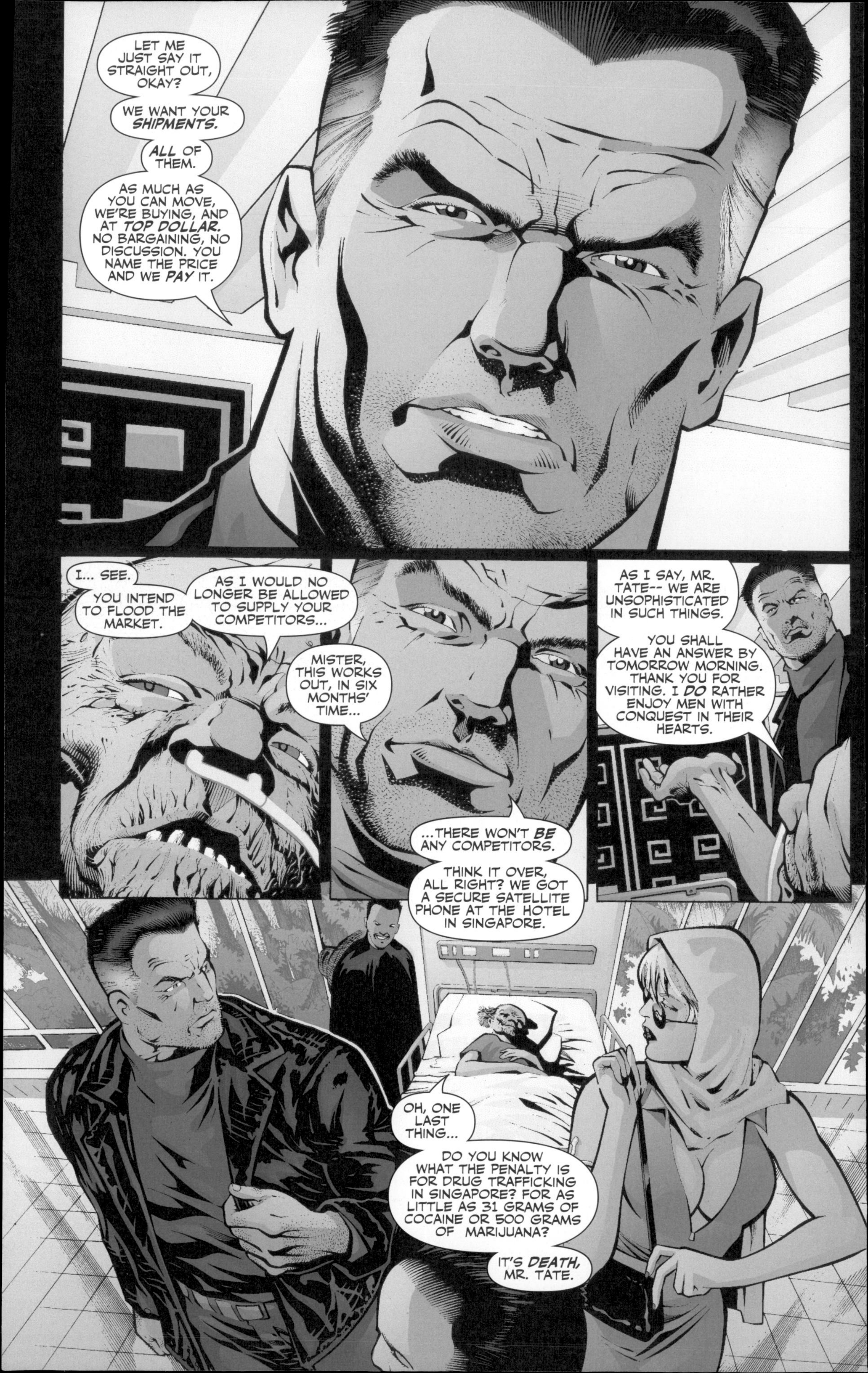
LET ME JUST SAY IT STRAIGHT OUT, OKAY?
WE WANT YOUR *SHIPMENTS.*
ALL OF THEM.
AS MUCH AS YOU CAN MOVE, WE'RE BUYING, AND AT *TOP DOLLAR.* NO BARGAINING, NO DISCUSSION. YOU NAME THE PRICE AND WE *PAY* IT.
I... SEE.
YOU INTEND TO FLOOD THE MARKET.
AS I WOULD NO LONGER BE ALLOWED TO SUPPLY YOUR COMPETITORS...
MISTER, THIS WORKS OUT, IN SIX MONTHS' TIME...
...THERE WON'T *BE* ANY COMPETITORS.
THINK IT OVER, ALL RIGHT? WE GOT A SECURE SATELLITE PHONE AT THE HOTEL IN SINGAPORE.
AS I SAY, MR. TATE-- WE ARE UNSOPHISTICATED IN SUCH THINGS.
YOU SHALL HAVE AN ANSWER BY TOMORROW MORNING. THANK YOU FOR VISITING. I *DO* RATHER ENJOY MEN WITH CONQUEST IN THEIR HEARTS.
OH, ONE LAST THING...
DO YOU KNOW WHAT THE PENALTY IS FOR DRUG TRAFFICKING IN SINGAPORE? FOR AS LITTLE AS 31 GRAMS OF COCAINE OR 500 GRAMS OF MARIJUANA?
IT'S *DEATH,* MR. TATE.

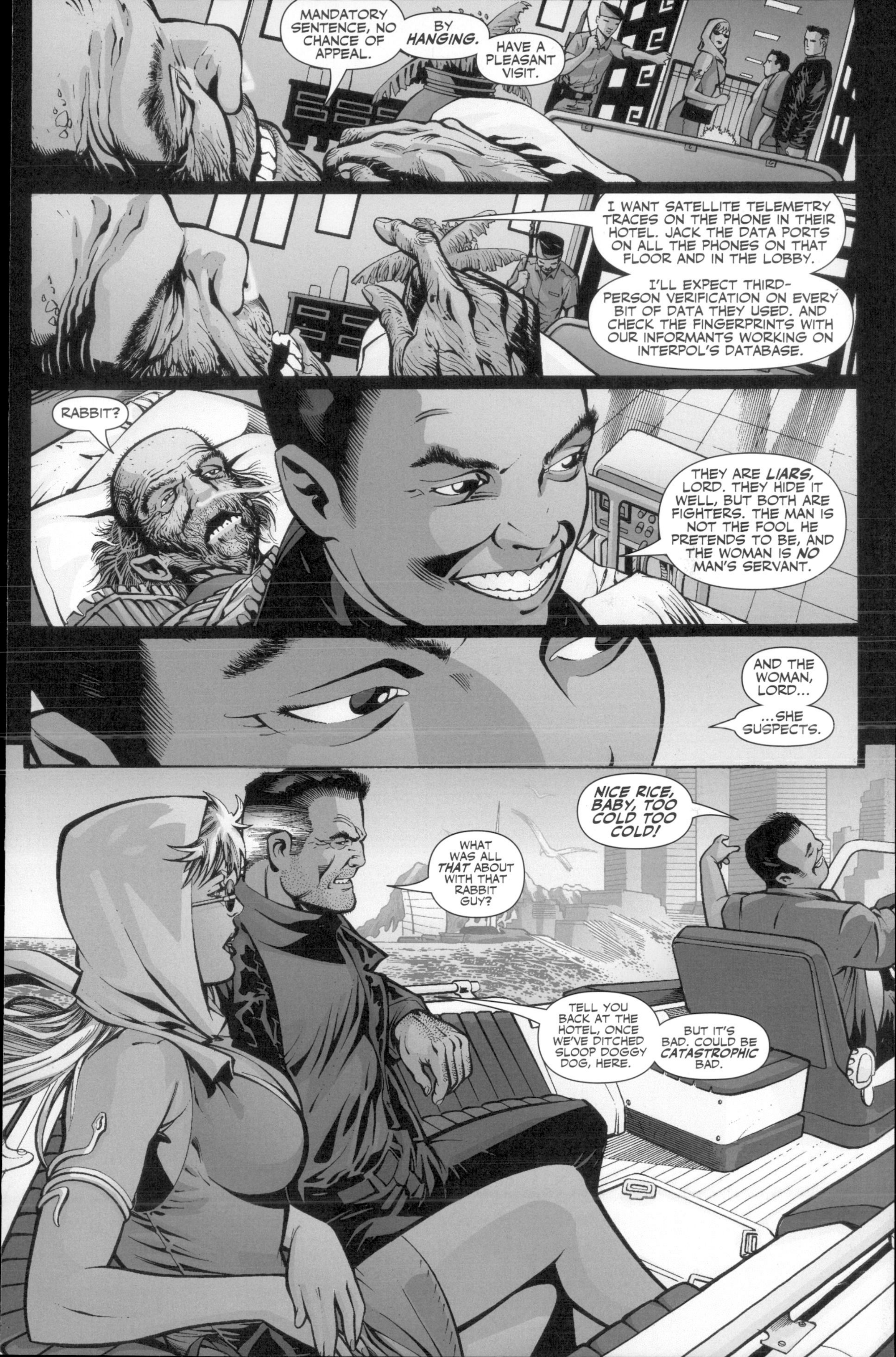
MANDATORY SENTENCE, NO CHANCE OF APPEAL.
BY *HANGING.*
HAVE A PLEASANT VISIT.
I WANT SATELLITE TELEMETRY TRACES ON THE PHONE IN THEIR HOTEL. JACK THE DATA PORTS ON ALL THE PHONES ON THAT FLOOR AND IN THE LOBBY.
I'LL EXPECT THIRD-PERSON VERIFICATION ON EVERY BIT OF DATA THEY USED. AND CHECK THE FINGERPRINTS WITH OUR INFORMANTS WORKING ON INTERPOL'S DATABASE.
RABBIT?
THEY ARE *LIARS,* LORD. THEY HIDE IT WELL, BUT BOTH ARE FIGHTERS. THE MAN IS NOT THE FOOL HE PRETENDS TO BE, AND THE WOMAN IS *NO* MAN'S SERVANT.
AND THE WOMAN, LORD...
...SHE SUSPECTS.
NICE RICE, BABY, TOO COLD TOO COLD!
WHAT WAS ALL *THAT* ABOUT WITH THAT RABBIT GUY?
TELL YOU BACK AT THE HOTEL, ONCE WE'VE DITCHED SLOOP DOGGY DOG, HERE.
BUT IT'S BAD. COULD BE *CATASTROPHIC* BAD.

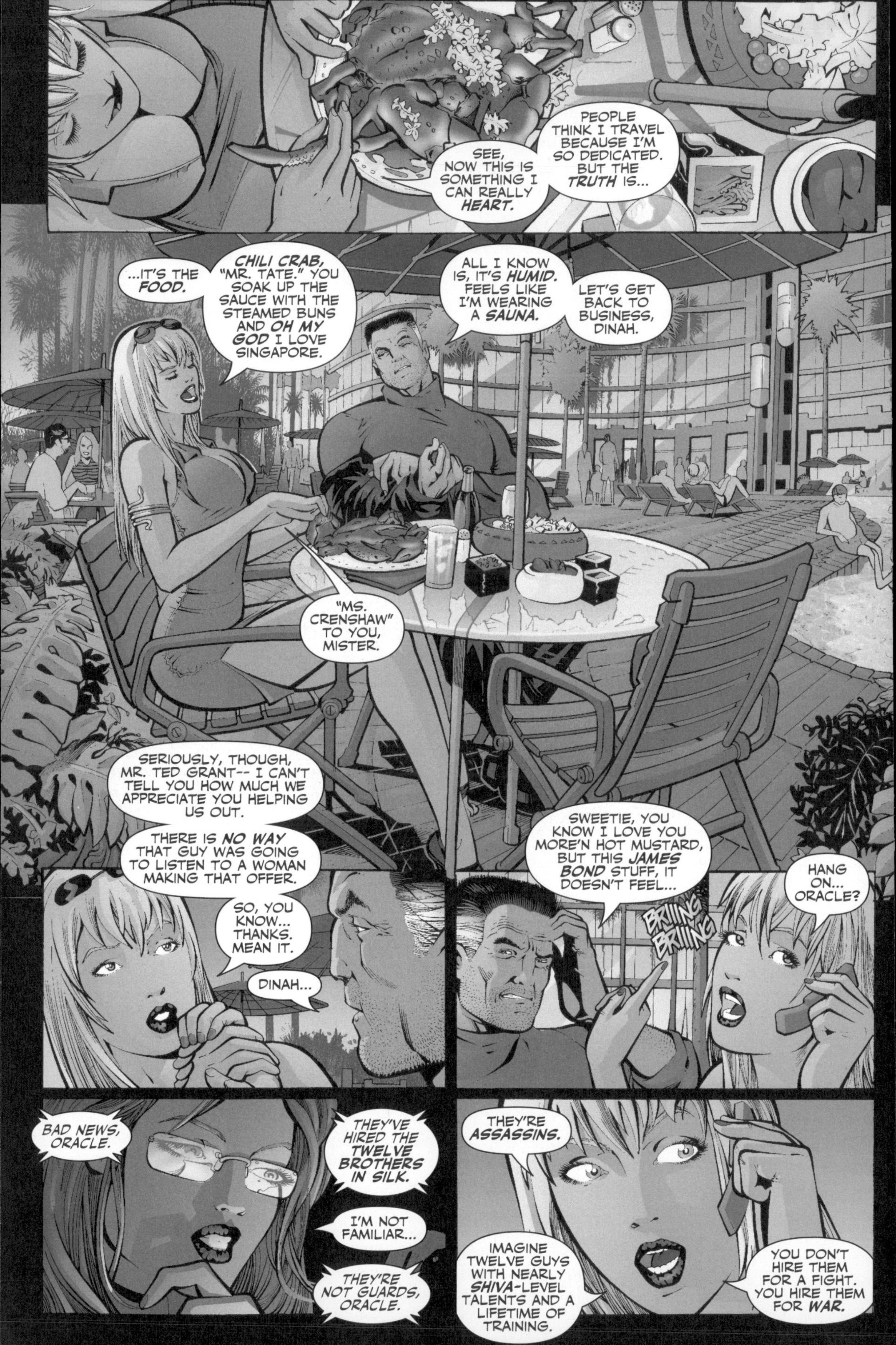
SEE, NOW THIS IS SOMETHING I CAN REALLY HEART.
PEOPLE THINK I TRAVEL BECAUSE I'M SO DEDICATED. BUT THE TRUTH IS...
...IT'S THE FOOD.
CHILI CRAB, "MR. TATE." YOU SOAK UP THE SAUCE WITH THE STEAMED BUNS AND OH MY GOD I LOVE SINGAPORE.
ALL I KNOW IS, IT'S HUMID. FEELS LIKE I'M WEARING A SAUNA.
LET'S GET BACK TO BUSINESS, DINAH.
"MS. CRENSHAW" TO YOU, MISTER.
SERIOUSLY, THOUGH, MR. TED GRANT-- I CAN'T TELL YOU HOW MUCH WE APPRECIATE YOU HELPING US OUT.
THERE IS NO WAY THAT GUY WAS GOING TO LISTEN TO A WOMAN MAKING THAT OFFER.
SO, YOU KNOW... THANKS. MEAN IT.
DINAH...
SWEETIE, YOU KNOW I LOVE YOU MORE'N HOT MUSTARD, BUT THIS JAMES BOND STUFF, IT DOESN'T FEEL...
BRIIING BRIIING
HANG ON... ORACLE?
BAD NEWS, ORACLE.
THEY'VE HIRED THE TWELVE BROTHERS IN SILK.
I'M NOT FAMILIAR...
THEY'RE NOT GUARDS, ORACLE.
THEY'RE ASSASSINS.
IMAGINE TWELVE GUYS WITH NEARLY SHIVA-LEVEL TALENTS AND A LIFETIME OF TRAINING.
YOU DON'T HIRE THEM FOR A FIGHT. YOU HIRE THEM FOR WAR.

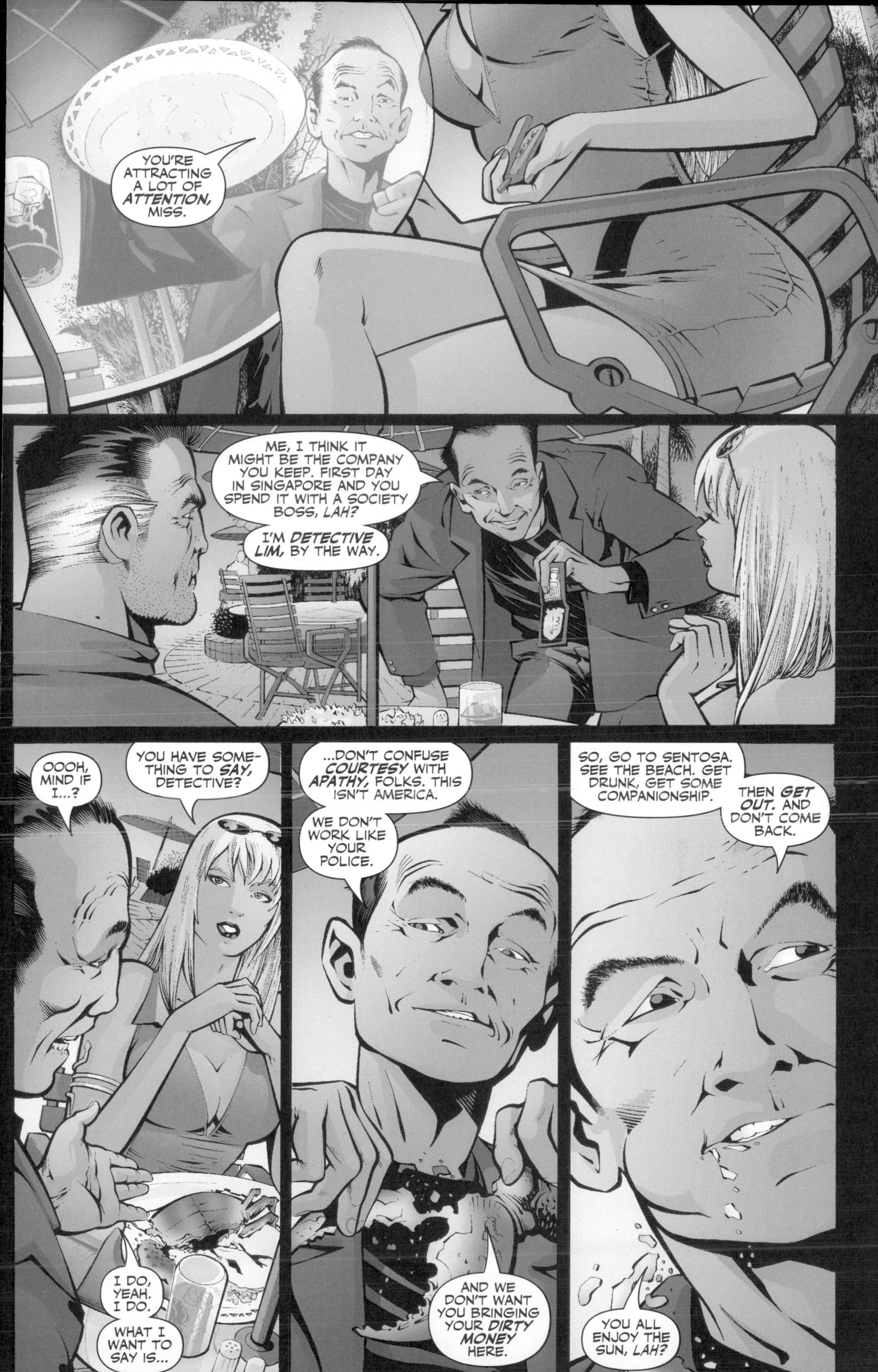
YOU'RE ATTRACTING A LOT OF ATTENTION, MISS.
ME, I THINK IT MIGHT BE THE COMPANY YOU KEEP. FIRST DAY IN SINGAPORE AND YOU SPEND IT WITH A SOCIETY BOSS, LAH?
I'M DETECTIVE LIM, BY THE WAY.
OOOH, MIND IF I...?
YOU HAVE SOME-THING TO SAY, DETECTIVE?
I DO, YEAH. I DO.
WHAT I WANT TO SAY IS...
...DON'T CONFUSE COURTESY WITH APATHY, FOLKS. THIS ISN'T AMERICA.
WE DON'T WORK LIKE YOUR POLICE.
AND WE DON'T WANT YOU BRINGING YOUR DIRTY MONEY HERE.
SO, GO TO SENTOSA. SEE THE BEACH. GET DRUNK, GET SOME COMPANIONSHIP.
THEN GET OUT. AND DON'T COME BACK.
YOU ALL ENJOY THE SUN, LAH?

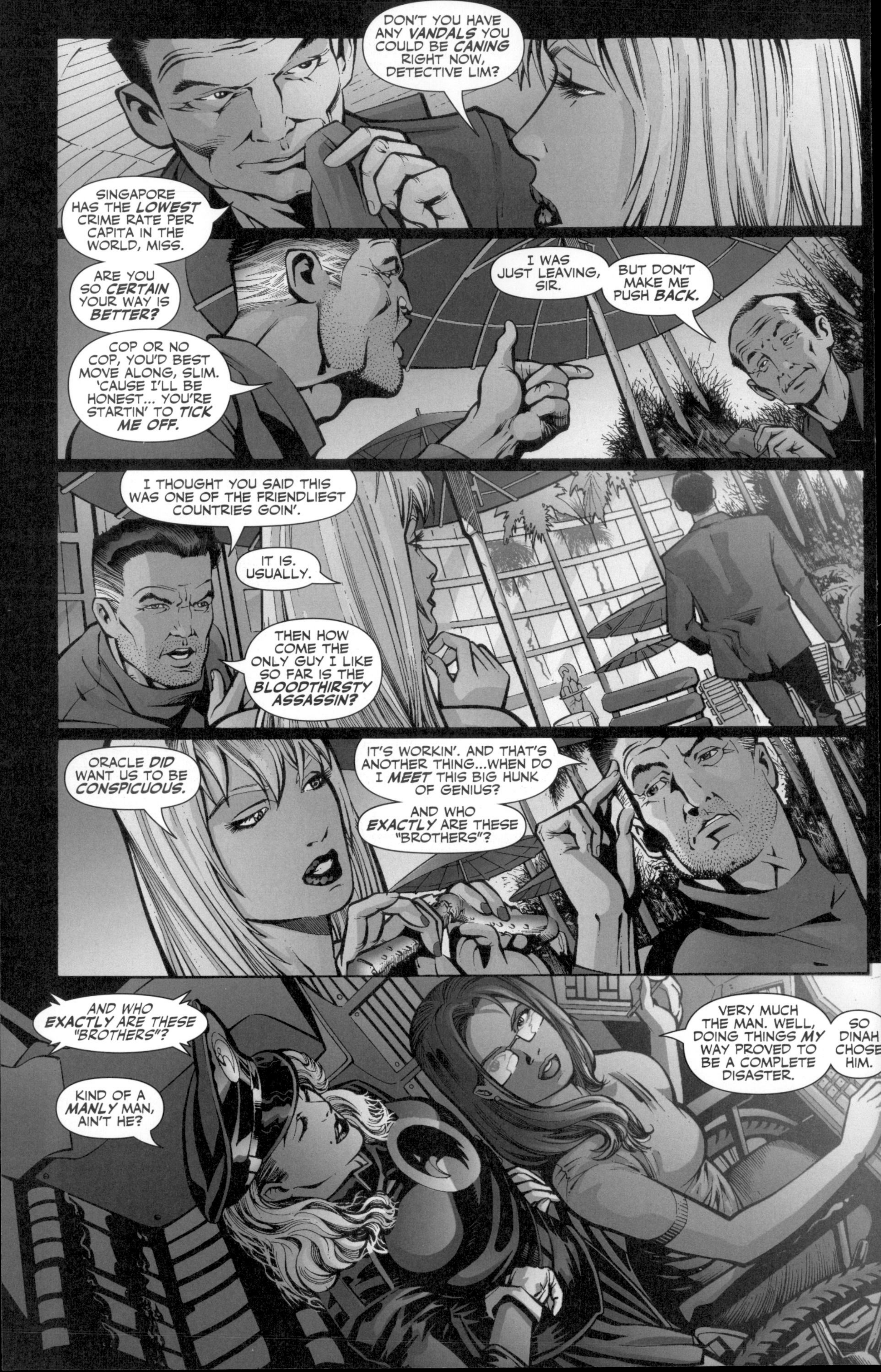
DON'T YOU HAVE ANY VANDALS YOU COULD BE CANING RIGHT NOW, DETECTIVE LIM?
SINGAPORE HAS THE LOWEST CRIME RATE PER CAPITA IN THE WORLD, MISS.
ARE YOU SO CERTAIN YOUR WAY IS BETTER?
COP OR NO COP, YOU'D BEST MOVE ALONG, SLIM. 'CAUSE I'LL BE HONEST... YOU'RE STARTIN' TO TICK ME OFF.
I WAS JUST LEAVING, SIR.
BUT DON'T MAKE ME PUSH BACK.
I THOUGHT YOU SAID THIS WAS ONE OF THE FRIENDLIEST COUNTRIES GOIN'.
IT IS. USUALLY.
THEN HOW COME THE ONLY GUY I LIKE SO FAR IS THE BLOODTHIRSTY ASSASSIN?
ORACLE DID WANT US TO BE CONSPICUOUS.
IT'S WORKIN'. AND THAT'S ANOTHER THING...WHEN DO I MEET THIS BIG HUNK OF GENIUS?
AND WHO EXACTLY ARE THESE "BROTHERS"?
AND WHO EXACTLY ARE THESE "BROTHERS"?
KIND OF A MANLY MAN, AIN'T HE?
VERY MUCH THE MAN. WELL, DOING THINGS MY WAY PROVED TO BE A COMPLETE DISASTER.
SO DINAH CHOSE HIM.

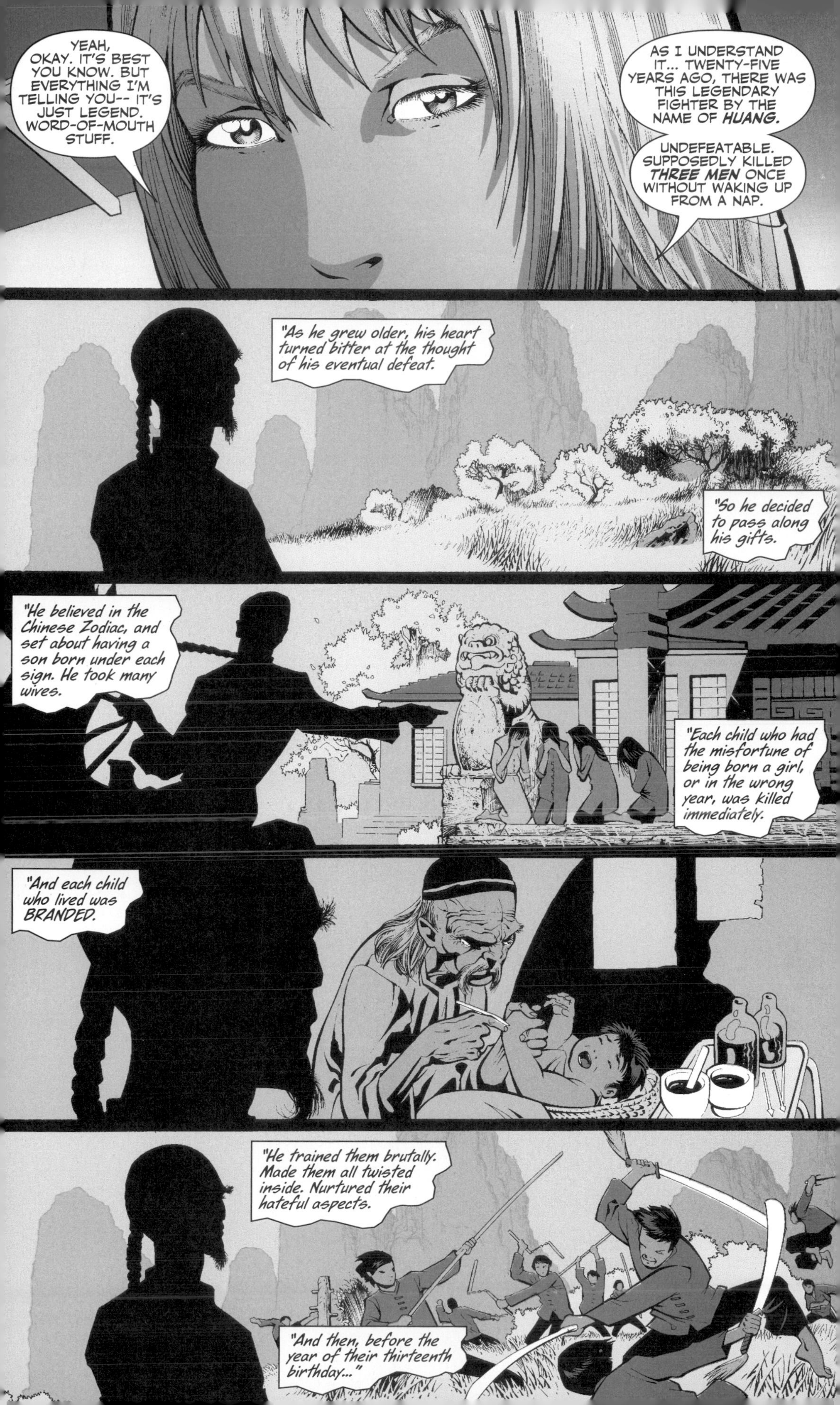
YEAH, OKAY. IT'S BEST YOU KNOW. BUT EVERYTHING I'M TELLING YOU-- IT'S JUST LEGEND. WORD-OF-MOUTH STUFF.
AS I UNDERSTAND IT... TWENTY-FIVE YEARS AGO, THERE WAS THIS LEGENDARY FIGHTER BY THE NAME OF HUANG.
UNDEFEATABLE. SUPPOSEDLY KILLED THREE MEN ONCE WITHOUT WAKING UP FROM A NAP.
"As he grew older, his heart turned bitter at the thought of his eventual defeat.
"So he decided to pass along his gifts.
"He believed in the Chinese Zodiac, and set about having a son born under each sign. He took many wives.
"Each child who had the misfortune of being born a girl, or in the wrong year, was killed immediately.
"And each child who lived was BRANDED.
"He trained them brutally. Made them all twisted inside. Nurtured their hateful aspects.
"And then, before the year of their thirteenth birthday..."

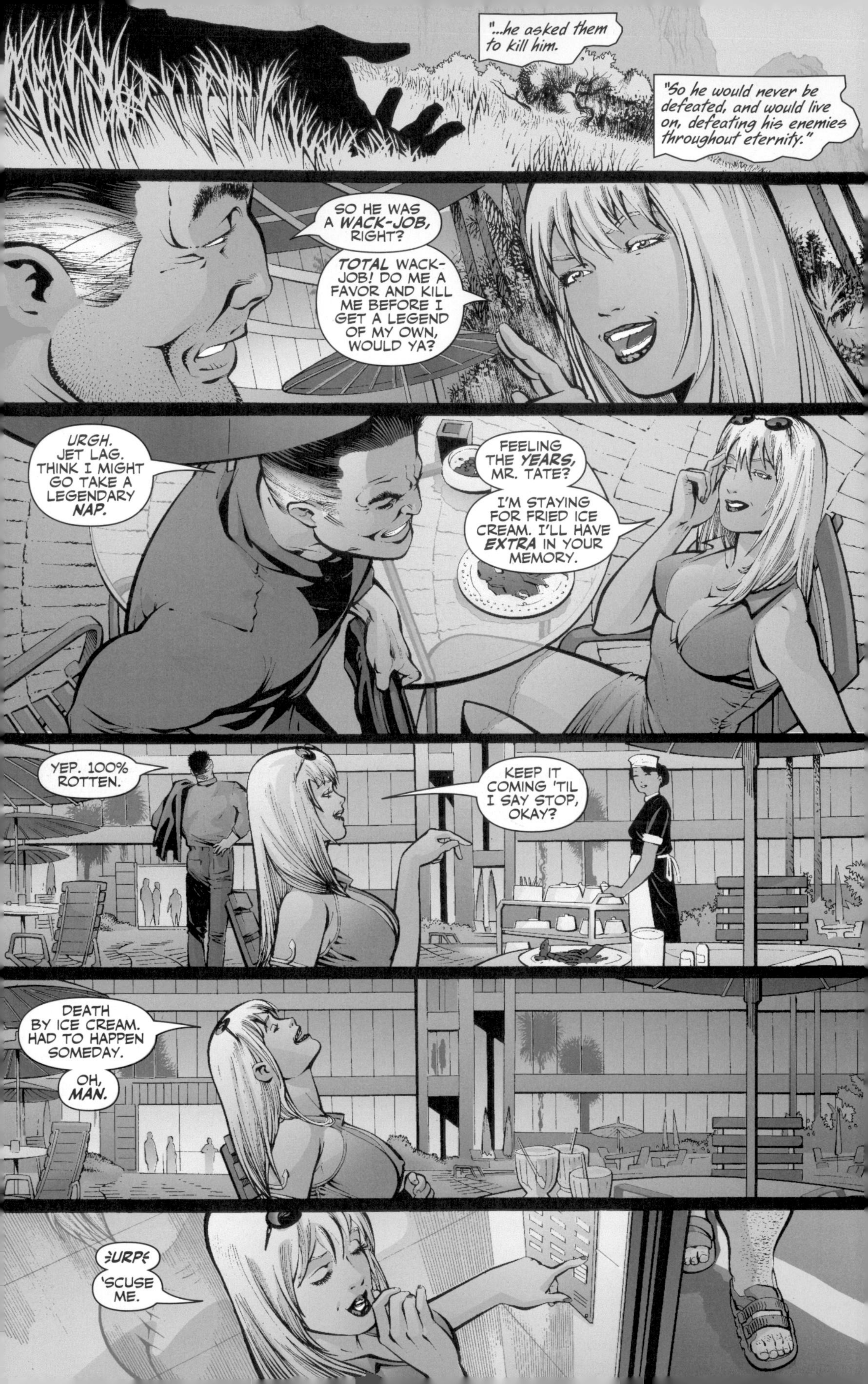
"...he asked them to kill him.
"So he would never be defeated, and would live on, defeating his enemies throughout eternity."
SO HE WAS A WACK-JOB, RIGHT?
TOTAL WACK-JOB! DO ME A FAVOR AND KILL ME BEFORE I GET A LEGEND OF MY OWN, WOULD YA?
URGH. JET LAG. THINK I MIGHT GO TAKE A LEGENDARY NAP.
FEELING THE YEARS, MR. TATE?
I'M STAYING FOR FRIED ICE CREAM. I'LL HAVE EXTRA IN YOUR MEMORY.
YEP. 100% ROTTEN.
KEEP IT COMING 'TIL I SAY STOP, OKAY?
DEATH BY ICE CREAM. HAD TO HAPPEN SOMEDAY.
OH, MAN.
URP
'SCUSE ME.

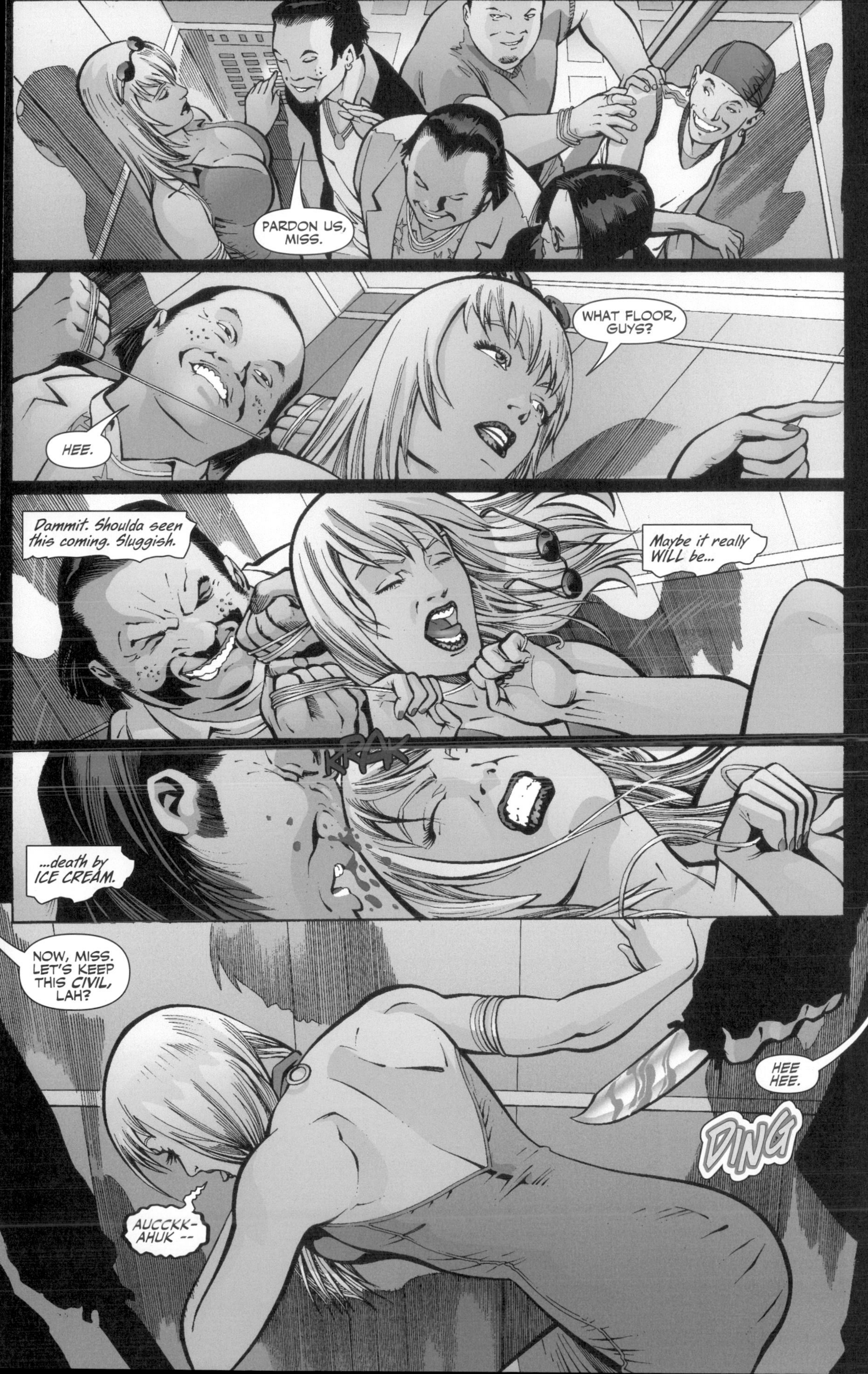

PARDON US, MISS.
WHAT FLOOR, GUYS?
HEE.
Dammit. Shoulda seen this coming. Sluggish.
Maybe it really WILL be...
KRAK
...death by ICE CREAM.
NOW, MISS. LET'S KEEP THIS CIVIL, LAH?
HEE HEE.
DING
AUCCKK-AHUK --

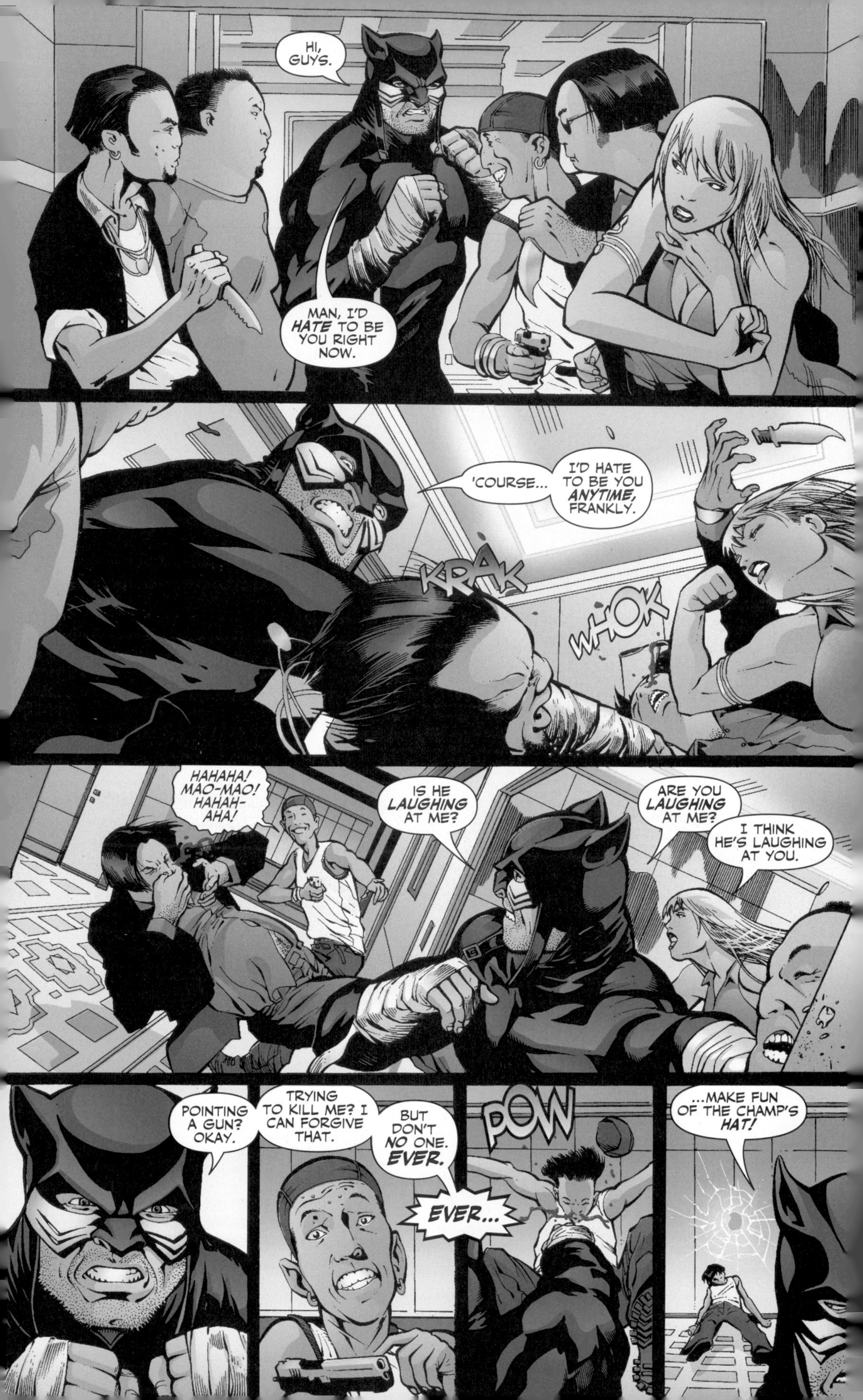
HI, GUYS.
MAN, I'D HATE TO BE YOU RIGHT NOW.
'COURSE...
I'D HATE TO BE YOU ANYTIME, FRANKLY.
KRAK
WHOK
HAHAHA! MAO-MAO! HAHAH-AHA!
IS HE LAUGHING AT ME?
ARE YOU LAUGHING AT ME?
I THINK HE'S LAUGHING AT YOU.
POINTING A GUN? OKAY.
TRYING TO KILL ME? I CAN FORGIVE THAT.
BUT DON'T NO ONE. EVER.
EVER...
POW
...MAKE FUN OF THE CHAMP'S HAT!

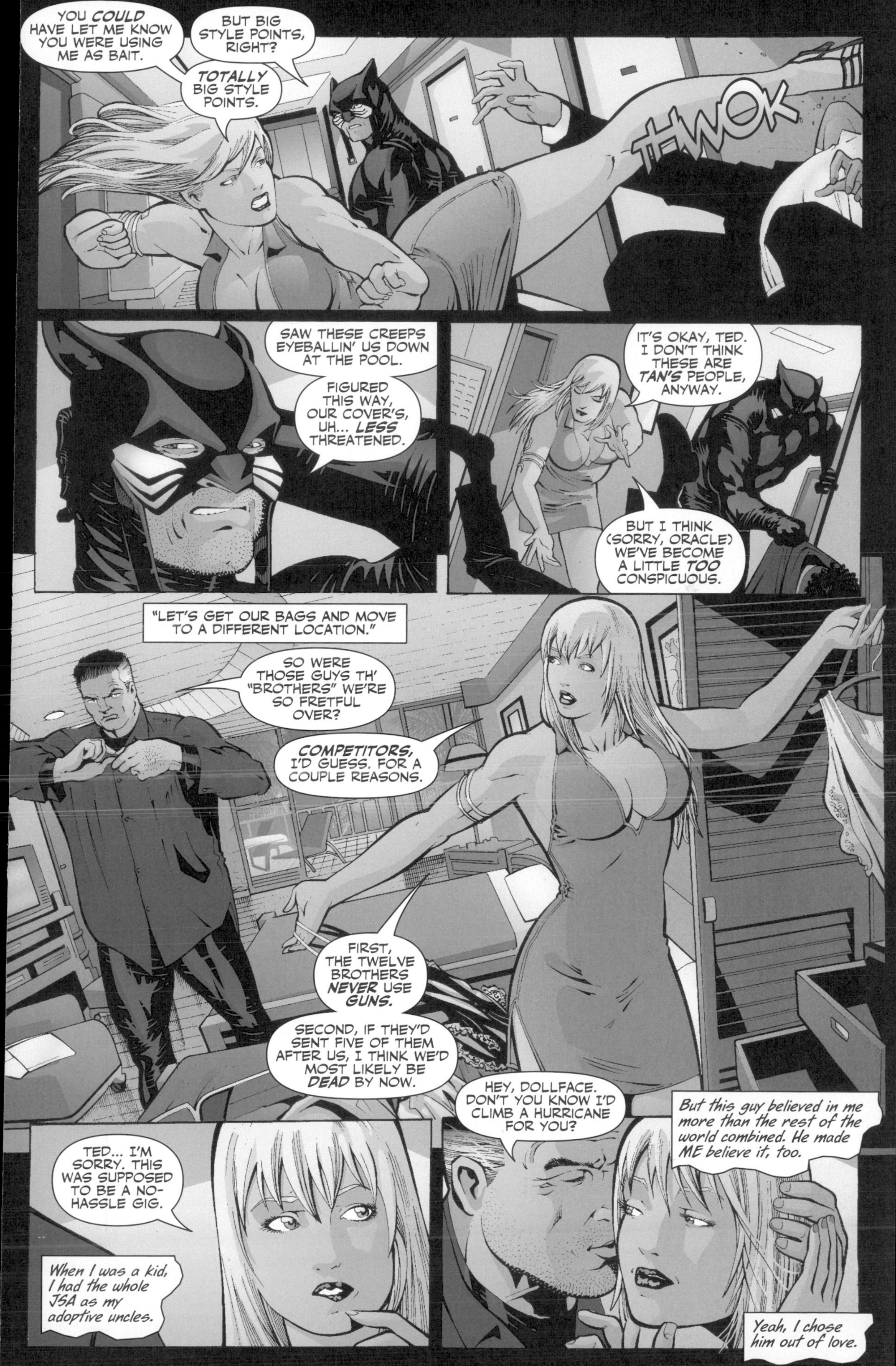

YOU COULD HAVE LET ME KNOW YOU WERE USING ME AS BAIT.
BUT BIG STYLE POINTS, RIGHT?
TOTALLY BIG STYLE POINTS.
THWOK
SAW THESE CREEPS EYEBALLIN' US DOWN AT THE POOL.
FIGURED THIS WAY, OUR COVER'S, UH... LESS THREATENED.
IT'S OKAY, TED. I DON'T THINK THESE ARE TAN'S PEOPLE, ANYWAY.
BUT I THINK (SORRY, ORACLE) WE'VE BECOME A LITTLE TOO CONSPICUOUS.
"LET'S GET OUR BAGS AND MOVE TO A DIFFERENT LOCATION."
SO WERE THOSE GUYS TH' "BROTHERS" WE'RE SO FRETFUL OVER?
COMPETITORS, I'D GUESS. FOR A COUPLE REASONS.
FIRST, THE TWELVE BROTHERS NEVER USE GUNS.
SECOND, IF THEY'D SENT FIVE OF THEM AFTER US, I THINK WE'D MOST LIKELY BE DEAD BY NOW.
TED... I'M SORRY. THIS WAS SUPPOSED TO BE A NO-HASSLE GIG.
When I was a kid, I had the whole JSA as my adoptive uncles.
HEY, DOLLFACE. DON'T YOU KNOW I'D CLIMB A HURRICANE FOR YOU?
But this guy believed in me more than the rest of the world combined. He made ME believe it, too.
Yeah, I chose him out of love.

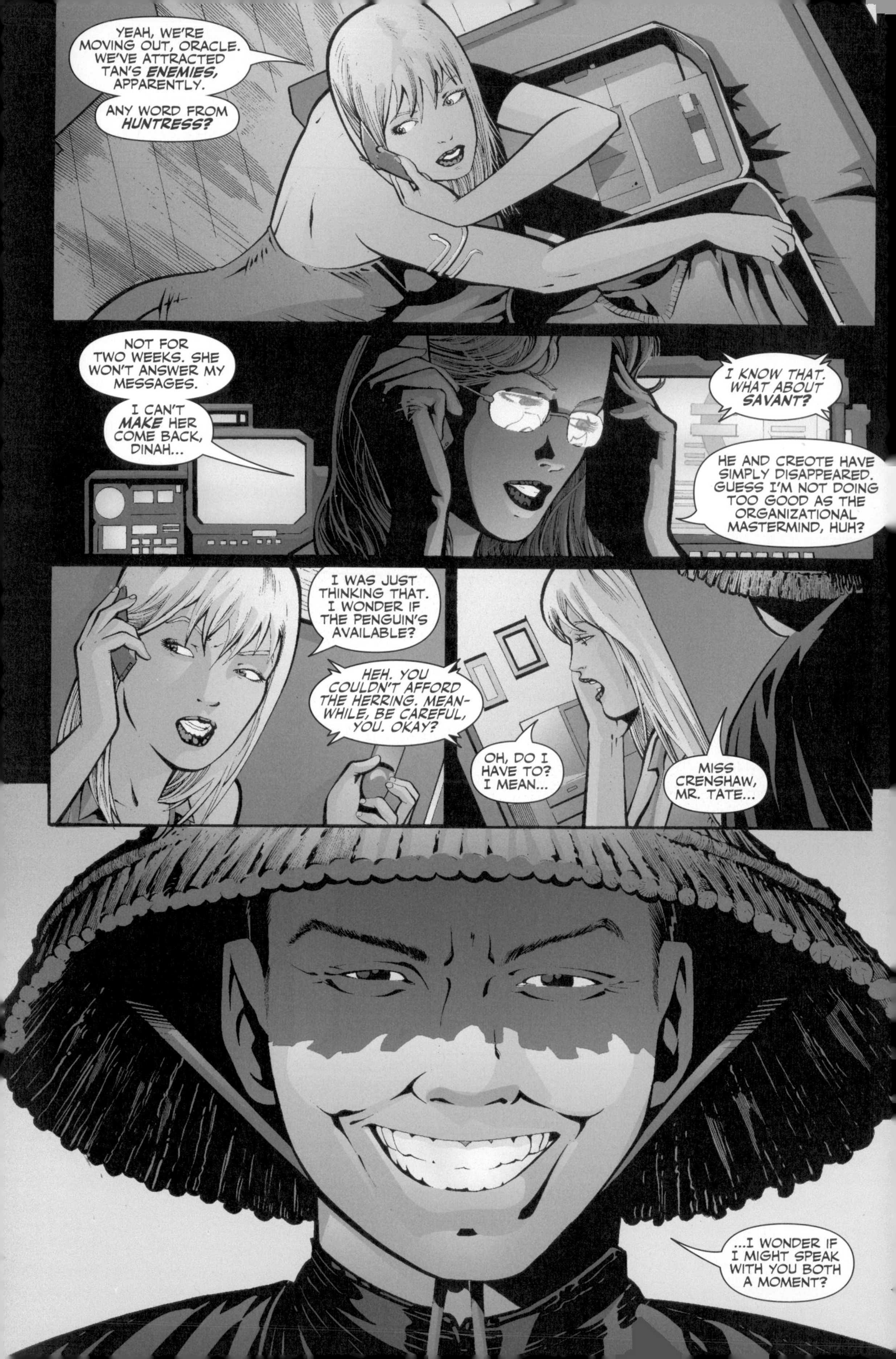
YEAH, WE'RE MOVING OUT, ORACLE. WE'VE ATTRACTED TAN'S ENEMIES, APPARENTLY.
ANY WORD FROM HUNTRESS?
NOT FOR TWO WEEKS. SHE WON'T ANSWER MY MESSAGES.
I CAN'T MAKE HER COME BACK, DINAH...
I KNOW THAT. WHAT ABOUT SAVANT?
HE AND CREOTE HAVE SIMPLY DISAPPEARED. GUESS I'M NOT DOING TOO GOOD AS THE ORGANIZATIONAL MASTERMIND, HUH?
I WAS JUST THINKING THAT. I WONDER IF THE PENGUIN'S AVAILABLE?
HEH. YOU COULDN'T AFFORD THE HERRING. MEAN-WHILE, BE CAREFUL, YOU. OKAY?
OH, DO I HAVE TO? I MEAN...
MISS CRENSHAW, MR. TATE...
...I WONDER IF I MIGHT SPEAK WITH YOU BOTH A MOMENT?

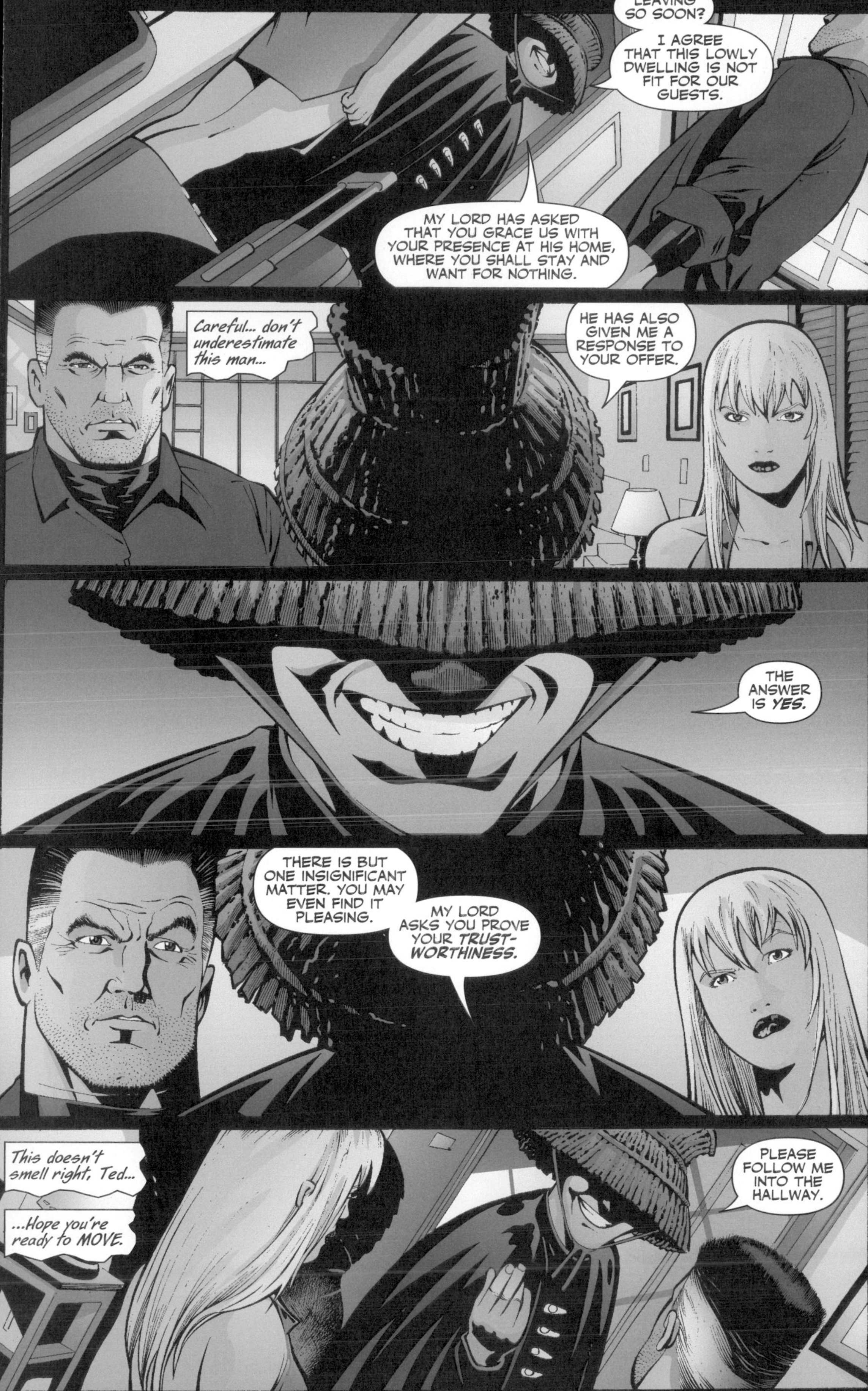

LEAVING SO SOON?
I AGREE THAT THIS LOWLY DWELLING IS NOT FIT FOR OUR GUESTS.
MY LORD HAS ASKED THAT YOU GRACE US WITH YOUR PRESENCE AT HIS HOME, WHERE YOU SHALL STAY AND WANT FOR NOTHING.
Careful... don't underestimate this man...
HE HAS ALSO GIVEN ME A RESPONSE TO YOUR OFFER.
THE ANSWER IS *YES.*
THERE IS BUT ONE INSIGNIFICANT MATTER. YOU MAY EVEN FIND IT PLEASING.
MY LORD ASKS YOU PROVE YOUR *TRUST-WORTHINESS.*
This doesn't smell right, Ted...
...Hope you're ready to MOVE.
PLEASE FOLLOW ME INTO THE HALLWAY.

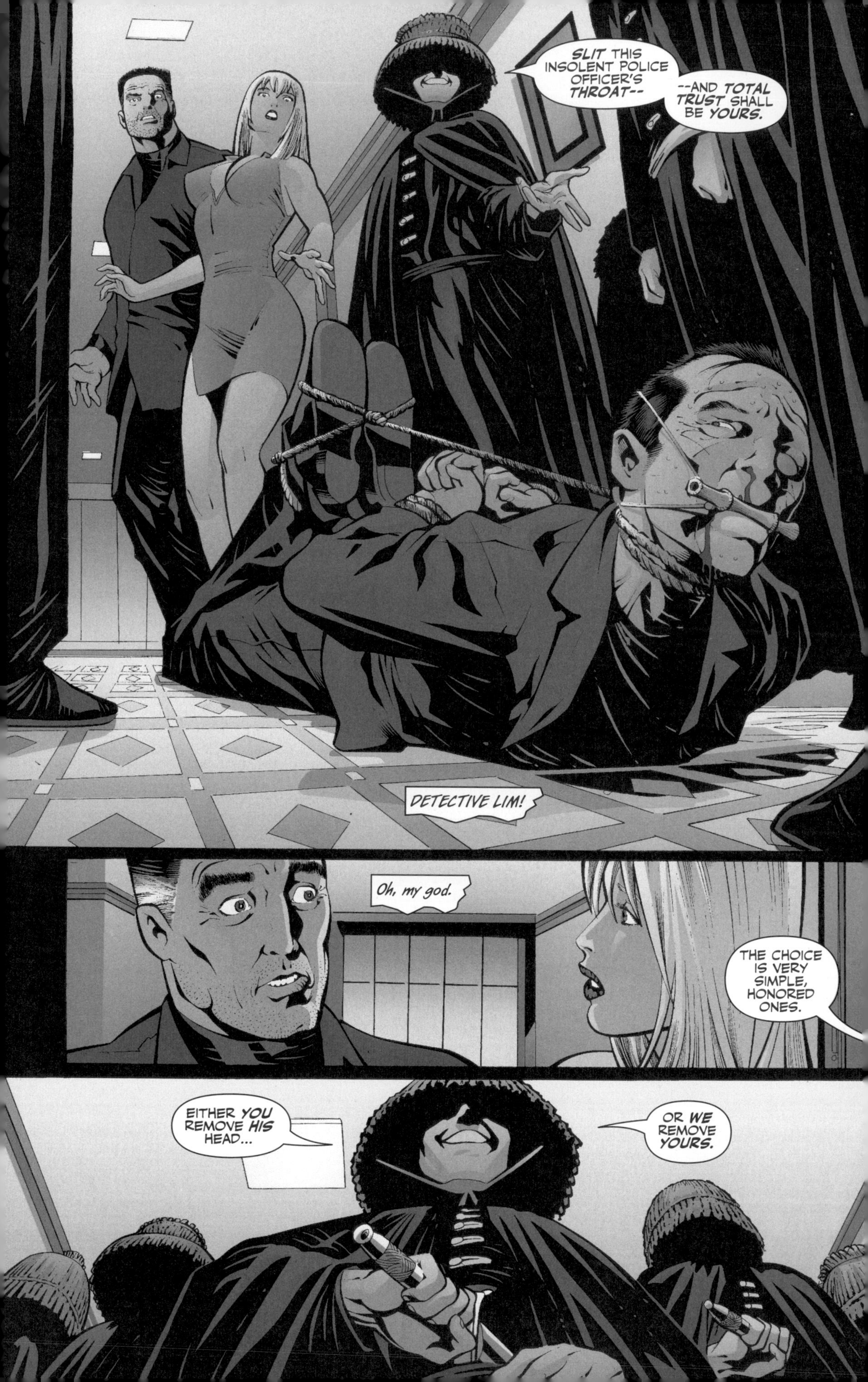
SLIT THIS INSOLENT POLICE OFFICER'S THROAT--
--AND TOTAL TRUST SHALL BE YOURS.
DETECTIVE LIM!
Oh, my god.
THE CHOICE IS VERY SIMPLE, HONORED ONES.
EITHER YOU REMOVE HIS HEAD...
OR WE REMOVE YOURS.

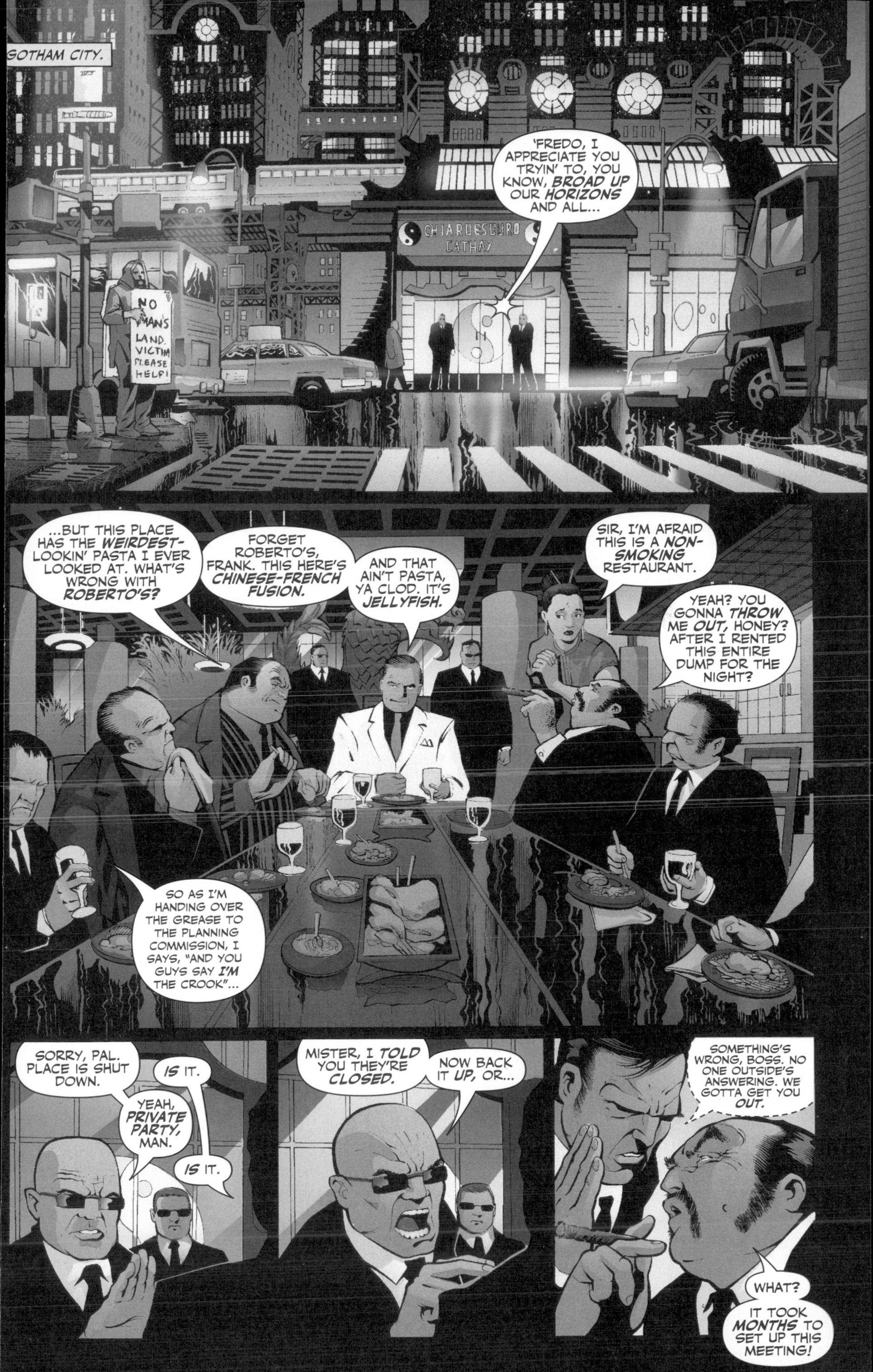
GOTHAM CITY.
NO MAN'S LAND. VICTIM PLEASE HELP!
CHIAROSCURO CATHAY
'FREDO, I APPRECIATE YOU TRYIN' TO, YOU KNOW, BROAD UP OUR HORIZONS AND ALL...
...BUT THIS PLACE HAS THE WEIRDEST-LOOKIN' PASTA I EVER LOOKED AT. WHAT'S WRONG WITH ROBERTO'S?
FORGET ROBERTO'S, FRANK. THIS HERE'S CHINESE-FRENCH FUSION.
AND THAT AIN'T PASTA, YA CLOD. IT'S JELLYFISH.
SIR, I'M AFRAID THIS IS A NON-SMOKING RESTAURANT.
YEAH? YOU GONNA THROW ME OUT, HONEY? AFTER I RENTED THIS ENTIRE DUMP FOR THE NIGHT?
SO AS I'M HANDING OVER THE GREASE TO THE PLANNING COMMISSION, I SAYS, "AND YOU GUYS SAY I'M THE CROOK"...
SORRY, PAL. PLACE IS SHUT DOWN.
IS IT.
YEAH, PRIVATE PARTY, MAN.
IS IT.
MISTER, I TOLD YOU THEY'RE CLOSED.
NOW BACK IT UP, OR...
SOMETHING'S WRONG, BOSS. NO ONE OUTSIDE'S ANSWERING. WE GOTTA GET YOU OUT.
WHAT?
IT TOOK MONTHS TO SET UP THIS MEETING!

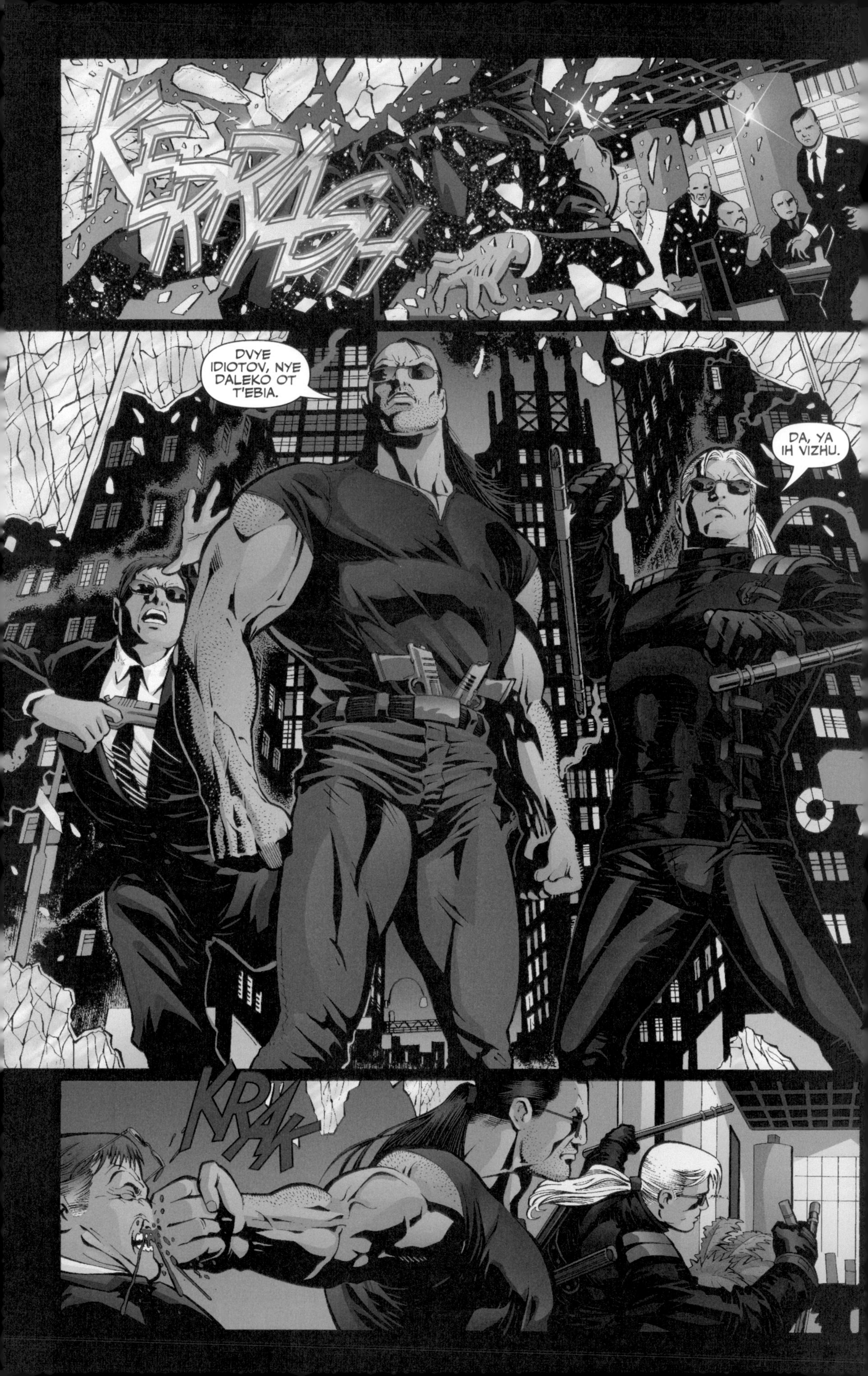
KERRASH
DVYE IDIOTOV, NYE DALEKO OT T'EBIA.
DA, YA IH VIZHU.
KRAK

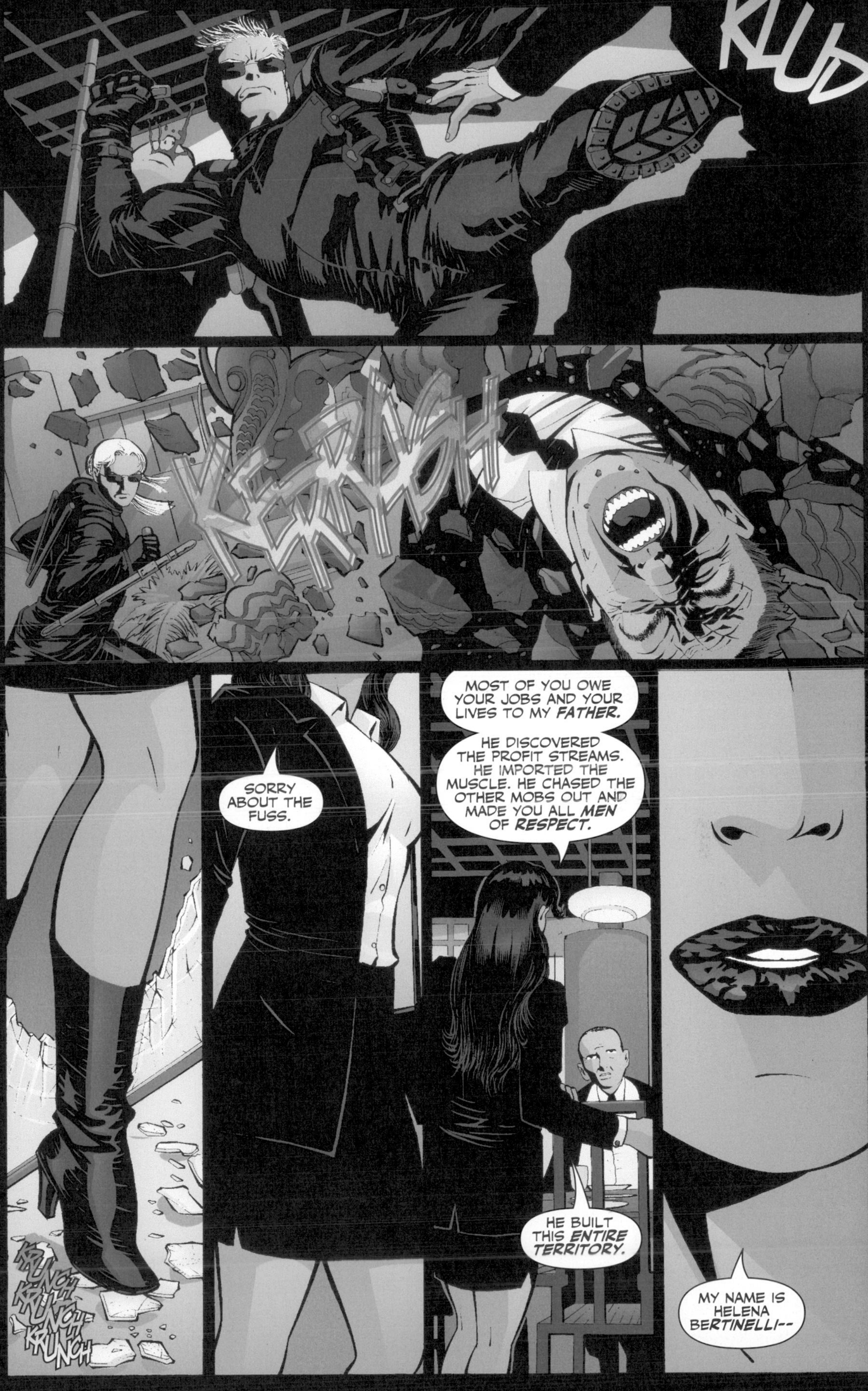
KLUD
KRASH
SORRY ABOUT THE FUSS.
MOST OF YOU OWE YOUR JOBS AND YOUR LIVES TO MY *FATHER.*
HE DISCOVERED THE PROFIT STREAMS. HE IMPORTED THE MUSCLE. HE CHASED THE OTHER MOBS OUT AND MADE YOU ALL *MEN* OF *RESPECT.*
KRUNCH KRUNCH KRUNCH
HE BUILT THIS *ENTIRE TERRITORY.*
MY NAME IS HELENA BE*RTINELLI--*

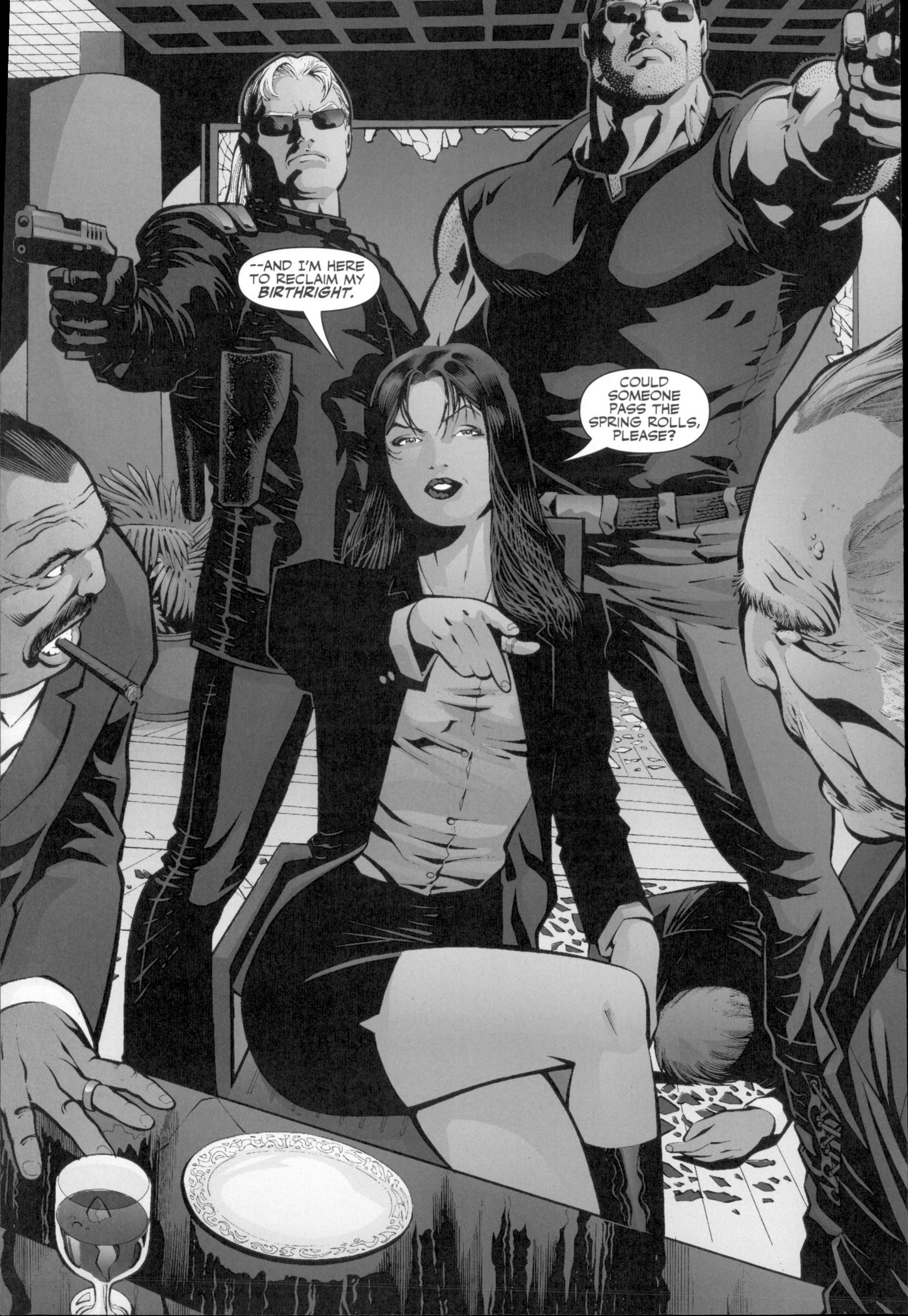
--AND I'M HERE TO RECLAIM MY *BIRTHRIGHT.*
COULD SOMEONE PASS THE SPRING ROLLS, PLEASE?

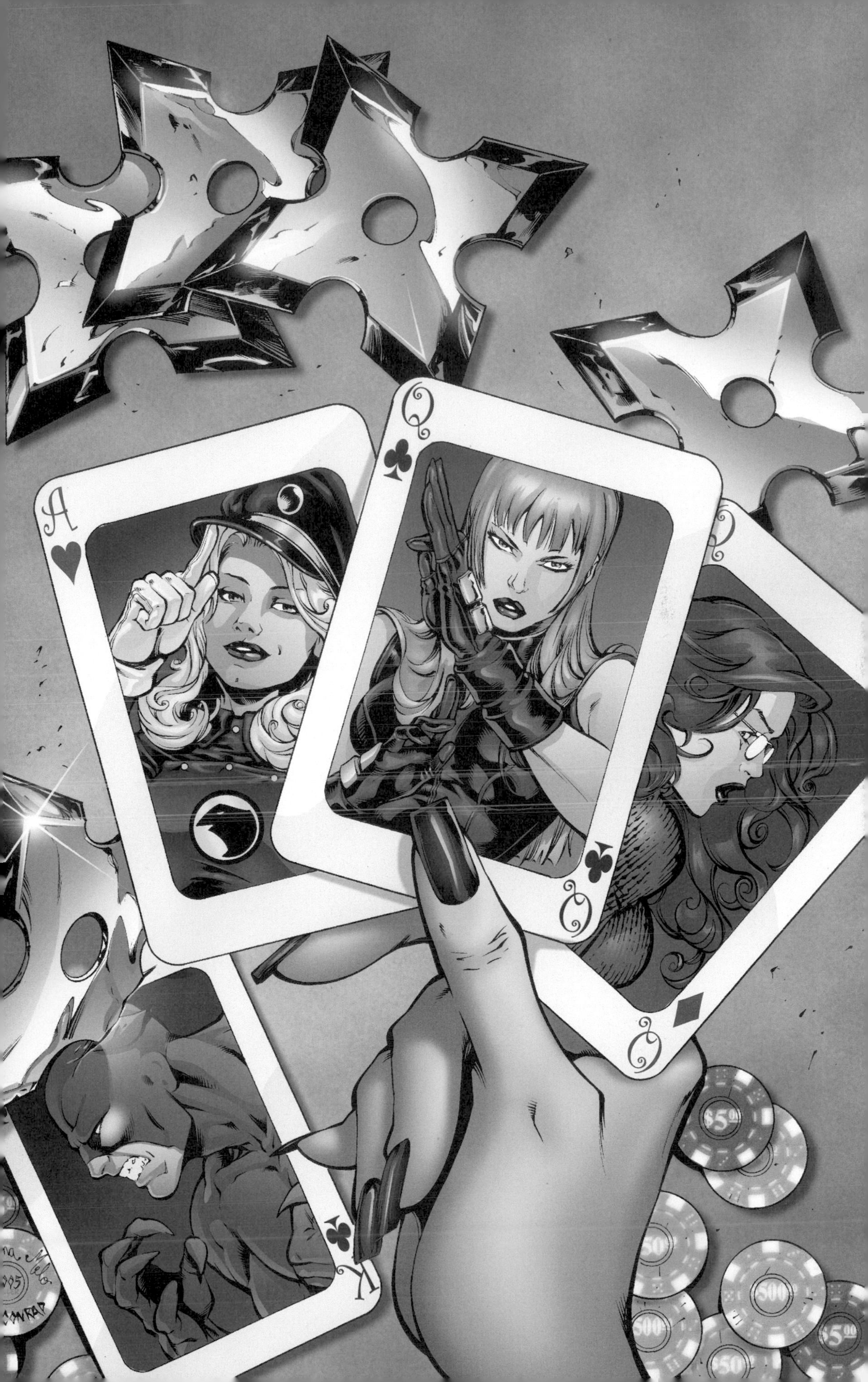

Cover art by
ADRIANA MELO
and WILL CONRAD

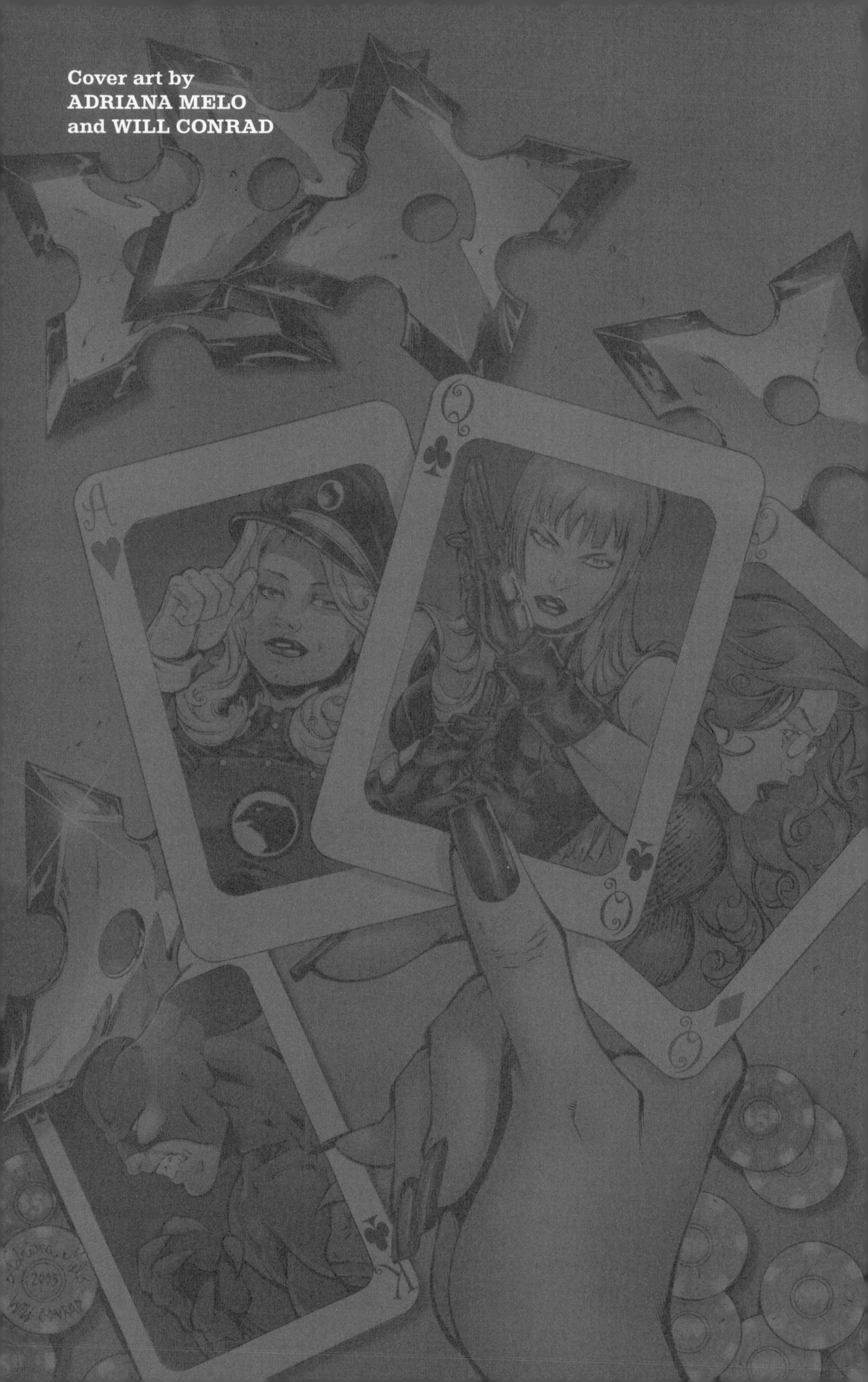

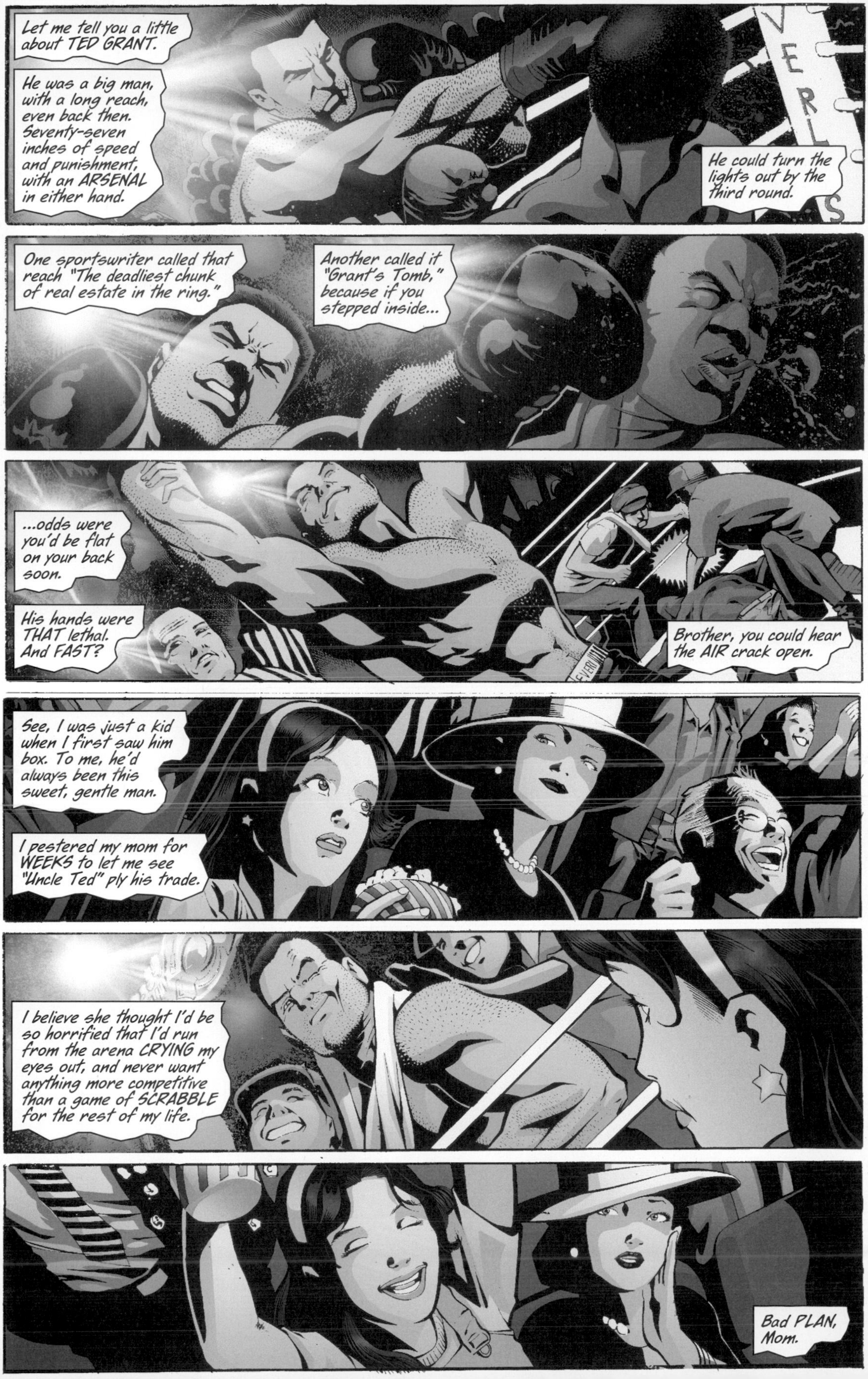

Let me tell you a little about TED GRANT.
He was a big man, with a long reach, even back then. Seventy-seven inches of speed and punishment, with an ARSENAL in either hand.
He could turn the lights out by the third round.
One sportswriter called that reach "The deadliest chunk of real estate in the ring."
Another called it "Grant's Tomb," because if you stepped inside...
...odds were you'd be flat on your back soon.
His hands were THAT lethal. And FAST?
Brother, you could hear the AIR crack open.
See, I was just a kid when I first saw him box. To me, he'd always been this sweet, gentle man.
I pestered my mom for WEEKS to let me see "Uncle Ted" ply his trade.
I believe she thought I'd be so horrified that I'd run from the arena CRYING my eyes out, and never want anything more competitive than a game of SCRABBLE for the rest of my life.
Bad PLAN, Mom.

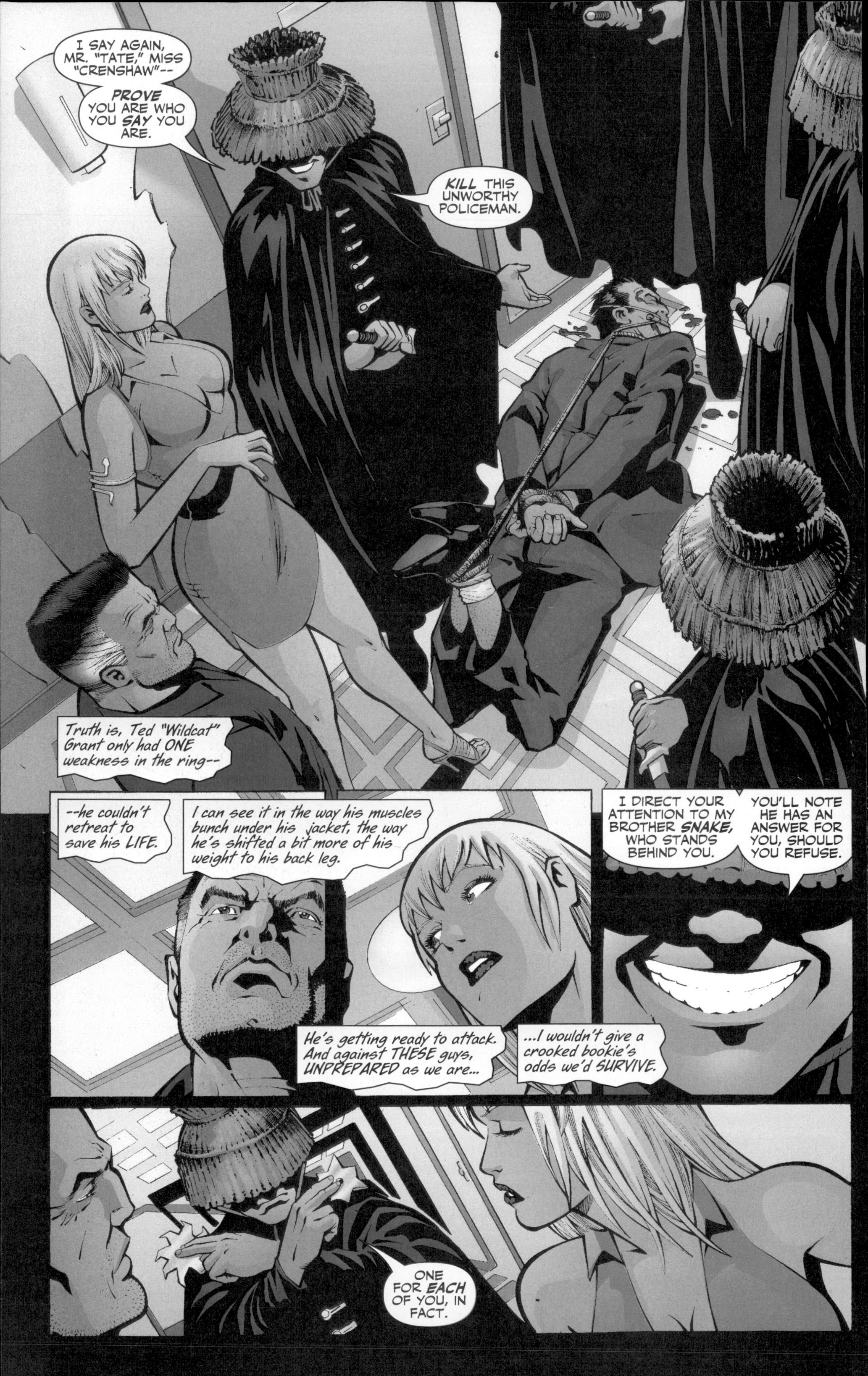
I SAY AGAIN, MR. "TATE," MISS "CRENSHAW"--
PROVE YOU ARE WHO YOU SAY YOU ARE.
KILL THIS UNWORTHY POLICEMAN.
Truth is, Ted "Wildcat" Grant only had ONE weakness in the ring--
--he couldn't retreat to save his LIFE.
I can see it in the way his muscles bunch under his jacket, the way he's shifted a bit more of his weight to his back leg.
He's getting ready to attack. And against THESE guys, UNPREPARED as we are...
...I wouldn't give a crooked bookie's odds we'd SURVIVE.
I DIRECT YOUR ATTENTION TO MY BROTHER SNAKE, WHO STANDS BEHIND YOU.
YOU'LL NOTE HE HAS AN ANSWER FOR YOU, SHOULD YOU REFUSE.
ONE FOR EACH OF YOU, IN FACT.

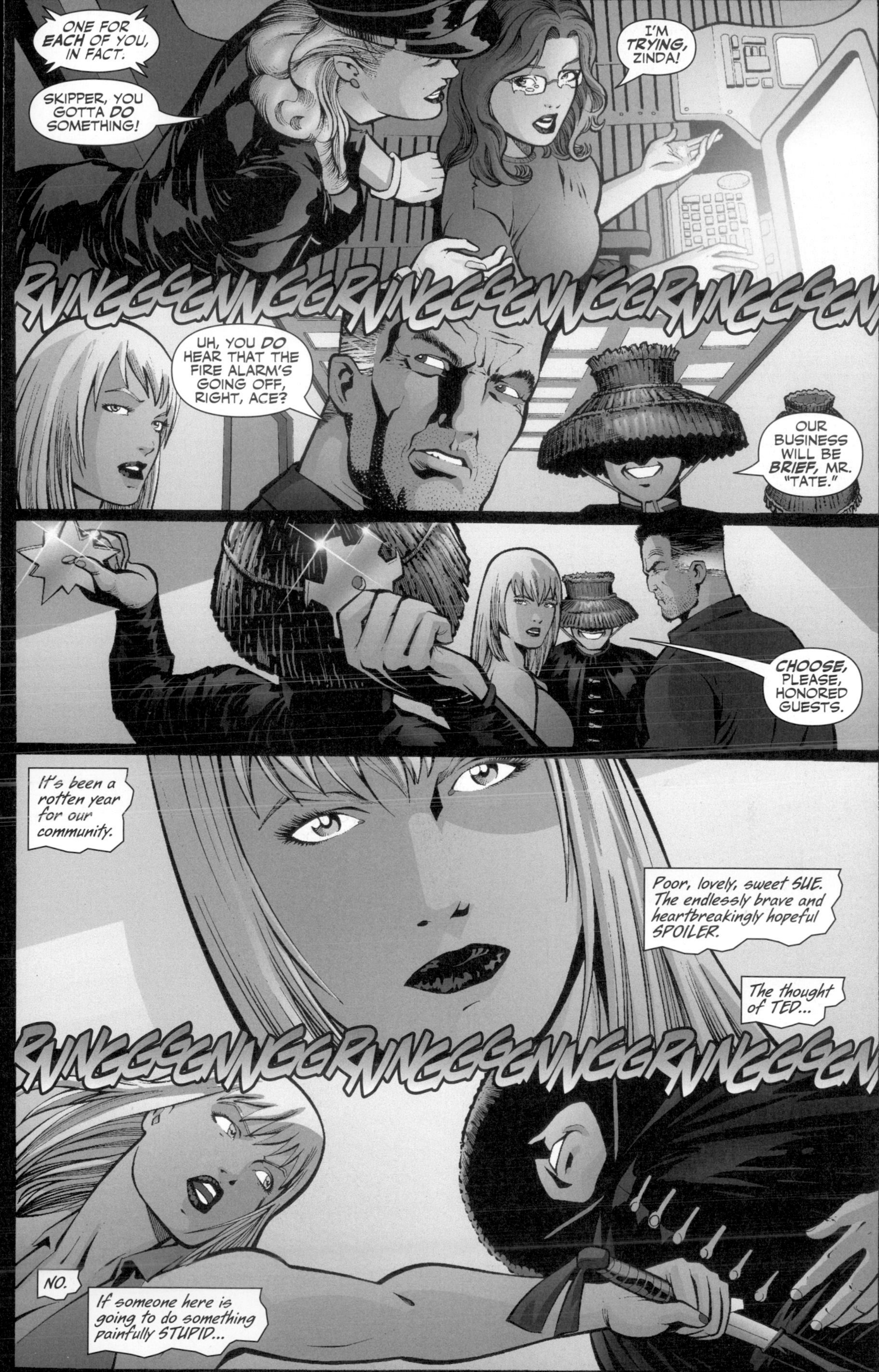
ONE FOR EACH OF YOU, IN FACT.
SKIPPER, YOU GOTTA DO SOMETHING!
I'M TRYING, ZINDA!
RNNGGGNNGGRNNGGGNNGGRNNGGG
UH, YOU DO HEAR THAT THE FIRE ALARM'S GOING OFF, RIGHT, ACE?
OUR BUSINESS WILL BE BRIEF, MR. "TATE."
CHOOSE, PLEASE, HONORED GUESTS.
It's been a rotten year for our community.
Poor, lovely, sweet SUE. The endlessly brave and heartbreakingly hopeful SPOILER.
The thought of TED...
RNNGGGNNGGRNNGGGNNGGRNNGGG
NO.
If someone here is going to do something painfully STUPID...

RVNGGGENNGGRVNGGGENNGGRVNGGGENN

...it sure as HELL is gonna be ME.

KRACK

THE BATTLE WITHIN: PART TWO
THE LONG COUNT

GAIL SIMONE
writer

JOE BENNETT
penciller

JACK JADSON
inker

HI-FI DESIGN colorist   JARED K. FLETCHER letterer

RACHEL GLUCKSTERN asst. editor   JOAN HILTY editor

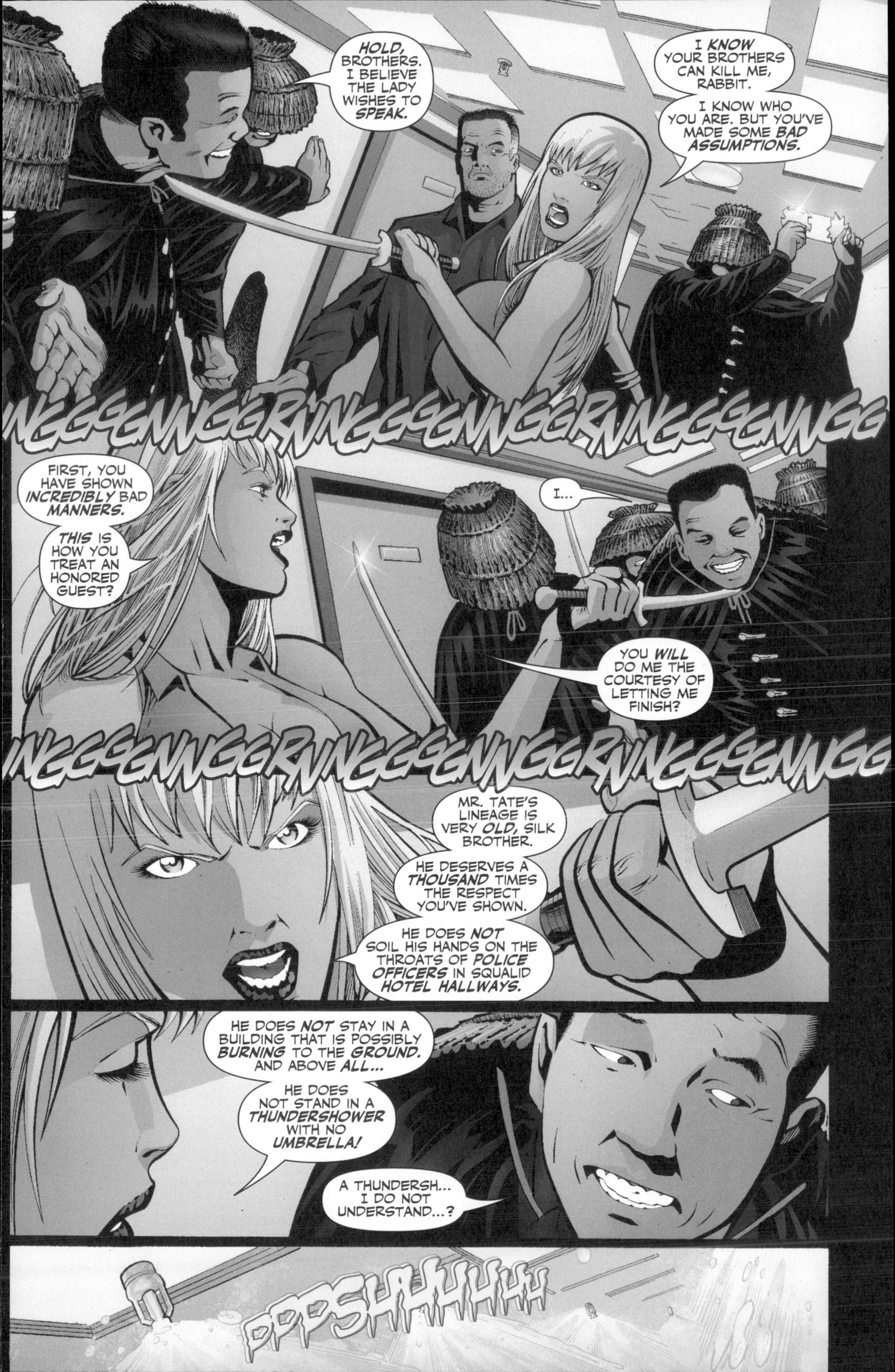
HOLD, BROTHERS. I BELIEVE THE LADY WISHES TO SPEAK.
I KNOW YOUR BROTHERS CAN KILL ME, RABBIT.
I KNOW WHO YOU ARE. BUT YOU'VE MADE SOME BAD ASSUMPTIONS.
NGGGGNNGGRNNGGGGNNGGRNNGGGGNNGG
FIRST, YOU HAVE SHOWN INCREDIBLY BAD MANNERS.
THIS IS HOW YOU TREAT AN HONORED GUEST?
I...
YOU WILL DO ME THE COURTESY OF LETTING ME FINISH?
NGGGGNNGGRNNGGGGNNGGRNNGGGGNNGG
MR. TATE'S LINEAGE IS VERY OLD, SILK BROTHER.
HE DESERVES A THOUSAND TIMES THE RESPECT YOU'VE SHOWN.
HE DOES NOT SOIL HIS HANDS ON THE THROATS OF POLICE OFFICERS IN SQUALID HOTEL HALLWAYS.
HE DOES NOT STAY IN A BUILDING THAT IS POSSIBLY BURNING TO THE GROUND. AND ABOVE ALL...
HE DOES NOT STAND IN A THUNDERSHOWER WITH NO UMBRELLA!
A THUNDERSH... I DO NOT UNDERSTAND...?
DDDSHHHHHH

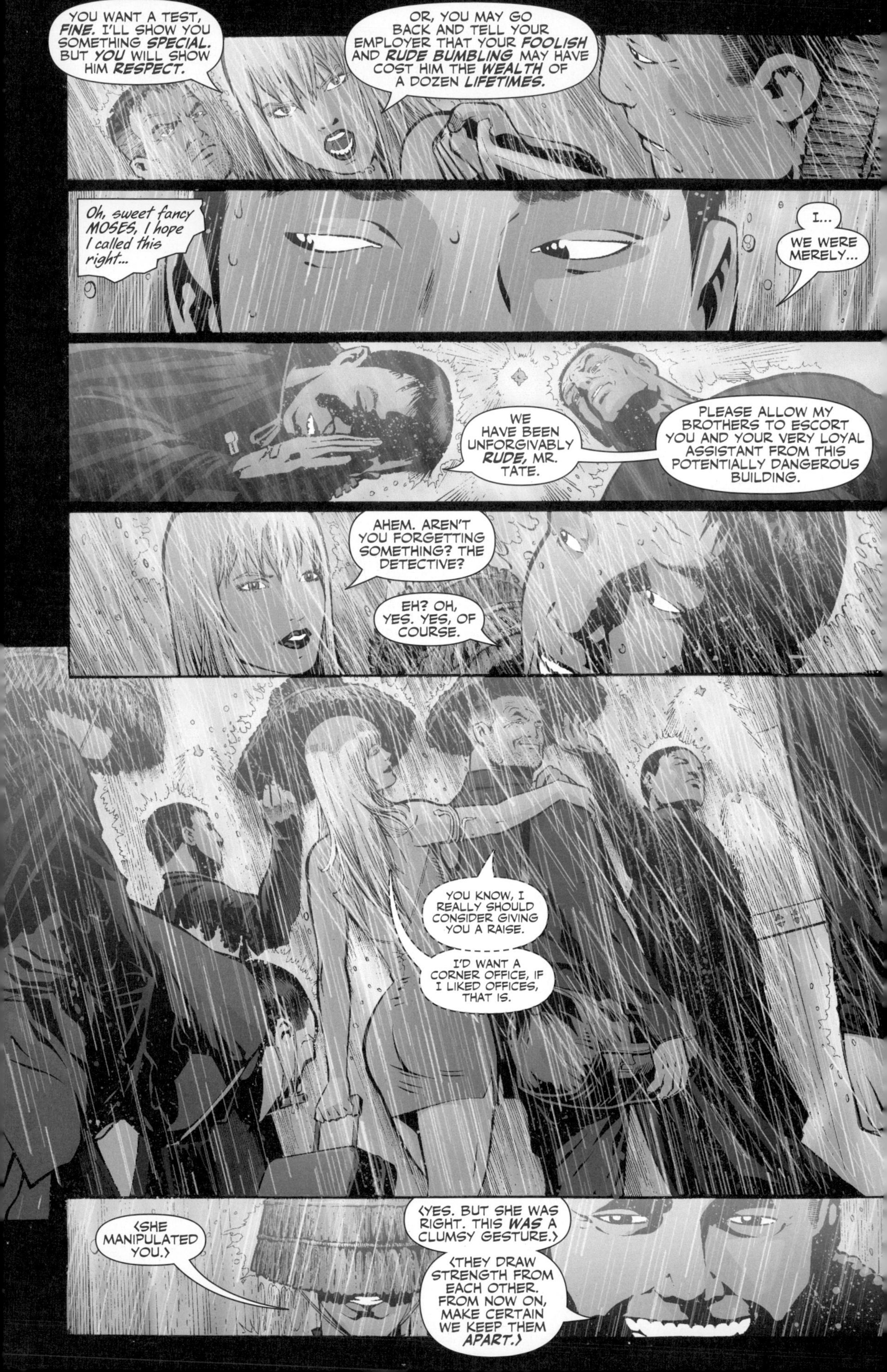
YOU WANT A TEST, FINE. I'LL SHOW YOU SOMETHING SPECIAL. BUT YOU WILL SHOW HIM RESPECT.
OR, YOU MAY GO BACK AND TELL YOUR EMPLOYER THAT YOUR FOOLISH AND RUDE BUMBLING MAY HAVE COST HIM THE WEALTH OF A DOZEN LIFETIMES.
Oh, sweet fancy MOSES, I hope I called this right...
I...
WE WERE MERELY...
WE HAVE BEEN UNFORGIVABLY RUDE, MR. TATE.
PLEASE ALLOW MY BROTHERS TO ESCORT YOU AND YOUR VERY LOYAL ASSISTANT FROM THIS POTENTIALLY DANGEROUS BUILDING.
AHEM. AREN'T YOU FORGETTING SOMETHING? THE DETECTIVE?
EH? OH, YES. YES, OF COURSE.
YOU KNOW, I REALLY SHOULD CONSIDER GIVING YOU A RAISE.
I'D WANT A CORNER OFFICE, IF I LIKED OFFICES, THAT IS.
<SHE MANIPULATED YOU.>
<YES. BUT SHE WAS RIGHT. THIS WAS A CLUMSY GESTURE.>
<THEY DRAW STRENGTH FROM EACH OTHER. FROM NOW ON, MAKE CERTAIN WE KEEP THEM APART.>

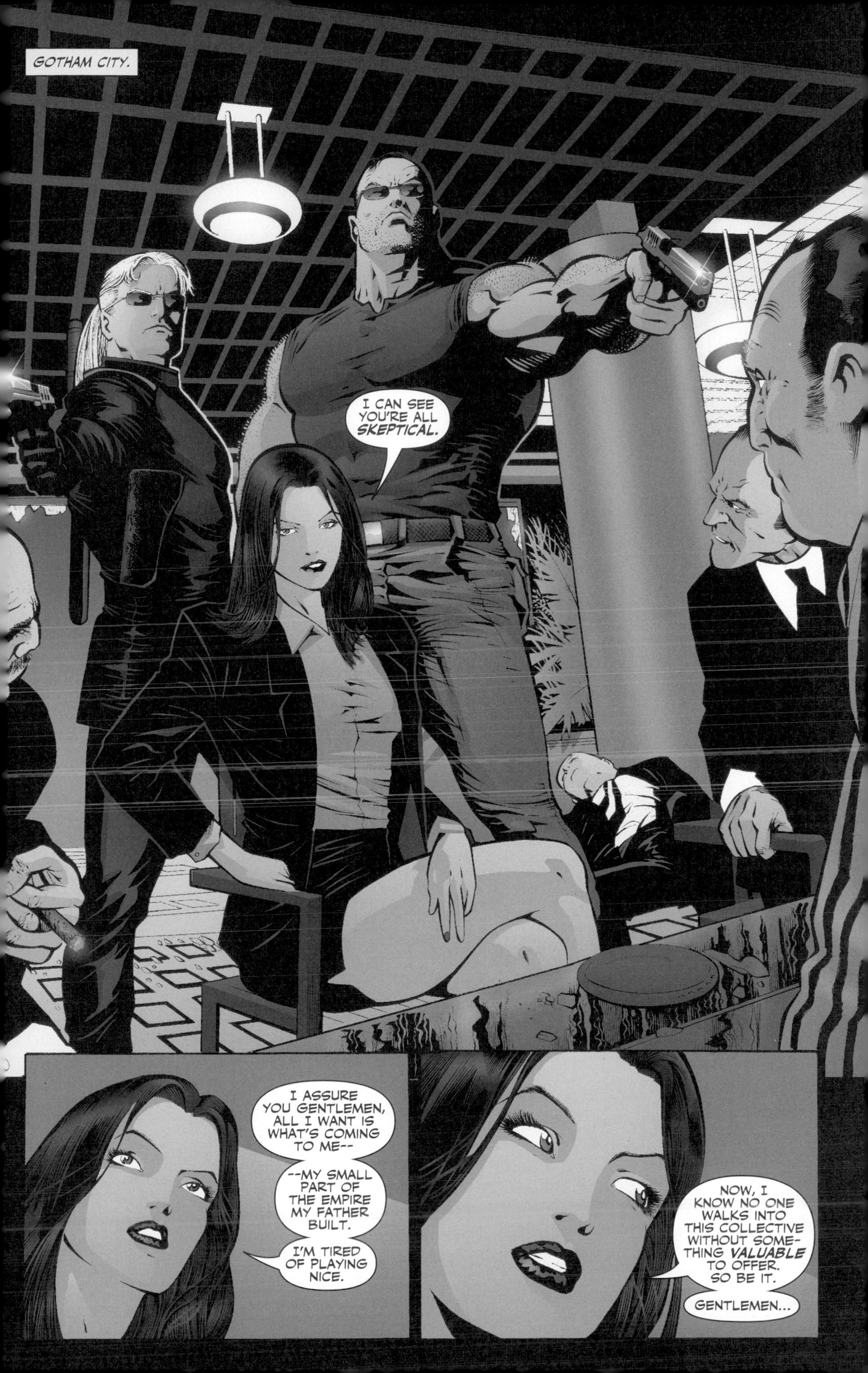
GOTHAM CITY.
I CAN SEE YOU'RE ALL SKEPTICAL.
I ASSURE YOU GENTLEMEN, ALL I WANT IS WHAT'S COMING TO ME--
--MY SMALL PART OF THE EMPIRE MY FATHER BUILT.
I'M TIRED OF PLAYING NICE.
NOW, I KNOW NO ONE WALKS INTO THIS COLLECTIVE WITHOUT SOME-THING VALUABLE TO OFFER. SO BE IT.
GENTLEMEN...

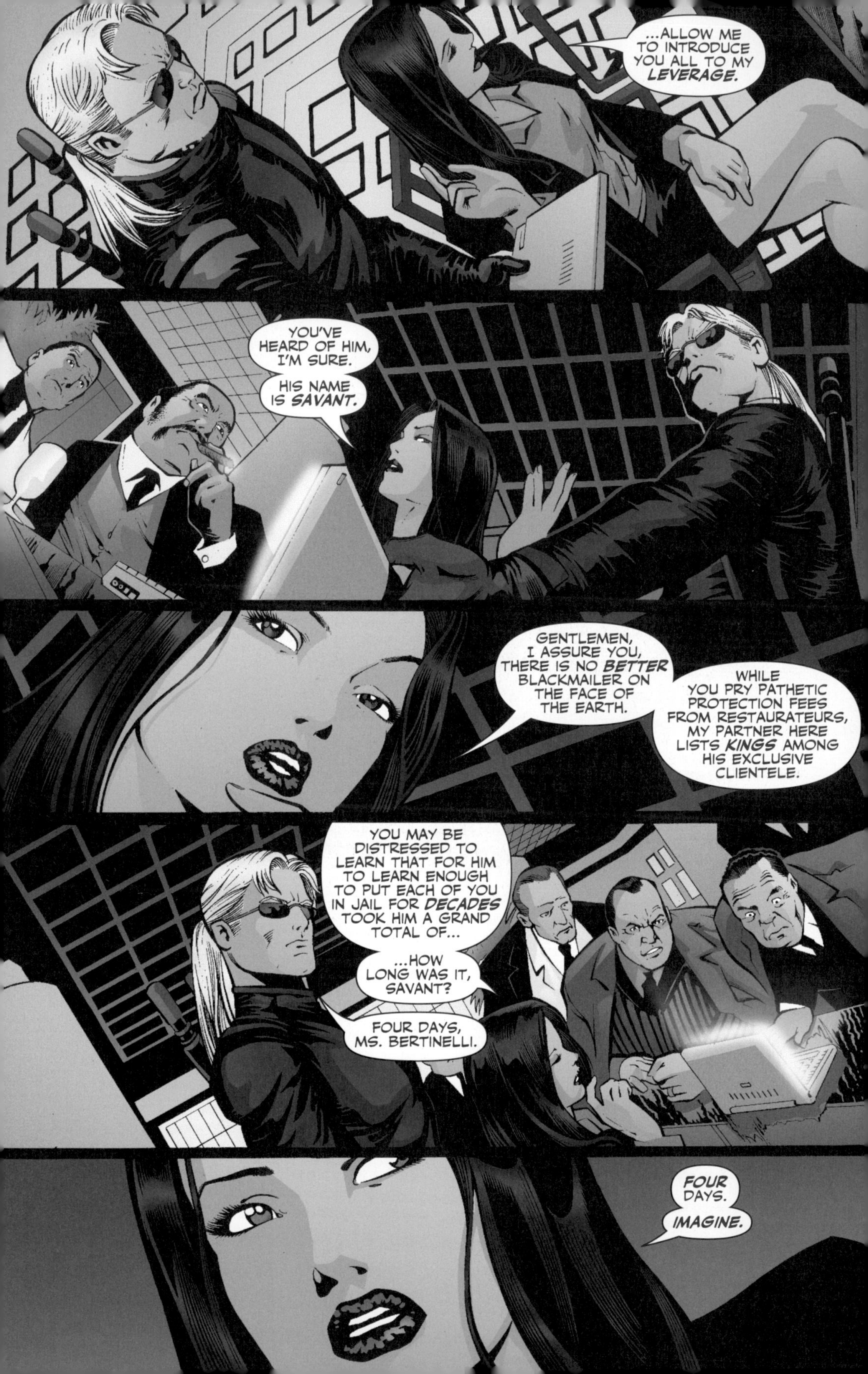
...ALLOW ME TO INTRODUCE YOU ALL TO MY *LEVERAGE.*
YOU'VE HEARD OF HIM, I'M SURE.
HIS NAME IS *SAVANT.*
GENTLEMEN, I ASSURE YOU, THERE IS NO *BETTER* BLACKMAILER ON THE FACE OF THE EARTH.
WHILE YOU PRY PATHETIC PROTECTION FEES FROM RESTAURATEURS, MY PARTNER HERE LISTS *KINGS* AMONG HIS EXCLUSIVE CLIENTELE.
YOU MAY BE DISTRESSED TO LEARN THAT FOR HIM TO LEARN ENOUGH TO PUT EACH OF YOU IN JAIL FOR *DECADES* TOOK HIM A GRAND TOTAL OF...
...HOW LONG WAS IT, SAVANT?
FOUR DAYS, MS. BERTINELLI.
FOUR DAYS.
IMAGINE.

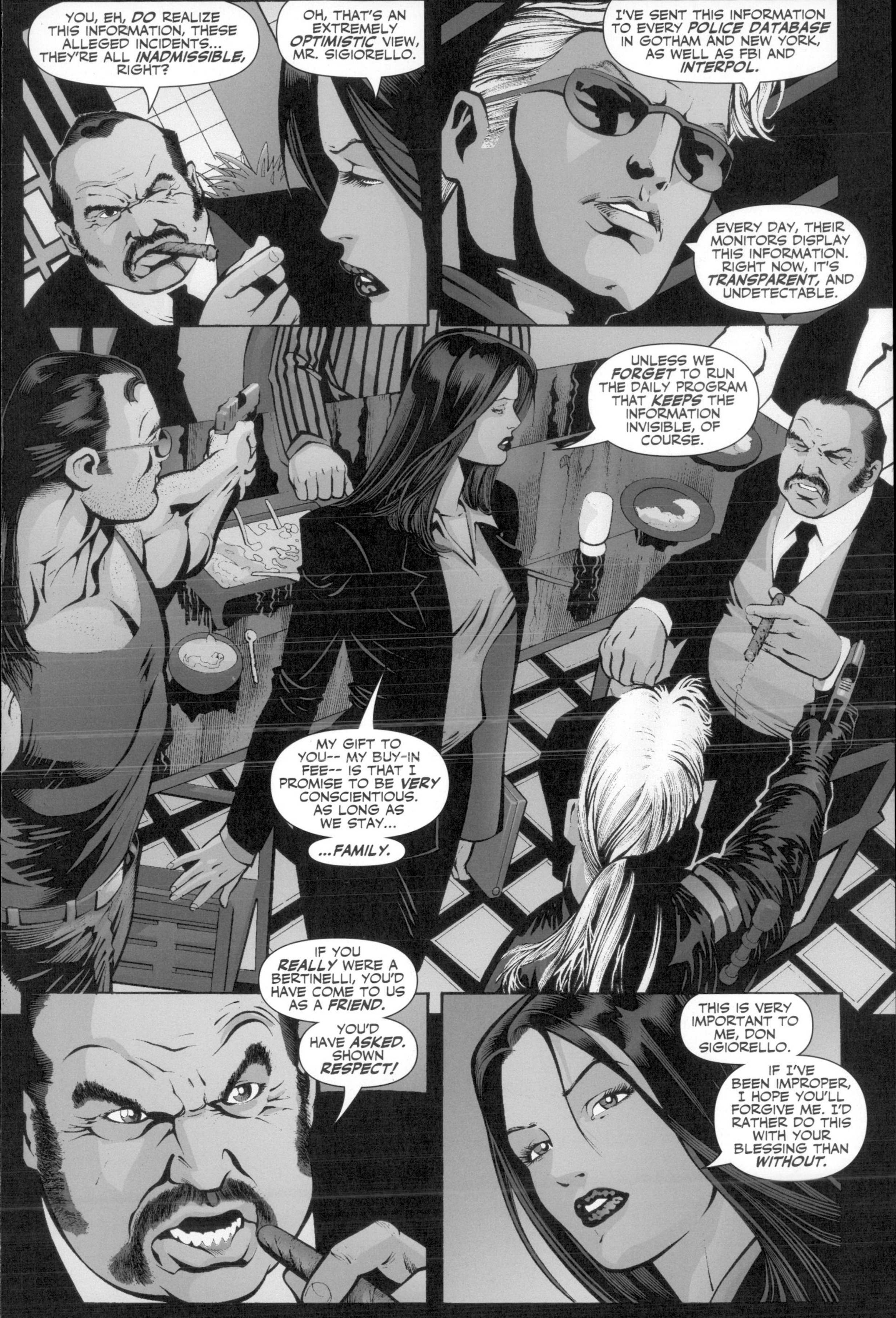
YOU, EH, DO REALIZE THIS INFORMATION, THESE ALLEGED INCIDENTS... THEY'RE ALL INADMISSIBLE, RIGHT?
OH, THAT'S AN EXTREMELY OPTIMISTIC VIEW, MR. SIGIORELLO.
I'VE SENT THIS INFORMATION TO EVERY POLICE DATABASE IN GOTHAM AND NEW YORK, AS WELL AS FBI AND INTERPOL.
EVERY DAY, THEIR MONITORS DISPLAY THIS INFORMATION. RIGHT NOW, IT'S TRANSPARENT, AND UNDETECTABLE.
UNLESS WE FORGET TO RUN THE DAILY PROGRAM THAT KEEPS THE INFORMATION INVISIBLE, OF COURSE.
MY GIFT TO YOU-- MY BUY-IN FEE-- IS THAT I PROMISE TO BE VERY CONSCIENTIOUS. AS LONG AS WE STAY...
...FAMILY.
IF YOU REALLY WERE A BERTINELLI, YOU'D HAVE COME TO US AS A FRIEND.
YOU'D HAVE ASKED. SHOWN RESPECT!
THIS IS VERY IMPORTANT TO ME, DON SIGIORELLO.
IF I'VE BEEN IMPROPER, I HOPE YOU'LL FORGIVE ME. I'D RATHER DO THIS WITH YOUR BLESSING THAN WITHOUT.

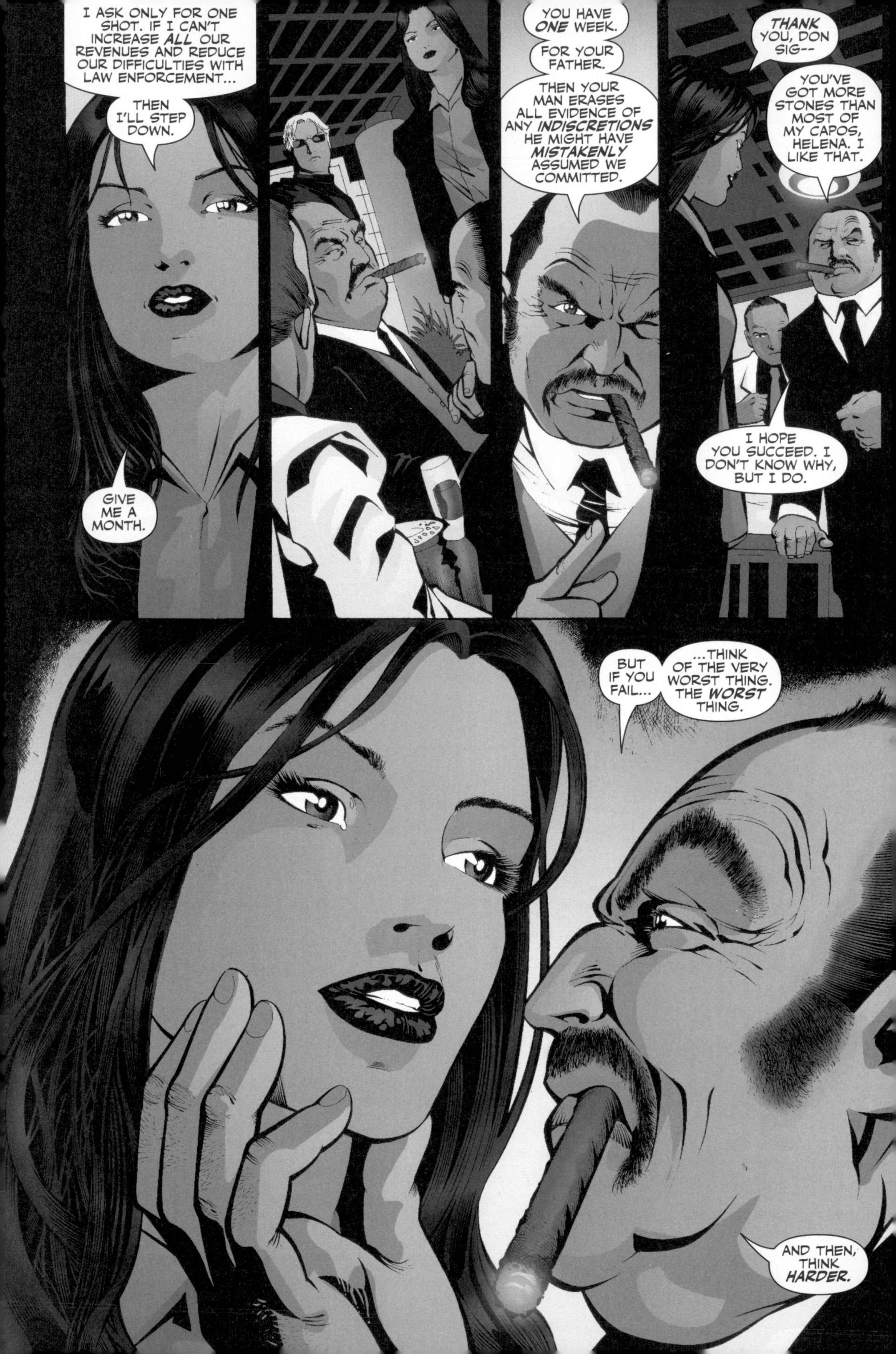
I ASK ONLY FOR ONE SHOT. IF I CAN'T INCREASE ALL OUR REVENUES AND REDUCE OUR DIFFICULTIES WITH LAW ENFORCEMENT...
THEN I'LL STEP DOWN.
GIVE ME A MONTH.
YOU HAVE ONE WEEK.
FOR YOUR FATHER.
THEN YOUR MAN ERASES ALL EVIDENCE OF ANY INDISCRETIONS HE MIGHT HAVE MISTAKENLY ASSUMED WE COMMITTED.
THANK YOU, DON SIG--
YOU'VE GOT MORE STONES THAN MOST OF MY CAPOS, HELENA. I LIKE THAT.
I HOPE YOU SUCCEED. I DON'T KNOW WHY, BUT I DO.
BUT IF YOU FAIL...
...THINK OF THE VERY WORST THING. THE WORST THING.
AND THEN, THINK HARDER.

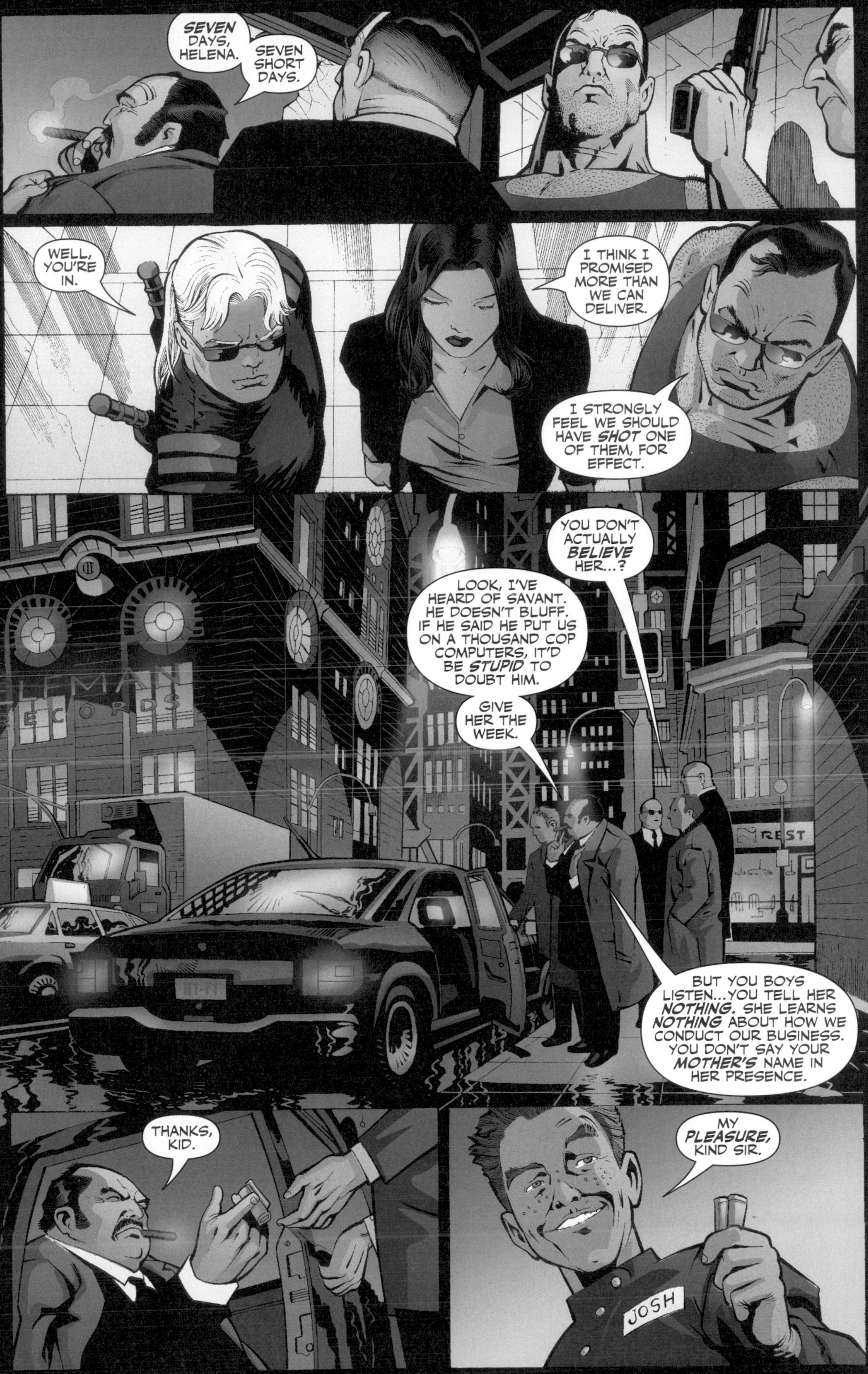
SEVEN DAYS, HELENA.
SEVEN SHORT DAYS.
WELL, YOU'RE IN.
I THINK I PROMISED MORE THAN WE CAN DELIVER.
I STRONGLY FEEL WE SHOULD HAVE SHOT ONE OF THEM, FOR EFFECT.
YOU DON'T ACTUALLY BELIEVE HER...?
LOOK, I'VE HEARD OF SAVANT. HE DOESN'T BLUFF. IF HE SAID HE PUT US ON A THOUSAND COP COMPUTERS, IT'D BE STUPID TO DOUBT HIM.
GIVE HER THE WEEK.
REST
BUT YOU BOYS LISTEN...YOU TELL HER NOTHING. SHE LEARNS NOTHING ABOUT HOW WE CONDUCT OUR BUSINESS. YOU DON'T SAY YOUR MOTHER'S NAME IN HER PRESENCE.
THANKS, KID.
MY PLEASURE, KIND SIR.
JOSH

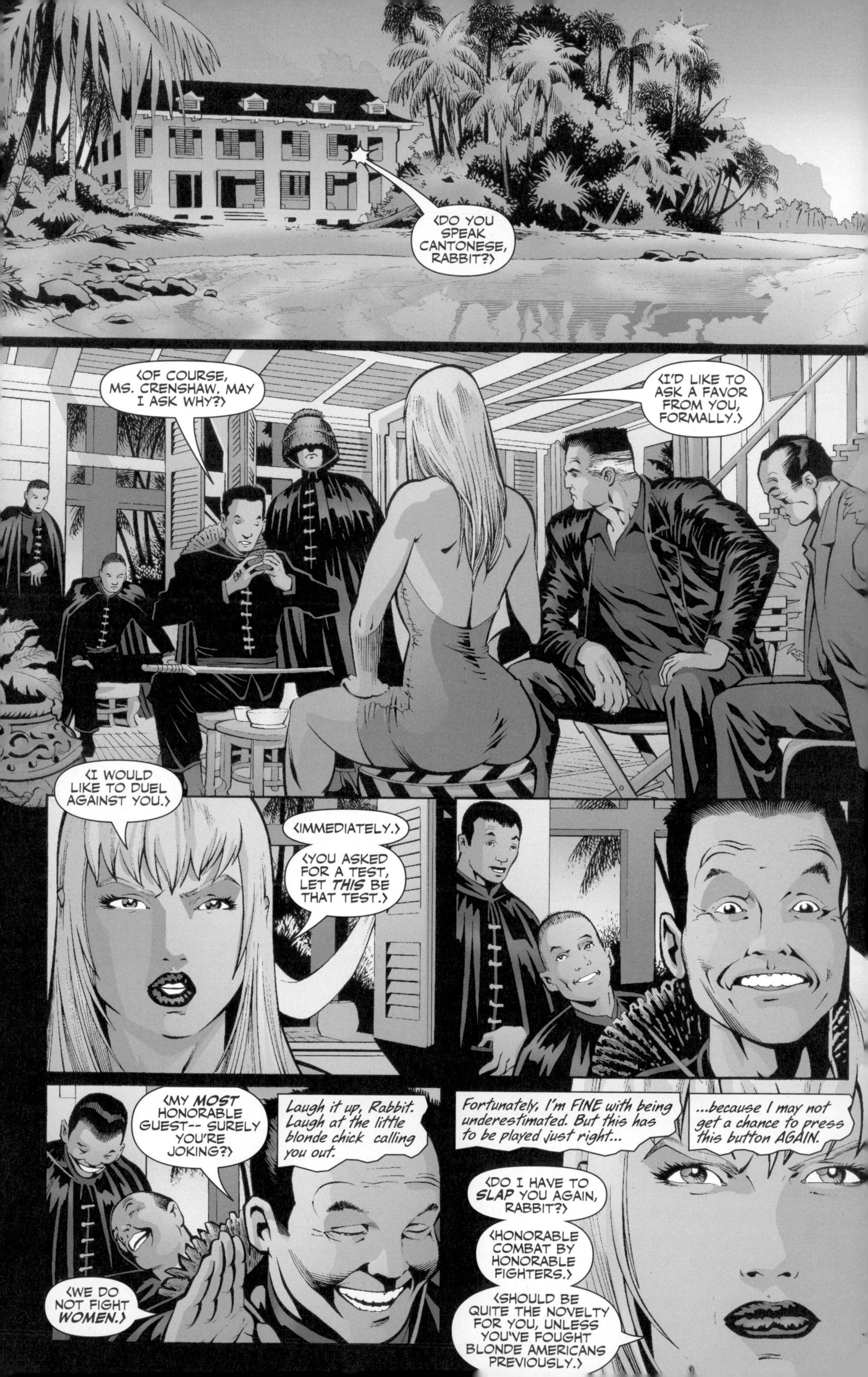

<DO YOU SPEAK CANTONESE, RABBIT?>
<OF COURSE, MS. CRENSHAW. MAY I ASK WHY?>
<I'D LIKE TO ASK A FAVOR FROM YOU, FORMALLY.>
<I WOULD LIKE TO DUEL AGAINST YOU.>
<IMMEDIATELY.>
<YOU ASKED FOR A TEST, LET *THIS* BE THAT TEST.>
<MY *MOST* HONORABLE GUEST-- SURELY YOU'RE JOKING?>
<WE DO NOT FIGHT *WOMEN.*>
Laugh it up, Rabbit. Laugh at the little blonde chick calling you out.
Fortunately, I'm FINE with being underestimated. But this has to be played just right...
...because I may not get a chance to press this button AGAIN.
<DO I HAVE TO *SLAP* YOU AGAIN, RABBIT?>
<HONORABLE COMBAT BY HONORABLE FIGHTERS.>
<SHOULD BE QUITE THE NOVELTY FOR YOU, UNLESS YOU'VE FOUGHT BLONDE AMERICANS PREVIOUSLY.>

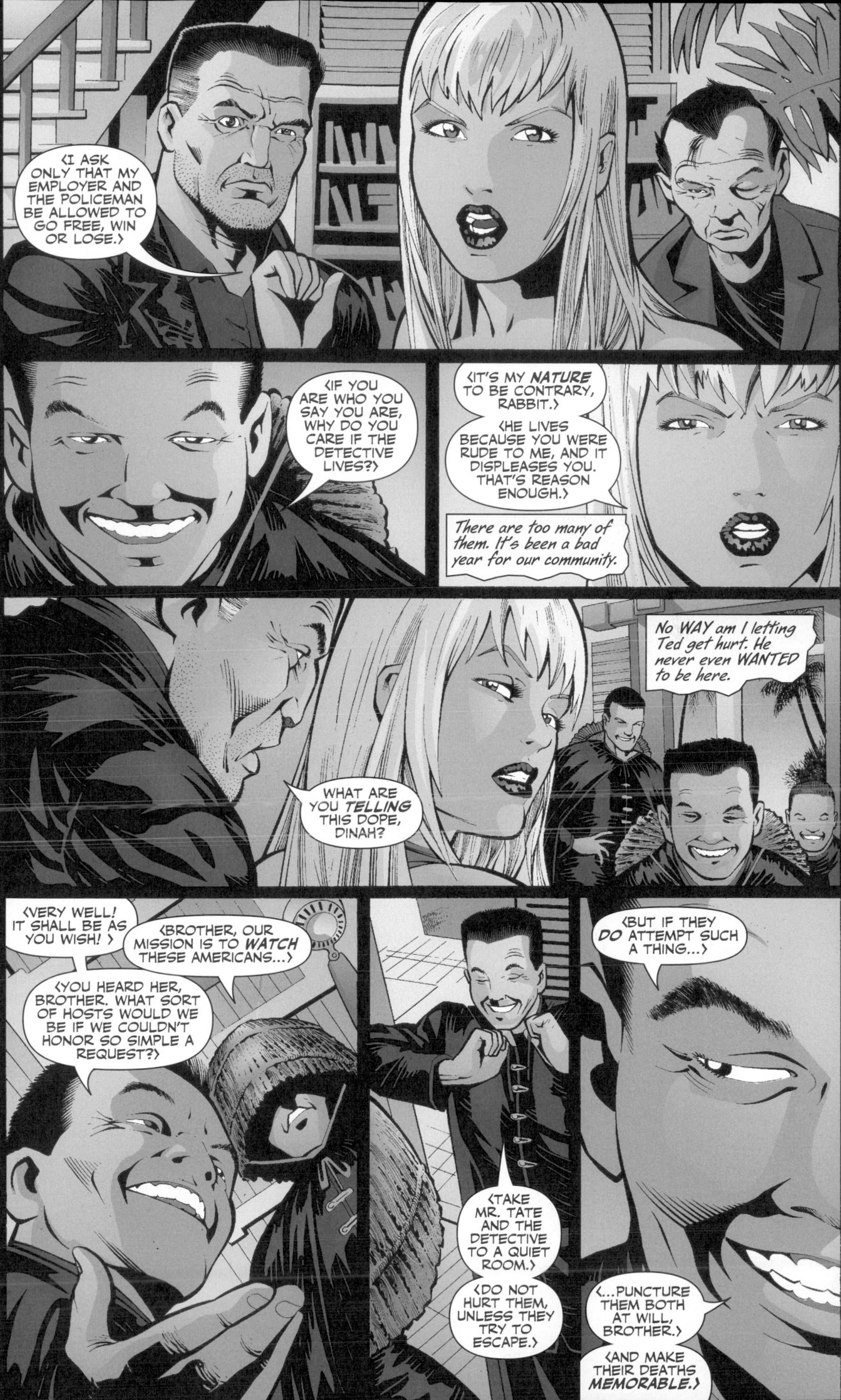

<I ASK ONLY THAT MY EMPLOYER AND THE POLICEMAN BE ALLOWED TO GO FREE, WIN OR LOSE.>
<IF YOU ARE WHO YOU SAY YOU ARE, WHY DO YOU CARE IF THE DETECTIVE LIVES?>
<IT'S MY NATURE TO BE CONTRARY, RABBIT.>
<HE LIVES BECAUSE YOU WERE RUDE TO ME, AND IT DISPLEASES YOU. THAT'S REASON ENOUGH.>
There are too many of them. It's been a bad year for our community.
No WAY am I letting Ted get hurt. He never even WANTED to be here.
WHAT ARE YOU TELLING THIS DOPE, DINAH?
<VERY WELL! IT SHALL BE AS YOU WISH! >
<BROTHER, OUR MISSION IS TO WATCH THESE AMERICANS...>
<YOU HEARD HER, BROTHER. WHAT SORT OF HOSTS WOULD WE BE IF WE COULDN'T HONOR SO SIMPLE A REQUEST?>
<TAKE MR. TATE AND THE DETECTIVE TO A QUIET ROOM.>
<DO NOT HURT THEM, UNLESS THEY TRY TO ESCAPE.>
<BUT IF THEY DO ATTEMPT SUCH A THING...>
<...PUNCTURE THEM BOTH AT WILL, BROTHER.>
<AND MAKE THEIR DEATHS MEMORABLE.>

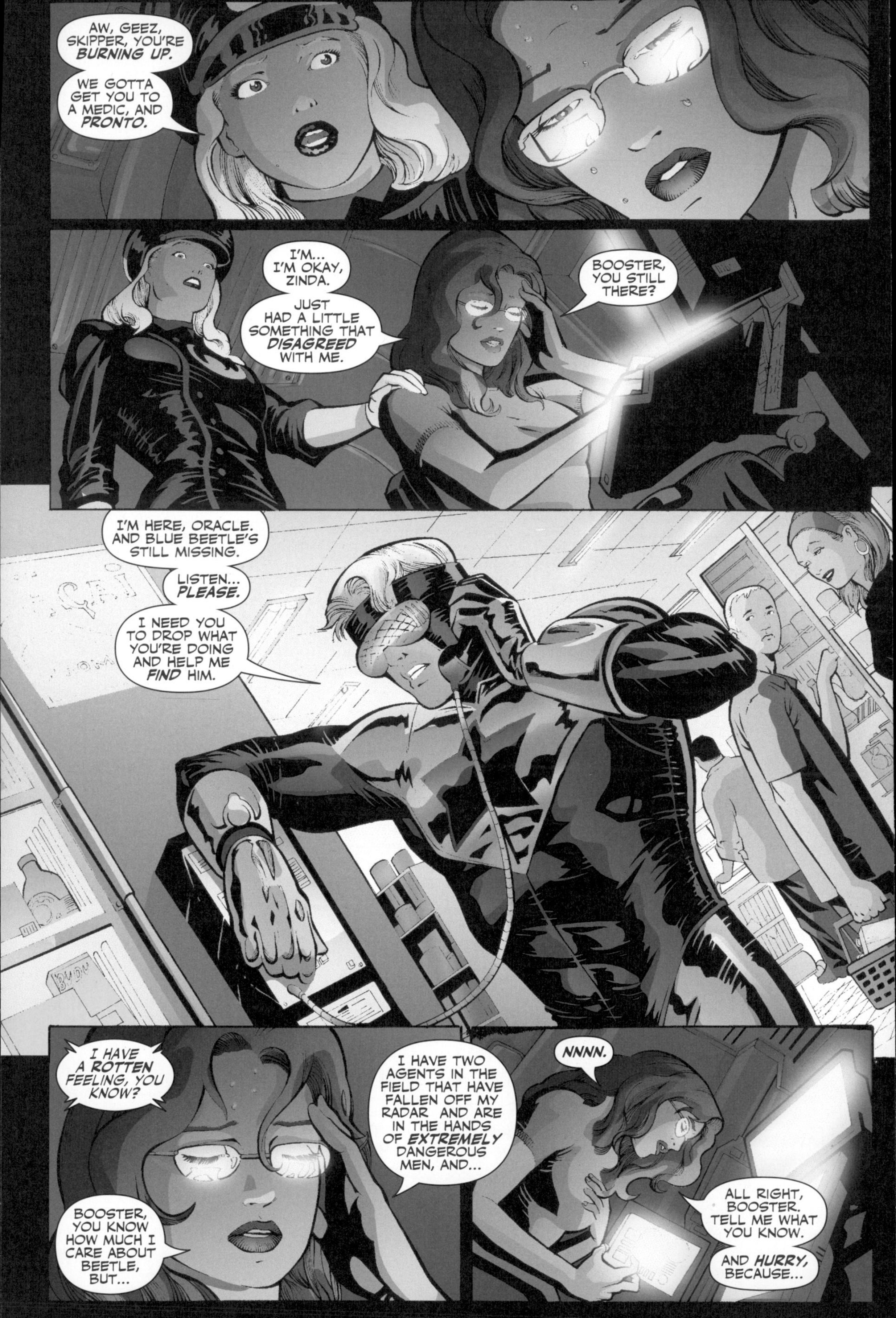
AW, GEEZ, SKIPPER, YOU'RE *BURNING UP.*
WE GOTTA GET YOU TO A MEDIC, AND *PRONTO.*
I'M... I'M OKAY, ZINDA.
JUST HAD A LITTLE SOMETHING THAT *DISAGREED* WITH ME.
BOOSTER, YOU STILL THERE?
I'M HERE, ORACLE. AND BLUE BEETLE'S STILL MISSING.
LISTEN... *PLEASE.*
I NEED YOU TO DROP WHAT YOU'RE DOING AND HELP ME *FIND* HIM.
I HAVE A ROTTEN FEELING, YOU KNOW?
BOOSTER, YOU KNOW HOW MUCH I CARE ABOUT BEETLE, BUT...
I HAVE TWO AGENTS IN THE FIELD THAT HAVE FALLEN OFF MY RADAR AND ARE IN THE HANDS OF *EXTREMELY* DANGEROUS MEN, AND...
NNNN.
ALL RIGHT, BOOSTER. TELL ME WHAT YOU KNOW.
AND *HURRY,* BECAUSE...

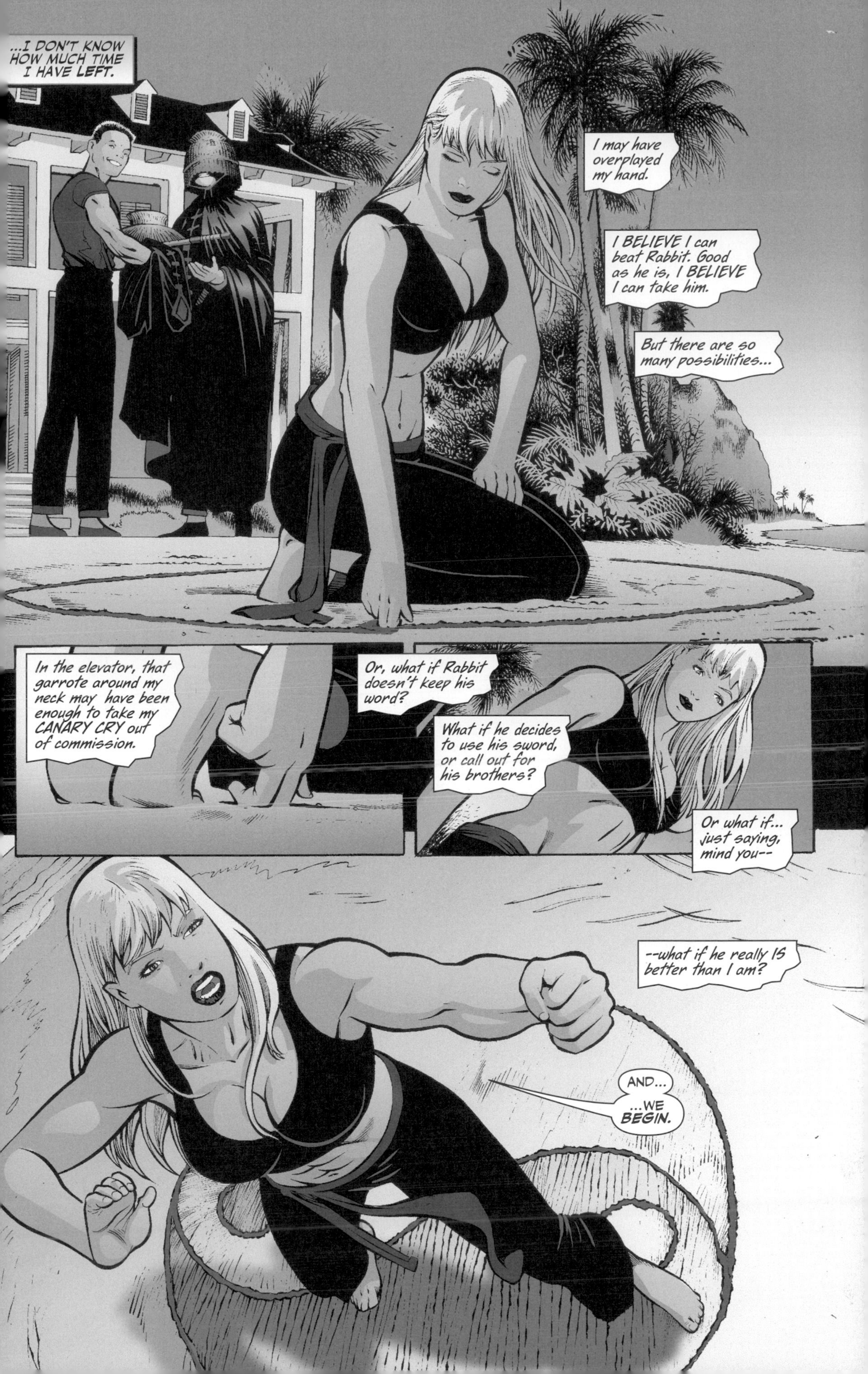
...I DON'T KNOW HOW MUCH TIME I HAVE LEFT.
I may have overplayed my hand.
I BELIEVE I can beat Rabbit. Good as he is, I BELIEVE I can take him.
But there are so many possibilities...
In the elevator, that garrote around my neck may have been enough to take my CANARY CRY out of commission.
Or, what if Rabbit doesn't keep his word?
What if he decides to use his sword, or call out for his brothers?
Or what if... just saying, mind you--
--what if he really IS better than I am?
AND...
...WE BEGIN.

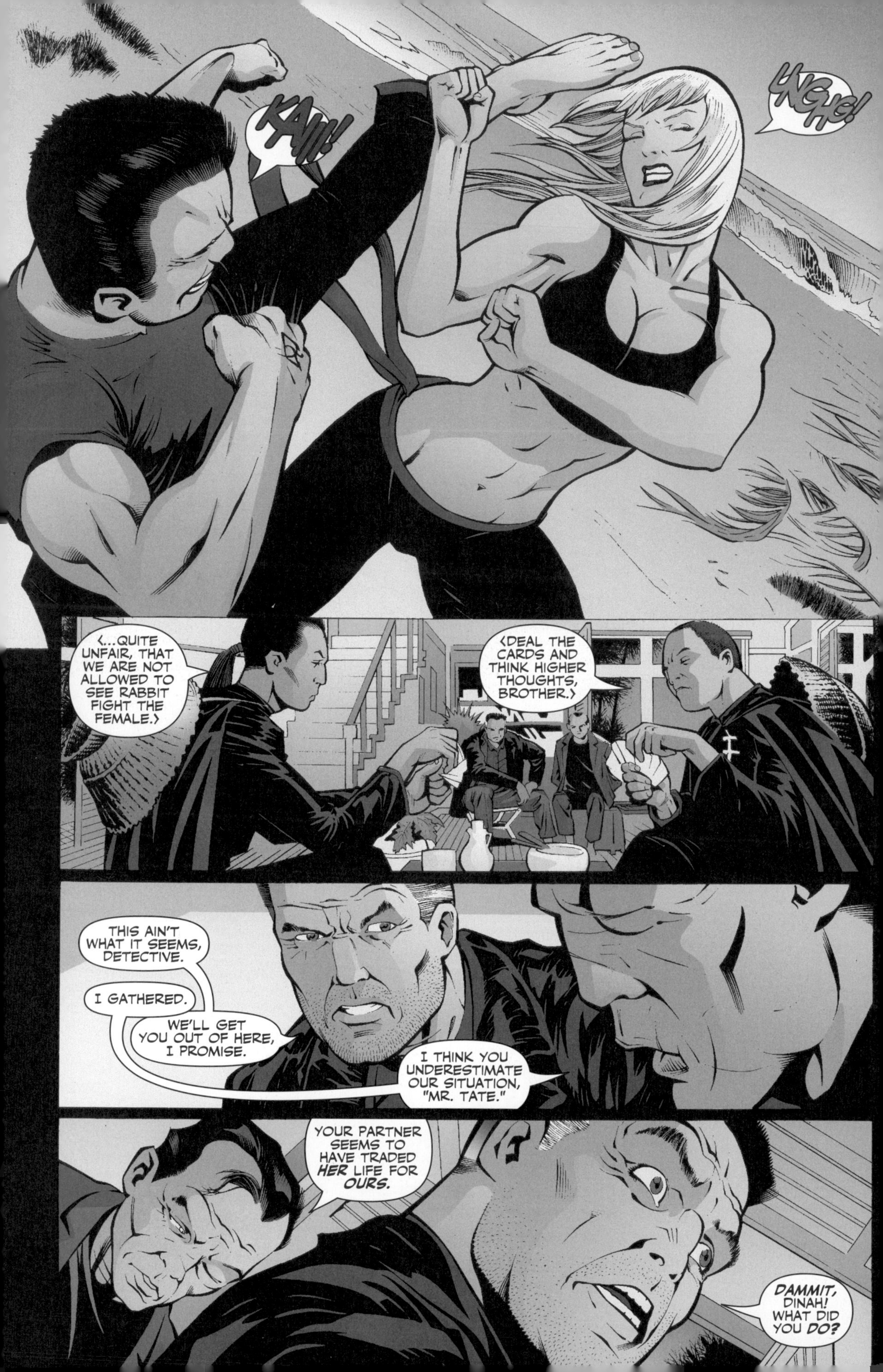

KAIII!
UNGHH!
<...QUITE UNFAIR, THAT WE ARE NOT ALLOWED TO SEE RABBIT FIGHT THE FEMALE.>
<DEAL THE CARDS AND THINK HIGHER THOUGHTS, BROTHER.>
THIS AIN'T WHAT IT SEEMS, DETECTIVE.
I GATHERED.
WE'LL GET YOU OUT OF HERE, I PROMISE.
I THINK YOU UNDERESTIMATE OUR SITUATION, "MR. TATE."
YOUR PARTNER SEEMS TO HAVE TRADED *HER* LIFE FOR *OURS.*
DAMMIT, DINAH! WHAT DID YOU *DO?*

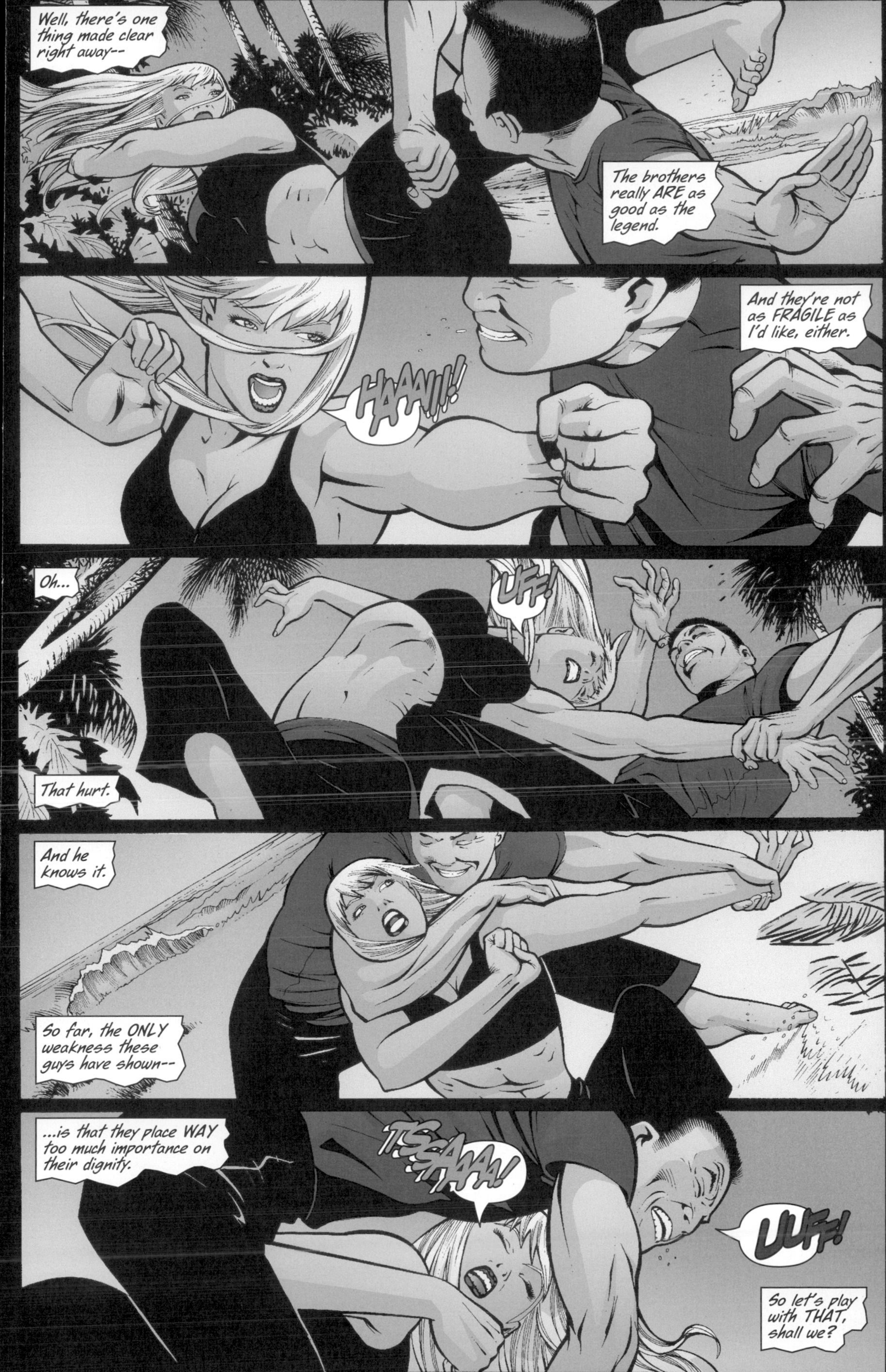
Well, there's one thing made clear right away--
The brothers really ARE as good as the legend.
And they're not as FRAGILE as I'd like, either.
HAAAII!!
Oh...
UFF!
That hurt.
And he knows it.
So far, the ONLY weakness these guys have shown--
...is that they place WAY too much importance on their dignity.
TSSAAAA!
UUFF!
So let's play with THAT, shall we?

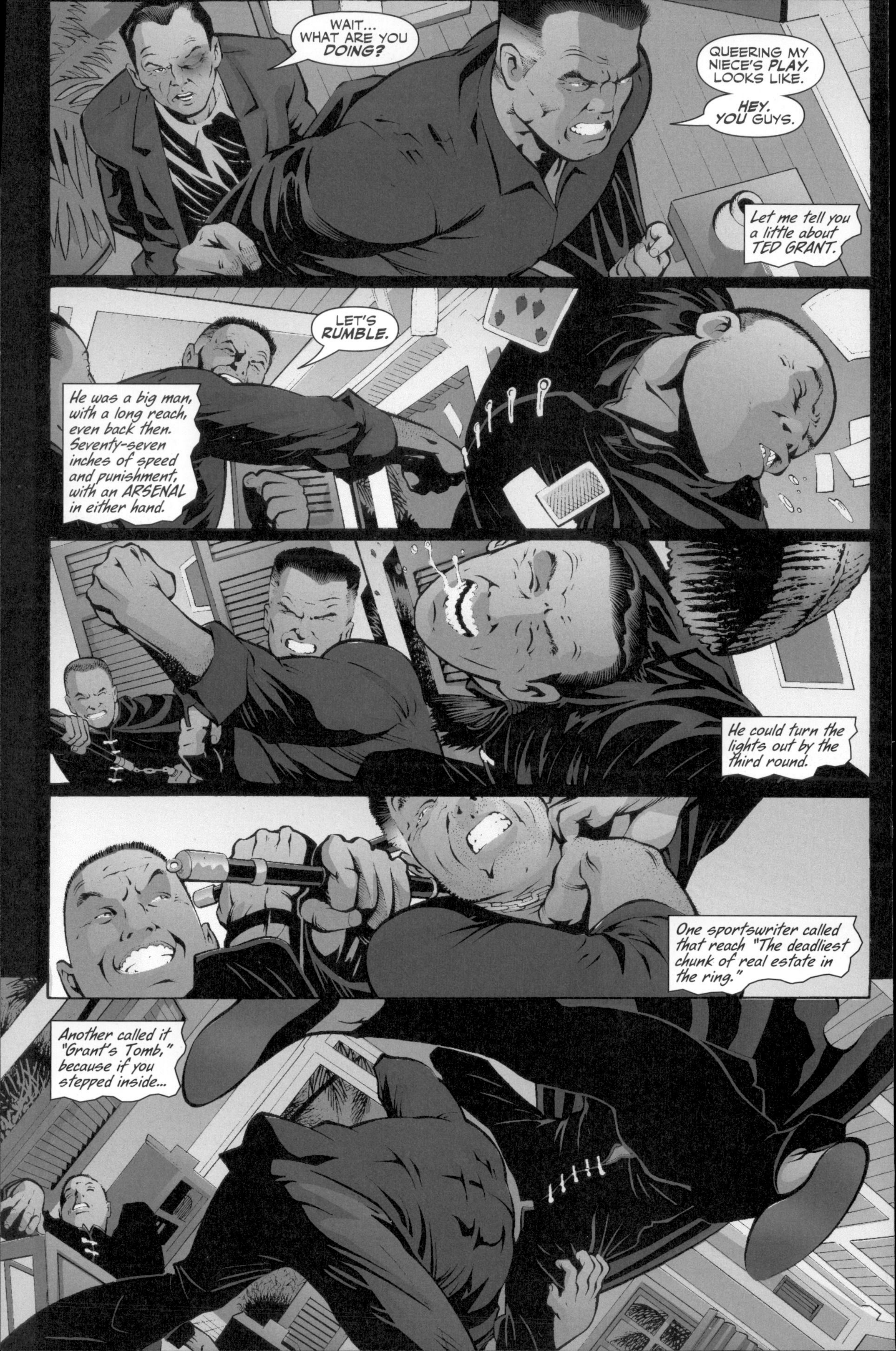
WAIT... WHAT ARE YOU DOING?
QUEERING MY NIECE'S PLAY, LOOKS LIKE.
HEY. YOU GUYS.
Let me tell you a little about TED GRANT.
LET'S RUMBLE.
He was a big man, with a long reach, even back then. Seventy-seven inches of speed and punishment, with an ARSENAL in either hand.
He could turn the lights out by the third round.
One sportswriter called that reach "The deadliest chunk of real estate in the ring."
Another called it "Grant's Tomb," because if you stepped inside...

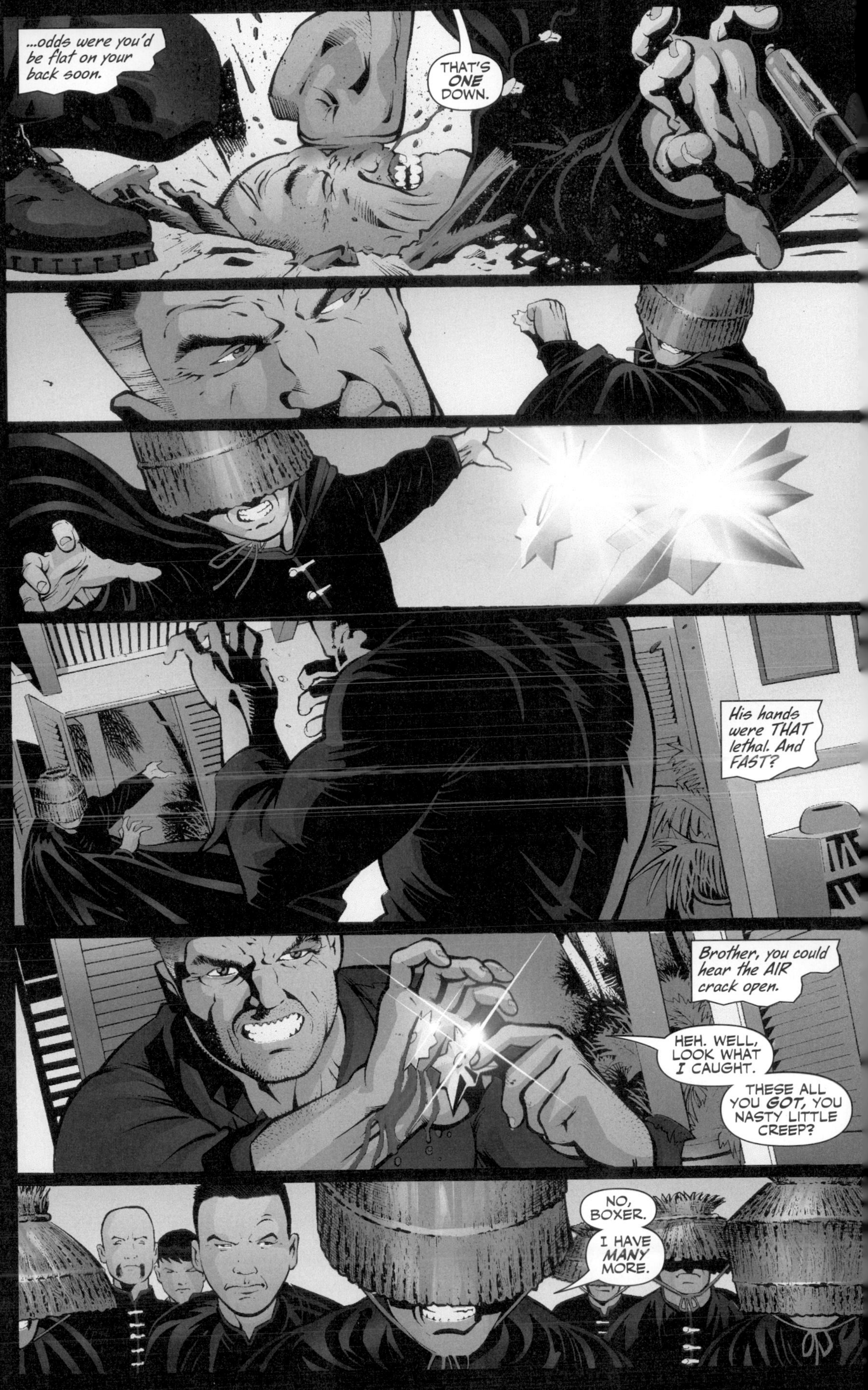
...odds were you'd be flat on your back soon.
THAT'S ONE DOWN.
His hands were THAT lethal. And FAST?
Brother, you could hear the AIR crack open.
HEH. WELL, LOOK WHAT I CAUGHT.
THESE ALL YOU GOT, YOU NASTY LITTLE CREEP?
NO, BOXER.
I HAVE MANY MORE.

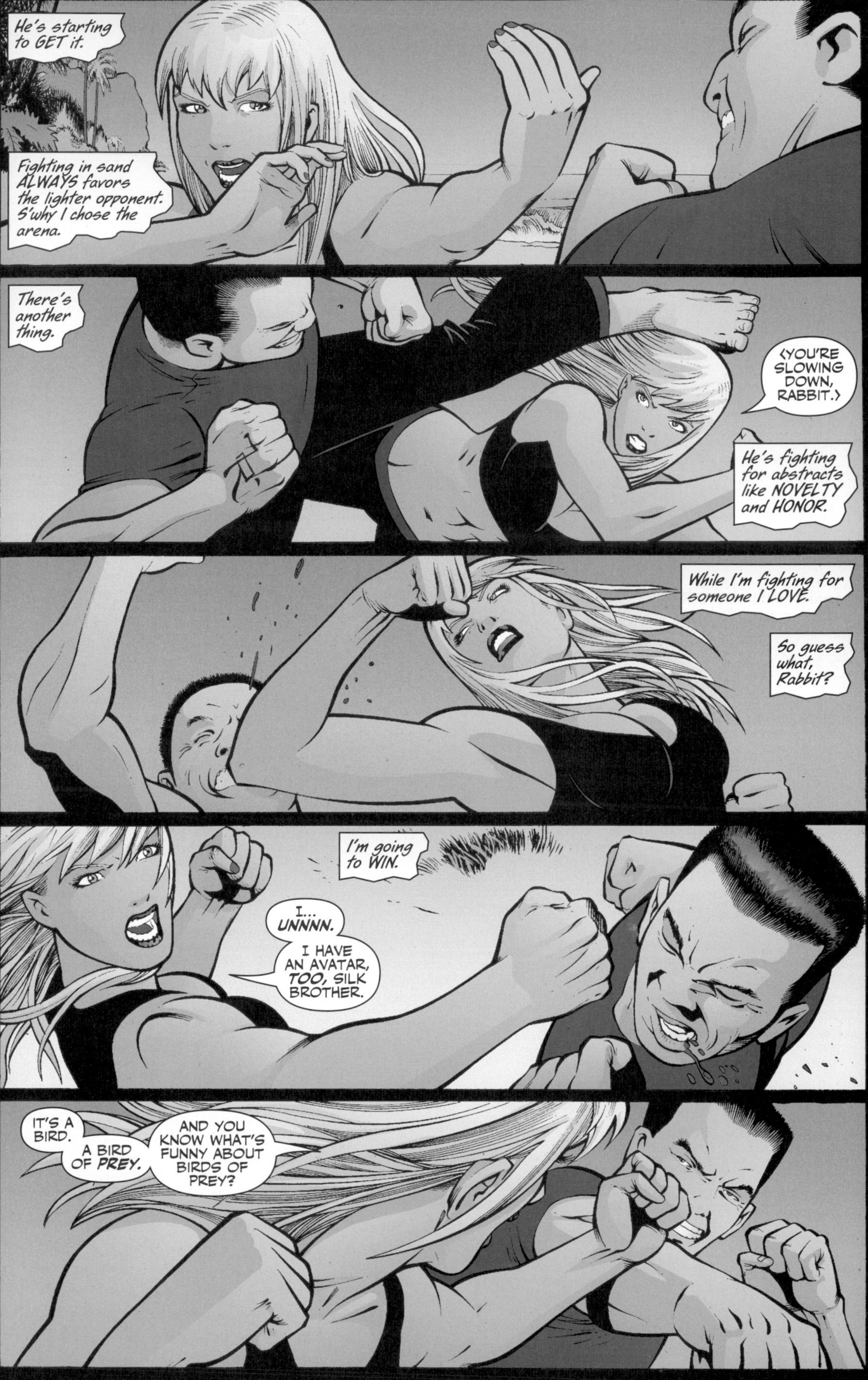
He's starting to GET it.
Fighting in sand ALWAYS favors the lighter opponent. S'why I chose the arena.
There's another thing.
‹YOU'RE SLOWING DOWN, RABBIT.›
He's fighting for abstracts like NOVELTY and HONOR.
While I'm fighting for someone I LOVE.
So guess what, Rabbit?
I'm going to WIN.
I... UNNNN.
I HAVE AN AVATAR, TOO, SILK BROTHER.
IT'S A BIRD.
A BIRD OF PREY.
AND YOU KNOW WHAT'S FUNNY ABOUT BIRDS OF PREY?

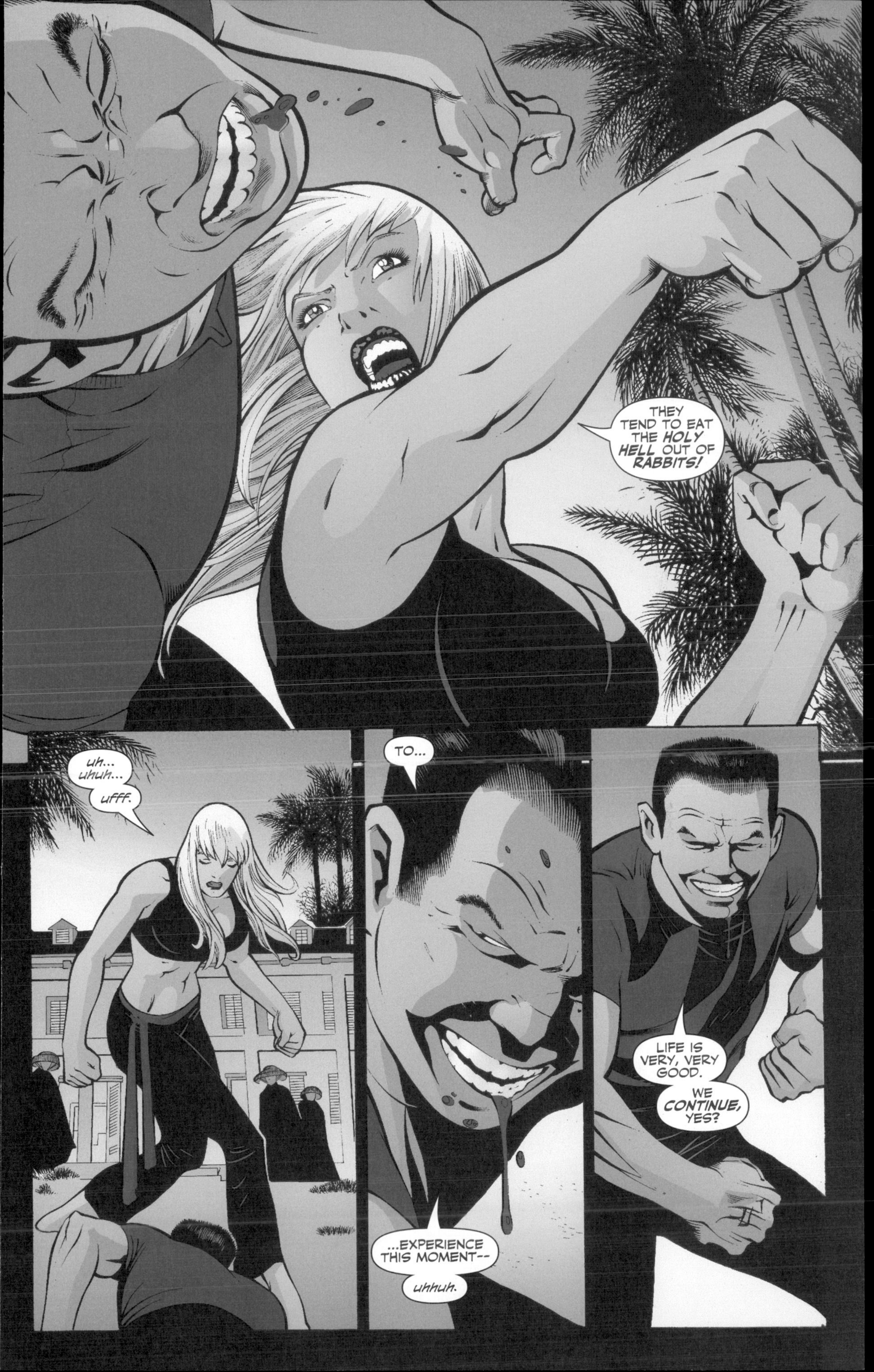
THEY TEND TO EAT THE HOLY HELL OUT OF RABBITS!
uh... uhuh... ufff.
TO...
...EXPERIENCE THIS MOMENT--
uhhuh.
LIFE IS VERY, VERY GOOD.
WE CONTINUE, YES?

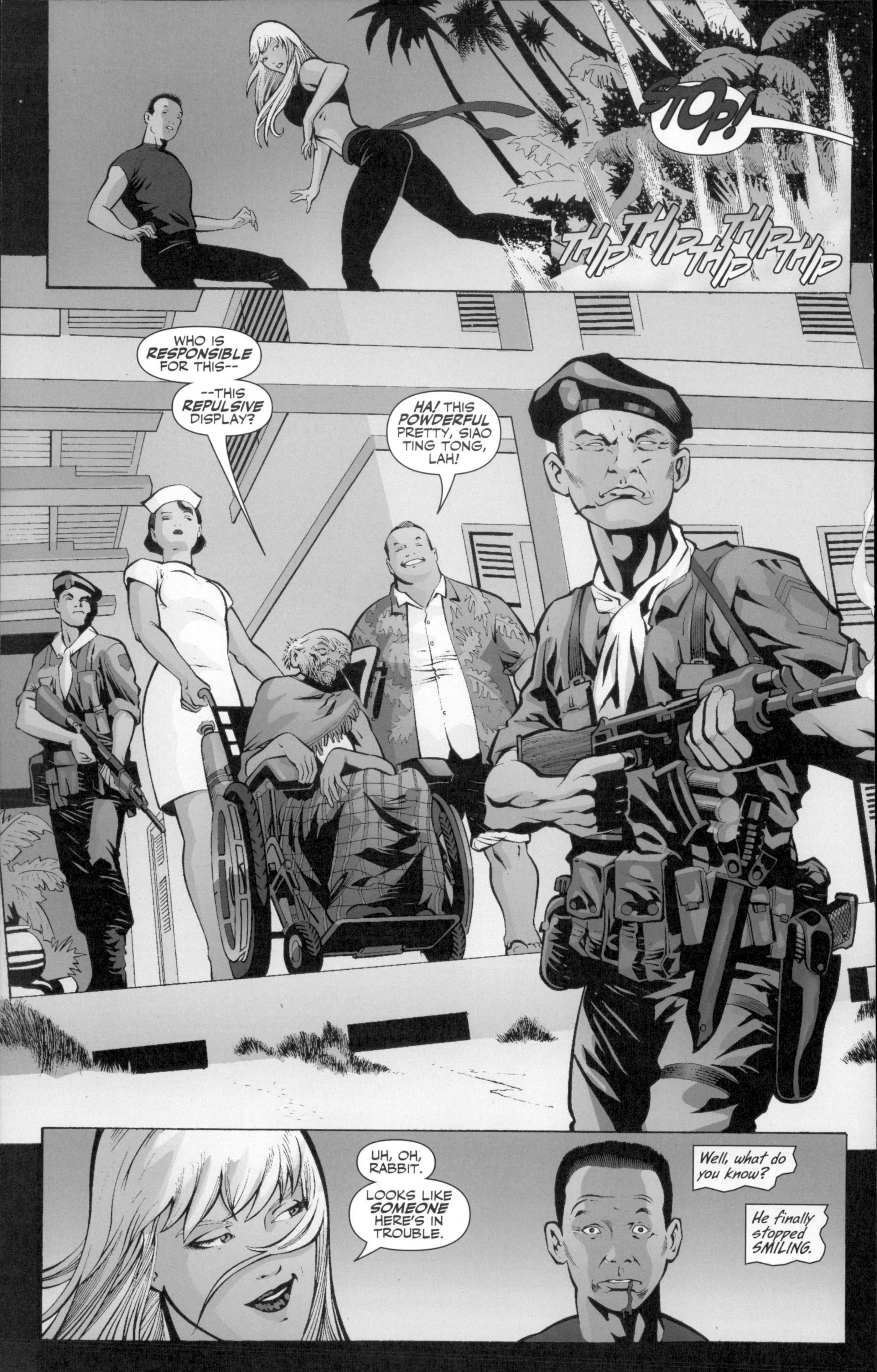
STOP!
THP THP THP THP THP THP THP
WHO IS RESPONSIBLE FOR THIS--
--THIS REPULSIVE DISPLAY?
HA! THIS POWDERFUL PRETTY, SIAO TING TONG, LAH!
UH, OH, RABBIT.
LOOKS LIKE SOMEONE HERE'S IN TROUBLE.
Well, what do you know?
He finally stopped SMILING.

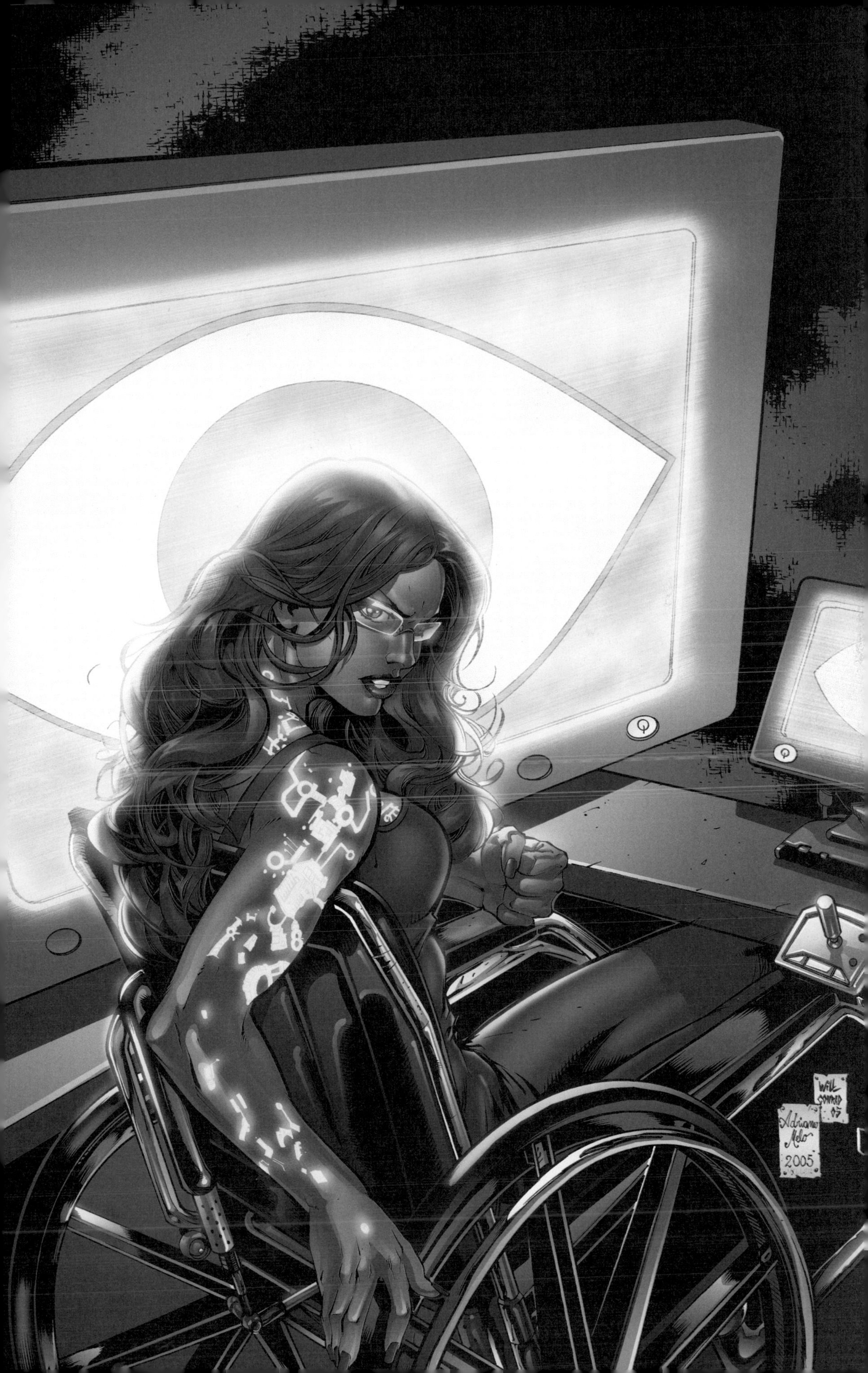
WILL CONRAD 05
Adriano Melo
2005

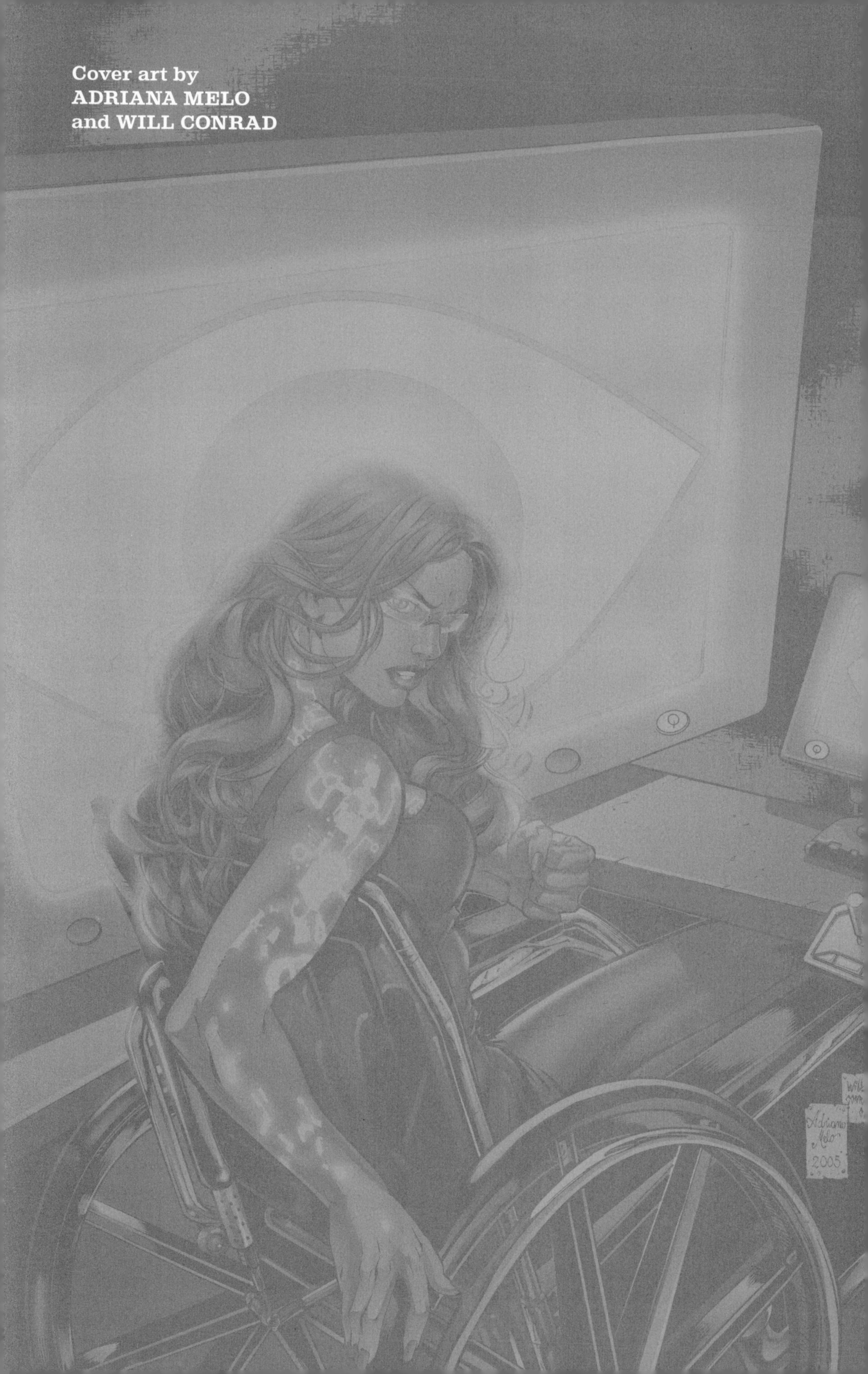
Adriana Melo
2005

Cover art by
ADRIANA MELO
and WILL CONRAD

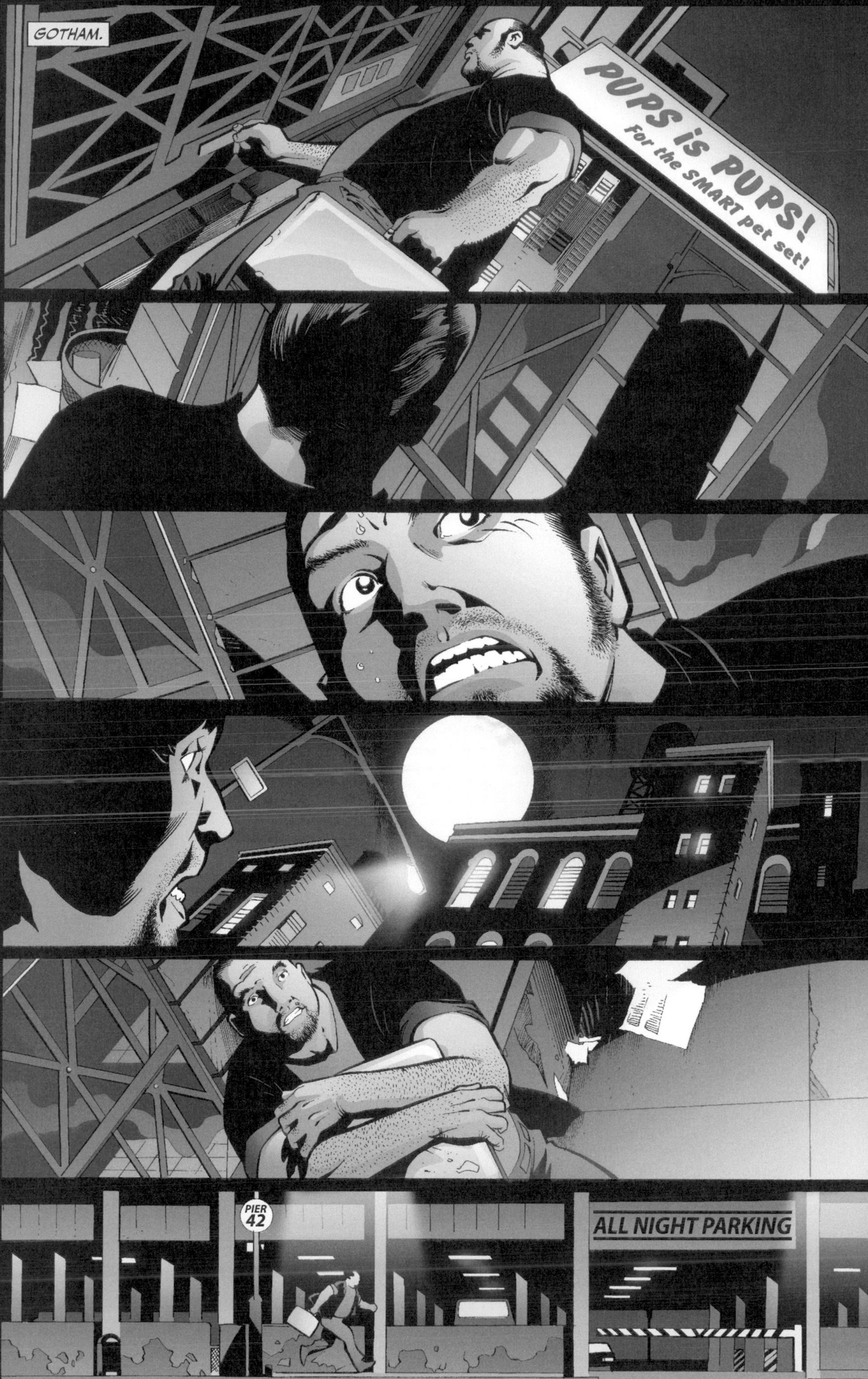
GOTHAM.
PUPS is PUPS!
For the SMART pet set!
PIER
42
ALL NIGHT PARKING

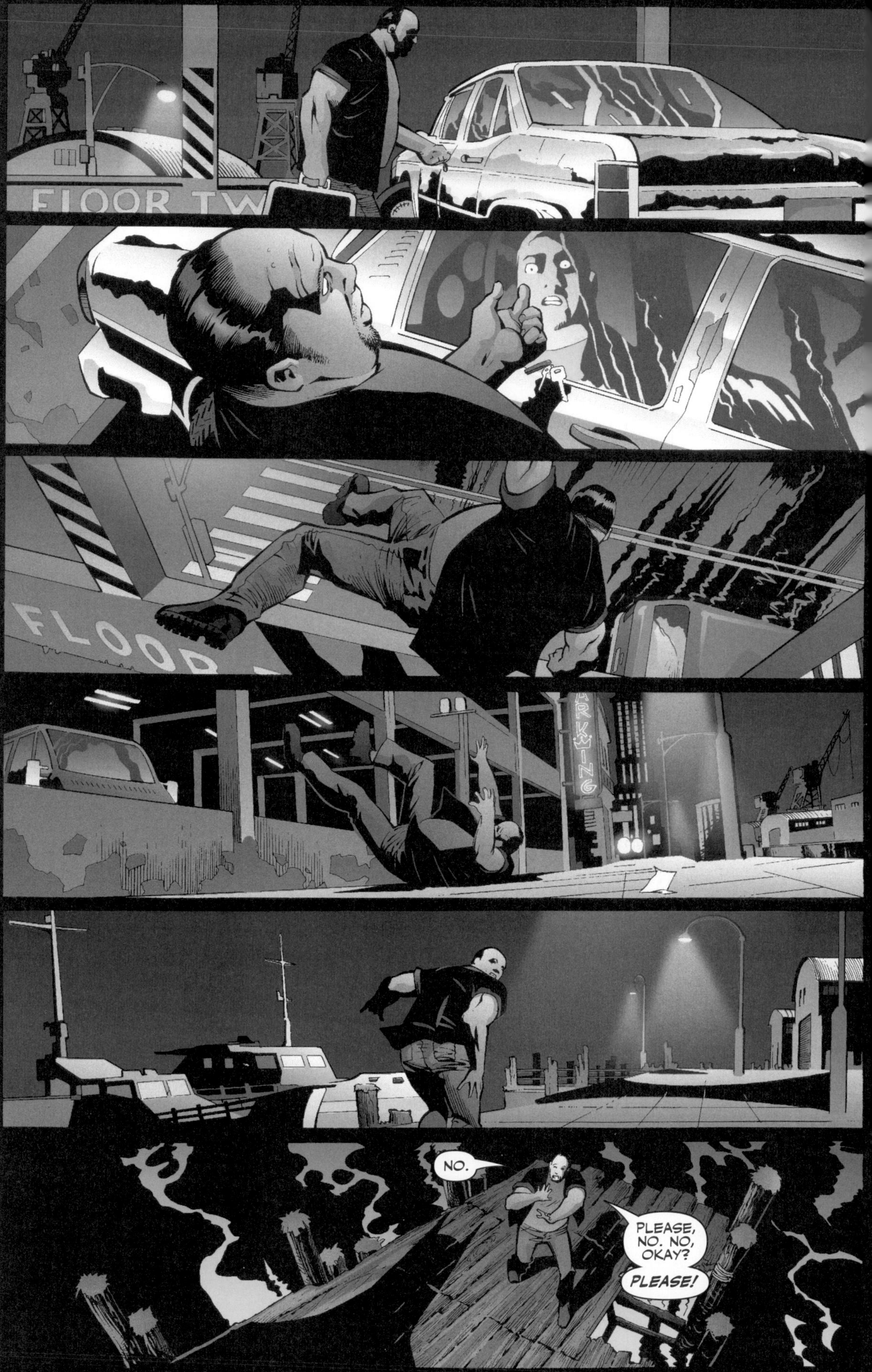
FLOOR TW
FLOOR
ARKING
NO.
PLEASE, NO. NO, OKAY?
PLEASE!

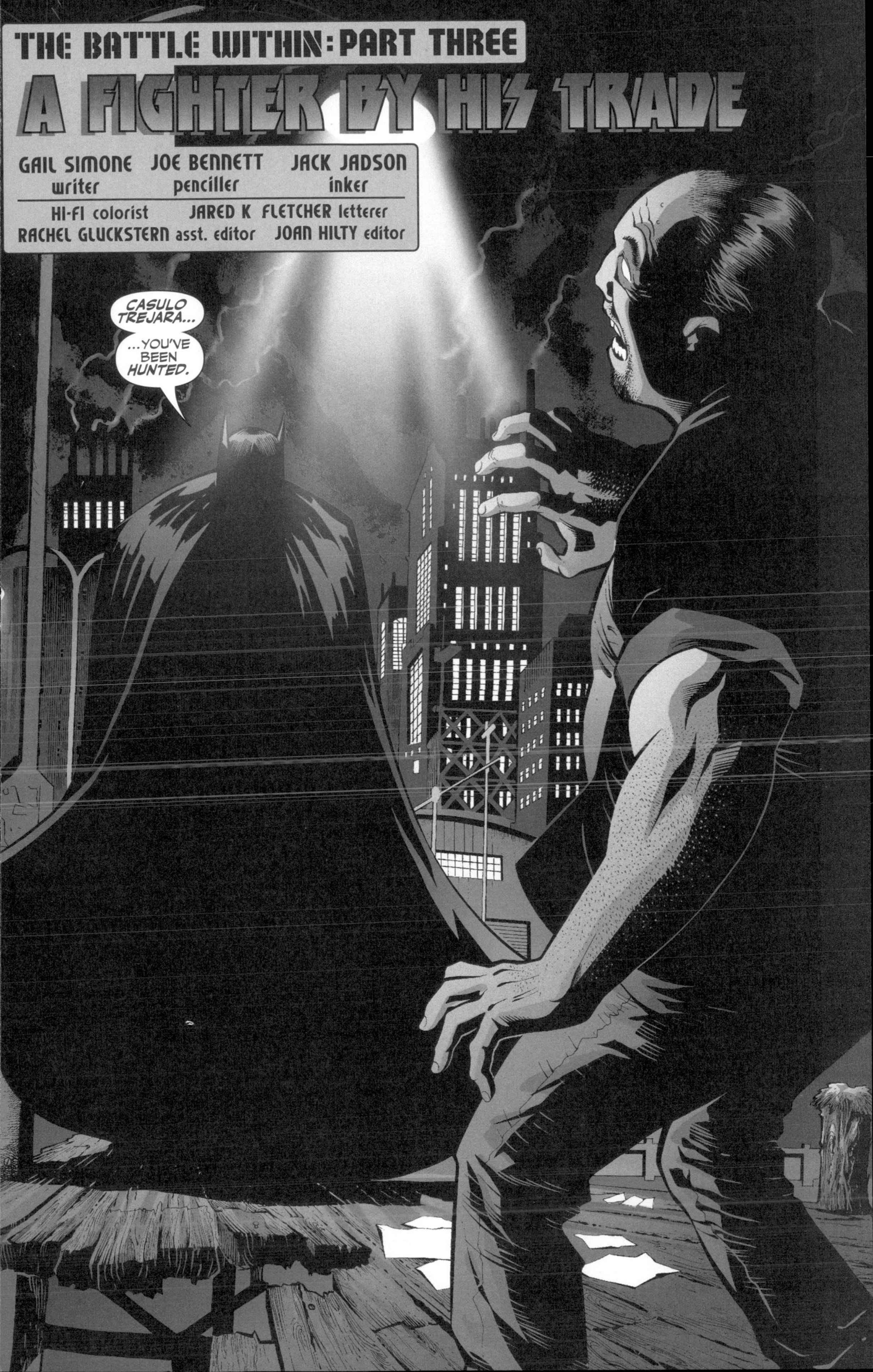
THE BATTLE WITHIN: PART THREE
A FIGHTER BY HIS TRADE
GAIL SIMONE writer JOE BENNETT penciller JACK JADSON inker
HI-FI colorist JARED K FLETCHER letterer
RACHEL GLUCKSTERN asst. editor JOAN HILTY editor
CASULO TREJARA...
...YOU'VE BEEN HUNTED.

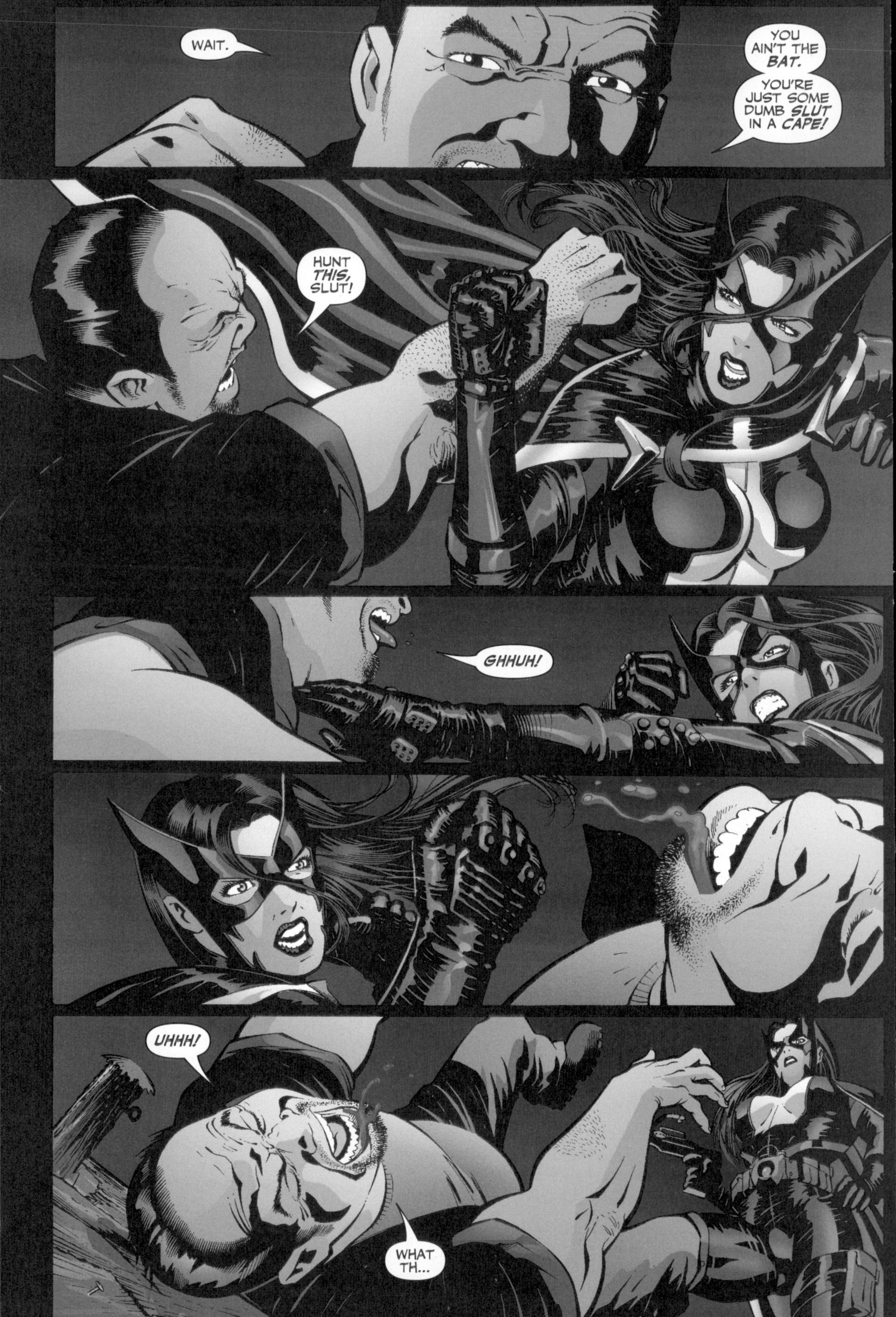
WAIT.
YOU AIN'T THE *BAT.*
YOU'RE JUST SOME DUMB *SLUT* IN A *CAPE!*
HUNT *THIS,* SLUT!
GHHUH!
UHHH!
WHAT TH...

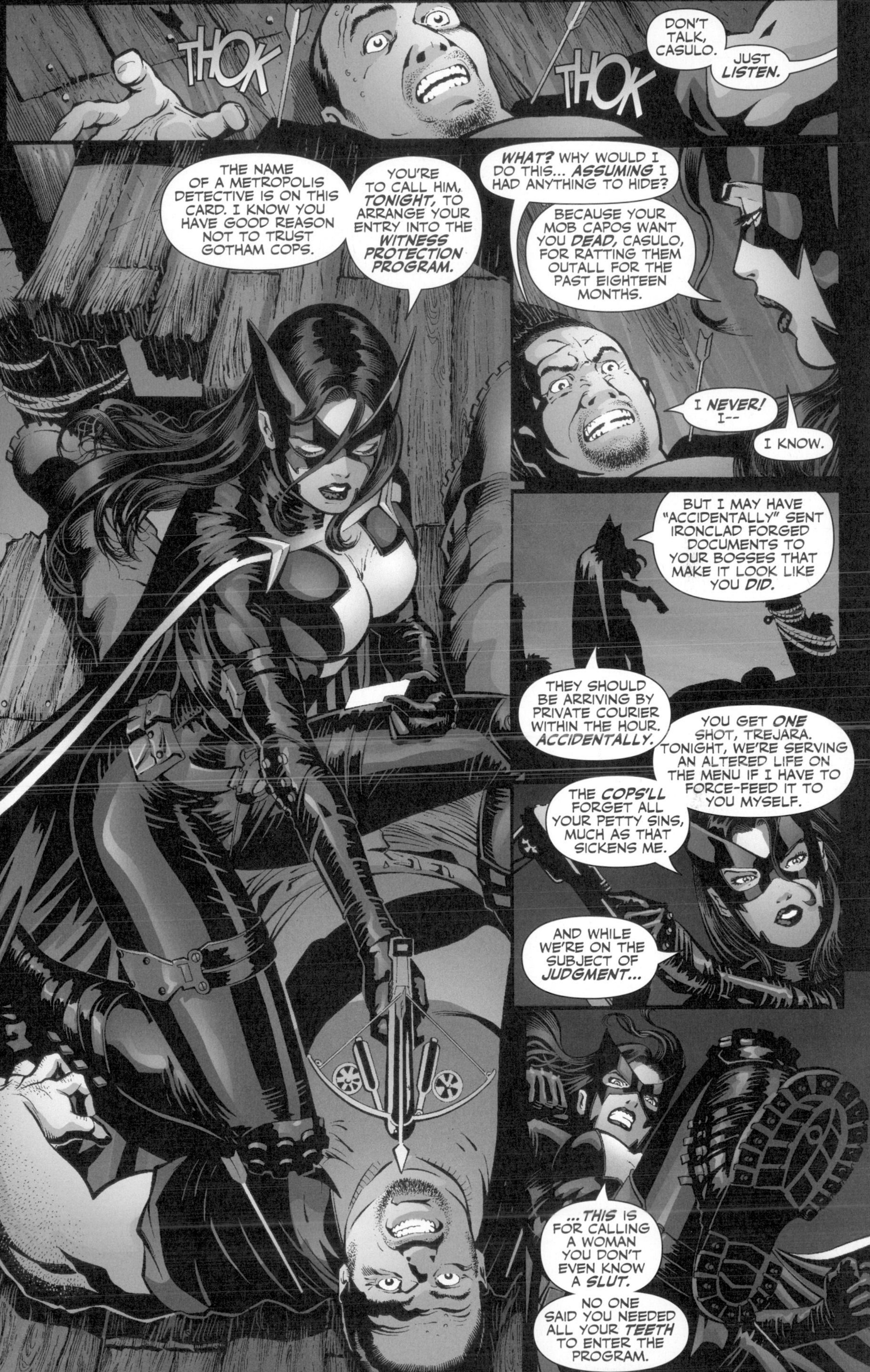
THOK
THOK
DON'T TALK, CASULO.
JUST LISTEN.
THE NAME OF A METROPOLIS DETECTIVE IS ON THIS CARD. I KNOW YOU HAVE GOOD REASON NOT TO TRUST GOTHAM COPS.
YOU'RE TO CALL HIM, TONIGHT, TO ARRANGE YOUR ENTRY INTO THE WITNESS PROTECTION PROGRAM.
WHAT? WHY WOULD I DO THIS... ASSUMING I HAD ANYTHING TO HIDE?
BECAUSE YOUR MOB CAPOS WANT YOU DEAD, CASULO, FOR RATTING THEM OUTALL FOR THE PAST EIGHTEEN MONTHS.
I NEVER! I--
I KNOW.
BUT I MAY HAVE "ACCIDENTALLY" SENT IRONCLAD FORGED DOCUMENTS TO YOUR BOSSES THAT MAKE IT LOOK LIKE YOU DID.
THEY SHOULD BE ARRIVING BY PRIVATE COURIER WITHIN THE HOUR. ACCIDENTALLY.
YOU GET ONE SHOT, TREJARA. TONIGHT, WE'RE SERVING AN ALTERED LIFE ON THE MENU IF I HAVE TO FORCE-FEED IT TO YOU MYSELF.
THE COPS'LL FORGET ALL YOUR PETTY SINS, MUCH AS THAT SICKENS ME.
AND WHILE WE'RE ON THE SUBJECT OF JUDGMENT...
...THIS IS FOR CALLING A WOMAN YOU DON'T EVEN KNOW A SLUT.
NO ONE SAID YOU NEEDED ALL YOUR TEETH TO ENTER THE PROGRAM.

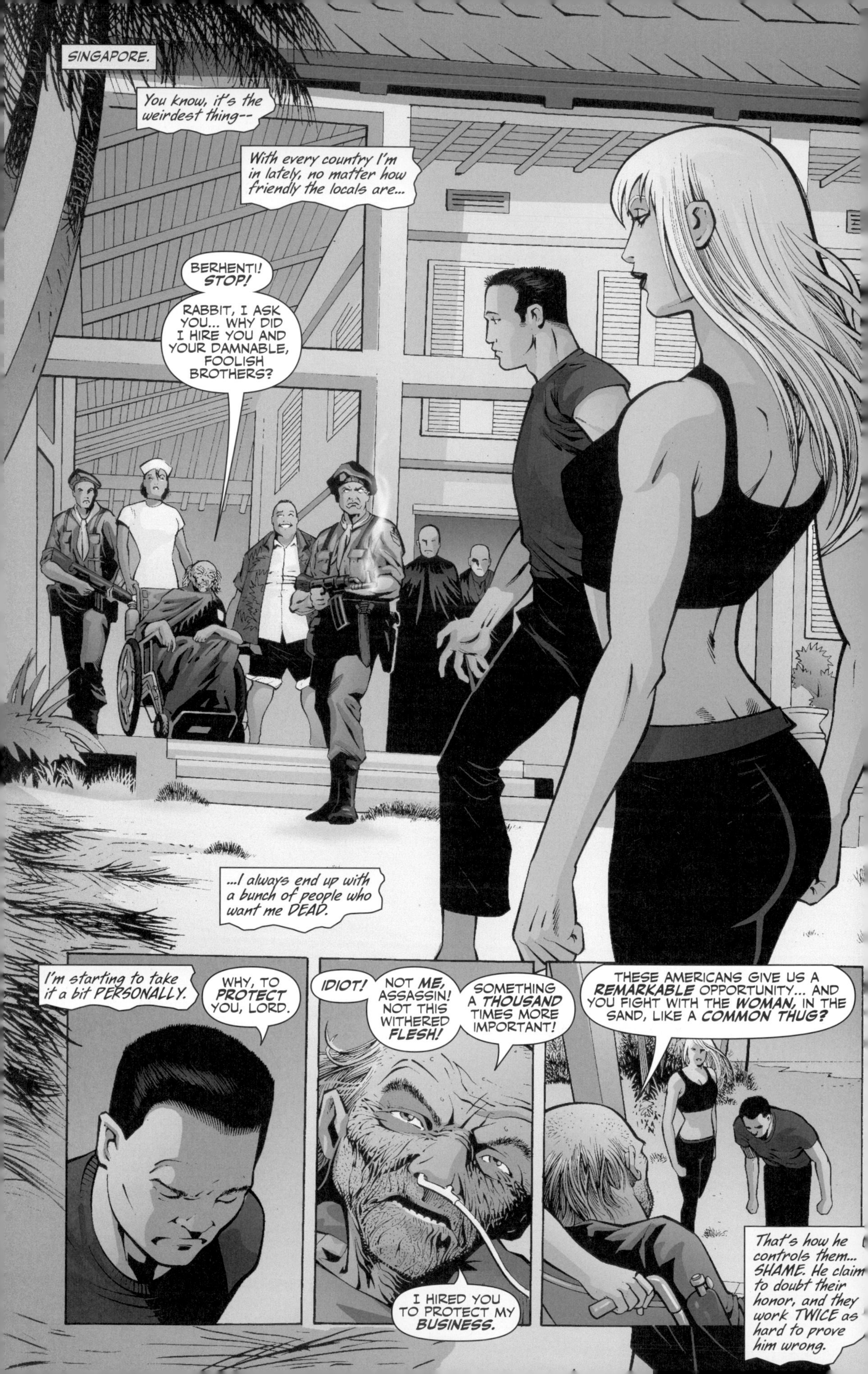

SINGAPORE.
You know, it's the weirdest thing--
With every country I'm in lately, no matter how friendly the locals are...
BERHENTI! STOP!
RABBIT, I ASK YOU... WHY DID I HIRE YOU AND YOUR DAMNABLE, FOOLISH BROTHERS?
...I always end up with a bunch of people who want me DEAD.
I'm starting to take it a bit PERSONALLY.
WHY, TO PROTECT YOU, LORD.
IDIOT!
NOT ME, ASSASSIN! NOT THIS WITHERED FLESH!
SOMETHING A THOUSAND TIMES MORE IMPORTANT!
I HIRED YOU TO PROTECT MY BUSINESS.
THESE AMERICANS GIVE US A REMARKABLE OPPORTUNITY... AND YOU FIGHT WITH THE WOMAN, IN THE SAND, LIKE A COMMON THUG?
That's how he controls them... SHAME. He claim to doubt their honor, and they work TWICE as hard to prove him wrong.

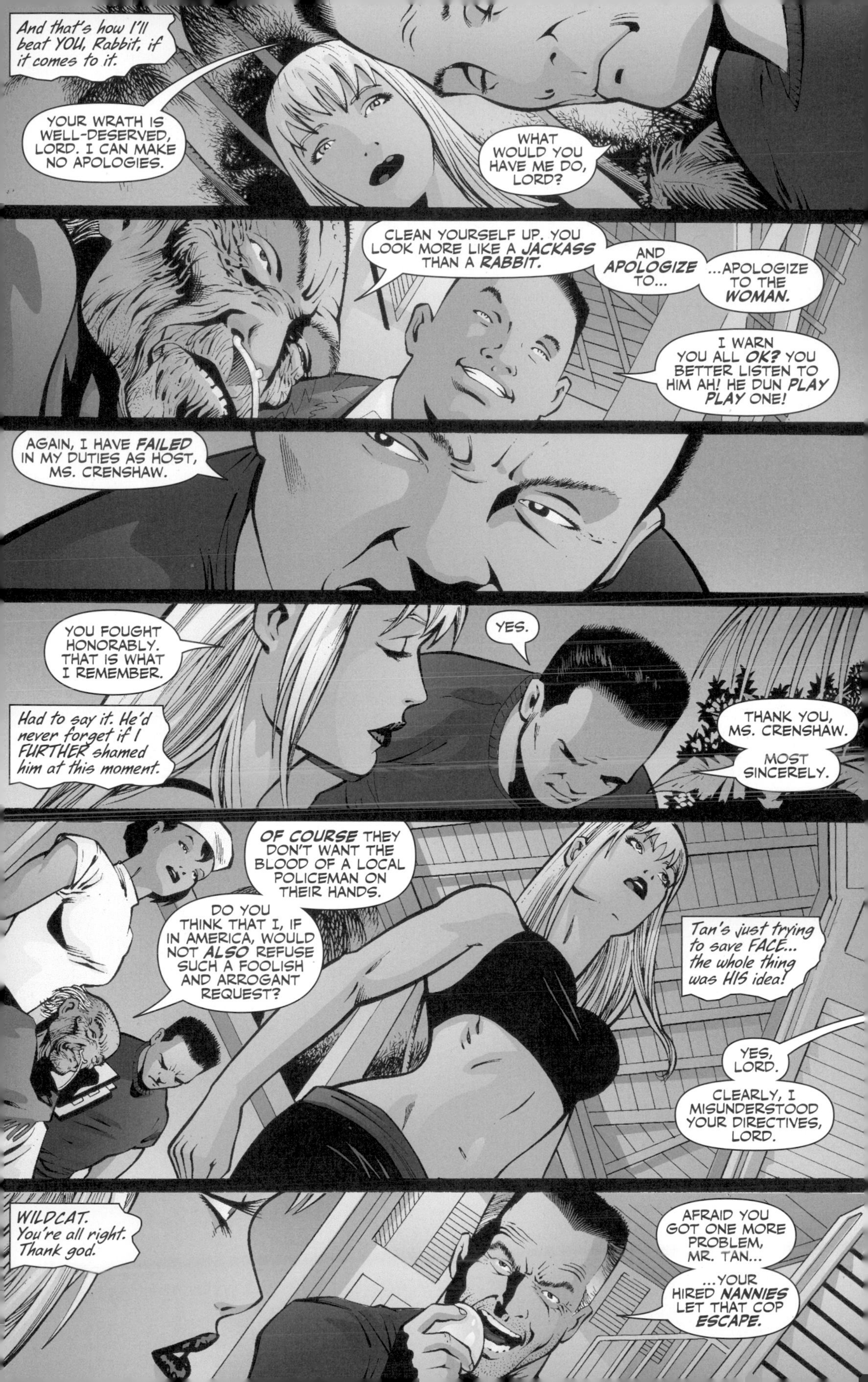
And that's how I'll beat YOU, Rabbit, if it comes to it.
YOUR WRATH IS WELL-DESERVED, LORD. I CAN MAKE NO APOLOGIES.
WHAT WOULD YOU HAVE ME DO, LORD?
CLEAN YOURSELF UP. YOU LOOK MORE LIKE A JACKASS THAN A RABBIT.
AND APOLOGIZE TO...
...APOLOGIZE TO THE WOMAN.
I WARN YOU ALL OK? YOU BETTER LISTEN TO HIM AH! HE DUN PLAY PLAY ONE!
AGAIN, I HAVE FAILED IN MY DUTIES AS HOST, MS. CRENSHAW.
YOU FOUGHT HONORABLY. THAT IS WHAT I REMEMBER.
YES.
Had to say it. He'd never forget if I FURTHER shamed him at this moment.
THANK YOU, MS. CRENSHAW.
MOST SINCERELY.
OF COURSE THEY DON'T WANT THE BLOOD OF A LOCAL POLICEMAN ON THEIR HANDS.
DO YOU THINK THAT I, IF IN AMERICA, WOULD NOT ALSO REFUSE SUCH A FOOLISH AND ARROGANT REQUEST?
Tan's just trying to save FACE... the whole thing was HIS idea!
YES, LORD.
CLEARLY, I MISUNDERSTOOD YOUR DIRECTIVES, LORD.
WILDCAT. You're all right. Thank god.
AFRAID YOU GOT ONE MORE PROBLEM, MR. TAN...
...YOUR HIRED NANNIES LET THAT COP ESCAPE.

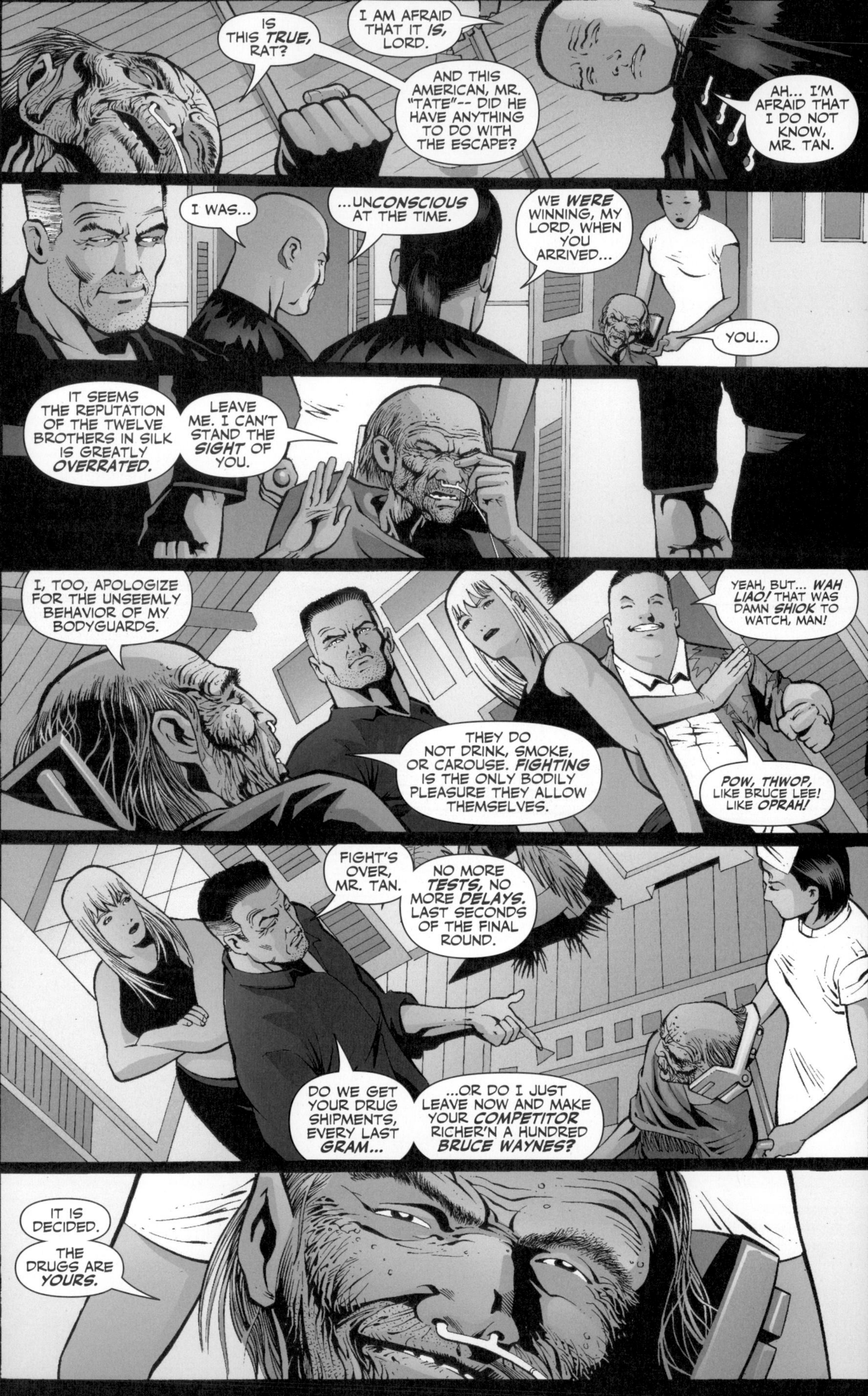
IS THIS TRUE, RAT?
I AM AFRAID THAT IT IS, LORD.
AND THIS AMERICAN, MR. "TATE"-- DID HE HAVE ANYTHING TO DO WITH THE ESCAPE?
AH... I'M AFRAID THAT I DO NOT KNOW, MR. TAN.
I WAS...
...UNCONSCIOUS AT THE TIME.
WE WERE WINNING, MY LORD, WHEN YOU ARRIVED...
YOU...
IT SEEMS THE REPUTATION OF THE TWELVE BROTHERS IN SILK IS GREATLY OVERRATED.
LEAVE ME. I CAN'T STAND THE SIGHT OF YOU.
I, TOO, APOLOGIZE FOR THE UNSEEMLY BEHAVIOR OF MY BODYGUARDS.
YEAH, BUT... WAH LIAO! THAT WAS DAMN SHIOK TO WATCH, MAN!
THEY DO NOT DRINK, SMOKE, OR CAROUSE. FIGHTING IS THE ONLY BODILY PLEASURE THEY ALLOW THEMSELVES.
POW, THWOP, LIKE BRUCE LEE! LIKE OPRAH!
FIGHT'S OVER, MR. TAN.
NO MORE TESTS, NO MORE DELAYS. LAST SECONDS OF THE FINAL ROUND.
DO WE GET YOUR DRUG SHIPMENTS, EVERY LAST GRAM...
...OR DO I JUST LEAVE NOW AND MAKE YOUR COMPETITOR RICHER'N A HUNDRED BRUCE WAYNES?
IT IS DECIDED.
THE DRUGS ARE YOURS.

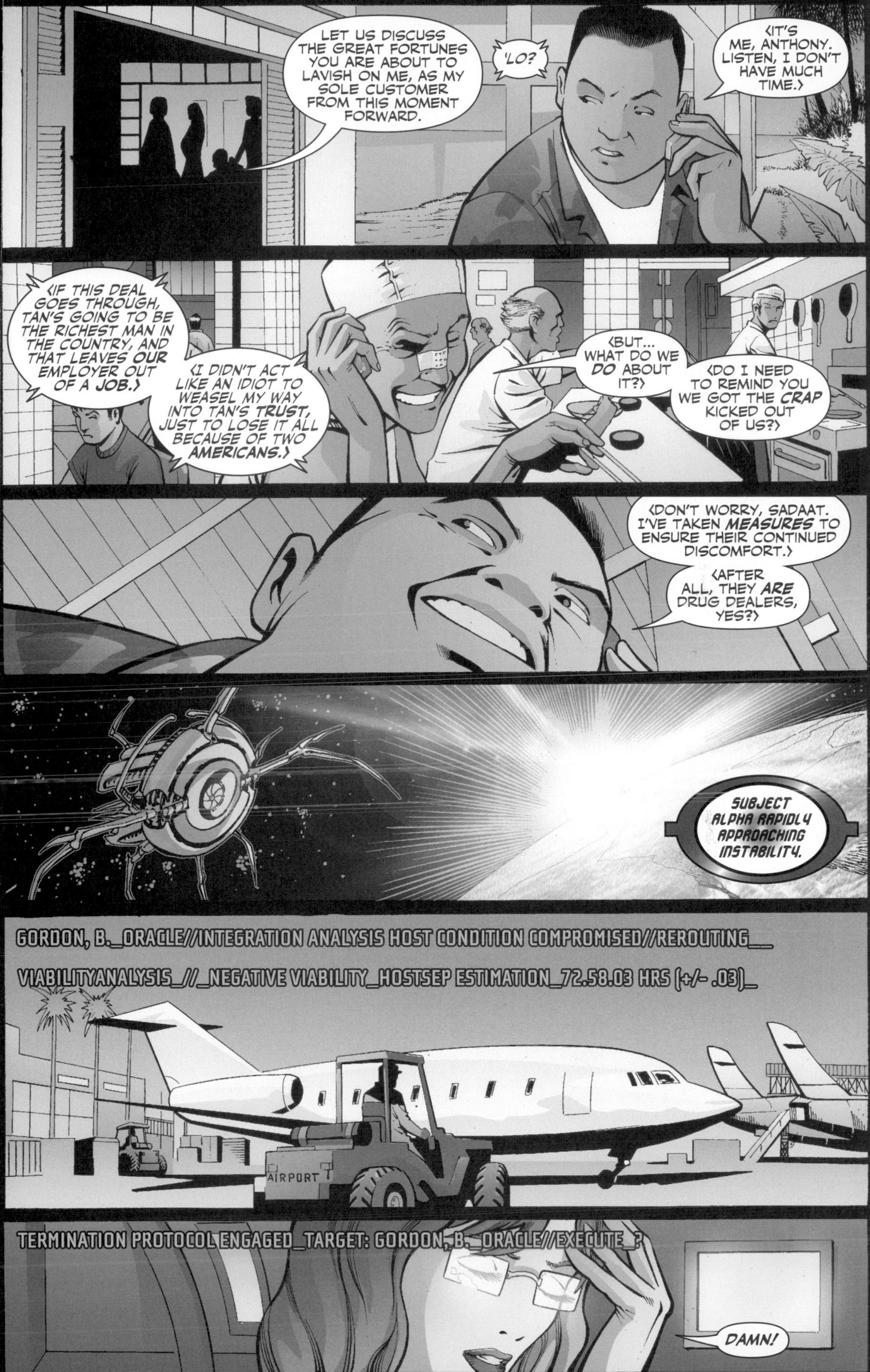
LET US DISCUSS THE GREAT FORTUNES YOU ARE ABOUT TO LAVISH ON ME, AS MY SOLE CUSTOMER FROM THIS MOMENT FORWARD.
'LO?
‹IT'S ME, ANTHONY. LISTEN, I DON'T HAVE MUCH TIME.›
‹IF THIS DEAL GOES THROUGH, TAN'S GOING TO BE THE RICHEST MAN IN THE COUNTRY, AND THAT LEAVES OUR EMPLOYER OUT OF A JOB.›
‹I DIDN'T ACT LIKE AN IDIOT TO WEASEL MY WAY INTO TAN'S TRUST, JUST TO LOSE IT ALL BECAUSE OF TWO AMERICANS.›
‹BUT... WHAT DO WE DO ABOUT IT?›
‹DO I NEED TO REMIND YOU WE GOT THE CRAP KICKED OUT OF US?›
‹DON'T WORRY, SADAAT. I'VE TAKEN MEASURES TO ENSURE THEIR CONTINUED DISCOMFORT.›
‹AFTER ALL, THEY ARE DRUG DEALERS, YES?›
SUBJECT ALPHA RAPIDLY APPROACHING INSTABILITY.
GORDON, B._ORACLE//INTEGRATION ANALYSIS HOST CONDITION COMPROMISED//REROUTING__
VIABILITYANALYSIS_//_NEGATIVE VIABILITY_HOSTSEP ESTIMATION_72.58.03 HRS (+/- .03)_
AIRPORT
TERMINATION PROTOCOL ENGAGED_TARGET: GORDON, B._ORACLE//EXECUTE_?
DAMN!

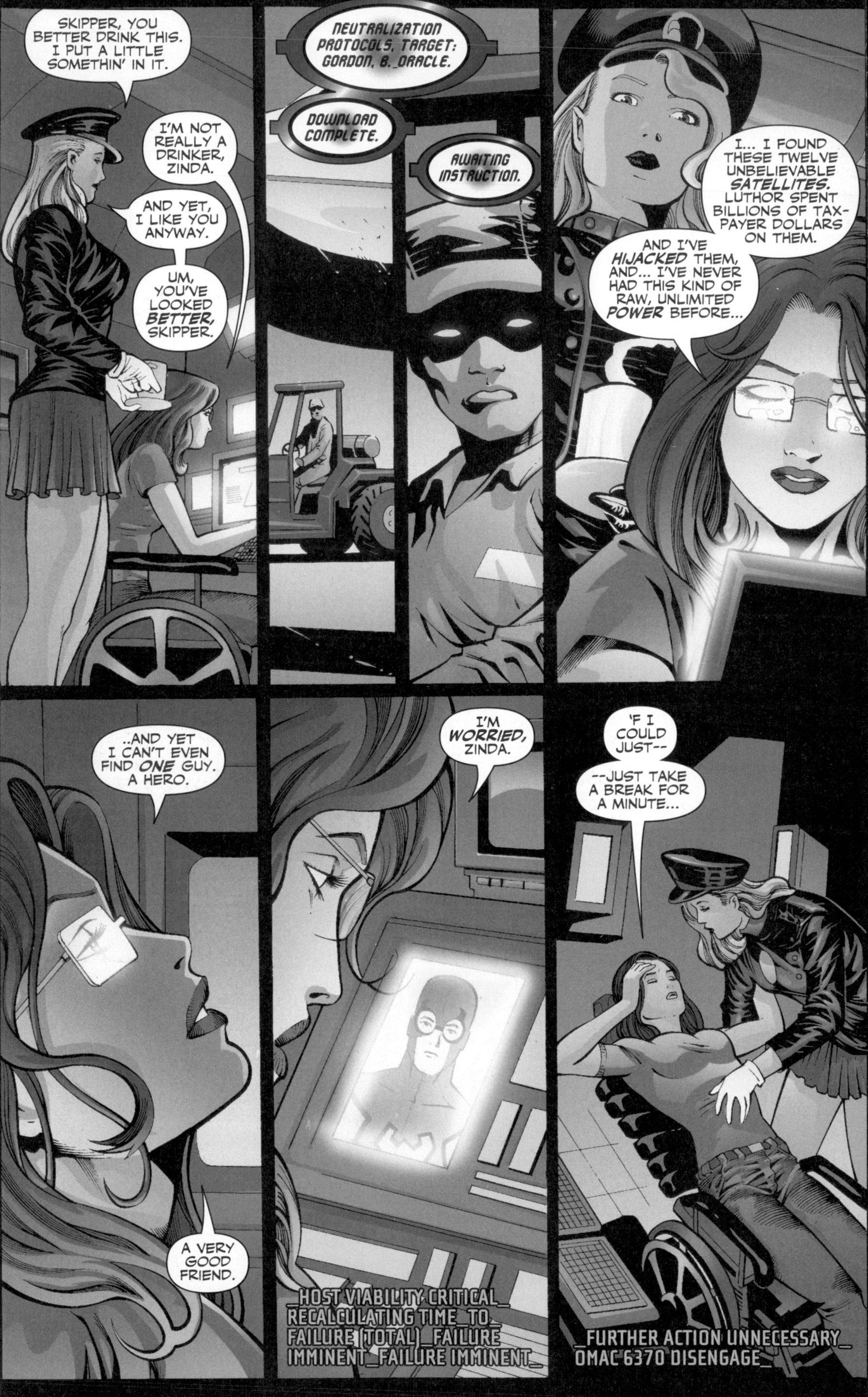
SKIPPER, YOU BETTER DRINK THIS. I PUT A LITTLE SOMETHIN' IN IT.
I'M NOT REALLY A DRINKER, ZINDA.
AND YET, I LIKE YOU ANYWAY.
UM, YOU'VE LOOKED BETTER, SKIPPER.
NEUTRALIZATION PROTOCOLS, TARGET: GORDON, B._ORACLE.
DOWNLOAD COMPLETE.
AWAITING INSTRUCTION.
I... I FOUND THESE TWELVE UNBELIEVABLE SATELLITES. LUTHOR SPENT BILLIONS OF TAX-PAYER DOLLARS ON THEM.
AND I'VE HIJACKED THEM, AND... I'VE NEVER HAD THIS KIND OF RAW, UNLIMITED POWER BEFORE...
..AND YET I CAN'T EVEN FIND ONE GUY. A HERO.
A VERY GOOD FRIEND.
I'M WORRIED, ZINDA.
HOST VIABILITY CRITICAL RECALCULATING TIME_TO_ FAILURE (TOTAL)_FAILURE IMMINENT_FAILURE IMMINENT_
'F I COULD JUST--
--JUST TAKE A BREAK FOR A MINUTE...
FURTHER ACTION UNNECESSARY OMAC 6370 DISENGAGE_

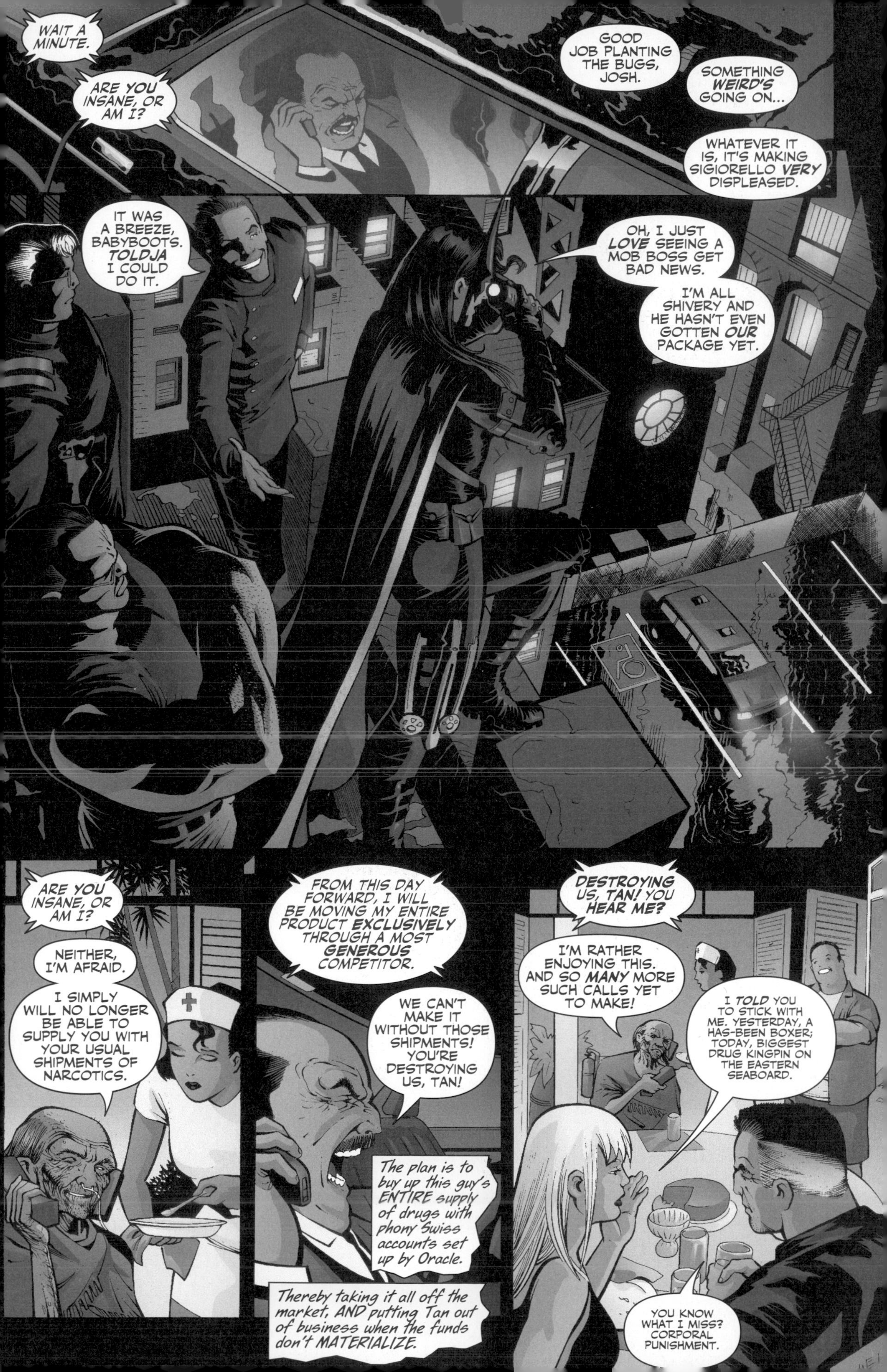
WAIT A MINUTE.
ARE YOU INSANE, OR AM I?
GOOD JOB PLANTING THE BUGS, JOSH.
SOMETHING WEIRD'S GOING ON...
WHATEVER IT IS, IT'S MAKING SIGIORELLO VERY DISPLEASED.
IT WAS A BREEZE, BABYBOOTS. TOLDJA I COULD DO IT.
OH, I JUST LOVE SEEING A MOB BOSS GET BAD NEWS.
I'M ALL SHIVERY AND HE HASN'T EVEN GOTTEN OUR PACKAGE YET.
ARE YOU INSANE, OR AM I?
NEITHER, I'M AFRAID.
I SIMPLY WILL NO LONGER BE ABLE TO SUPPLY YOU WITH YOUR USUAL SHIPMENTS OF NARCOTICS.
FROM THIS DAY FORWARD, I WILL BE MOVING MY ENTIRE PRODUCT EXCLUSIVELY THROUGH A MOST GENEROUS COMPETITOR.
WE CAN'T MAKE IT WITHOUT THOSE SHIPMENTS! YOU'RE DESTROYING US, TAN!
The plan is to buy up this guy's ENTIRE supply of drugs with phony Swiss accounts set up by Oracle.
Thereby taking it all off the market, AND putting Tan out of business when the funds don't MATERIALIZE.
DESTROYING US, TAN! YOU HEAR ME?
I'M RATHER ENJOYING THIS. AND SO MANY MORE SUCH CALLS YET TO MAKE!
I TOLD YOU TO STICK WITH ME. YESTERDAY, A HAS-BEEN BOXER; TODAY, BIGGEST DRUG KINGPIN ON THE EASTERN SEABOARD.
YOU KNOW WHAT I MISS? CORPORAL PUNISHMENT.

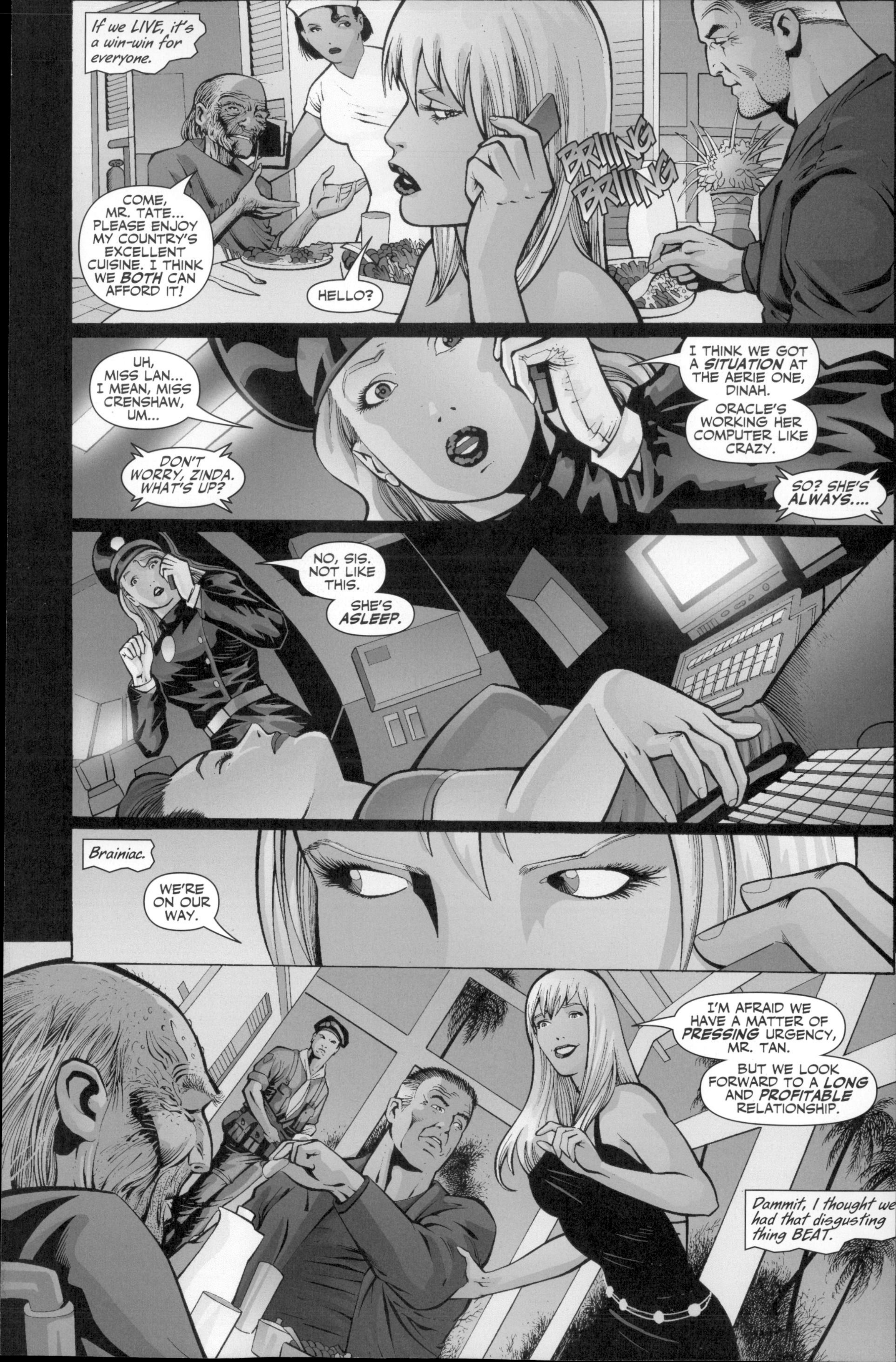
If we LIVE, it's a win-win for everyone.
COME, MR. TATE... PLEASE ENJOY MY COUNTRY'S EXCELLENT CUISINE. I THINK WE BOTH CAN AFFORD IT!
HELLO?
BRIIING BRIIING
UH, MISS LAN... I MEAN, MISS CRENSHAW, UM...
DON'T WORRY, ZINDA. WHAT'S UP?
I THINK WE GOT A SITUATION AT THE AERIE ONE, DINAH.
ORACLE'S WORKING HER COMPUTER LIKE CRAZY.
SO? SHE'S ALWAYS....
NO, SIS. NOT LIKE THIS.
SHE'S ASLEEP.
Brainiac.
WE'RE ON OUR WAY.
I'M AFRAID WE HAVE A MATTER OF PRESSING URGENCY, MR. TAN.
BUT WE LOOK FORWARD TO A LONG AND PROFITABLE RELATIONSHIP.
Dammit, I thought we had that disgusting thing BEAT.

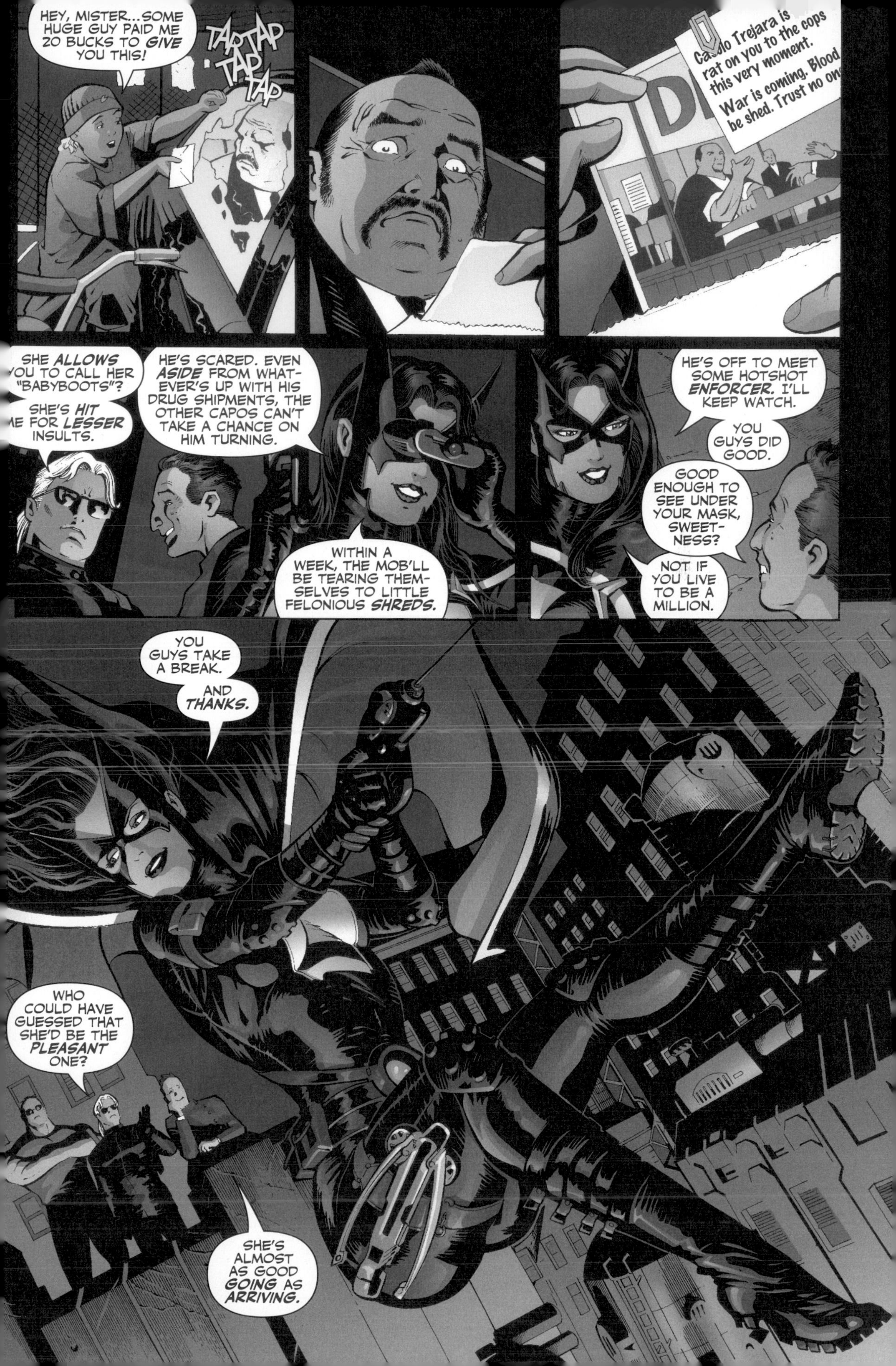

HEY, MISTER...SOME HUGE GUY PAID ME 20 BUCKS TO GIVE YOU THIS!
TAP TAP TAP TAP
Casslo Trejara is rat on you to the cops this very moment.
War is coming. Blood be shed. Trust no on
SHE ALLOWS YOU TO CALL HER "BABYBOOTS"?
SHE'S HIT ME FOR LESSER INSULTS.
HE'S SCARED. EVEN ASIDE FROM WHAT-EVER'S UP WITH HIS DRUG SHIPMENTS, THE OTHER CAPOS CAN'T TAKE A CHANCE ON HIM TURNING.
WITHIN A WEEK, THE MOB'LL BE TEARING THEM-SELVES TO LITTLE FELONIOUS SHREDS.
HE'S OFF TO MEET SOME HOTSHOT ENFORCER. I'LL KEEP WATCH.
YOU GUYS DID GOOD.
GOOD ENOUGH TO SEE UNDER YOUR MASK, SWEET-NESS?
NOT IF YOU LIVE TO BE A MILLION.
YOU GUYS TAKE A BREAK.
AND THANKS.
WHO COULD HAVE GUESSED THAT SHE'D BE THE PLEASANT ONE?
SHE'S ALMOST AS GOOD GOING AS ARRIVING.

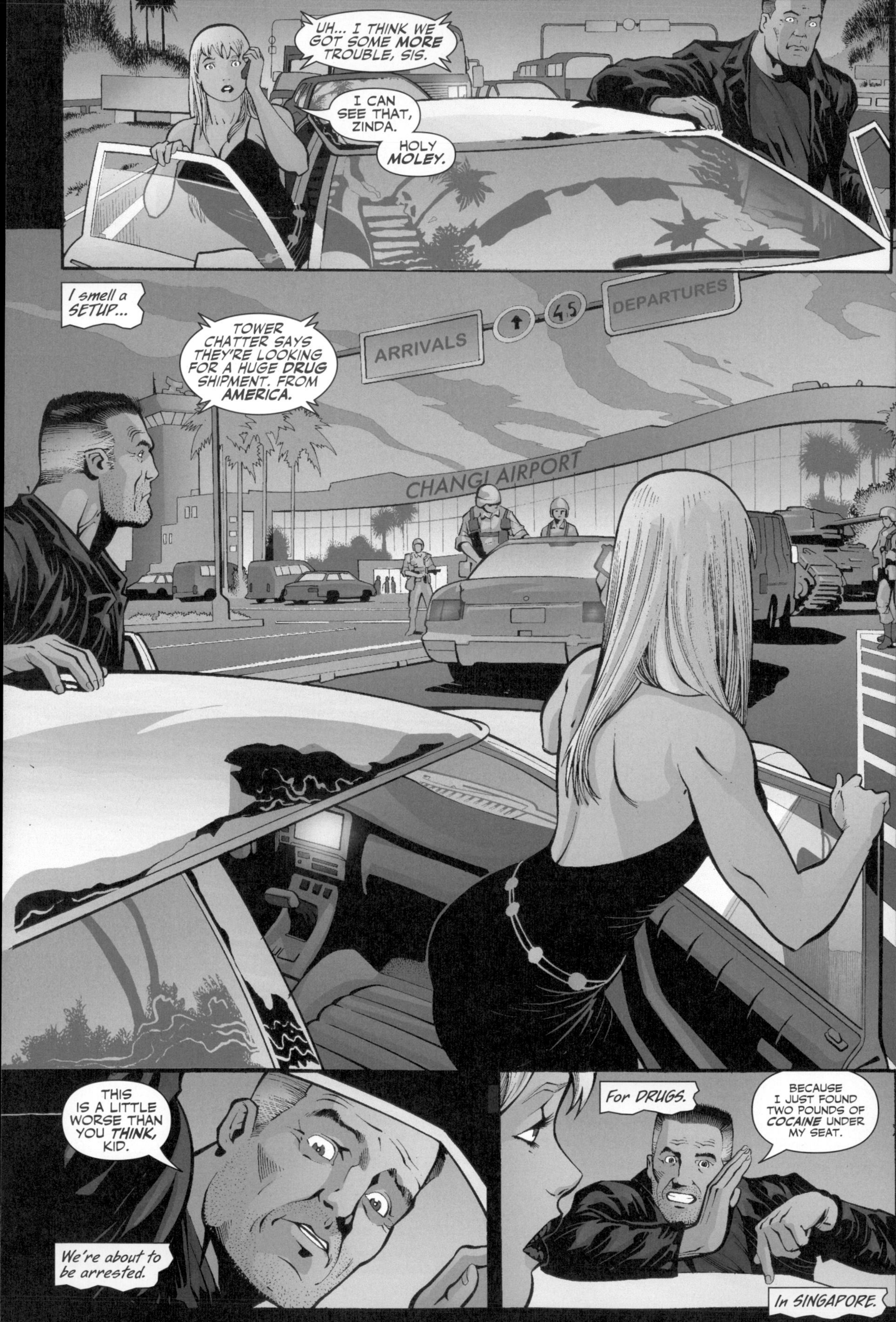
UH... I THINK WE GOT SOME MORE TROUBLE, SIS.
I CAN SEE THAT, ZINDA.
HOLY MOLEY.
I smell a SETUP...
DEPARTURES
45
ARRIVALS
TOWER CHATTER SAYS THEY'RE LOOKING FOR A HUGE DRUG SHIPMENT. FROM AMERICA.
CHANGI AIRPORT
THIS IS A LITTLE WORSE THAN YOU THINK, KID.
We're about to be arrested.
For DRUGS.
BECAUSE I JUST FOUND TWO POUNDS OF COCAINE UNDER MY SEAT.
In SINGAPORE.

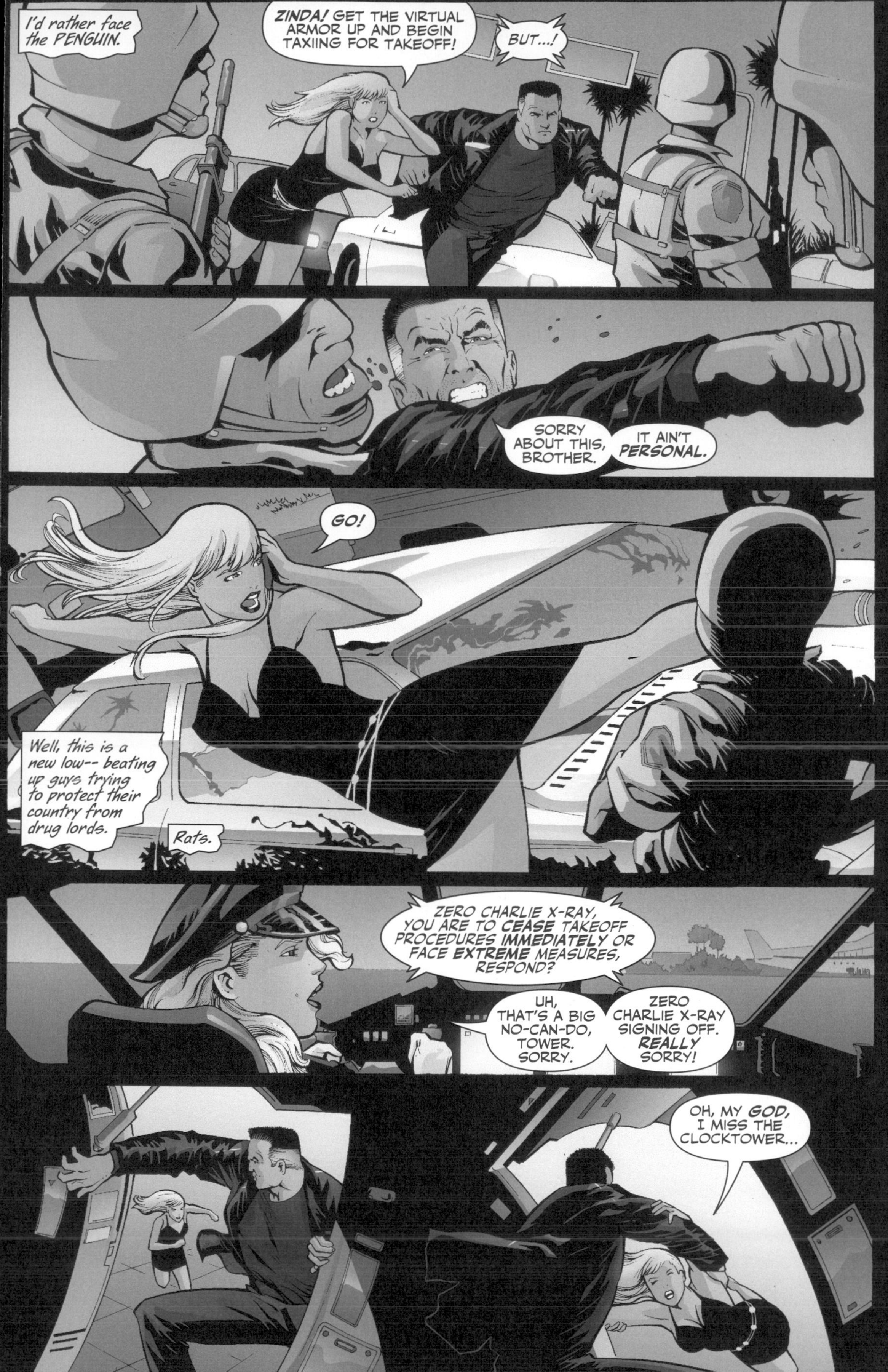
I'd rather face the PENGUIN.
ZINDA! GET THE VIRTUAL ARMOR UP AND BEGIN TAXIING FOR TAKEOFF!
BUT...!
SORRY ABOUT THIS, BROTHER.
IT AIN'T PERSONAL.
GO!
Well, this is a new low-- beating up guys trying to protect their country from drug lords.
Rats.
ZERO CHARLIE X-RAY, YOU ARE TO CEASE TAKEOFF PROCEDURES IMMEDIATELY OR FACE EXTREME MEASURES, RESPOND?
UH, THAT'S A BIG NO-CAN-DO, TOWER. SORRY.
ZERO CHARLIE X-RAY SIGNING OFF. REALLY SORRY!
OH, MY GOD, I MISS THE CLOCKTOWER...

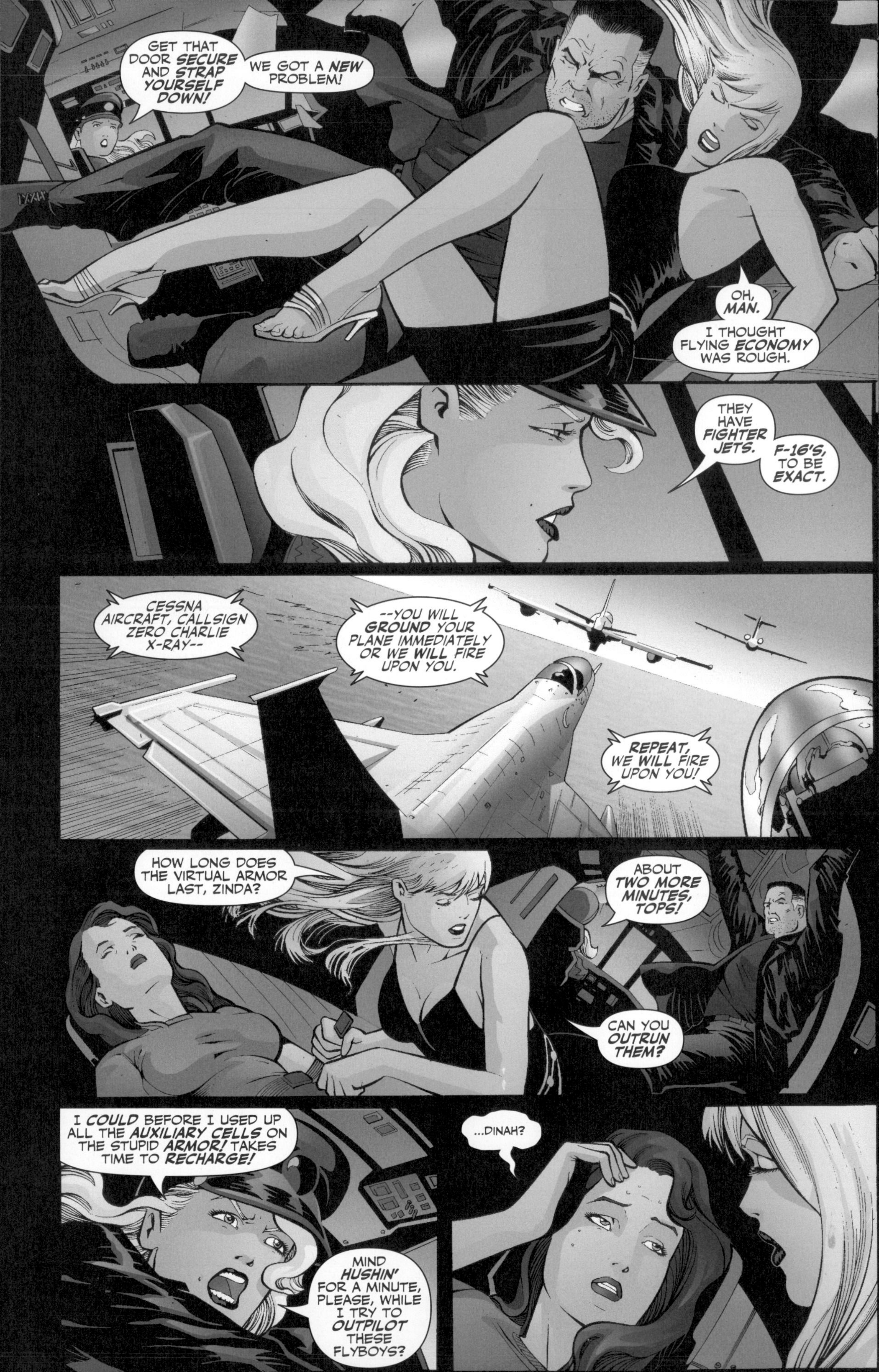
GET THAT DOOR SECURE AND STRAP YOURSELF DOWN!
WE GOT A NEW PROBLEM!
OH, MAN.
I THOUGHT FLYING ECONOMY WAS ROUGH.
THEY HAVE FIGHTER JETS.
F-16'S, TO BE EXACT.
CESSNA AIRCRAFT, CALLSIGN ZERO CHARLIE X-RAY--
--YOU WILL GROUND YOUR PLANE IMMEDIATELY OR WE WILL FIRE UPON YOU.
REPEAT, WE WILL FIRE UPON YOU!
HOW LONG DOES THE VIRTUAL ARMOR LAST, ZINDA?
ABOUT TWO MORE MINUTES, TOPS!
CAN YOU OUTRUN THEM?
I COULD BEFORE I USED UP ALL THE AUXILIARY CELLS ON THE STUPID ARMOR! TAKES TIME TO RECHARGE!
MIND HUSHIN' FOR A MINUTE, PLEASE, WHILE I TRY TO OUTPILOT THESE FLYBOYS?
...DINAH?

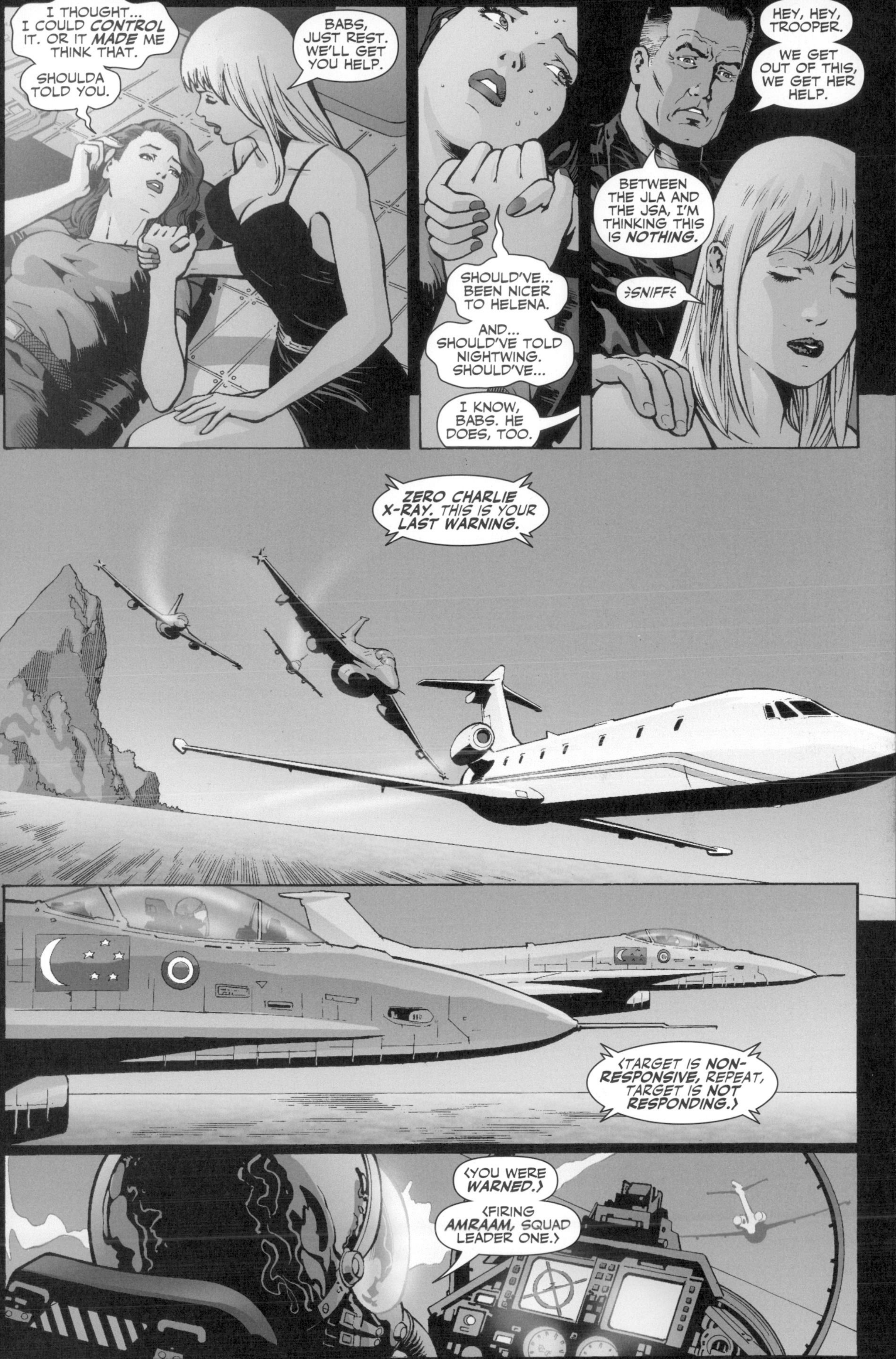
I THOUGHT... I COULD CONTROL IT. OR IT MADE ME THINK THAT.
SHOULDA TOLD YOU.
BABS, JUST REST. WE'LL GET YOU HELP.
SHOULD'VE... BEEN NICER TO HELENA.
AND... SHOULD'VE TOLD NIGHTWING. SHOULD'VE...
I KNOW, BABS. HE DOES, TOO.
HEY, HEY, TROOPER.
WE GET OUT OF THIS, WE GET HER HELP.
BETWEEN THE JLA AND THE JSA, I'M THINKING THIS IS NOTHING.
SNIFF
ZERO CHARLIE X-RAY. THIS IS YOUR LAST WARNING.
‹TARGET IS NON-RESPONSIVE, REPEAT, TARGET IS NOT RESPONDING.›
‹YOU WERE WARNED.›
‹FIRING AMRAAM, SQUAD LEADER ONE.›

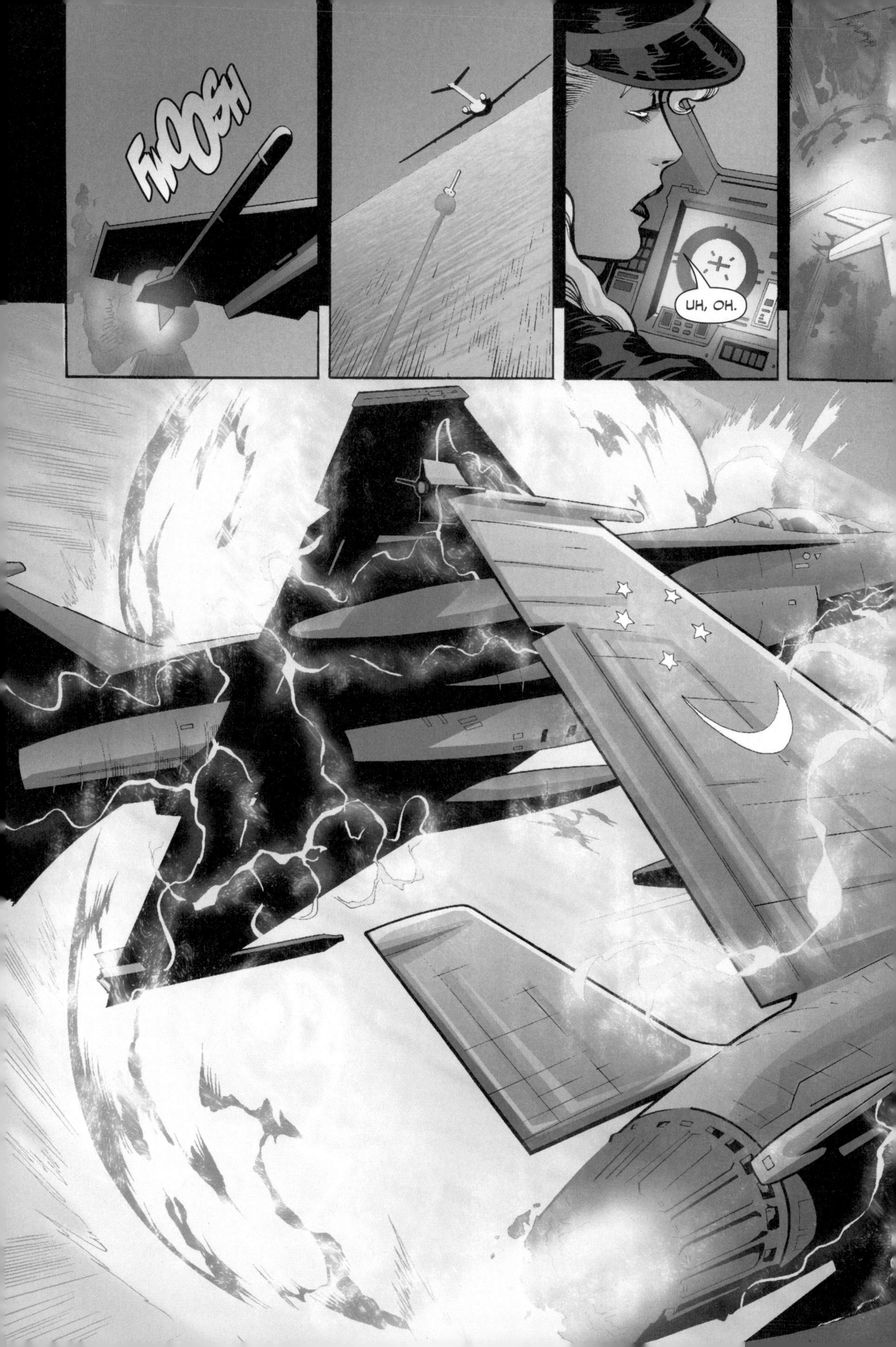
FWOOSH
UH, OH.

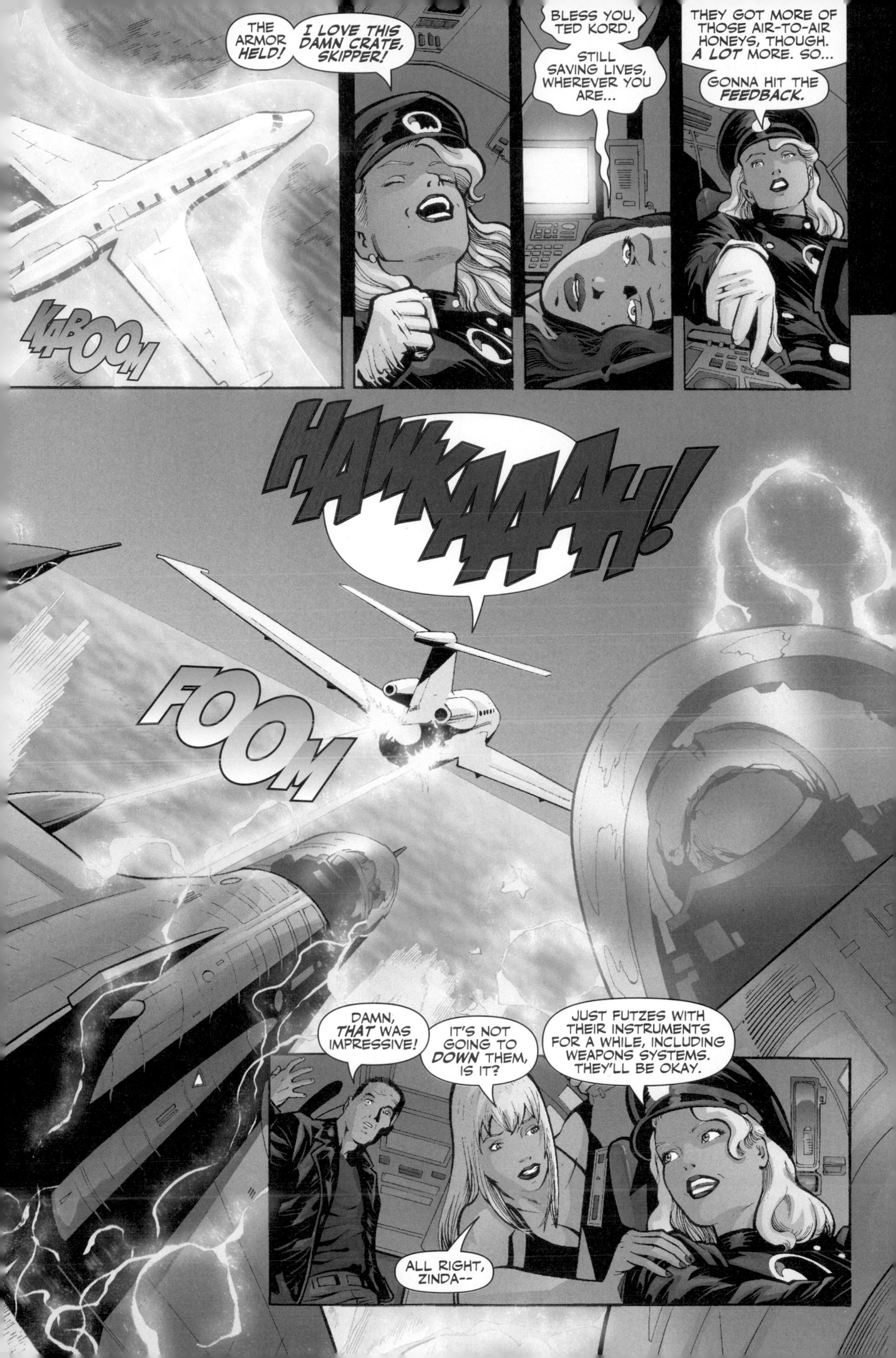

THE ARMOR HELD!
I LOVE THIS DAMN CRATE, SKIPPER!
KABOOM
BLESS YOU, TED KORD.
STILL SAVING LIVES, WHEREVER YOU ARE...
THEY GOT MORE OF THOSE AIR-TO-AIR HONEYS, THOUGH. A LOT MORE. SO...
GONNA HIT THE FEEDBACK.
HAWKAAAH!
FOOOM
DAMN, THAT WAS IMPRESSIVE!
IT'S NOT GOING TO DOWN THEM, IS IT?
JUST FUTZES WITH THEIR INSTRUMENTS FOR A WHILE, INCLUDING WEAPONS SYSTEMS. THEY'LL BE OKAY.
ALL RIGHT, ZINDA--

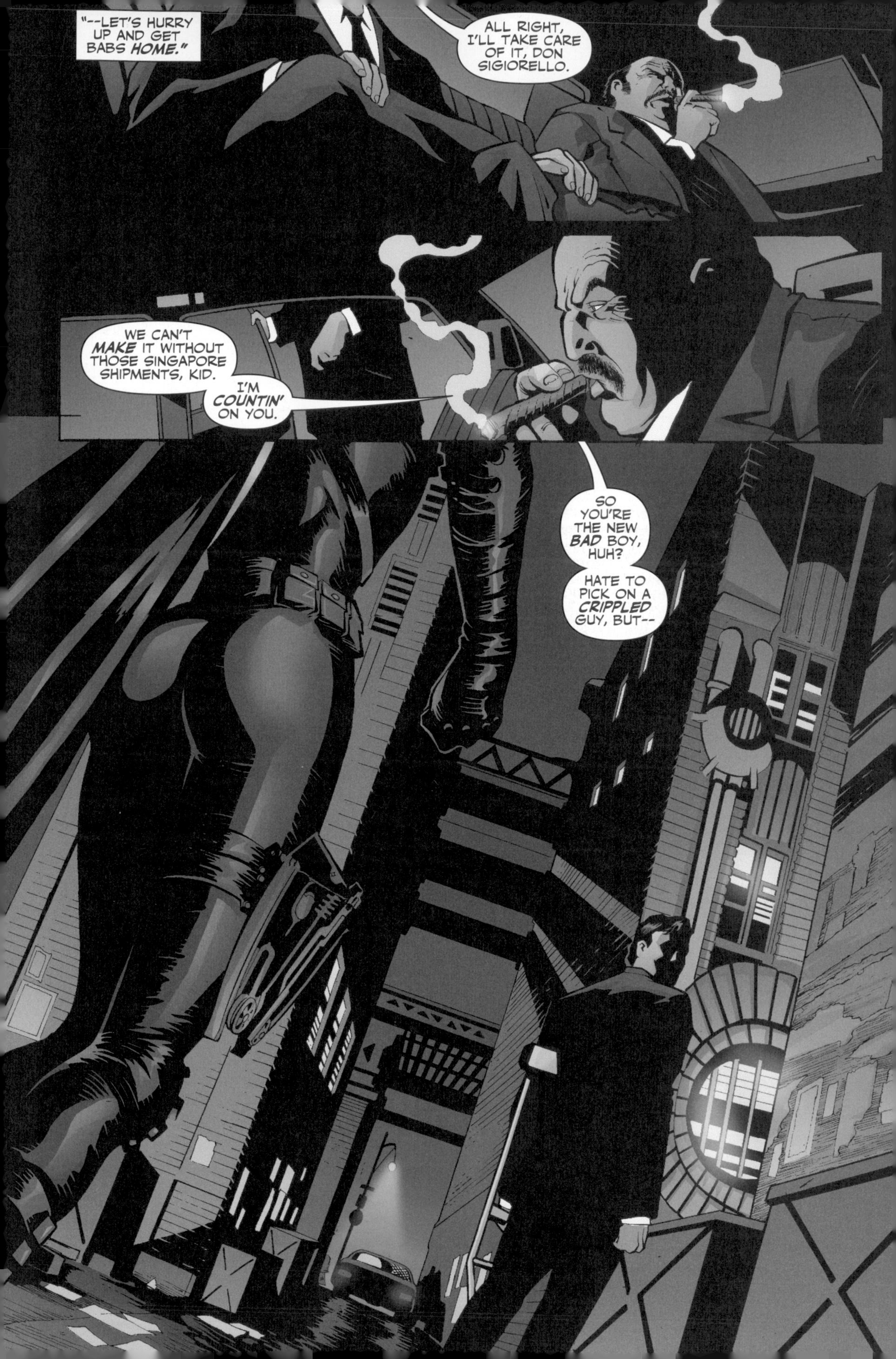
"--LET'S HURRY UP AND GET BABS *HOME.*"
ALL RIGHT, I'LL TAKE CARE OF IT, DON SIGIORELLO.
WE CAN'T *MAKE* IT WITHOUT THOSE SINGAPORE SHIPMENTS, KID.
I'M *COUNTIN'* ON YOU.
SO YOU'RE THE NEW *BAD* BOY, HUH?
HATE TO PICK ON A *CRIPPLED* GUY, BUT--

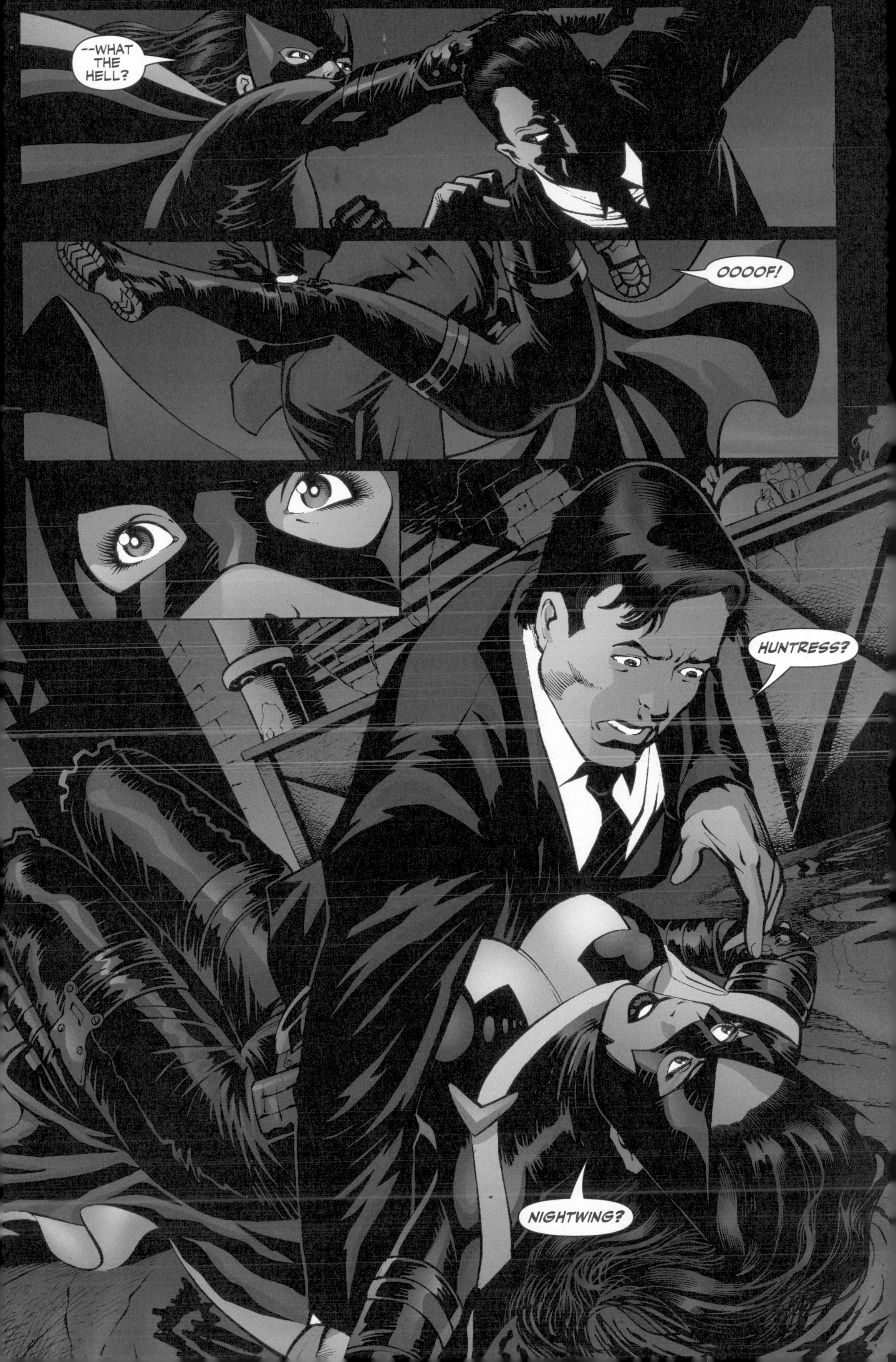
--WHAT THE HELL?
OOOOF!
HUNTRESS?
NIGHTWING?

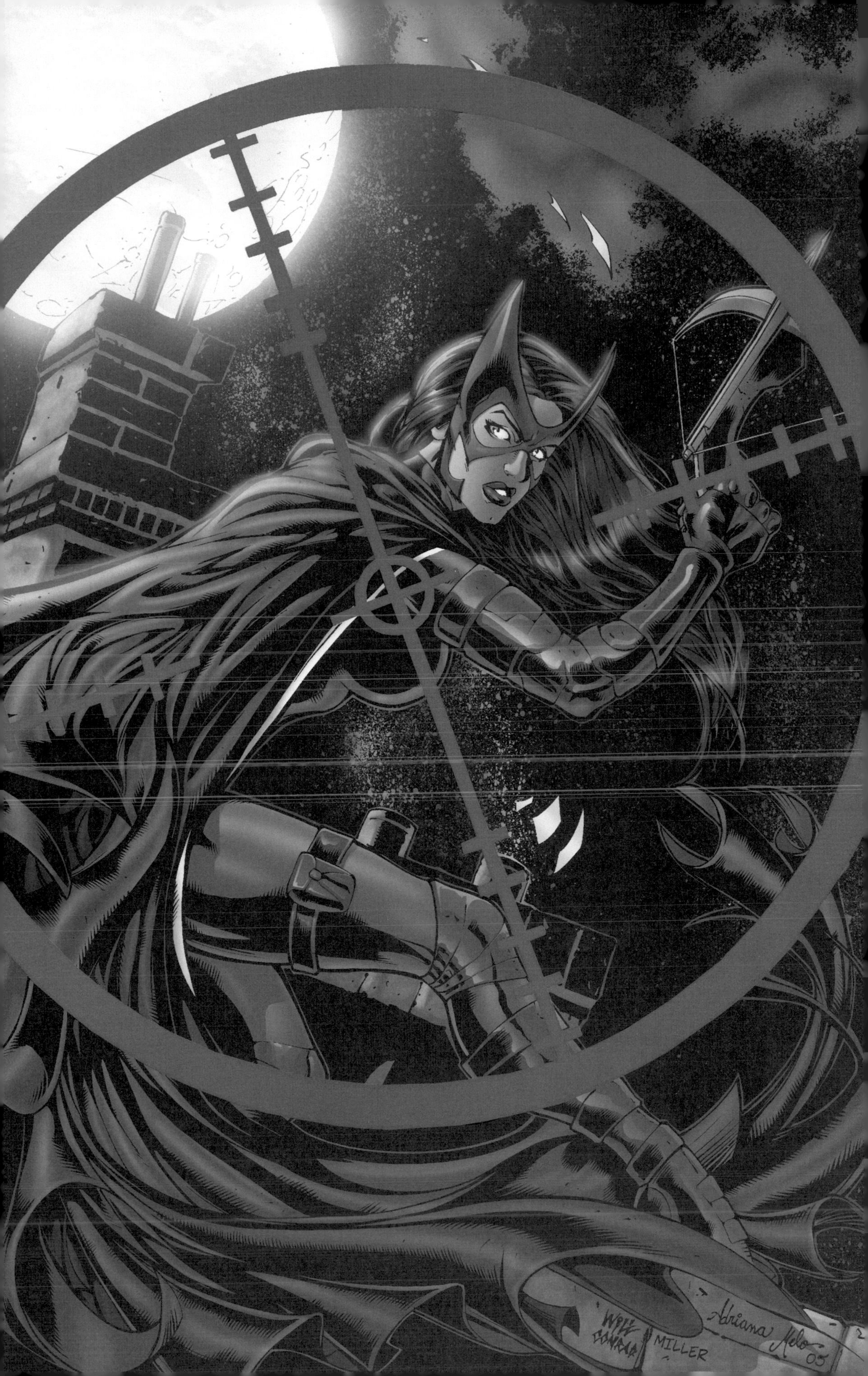
WILL CONRAD
MILLER
Adriana Melo 05

Cover art by
ADRIANA MELO
and WILL CONRAD

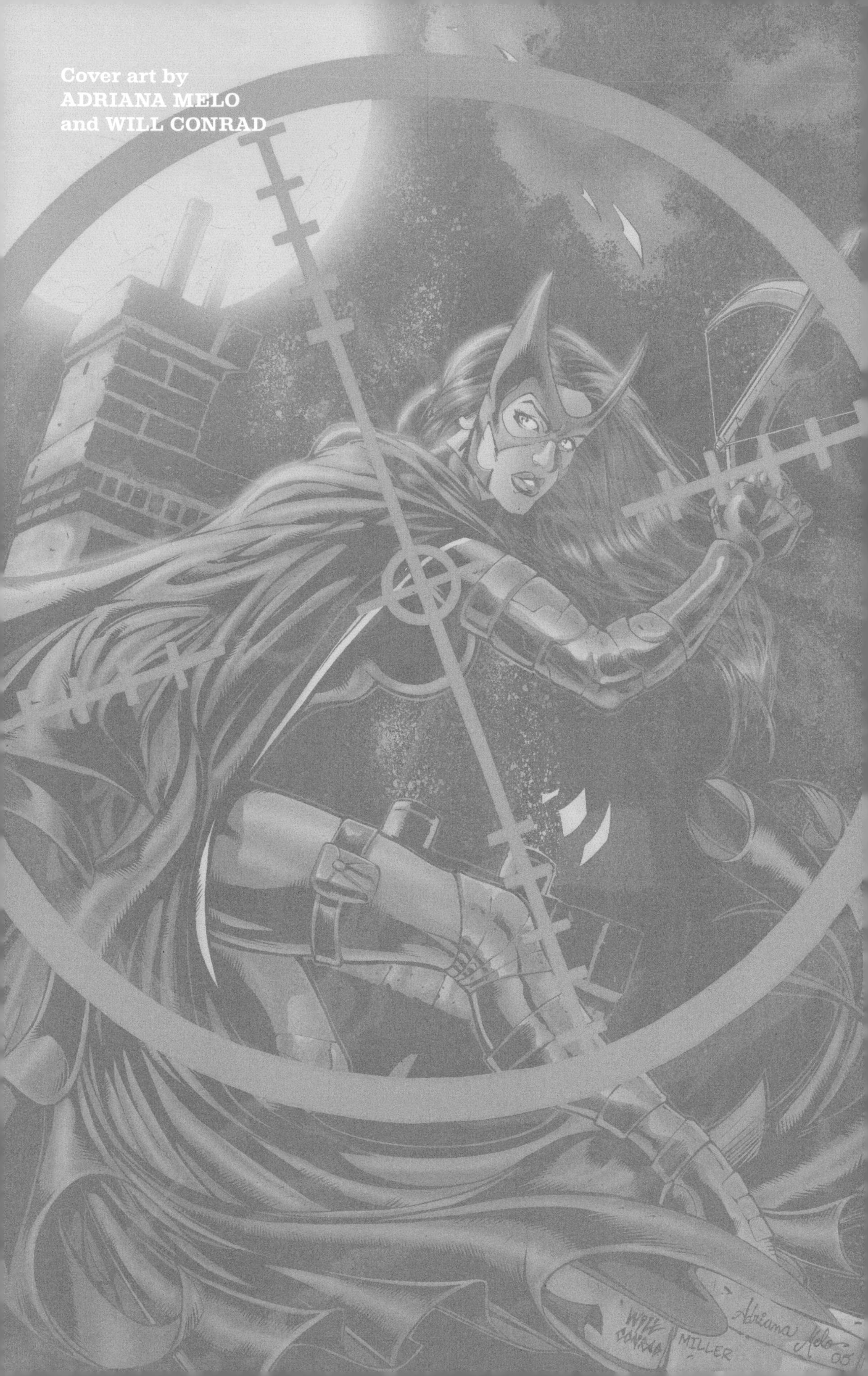
WILL CONRAD
MILLER
Adriana Melo
05

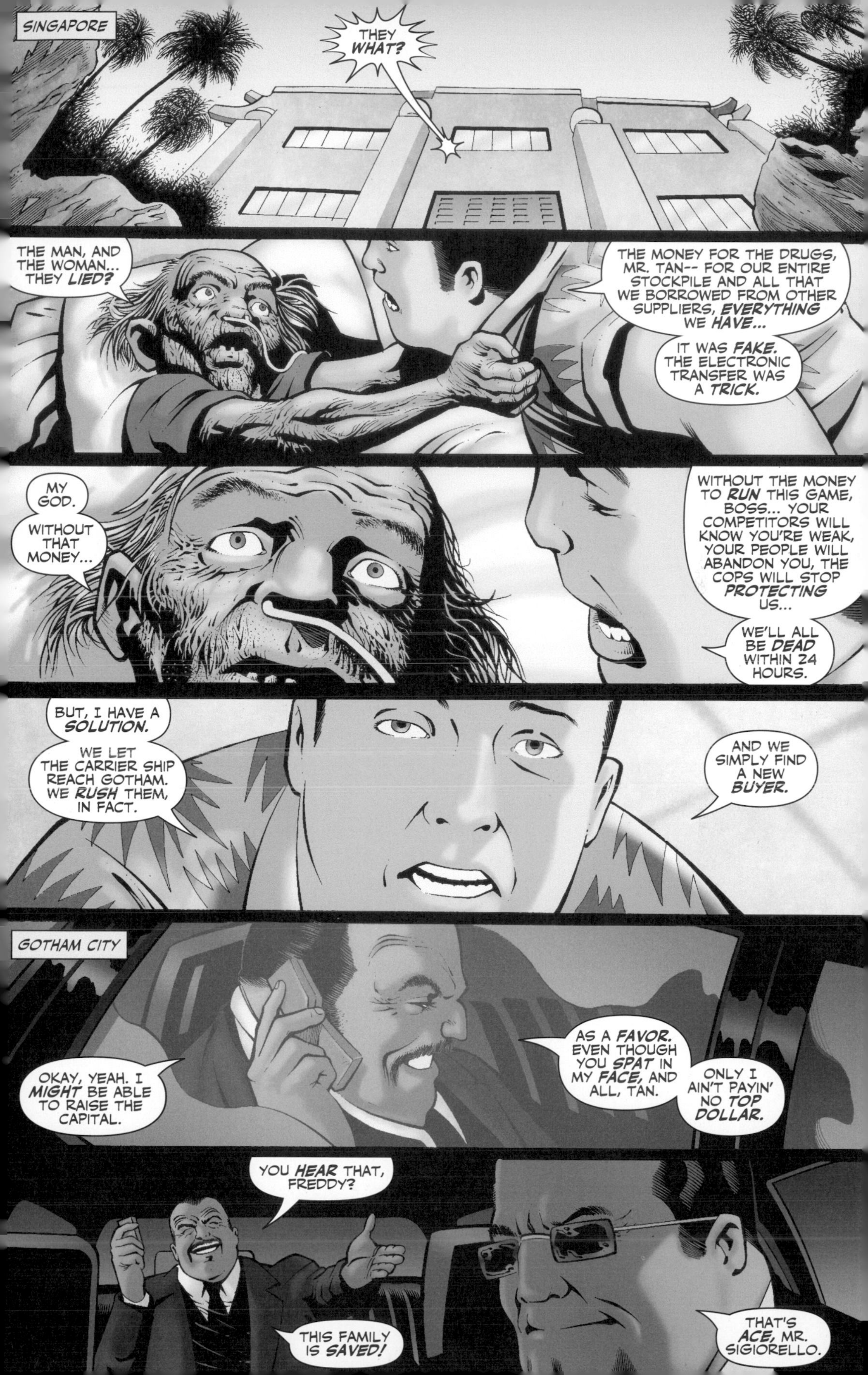
SINGAPORE
THEY WHAT?
THE MAN, AND THE WOMAN... THEY LIED?
THE MONEY FOR THE DRUGS, MR. TAN-- FOR OUR ENTIRE STOCKPILE AND ALL THAT WE BORROWED FROM OTHER SUPPLIERS, EVERYTHING WE HAVE...
IT WAS FAKE. THE ELECTRONIC TRANSFER WAS A TRICK.
MY GOD.
WITHOUT THAT MONEY...
WITHOUT THE MONEY TO RUN THIS GAME, BOSS... YOUR COMPETITORS WILL KNOW YOU'RE WEAK, YOUR PEOPLE WILL ABANDON YOU, THE COPS WILL STOP PROTECTING US...
WE'LL ALL BE DEAD WITHIN 24 HOURS.
BUT, I HAVE A SOLUTION.
WE LET THE CARRIER SHIP REACH GOTHAM. WE RUSH THEM, IN FACT.
AND WE SIMPLY FIND A NEW BUYER.
GOTHAM CITY
OKAY, YEAH. I MIGHT BE ABLE TO RAISE THE CAPITAL.
AS A FAVOR. EVEN THOUGH YOU SPAT IN MY FACE, AND ALL, TAN.
ONLY I AIN'T PAYIN' NO TOP DOLLAR.
YOU HEAR THAT, FREDDY?
THIS FAMILY IS SAVED!
THAT'S ACE, MR. SIGIORELLO.

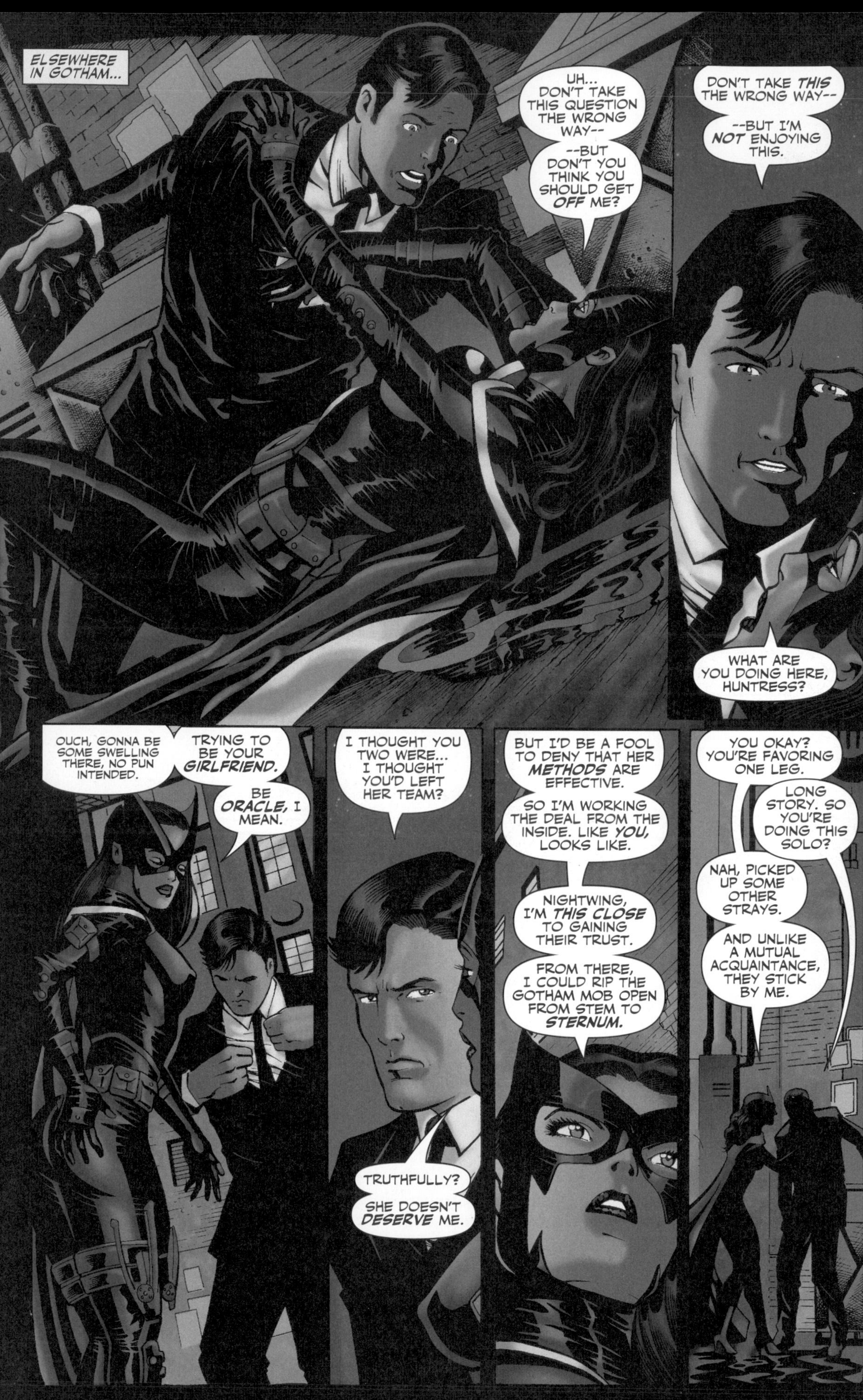

ELSEWHERE IN GOTHAM...
UH... DON'T TAKE THIS QUESTION THE WRONG WAY--
--BUT DON'T YOU THINK YOU SHOULD GET OFF ME?
DON'T TAKE THIS THE WRONG WAY--
--BUT I'M NOT ENJOYING THIS.
WHAT ARE YOU DOING HERE, HUNTRESS?
OUCH, GONNA BE SOME SWELLING THERE, NO PUN INTENDED.
TRYING TO BE YOUR GIRLFRIEND.
BE ORACLE, I MEAN.
I THOUGHT YOU TWO WERE... I THOUGHT YOU'D LEFT HER TEAM?
TRUTHFULLY?
SHE DOESN'T DESERVE ME.
BUT I'D BE A FOOL TO DENY THAT HER METHODS ARE EFFECTIVE.
SO I'M WORKING THE DEAL FROM THE INSIDE. LIKE YOU, LOOKS LIKE.
NIGHTWING, I'M THIS CLOSE TO GAINING THEIR TRUST.
FROM THERE, I COULD RIP THE GOTHAM MOB OPEN FROM STEM TO STERNUM.
YOU OKAY? YOU'RE FAVORING ONE LEG.
LONG STORY. SO YOU'RE DOING THIS SOLO?
NAH, PICKED UP SOME OTHER STRAYS.
AND UNLIKE A MUTUAL ACQUAINTANCE, THEY STICK BY ME.

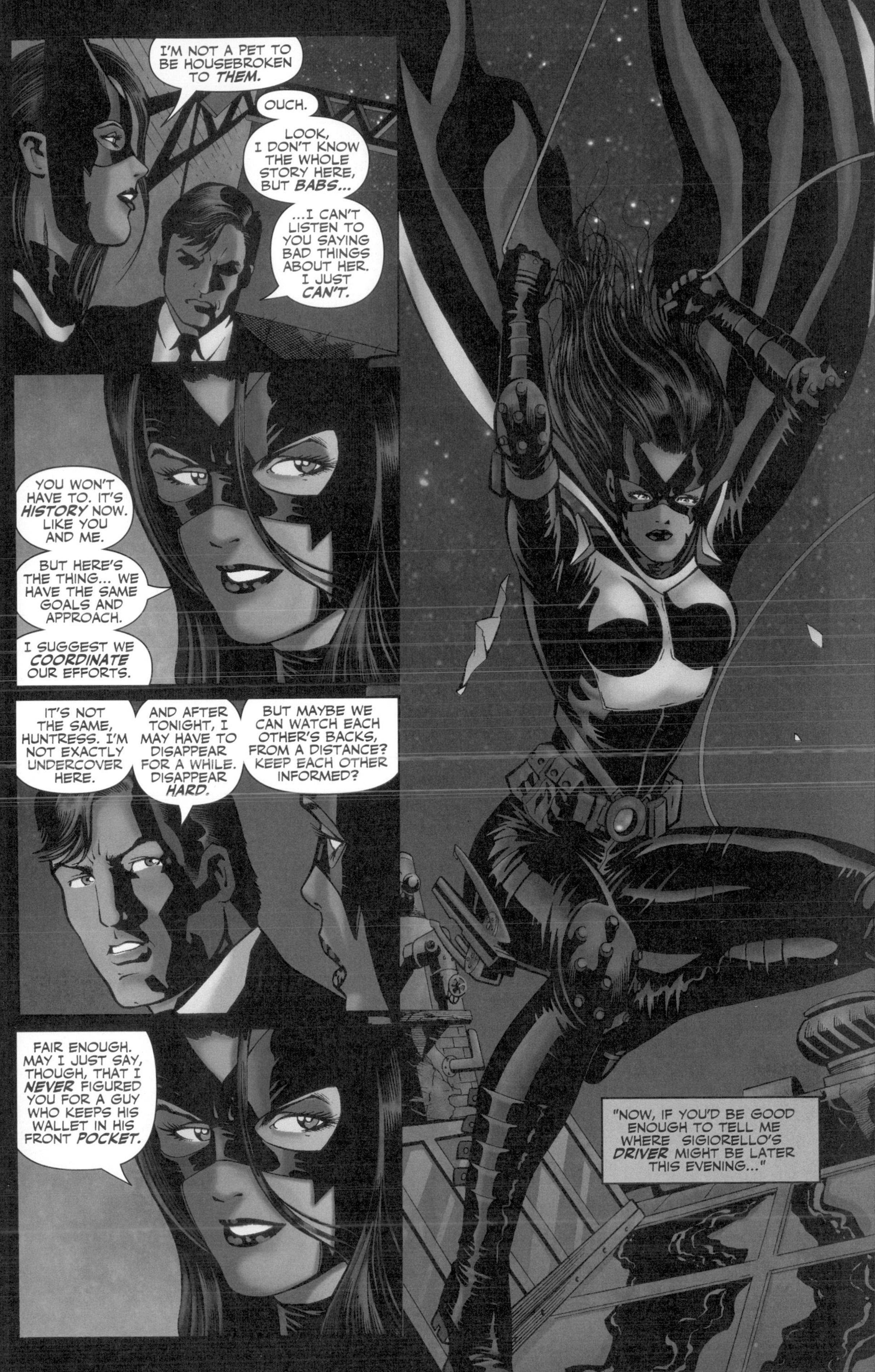
I'M NOT A PET TO BE HOUSEBROKEN TO *THEM.*
OUCH.
LOOK, I DON'T KNOW THE WHOLE STORY HERE, BUT *BABS...*
...I CAN'T LISTEN TO YOU SAYING BAD THINGS ABOUT HER. I JUST *CAN'T.*
YOU WON'T HAVE TO. IT'S *HISTORY* NOW. LIKE YOU AND ME.
BUT HERE'S THE THING... WE HAVE THE SAME GOALS AND APPROACH.
I SUGGEST WE *COORDINATE* OUR EFFORTS.
IT'S NOT THE SAME, HUNTRESS. I'M NOT EXACTLY UNDERCOVER HERE.
AND AFTER TONIGHT, I MAY HAVE TO DISAPPEAR FOR A WHILE. DISAPPEAR *HARD.*
BUT MAYBE WE CAN WATCH EACH OTHER'S BACKS, FROM A DISTANCE? KEEP EACH OTHER INFORMED?
FAIR ENOUGH. MAY I JUST SAY, THOUGH, THAT I *NEVER* FIGURED YOU FOR A GUY WHO KEEPS HIS WALLET IN HIS FRONT *POCKET.*
"NOW, IF YOU'D BE GOOD ENOUGH TO TELL ME WHERE SIGIORELLO'S *DRIVER* MIGHT BE LATER THIS EVENING..."

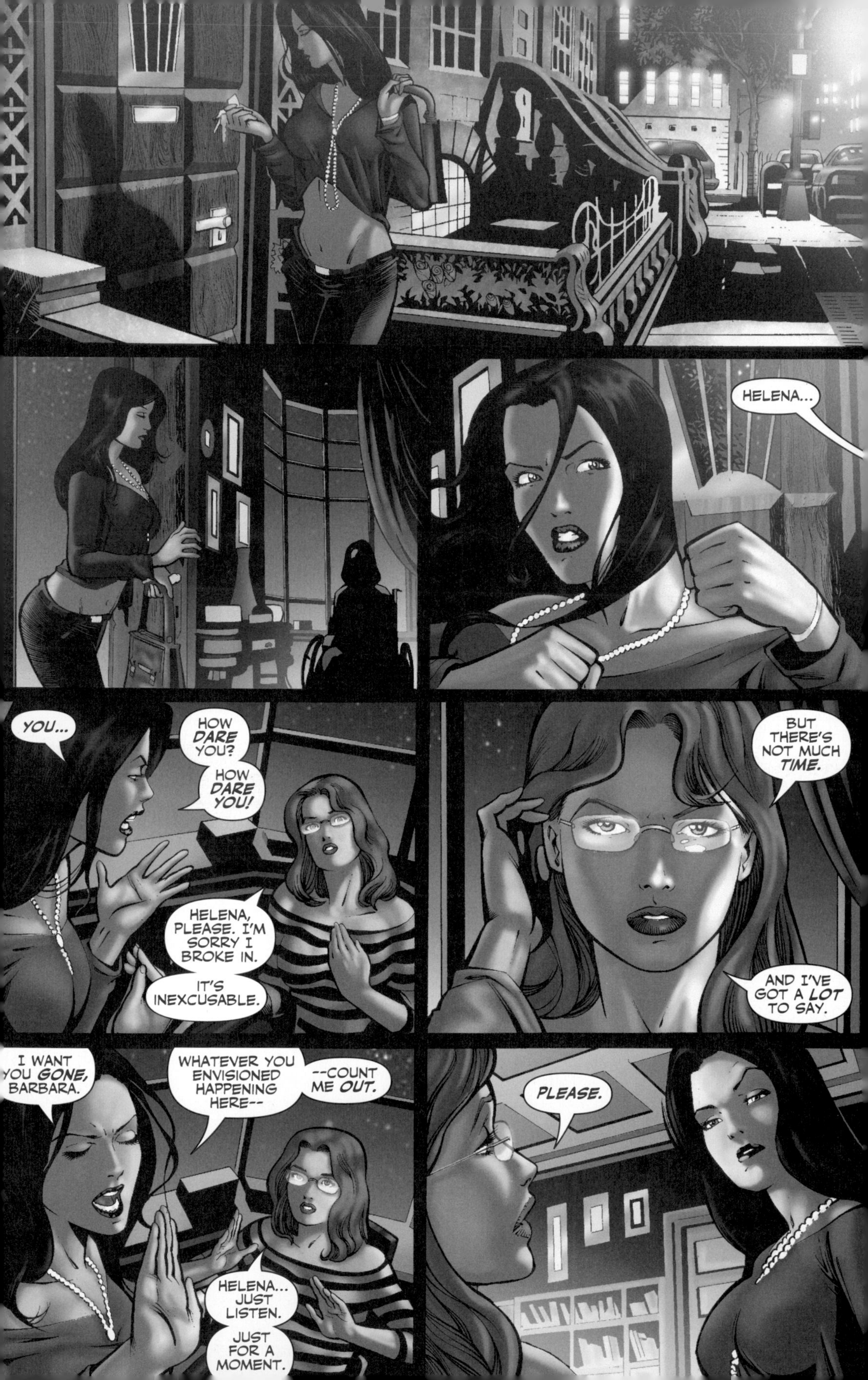
HELENA...
YOU...
HOW *DARE* YOU?
HOW *DARE* YOU!
HELENA, PLEASE. I'M SORRY I BROKE IN.
IT'S INEXCUSABLE.
BUT THERE'S NOT MUCH *TIME.*
AND I'VE GOT A *LOT* TO SAY.
I WANT YOU *GONE,* BARBARA.
WHATEVER YOU ENVISIONED HAPPENING HERE--
--COUNT ME *OUT.*
HELENA... JUST LISTEN.
JUST FOR A MOMENT.
PLEASE.

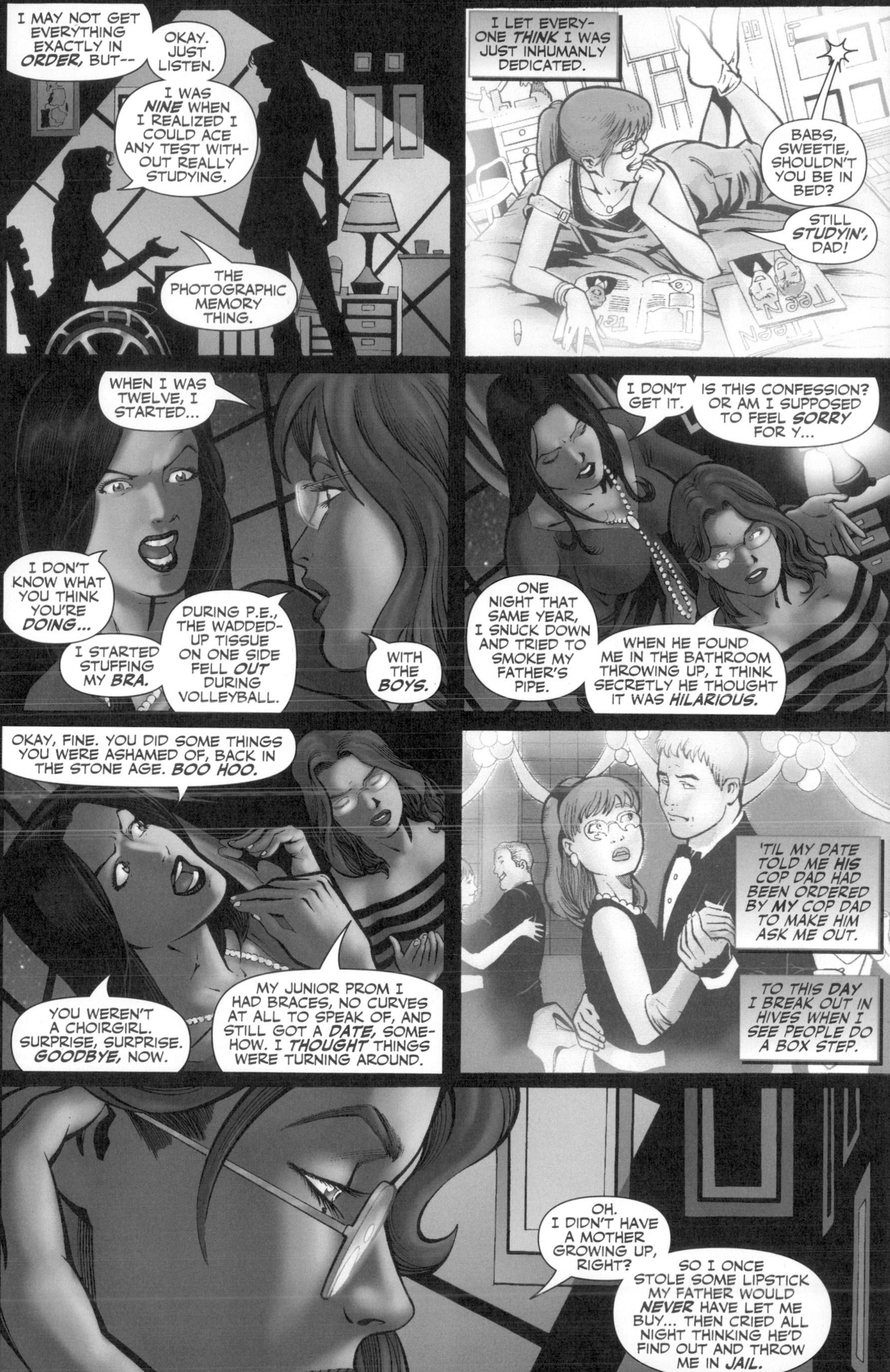
I MAY NOT GET EVERYTHING EXACTLY IN ORDER, BUT--
OKAY. JUST LISTEN.
I WAS NINE WHEN I REALIZED I COULD ACE ANY TEST WITH-OUT REALLY STUDYING.
THE PHOTOGRAPHIC MEMORY THING.
I LET EVERY-ONE THINK I WAS JUST INHUMANLY DEDICATED.
BABS, SWEETIE, SHOULDN'T YOU BE IN BED?
STILL STUDYIN', DAD!
TEEN
WHEN I WAS TWELVE, I STARTED...
I DON'T KNOW WHAT YOU THINK YOU'RE DOING...
I STARTED STUFFING MY BRA.
DURING P.E., THE WADDED-UP TISSUE ON ONE SIDE FELL OUT DURING VOLLEYBALL.
WITH THE BOYS.
I DON'T GET IT.
IS THIS CONFESSION? OR AM I SUPPOSED TO FEEL SORRY FOR Y...
ONE NIGHT THAT SAME YEAR, I SNUCK DOWN AND TRIED TO SMOKE MY FATHER'S PIPE.
WHEN HE FOUND ME IN THE BATHROOM THROWING UP, I THINK SECRETLY HE THOUGHT IT WAS HILARIOUS.
OKAY, FINE. YOU DID SOME THINGS YOU WERE ASHAMED OF, BACK IN THE STONE AGE. BOO HOO.
YOU WEREN'T A CHOIRGIRL. SURPRISE, SURPRISE. GOODBYE, NOW.
MY JUNIOR PROM I HAD BRACES, NO CURVES AT ALL TO SPEAK OF, AND STILL GOT A DATE, SOME-HOW. I THOUGHT THINGS WERE TURNING AROUND.
'TIL MY DATE TOLD ME HIS COP DAD HAD BEEN ORDERED BY MY COP DAD TO MAKE HIM ASK ME OUT.
TO THIS DAY I BREAK OUT IN HIVES WHEN I SEE PEOPLE DO A BOX STEP.
OH. I DIDN'T HAVE A MOTHER GROWING UP, RIGHT?
SO I ONCE STOLE SOME LIPSTICK MY FATHER WOULD NEVER HAVE LET ME BUY... THEN CRIED ALL NIGHT THINKING HE'D FIND OUT AND THROW ME IN JAIL.

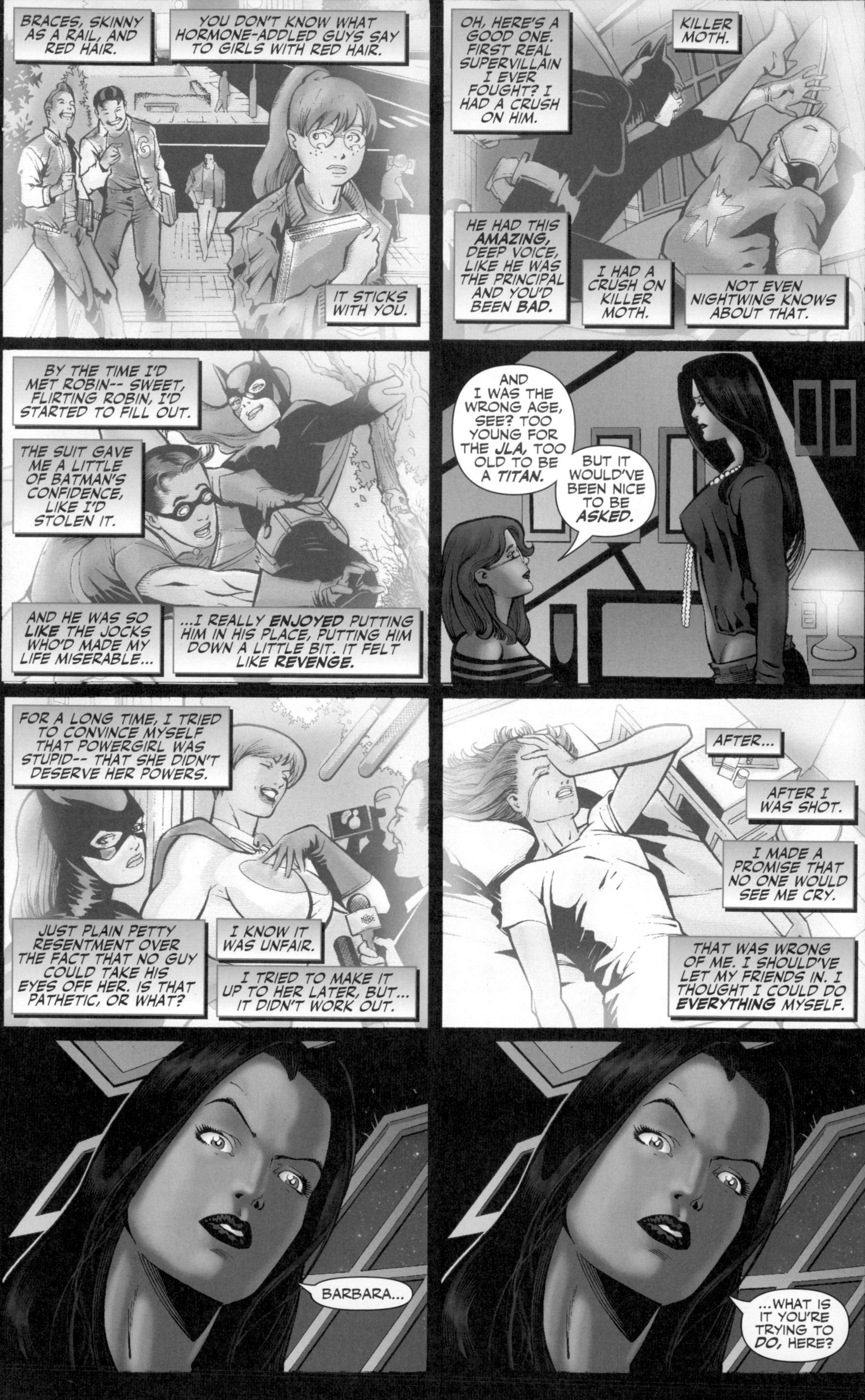
BRACES, SKINNY AS A RAIL, AND RED HAIR.
YOU DON'T KNOW WHAT HORMONE-ADDLED GUYS SAY TO GIRLS WITH RED HAIR.
IT STICKS WITH YOU.
OH, HERE'S A GOOD ONE. FIRST REAL SUPERVILLAIN I EVER FOUGHT? I HAD A CRUSH ON HIM.
KILLER MOTH.
HE HAD THIS AMAZING, DEEP VOICE, LIKE HE WAS THE PRINCIPAL AND YOU'D BEEN BAD.
I HAD A CRUSH ON KILLER MOTH.
NOT EVEN NIGHTWING KNOWS ABOUT THAT.
BY THE TIME I'D MET ROBIN-- SWEET, FLIRTING ROBIN, I'D STARTED TO FILL OUT.
THE SUIT GAVE ME A LITTLE OF BATMAN'S CONFIDENCE, LIKE I'D STOLEN IT.
AND HE WAS SO LIKE THE JOCKS WHO'D MADE MY LIFE MISERABLE...
...I REALLY ENJOYED PUTTING HIM IN HIS PLACE, PUTTING HIM DOWN A LITTLE BIT. IT FELT LIKE REVENGE.
AND I WAS THE WRONG AGE, SEE? TOO YOUNG FOR THE JLA, TOO OLD TO BE A TITAN.
BUT IT WOULD'VE BEEN NICE TO BE ASKED.
FOR A LONG TIME, I TRIED TO CONVINCE MYSELF THAT POWERGIRL WAS STUPID-- THAT SHE DIDN'T DESERVE HER POWERS.
JUST PLAIN PETTY RESENTMENT OVER THE FACT THAT NO GUY COULD TAKE HIS EYES OFF HER. IS THAT PATHETIC, OR WHAT?
I KNOW IT WAS UNFAIR.
I TRIED TO MAKE IT UP TO HER LATER, BUT... IT DIDN'T WORK OUT.
AFTER...
AFTER I WAS SHOT.
I MADE A PROMISE THAT NO ONE WOULD SEE ME CRY.
THAT WAS WRONG OF ME. I SHOULD'VE LET MY FRIENDS IN. I THOUGHT I COULD DO EVERYTHING MYSELF.
BARBARA...
...WHAT IS IT YOU'RE TRYING TO DO, HERE?

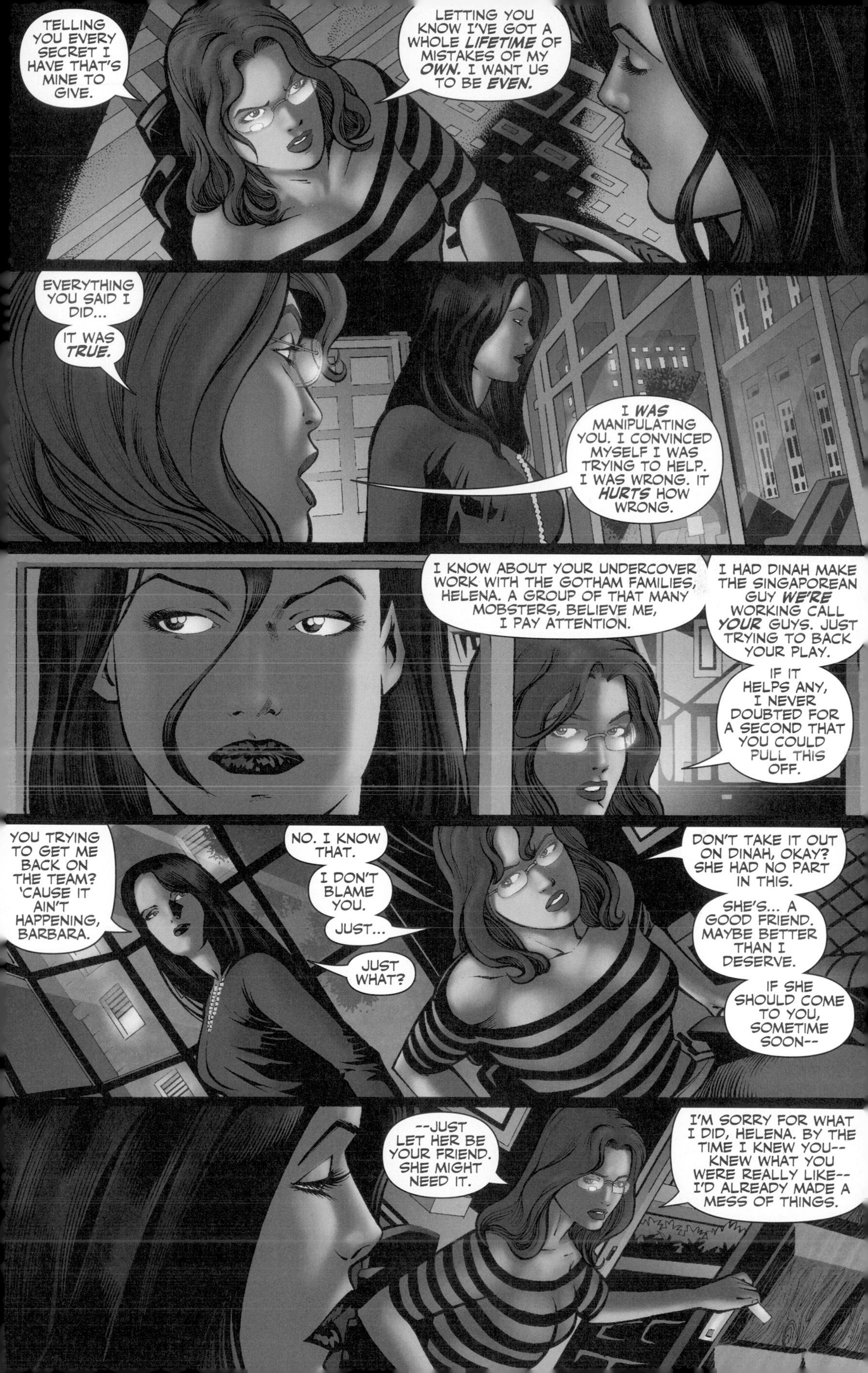
TELLING YOU EVERY SECRET I HAVE THAT'S MINE TO GIVE.
LETTING YOU KNOW I'VE GOT A WHOLE *LIFETIME* OF MISTAKES OF MY *OWN.* I WANT US TO BE *EVEN.*
EVERYTHING YOU SAID I DID...
IT WAS *TRUE.*
I *WAS* MANIPULATING YOU. I CONVINCED MYSELF I WAS TRYING TO HELP. I WAS WRONG. IT *HURTS* HOW WRONG.
I KNOW ABOUT YOUR UNDERCOVER WORK WITH THE GOTHAM FAMILIES, HELENA. A GROUP OF THAT MANY MOBSTERS, BELIEVE ME, I PAY ATTENTION.
I HAD DINAH MAKE THE SINGAPOREAN GUY *WE'RE* WORKING CALL *YOUR* GUYS. JUST TRYING TO BACK YOUR PLAY.
IF IT HELPS ANY, I NEVER DOUBTED FOR A SECOND THAT YOU COULD PULL THIS OFF.
YOU TRYING TO GET ME BACK ON THE TEAM? 'CAUSE IT AIN'T HAPPENING, BARBARA.
NO. I KNOW THAT.
I DON'T BLAME YOU.
JUST...
JUST WHAT?
DON'T TAKE IT OUT ON DINAH, OKAY? SHE HAD NO PART IN THIS.
SHE'S... A GOOD FRIEND. MAYBE BETTER THAN I DESERVE.
IF SHE SHOULD COME TO YOU, SOMETIME SOON--
--JUST LET HER BE YOUR FRIEND. SHE MIGHT NEED IT.
I'M SORRY FOR WHAT I DID, HELENA. BY THE TIME I KNEW YOU-- KNEW WHAT YOU WERE REALLY LIKE-- I'D ALREADY MADE A MESS OF THINGS.

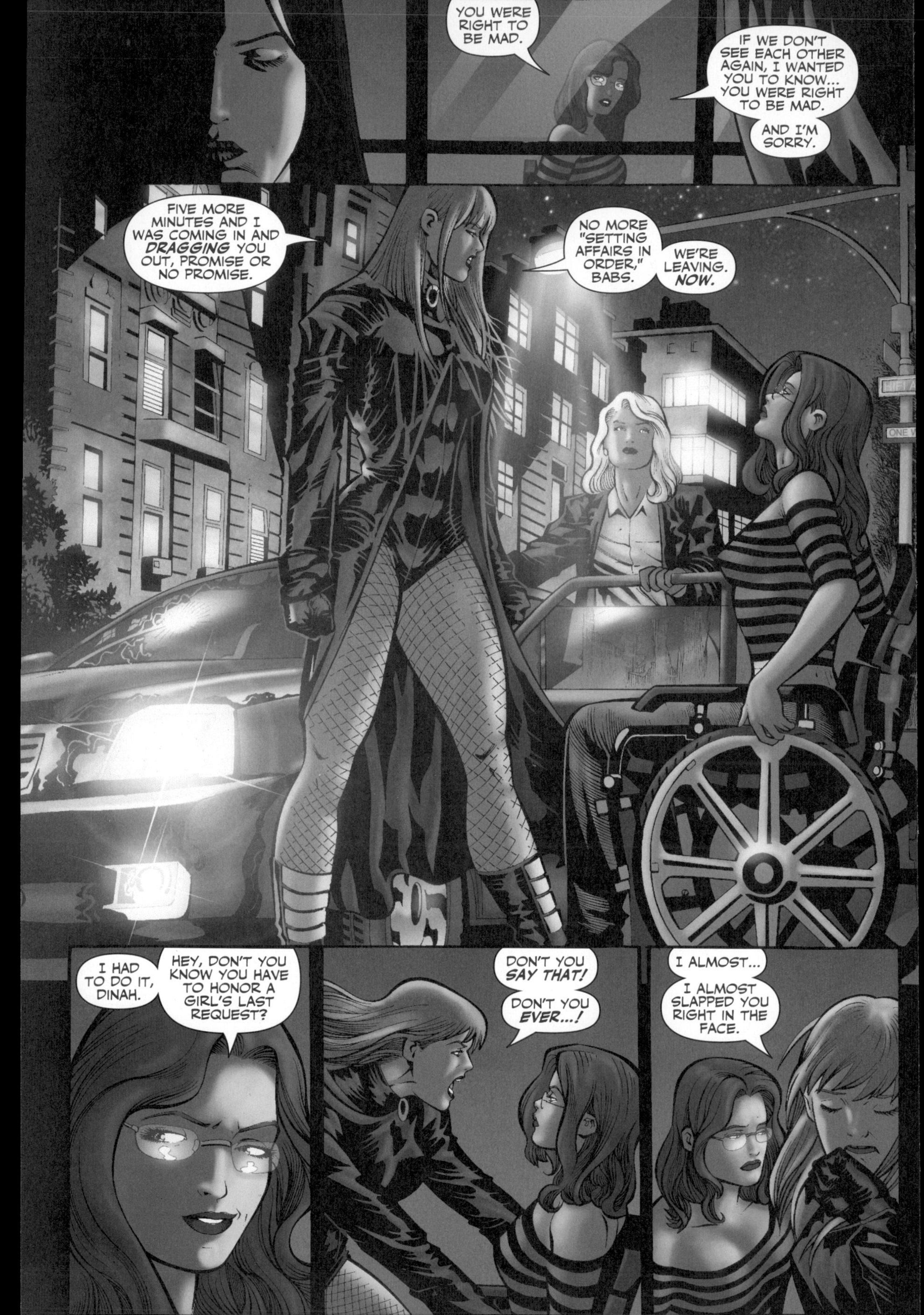
YOU WERE RIGHT TO BE MAD.
IF WE DON'T SEE EACH OTHER AGAIN, I WANTED YOU TO KNOW... YOU WERE RIGHT TO BE MAD.
AND I'M SORRY.
FIVE MORE MINUTES AND I WAS COMING IN AND DRAGGING YOU OUT, PROMISE OR NO PROMISE.
NO MORE "SETTING AFFAIRS IN ORDER," BABS.
WE'RE LEAVING. NOW.
ONE W
I HAD TO DO IT, DINAH.
HEY, DON'T YOU KNOW YOU HAVE TO HONOR A GIRL'S LAST REQUEST?
DON'T YOU SAY THAT!
DON'T YOU EVER...!
I ALMOST...
I ALMOST SLAPPED YOU RIGHT IN THE FACE.

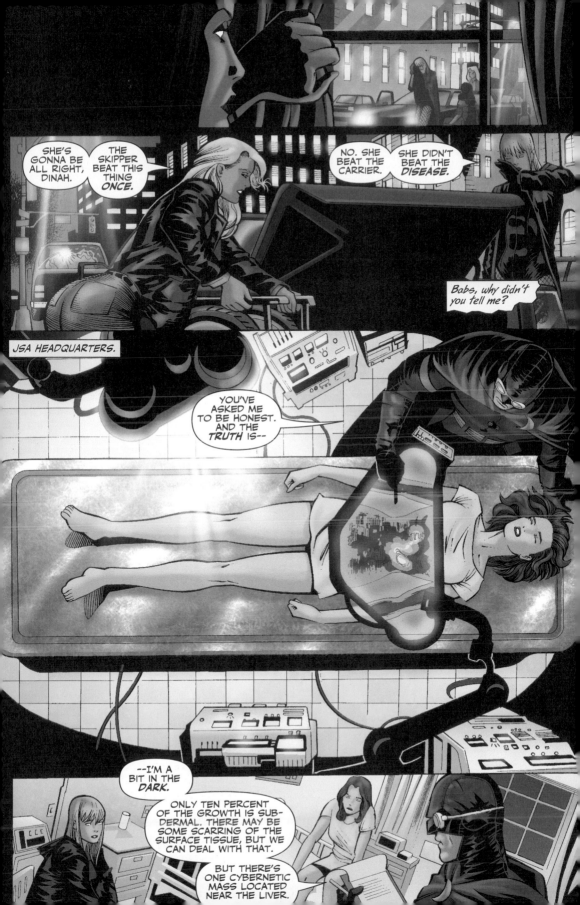

SHE'S GONNA BE ALL RIGHT, DINAH.

THE SKIPPER BEAT THIS THING *ONCE*.

NO. SHE BEAT THE CARRIER.

SHE DIDN'T BEAT THE *DISEASE*.

Babs, why didn't you tell me?

JSA HEADQUARTERS.

YOU'VE ASKED ME TO BE HONEST. AND THE *TRUTH* IS--

--I'M A BIT IN THE *DARK*.

ONLY TEN PERCENT OF THE GROWTH IS SUB-DERMAL. THERE MAY BE SOME SCARRING OF THE SURFACE TISSUE, BUT WE CAN DEAL WITH THAT.

BUT THERE'S ONE CYBERNETIC MASS LOCATED NEAR THE LIVER.

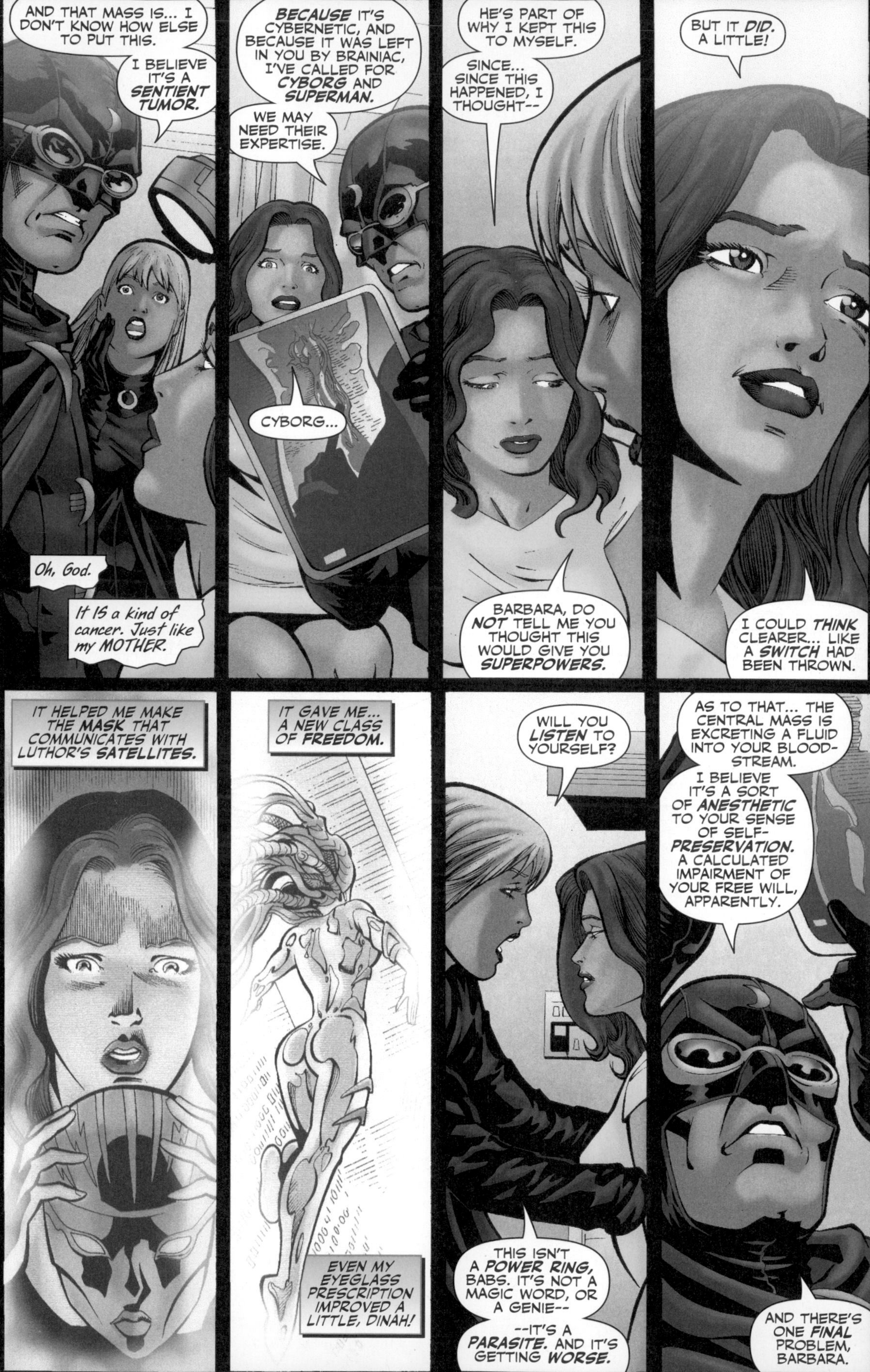
AND THAT MASS IS... I DON'T KNOW HOW ELSE TO PUT THIS.
I BELIEVE IT'S A SENTIENT TUMOR.
Oh, God.
It IS a kind of cancer. Just like my MOTHER.
BECAUSE IT'S CYBERNETIC, AND BECAUSE IT WAS LEFT IN YOU BY BRAINIAC, I'VE CALLED FOR CYBORG AND SUPERMAN.
WE MAY NEED THEIR EXPERTISE.
CYBORG...
HE'S PART OF WHY I KEPT THIS TO MYSELF.
SINCE... SINCE THIS HAPPENED, I THOUGHT--
BARBARA, DO NOT TELL ME YOU THOUGHT THIS WOULD GIVE YOU SUPERPOWERS.
BUT IT DID. A LITTLE!
I COULD THINK CLEARER... LIKE A SWITCH HAD BEEN THROWN.
IT HELPED ME MAKE THE MASK THAT COMMUNICATES WITH LUTHOR'S SATELLITES.
IT GAVE ME... A NEW CLASS OF FREEDOM.
EVEN MY EYEGLASS PRESCRIPTION IMPROVED A LITTLE, DINAH!
WILL YOU LISTEN TO YOURSELF?
THIS ISN'T A POWER RING, BABS. IT'S NOT A MAGIC WORD, OR A GENIE--
--IT'S A PARASITE. AND IT'S GETTING WORSE.
AS TO THAT... THE CENTRAL MASS IS EXCRETING A FLUID INTO YOUR BLOODSTREAM.
I BELIEVE IT'S A SORT OF ANESTHETIC TO YOUR SENSE OF SELF-PRESERVATION. A CALCULATED IMPAIRMENT OF YOUR FREE WILL, APPARENTLY.
AND THERE'S ONE FINAL PROBLEM, BARBARA.

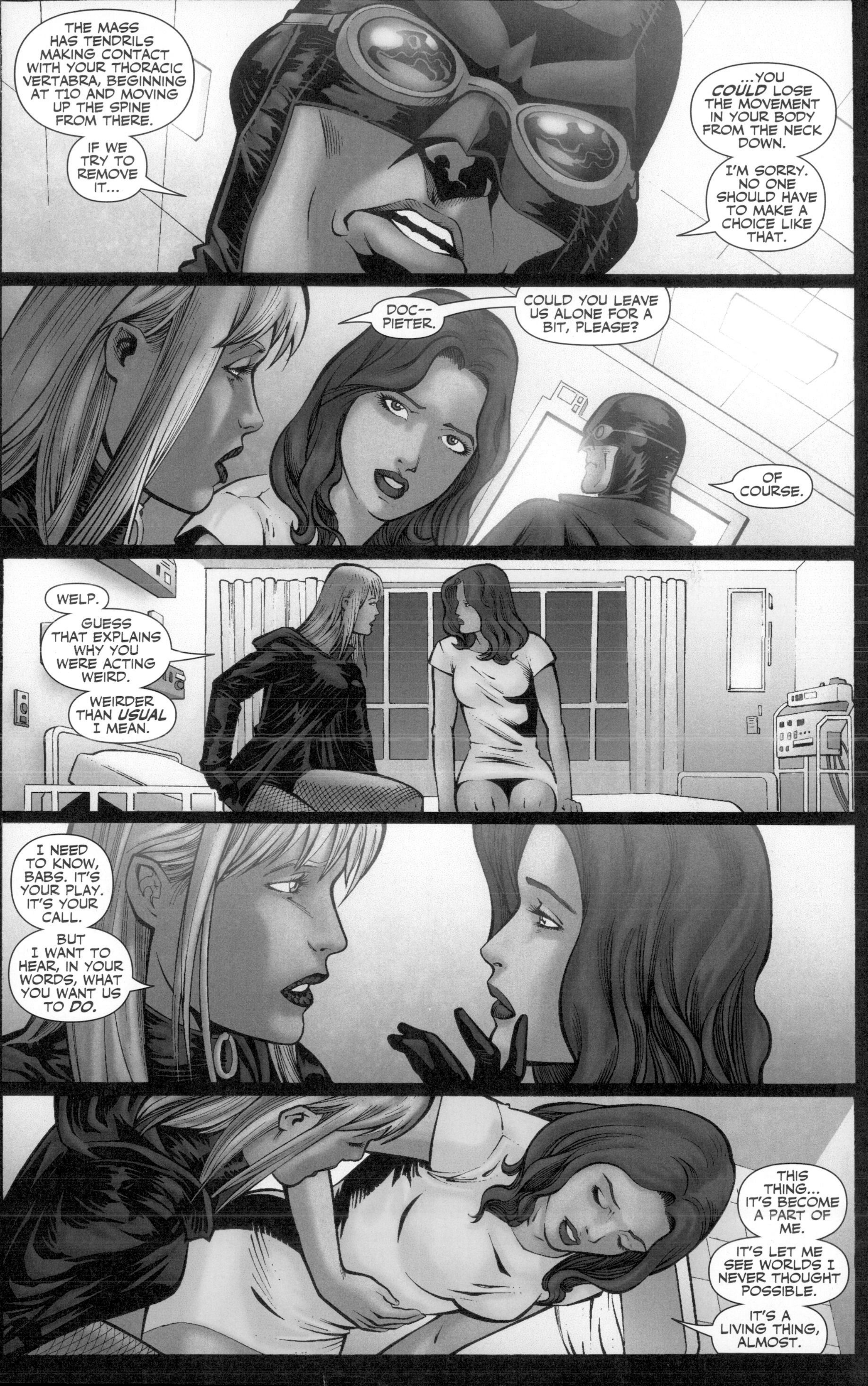
THE MASS HAS TENDRILS MAKING CONTACT WITH YOUR THORACIC VERTABRA, BEGINNING AT T10 AND MOVING UP THE SPINE FROM THERE.
IF WE TRY TO REMOVE IT...
...YOU *COULD* LOSE THE MOVEMENT IN YOUR BODY FROM THE NECK DOWN.
I'M SORRY. NO ONE SHOULD HAVE TO MAKE A CHOICE LIKE THAT.
DOC-- PIETER.
COULD YOU LEAVE US ALONE FOR A BIT, PLEASE?
OF COURSE.
WELP.
GUESS THAT EXPLAINS WHY YOU WERE ACTING WEIRD.
WEIRDER THAN *USUAL* I MEAN.
I NEED TO KNOW, BABS. IT'S YOUR PLAY. IT'S YOUR CALL.
BUT I WANT TO HEAR, IN YOUR WORDS, WHAT YOU WANT US TO *DO*.
THIS THING... IT'S BECOME A PART OF ME.
IT'S LET ME SEE WORLDS I NEVER THOUGHT POSSIBLE.
IT'S A LIVING THING, ALMOST.

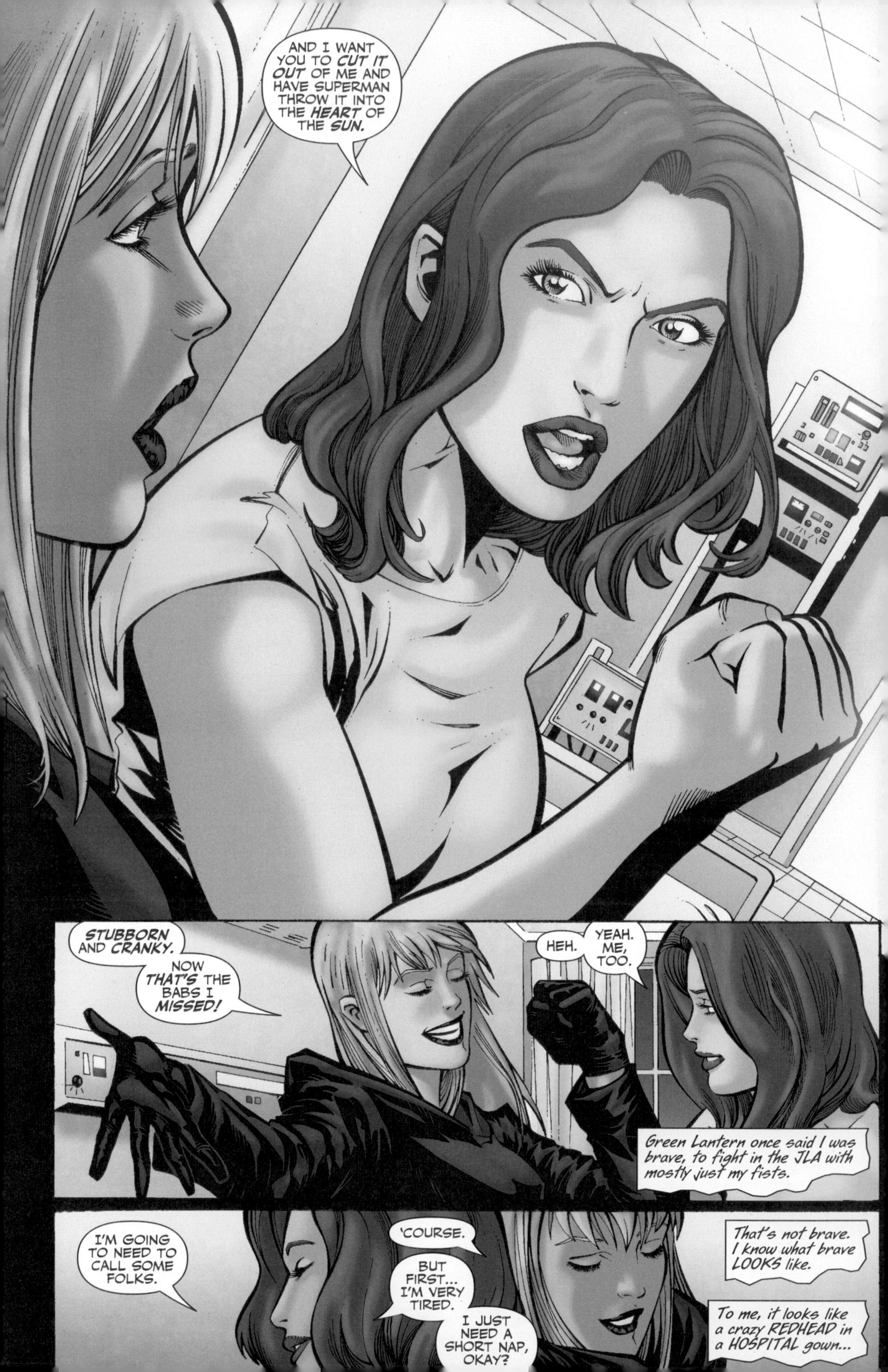
AND I WANT YOU TO CUT IT OUT OF ME AND HAVE SUPERMAN THROW IT INTO THE HEART OF THE SUN.
STUBBORN AND CRANKY.
NOW THAT'S THE BABS I MISSED!
HEH.
YEAH. ME, TOO.
Green Lantern once said I was brave, to fight in the JLA with mostly just my fists.
I'M GOING TO NEED TO CALL SOME FOLKS.
'COURSE.
BUT FIRST... I'M VERY TIRED.
I JUST NEED A SHORT NAP, OKAY?
That's not brave. I know what brave LOOKS like.
To me, it looks like a crazy REDHEAD in a HOSPITAL gown...

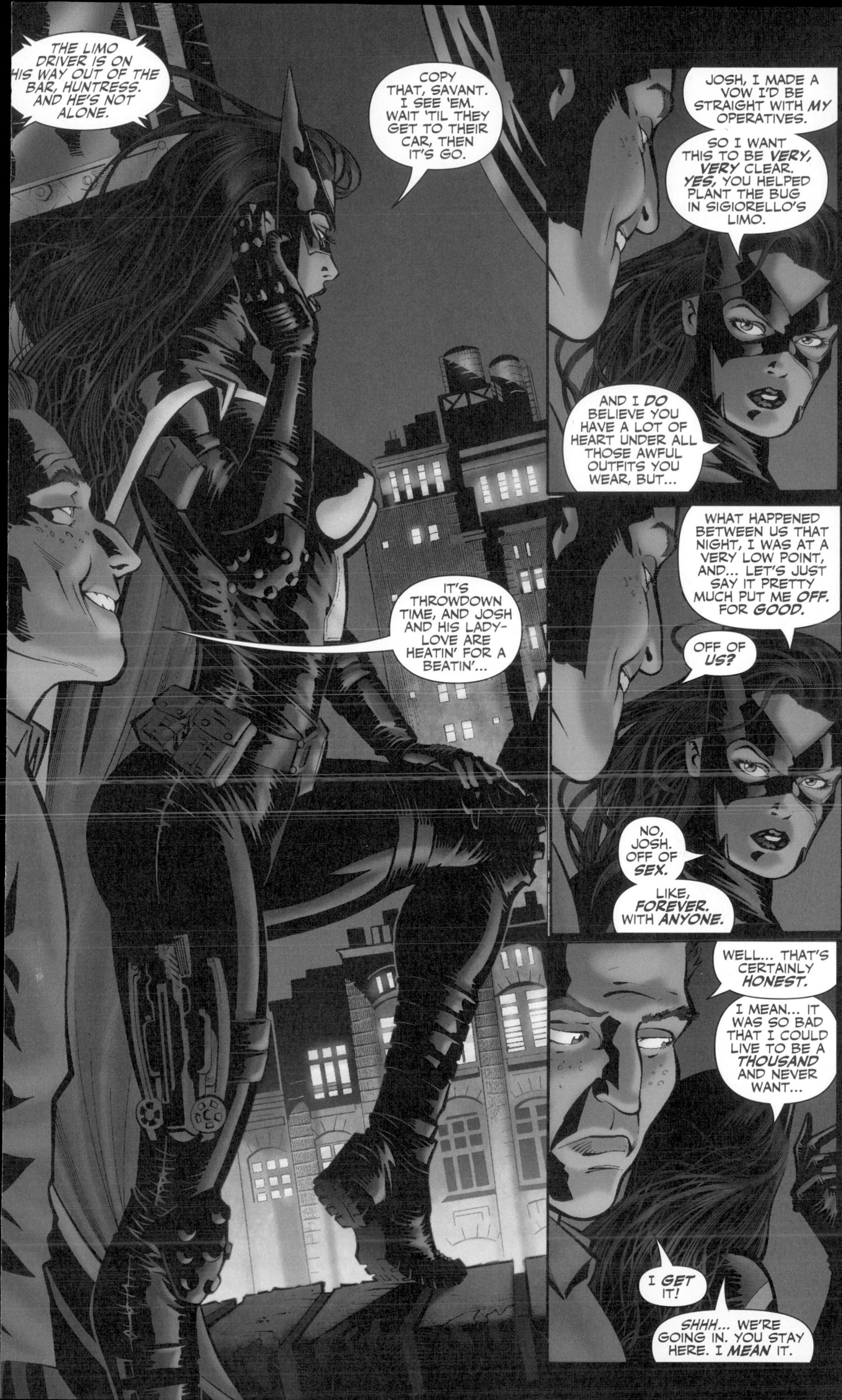
THE LIMO DRIVER IS ON HIS WAY OUT OF THE BAR, HUNTRESS. AND HE'S NOT ALONE.
COPY THAT, SAVANT. I SEE 'EM. WAIT 'TIL THEY GET TO THEIR CAR, THEN IT'S GO.
IT'S THROWDOWN TIME, AND JOSH AND HIS LADY-LOVE ARE HEATIN' FOR A BEATIN'...
JOSH, I MADE A VOW I'D BE STRAIGHT WITH MY OPERATIVES.
SO I WANT THIS TO BE VERY, VERY CLEAR. YES, YOU HELPED PLANT THE BUG IN SIGIORELLO'S LIMO.
AND I DO BELIEVE YOU HAVE A LOT OF HEART UNDER ALL THOSE AWFUL OUTFITS YOU WEAR, BUT...
WHAT HAPPENED BETWEEN US THAT NIGHT, I WAS AT A VERY LOW POINT, AND... LET'S JUST SAY IT PRETTY MUCH PUT ME OFF. FOR GOOD.
OFF OF US?
NO, JOSH. OFF OF SEX.
LIKE, FOREVER. WITH ANYONE.
WELL... THAT'S CERTAINLY HONEST.
I MEAN... IT WAS SO BAD THAT I COULD LIVE TO BE A THOUSAND AND NEVER WANT...
I GET IT!
SHHH... WE'RE GOING IN. YOU STAY HERE. I MEAN IT.

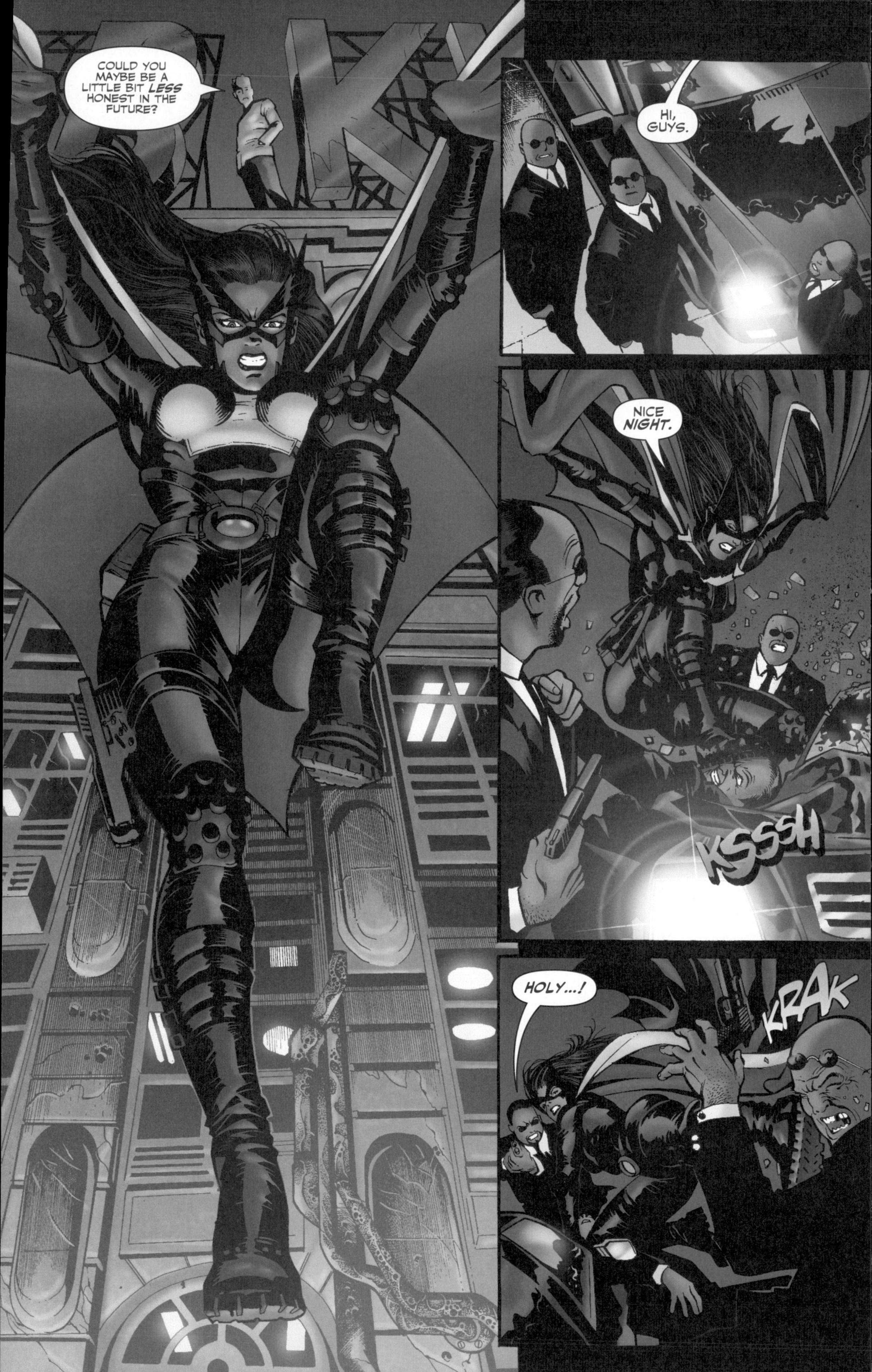
COULD YOU MAYBE BE A LITTLE BIT *LESS* HONEST IN THE FUTURE?
HI, GUYS.
NICE *NIGHT*.
KSSSH
HOLY...!
KRAK

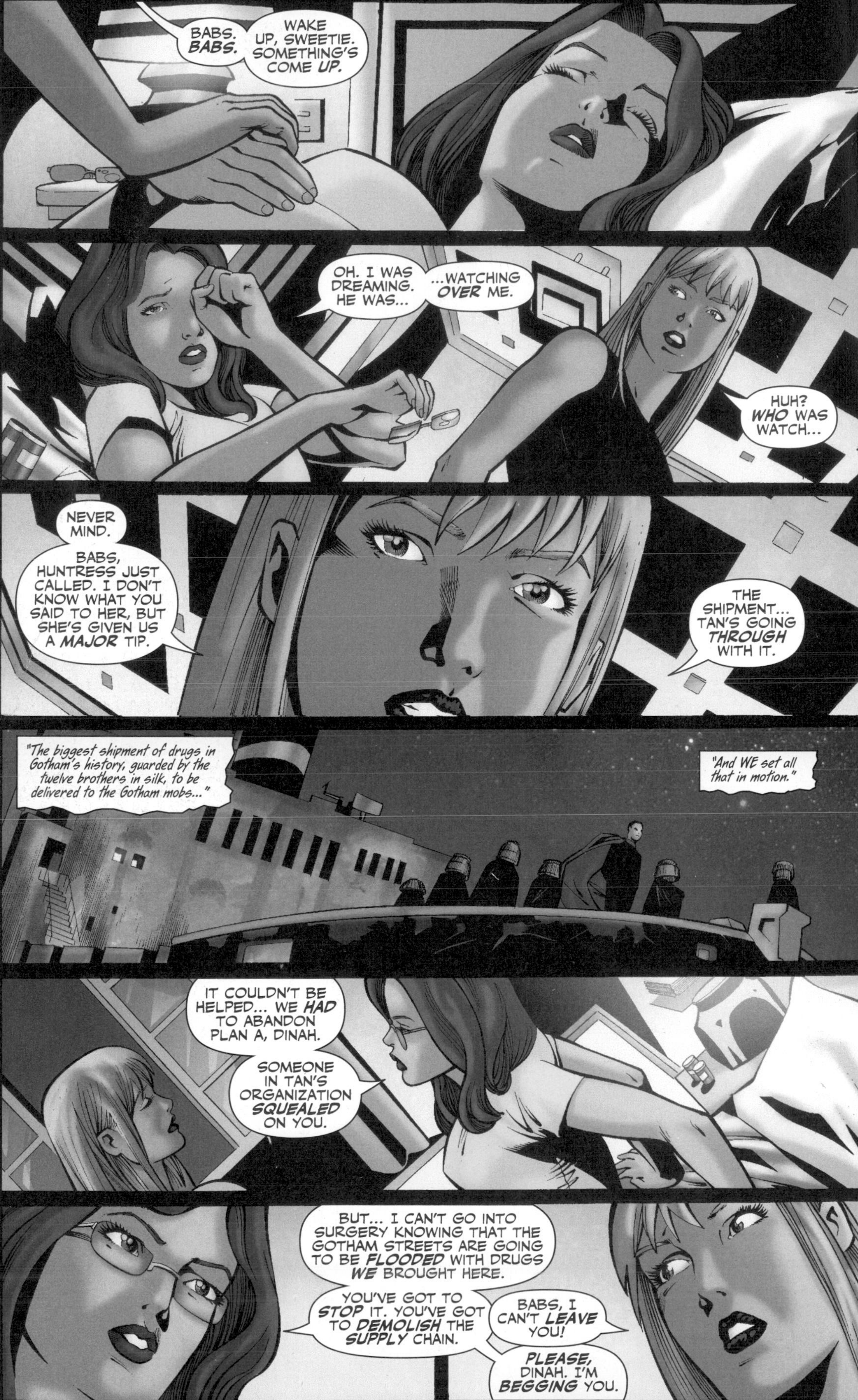

BABS. BABS.
WAKE UP, SWEETIE. SOMETHING'S COME UP.
OH. I WAS DREAMING. HE WAS...
...WATCHING OVER ME.
HUH? WHO WAS WATCH...
NEVER MIND.
BABS, HUNTRESS JUST CALLED. I DON'T KNOW WHAT YOU SAID TO HER, BUT SHE'S GIVEN US A MAJOR TIP.
THE SHIPMENT... TAN'S GOING THROUGH WITH IT.
"The biggest shipment of drugs in Gotham's history, guarded by the twelve brothers in silk, to be delivered to the Gotham mobs..."
"And WE set all that in motion."
IT COULDN'T BE HELPED... WE HAD TO ABANDON PLAN A, DINAH.
SOMEONE IN TAN'S ORGANIZATION SQUEALED ON YOU.
BUT... I CAN'T GO INTO SURGERY KNOWING THAT THE GOTHAM STREETS ARE GOING TO BE FLOODED WITH DRUGS WE BROUGHT HERE.
YOU'VE GOT TO STOP IT. YOU'VE GOT TO DEMOLISH THE SUPPLY CHAIN.
BABS, I CAN'T LEAVE YOU!
PLEASE, DINAH. I'M BEGGING YOU.

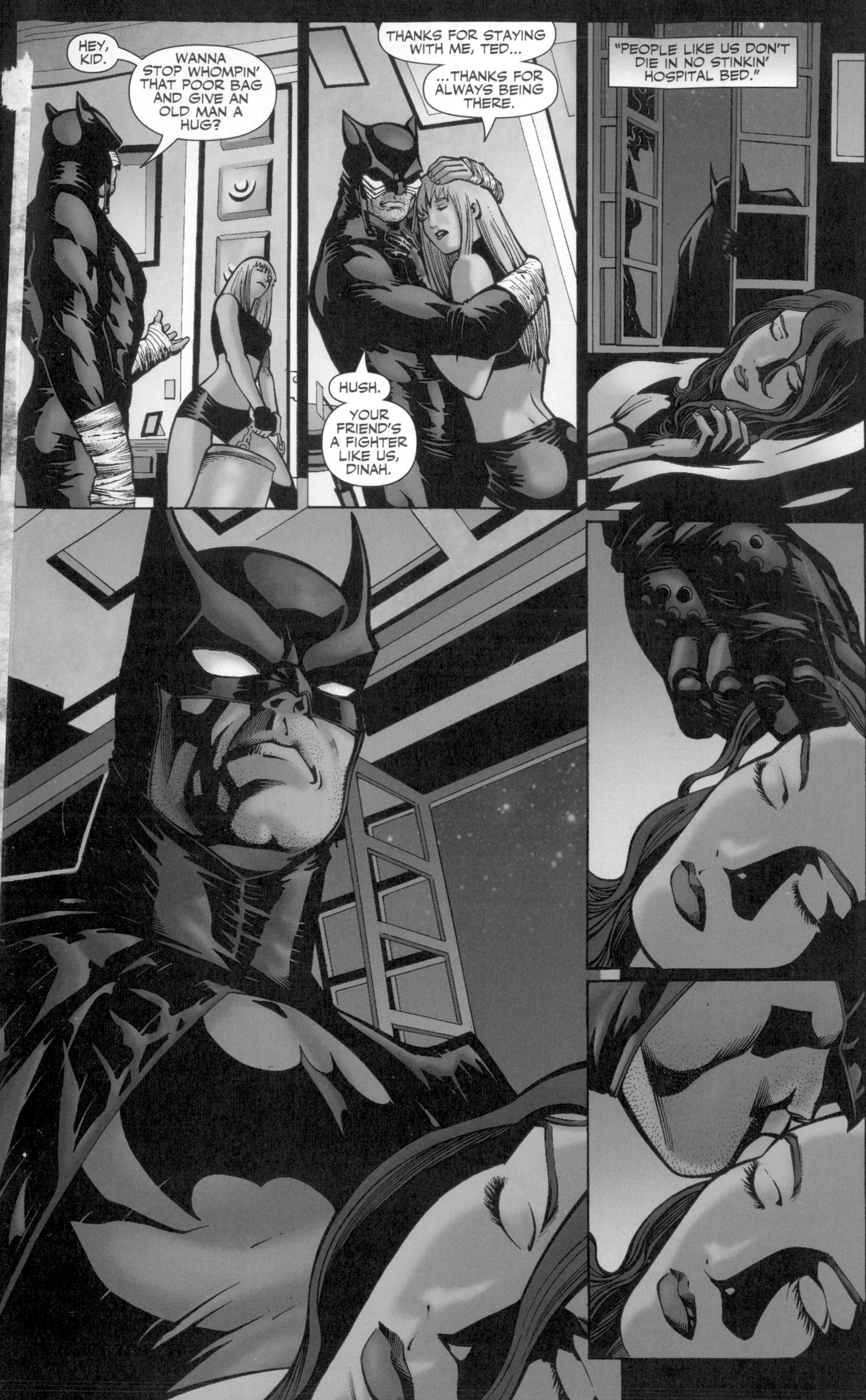
HEY, KID.
WANNA STOP WHOMPIN' THAT POOR BAG AND GIVE AN OLD MAN A HUG?
THANKS FOR STAYING WITH ME, TED...
...THANKS FOR ALWAYS BEING THERE.
HUSH.
YOUR FRIEND'S A FIGHTER LIKE US, DINAH.
"PEOPLE LIKE US DON'T DIE IN NO STINKIN' HOSPITAL BED."

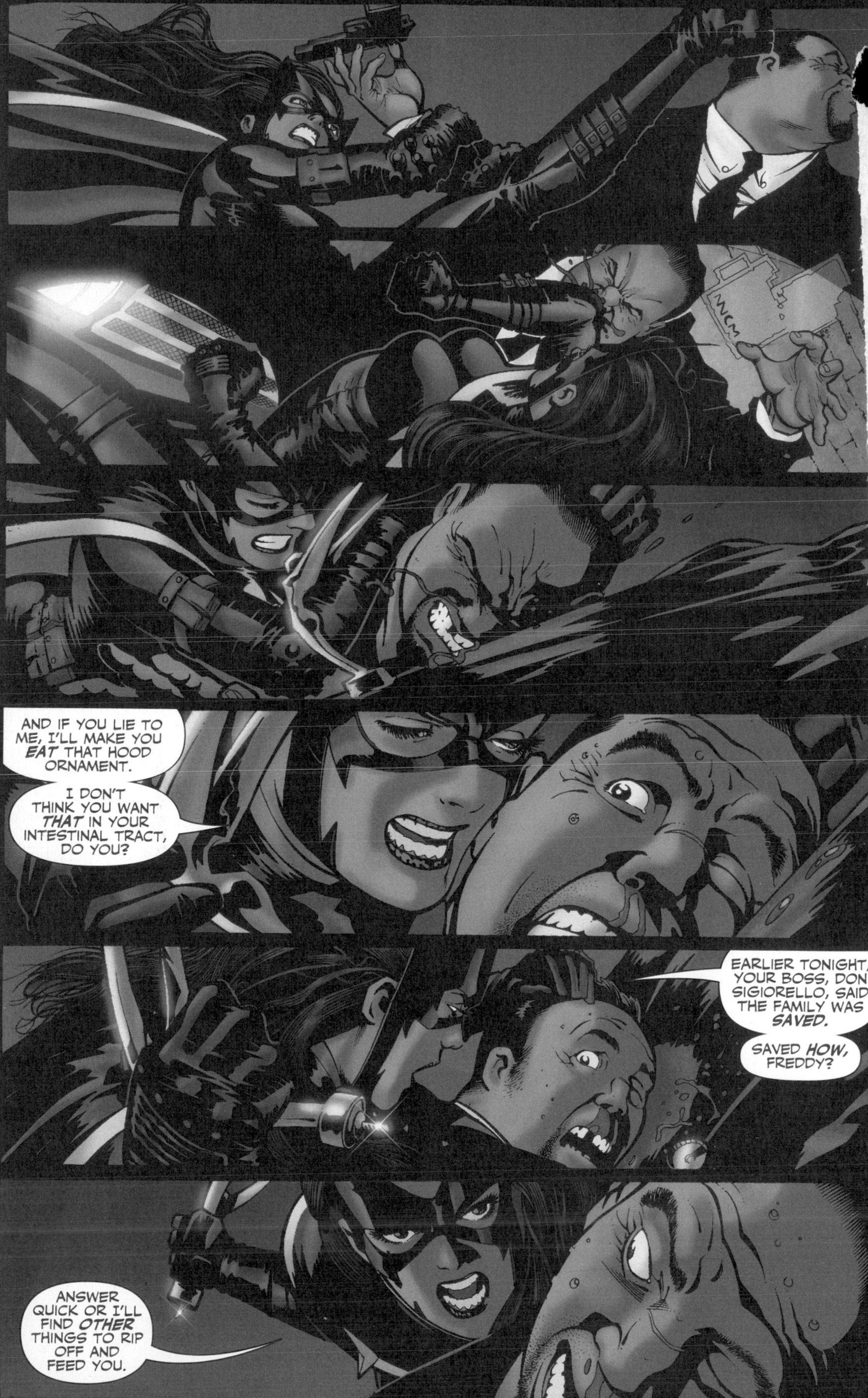
AND IF YOU LIE TO ME, I'LL MAKE YOU *EAT* THAT HOOD ORNAMENT.
I DON'T THINK YOU WANT *THAT* IN YOUR INTESTINAL TRACT, DO YOU?
EARLIER TONIGHT, YOUR BOSS, DON SIGIORELLO, SAID THE FAMILY WAS *SAVED*.
SAVED *HOW*, FREDDY?
ANSWER QUICK OR I'LL FIND *OTHER* THINGS TO RIP OFF AND FEED YOU.

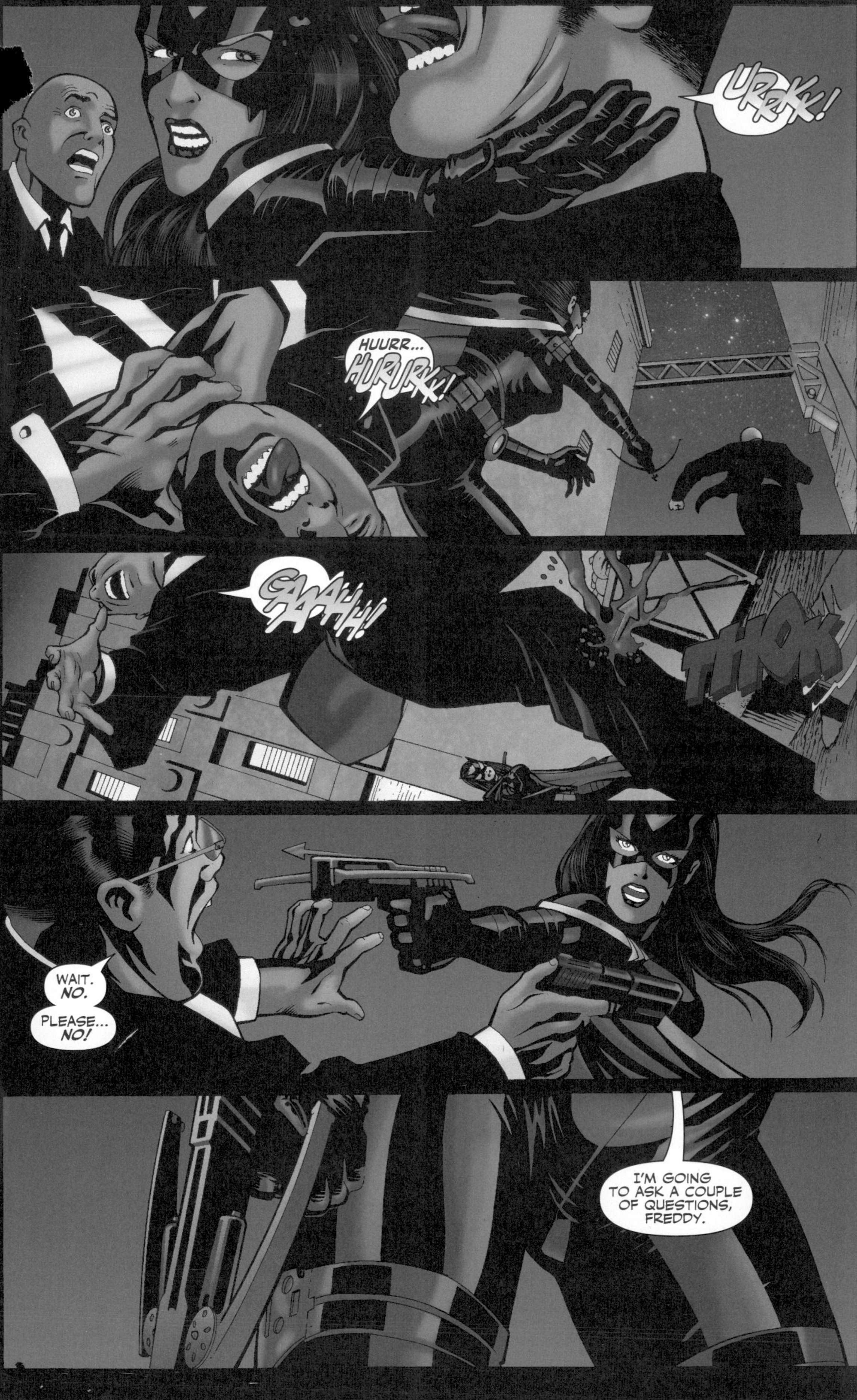
URRKK!
HUURR... HURURKK!
GAAAHH!
THOK
WAIT. NO.
PLEASE... NO!
I'M GOING TO ASK A COUPLE OF QUESTIONS, FREDDY.

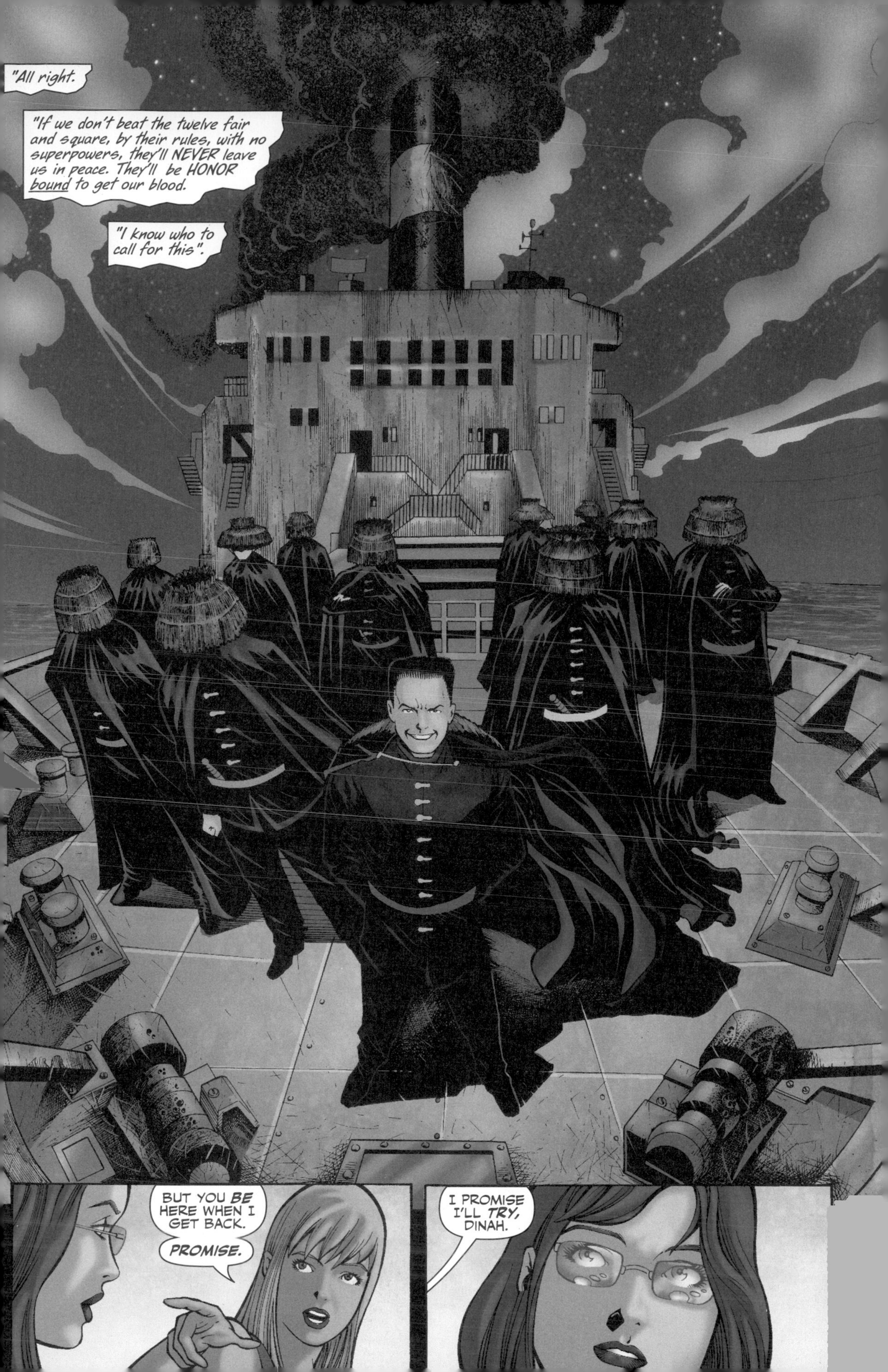
"All right.
"If we don't beat the twelve fair and square, by their rules, with no superpowers, they'll NEVER leave us in peace. They'll be HONOR bound to get our blood.
"I know who to call for this".
BUT YOU BE HERE WHEN I GET BACK.
PROMISE.
I PROMISE I'LL TRY, DINAH.

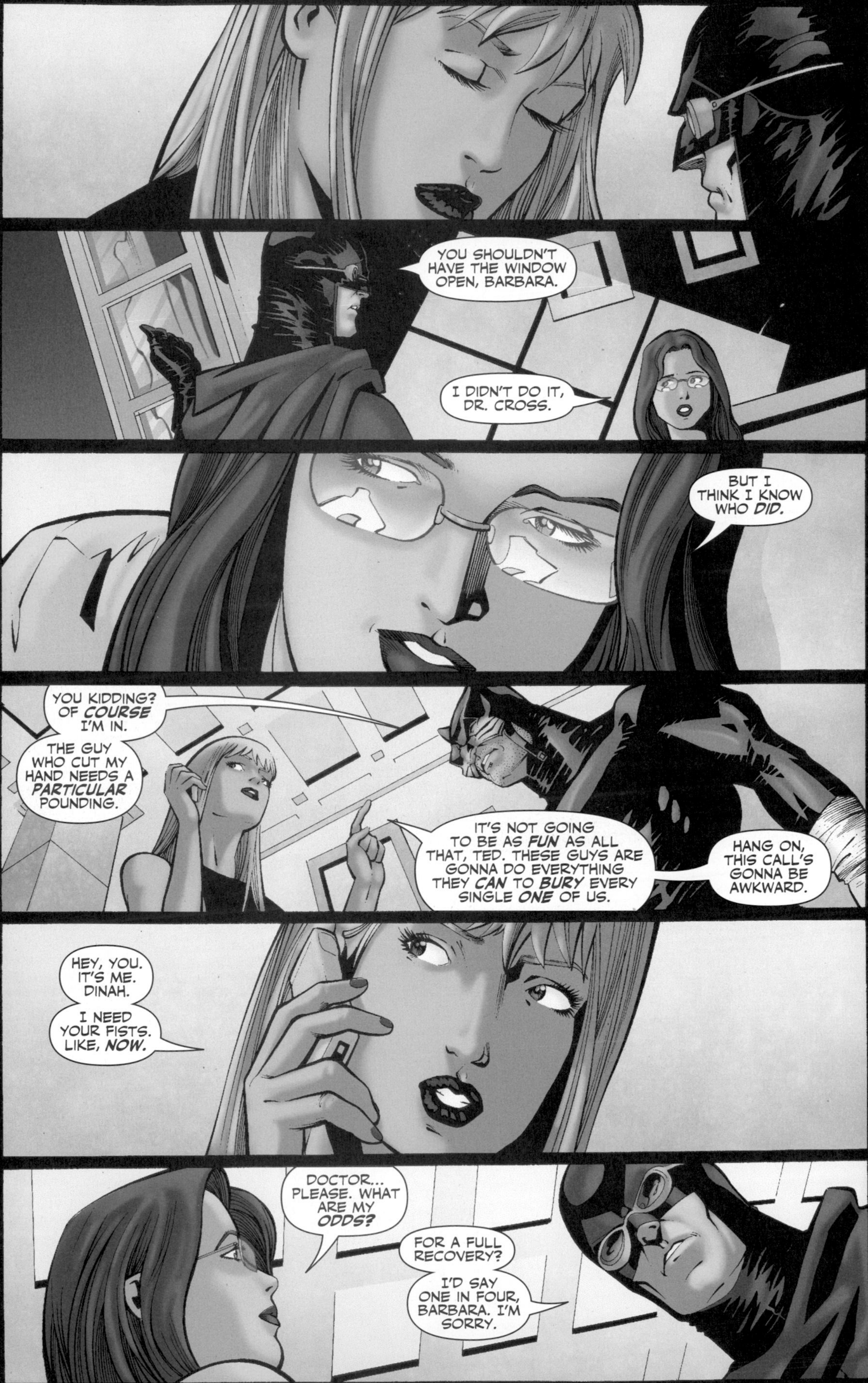

YOU SHOULDN'T HAVE THE WINDOW OPEN, BARBARA.
I DIDN'T DO IT, DR. CROSS.
BUT I THINK I KNOW WHO *DID.*
YOU KIDDING? OF *COURSE* I'M IN.
THE GUY WHO CUT MY HAND NEEDS A *PARTICULAR* POUNDING.
IT'S NOT GOING TO BE AS *FUN* AS ALL THAT, TED. THESE GUYS ARE GONNA DO EVERYTHING THEY *CAN* TO *BURY* EVERY SINGLE *ONE* OF US.
HANG ON, THIS CALL'S GONNA BE AWKWARD.
HEY, YOU. IT'S ME. DINAH.
I NEED YOUR FISTS. LIKE, *NOW.*
DOCTOR... PLEASE. WHAT ARE MY *ODDS?*
FOR A FULL RECOVERY?
I'D SAY ONE IN FOUR, BARBARA. I'M SORRY.

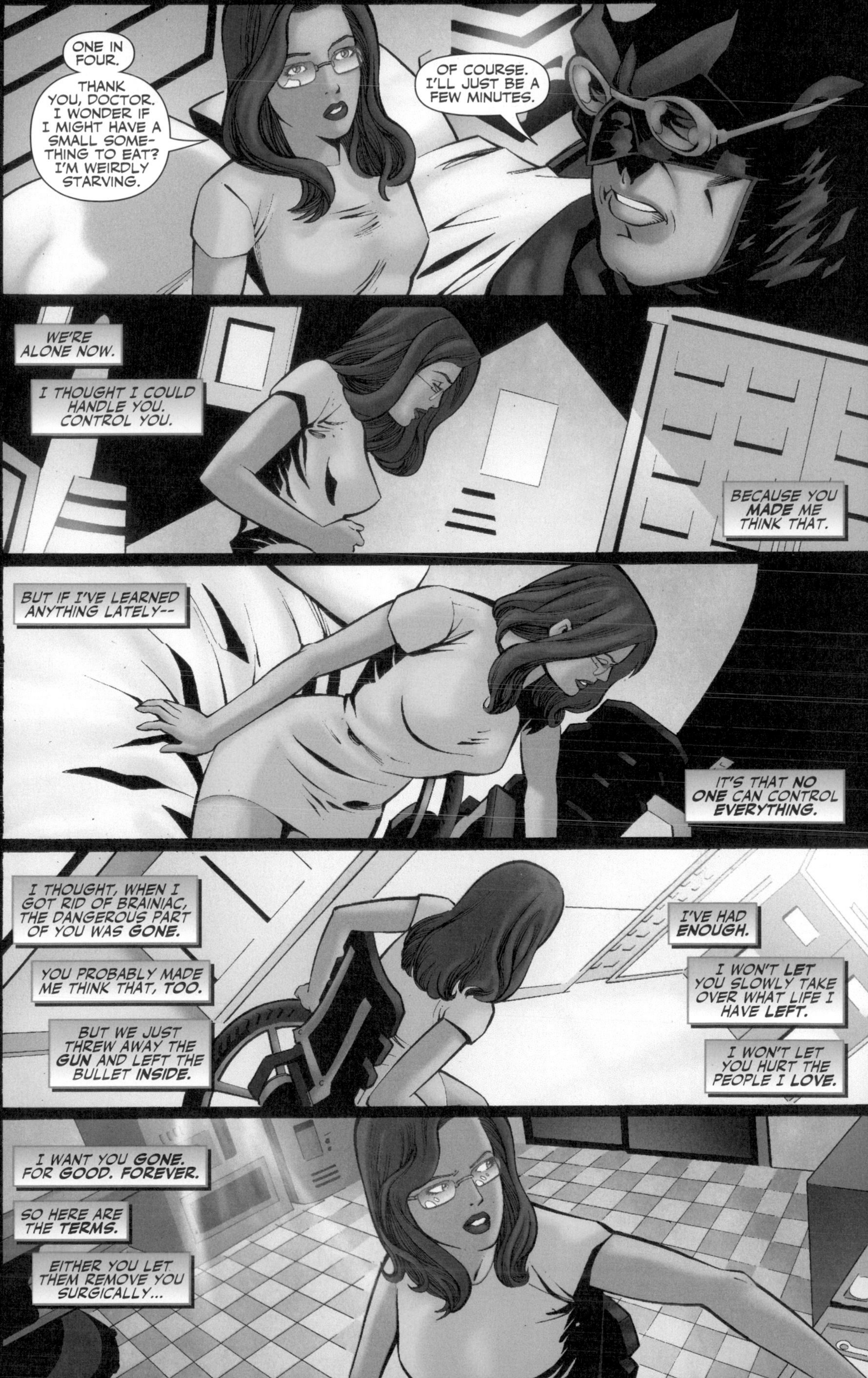
ONE IN FOUR.
THANK YOU, DOCTOR. I WONDER IF I MIGHT HAVE A SMALL SOME-THING TO EAT? I'M WEIRDLY STARVING.
OF COURSE. I'LL JUST BE A FEW MINUTES.
WE'RE ALONE NOW.
I THOUGHT I COULD HANDLE YOU. CONTROL YOU.
BECAUSE YOU MADE ME THINK THAT.
BUT IF I'VE LEARNED ANYTHING LATELY--
IT'S THAT NO ONE CAN CONTROL EVERYTHING.
I THOUGHT, WHEN I GOT RID OF BRAINIAC, THE DANGEROUS PART OF YOU WAS GONE.
YOU PROBABLY MADE ME THINK THAT, TOO.
BUT WE JUST THREW AWAY THE GUN AND LEFT THE BULLET INSIDE.
I'VE HAD ENOUGH.
I WON'T LET YOU SLOWLY TAKE OVER WHAT LIFE I HAVE LEFT.
I WON'T LET YOU HURT THE PEOPLE I LOVE.
I WANT YOU GONE. FOR GOOD. FOREVER.
SO HERE ARE THE TERMS.
EITHER YOU LET THEM REMOVE YOU SURGICALLY...

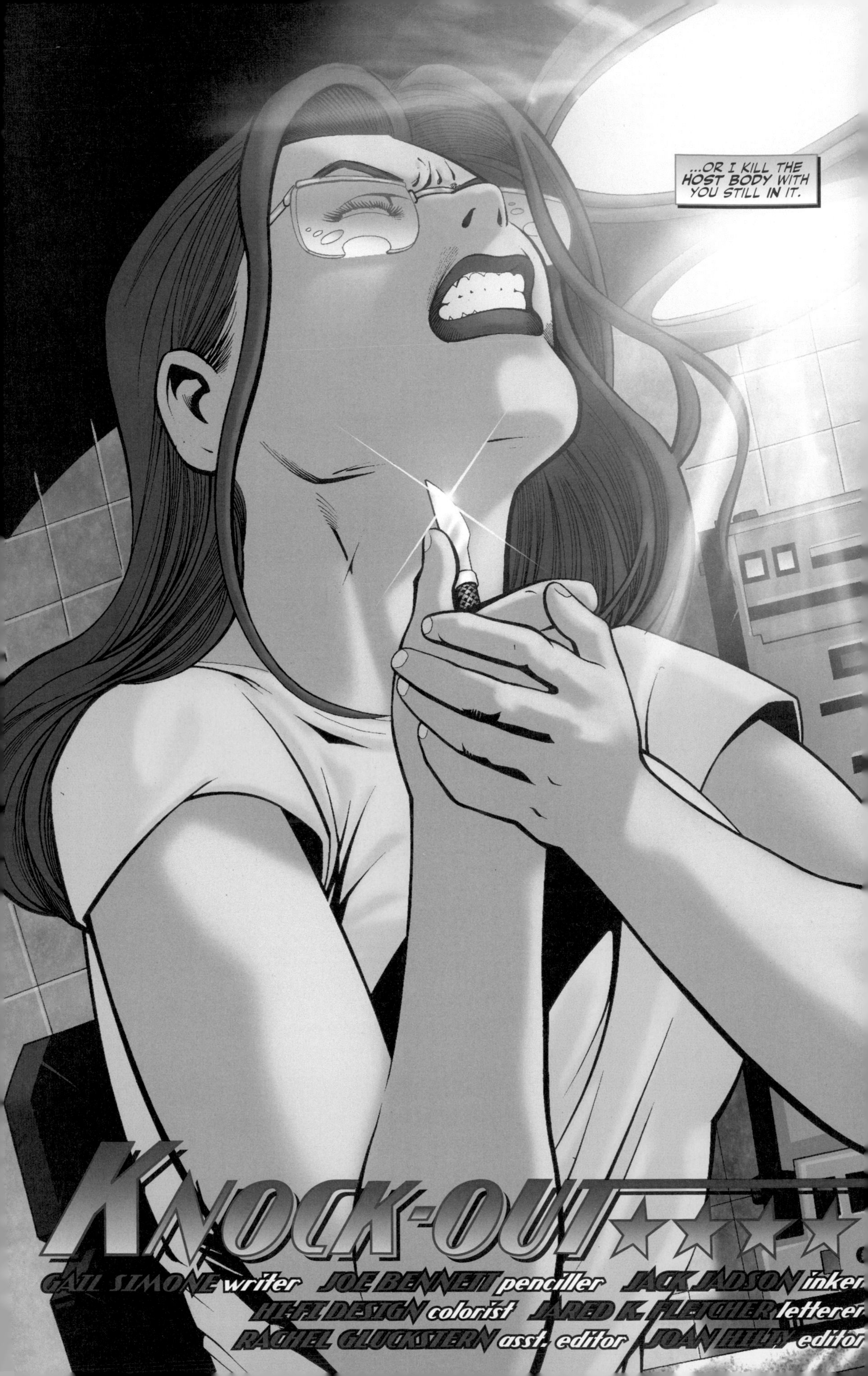
...OR I KILL THE HOST BODY WITH YOU STILL IN IT.
KNOCK-OUT
GAIL SIMONE writer JOE BENNETT penciller JACK JADSON inker
HI-FI DESIGN colorist JARED K. FLETCHER letterer
RACHEL GLUCKSTERN asst. editor JOAN HILTY editor

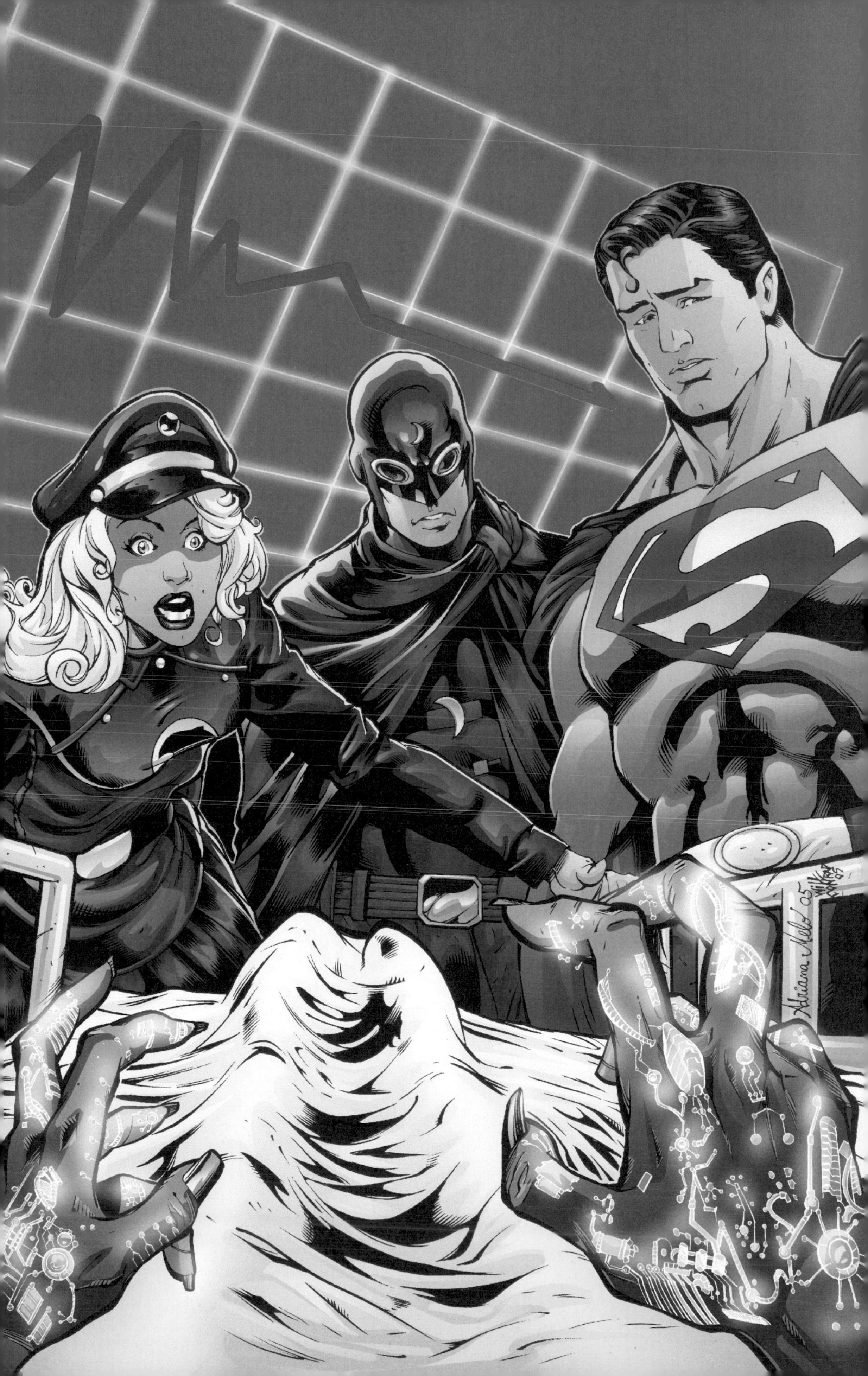

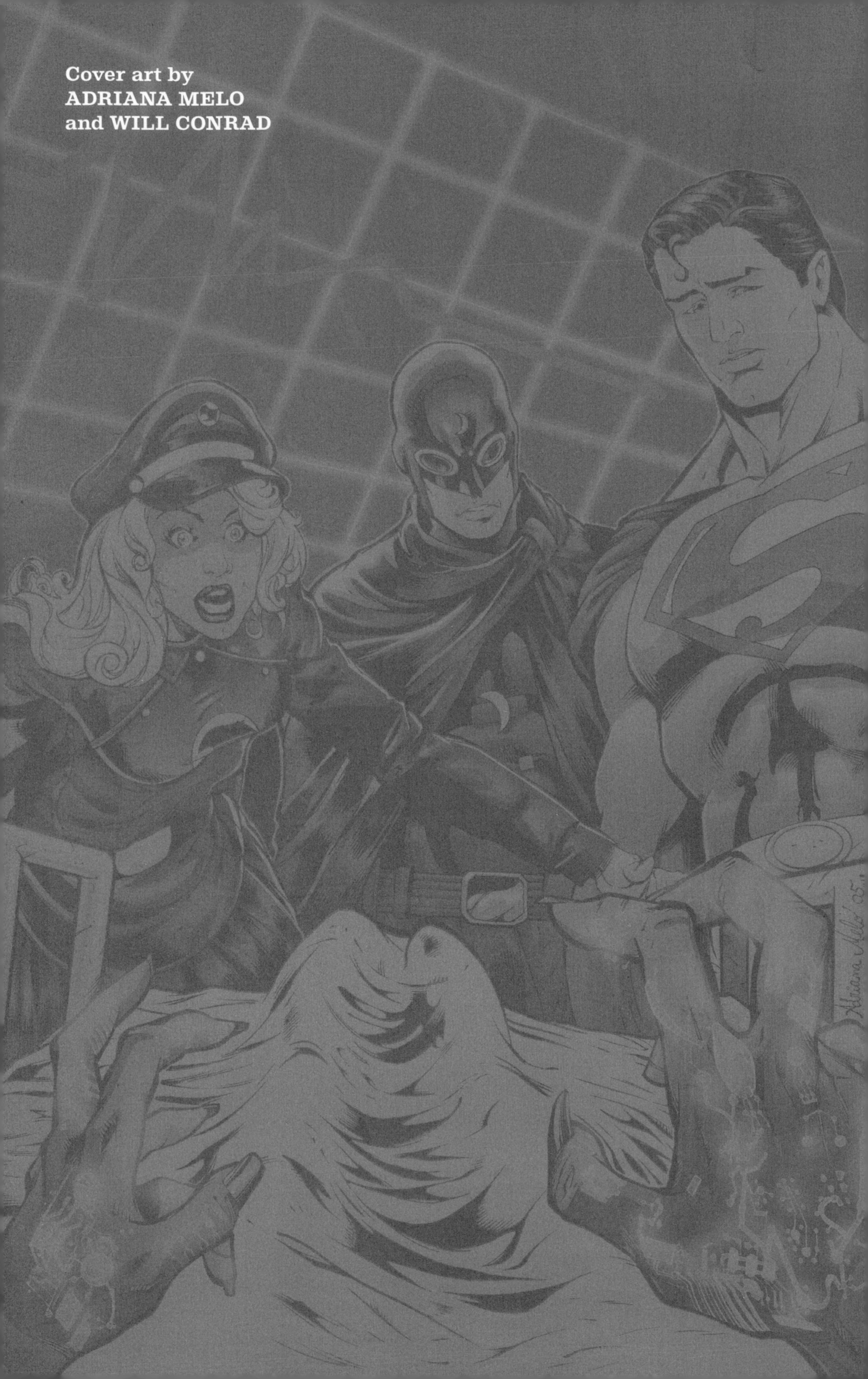

Cover art by
ADRIANA MELO
and WILL CONRAD

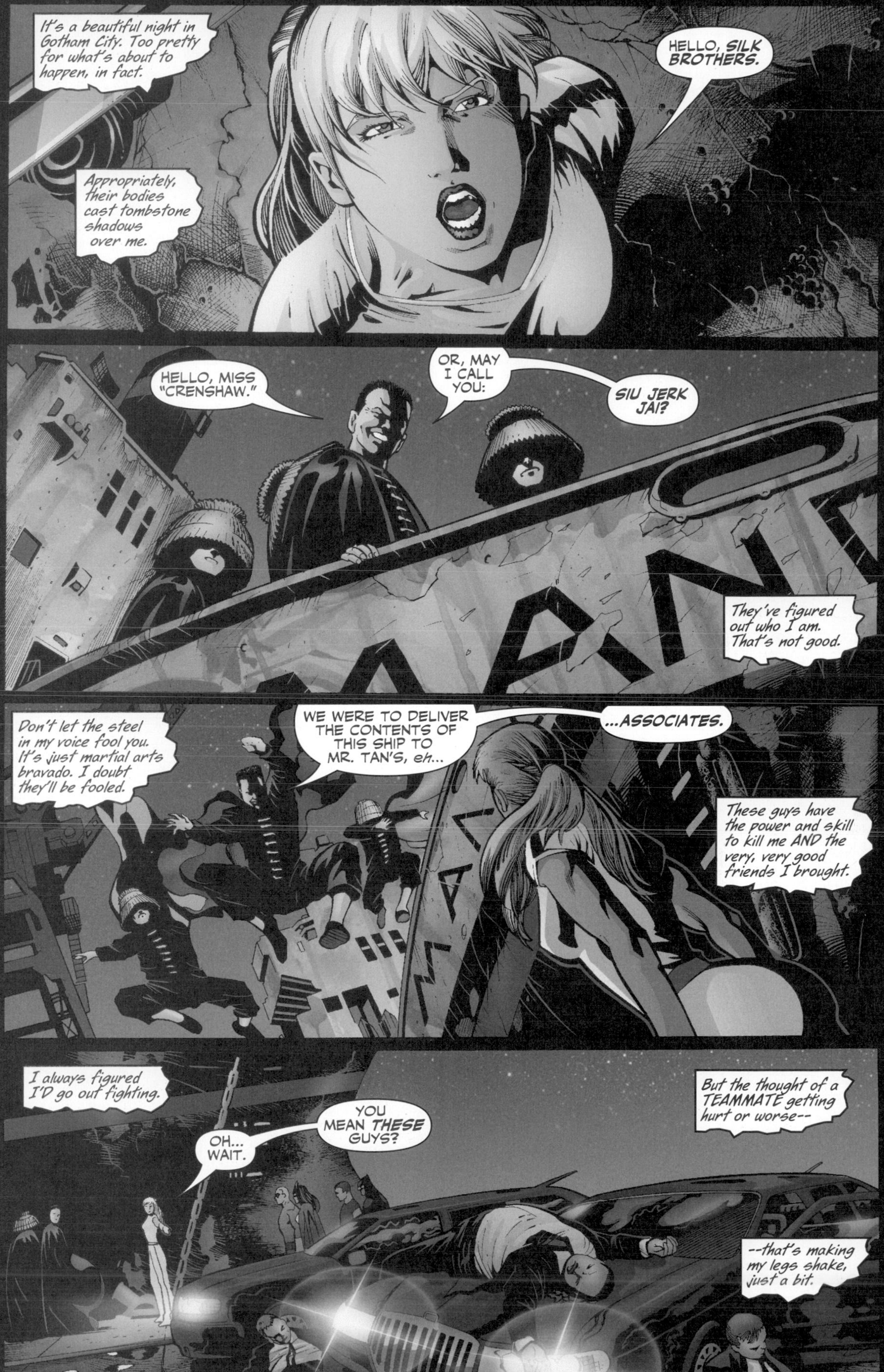
It's a beautiful night in Gotham City. Too pretty for what's about to happen, in fact.
HELLO, SILK BROTHERS.
Appropriately, their bodies cast tombstone shadows over me.
HELLO, MISS "CRENSHAW."
OR, MAY I CALL YOU:
SIU JERK JAI?
They've figured out who I am. That's not good.
Don't let the steel in my voice fool you. It's just martial arts bravado. I doubt they'll be fooled.
WE WERE TO DELIVER THE CONTENTS OF THIS SHIP TO MR. TAN'S, eh...
...ASSOCIATES.
These guys have the power and skill to kill me AND the very, very good friends I brought.
I always figured I'D go out fighting.
OH... WAIT.
YOU MEAN THESE GUYS?
But the thought of a TEAMMATE getting hurt or worse--
--that's making my legs shake, just a bit.

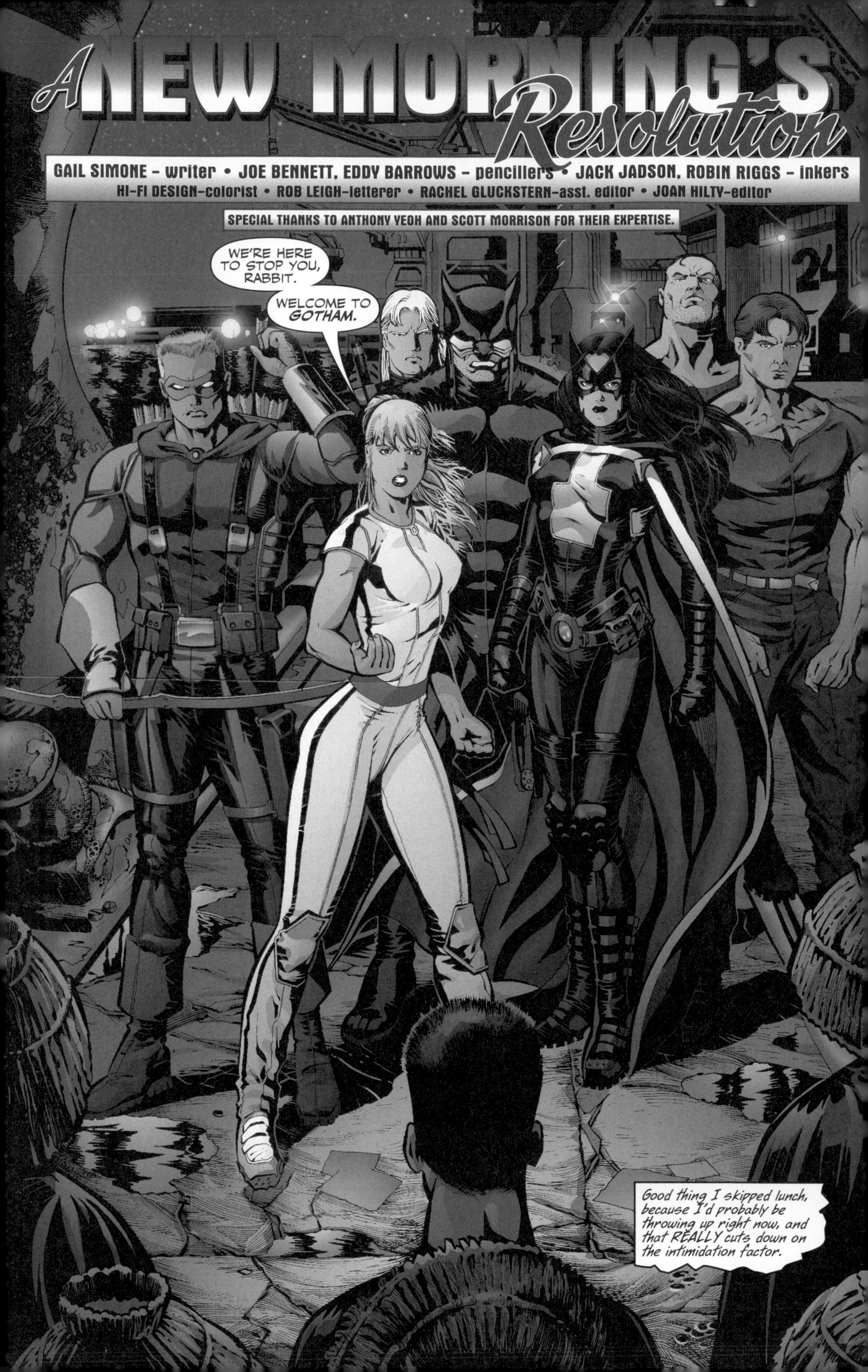
A NEW MORNING'S Resolution
GAIL SIMONE - writer • JOE BENNETT, EDDY BARROWS - pencillers • JACK JADSON, ROBIN RIGGS - inkers
HI-FI DESIGN-colorist • ROB LEIGH-letterer • RACHEL GLUCKSTERN-asst. editor • JOAN HILTY-editor
SPECIAL THANKS TO ANTHONY YEOH AND SCOTT MORRISON FOR THEIR EXPERTISE.
WE'RE HERE TO STOP YOU, RABBIT.
WELCOME TO GOTHAM.
Good thing I skipped lunch, because I'd probably be throwing up right now, and that REALLY cuts down on the intimidation factor.

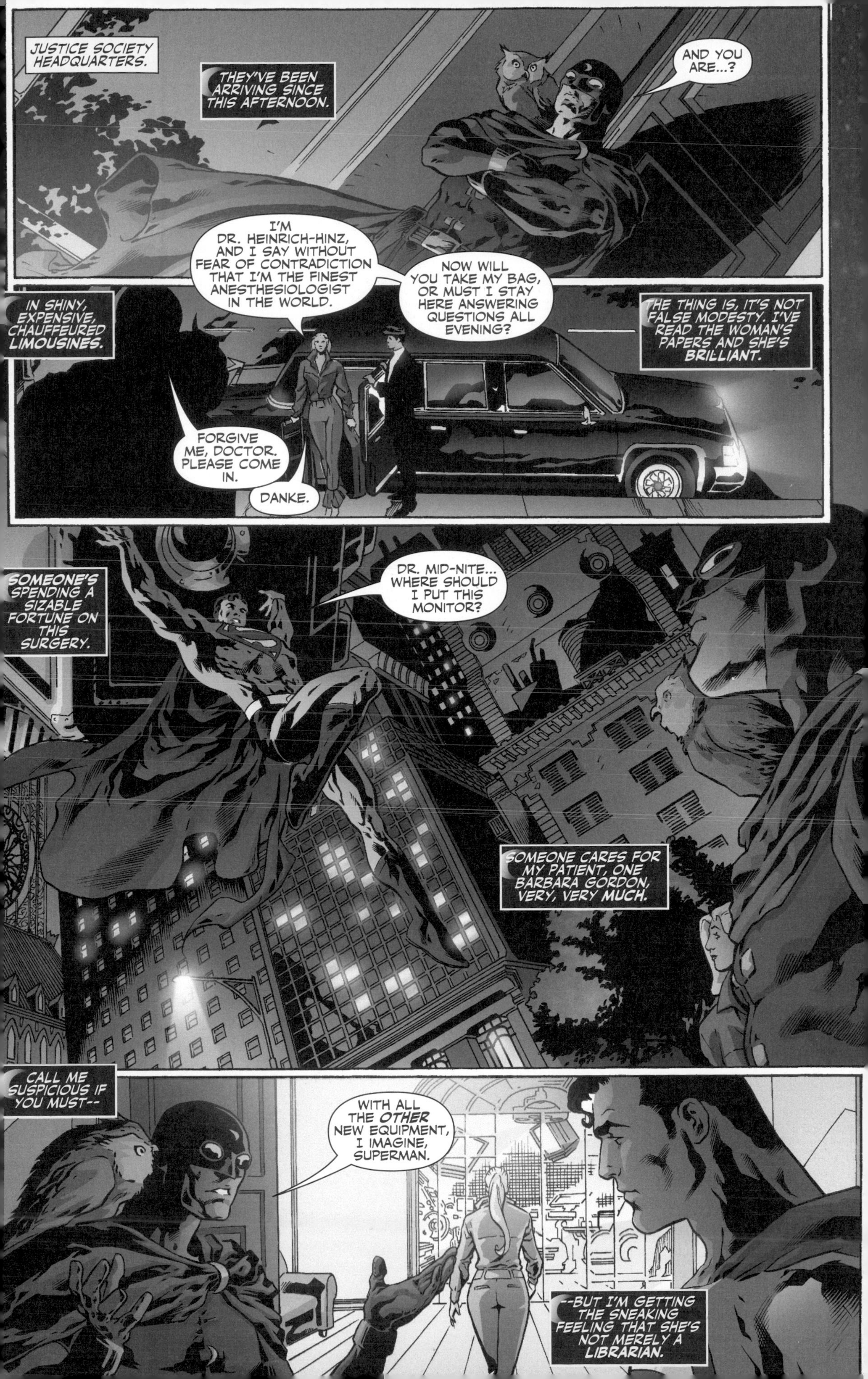
JUSTICE SOCIETY HEADQUARTERS.
THEY'VE BEEN ARRIVING SINCE THIS AFTERNOON.
AND YOU ARE...?
IN SHINY, EXPENSIVE, CHAUFFEURED LIMOUSINES.
I'M DR. HEINRICH-HINZ, AND I SAY WITHOUT FEAR OF CONTRADICTION THAT I'M THE FINEST ANESTHESIOLOGIST IN THE WORLD.
NOW WILL YOU TAKE MY BAG, OR MUST I STAY HERE ANSWERING QUESTIONS ALL EVENING?
THE THING IS, IT'S NOT FALSE MODESTY. I'VE READ THE WOMAN'S PAPERS AND SHE'S BRILLIANT.
FORGIVE ME, DOCTOR. PLEASE COME IN.
DANKE.
SOMEONE'S SPENDING A SIZABLE FORTUNE ON THIS SURGERY.
DR. MID-NITE... WHERE SHOULD I PUT THIS MONITOR?
SOMEONE CARES FOR MY PATIENT, ONE BARBARA GORDON, VERY, VERY MUCH.
CALL ME SUSPICIOUS IF YOU MUST--
WITH ALL THE OTHER NEW EQUIPMENT, I IMAGINE, SUPERMAN.
--BUT I'M GETTING THE SNEAKING FEELING THAT SHE'S NOT MERELY A LIBRARIAN.

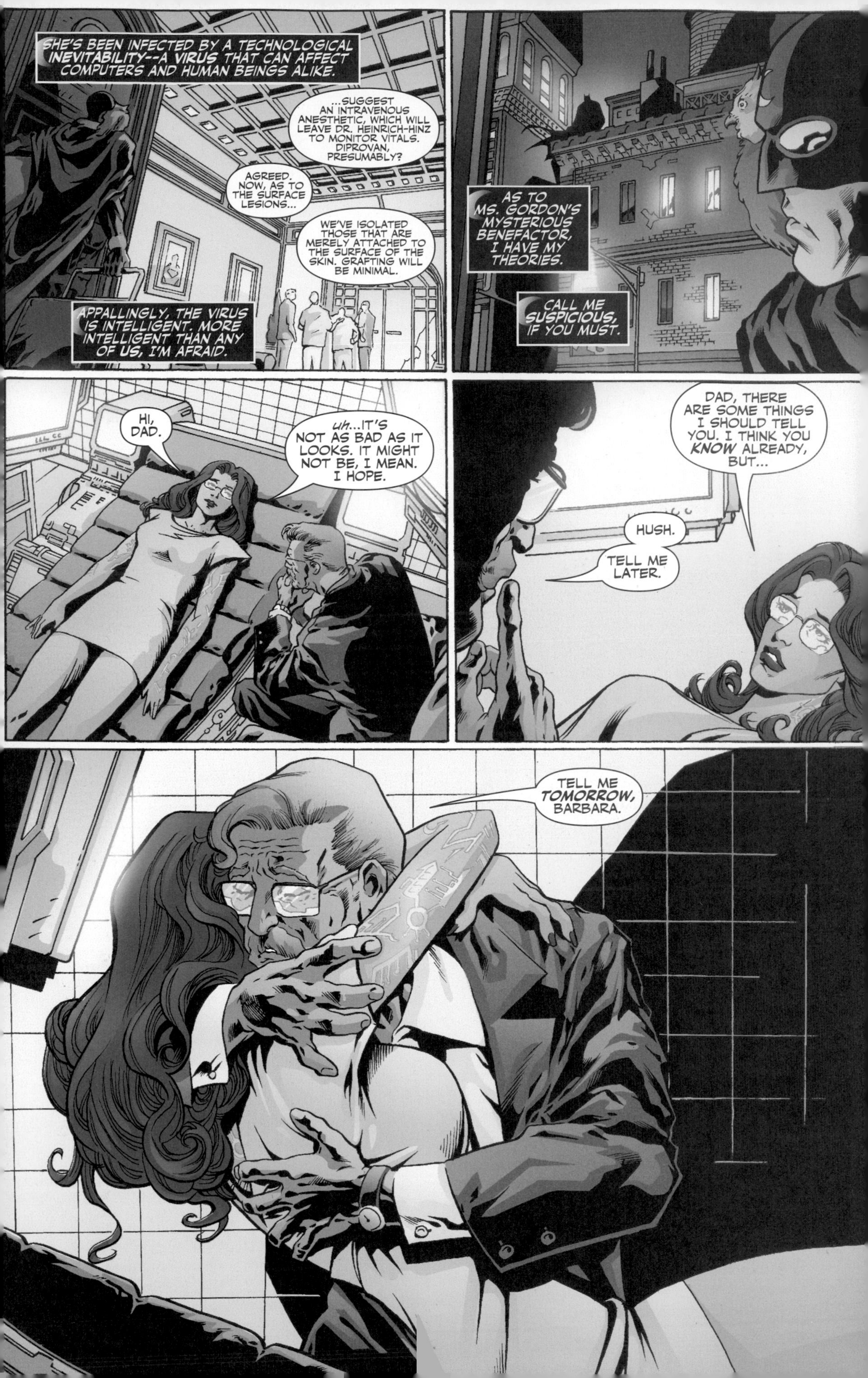
SHE'S BEEN INFECTED BY A TECHNOLOGICAL INEVITABILITY--A VIRUS THAT CAN AFFECT COMPUTERS AND HUMAN BEINGS ALIKE.
...SUGGEST AN INTRAVENOUS ANESTHETIC, WHICH WILL LEAVE DR. HEINRICH-HINZ TO MONITOR VITALS. DIPROVAN, PRESUMABLY?
AGREED. NOW, AS TO THE SURFACE LESIONS...
WE'VE ISOLATED THOSE THAT ARE MERELY ATTACHED TO THE SURFACE OF THE SKIN. GRAFTING WILL BE MINIMAL.
APPALLINGLY, THE VIRUS IS INTELLIGENT. MORE INTELLIGENT THAN ANY OF US, I'M AFRAID.
AS TO MS. GORDON'S MYSTERIOUS BENEFACTOR, I HAVE MY THEORIES.
CALL ME SUSPICIOUS, IF YOU MUST.
HI, DAD.
uh...IT'S NOT AS BAD AS IT LOOKS. IT MIGHT NOT BE, I MEAN. I HOPE.
DAD, THERE ARE SOME THINGS I SHOULD TELL YOU. I THINK YOU KNOW ALREADY, BUT...
HUSH.
TELL ME LATER.
TELL ME TOMORROW, BARBARA.

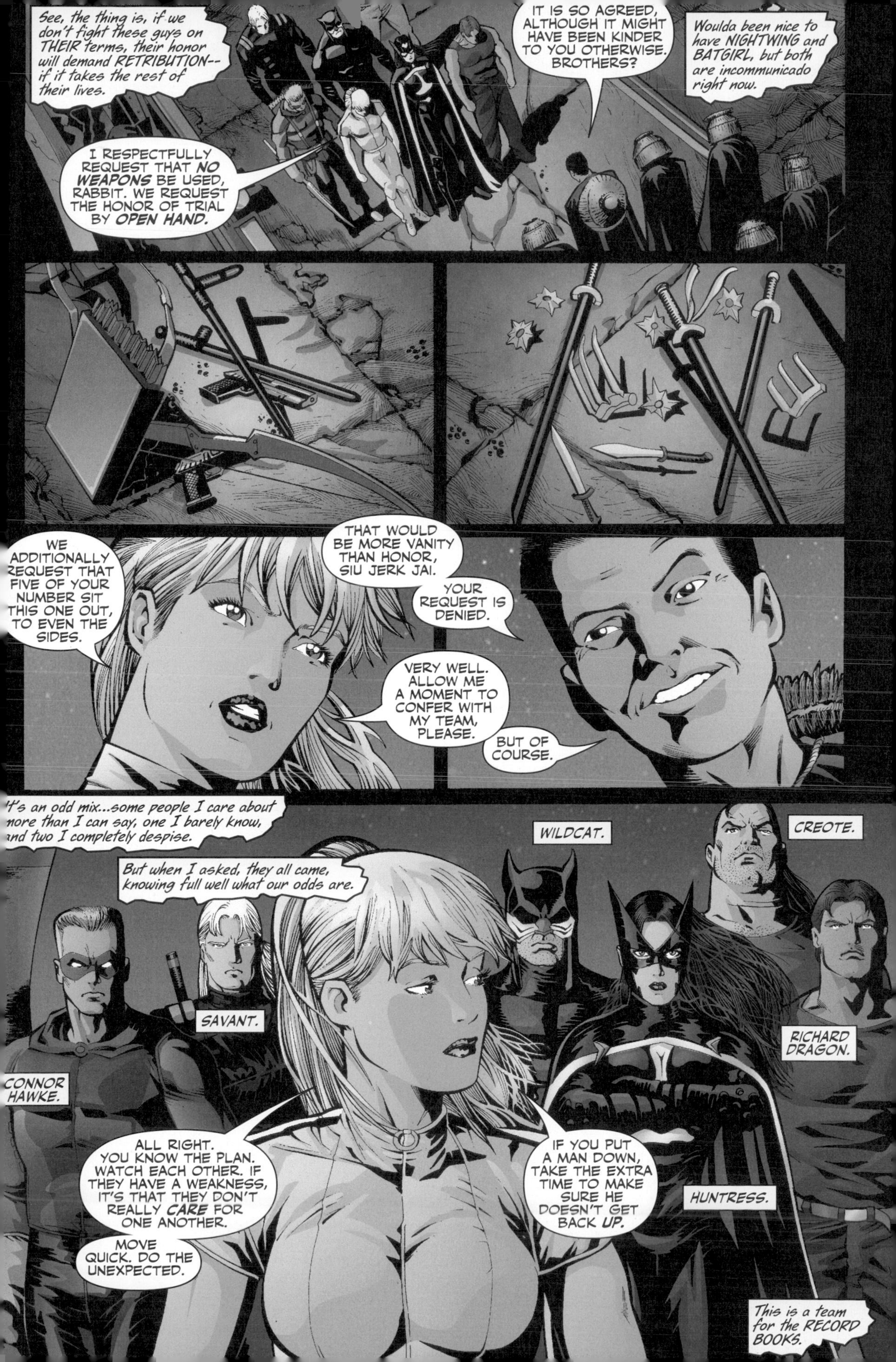

See, the thing is, if we don't fight these guys on THEIR terms, their honor will demand RETRIBUTION-- if it takes the rest of their lives.
IT IS SO AGREED, ALTHOUGH IT MIGHT HAVE BEEN KINDER TO YOU OTHERWISE. BROTHERS?
Woulda been nice to have NIGHTWING and BATGIRL, but both are incommunicado right now.
I RESPECTFULLY REQUEST THAT NO WEAPONS BE USED, RABBIT. WE REQUEST THE HONOR OF TRIAL BY OPEN HAND.
WE ADDITIONALLY REQUEST THAT FIVE OF YOUR NUMBER SIT THIS ONE OUT, TO EVEN THE SIDES.
THAT WOULD BE MORE VANITY THAN HONOR, SIU JERK JAI.
YOUR REQUEST IS DENIED.
VERY WELL. ALLOW ME A MOMENT TO CONFER WITH MY TEAM, PLEASE.
BUT OF COURSE.
It's an odd mix...some people I care about more than I can say, one I barely know, and two I completely despise.
But when I asked, they all came, knowing full well what our odds are.
WILDCAT.
CREOTE.
SAVANT.
RICHARD DRAGON.
CONNOR HAWKE.
HUNTRESS.
ALL RIGHT. YOU KNOW THE PLAN. WATCH EACH OTHER. IF THEY HAVE A WEAKNESS, IT'S THAT THEY DON'T REALLY CARE FOR ONE ANOTHER.
MOVE QUICK. DO THE UNEXPECTED.
IF YOU PUT A MAN DOWN, TAKE THE EXTRA TIME TO MAKE SURE HE DOESN'T GET BACK UP.
This is a team for the RECORD BOOKS.

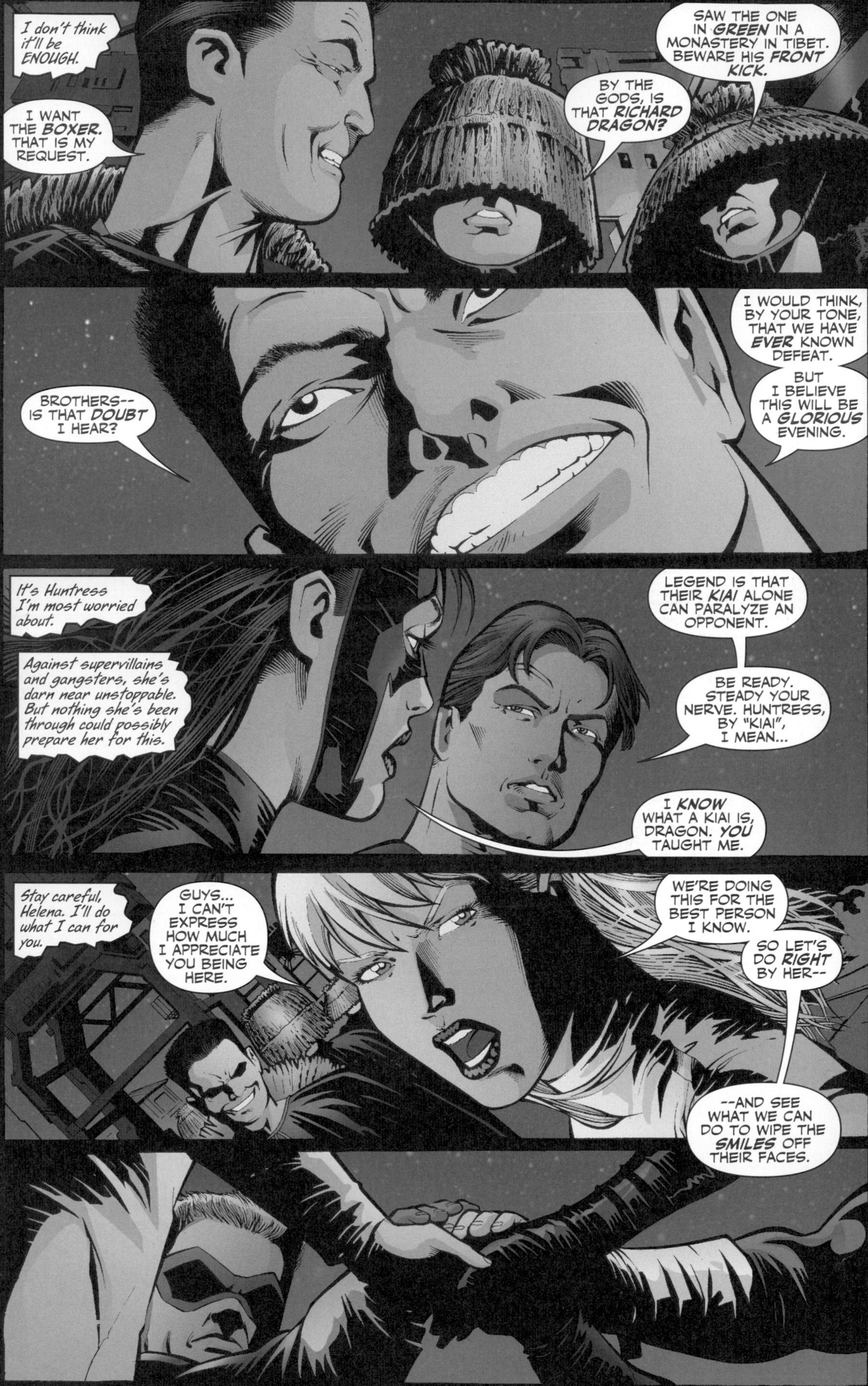

I don't think it'll be ENOUGH.
I WANT THE BOXER. THAT IS MY REQUEST.
BY THE GODS, IS THAT RICHARD DRAGON?
SAW THE ONE IN GREEN IN A MONASTERY IN TIBET. BEWARE HIS FRONT KICK.
BROTHERS-- IS THAT DOUBT I HEAR?
I WOULD THINK, BY YOUR TONE, THAT WE HAVE EVER KNOWN DEFEAT.
BUT I BELIEVE THIS WILL BE A GLORIOUS EVENING.
It's Huntress I'm most worried about.
Against supervillains and gangsters, she's darn near unstoppable. But nothing she's been through could possibly prepare her for this.
LEGEND IS THAT THEIR KIAI ALONE CAN PARALYZE AN OPPONENT.
BE READY. STEADY YOUR NERVE. HUNTRESS, BY "KIAI", I MEAN...
I KNOW WHAT A KIAI IS, DRAGON. YOU TAUGHT ME.
Stay careful, Helena. I'll do what I can for you.
GUYS... I CAN'T EXPRESS HOW MUCH I APPRECIATE YOU BEING HERE.
WE'RE DOING THIS FOR THE BEST PERSON I KNOW.
SO LET'S DO RIGHT BY HER--
--AND SEE WHAT WE CAN DO TO WIPE THE SMILES OFF THEIR FACES.

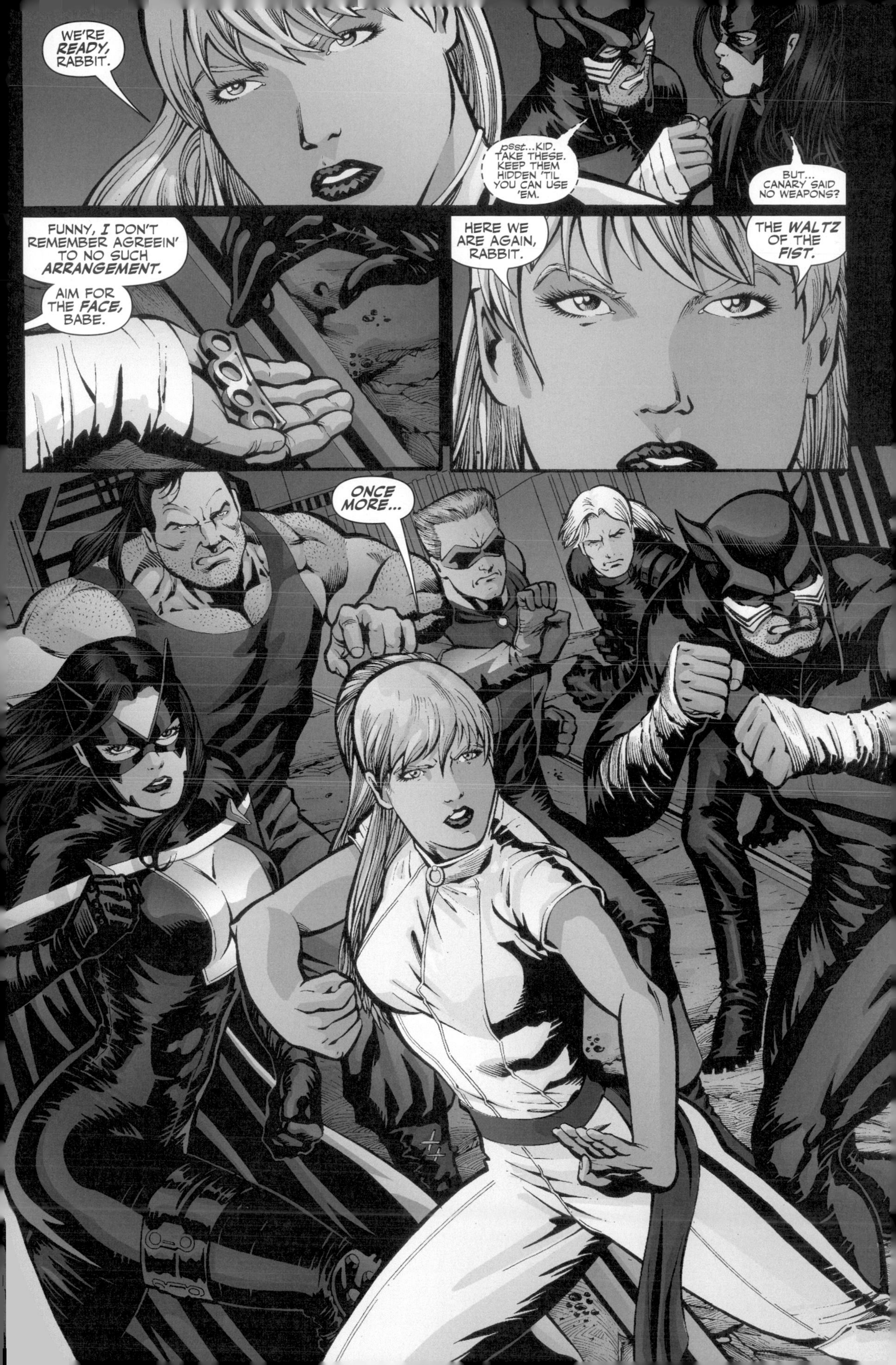
WE'RE READY, RABBIT.
pssst...KID. TAKE THESE. KEEP THEM HIDDEN 'TIL YOU CAN USE 'EM.
BUT... CANARY SAID NO WEAPONS?
FUNNY, I DON'T REMEMBER AGREEIN' TO NO SUCH ARRANGEMENT.
AIM FOR THE FACE, BABE.
HERE WE ARE AGAIN, RABBIT.
THE WALTZ OF THE FIST.
ONCE MORE...

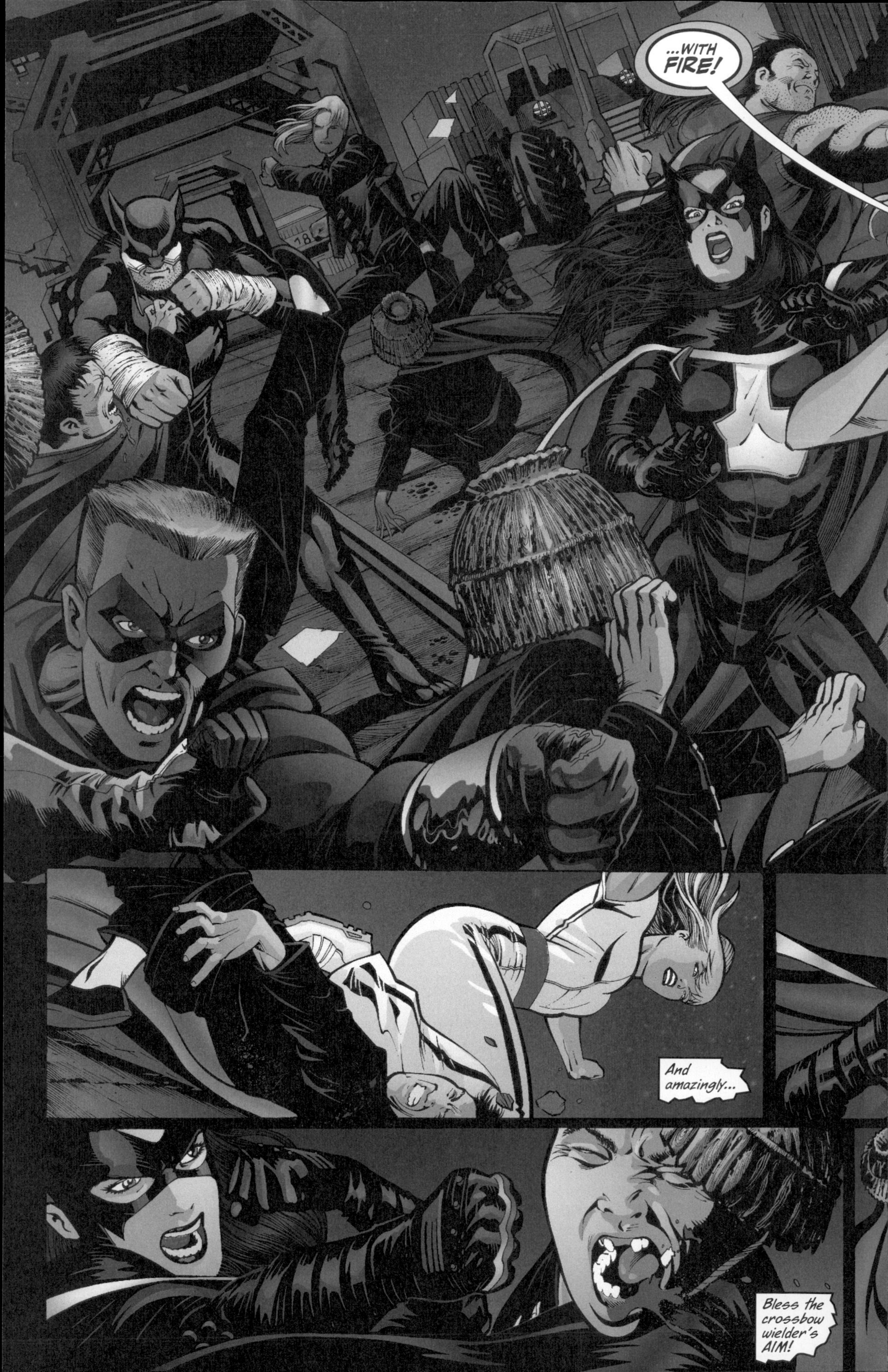
...WITH FIRE!
And amazingly...
Bless the crossbow wielder's AIM!

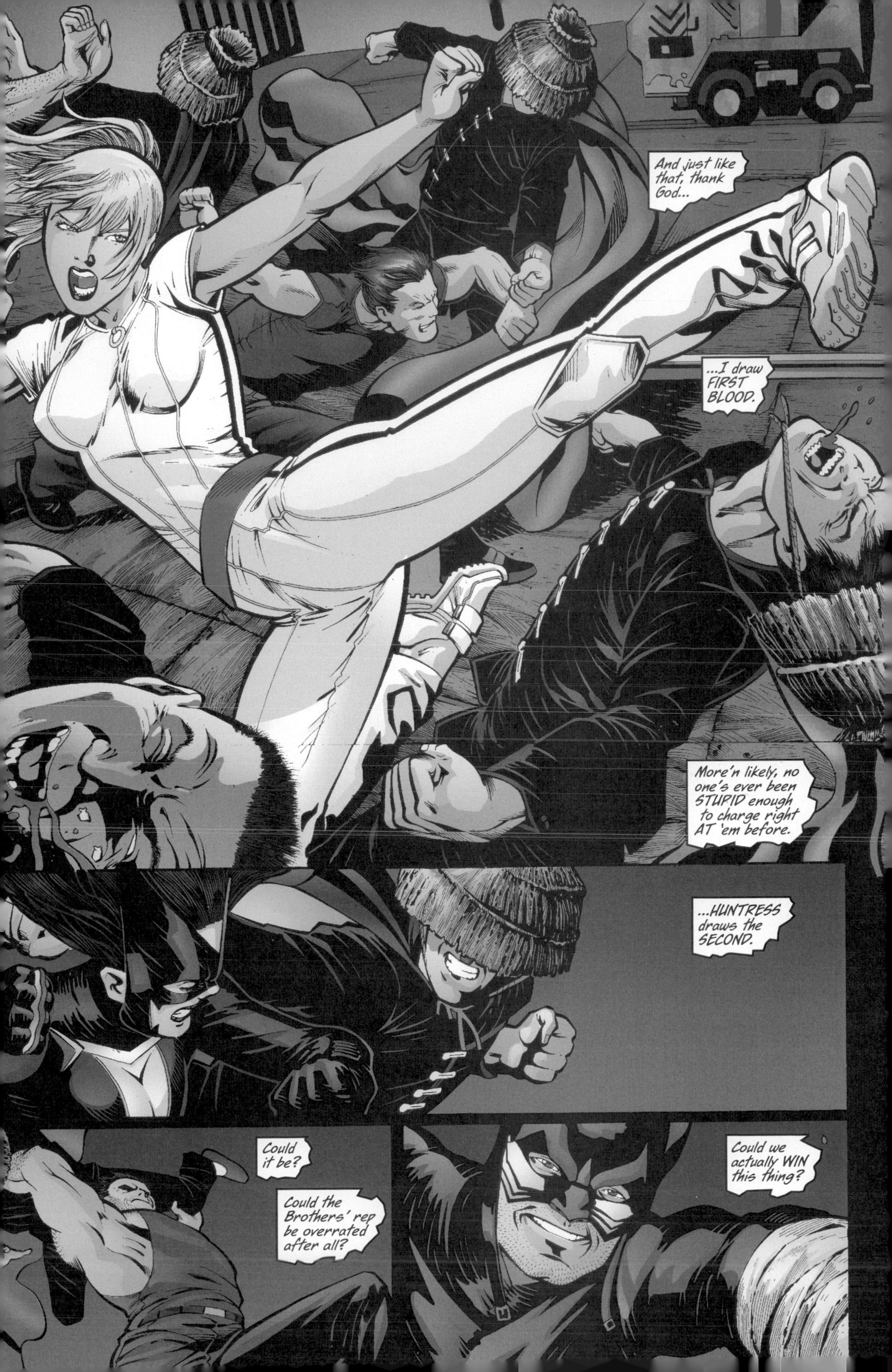
And just like that, thank God...
...I draw FIRST BLOOD.
More'n likely, no one's ever been STUPID enough to charge right AT 'em before.
...HUNTRESS draws the SECOND.
Could it be?
Could the Brothers' rep be overrated after all?
Could we actually WIN this thing?

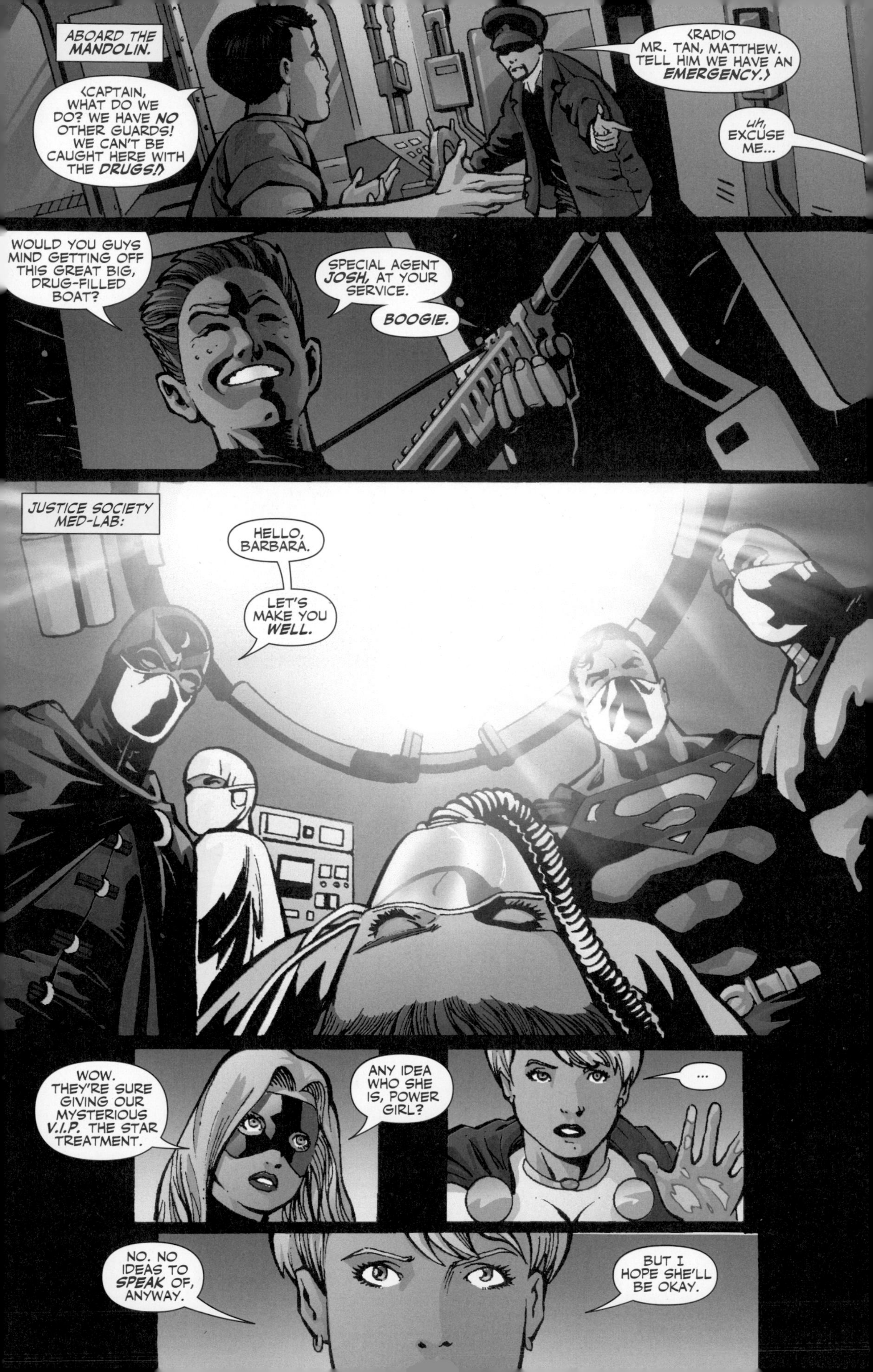

ABOARD THE MANDOLIN.
<CAPTAIN, WHAT DO WE DO? WE HAVE NO OTHER GUARDS! WE CAN'T BE CAUGHT HERE WITH THE DRUGS!>
<RADIO MR. TAN, MATTHEW. TELL HIM WE HAVE AN EMERGENCY.>
uh, EXCUSE ME...
WOULD YOU GUYS MIND GETTING OFF THIS GREAT BIG, DRUG-FILLED BOAT?
SPECIAL AGENT JOSH, AT YOUR SERVICE.
BOOGIE.
JUSTICE SOCIETY MED-LAB:
HELLO, BARBARA.
LET'S MAKE YOU WELL.
WOW. THEY'RE SURE GIVING OUR MYSTERIOUS V.I.P. THE STAR TREATMENT.
ANY IDEA WHO SHE IS, POWER GIRL?
...
NO. NO IDEAS TO SPEAK OF, ANYWAY.
BUT I HOPE SHE'LL BE OKAY.

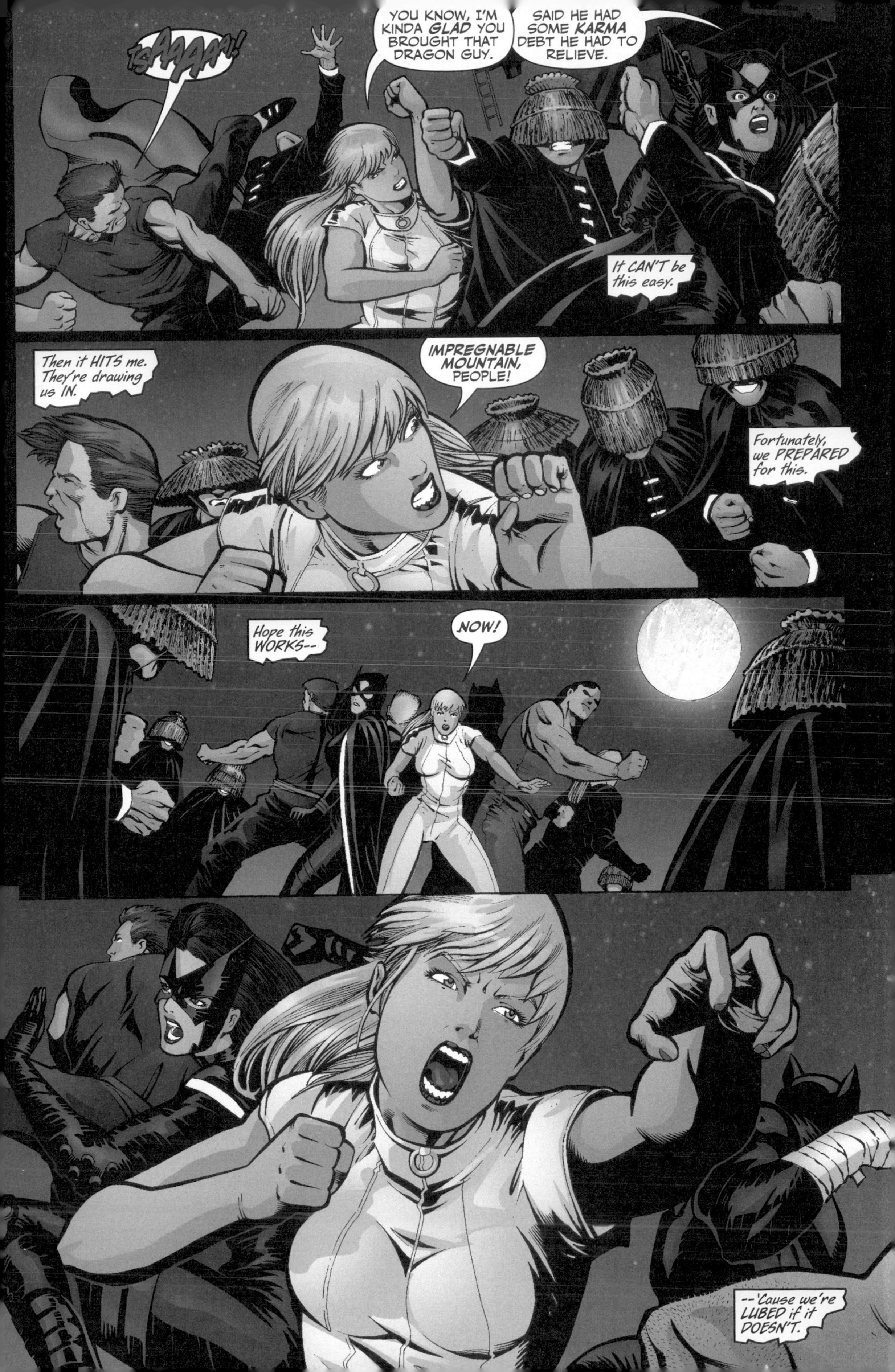
TSAAAAA!!
YOU KNOW, I'M KINDA GLAD YOU BROUGHT THAT DRAGON GUY.
SAID HE HAD SOME KARMA DEBT HE HAD TO RELIEVE.
It CAN'T be this easy.
Then it HITS me. They're drawing us IN.
IMPREGNABLE MOUNTAIN, PEOPLE!
Fortunately, we PREPARED for this.
Hope this WORKS--
NOW!
--'Cause we're LUBED if it DOESN'T.

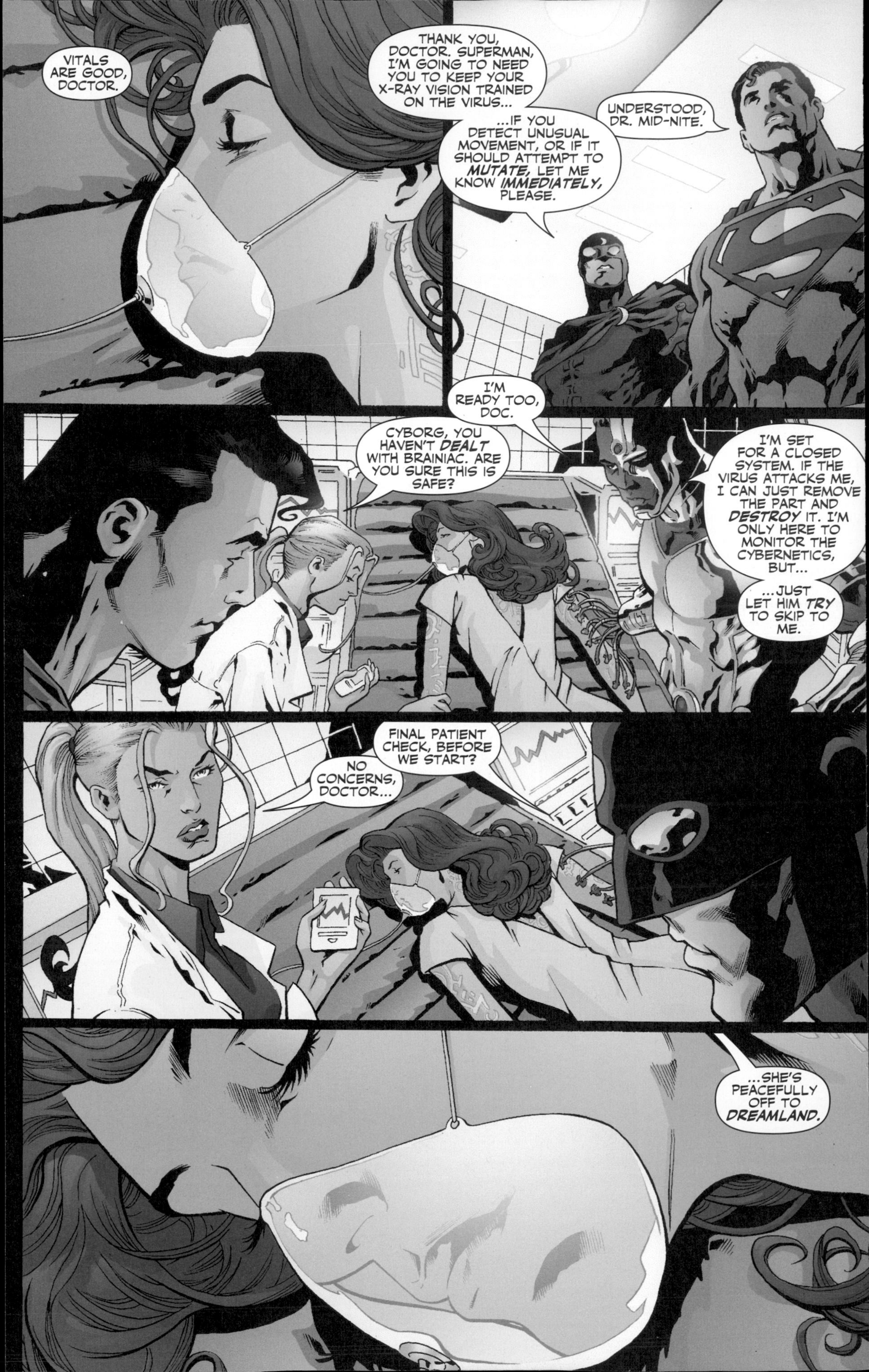
VITALS ARE GOOD, DOCTOR.
THANK YOU, DOCTOR. SUPERMAN, I'M GOING TO NEED YOU TO KEEP YOUR X-RAY VISION TRAINED ON THE VIRUS...
...IF YOU DETECT UNUSUAL MOVEMENT, OR IF IT SHOULD ATTEMPT TO *MUTATE,* LET ME KNOW *IMMEDIATELY,* PLEASE.
UNDERSTOOD, DR. MID-NITE.
I'M READY TOO, DOC.
CYBORG, YOU HAVEN'T *DEALT* WITH BRAINIAC. ARE YOU SURE THIS IS SAFE?
I'M SET FOR A CLOSED SYSTEM. IF THE VIRUS ATTACKS ME, I CAN JUST REMOVE THE PART AND *DESTROY* IT. I'M ONLY HERE TO MONITOR THE CYBERNETICS, BUT...
...JUST LET HIM *TRY* TO SKIP TO ME.
FINAL PATIENT CHECK, BEFORE WE START?
NO CONCERNS, DOCTOR...
...SHE'S PEACEFULLY OFF TO *DREAMLAND.*

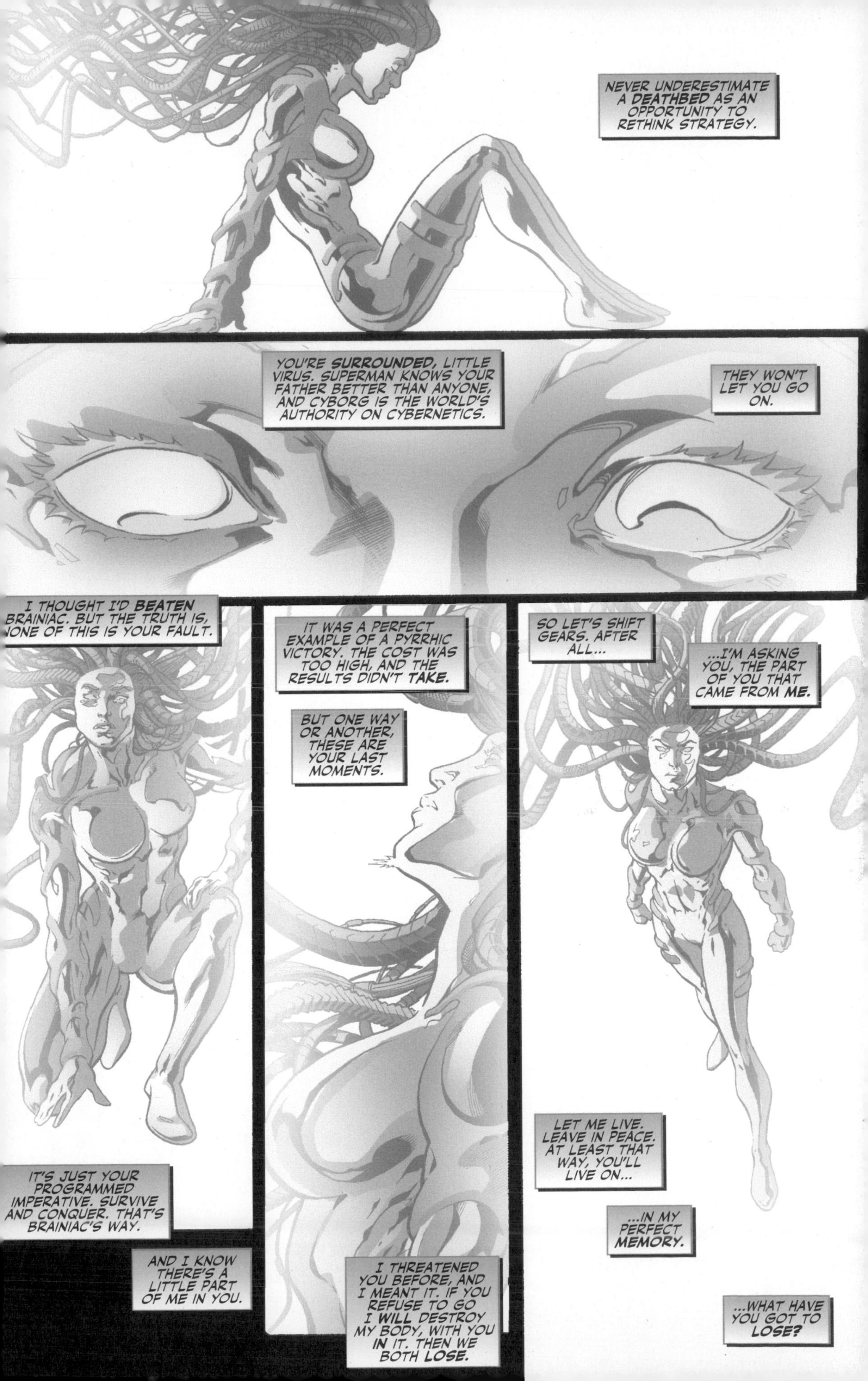
NEVER UNDERESTIMATE A DEATHBED AS AN OPPORTUNITY TO RETHINK STRATEGY.
YOU'RE SURROUNDED, LITTLE VIRUS. SUPERMAN KNOWS YOUR FATHER BETTER THAN ANYONE, AND CYBORG IS THE WORLD'S AUTHORITY ON CYBERNETICS.
THEY WON'T LET YOU GO ON.
I THOUGHT I'D BEATEN BRAINIAC. BUT THE TRUTH IS, NONE OF THIS IS YOUR FAULT.
IT'S JUST YOUR PROGRAMMED IMPERATIVE. SURVIVE AND CONQUER. THAT'S BRAINIAC'S WAY.
AND I KNOW THERE'S A LITTLE PART OF ME IN YOU.
IT WAS A PERFECT EXAMPLE OF A PYRRHIC VICTORY. THE COST WAS TOO HIGH, AND THE RESULTS DIDN'T TAKE.
BUT ONE WAY OR ANOTHER, THESE ARE YOUR LAST MOMENTS.
I THREATENED YOU BEFORE, AND I MEANT IT. IF YOU REFUSE TO GO I WILL DESTROY MY BODY, WITH YOU IN IT. THEN WE BOTH LOSE.
SO LET'S SHIFT GEARS. AFTER ALL...
...I'M ASKING YOU, THE PART OF YOU THAT CAME FROM ME.
LET ME LIVE. LEAVE IN PEACE. AT LEAST THAT WAY, YOU'LL LIVE ON...
...IN MY PERFECT MEMORY.
...WHAT HAVE YOU GOT TO LOSE?

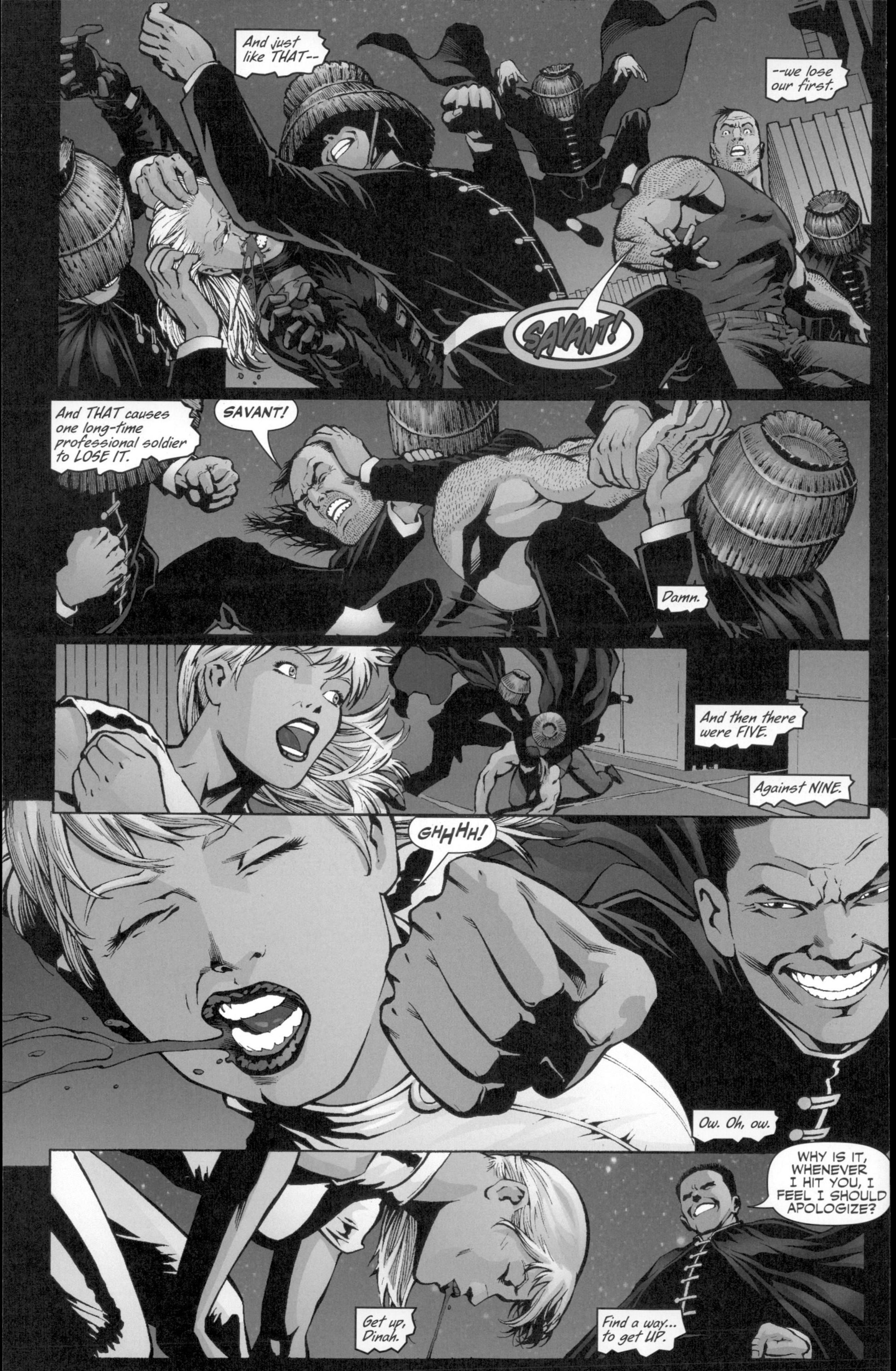
And just like THAT--
--we lose our first.
SAVANT!
And THAT causes one long-time professional soldier to LOSE IT.
SAVANT!
Damn.
And then there were FIVE.
Against NINE.
GHHHH!
Ow. Oh, ow.
WHY IS IT, WHENEVER I HIT YOU, I FEEL I SHOULD APOLOGIZE?
Get up, Dinah.
Find a way... to get UP.

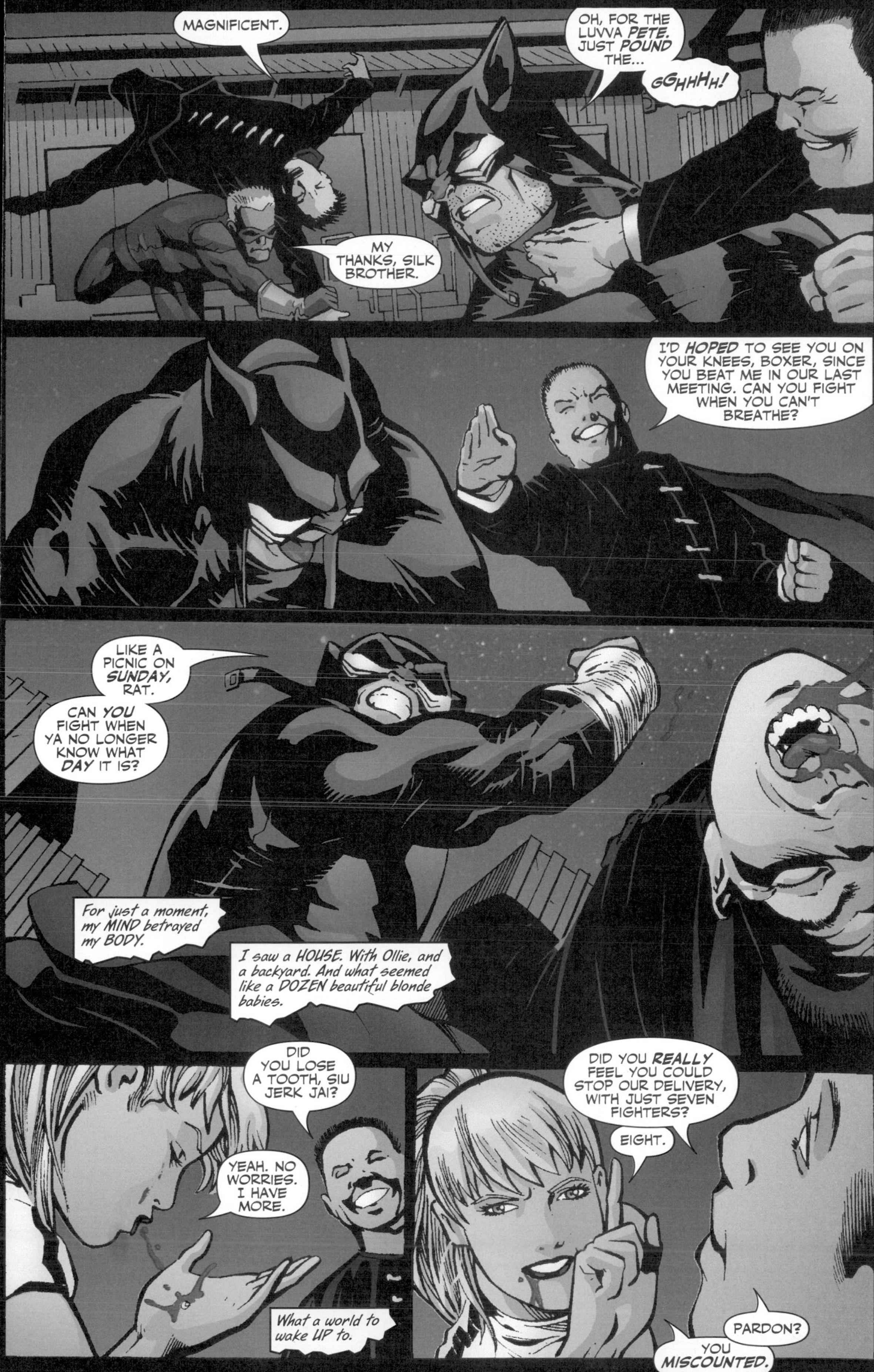

MAGNIFICENT.
OH, FOR THE LUVVA PETE. JUST POUND THE...
GGHHHH!
MY THANKS, SILK BROTHER.
I'D HOPED TO SEE YOU ON YOUR KNEES, BOXER, SINCE YOU BEAT ME IN OUR LAST MEETING. CAN YOU FIGHT WHEN YOU CAN'T BREATHE?
LIKE A PICNIC ON SUNDAY, RAT.
CAN YOU FIGHT WHEN YA NO LONGER KNOW WHAT DAY IT IS?
For just a moment, my MIND betrayed my BODY.
I saw a HOUSE. With Ollie, and a backyard. And what seemed like a DOZEN beautiful blonde babies.
DID YOU LOSE A TOOTH, SIU JERK JAI?
YEAH. NO WORRIES. I HAVE MORE.
What a world to wake UP to.
DID YOU REALLY FEEL YOU COULD STOP OUR DELIVERY, WITH JUST SEVEN FIGHTERS?
EIGHT.
PARDON?
YOU MISCOUNTED.

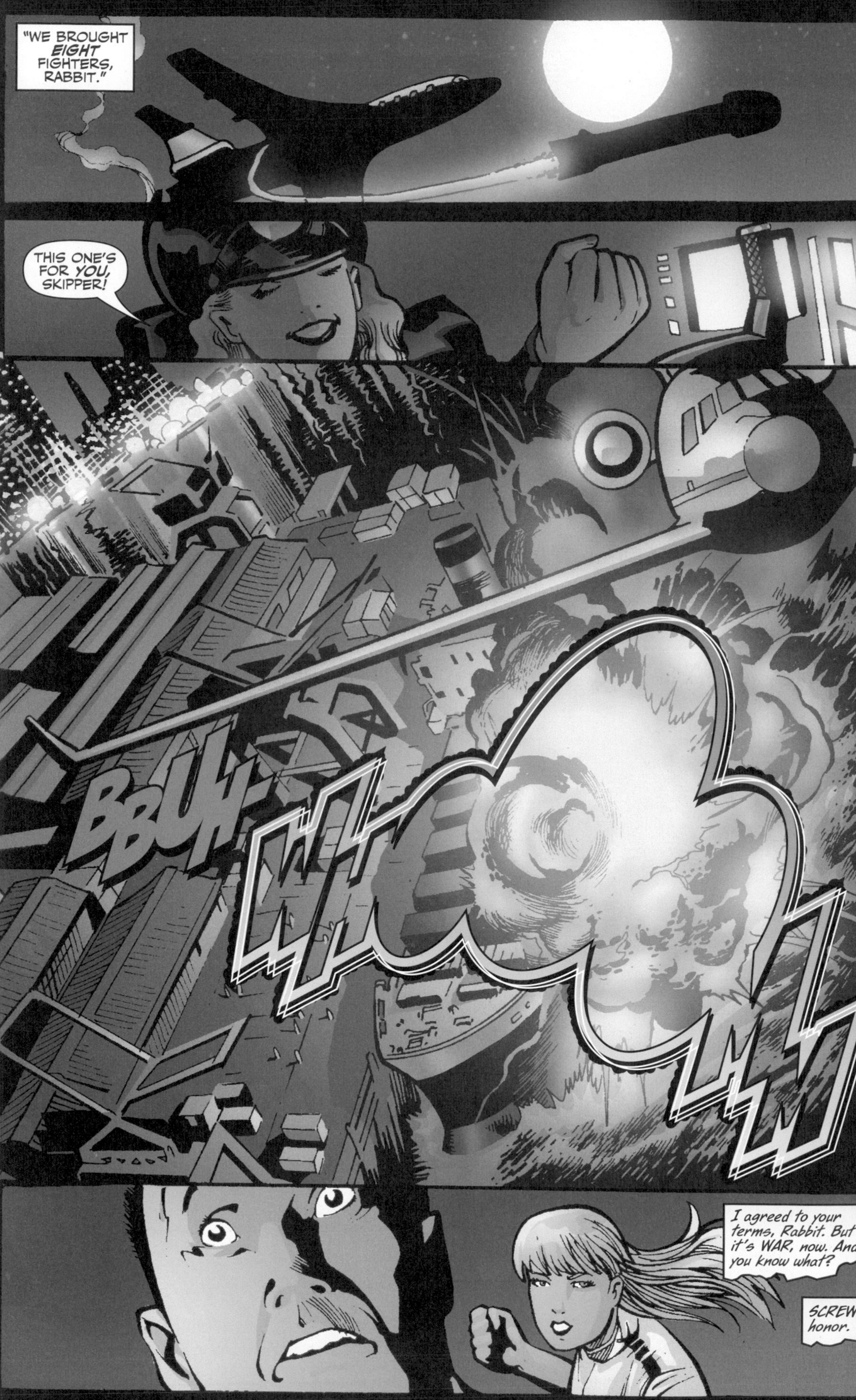
"WE BROUGHT EIGHT FIGHTERS, RABBIT."
THIS ONE'S FOR YOU, SKIPPER!
BBUH-WHOOM
I agreed to your terms, Rabbit. But it's WAR, now. And you know what?
SCREW honor.

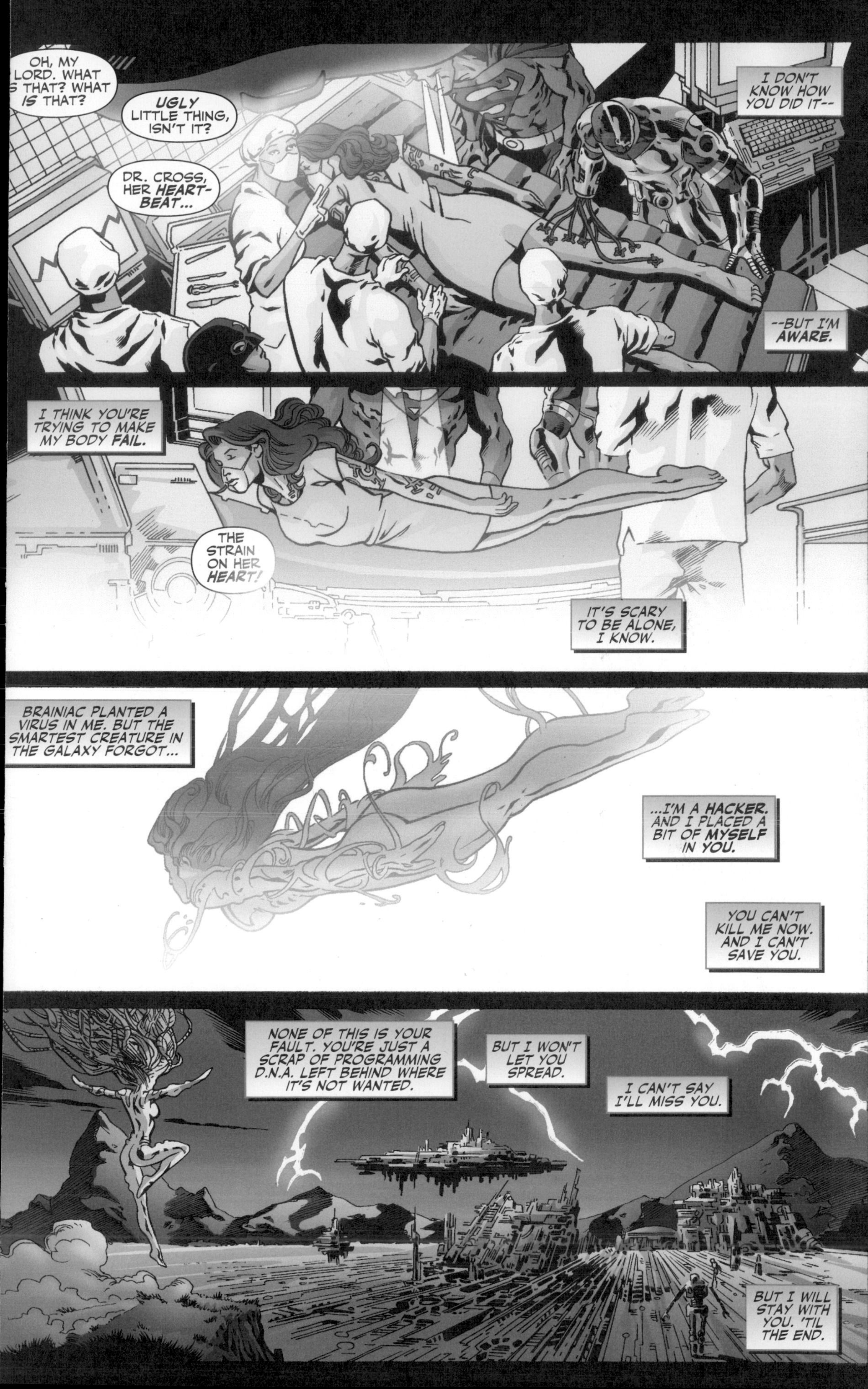

OH, MY LORD. WHAT IS THAT? WHAT IS THAT?
UGLY LITTLE THING, ISN'T IT?
DR. CROSS, HER HEART-BEAT...
I DON'T KNOW HOW YOU DID IT--
--BUT I'M AWARE.
I THINK YOU'RE TRYING TO MAKE MY BODY FAIL.
THE STRAIN ON HER HEART!
IT'S SCARY TO BE ALONE, I KNOW.
BRAINIAC PLANTED A VIRUS IN ME. BUT THE SMARTEST CREATURE IN THE GALAXY FORGOT...
...I'M A HACKER. AND I PLACED A BIT OF MYSELF IN YOU.
YOU CAN'T KILL ME NOW. AND I CAN'T SAVE YOU.
NONE OF THIS IS YOUR FAULT. YOU'RE JUST A SCRAP OF PROGRAMMING D.N.A. LEFT BEHIND WHERE IT'S NOT WANTED.
BUT I WON'T LET YOU SPREAD.
I CAN'T SAY I'LL MISS YOU.
BUT I WILL STAY WITH YOU. 'TIL THE END.

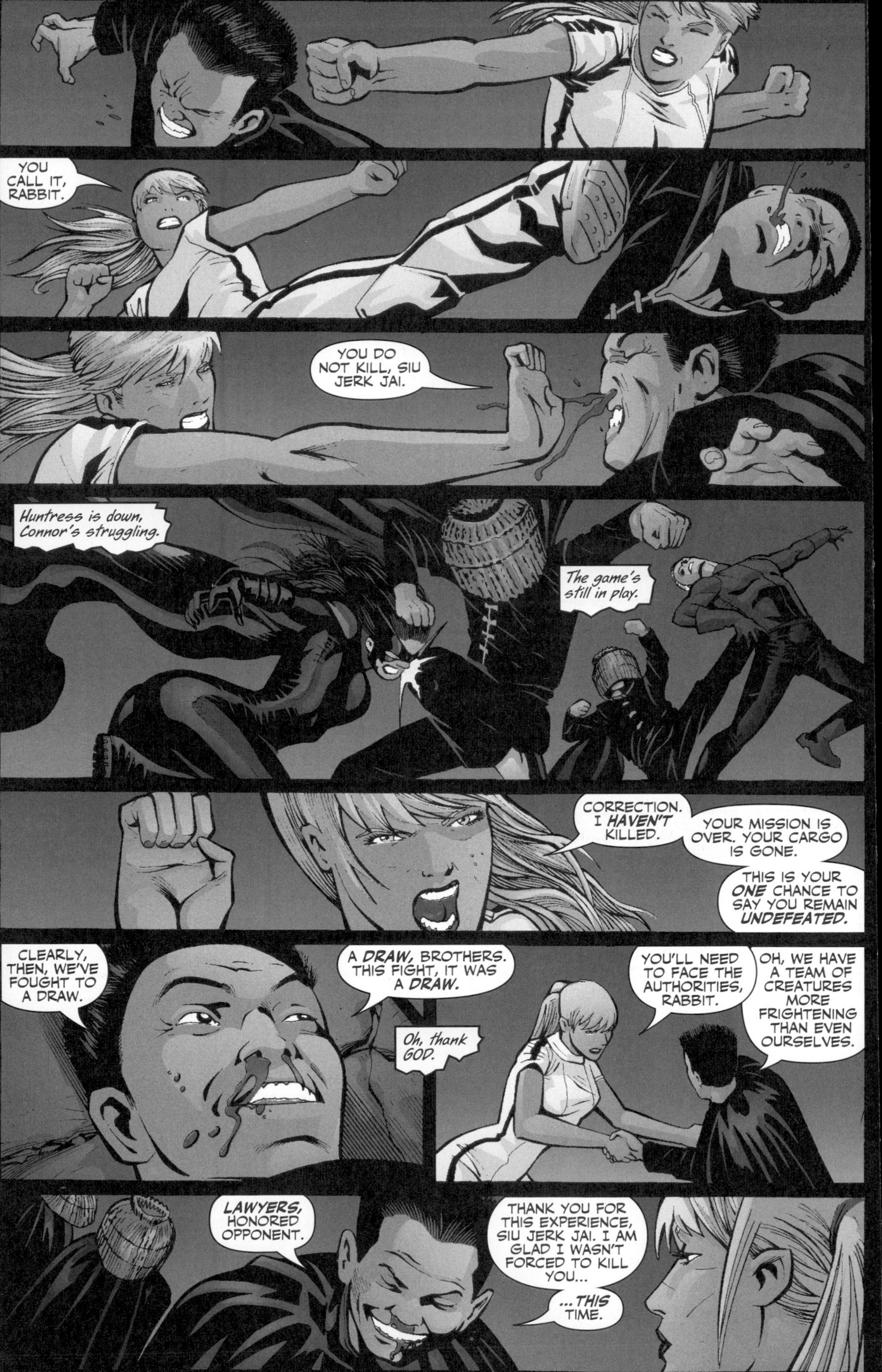
YOU CALL IT, RABBIT.
YOU DO NOT KILL, SIU JERK JAI.
Huntress is down, Connor's struggling.
The game's still in play.
CORRECTION. I HAVEN'T KILLED.
YOUR MISSION IS OVER. YOUR CARGO IS GONE.
THIS IS YOUR ONE CHANCE TO SAY YOU REMAIN UNDEFEATED.
CLEARLY, THEN, WE'VE FOUGHT TO A DRAW.
A DRAW, BROTHERS. THIS FIGHT, IT WAS A DRAW.
Oh, thank GOD.
YOU'LL NEED TO FACE THE AUTHORITIES, RABBIT.
OH, WE HAVE A TEAM OF CREATURES MORE FRIGHTENING THAN EVEN OURSELVES.
LAWYERS, HONORED OPPONENT.
THANK YOU FOR THIS EXPERIENCE, SIU JERK JAI. I AM GLAD I WASN'T FORCED TO KILL YOU...
...THIS TIME.

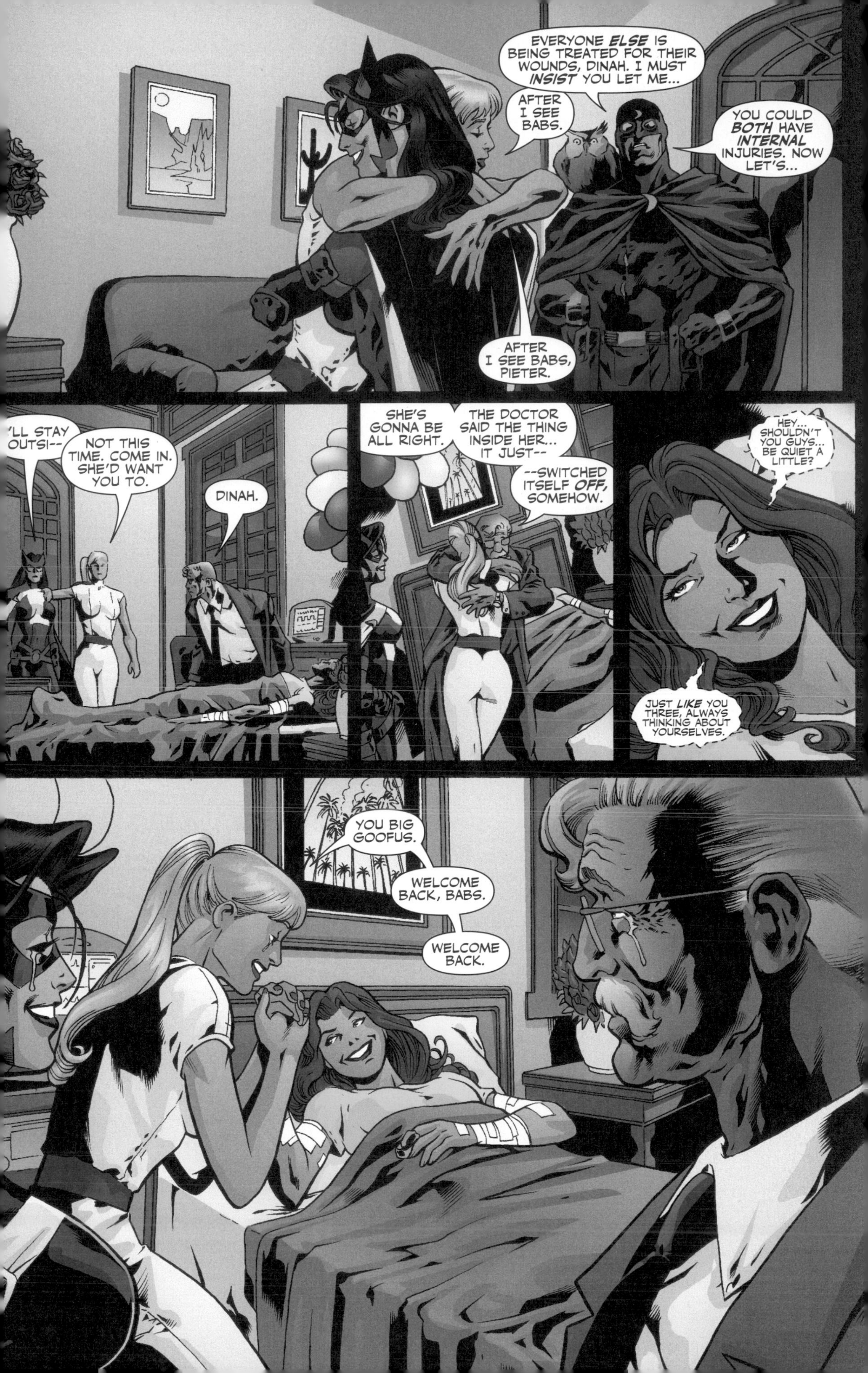
EVERYONE ELSE IS BEING TREATED FOR THEIR WOUNDS, DINAH. I MUST INSIST YOU LET ME...
AFTER I SEE BABS.
YOU COULD BOTH HAVE INTERNAL INJURIES. NOW LET'S...
AFTER I SEE BABS, PIETER.
'LL STAY OUTSI--
NOT THIS TIME. COME IN. SHE'D WANT YOU TO.
DINAH.
SHE'S GONNA BE ALL RIGHT.
THE DOCTOR SAID THE THING INSIDE HER... IT JUST--
--SWITCHED ITSELF OFF, SOMEHOW.
HEY... SHOULDN'T YOU GUYS... BE QUIET A LITTLE?
JUST LIKE YOU THREE, ALWAYS THINKING ABOUT YOURSELVES.
YOU BIG GOOFUS.
WELCOME BACK, BABS.
WELCOME BACK.

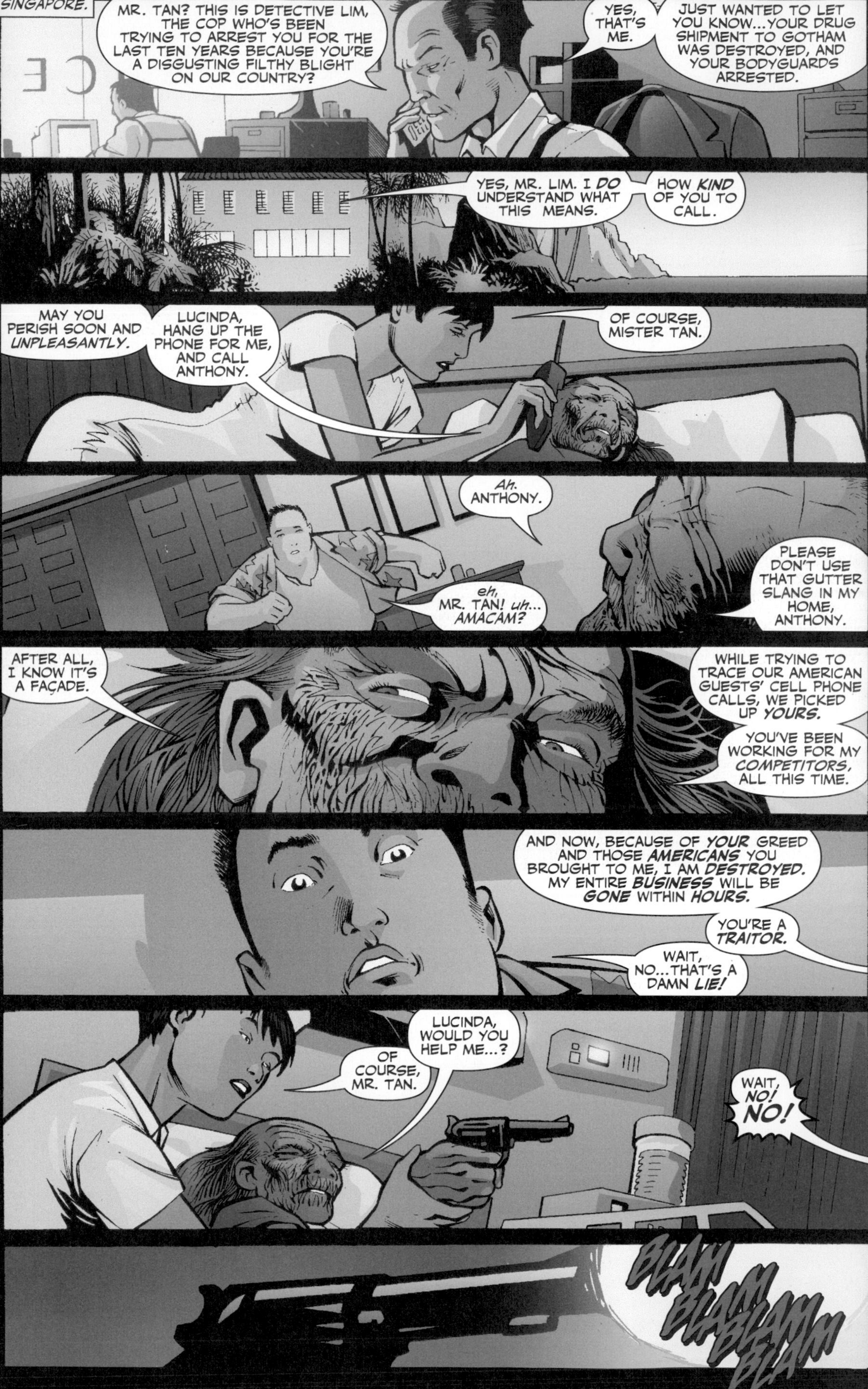
SINGAPORE.
MR. TAN? THIS IS DETECTIVE LIM, THE COP WHO'S BEEN TRYING TO ARREST YOU FOR THE LAST TEN YEARS BECAUSE YOU'RE A DISGUSTING FILTHY BLIGHT ON OUR COUNTRY?
YES, THAT'S ME.
JUST WANTED TO LET YOU KNOW...YOUR DRUG SHIPMENT TO GOTHAM WAS DESTROYED, AND YOUR BODYGUARDS ARRESTED.
YES, MR. LIM. I DO UNDERSTAND WHAT THIS MEANS.
HOW KIND OF YOU TO CALL.
MAY YOU PERISH SOON AND UNPLEASANTLY.
LUCINDA, HANG UP THE PHONE FOR ME, AND CALL ANTHONY.
OF COURSE, MISTER TAN.
Ah. ANTHONY.
eh, MR. TAN! uh... AMACAM?
PLEASE DON'T USE THAT GUTTER SLANG IN MY HOME, ANTHONY.
AFTER ALL, I KNOW IT'S A FAÇADE.
WHILE TRYING TO TRACE OUR AMERICAN GUESTS' CELL PHONE CALLS, WE PICKED UP YOURS.
YOU'VE BEEN WORKING FOR MY COMPETITORS, ALL THIS TIME.
AND NOW, BECAUSE OF YOUR GREED AND THOSE AMERICANS YOU BROUGHT TO ME, I AM DESTROYED. MY ENTIRE BUSINESS WILL BE GONE WITHIN HOURS.
YOU'RE A TRAITOR.
WAIT, NO...THAT'S A DAMN LIE!
LUCINDA, WOULD YOU HELP ME...?
OF COURSE, MR. TAN.
WAIT, NO! NO!
BLAM BLAM BLABLAM BLAM

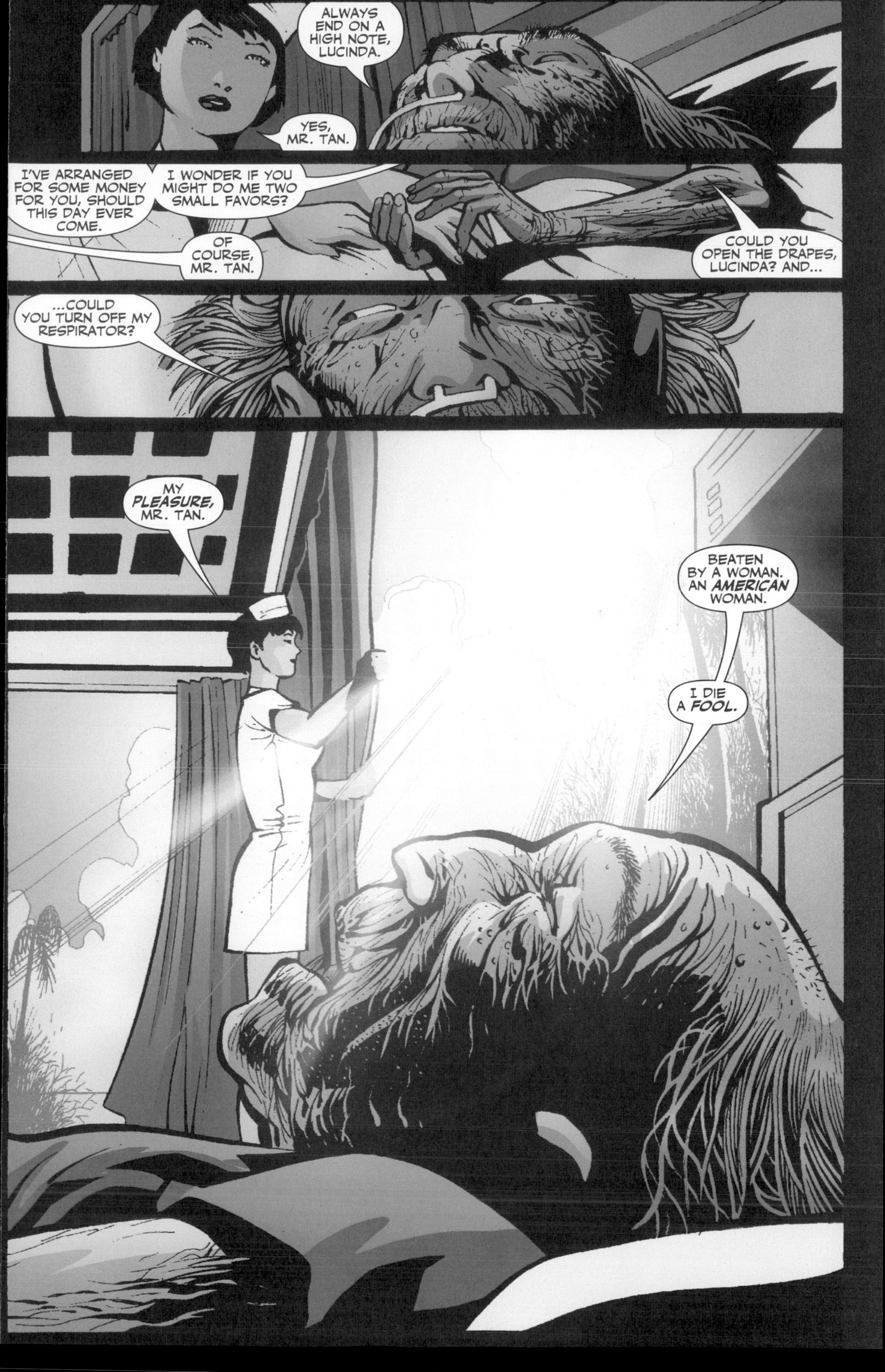
ALWAYS END ON A HIGH NOTE, LUCINDA.
YES, MR. TAN.
I'VE ARRANGED FOR SOME MONEY FOR YOU, SHOULD THIS DAY EVER COME.
OF COURSE, MR. TAN.
I WONDER IF YOU MIGHT DO ME TWO SMALL FAVORS?
COULD YOU OPEN THE DRAPES, LUCINDA? AND...
...COULD YOU TURN OFF MY RESPIRATOR?
MY PLEASURE, MR. TAN.
BEATEN BY A WOMAN. AN AMERICAN WOMAN.
I DIE A FOOL.

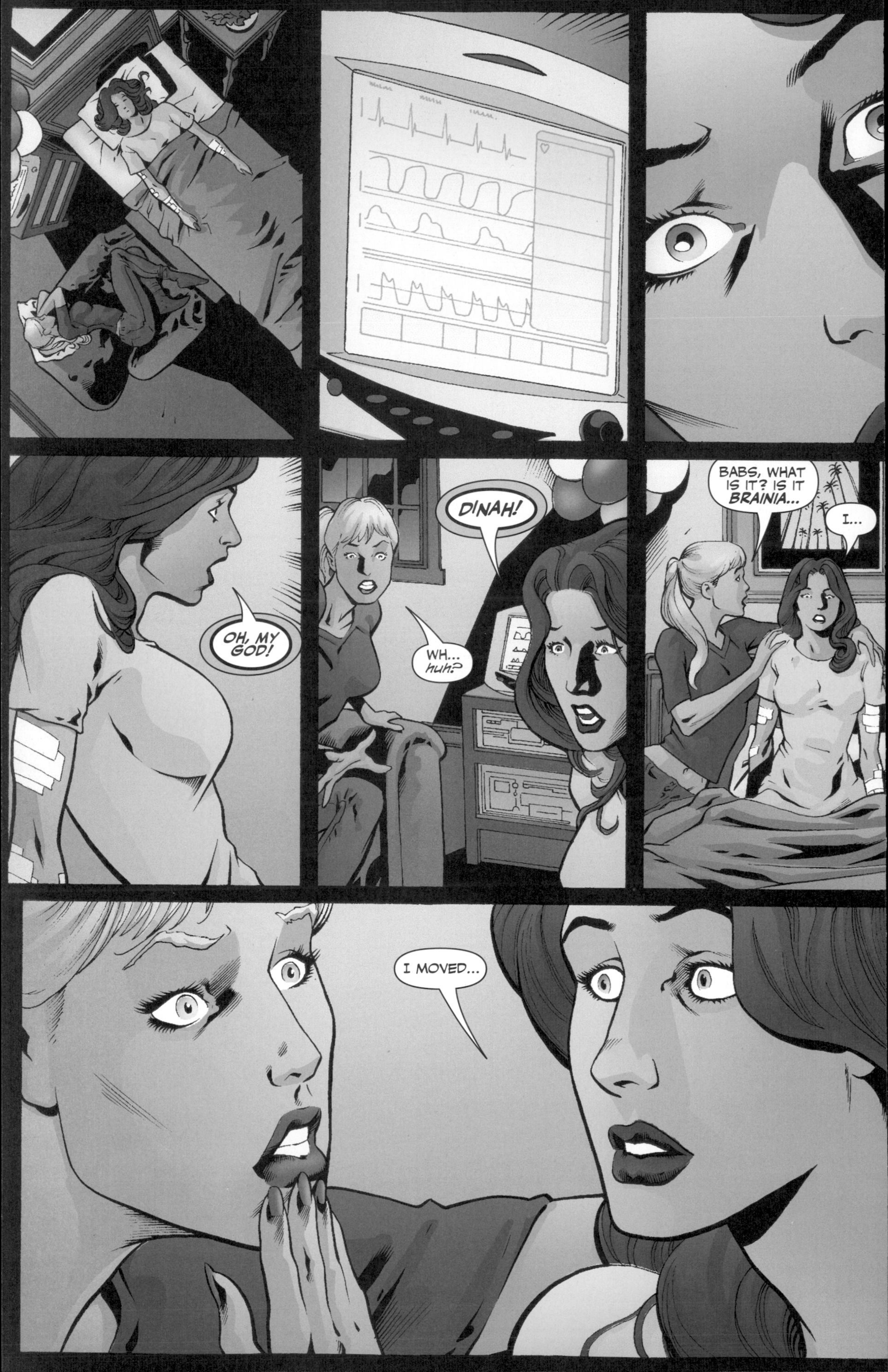
OH, MY GOD!
DINAH!
WH... huh?
BABS, WHAT IS IT? IS IT BRAINIA...
I...
I MOVED...

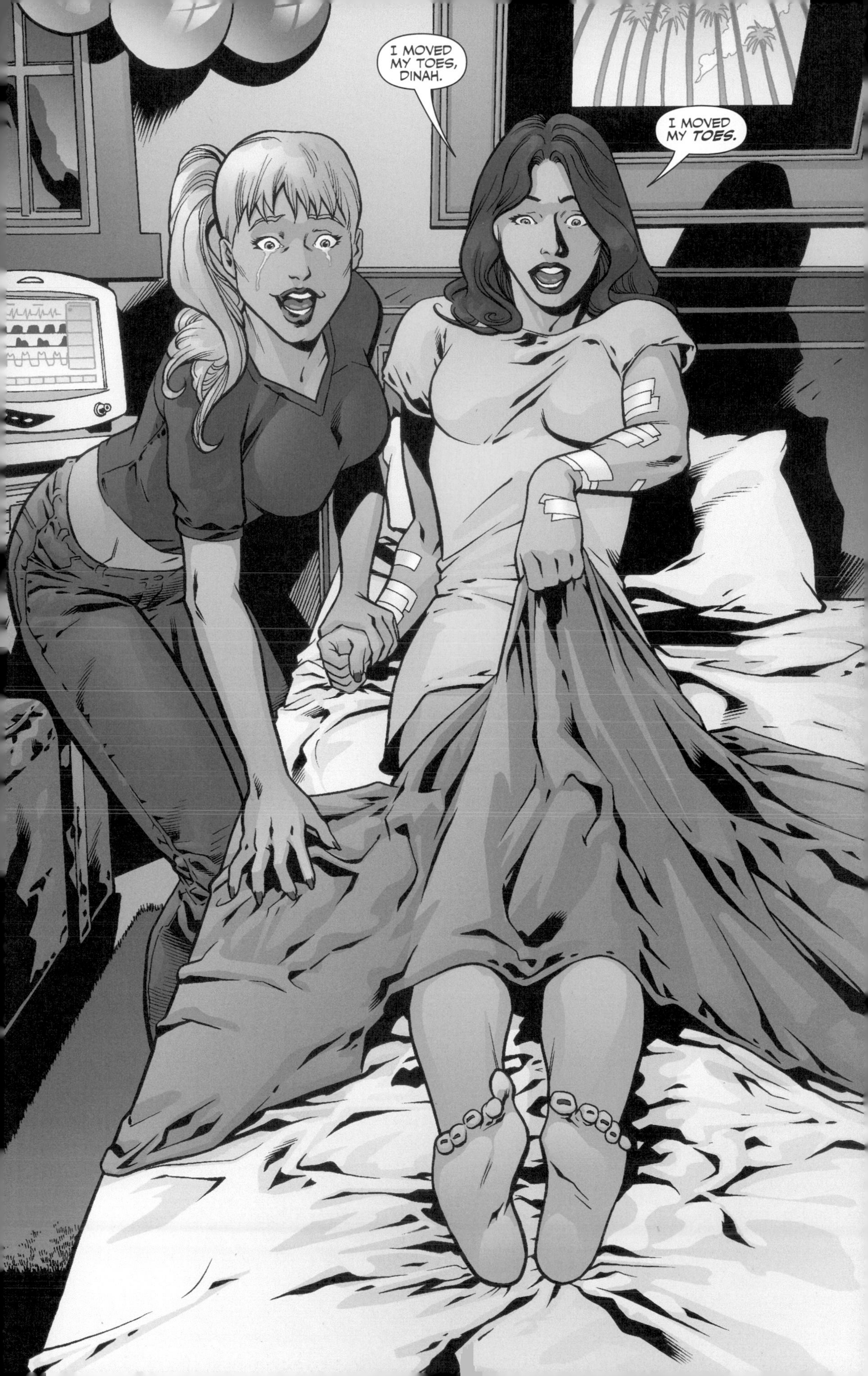
I MOVED MY TOES, DINAH.
I MOVED MY *TOES*.

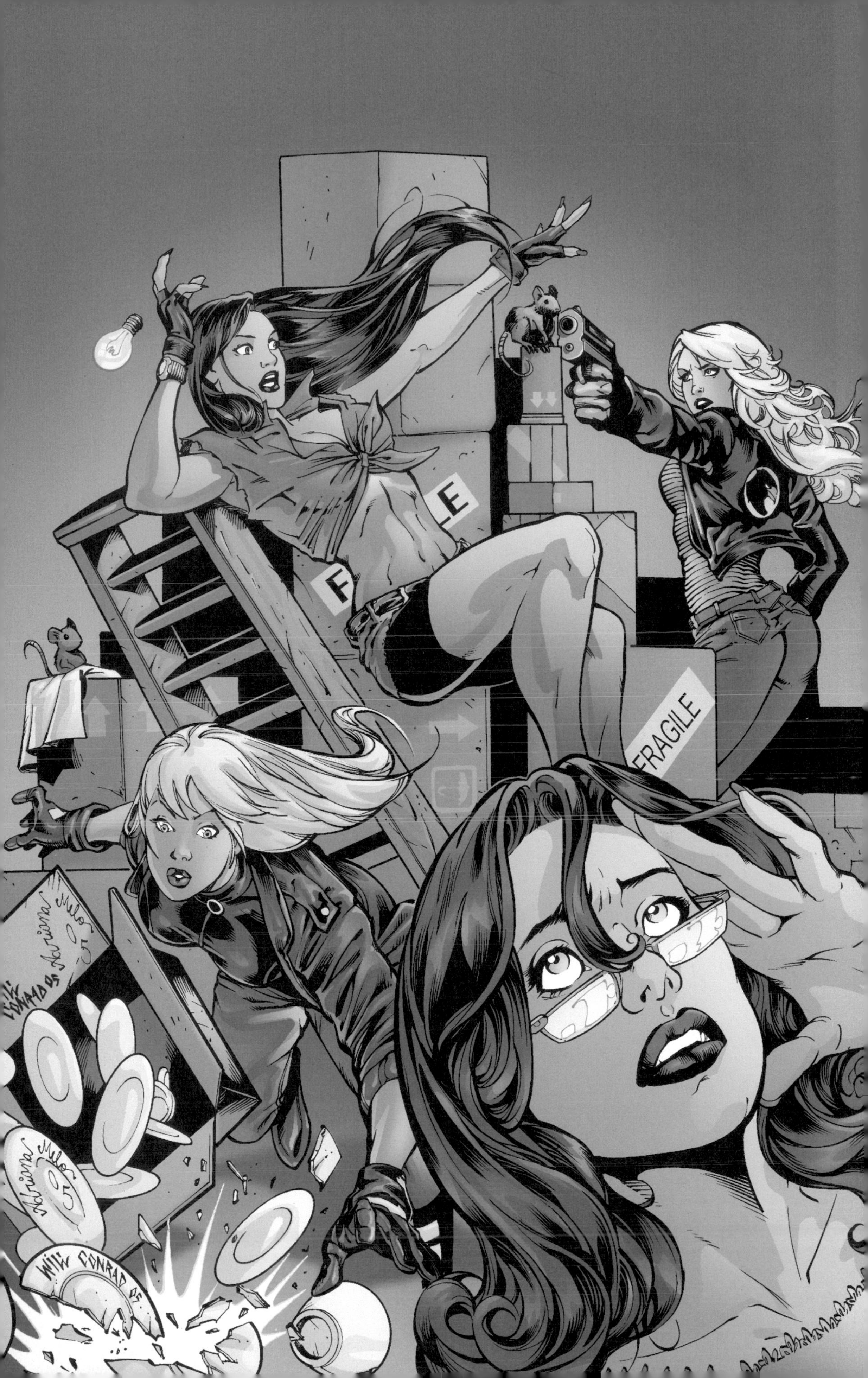

E
F
FRAGILE

Cover art by
ADRIANA MELO
and WILL CONRAD

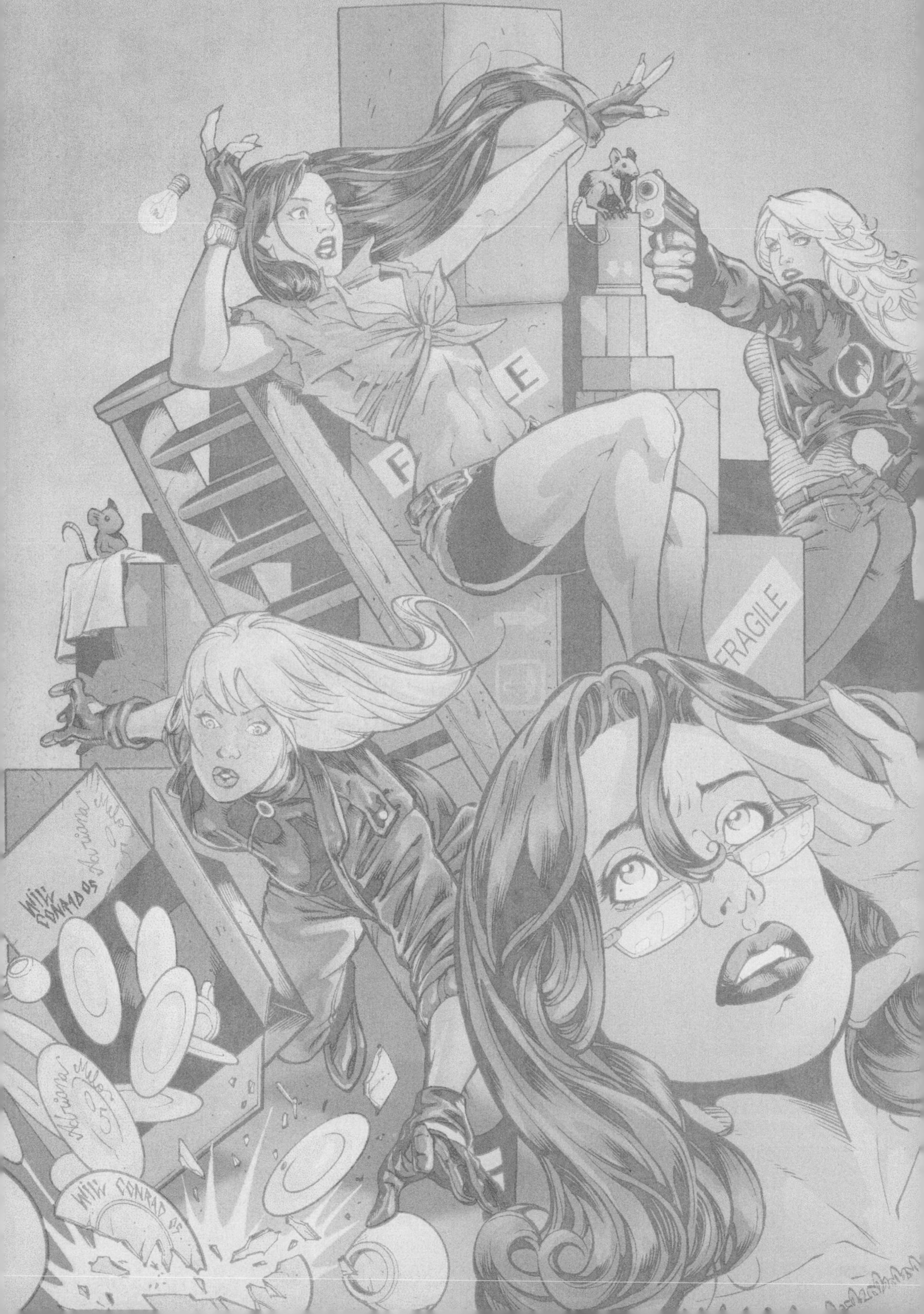
E
F
FRAGILE
Will Conrad 05
Adriana Melo 05
Adriana Melo 05
Will Conrad 05

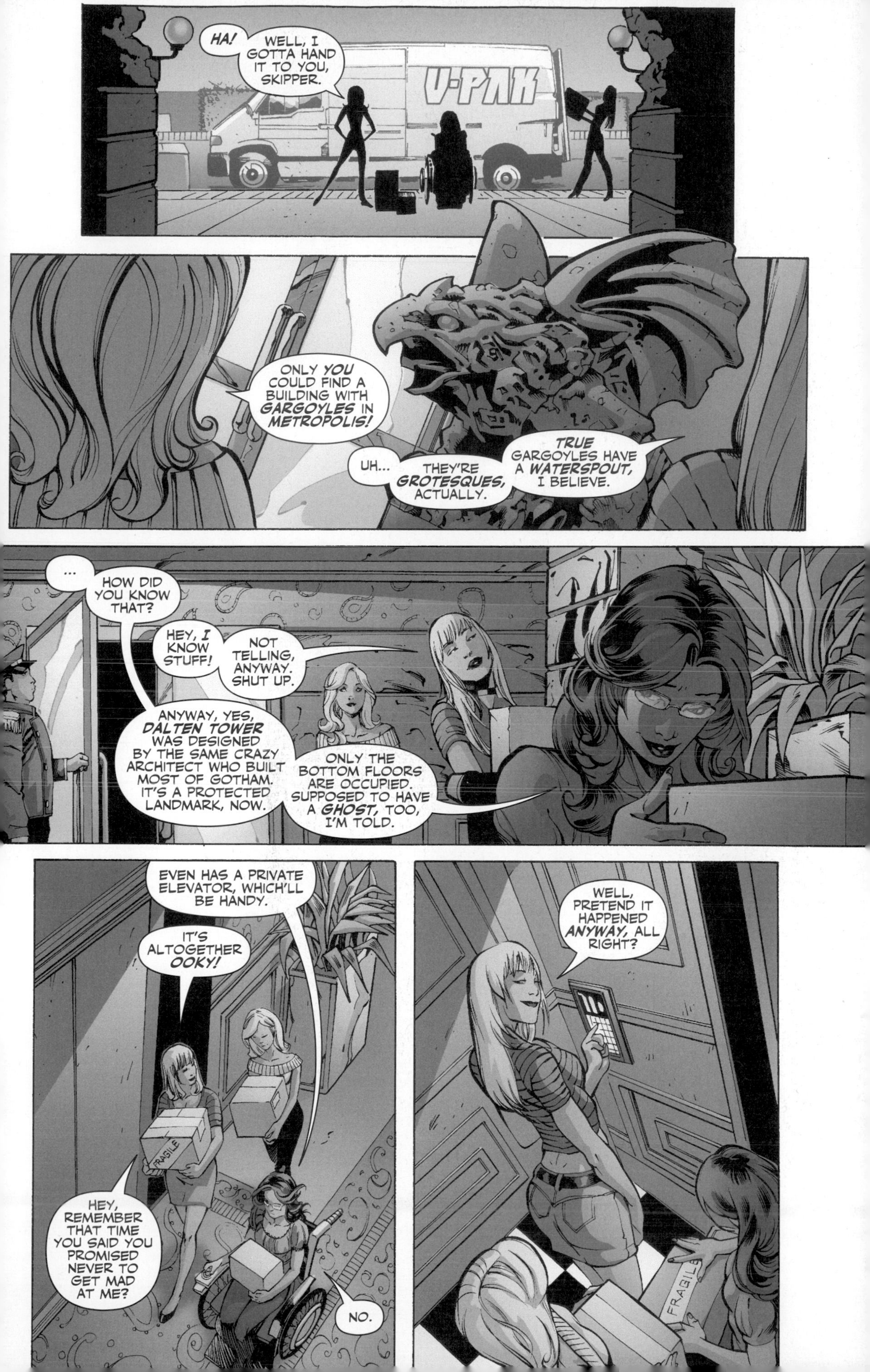
HA!
WELL, I GOTTA HAND IT TO YOU, SKIPPER.
V-PAK
ONLY YOU COULD FIND A BUILDING WITH GARGOYLES IN METROPOLIS!
UH...
THEY'RE GROTESQUES, ACTUALLY.
TRUE GARGOYLES HAVE A WATERSPOUT, I BELIEVE.
...
HOW DID YOU KNOW THAT?
HEY, I KNOW STUFF!
NOT TELLING, ANYWAY. SHUT UP.
ANYWAY, YES, DALTEN TOWER WAS DESIGNED BY THE SAME CRAZY ARCHITECT WHO BUILT MOST OF GOTHAM. IT'S A PROTECTED LANDMARK, NOW.
ONLY THE BOTTOM FLOORS ARE OCCUPIED. SUPPOSED TO HAVE A GHOST, TOO, I'M TOLD.
EVEN HAS A PRIVATE ELEVATOR, WHICH'LL BE HANDY.
IT'S ALTOGETHER OOKY!
FRAGILE
HEY, REMEMBER THAT TIME YOU SAID YOU PROMISED NEVER TO GET MAD AT ME?
NO.
WELL, PRETEND IT HAPPENED ANYWAY, ALL RIGHT?
FRAGILE

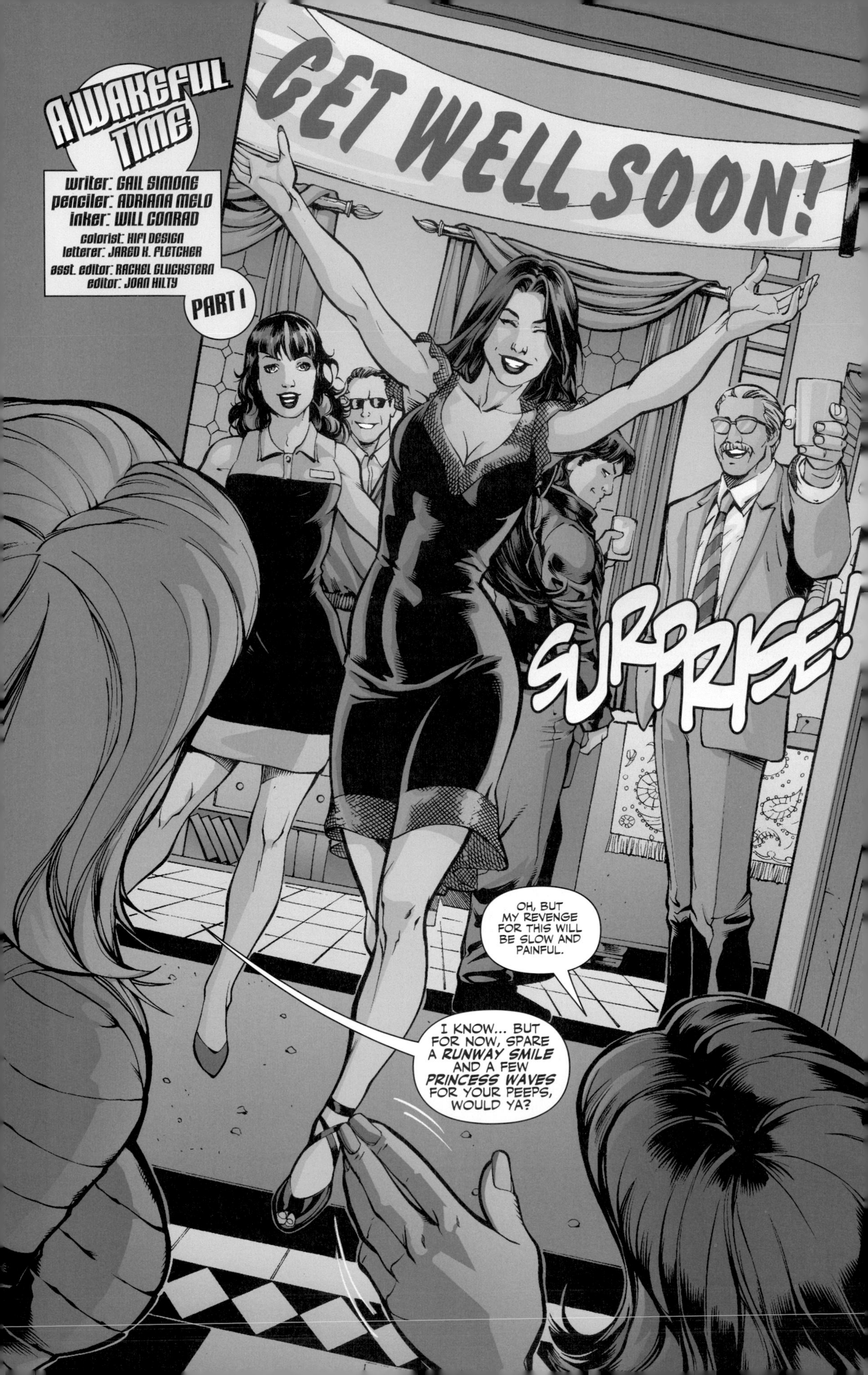
A WAKEFUL TIME
writer: GAIL SIMONE
penciler: ADRIANA MELO
inker: WILL CONRAD
colorist: HIFI DESIGN
letterer: JARED K. FLETCHER
asst. editor: RACHEL GLUCKSTERN
editor: JOAN HILTY
PART 1
GET WELL SOON!
SURPRISE!
OH, BUT MY REVENGE FOR THIS WILL BE SLOW AND PAINFUL.
I KNOW... BUT FOR NOW, SPARE A RUNWAY SMILE AND A FEW PRINCESS WAVES FOR YOUR PEEPS, WOULD YA?

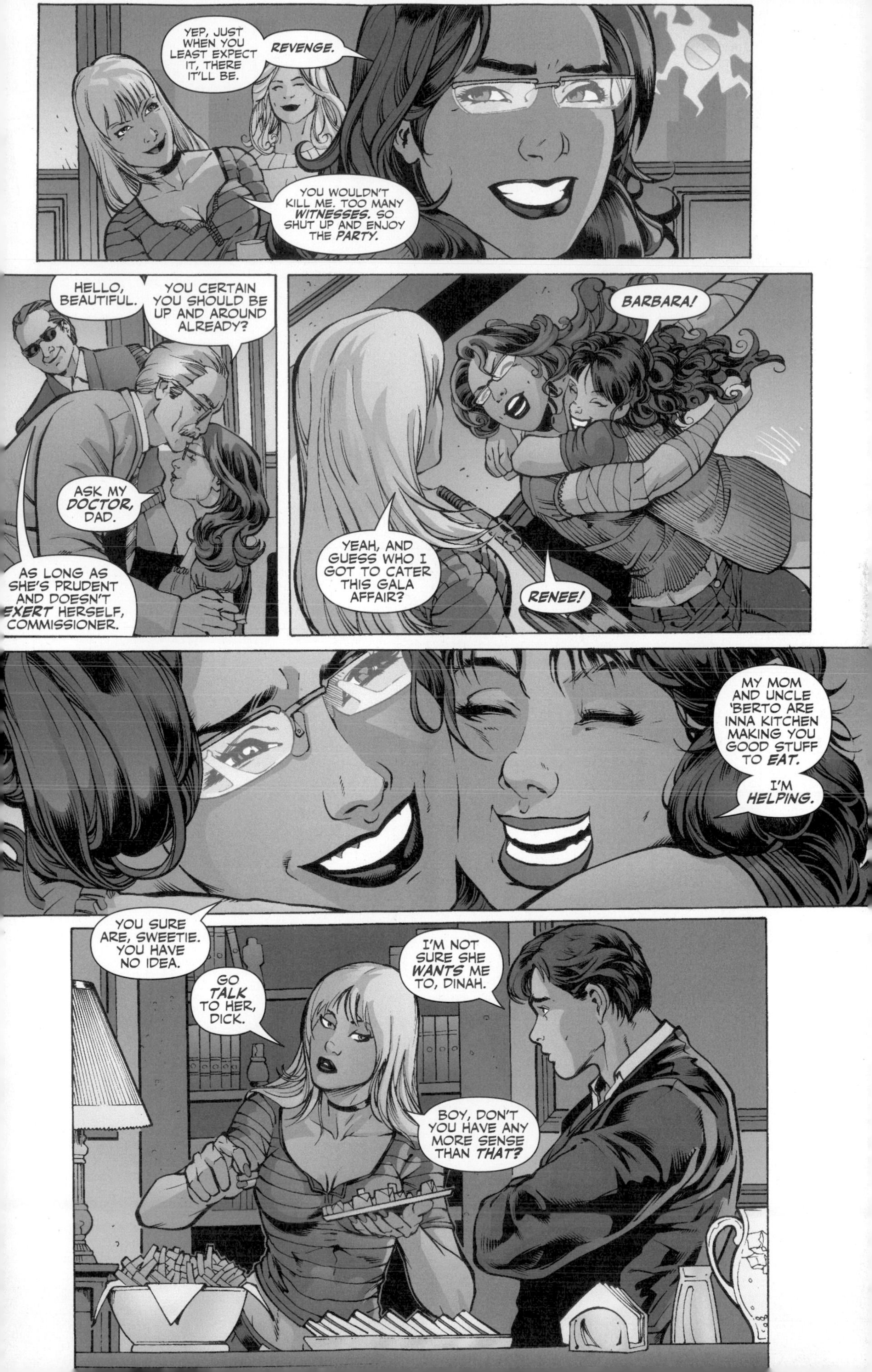
YEP, JUST WHEN YOU LEAST EXPECT IT, THERE IT'LL BE.
REVENGE.
YOU WOULDN'T KILL ME. TOO MANY WITNESSES. SO SHUT UP AND ENJOY THE PARTY.
HELLO, BEAUTIFUL.
YOU CERTAIN YOU SHOULD BE UP AND AROUND ALREADY?
ASK MY DOCTOR, DAD.
AS LONG AS SHE'S PRUDENT AND DOESN'T EXERT HERSELF, COMMISSIONER.
BARBARA!
RENEE!
YEAH, AND GUESS WHO I GOT TO CATER THIS GALA AFFAIR?
MY MOM AND UNCLE 'BERTO ARE INNA KITCHEN MAKING YOU GOOD STUFF TO EAT.
I'M HELPING.
YOU SURE ARE, SWEETIE. YOU HAVE NO IDEA.
GO TALK TO HER, DICK.
I'M NOT SURE SHE WANTS ME TO, DINAH.
BOY, DON'T YOU HAVE ANY MORE SENSE THAN THAT?

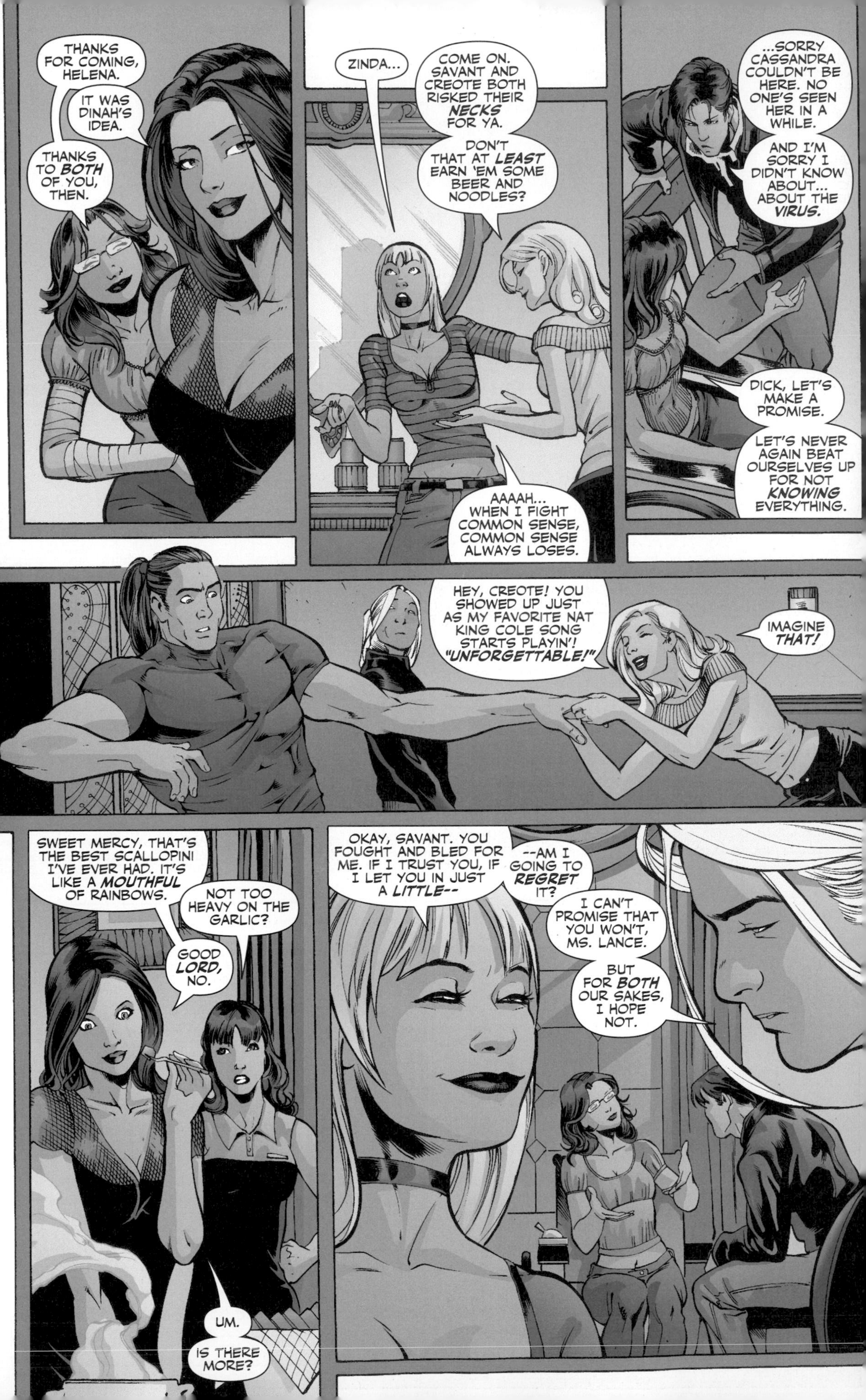
THANKS FOR COMING, HELENA.
IT WAS DINAH'S IDEA.
THANKS TO BOTH OF YOU, THEN.
ZINDA...
COME ON. SAVANT AND CREOTE BOTH RISKED THEIR NECKS FOR YA.
DON'T THAT AT LEAST EARN 'EM SOME BEER AND NOODLES?
AAAAH... WHEN I FIGHT COMMON SENSE, COMMON SENSE ALWAYS LOSES.
...SORRY CASSANDRA COULDN'T BE HERE. NO ONE'S SEEN HER IN A WHILE.
AND I'M SORRY I DIDN'T KNOW ABOUT... ABOUT THE VIRUS.
DICK, LET'S MAKE A PROMISE.
LET'S NEVER AGAIN BEAT OURSELVES UP FOR NOT KNOWING EVERYTHING.
HEY, CREOTE! YOU SHOWED UP JUST AS MY FAVORITE NAT KING COLE SONG STARTS PLAYIN'! "UNFORGETTABLE!"
IMAGINE THAT!
SWEET MERCY, THAT'S THE BEST SCALLOPINI I'VE EVER HAD. IT'S LIKE A MOUTHFUL OF RAINBOWS.
NOT TOO HEAVY ON THE GARLIC?
GOOD LORD, NO.
UM.
IS THERE MORE?
OKAY, SAVANT. YOU FOUGHT AND BLED FOR ME. IF I TRUST YOU, IF I LET YOU IN JUST A LITTLE--
--AM I GOING TO REGRET IT?
I CAN'T PROMISE THAT YOU WON'T, MS. LANCE.
BUT FOR BOTH OUR SAKES, I HOPE NOT.

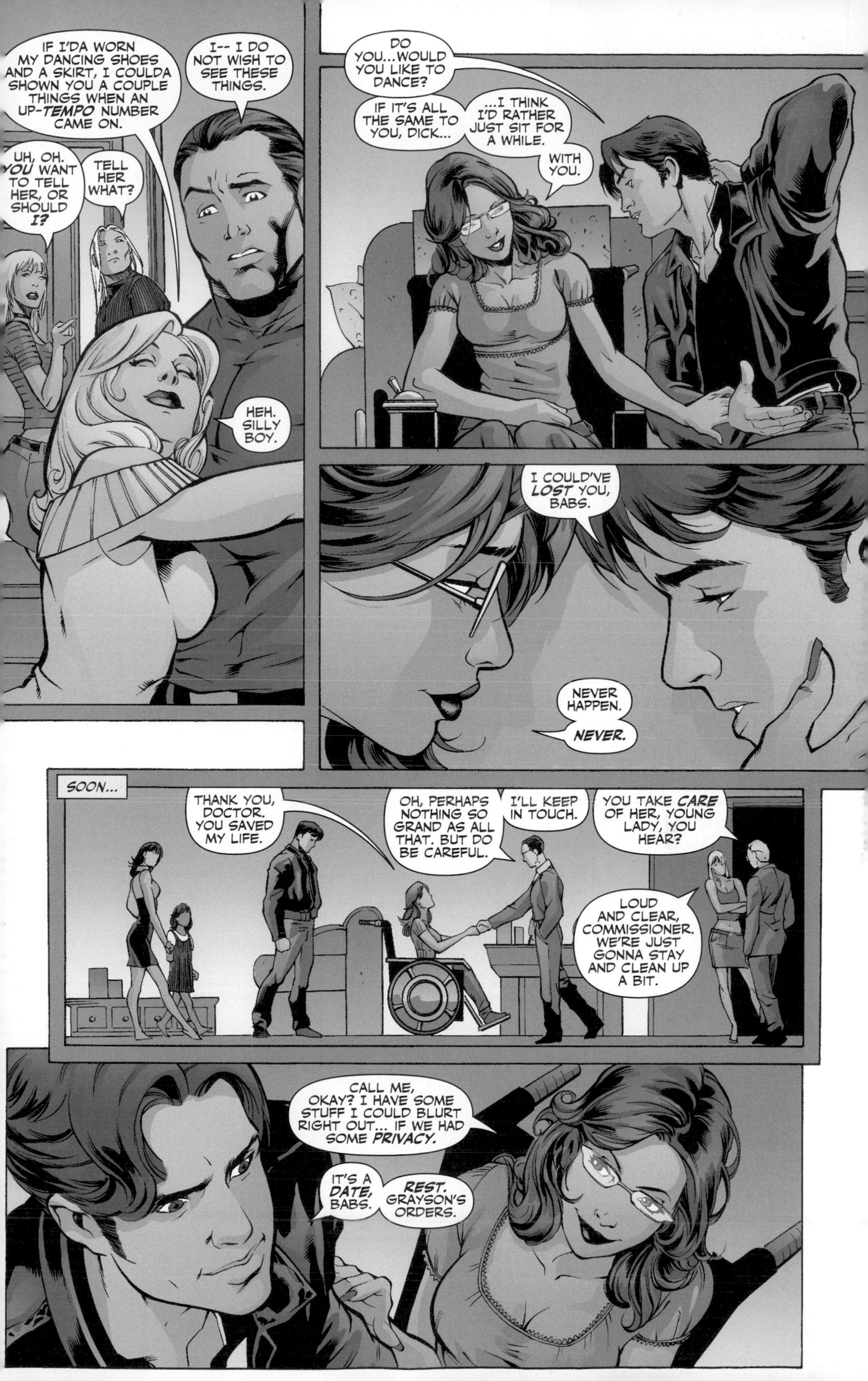
IF I'DA WORN MY DANCING SHOES AND A SKIRT, I COULDA SHOWN YOU A COUPLE THINGS WHEN AN UP-*TEMPO* NUMBER CAME ON.
I-- I DO NOT WISH TO SEE THESE THINGS.
UH, OH. *YOU* WANT TO TELL HER, OR SHOULD *I?*
TELL HER WHAT?
HEH. SILLY BOY.
DO YOU...WOULD YOU LIKE TO DANCE?
IF IT'S ALL THE SAME TO YOU, DICK...
...I THINK I'D RATHER JUST SIT FOR A WHILE.
WITH YOU.
I COULD'VE *LOST* YOU, BABS.
NEVER HAPPEN.
NEVER.
SOON...
THANK YOU, DOCTOR. YOU SAVED MY LIFE.
OH, PERHAPS NOTHING SO GRAND AS ALL THAT. BUT DO BE CAREFUL.
I'LL KEEP IN TOUCH.
YOU TAKE *CARE* OF HER, YOUNG LADY, YOU HEAR?
LOUD AND CLEAR, COMMISSIONER. WE'RE JUST GONNA STAY AND CLEAN UP A BIT.
CALL ME, OKAY? I HAVE SOME STUFF I COULD BLURT RIGHT OUT... IF WE HAD SOME *PRIVACY.*
IT'S A *DATE,* BABS.
REST. GRAYSON'S ORDERS.

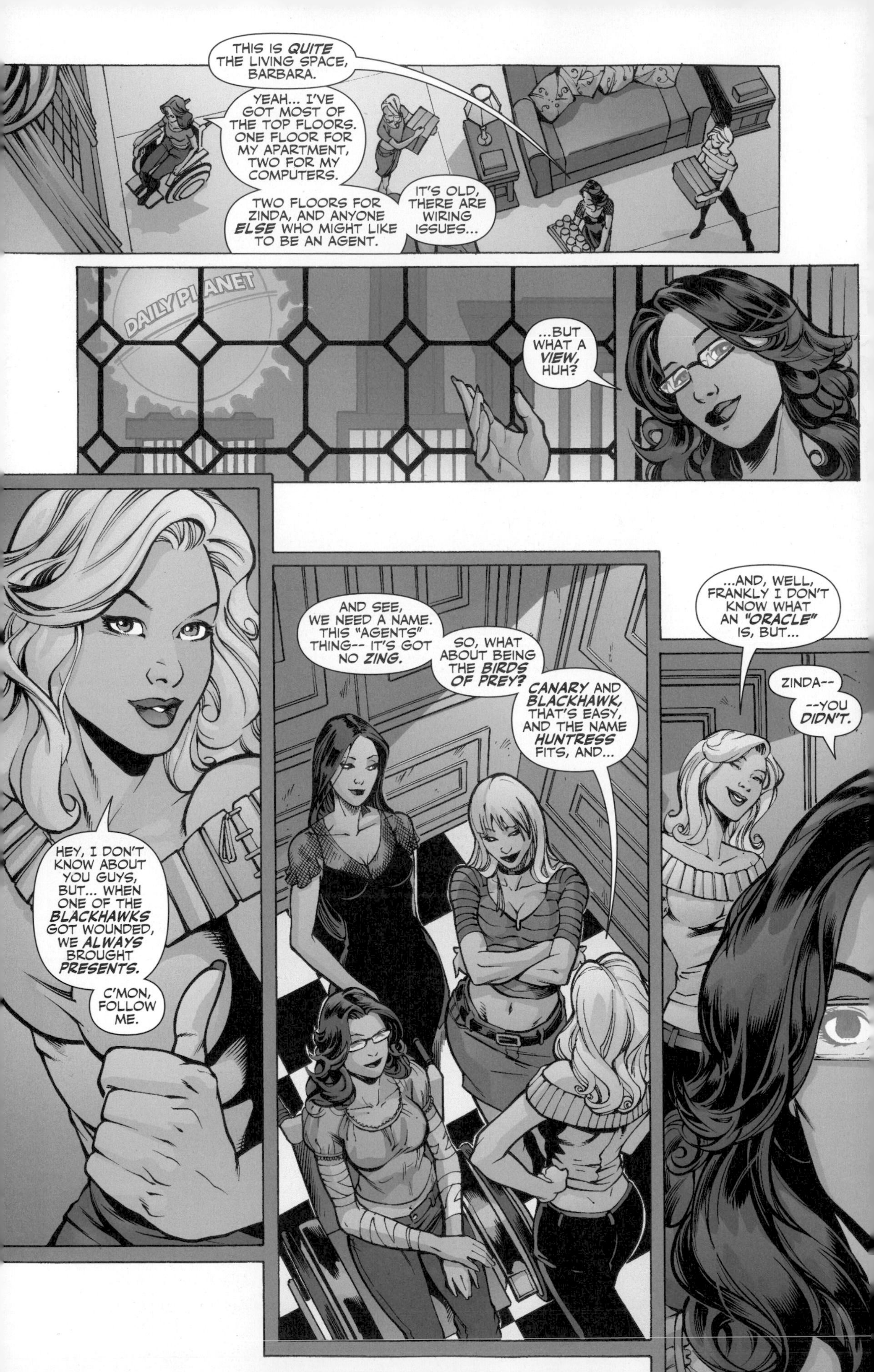

THIS IS QUITE THE LIVING SPACE, BARBARA.
YEAH... I'VE GOT MOST OF THE TOP FLOORS. ONE FLOOR FOR MY APARTMENT, TWO FOR MY COMPUTERS.
TWO FLOORS FOR ZINDA, AND ANYONE ELSE WHO MIGHT LIKE TO BE AN AGENT.
IT'S OLD, THERE ARE WIRING ISSUES...
DAILY PLANET
...BUT WHAT A VIEW, HUH?
HEY, I DON'T KNOW ABOUT YOU GUYS, BUT... WHEN ONE OF THE BLACKHAWKS GOT WOUNDED, WE ALWAYS BROUGHT PRESENTS.
C'MON, FOLLOW ME.
AND SEE, WE NEED A NAME. THIS "AGENTS" THING-- IT'S GOT NO ZING.
SO, WHAT ABOUT BEING THE BIRDS OF PREY?
CANARY AND BLACKHAWK, THAT'S EASY, AND THE NAME HUNTRESS FITS, AND...
...AND, WELL, FRANKLY I DON'T KNOW WHAT AN "ORACLE" IS, BUT...
ZINDA--
--YOU DIDN'T.

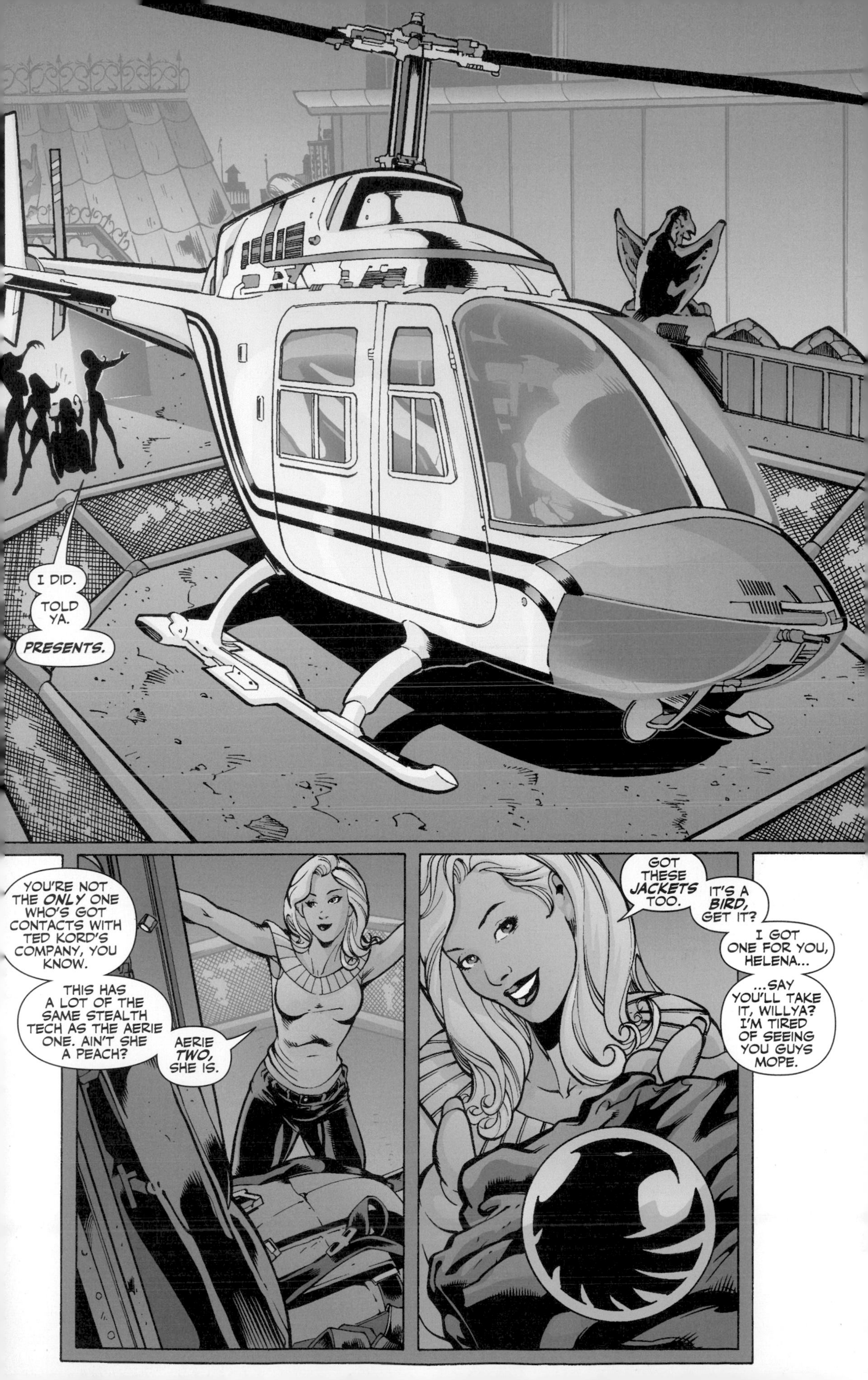
I DID.
TOLD YA.
PRESENTS.
YOU'RE NOT THE *ONLY* ONE WHO'S GOT CONTACTS WITH TED KORD'S COMPANY, YOU KNOW.
THIS HAS A LOT OF THE SAME STEALTH TECH AS THE AERIE ONE. AIN'T SHE A PEACH?
AERIE *TWO,* SHE IS.
GOT THESE *JACKETS* TOO.
IT'S A *BIRD,* GET IT?
I GOT ONE FOR YOU, HELENA...
...SAY YOU'LL TAKE IT, WILLYA? I'M TIRED OF SEEING YOU GUYS MOPE.

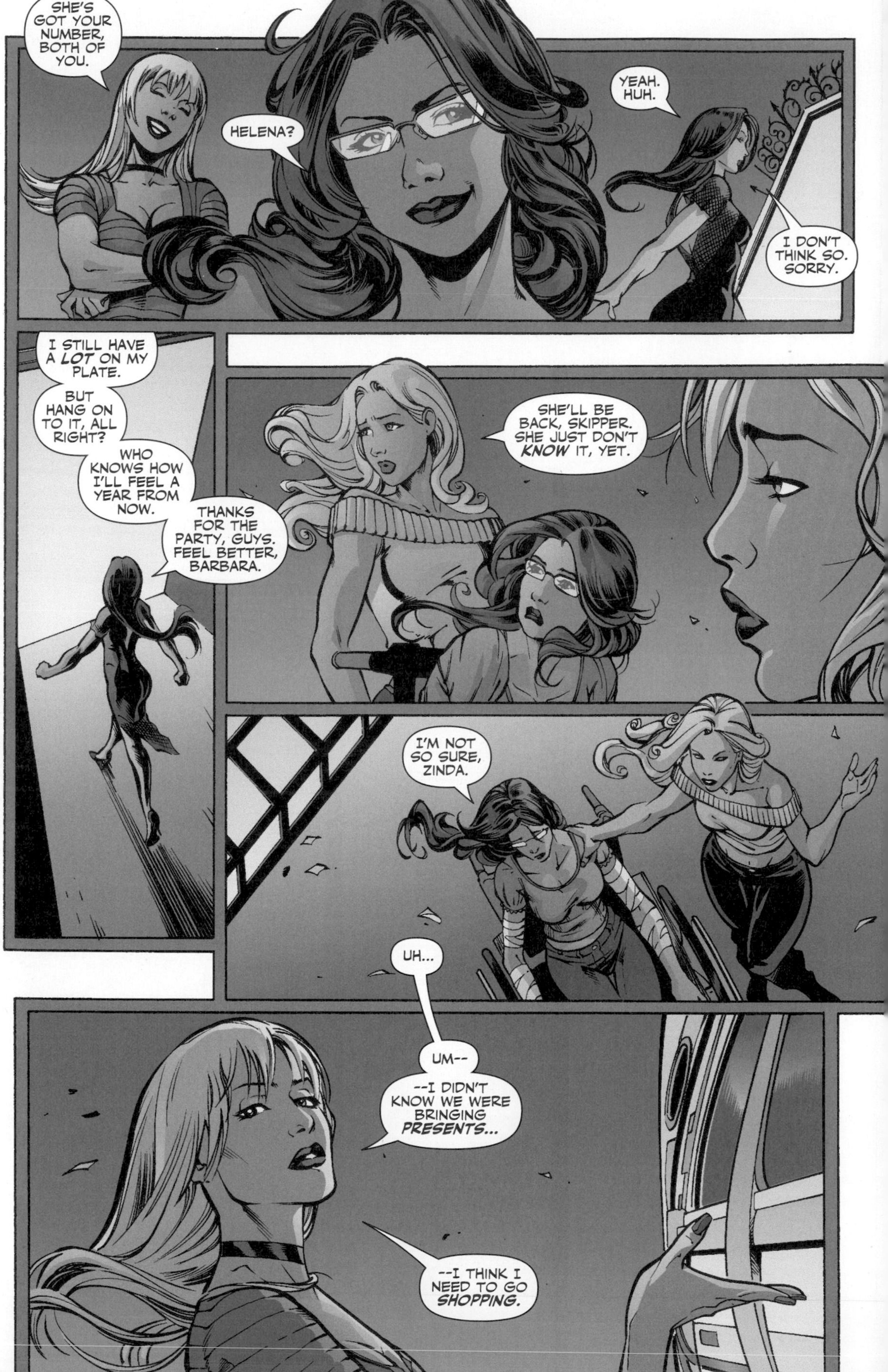

SHE'S GOT YOUR NUMBER, BOTH OF YOU.
HELENA?
YEAH. HUH.
I DON'T THINK SO. SORRY.
I STILL HAVE A LOT ON MY PLATE.
BUT HANG ON TO IT, ALL RIGHT?
WHO KNOWS HOW I'LL FEEL A YEAR FROM NOW.
THANKS FOR THE PARTY, GUYS. FEEL BETTER, BARBARA.
SHE'LL BE BACK, SKIPPER. SHE JUST DON'T KNOW IT, YET.
I'M NOT SO SURE, ZINDA.
UH...
UM--
--I DIDN'T KNOW WE WERE BRINGING PRESENTS...
--I THINK I NEED TO GO SHOPPING.

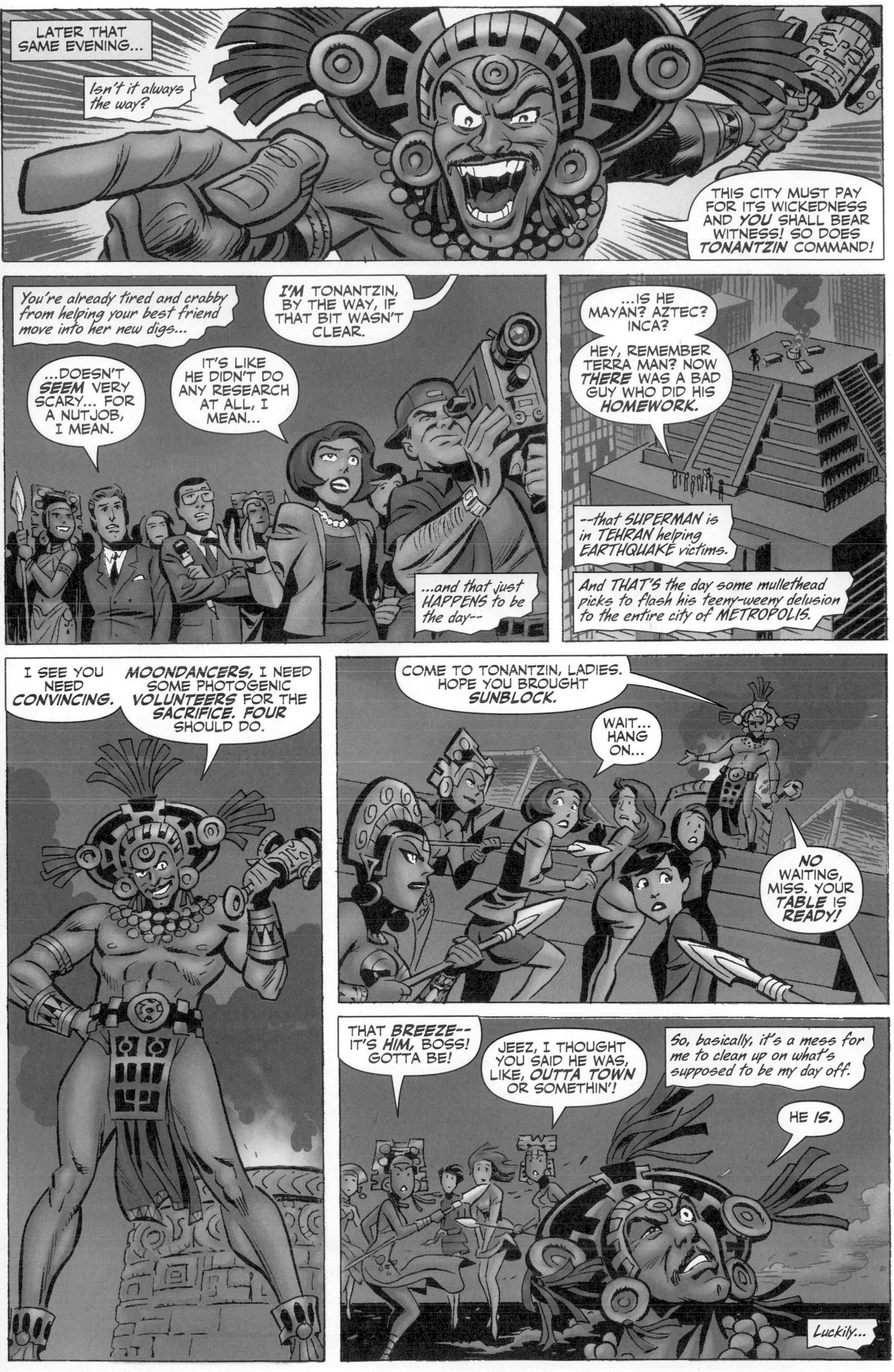
LATER THAT SAME EVENING...
Isn't it always the way?
THIS CITY MUST PAY FOR ITS WICKEDNESS AND YOU SHALL BEAR WITNESS! SO DOES TONANTZIN COMMAND!
You're already tired and crabby from helping your best friend move into her new digs...
I'M TONANTZIN, BY THE WAY, IF THAT BIT WASN'T CLEAR.
...DOESN'T SEEM VERY SCARY... FOR A NUTJOB, I MEAN.
IT'S LIKE HE DIDN'T DO ANY RESEARCH AT ALL, I MEAN...
...and that just HAPPENS to be the day--
...IS HE MAYAN? AZTEC? INCA?
HEY, REMEMBER TERRA MAN? NOW THERE WAS A BAD GUY WHO DID HIS HOMEWORK.
--that SUPERMAN is in TEHRAN helping EARTHQUAKE victims.
And THAT'S the day some mullethead picks to flash his teeny-weeny delusion to the entire city of METROPOLIS.
I SEE YOU NEED CONVINCING.
MOONDANCERS, I NEED SOME PHOTOGENIC VOLUNTEERS FOR THE SACRIFICE. FOUR SHOULD DO.
COME TO TONANTZIN, LADIES. HOPE YOU BROUGHT SUNBLOCK.
WAIT... HANG ON...
NO WAITING, MISS. YOUR TABLE IS READY!
THAT BREEZE-- IT'S HIM, BOSS! GOTTA BE!
JEEZ, I THOUGHT YOU SAID HE WAS, LIKE, OUTTA TOWN OR SOMETHIN'!
So, basically, it's a mess for me to clean up on what's supposed to be my day off.
HE IS.
Luckily...

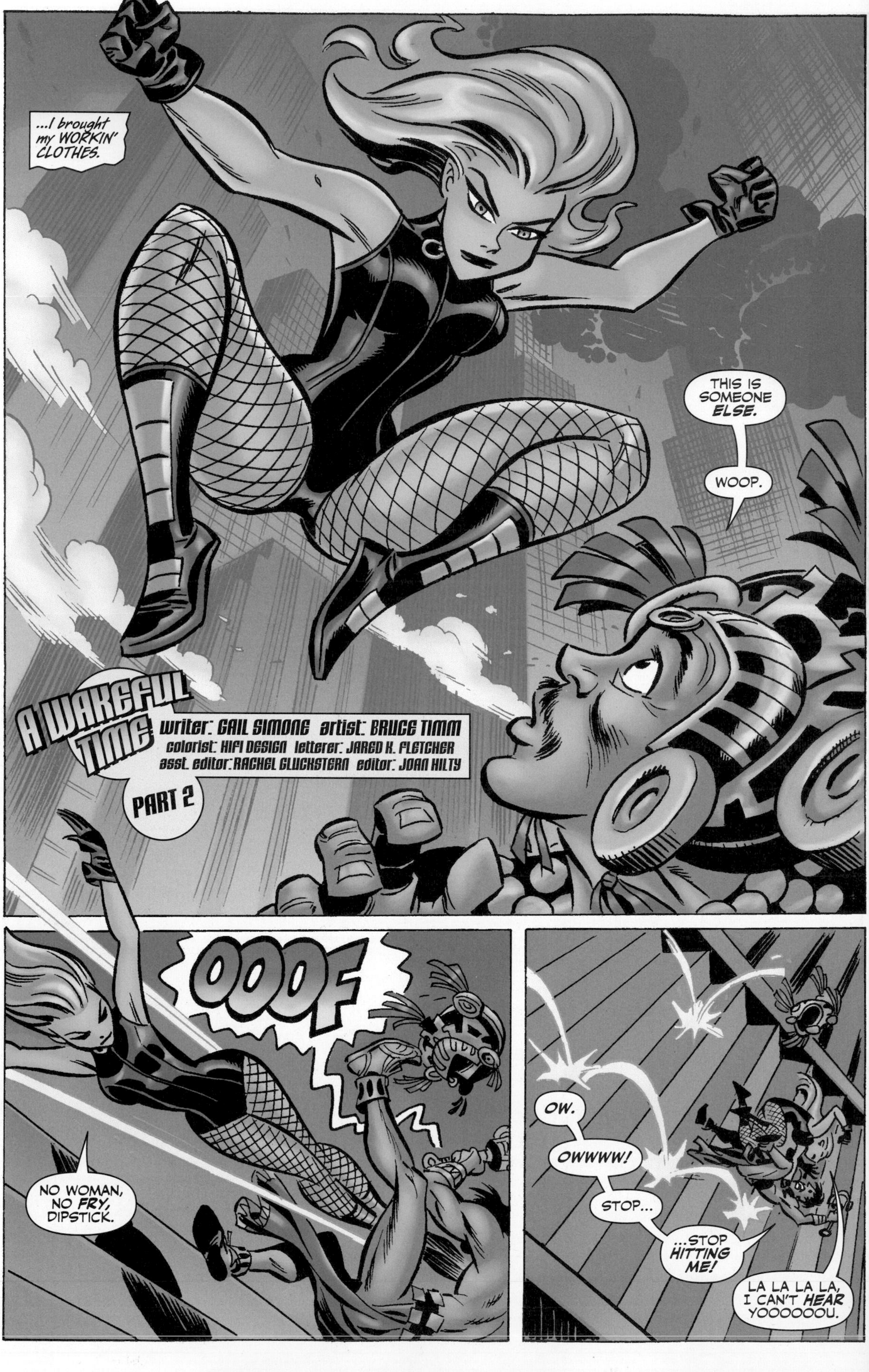
...I brought my WORKIN' CLOTHES.
THIS IS SOMEONE ELSE.
WOOP.
A WAKEFUL TIME
writer: GAIL SIMONE artist: BRUCE TIMM
colorist: HIFI DESIGN letterer: JARED K. FLETCHER
asst. editor: RACHEL GLUCKSTERN editor: JOAN HILTY
PART 2
OOOF
NO WOMAN, NO FRY, DIPSTICK.
OW.
OWWWW!
STOP...
...STOP HITTING ME!
LA LA LA LA, I CAN'T HEAR YOOOOOOU.

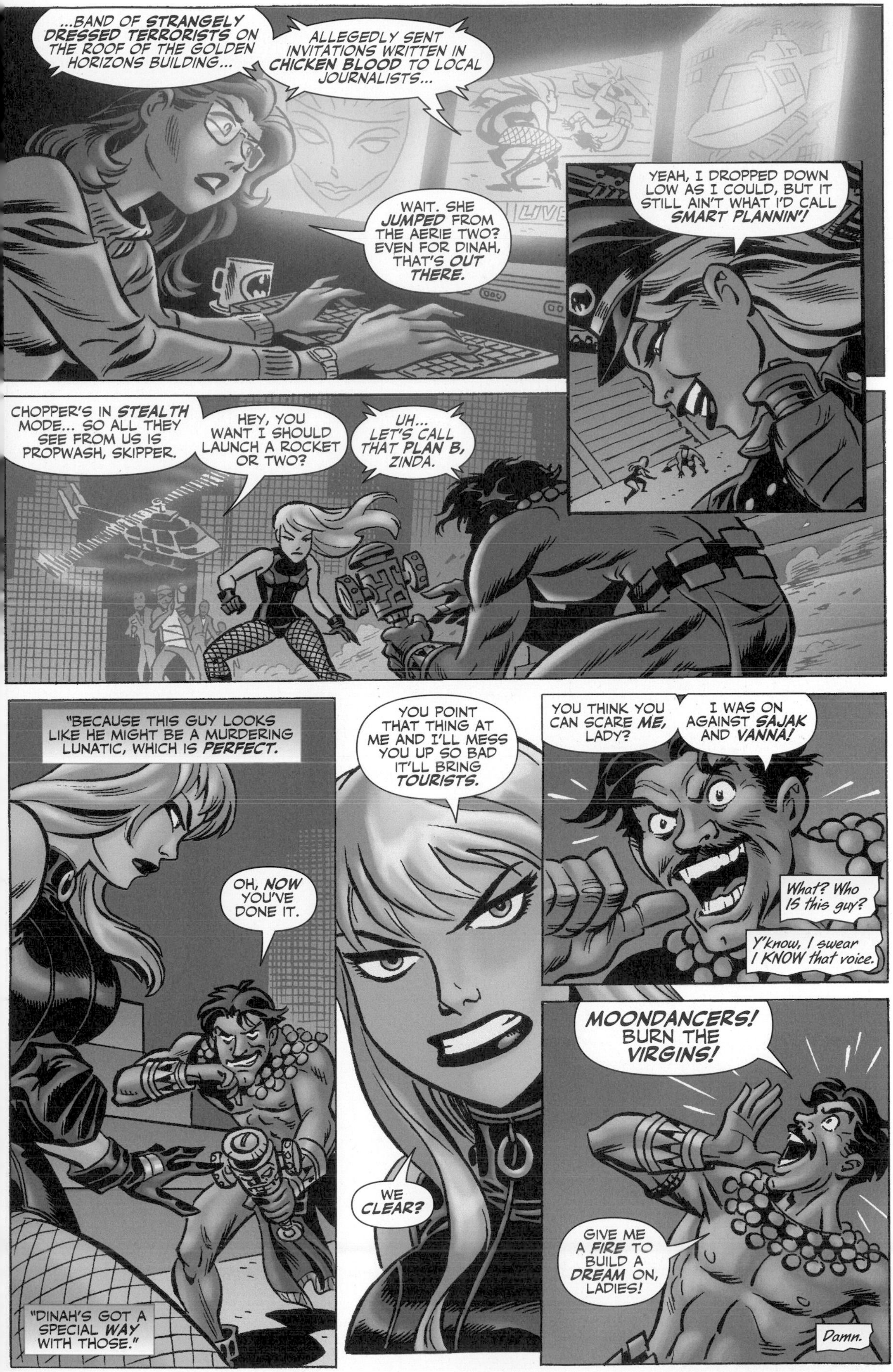
...BAND OF STRANGELY DRESSED TERRORISTS ON THE ROOF OF THE GOLDEN HORIZONS BUILDING...
ALLEGEDLY SENT INVITATIONS WRITTEN IN CHICKEN BLOOD TO LOCAL JOURNALISTS...
WAIT. SHE JUMPED FROM THE AERIE TWO? EVEN FOR DINAH, THAT'S OUT THERE.
YEAH, I DROPPED DOWN LOW AS I COULD, BUT IT STILL AIN'T WHAT I'D CALL SMART PLANNIN'!
CHOPPER'S IN STEALTH MODE... SO ALL THEY SEE FROM US IS PROPWASH, SKIPPER.
HEY, YOU WANT I SHOULD LAUNCH A ROCKET OR TWO?
UH... LET'S CALL THAT PLAN B, ZINDA.
"BECAUSE THIS GUY LOOKS LIKE HE MIGHT BE A MURDERING LUNATIC, WHICH IS PERFECT.
OH, NOW YOU'VE DONE IT.
"DINAH'S GOT A SPECIAL WAY WITH THOSE."
YOU POINT THAT THING AT ME AND I'LL MESS YOU UP SO BAD IT'LL BRING TOURISTS.
WE CLEAR?
YOU THINK YOU CAN SCARE ME, LADY?
I WAS ON AGAINST SAJAK AND VANNA!
What? Who IS this guy?
Y'know, I swear I KNOW that voice.
MOONDANCERS! BURN THE VIRGINS!
GIVE ME A FIRE TO BUILD A DREAM ON, LADIES!
Damn.

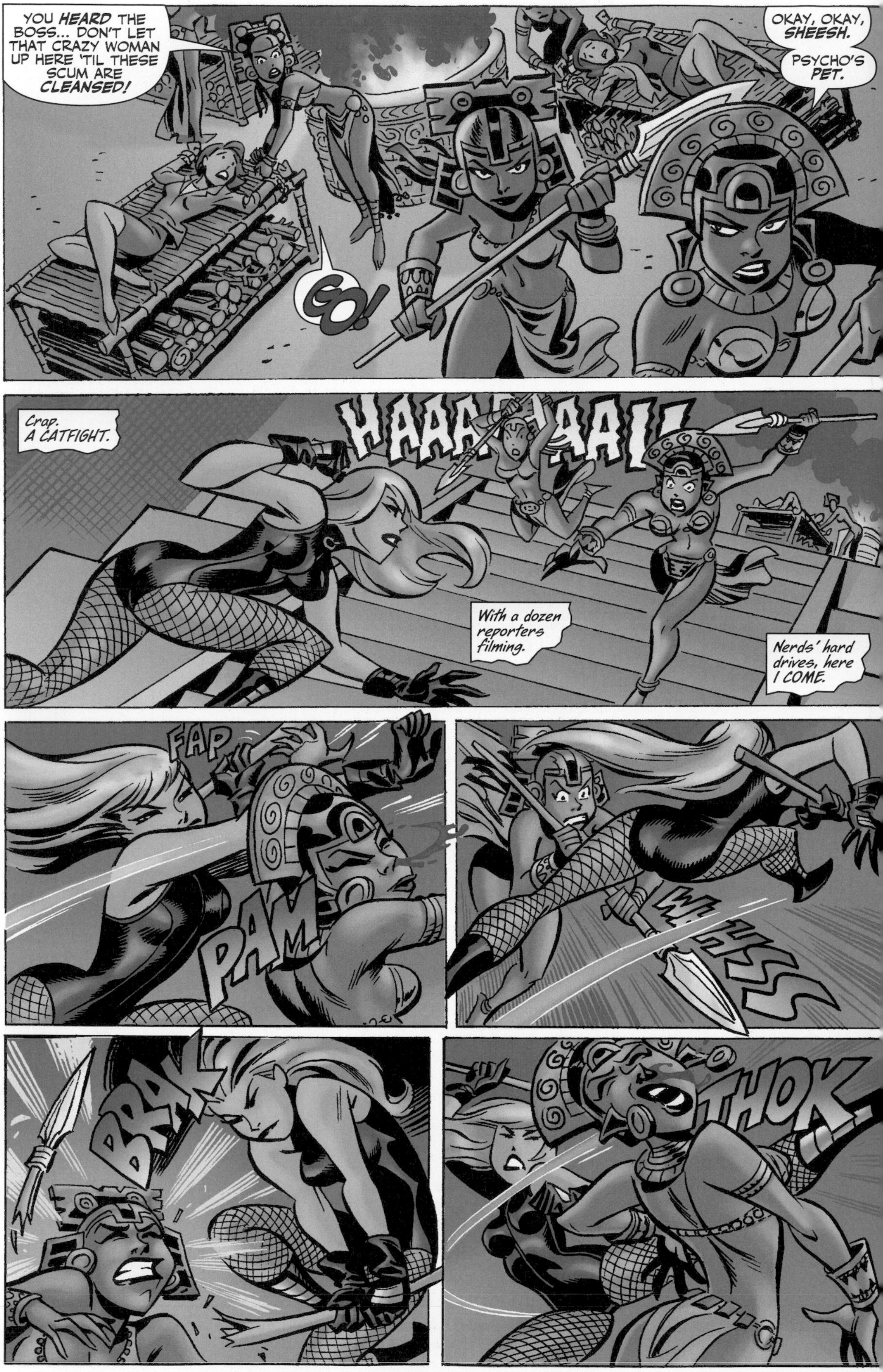
YOU **HEARD** THE BOSS... DON'T LET THAT CRAZY WOMAN UP HERE 'TIL THESE SCUM ARE **CLEANSED!**
OKAY, OKAY, **SHEESH.**
PSYCHO'S **PET.**
GO!
Crap. A CATFIGHT.
HAAAHAAI!
With a dozen reporters filming.
Nerds' hard drives, here I COME.
FAP
PAM
WHSSS
BRAK
THOK

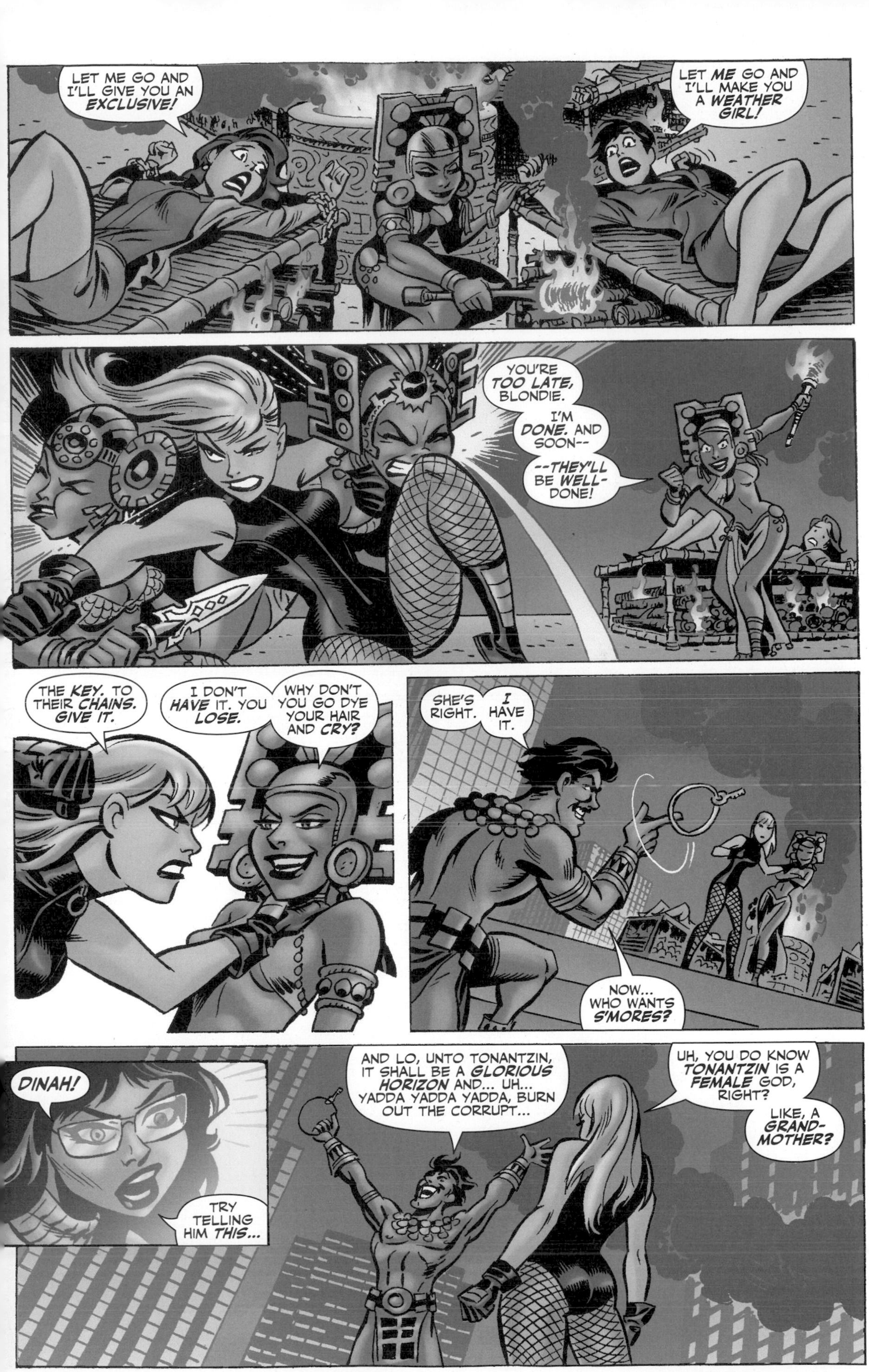
LET ME GO AND I'LL GIVE YOU AN EXCLUSIVE!
LET ME GO AND I'LL MAKE YOU A WEATHER GIRL!
YOU'RE TOO LATE, BLONDIE.
I'M DONE. AND SOON--
--THEY'LL BE WELL-DONE!
THE KEY. TO THEIR CHAINS. GIVE IT.
I DON'T HAVE IT. YOU LOSE.
WHY DON'T YOU GO DYE YOUR HAIR AND CRY?
SHE'S RIGHT.
I HAVE IT.
NOW... WHO WANTS S'MORES?
DINAH!
TRY TELLING HIM THIS...
AND LO, UNTO TONANTZIN, IT SHALL BE A GLORIOUS HORIZON AND... UH... YADDA YADDA YADDA, BURN OUT THE CORRUPT...
UH, YOU DO KNOW TONANTZIN IS A FEMALE GOD, RIGHT?
LIKE, A GRAND-MOTHER?

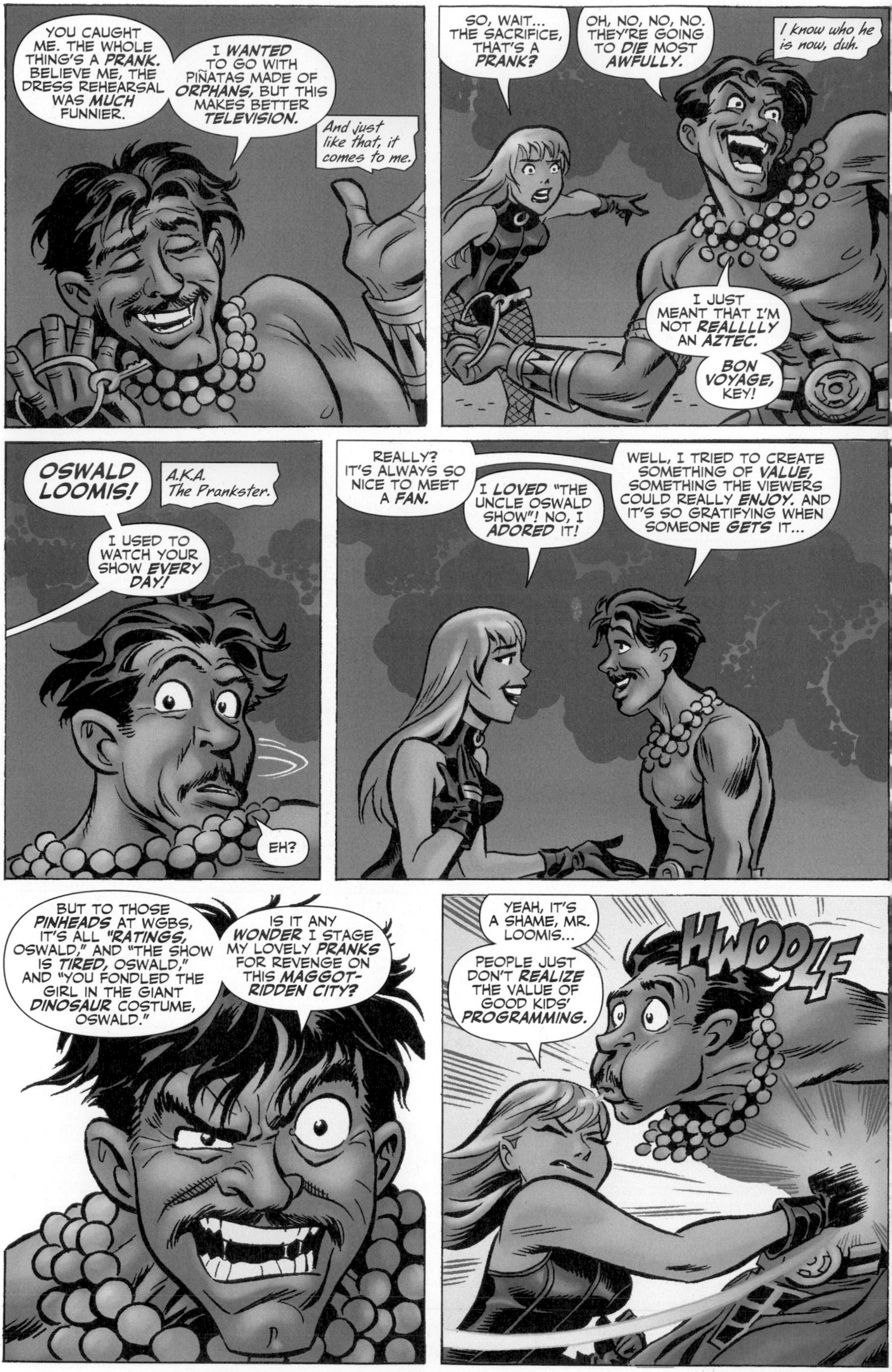
YOU CAUGHT ME. THE WHOLE THING'S A PRANK. BELIEVE ME, THE DRESS REHEARSAL WAS MUCH FUNNIER.
I WANTED TO GO WITH PIÑATAS MADE OF ORPHANS, BUT THIS MAKES BETTER TELEVISION.
And just like that, it comes to me.
SO, WAIT... THE SACRIFICE, THAT'S A PRANK?
OH, NO, NO, NO. THEY'RE GOING TO DIE MOST AWFULLY.
I know who he is now, duh.
I JUST MEANT THAT I'M NOT REALLLLY AN AZTEC.
BON VOYAGE, KEY!
OSWALD LOOMIS!
A.K.A. The Prankster.
I USED TO WATCH YOUR SHOW EVERY DAY!
EH?
REALLY? IT'S ALWAYS SO NICE TO MEET A FAN.
I LOVED "THE UNCLE OSWALD SHOW"! NO, I ADORED IT!
WELL, I TRIED TO CREATE SOMETHING OF VALUE, SOMETHING THE VIEWERS COULD REALLY ENJOY. AND IT'S SO GRATIFYING WHEN SOMEONE GETS IT...
BUT TO THOSE PINHEADS AT WGBS, IT'S ALL "RATINGS, OSWALD," AND "THE SHOW IS TIRED, OSWALD," AND "YOU FONDLED THE GIRL IN THE GIANT DINOSAUR COSTUME, OSWALD."
IS IT ANY WONDER I STAGE MY LOVELY PRANKS FOR REVENGE ON THIS MAGGOT-RIDDEN CITY?
YEAH, IT'S A SHAME, MR. LOOMIS...
PEOPLE JUST DON'T REALIZE THE VALUE OF GOOD KIDS' PROGRAMMING.
HWOOLF

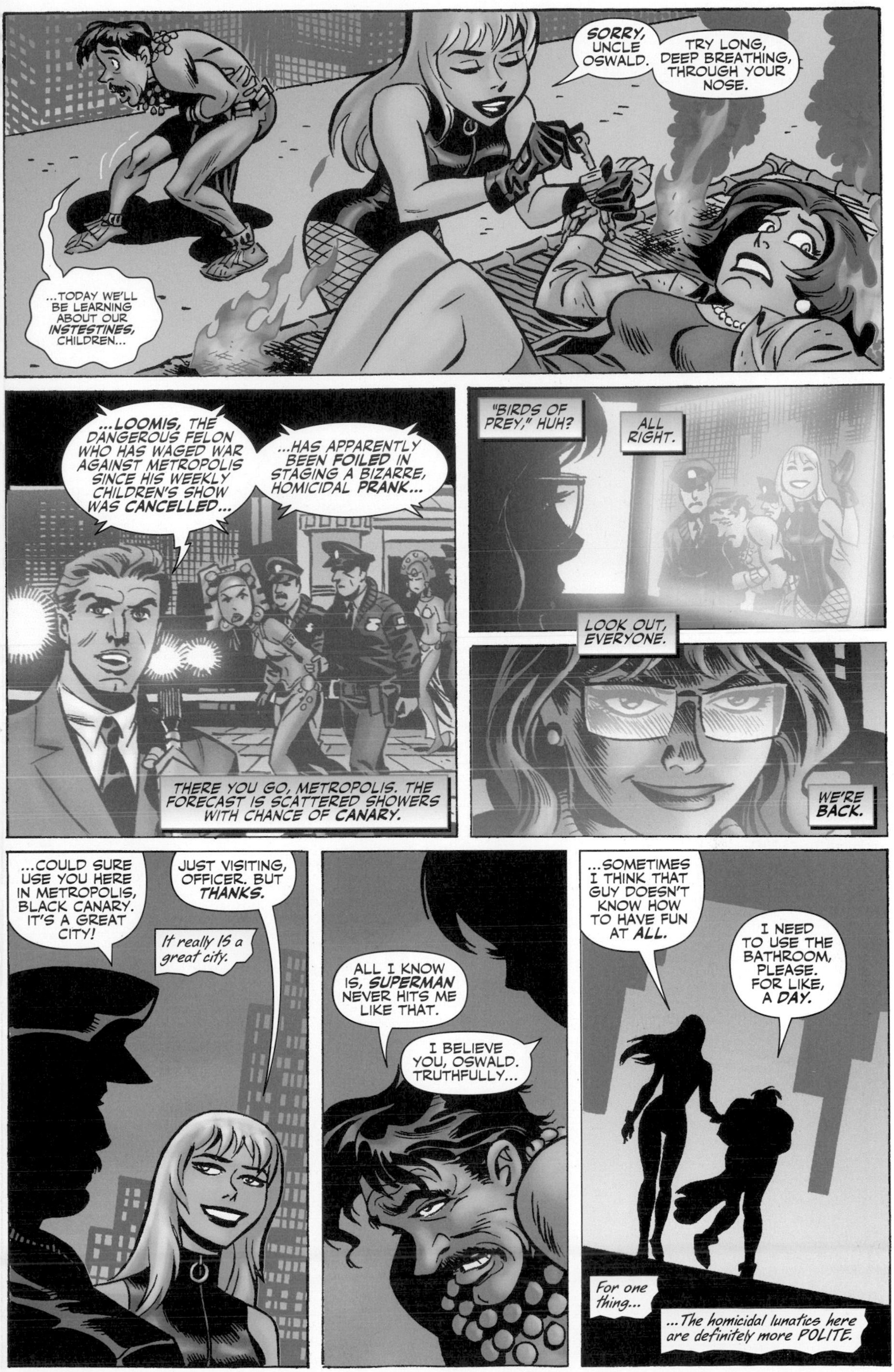
SORRY, UNCLE OSWALD.
TRY LONG, DEEP BREATHING, THROUGH YOUR NOSE.
...TODAY WE'LL BE LEARNING ABOUT OUR INSTESTINES, CHILDREN...
...LOOMIS, THE DANGEROUS FELON WHO HAS WAGED WAR AGAINST METROPOLIS SINCE HIS WEEKLY CHILDREN'S SHOW WAS CANCELLED...
...HAS APPARENTLY BEEN FOILED IN STAGING A BIZARRE, HOMICIDAL PRANK...
THERE YOU GO, METROPOLIS. THE FORECAST IS SCATTERED SHOWERS WITH CHANCE OF CANARY.
"BIRDS OF PREY," HUH?
ALL RIGHT.
LOOK OUT, EVERYONE.
WE'RE BACK.
...COULD SURE USE YOU HERE IN METROPOLIS, BLACK CANARY. IT'S A GREAT CITY!
JUST VISITING, OFFICER. BUT THANKS.
It really IS a great city.
ALL I KNOW IS, SUPERMAN NEVER HITS ME LIKE THAT.
I BELIEVE YOU, OSWALD. TRUTHFULLY...
...SOMETIMES I THINK THAT GUY DOESN'T KNOW HOW TO HAVE FUN AT ALL.
I NEED TO USE THE BATHROOM, PLEASE. FOR LIKE, A DAY.
For one thing...
...The homicidal lunatics here are definitely more POLITE.

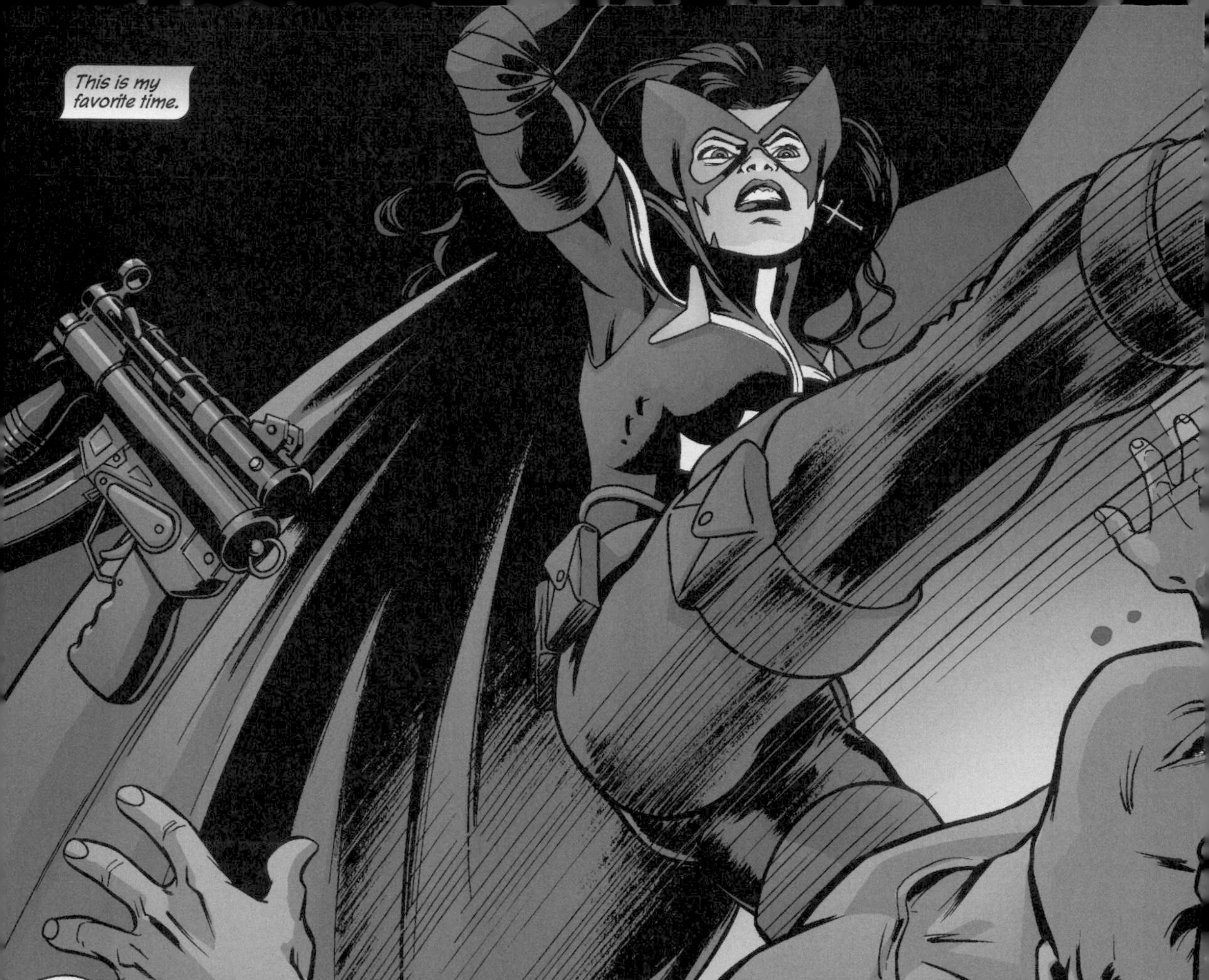
This is my favorite time.
A WAKEFUL TIME
writer: GAIL SIMONE penciler: DAVID LOPEZ
inker: FERNANDO BLANCO
colorist: HIFI DESIGN letterer: JARED K. FLETCHER
asst. editor: RACHEL GLUCKSTERN editor: JOAN HILTY
PART 3

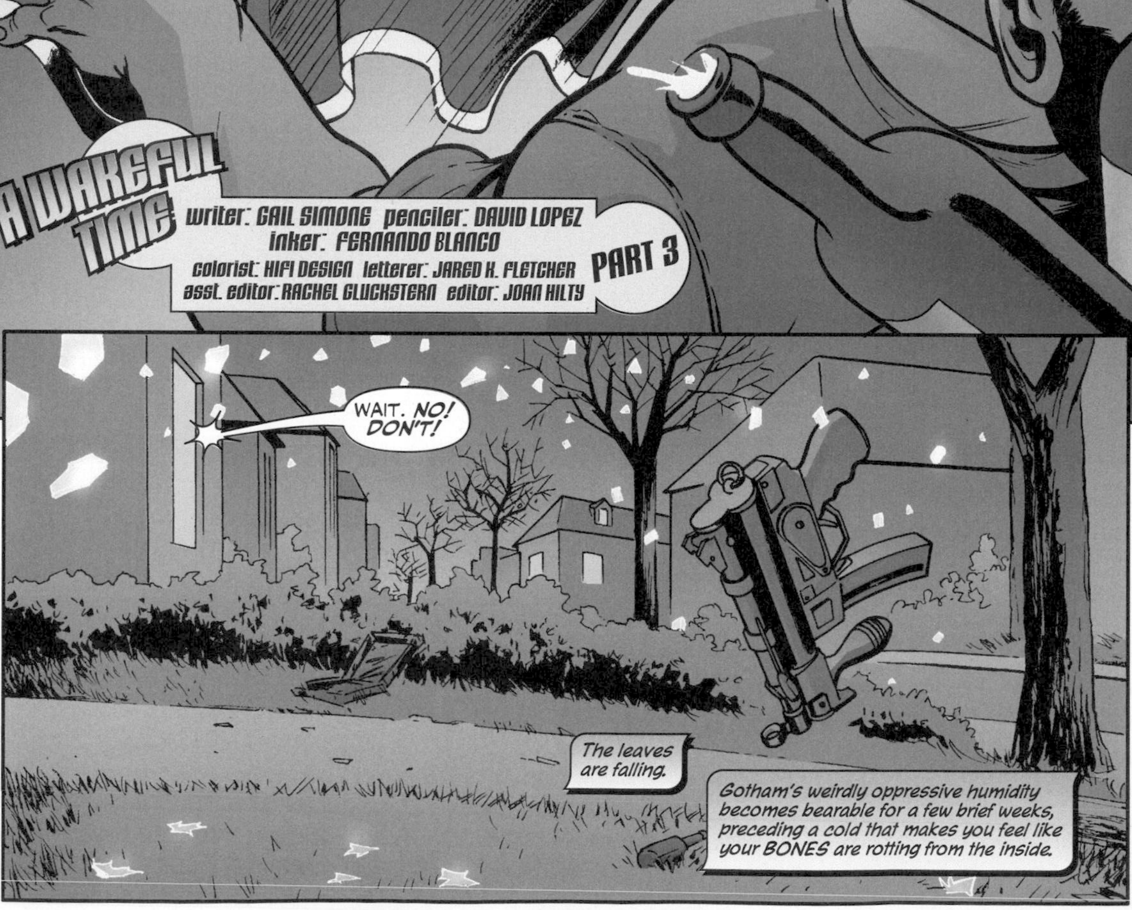
WAIT. NO! DON'T!
The leaves are falling.
Gotham's weirdly oppressive humidity becomes bearable for a few brief weeks, preceding a cold that makes you feel like your BONES are rotting from the inside.

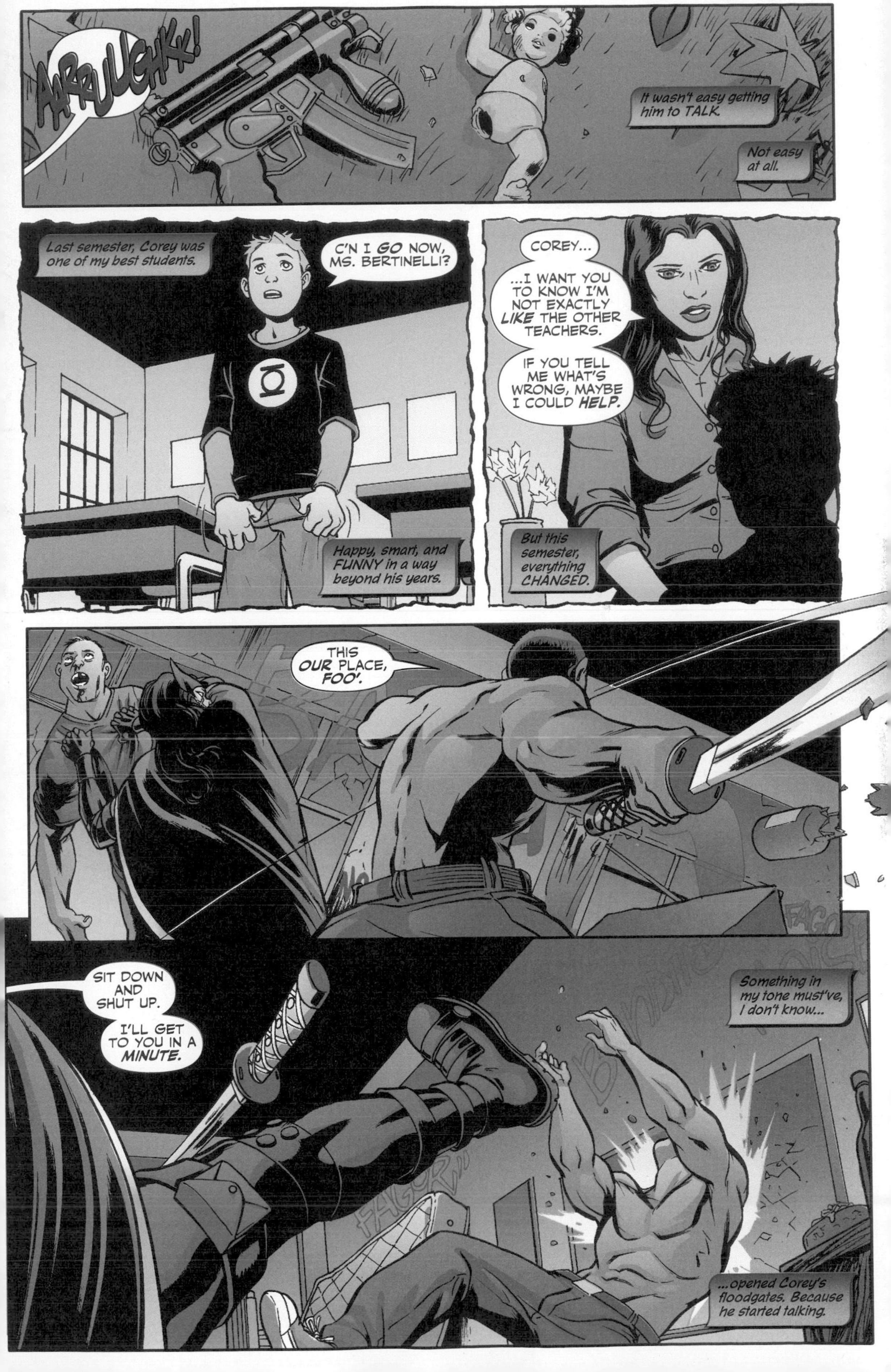
AARRUUGHKK!
It wasn't easy getting him to TALK.
Not easy at all.
Last semester, Corey was one of my best students.
C'N I GO NOW, MS. BERTINELLI?
Happy, smart, and FUNNY in a way beyond his years.
COREY...
...I WANT YOU TO KNOW I'M NOT EXACTLY LIKE THE OTHER TEACHERS.
IF YOU TELL ME WHAT'S WRONG, MAYBE I COULD HELP.
But this semester, everything CHANGED.
THIS OUR PLACE, FOO'.
SIT DOWN AND SHUT UP.
I'LL GET TO YOU IN A MINUTE.
Something in my tone must've, I don't know...
...opened Corey's floodgates. Because he started talking.

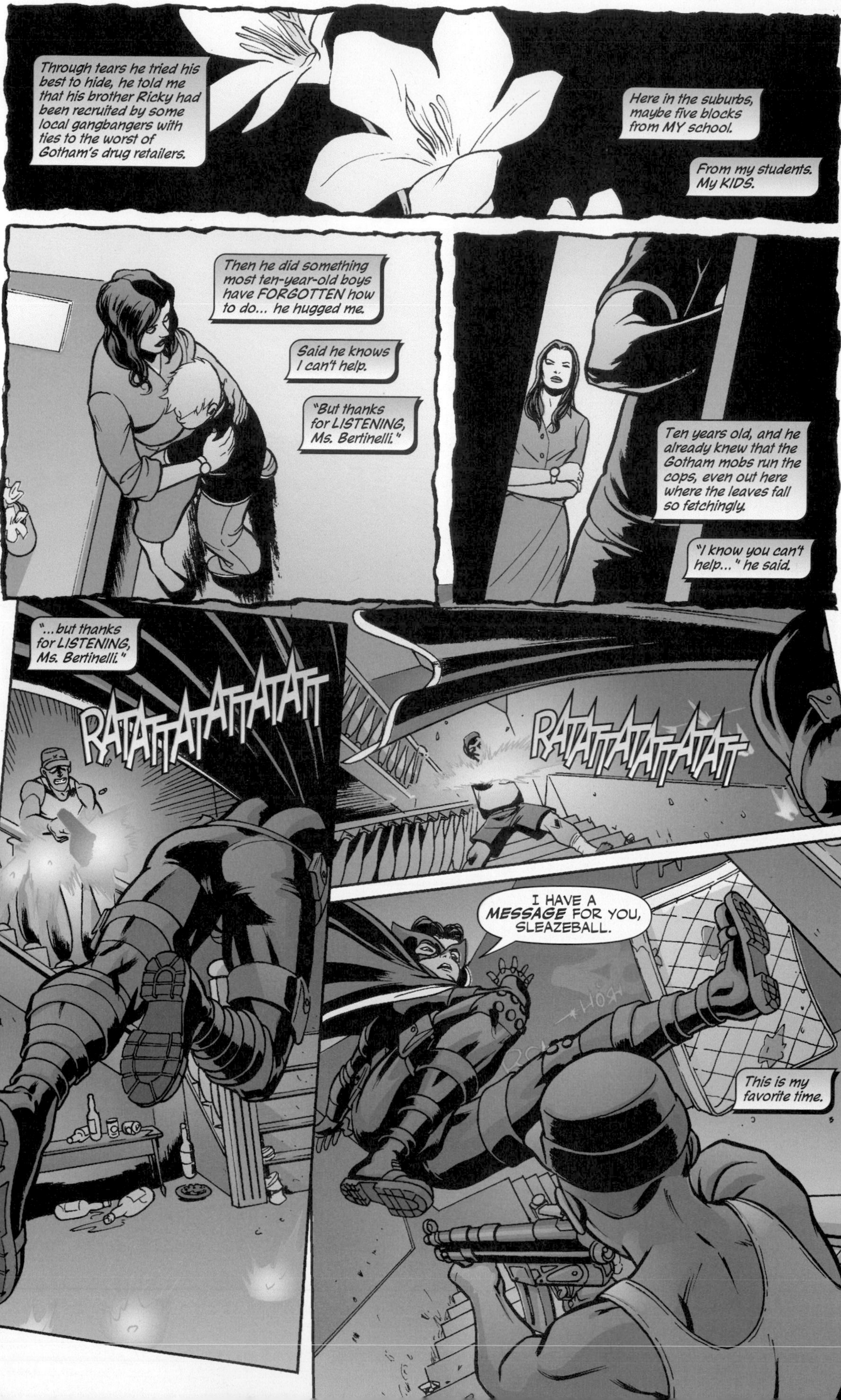
Through tears he tried his best to hide, he told me that his brother Ricky had been recruited by some local gangbangers with ties to the worst of Gotham's drug retailers.
Here in the suburbs, maybe five blocks from MY school.
From my students. My KIDS.
Then he did something most ten-year-old boys have FORGOTTEN how to do... he hugged me.
Said he knows I can't help.
"But thanks for LISTENING, Ms. Bertinelli."
Ten years old, and he already knew that the Gotham mobs run the cops, even out here where the leaves fall so fetchingly.
"I know you can't help..." he said.
"...but thanks for LISTENING, Ms. Bertinelli."
RATATTATATTATATT
RATATTATATTATATT
I HAVE A MESSAGE FOR YOU, SLEAZEBALL.
This is my favorite time.

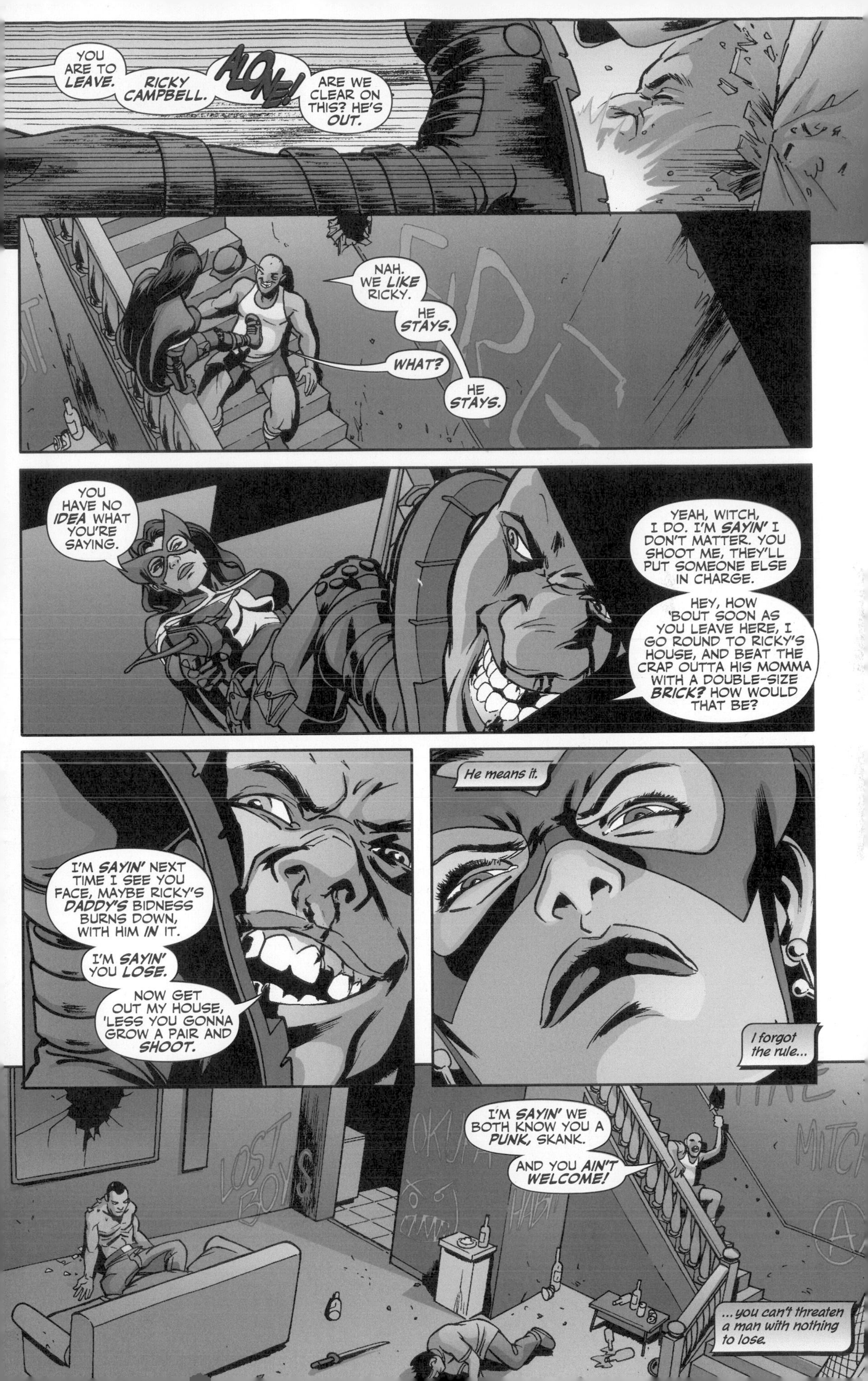
YOU ARE TO LEAVE.
RICKY CAMPBELL.
ALONE!
ARE WE CLEAR ON THIS? HE'S OUT.
NAH. WE LIKE RICKY.
HE STAYS.
WHAT?
HE STAYS.
YOU HAVE NO IDEA WHAT YOU'RE SAYING.
YEAH, WITCH, I DO. I'M SAYIN' I DON'T MATTER. YOU SHOOT ME, THEY'LL PUT SOMEONE ELSE IN CHARGE.
HEY, HOW 'BOUT SOON AS YOU LEAVE HERE, I GO ROUND TO RICKY'S HOUSE, AND BEAT THE CRAP OUTTA HIS MOMMA WITH A DOUBLE-SIZE BRICK? HOW WOULD THAT BE?
I'M SAYIN' NEXT TIME I SEE YOU FACE, MAYBE RICKY'S DADDY'S BIDNESS BURNS DOWN, WITH HIM IN IT.
I'M SAYIN' YOU LOSE.
NOW GET OUT MY HOUSE, 'LESS YOU GONNA GROW A PAIR AND SHOOT.
He means it.
I forgot the rule...
I'M SAYIN' WE BOTH KNOW YOU A PUNK, SKANK.
AND YOU AIN'T WELCOME!
...you can't threaten a man with nothing to lose.
LOST BOYS

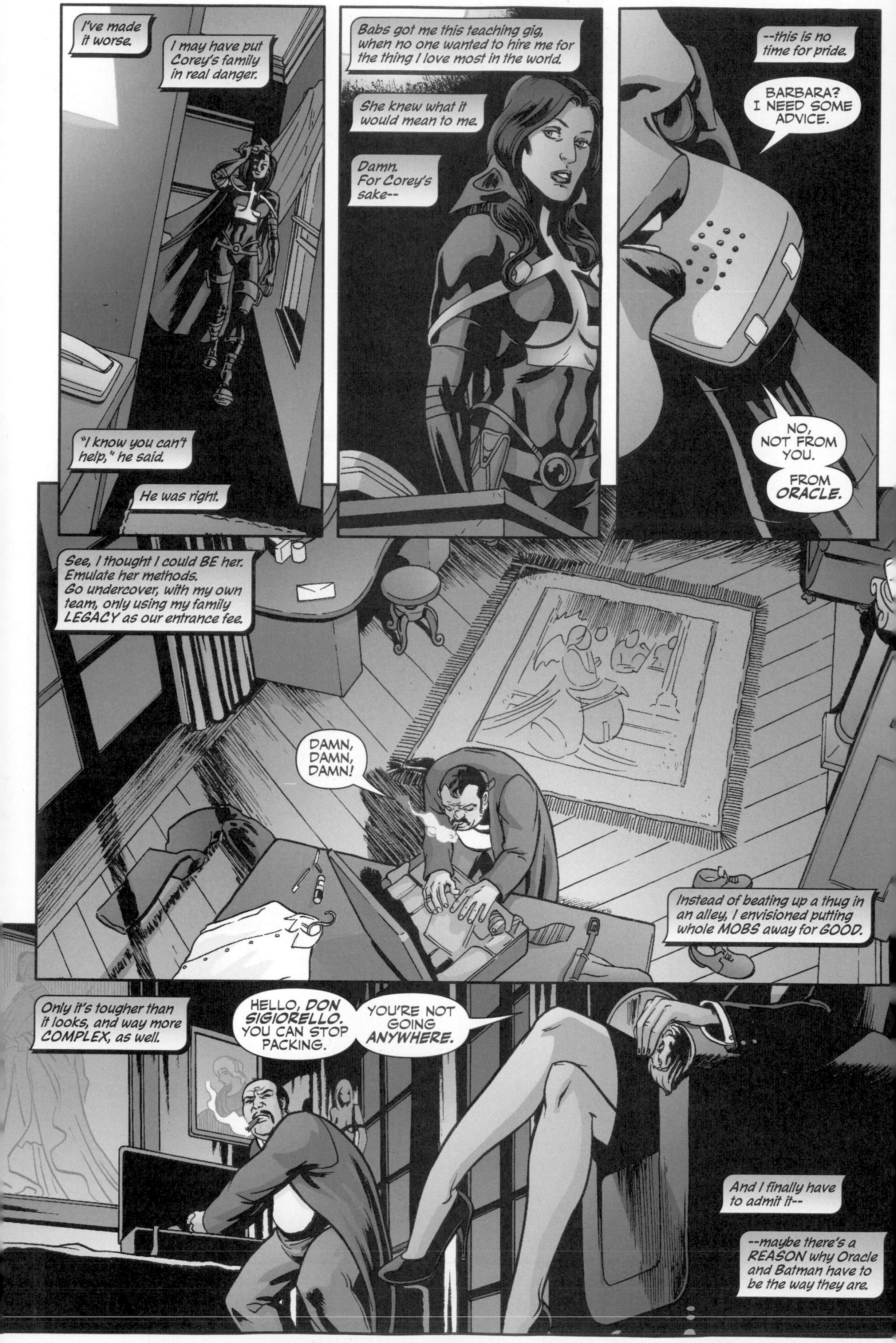

I've made it worse.
I may have put Corey's family in real danger.
"I know you can't help," he said.
He was right.
Babs got me this teaching gig, when no one wanted to hire me for the thing I love most in the world.
She knew what it would mean to me.
Damn. For Corey's sake--
--this is no time for pride.
BARBARA? I NEED SOME ADVICE.
NO, NOT FROM YOU.
FROM ORACLE.
See, I thought I could BE her. Emulate her methods. Go undercover, with my own team, only using my family LEGACY as our entrance fee.
DAMN, DAMN, DAMN!
Instead of beating up a thug in an alley, I envisioned putting whole MOBS away for GOOD.
Only it's tougher than it looks, and way more COMPLEX, as well.
HELLO, DON SIGIORELLO. YOU CAN STOP PACKING.
YOU'RE NOT GOING ANYWHERE.
And I finally have to admit it--
--maybe there's a REASON why Oracle and Batman have to be the way they are.

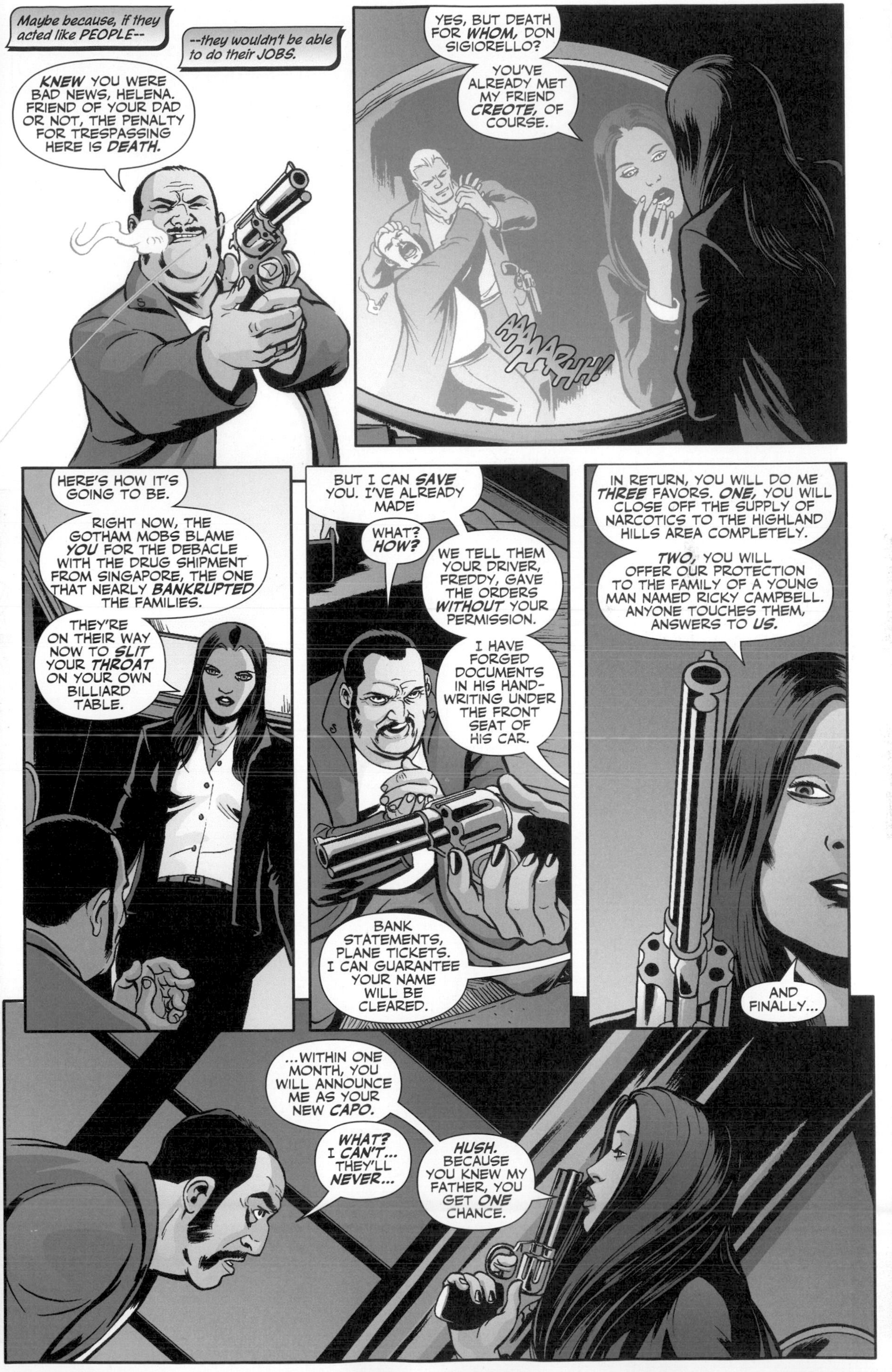

Maybe because, if they acted like PEOPLE--
--they wouldn't be able to do their JOBS.
KNEW YOU WERE BAD NEWS, HELENA. FRIEND OF YOUR DAD OR NOT, THE PENALTY FOR TRESPASSING HERE IS DEATH.
YES, BUT DEATH FOR WHOM, DON SIGIORELLO?
YOU'VE ALREADY MET MY FRIEND CREOTE, OF COURSE.
AAAAARRHH!
HERE'S HOW IT'S GOING TO BE.
RIGHT NOW, THE GOTHAM MOBS BLAME YOU FOR THE DEBACLE WITH THE DRUG SHIPMENT FROM SINGAPORE, THE ONE THAT NEARLY BANKRUPTED THE FAMILIES.
THEY'RE ON THEIR WAY NOW TO SLIT YOUR THROAT ON YOUR OWN BILLIARD TABLE.
BUT I CAN SAVE YOU. I'VE ALREADY MADE
WHAT? HOW?
WE TELL THEM YOUR DRIVER, FREDDY, GAVE THE ORDERS WITHOUT YOUR PERMISSION.
I HAVE FORGED DOCUMENTS IN HIS HAND-WRITING UNDER THE FRONT SEAT OF HIS CAR.
BANK STATEMENTS, PLANE TICKETS. I CAN GUARANTEE YOUR NAME WILL BE CLEARED.
IN RETURN, YOU WILL DO ME THREE FAVORS. ONE, YOU WILL CLOSE OFF THE SUPPLY OF NARCOTICS TO THE HIGHLAND HILLS AREA COMPLETELY.
TWO, YOU WILL OFFER OUR PROTECTION TO THE FAMILY OF A YOUNG MAN NAMED RICKY CAMPBELL. ANYONE TOUCHES THEM, ANSWERS TO US.
AND FINALLY...
...WITHIN ONE MONTH, YOU WILL ANNOUNCE ME AS YOUR NEW CAPO.
WHAT? I CAN'T... THEY'LL NEVER...
HUSH. BECAUSE YOU KNEW MY FATHER, YOU GET ONE CHANCE.

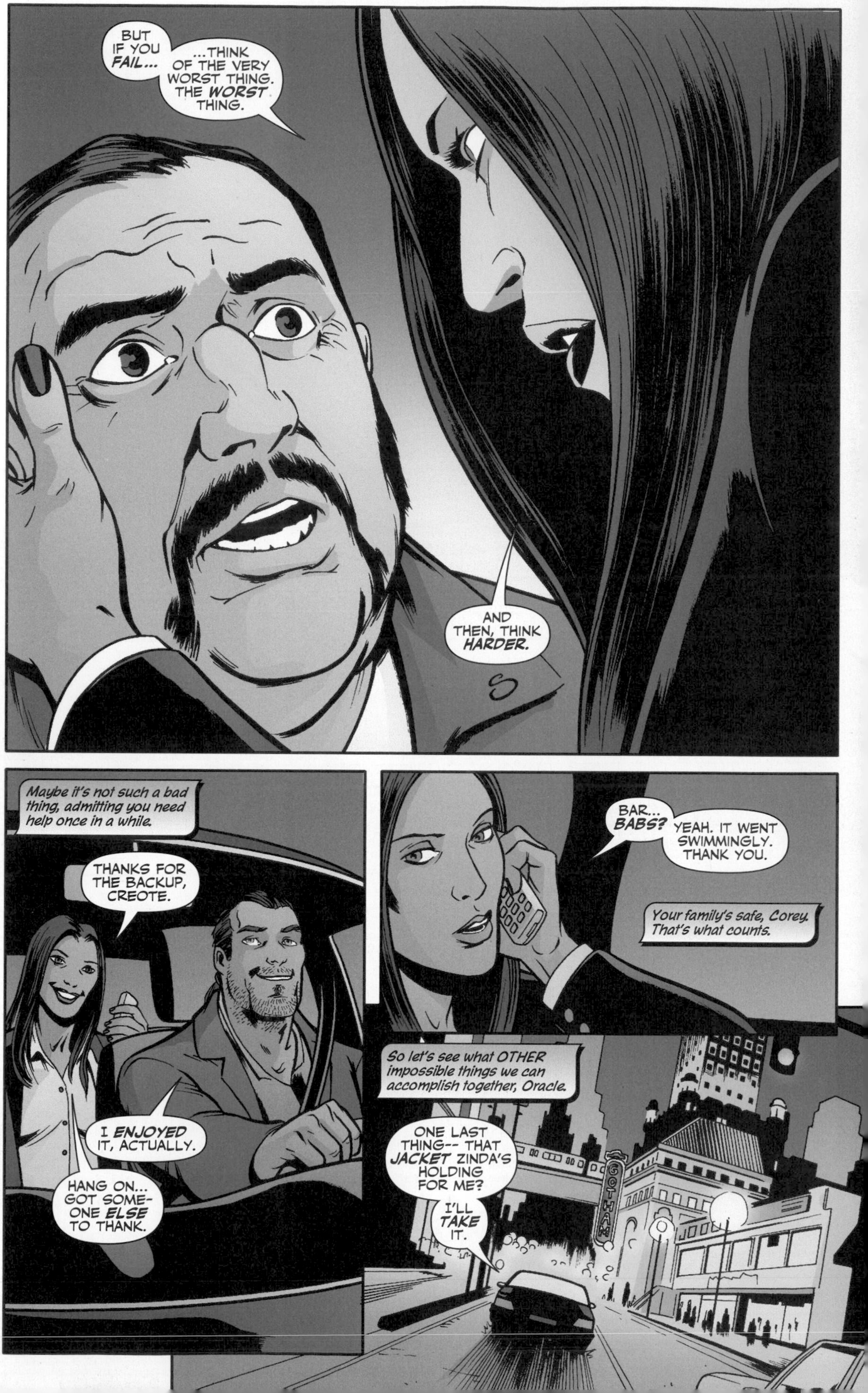
BUT IF YOU FAIL...
...THINK OF THE VERY WORST THING. THE WORST THING.
AND THEN, THINK HARDER.
Maybe it's not such a bad thing, admitting you need help once in a while.
THANKS FOR THE BACKUP, CREOTE.
I ENJOYED IT, ACTUALLY.
HANG ON... GOT SOME-ONE ELSE TO THANK.
BAR... BABS?
YEAH. IT WENT SWIMMINGLY. THANK YOU.
Your family's safe, Corey. That's what counts.
So let's see what OTHER impossible things we can accomplish together, Oracle.
ONE LAST THING-- THAT JACKET ZINDA'S HOLDING FOR ME?
I'LL TAKE IT.
GOTHAM

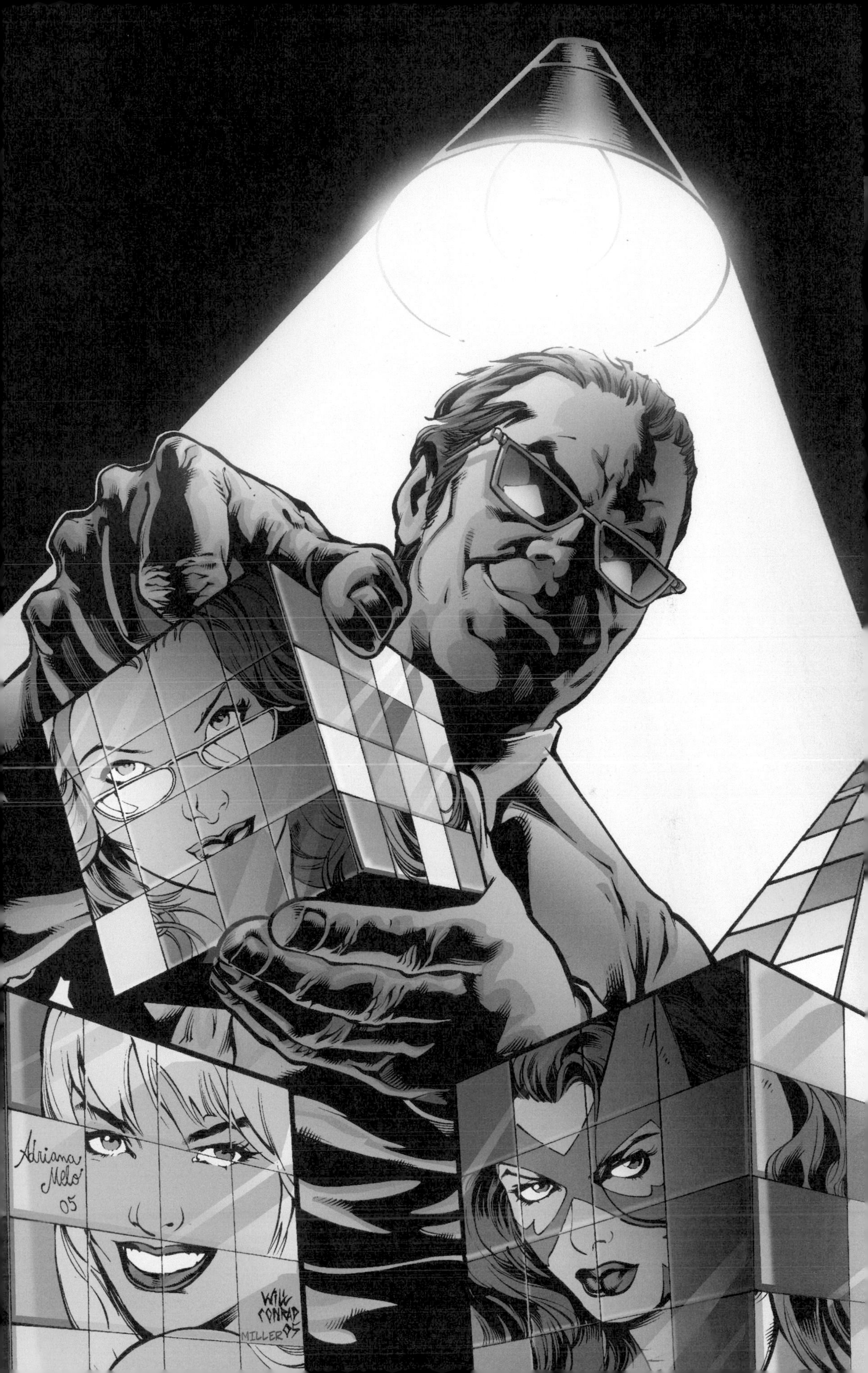
Adriana Melo 05
WILL CONRAD 05
MILLER

Cover art by
ADRIANA MELO
and WILL CONRAD

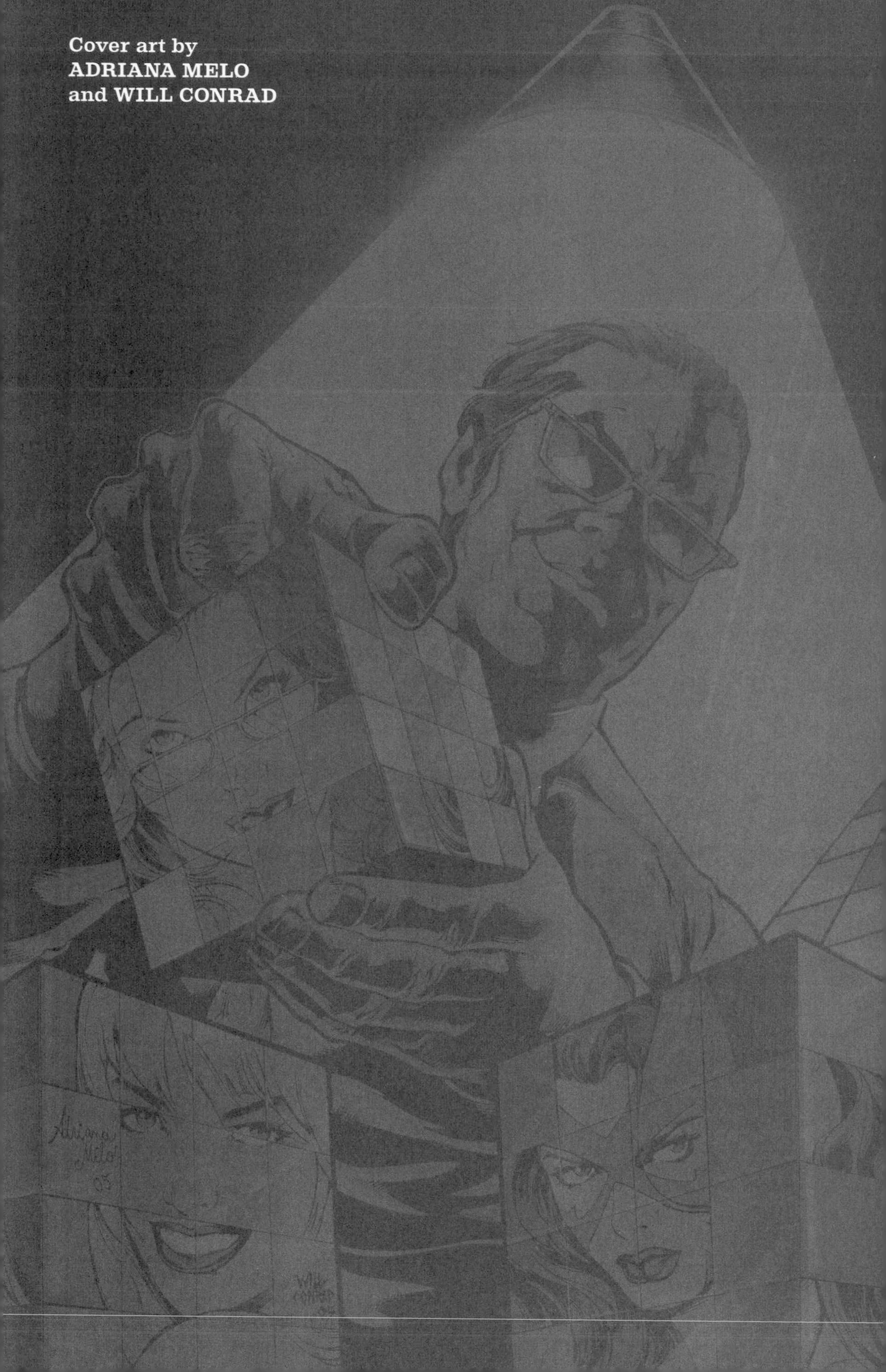
Adriana Melo 05

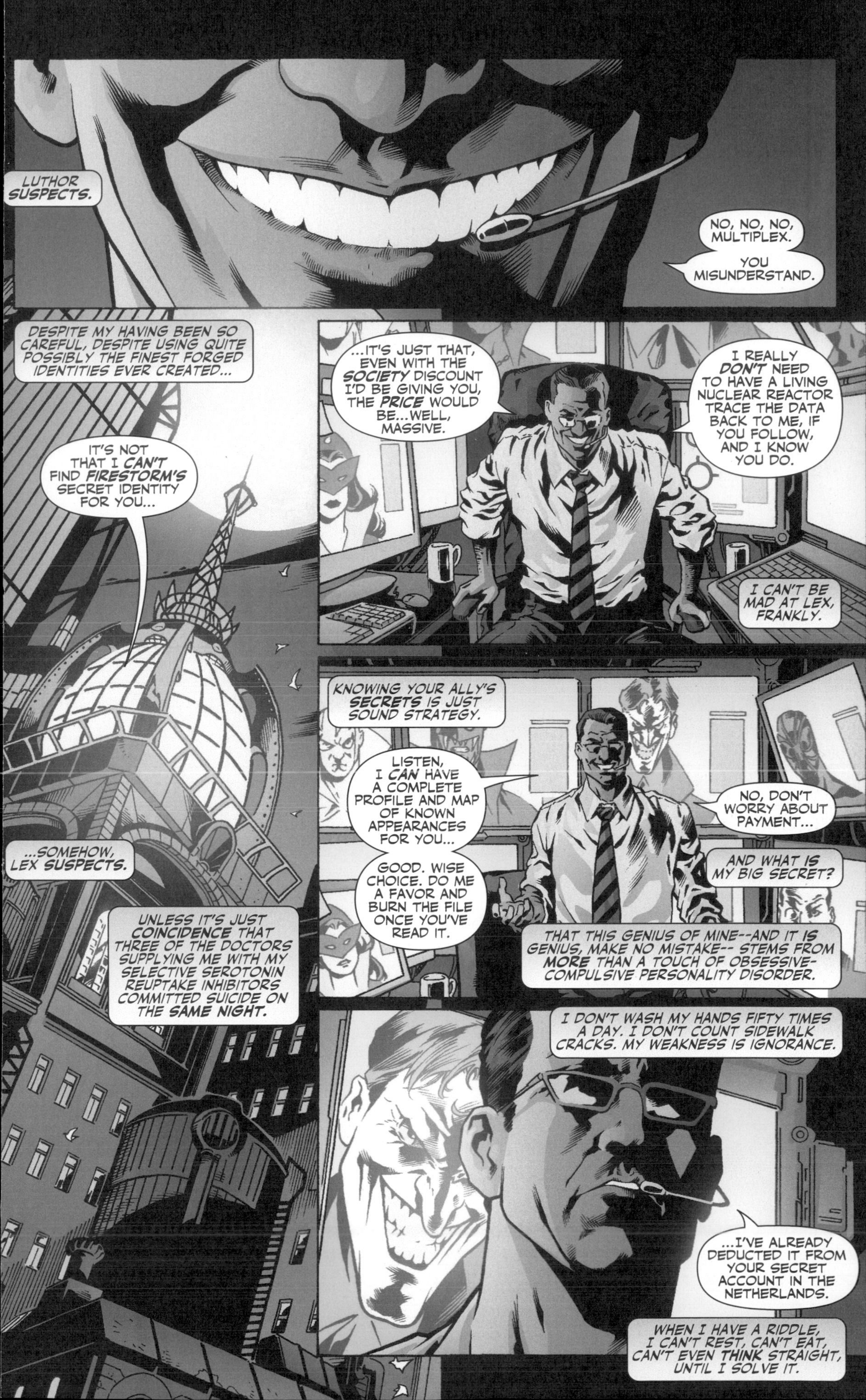
LUTHOR SUSPECTS.
NO, NO, NO, MULTIPLEX.
YOU MISUNDERSTAND.
DESPITE MY HAVING BEEN SO CAREFUL, DESPITE USING QUITE POSSIBLY THE FINEST FORGED IDENTITIES EVER CREATED...
IT'S NOT THAT I CAN'T FIND FIRESTORM'S SECRET IDENTITY FOR YOU...
...IT'S JUST THAT, EVEN WITH THE SOCIETY DISCOUNT I'D BE GIVING YOU, THE PRICE WOULD BE...WELL, MASSIVE.
I REALLY DON'T NEED TO HAVE A LIVING NUCLEAR REACTOR TRACE THE DATA BACK TO ME, IF YOU FOLLOW, AND I KNOW YOU DO.
I CAN'T BE MAD AT LEX, FRANKLY.
...SOMEHOW, LEX SUSPECTS.
UNLESS IT'S JUST COINCIDENCE THAT THREE OF THE DOCTORS SUPPLYING ME WITH MY SELECTIVE SEROTONIN REUPTAKE INHIBITORS COMMITTED SUICIDE ON THE SAME NIGHT.
KNOWING YOUR ALLY'S SECRETS IS JUST SOUND STRATEGY.
LISTEN, I CAN HAVE A COMPLETE PROFILE AND MAP OF KNOWN APPEARANCES FOR YOU...
NO, DON'T WORRY ABOUT PAYMENT...
GOOD. WISE CHOICE. DO ME A FAVOR AND BURN THE FILE ONCE YOU'VE READ IT.
AND WHAT IS MY BIG SECRET?
THAT THIS GENIUS OF MINE--AND IT IS GENIUS, MAKE NO MISTAKE-- STEMS FROM MORE THAN A TOUCH OF OBSESSIVE-COMPULSIVE PERSONALITY DISORDER.
I DON'T WASH MY HANDS FIFTY TIMES A DAY. I DON'T COUNT SIDEWALK CRACKS. MY WEAKNESS IS IGNORANCE.
...I'VE ALREADY DEDUCTED IT FROM YOUR SECRET ACCOUNT IN THE NETHERLANDS.
WHEN I HAVE A RIDDLE, I CAN'T REST, CAN'T EAT, CAN'T EVEN THINK STRAIGHT, UNTIL I SOLVE IT.

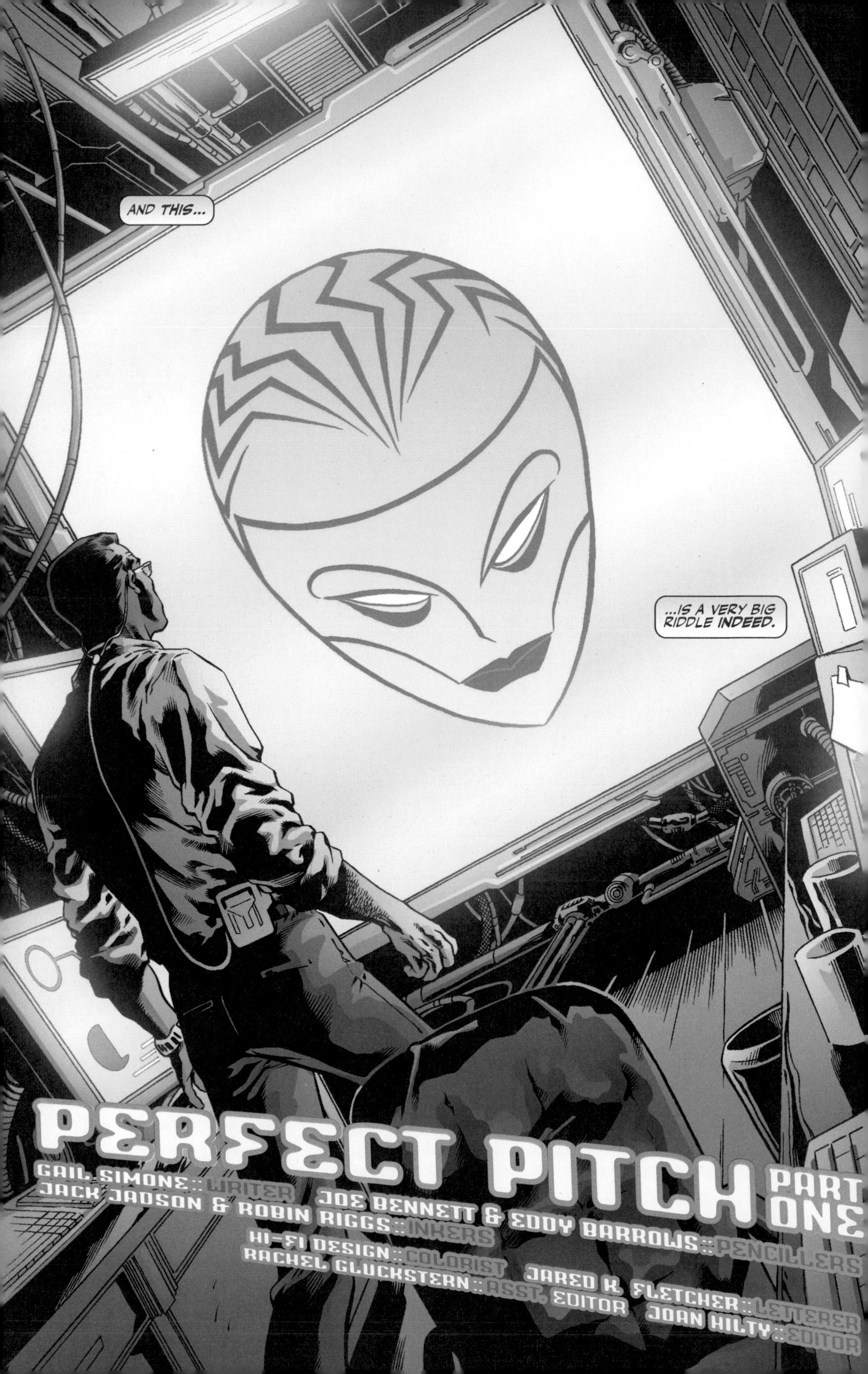
AND THIS...
...IS A VERY BIG RIDDLE INDEED.
PERFECT PITCH PART ONE
GAIL SIMONE::WRITER
JOE BENNETT & EDDY BARROWS::PENCILLERS
JACK JADSON & ROBIN RIGGS::INKERS
HI-FI DESIGN::COLORIST
JARED K. FLETCHER::LETTERER
RACHEL GLUCKSTERN::ASST. EDITOR
JOAN HILTY::EDITOR

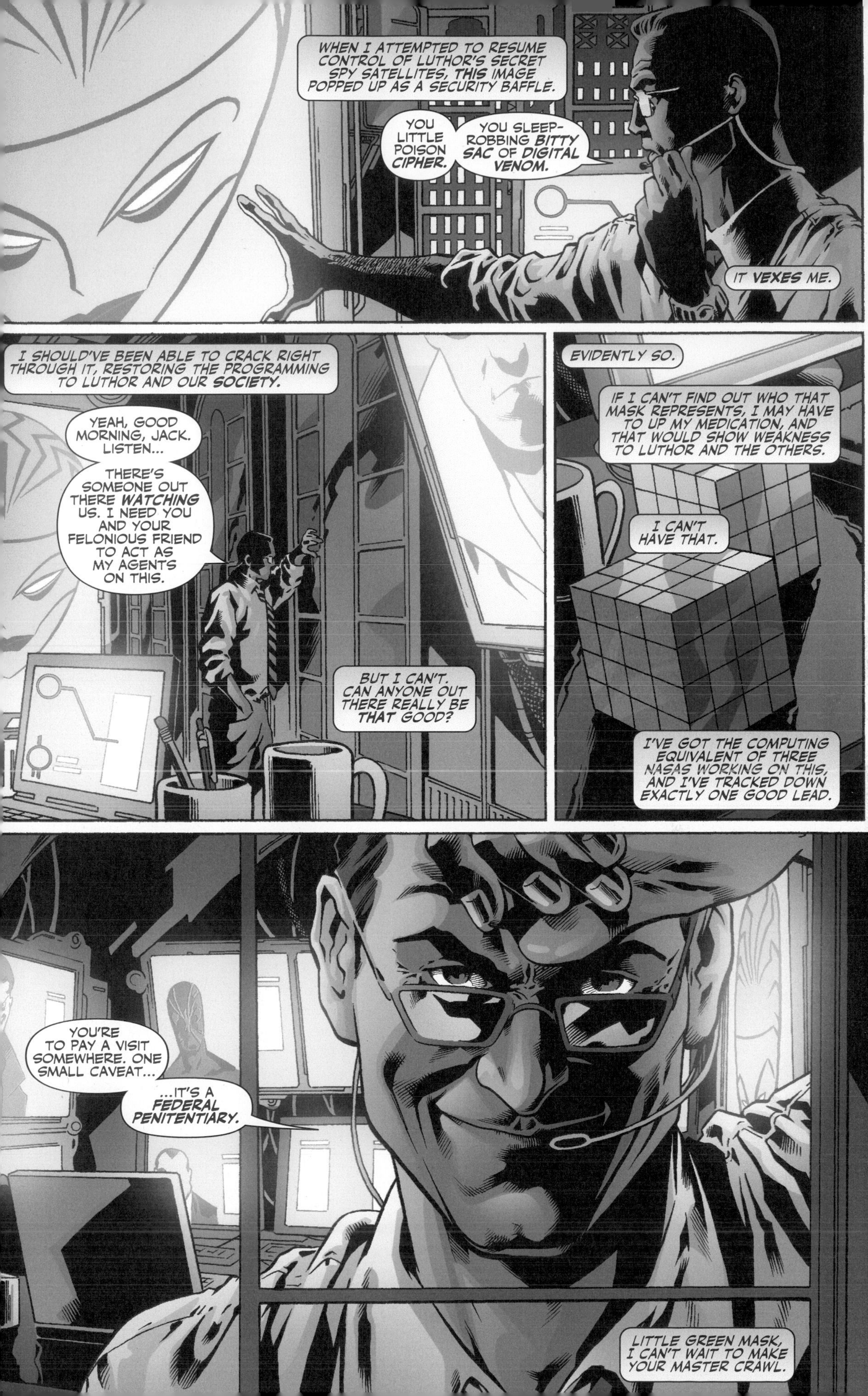

WHEN I ATTEMPTED TO RESUME CONTROL OF LUTHOR'S SECRET SPY SATELLITES, THIS IMAGE POPPED UP AS A SECURITY BAFFLE.
YOU LITTLE POISON CIPHER.
YOU SLEEP-ROBBING BITTY SAC OF DIGITAL VENOM.
IT VEXES ME.
I SHOULD'VE BEEN ABLE TO CRACK RIGHT THROUGH IT, RESTORING THE PROGRAMMING TO LUTHOR AND OUR SOCIETY.
YEAH, GOOD MORNING, JACK. LISTEN...
THERE'S SOMEONE OUT THERE WATCHING US. I NEED YOU AND YOUR FELONIOUS FRIEND TO ACT AS MY AGENTS ON THIS.
BUT I CAN'T. CAN ANYONE OUT THERE REALLY BE THAT GOOD?
EVIDENTLY SO.
IF I CAN'T FIND OUT WHO THAT MASK REPRESENTS, I MAY HAVE TO UP MY MEDICATION, AND THAT WOULD SHOW WEAKNESS TO LUTHOR AND THE OTHERS.
I CAN'T HAVE THAT.
I'VE GOT THE COMPUTING EQUIVALENT OF THREE NASAS WORKING ON THIS, AND I'VE TRACKED DOWN EXACTLY ONE GOOD LEAD.
YOU'RE TO PAY A VISIT SOMEWHERE. ONE SMALL CAVEAT...
...IT'S A FEDERAL PENITENTIARY.
LITTLE GREEN MASK, I CAN'T WAIT TO MAKE YOUR MASTER CRAWL.

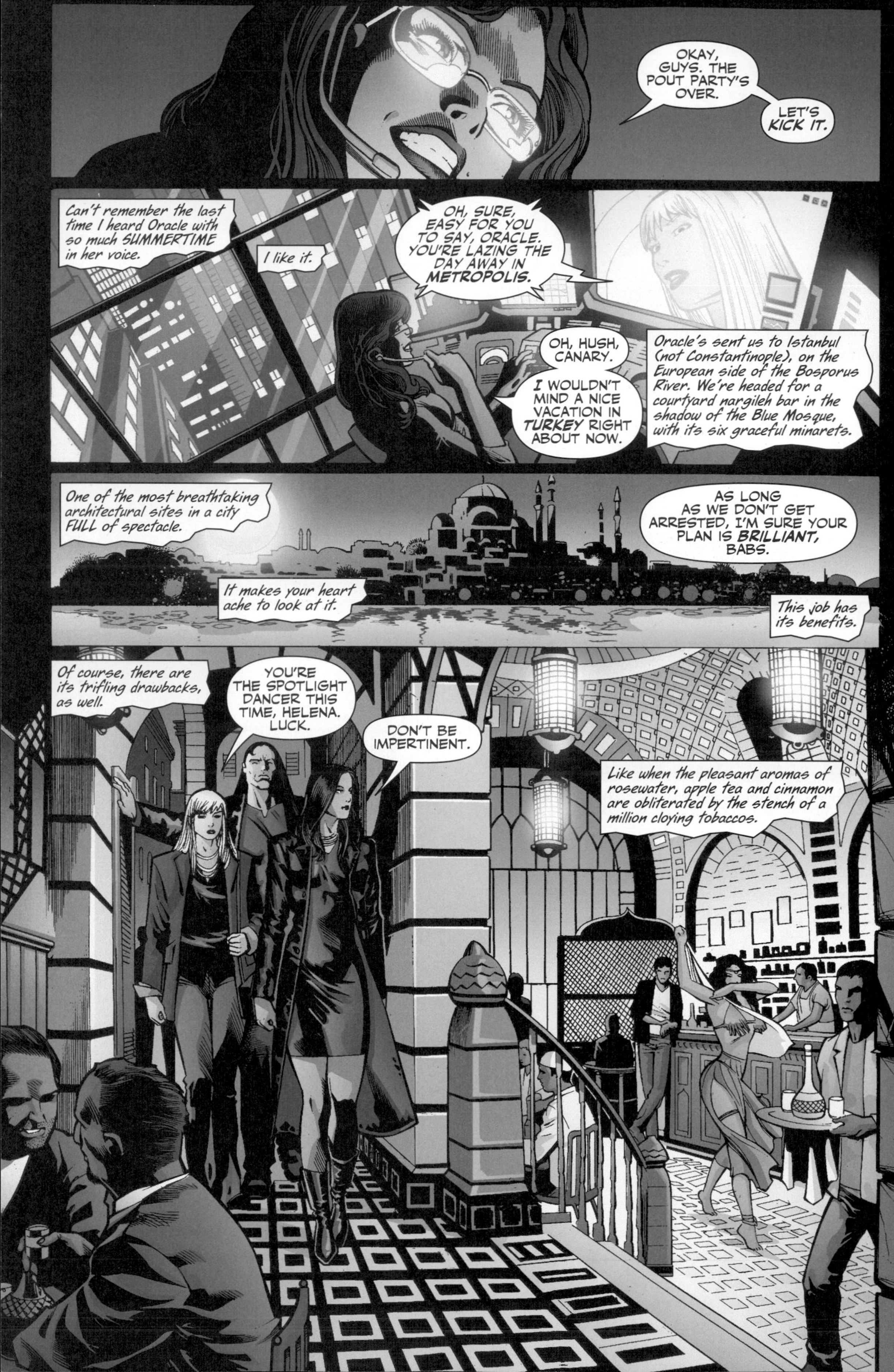
OKAY, GUYS. THE POUT PARTY'S OVER.
LET'S KICK IT.
Can't remember the last time I heard Oracle with so much SUMMERTIME in her voice.
I like it.
OH, SURE, EASY FOR YOU TO SAY, ORACLE. YOU'RE LAZING THE DAY AWAY IN METROPOLIS.
OH, HUSH, CANARY.
I WOULDN'T MIND A NICE VACATION IN TURKEY RIGHT ABOUT NOW.
Oracle's sent us to Istanbul (not Constantinople), on the European side of the Bosporus River. We're headed for a courtyard margileh bar in the shadow of the Blue Mosque, with its six graceful minarets.
One of the most breathtaking architectural sites in a city FULL of spectacle.
AS LONG AS WE DON'T GET ARRESTED, I'M SURE YOUR PLAN IS BRILLIANT, BABS.
It makes your heart ache to look at it.
This job has its benefits.
Of course, there are its trifling drawbacks, as well.
YOU'RE THE SPOTLIGHT DANCER THIS TIME, HELENA. LUCK.
DON'T BE IMPERTINENT.
Like when the pleasant aromas of rosewater, apple tea and cinnamon are obliterated by the stench of a million cloying tobaccos.

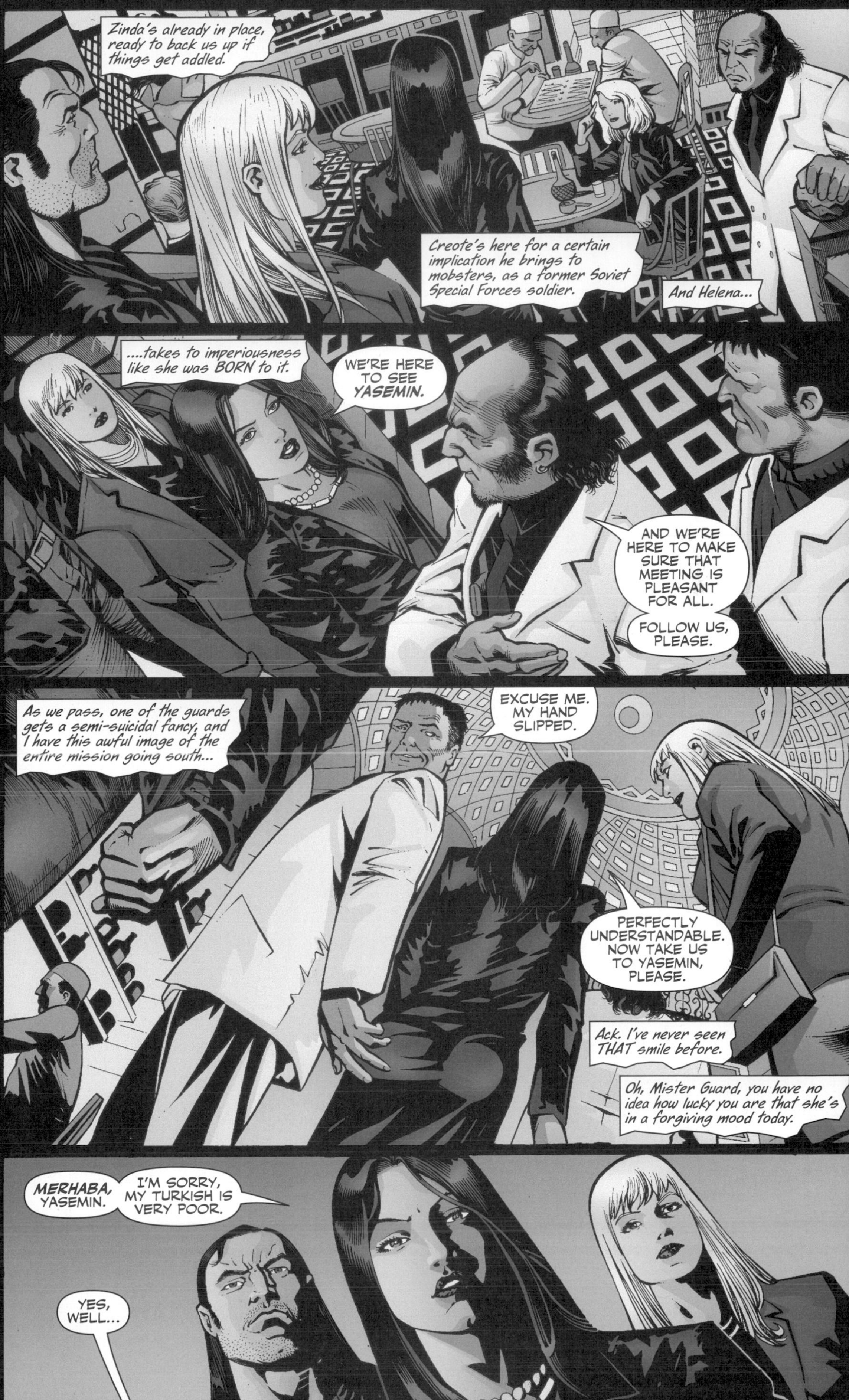

Zinda's already in place, ready to back us up if things get addled.
Creote's here for a certain implication he brings to mobsters, as a former Soviet Special Forces soldier.
And Helena...
....takes to imperiousness like she was BORN to it.
WE'RE HERE TO SEE YASEMIN.
AND WE'RE HERE TO MAKE SURE THAT MEETING IS PLEASANT FOR ALL.
FOLLOW US, PLEASE.
As we pass, one of the guards gets a semi-suicidal fancy, and I have this awful image of the entire mission going south...
EXCUSE ME. MY HAND SLIPPED.
PERFECTLY UNDERSTANDABLE. NOW TAKE US TO YASEMIN, PLEASE.
Ack. I've never seen THAT smile before.
Oh, Mister Guard, you have no idea how lucky you are that she's in a forgiving mood today.
MERHABA, YASEMIN.
I'M SORRY, MY TURKISH IS VERY POOR.
YES, WELL...

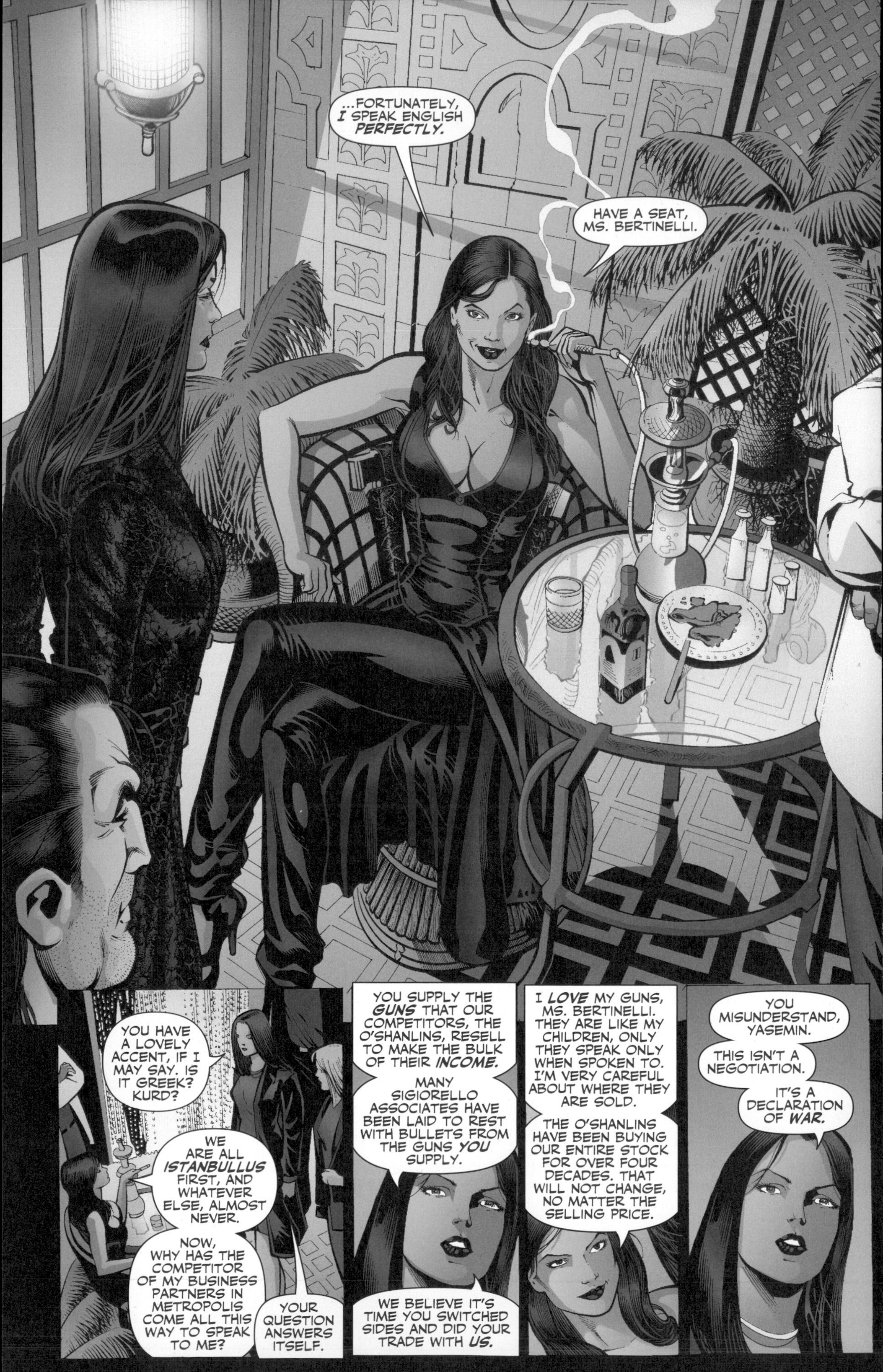
...FORTUNATELY, I SPEAK ENGLISH PERFECTLY.
HAVE A SEAT, MS. BERTINELLI.
YOU HAVE A LOVELY ACCENT, IF I MAY SAY. IS IT GREEK? KURD?
WE ARE ALL ISTANBULLUS FIRST, AND WHATEVER ELSE, ALMOST NEVER.
NOW, WHY HAS THE COMPETITOR OF MY BUSINESS PARTNERS IN METROPOLIS COME ALL THIS WAY TO SPEAK TO ME?
YOUR QUESTION ANSWERS ITSELF.
YOU SUPPLY THE GUNS THAT OUR COMPETITORS, THE O'SHANLINS, RESELL TO MAKE THE BULK OF THEIR INCOME.
MANY SIGIORELLO ASSOCIATES HAVE BEEN LAID TO REST WITH BULLETS FROM THE GUNS YOU SUPPLY.
WE BELIEVE IT'S TIME YOU SWITCHED SIDES AND DID YOUR TRADE WITH US.
I LOVE MY GUNS, MS. BERTINELLI. THEY ARE LIKE MY CHILDREN, ONLY THEY SPEAK ONLY WHEN SPOKEN TO. I'M VERY CAREFUL ABOUT WHERE THEY ARE SOLD.
THE O'SHANLINS HAVE BEEN BUYING OUR ENTIRE STOCK FOR OVER FOUR DECADES. THAT WILL NOT CHANGE, NO MATTER THE SELLING PRICE.
YOU MISUNDERSTAND, YASEMIN.
THIS ISN'T A NEGOTIATION.
IT'S A DECLARATION OF WAR.

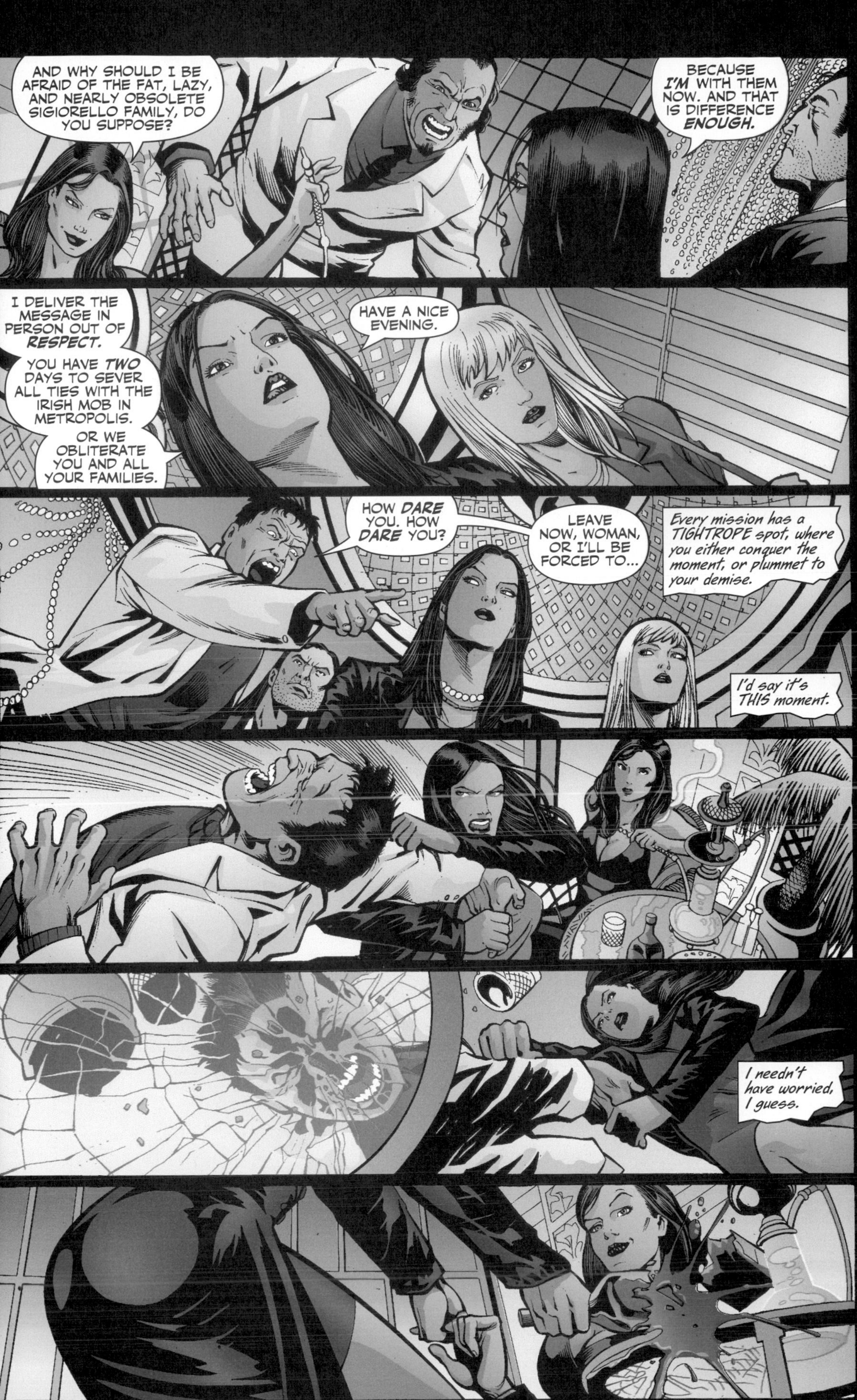
AND WHY SHOULD I BE AFRAID OF THE FAT, LAZY, AND NEARLY OBSOLETE SIGIORELLO FAMILY, DO YOU SUPPOSE?
BECAUSE I'M WITH THEM NOW. AND THAT IS DIFFERENCE ENOUGH.
I DELIVER THE MESSAGE IN PERSON OUT OF RESPECT.
YOU HAVE TWO DAYS TO SEVER ALL TIES WITH THE IRISH MOB IN METROPOLIS.
OR WE OBLITERATE YOU AND ALL YOUR FAMILIES.
HAVE A NICE EVENING.
HOW DARE YOU. HOW DARE YOU?
LEAVE NOW, WOMAN, OR I'LL BE FORCED TO...
Every mission has a TIGHTROPE spot, where you either conquer the moment, or plummet to your demise.
I'd say it's THIS moment.
I needn't have worried, I guess.

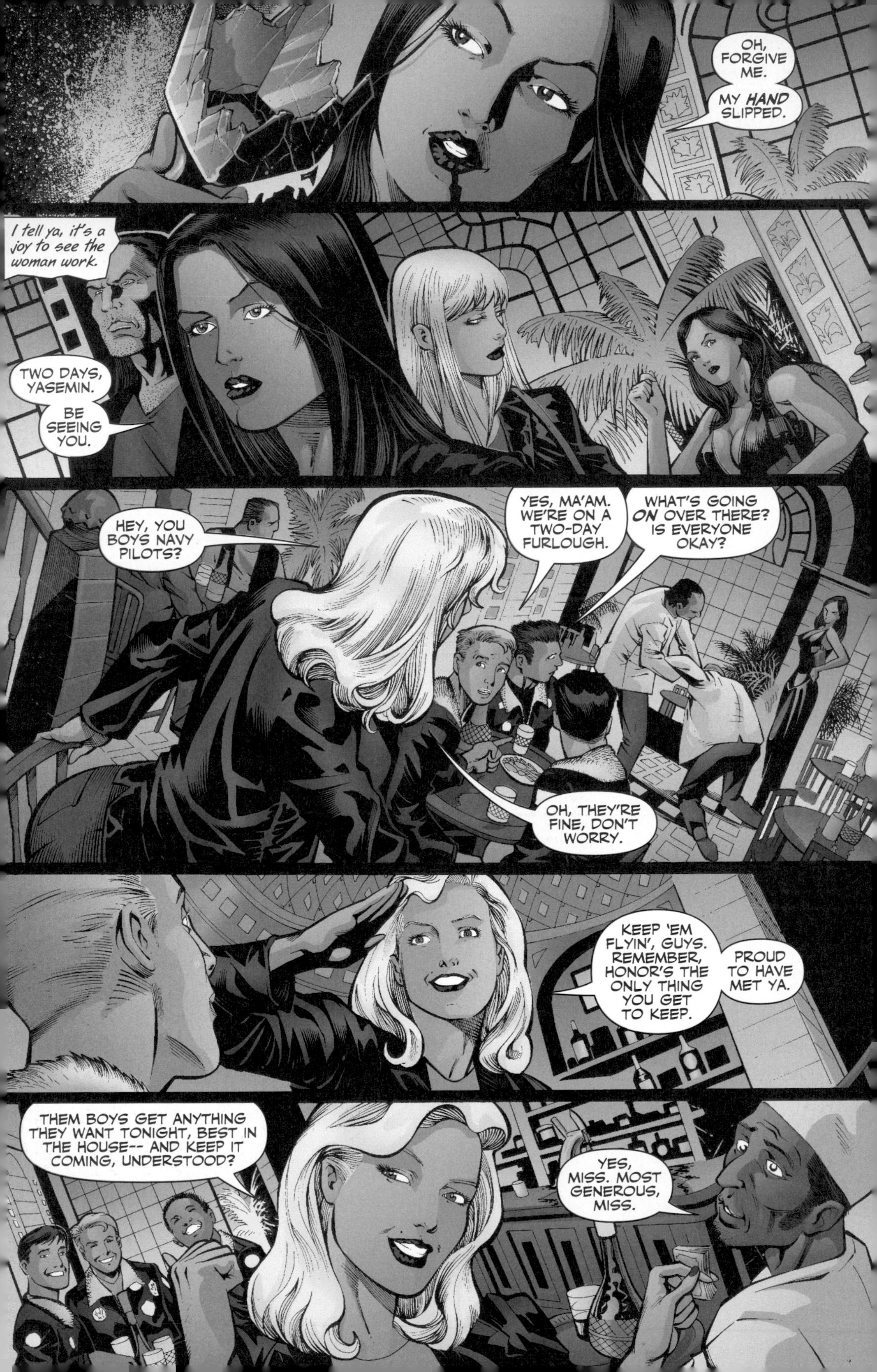
OH, FORGIVE ME.
MY HAND SLIPPED.
I tell ya, it's a joy to see the woman work.
TWO DAYS, YASEMIN.
BE SEEING YOU.
HEY, YOU BOYS NAVY PILOTS?
YES, MA'AM. WE'RE ON A TWO-DAY FURLOUGH.
WHAT'S GOING ON OVER THERE? IS EVERYONE OKAY?
OH, THEY'RE FINE, DON'T WORRY.
KEEP 'EM FLYIN', GUYS. REMEMBER, HONOR'S THE ONLY THING YOU GET TO KEEP.
PROUD TO HAVE MET YA.
THEM BOYS GET ANYTHING THEY WANT TONIGHT, BEST IN THE HOUSE-- AND KEEP IT COMING, UNDERSTOOD?
YES, MISS. MOST GENEROUS, MISS.

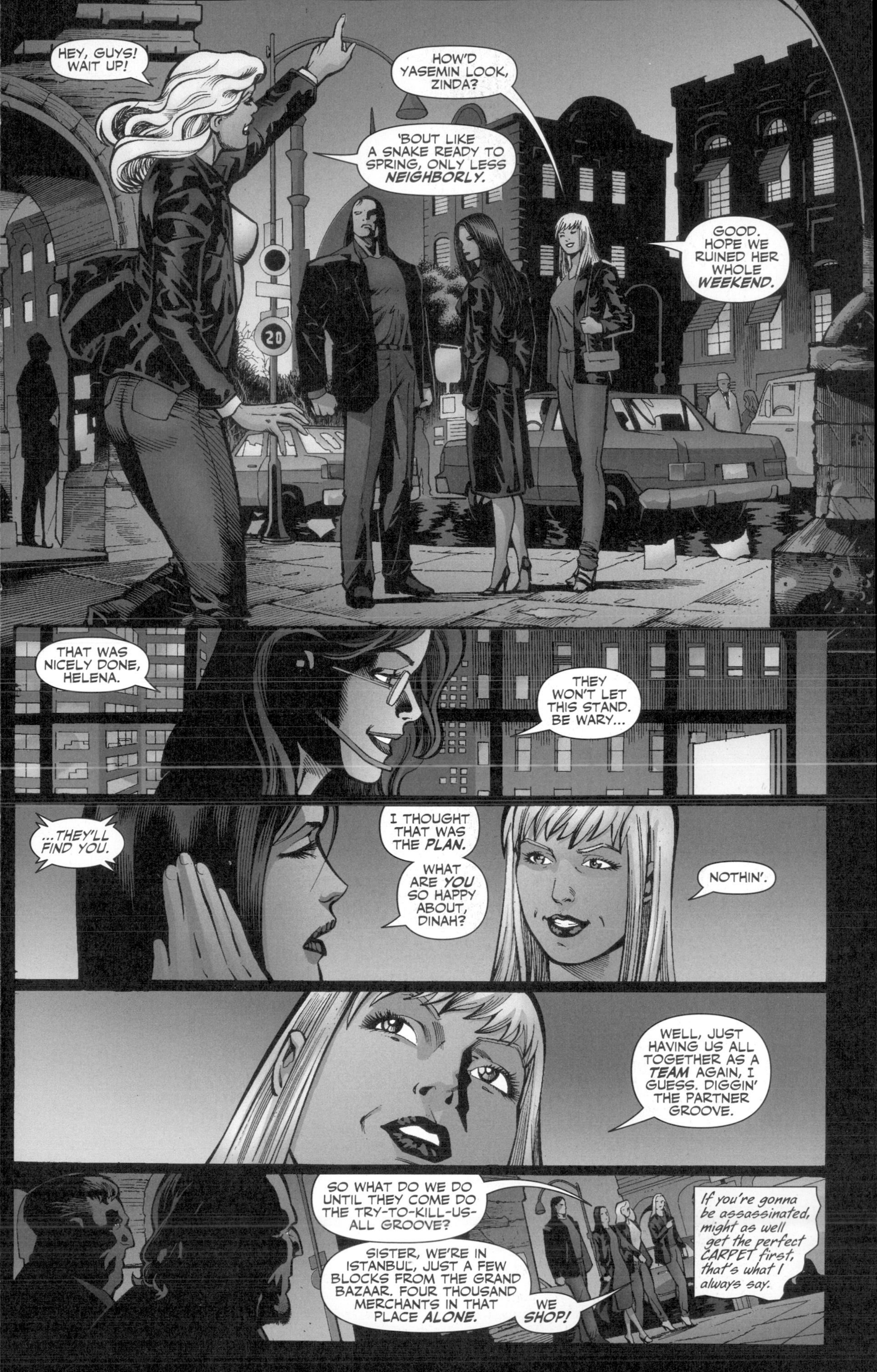
HEY, GUYS! WAIT UP!
HOW'D YASEMIN LOOK, ZINDA?
'BOUT LIKE A SNAKE READY TO SPRING, ONLY LESS NEIGHBORLY.
GOOD. HOPE WE RUINED HER WHOLE WEEKEND.
20
THAT WAS NICELY DONE, HELENA.
THEY WON'T LET THIS STAND. BE WARY...
...THEY'LL FIND YOU.
I THOUGHT THAT WAS THE PLAN.
WHAT ARE YOU SO HAPPY ABOUT, DINAH?
NOTHIN'.
WELL, JUST HAVING US ALL TOGETHER AS A TEAM AGAIN, I GUESS. DIGGIN' THE PARTNER GROOVE.
SO WHAT DO WE DO UNTIL THEY COME DO THE TRY-TO-KILL-US-ALL GROOVE?
SISTER, WE'RE IN ISTANBUL, JUST A FEW BLOCKS FROM THE GRAND BAZAAR. FOUR THOUSAND MERCHANTS IN THAT PLACE ALONE.
WE SHOP!
If you're gonna be assassinated, might as well get the perfect CARPET first, that's what I always say.

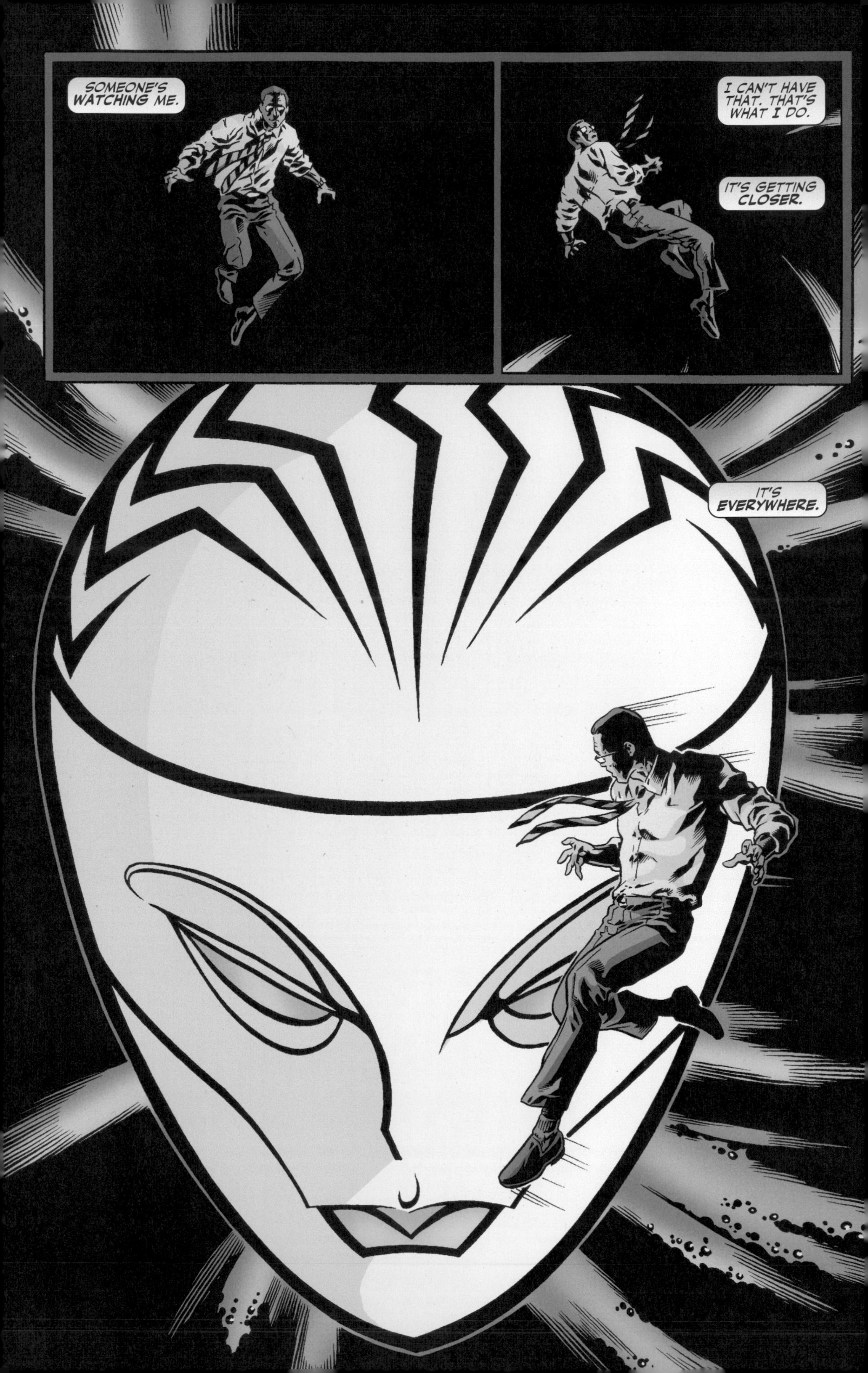
SOMEONE'S WATCHING ME.
I CAN'T HAVE THAT. THAT'S WHAT I DO.
IT'S GETTING CLOSER.
IT'S EVERYWHERE.

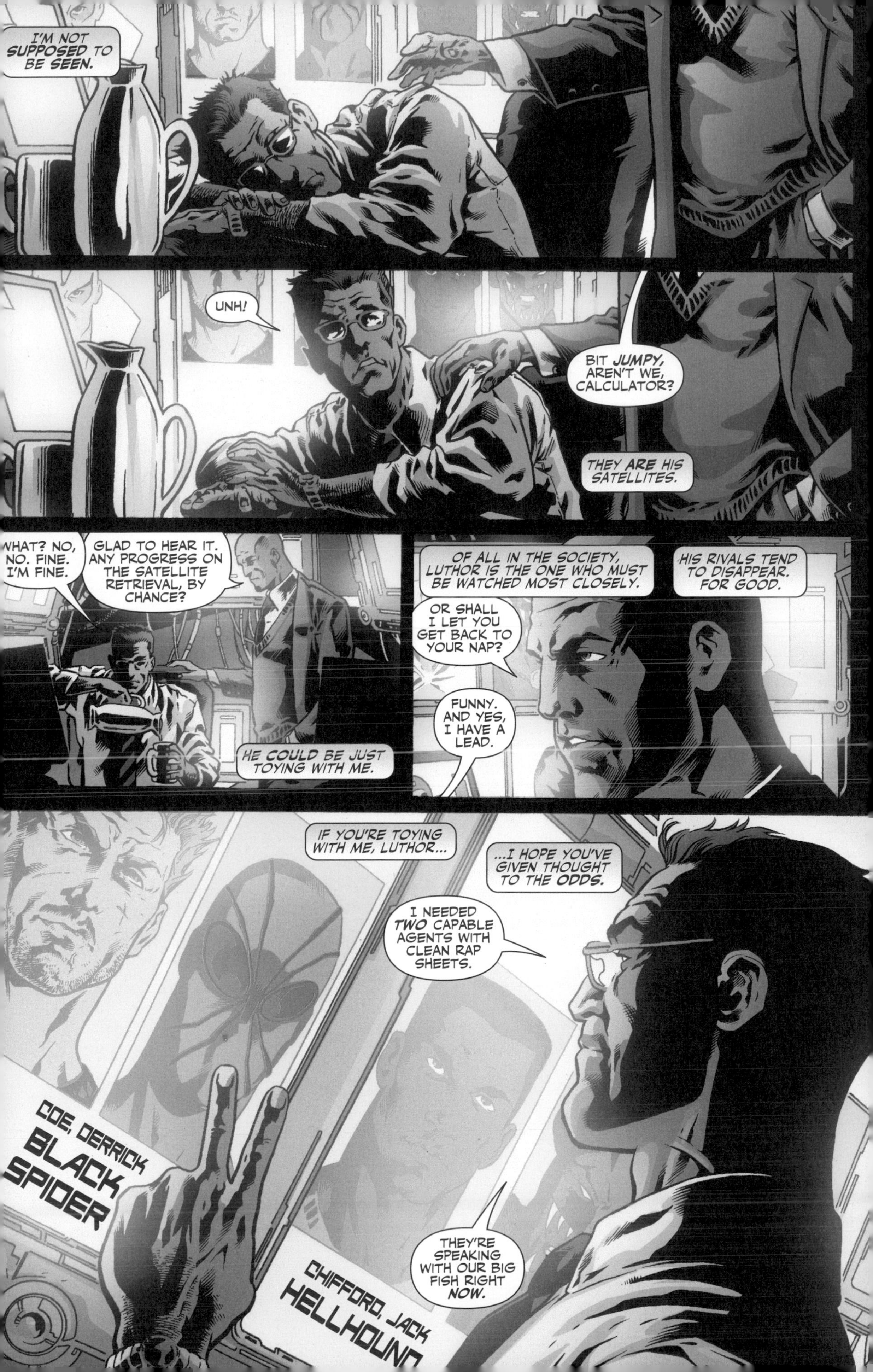
I'M NOT SUPPOSED TO BE SEEN.
UNH!
BIT JUMPY, AREN'T WE, CALCULATOR?
THEY ARE HIS SATELLITES.
WHAT? NO, NO. FINE. I'M FINE.
GLAD TO HEAR IT. ANY PROGRESS ON THE SATELLITE RETRIEVAL, BY CHANCE?
HE COULD BE JUST TOYING WITH ME.
OF ALL IN THE SOCIETY, LUTHOR IS THE ONE WHO MUST BE WATCHED MOST CLOSELY.
HIS RIVALS TEND TO DISAPPEAR. FOR GOOD.
OR SHALL I LET YOU GET BACK TO YOUR NAP?
FUNNY. AND YES, I HAVE A LEAD.
IF YOU'RE TOYING WITH ME, LUTHOR...
...I HOPE YOU'VE GIVEN THOUGHT TO THE ODDS.
I NEEDED TWO CAPABLE AGENTS WITH CLEAN RAP SHEETS.
COE, DERRICK
BLACK SPIDER
THEY'RE SPEAKING WITH OUR BIG FISH RIGHT NOW.
CHIFFORD, JACK
HELLHOUND

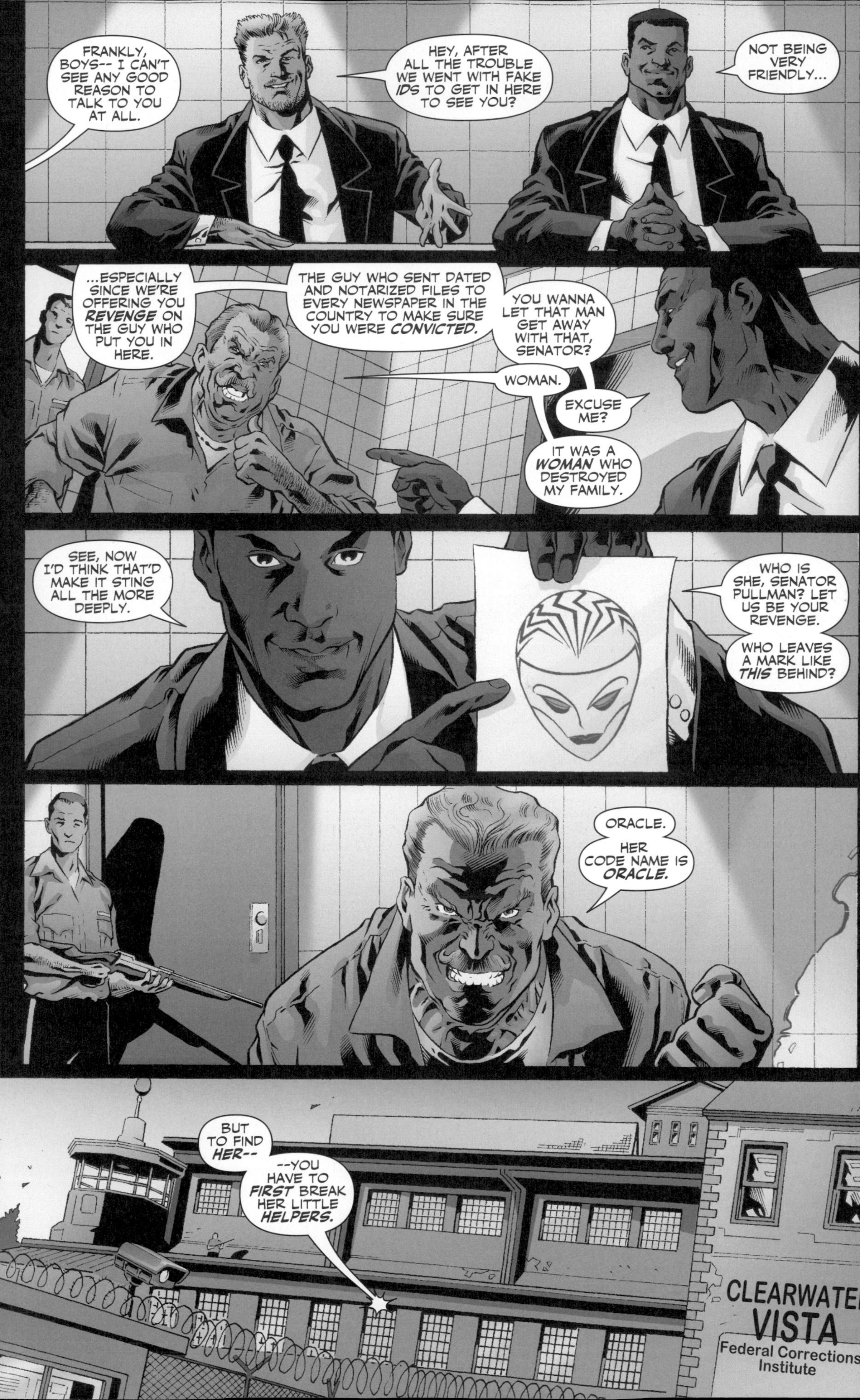

FRANKLY, BOYS-- I CAN'T SEE ANY GOOD REASON TO TALK TO YOU AT ALL.
HEY, AFTER ALL THE TROUBLE WE WENT WITH FAKE IDs TO GET IN HERE TO SEE YOU?
NOT BEING VERY FRIENDLY...
...ESPECIALLY SINCE WE'RE OFFERING YOU REVENGE ON THE GUY WHO PUT YOU IN HERE.
THE GUY WHO SENT DATED AND NOTARIZED FILES TO EVERY NEWSPAPER IN THE COUNTRY TO MAKE SURE YOU WERE CONVICTED.
YOU WANNA LET THAT MAN GET AWAY WITH THAT, SENATOR?
WOMAN.
EXCUSE ME?
IT WAS A WOMAN WHO DESTROYED MY FAMILY.
SEE, NOW I'D THINK THAT'D MAKE IT STING ALL THE MORE DEEPLY.
WHO IS SHE, SENATOR PULLMAN? LET US BE YOUR REVENGE.
WHO LEAVES A MARK LIKE THIS BEHIND?
ORACLE.
HER CODE NAME IS ORACLE.
BUT TO FIND HER--
--YOU HAVE TO FIRST BREAK HER LITTLE HELPERS.
CLEARWATE
VISTA
Federal Corrections
Institute

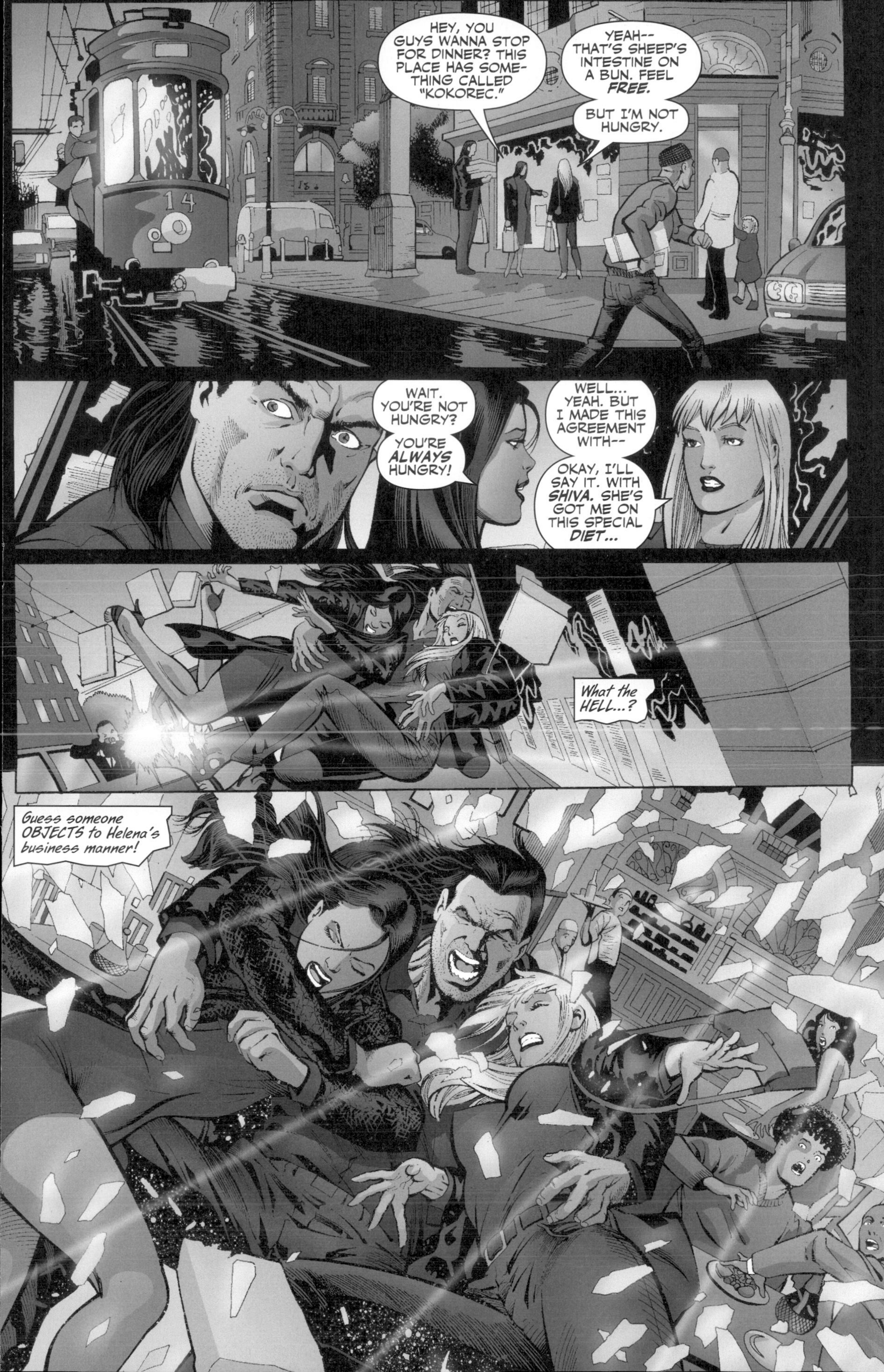

HEY, YOU GUYS WANNA STOP FOR DINNER? THIS PLACE HAS SOME-THING CALLED "KOKOREC."
YEAH-- THAT'S SHEEP'S INTESTINE ON A BUN. FEEL *FREE.*
BUT I'M NOT HUNGRY.
WAIT. YOU'RE NOT HUNGRY?
YOU'RE *ALWAYS* HUNGRY!
WELL... YEAH. BUT I MADE THIS AGREEMENT WITH--
OKAY, I'LL SAY IT. WITH *SHIVA.* SHE'S GOT ME ON THIS SPECIAL *DIET...*
What the *HELL...?*
Guess someone *OBJECTS* to Helena's business manner!

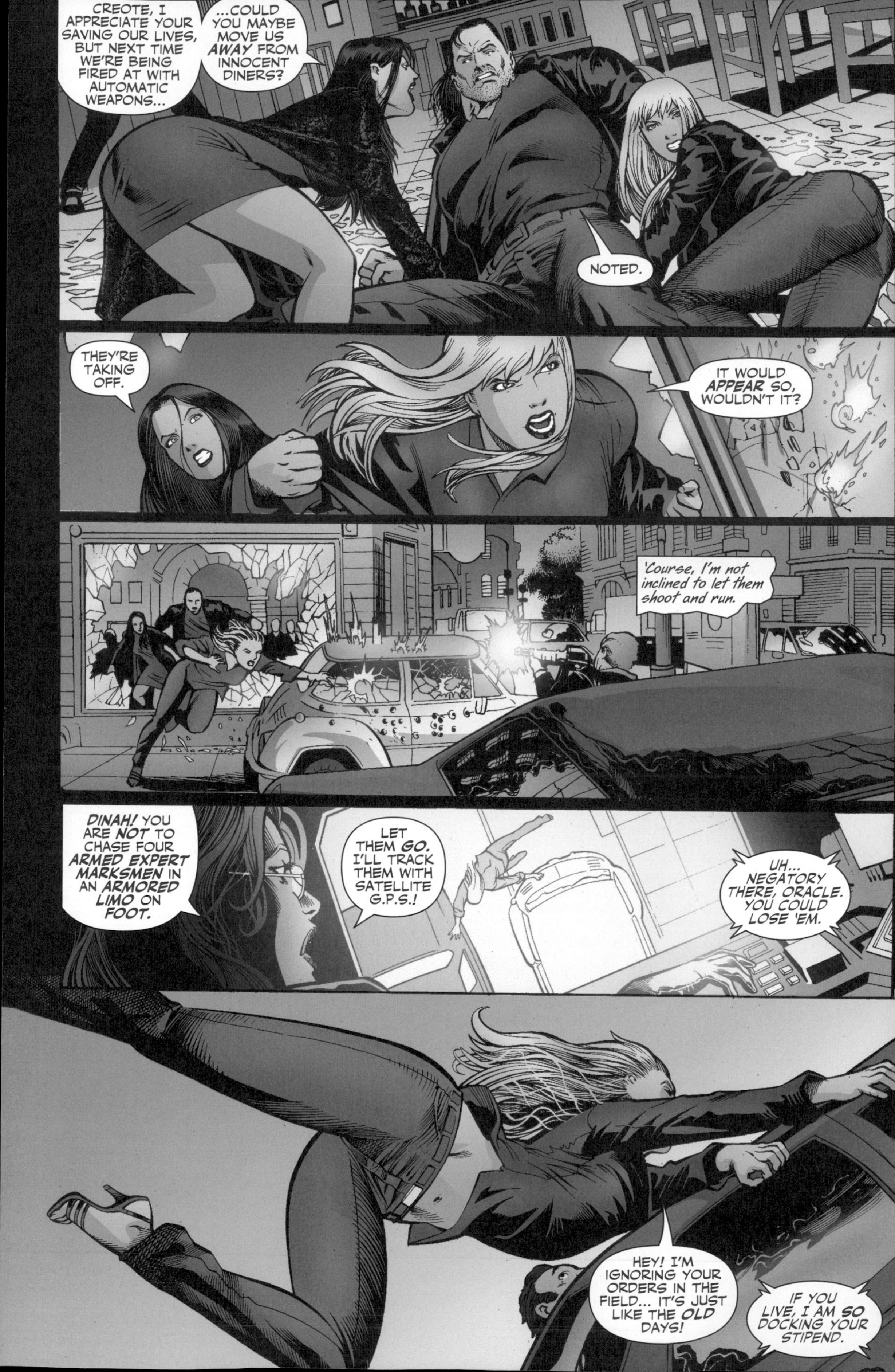
CREOTE, I APPRECIATE YOUR SAVING OUR LIVES, BUT NEXT TIME WE'RE BEING FIRED AT WITH AUTOMATIC WEAPONS...
...COULD YOU MAYBE MOVE US AWAY FROM INNOCENT DINERS?
NOTED.
THEY'RE TAKING OFF.
IT WOULD APPEAR SO, WOULDN'T IT?
'Course, I'm not inclined to let them shoot and run.
DINAH! YOU ARE NOT TO CHASE FOUR ARMED EXPERT MARKSMEN IN AN ARMORED LIMO ON FOOT.
LET THEM GO. I'LL TRACK THEM WITH SATELLITE G.P.S.!
UH... NEGATORY THERE, ORACLE. YOU COULD LOSE 'EM.
HEY! I'M IGNORING YOUR ORDERS IN THE FIELD... IT'S JUST LIKE THE OLD DAYS!
IF YOU LIVE, I AM SO DOCKING YOUR STIPEND.

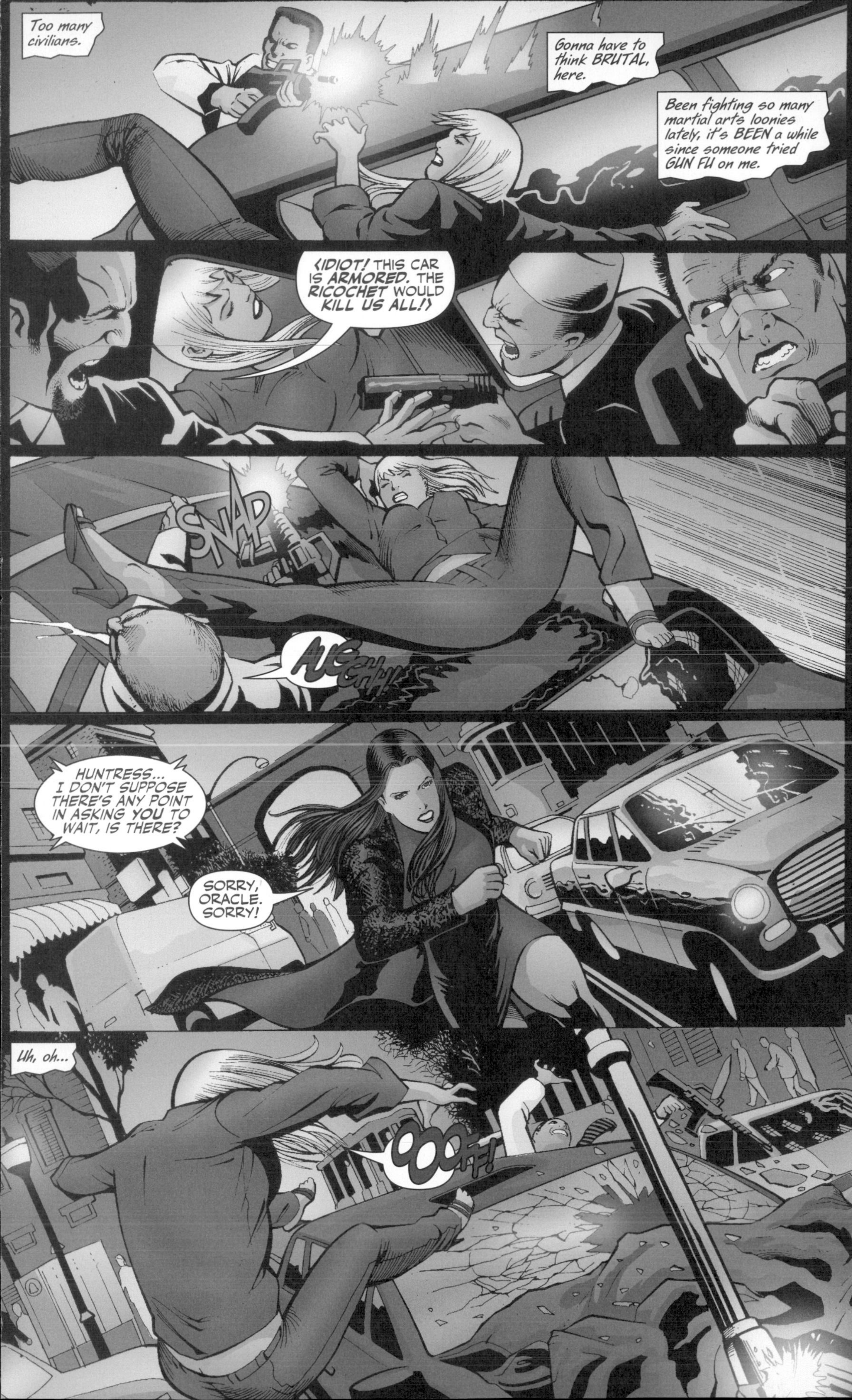
Too many civilians.
Gonna have to think BRUTAL, here.
Been fighting so many martial arts loonies lately, it's BEEN a while since someone tried GUN FU on me.
‹IDIOT! THIS CAR IS ARMORED. THE RICOCHET WOULD KILL US ALL!›
SNAP
AUGGHH!
HUNTRESS... I DON'T SUPPOSE THERE'S ANY POINT IN ASKING YOU TO WAIT, IS THERE?
SORRY, ORACLE. SORRY!
Uh, oh...
OOOFF!

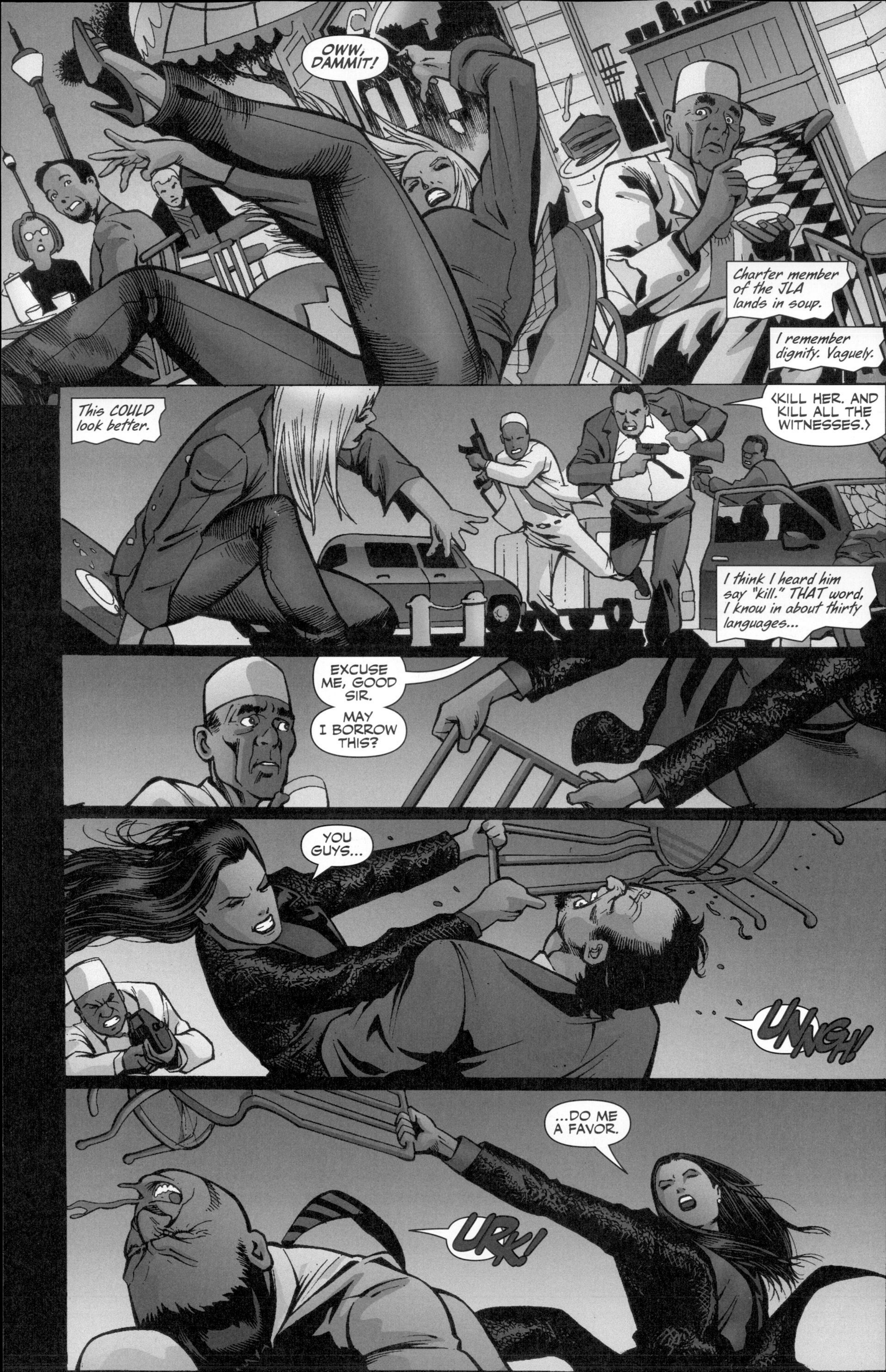
OWW, DAMMIT!
Charter member of the JLA lands in soup.
I remember dignity. Vaguely.
This COULD look better.
‹KILL HER. AND KILL ALL THE WITNESSES.›
I think I heard him say "kill." THAT word, I know in about thirty languages...
EXCUSE ME, GOOD SIR.
MAY I BORROW THIS?
YOU GUYS...
UNNGH!
...DO ME A FAVOR.
URK!

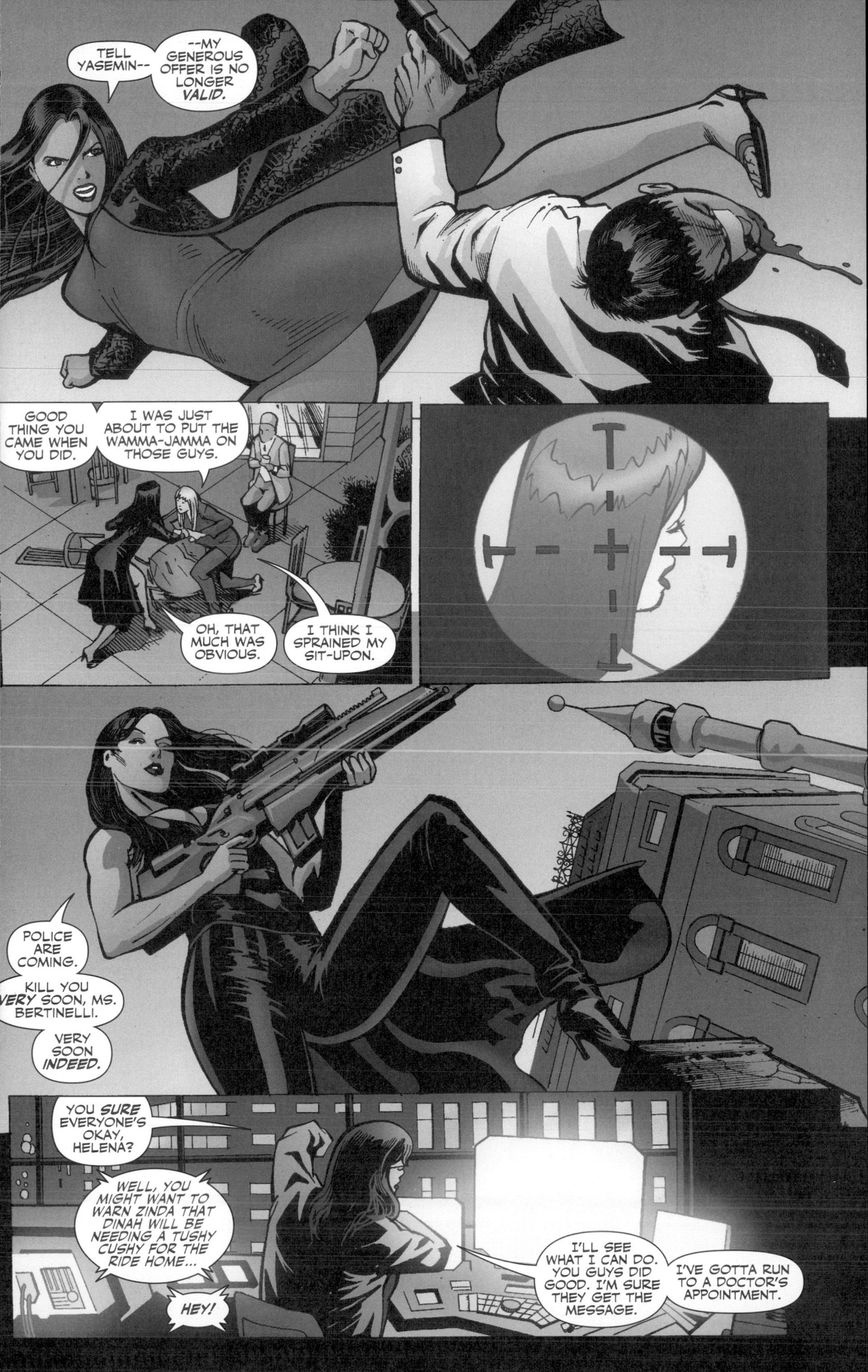
TELL YASEMIN--
--MY GENEROUS OFFER IS NO LONGER VALID.
GOOD THING YOU CAME WHEN YOU DID.
I WAS JUST ABOUT TO PUT THE WAMMA-JAMMA ON THOSE GUYS.
OH, THAT MUCH WAS OBVIOUS.
I THINK I SPRAINED MY SIT-UPON.
POLICE ARE COMING.
KILL YOU VERY SOON, MS. BERTINELLI.
VERY SOON INDEED.
YOU SURE EVERYONE'S OKAY, HELENA?
WELL, YOU MIGHT WANT TO WARN ZINDA THAT DINAH WILL BE NEEDING A TUSHY CUSHY FOR THE RIDE HOME...
HEY!
I'LL SEE WHAT I CAN DO. YOU GUYS DID GOOD. I'M SURE THEY GET THE MESSAGE.
I'VE GOTTA RUN TO A DOCTOR'S APPOINTMENT.

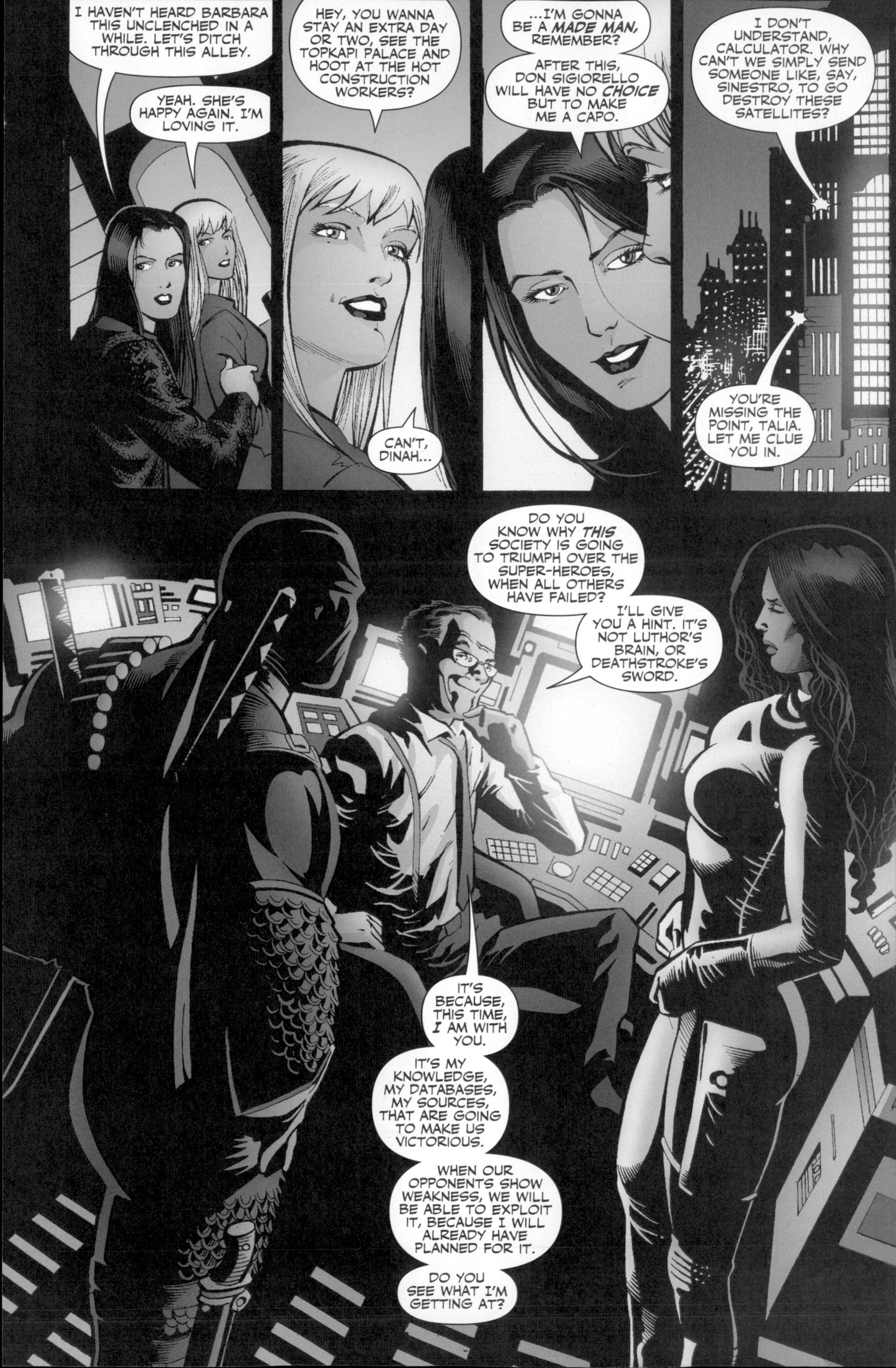

I HAVEN'T HEARD BARBARA THIS UNCLENCHED IN A WHILE. LET'S DITCH THROUGH THIS ALLEY.
YEAH. SHE'S HAPPY AGAIN. I'M LOVING IT.
HEY, YOU WANNA STAY AN EXTRA DAY OR TWO, SEE THE TOPKAPI PALACE AND HOOT AT THE HOT CONSTRUCTION WORKERS?
CAN'T, DINAH...
...I'M GONNA BE A *MADE MAN*, REMEMBER?
AFTER THIS, DON SIGIORELLO WILL HAVE NO *CHOICE* BUT TO MAKE ME A CAPO.
I DON'T UNDERSTAND, CALCULATOR. WHY CAN'T WE SIMPLY SEND SOMEONE LIKE, SAY, SINESTRO, TO GO DESTROY THESE SATELLITES?
YOU'RE MISSING THE POINT, TALIA. LET ME CLUE YOU IN.
DO YOU KNOW WHY *THIS* SOCIETY IS GOING TO TRIUMPH OVER THE SUPER-HEROES, WHEN ALL OTHERS HAVE FAILED?
I'LL GIVE YOU A HINT. IT'S NOT LUTHOR'S BRAIN, OR DEATHSTROKE'S SWORD.
IT'S BECAUSE, THIS TIME, *I* AM WITH YOU.
IT'S MY KNOWLEDGE, MY DATABASES, MY SOURCES, THAT ARE GOING TO MAKE US VICTORIOUS.
WHEN OUR OPPONENTS SHOW WEAKNESS, WE WILL BE ABLE TO EXPLOIT IT, BECAUSE I WILL ALREADY HAVE PLANNED FOR IT.
DO YOU SEE WHAT I'M GETTING AT?

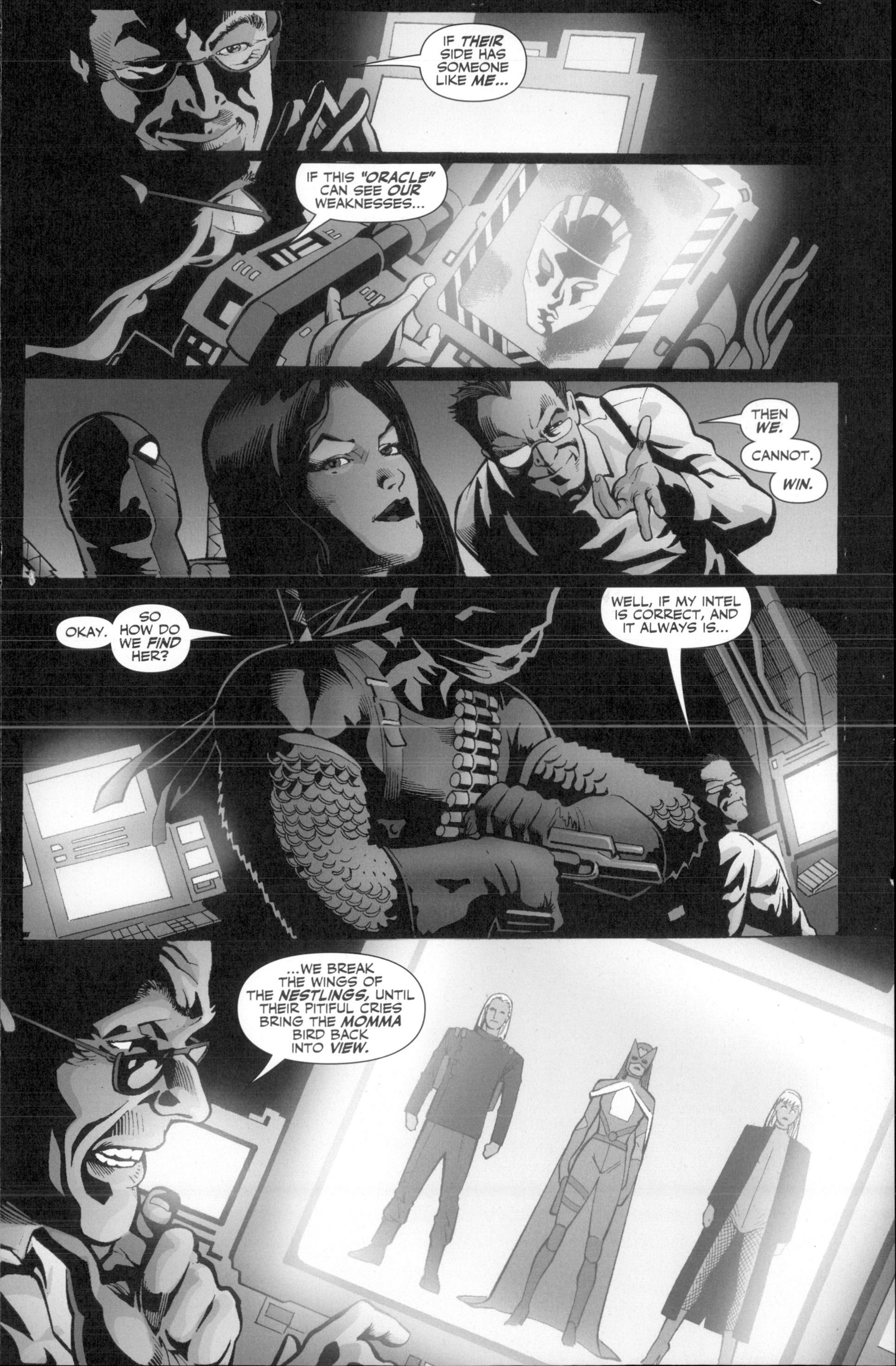
IF THEIR SIDE HAS SOMEONE LIKE ME...
IF THIS "ORACLE" CAN SEE OUR WEAKNESSES...
THEN WE.
CANNOT.
WIN.
OKAY.
SO HOW DO WE FIND HER?
WELL, IF MY INTEL IS CORRECT, AND IT ALWAYS IS...
...WE BREAK THE WINGS OF THE NESTLINGS, UNTIL THEIR PITIFUL CRIES BRING THE MOMMA BIRD BACK INTO VIEW.

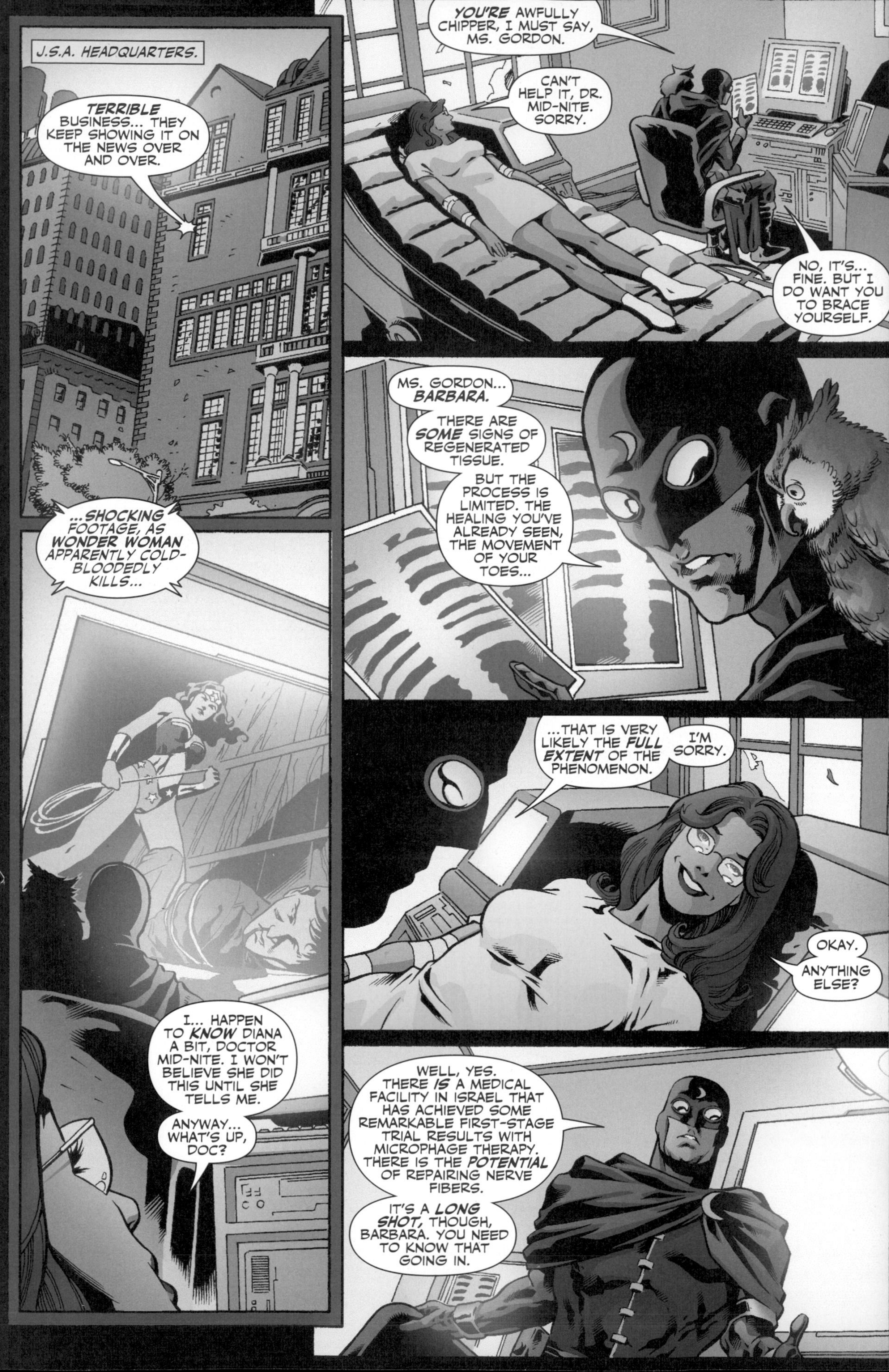
J.S.A. HEADQUARTERS.
TERRIBLE BUSINESS... THEY KEEP SHOWING IT ON THE NEWS OVER AND OVER.
YOU'RE AWFULLY CHIPPER, I MUST SAY, MS. GORDON.
CAN'T HELP IT, DR. MID-NITE. SORRY.
NO, IT'S... FINE. BUT I DO WANT YOU TO BRACE YOURSELF.
MS. GORDON... BARBARA.
THERE ARE SOME SIGNS OF REGENERATED TISSUE.
BUT THE PROCESS IS LIMITED. THE HEALING YOU'VE ALREADY SEEN, THE MOVEMENT OF YOUR TOES...
...SHOCKING FOOTAGE, AS WONDER WOMAN APPARENTLY COLD-BLOODEDLY KILLS...
...THAT IS VERY LIKELY THE FULL EXTENT OF THE PHENOMENON.
I'M SORRY.
OKAY.
ANYTHING ELSE?
I... HAPPEN TO KNOW DIANA A BIT, DOCTOR MID-NITE. I WON'T BELIEVE SHE DID THIS UNTIL SHE TELLS ME.
ANYWAY... WHAT'S UP, DOC?
WELL, YES. THERE IS A MEDICAL FACILITY IN ISRAEL THAT HAS ACHIEVED SOME REMARKABLE FIRST-STAGE TRIAL RESULTS WITH MICROPHAGE THERAPY. THERE IS THE POTENTIAL OF REPAIRING NERVE FIBERS.
IT'S A LONG SHOT, THOUGH, BARBARA. YOU NEED TO KNOW THAT GOING IN.

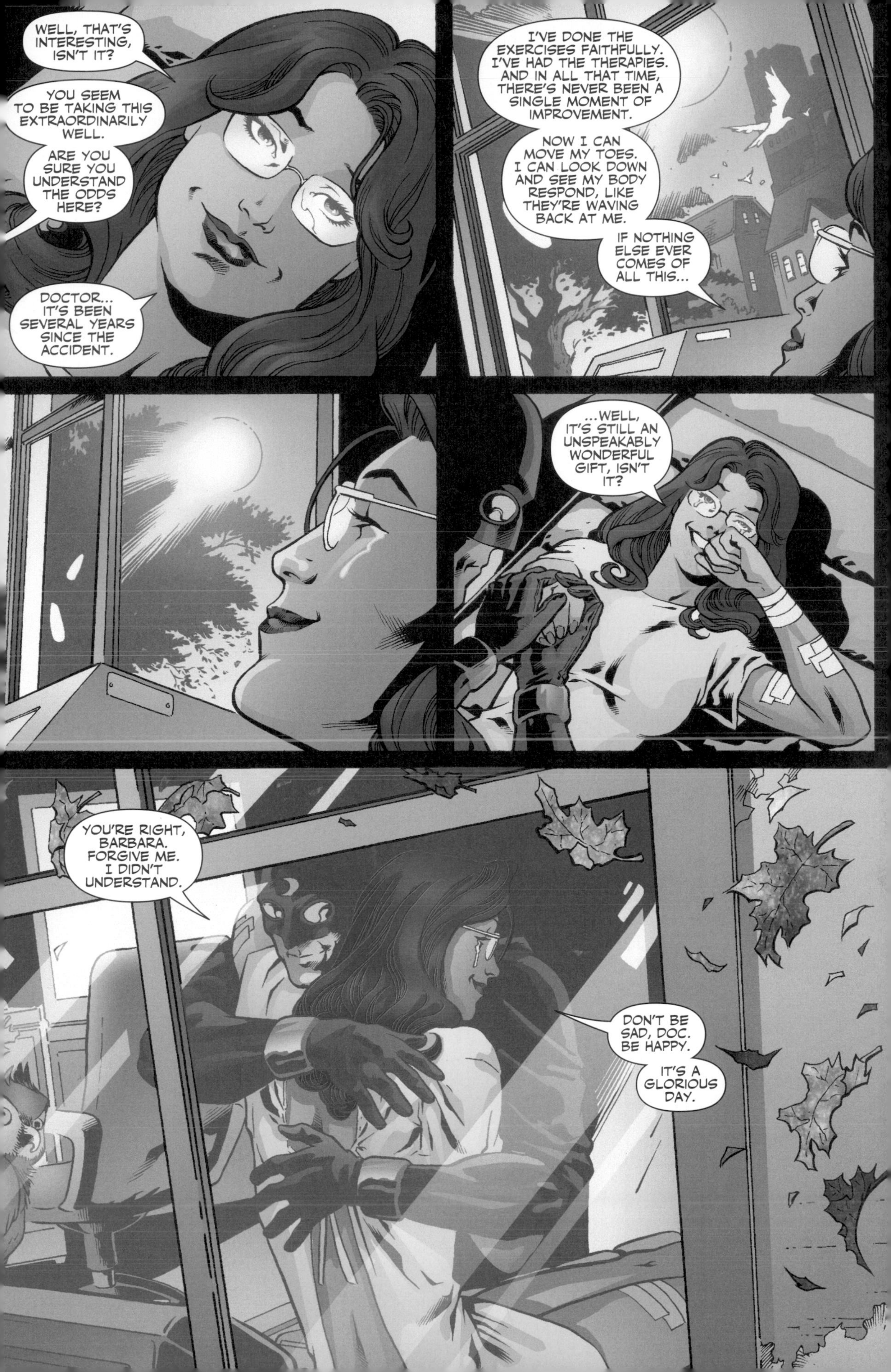

WELL, THAT'S INTERESTING, ISN'T IT?
YOU SEEM TO BE TAKING THIS EXTRAORDINARILY WELL.
ARE YOU SURE YOU UNDERSTAND THE ODDS HERE?
DOCTOR... IT'S BEEN SEVERAL YEARS SINCE THE ACCIDENT.
I'VE DONE THE EXERCISES FAITHFULLY. I'VE HAD THE THERAPIES. AND IN ALL THAT TIME, THERE'S NEVER BEEN A SINGLE MOMENT OF IMPROVEMENT.
NOW I CAN MOVE MY TOES. I CAN LOOK DOWN AND SEE MY BODY RESPOND, LIKE THEY'RE WAVING BACK AT ME.
IF NOTHING ELSE EVER COMES OF ALL THIS...
...WELL, IT'S STILL AN UNSPEAKABLY WONDERFUL GIFT, ISN'T IT?
YOU'RE RIGHT, BARBARA. FORGIVE ME. I DIDN'T UNDERSTAND.
DON'T BE SAD, DOC. BE HAPPY.
IT'S A GLORIOUS DAY.

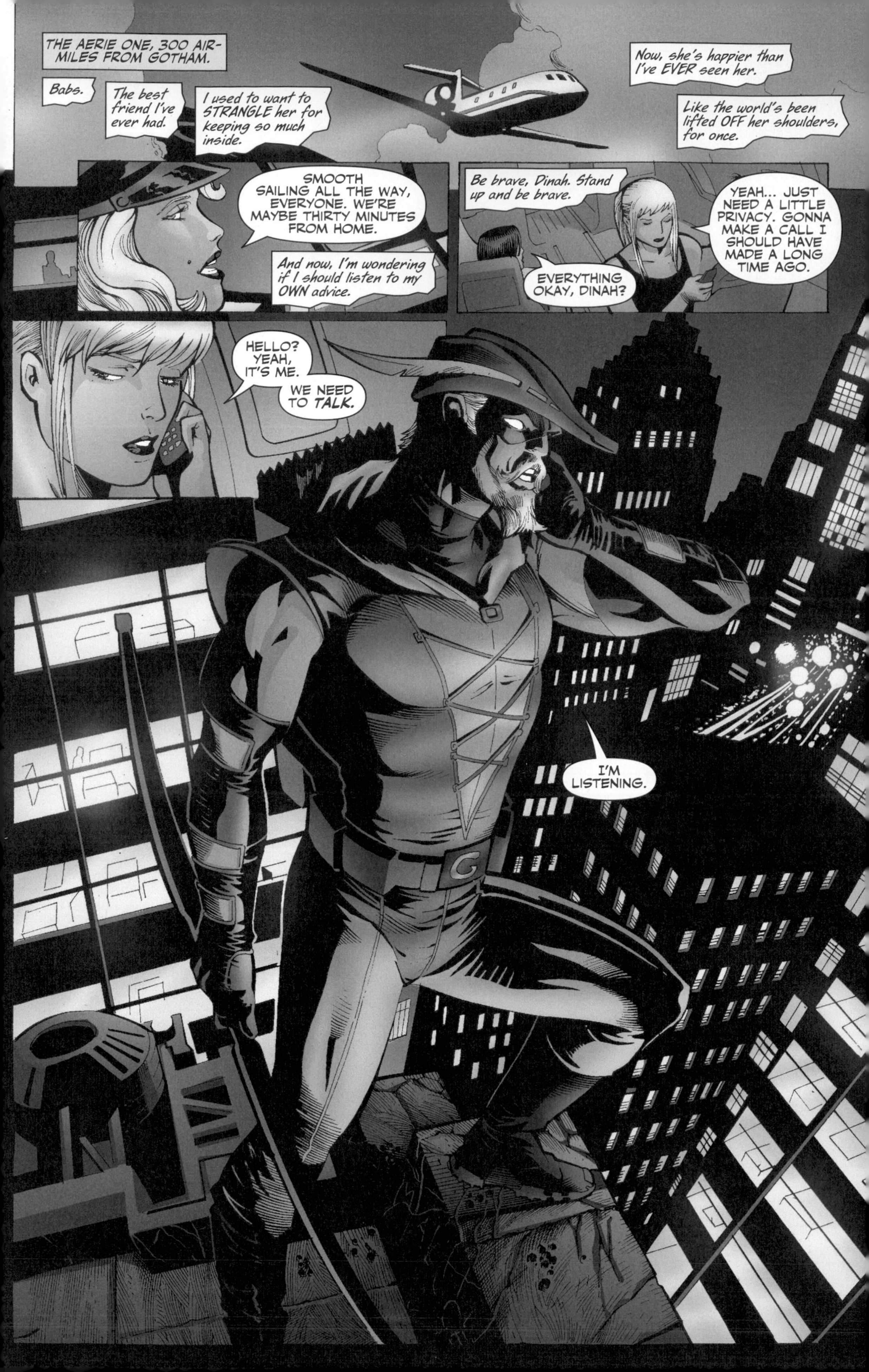
THE AERIE ONE, 300 AIR-MILES FROM GOTHAM.
Babs.
The best friend I've ever had.
I used to want to STRANGLE her for keeping so much inside.
Now, she's happier than I've EVER seen her.
Like the world's been lifted OFF her shoulders, for once.
SMOOTH SAILING ALL THE WAY, EVERYONE. WE'RE MAYBE THIRTY MINUTES FROM HOME.
And now, I'm wondering if I should listen to my OWN advice.
Be brave, Dinah. Stand up and be brave.
EVERYTHING OKAY, DINAH?
YEAH... JUST NEED A LITTLE PRIVACY. GONNA MAKE A CALL I SHOULD HAVE MADE A LONG TIME AGO.
HELLO? YEAH, IT'S ME.
WE NEED TO TALK.
I'M LISTENING.

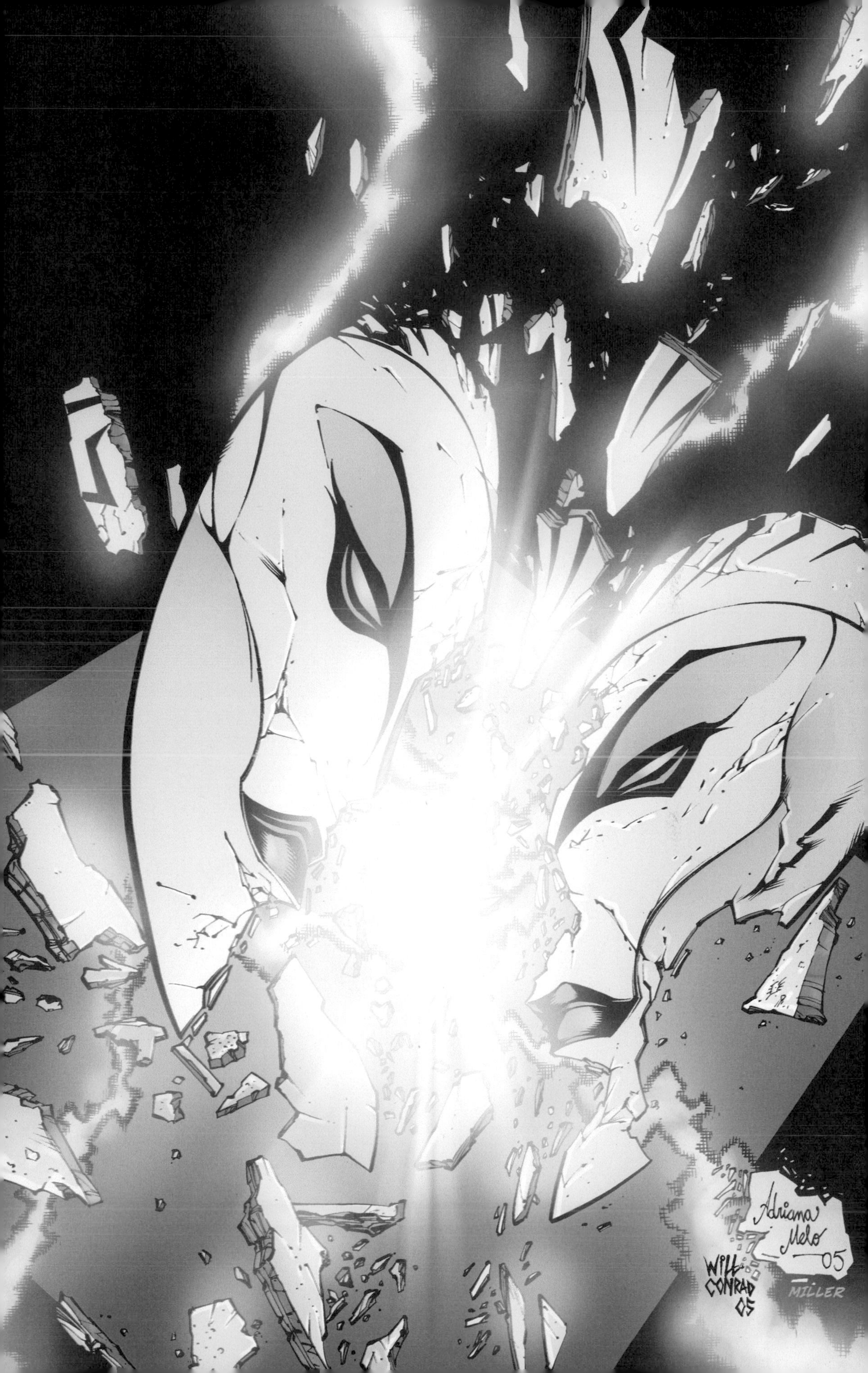
Adriana Melo 05
WILL CONRAD 05
MILLER

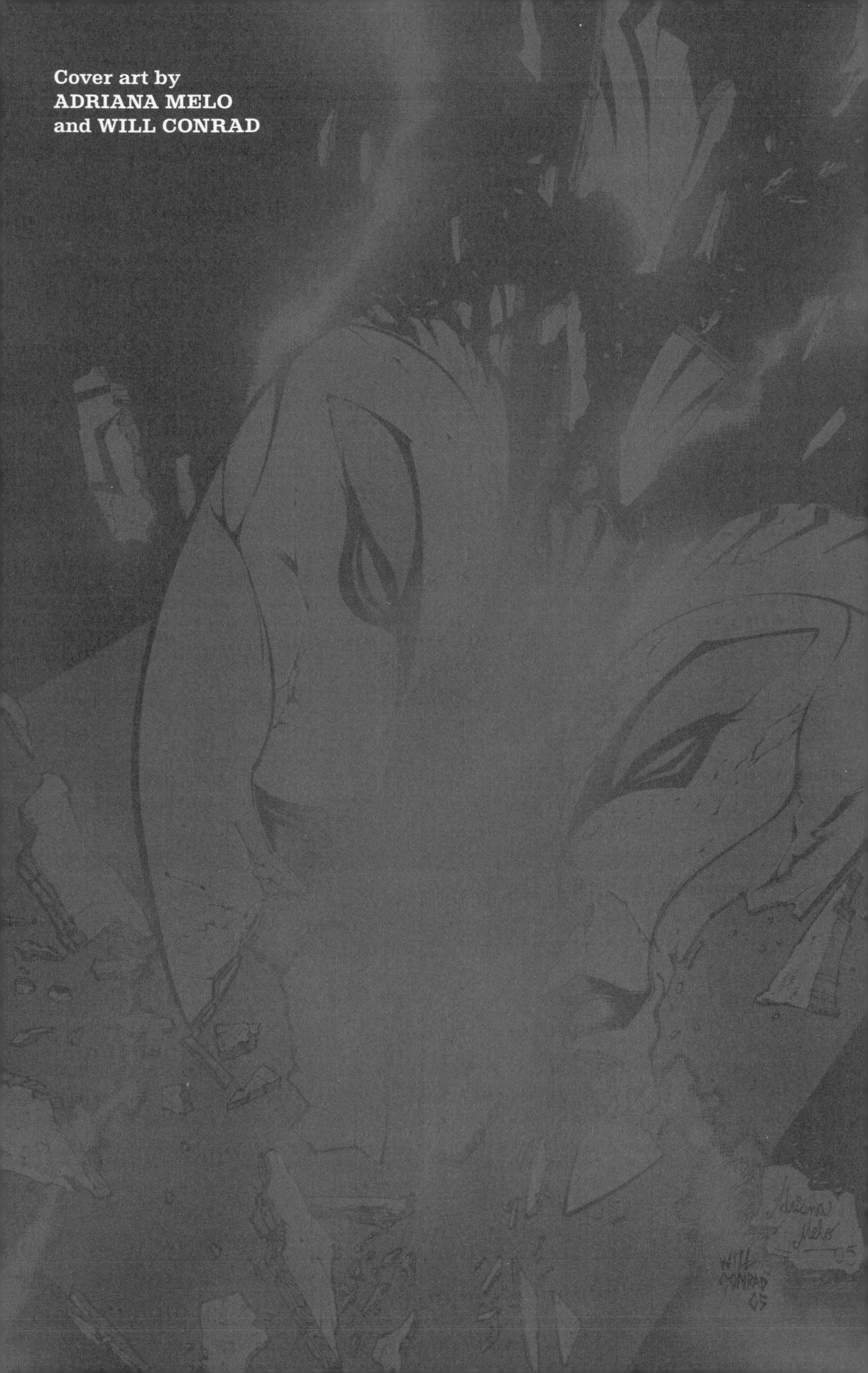
Adriana Melo 05
WILL CONRAD 05

Cover art by
ADRIANA MELO
and WILL CONRAD

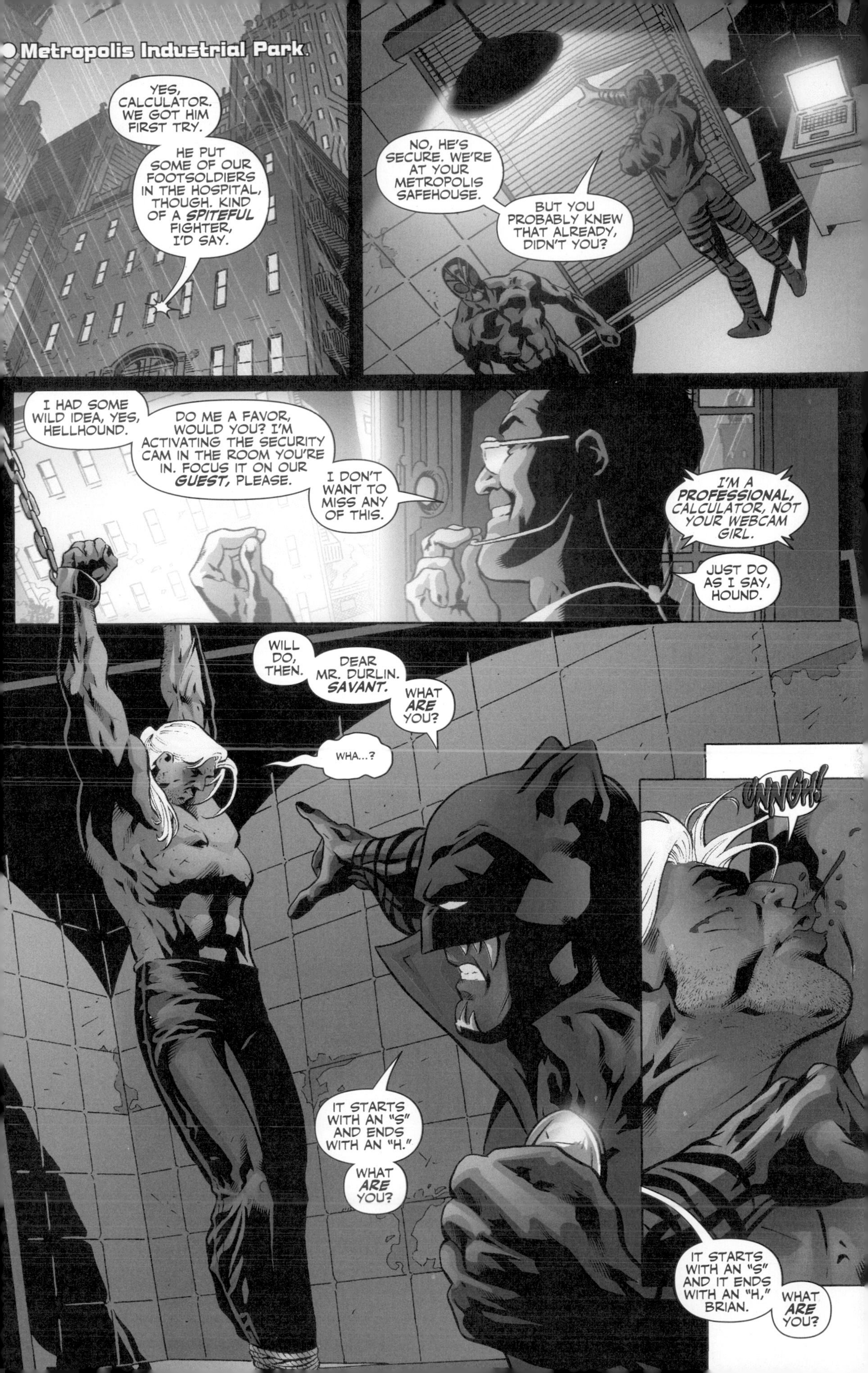
Metropolis Industrial Park.
YES, CALCULATOR. WE GOT HIM FIRST TRY.
HE PUT SOME OF OUR FOOTSOLDIERS IN THE HOSPITAL, THOUGH. KIND OF A *SPITEFUL* FIGHTER, I'D SAY.
NO, HE'S SECURE. WE'RE AT YOUR METROPOLIS SAFEHOUSE.
BUT YOU PROBABLY KNEW THAT ALREADY, DIDN'T YOU?
I HAD SOME WILD IDEA, YES, HELLHOUND.
DO ME A FAVOR, WOULD YOU? I'M ACTIVATING THE SECURITY CAM IN THE ROOM YOU'RE IN. FOCUS IT ON OUR *GUEST,* PLEASE.
I DON'T WANT TO MISS ANY OF THIS.
I'M A *PROFESSIONAL,* CALCULATOR, NOT YOUR WEBCAM GIRL.
JUST DO AS I SAY, HOUND.
WILL DO, THEN.
DEAR MR. DURLIN. *SAVANT.*
WHAT *ARE* YOU?
WHA...?
UNNGH!
IT STARTS WITH AN "S" AND ENDS WITH AN "H."
WHAT *ARE* YOU?
IT STARTS WITH AN "S" AND IT ENDS WITH AN "H," BRIAN.
WHAT *ARE* YOU?

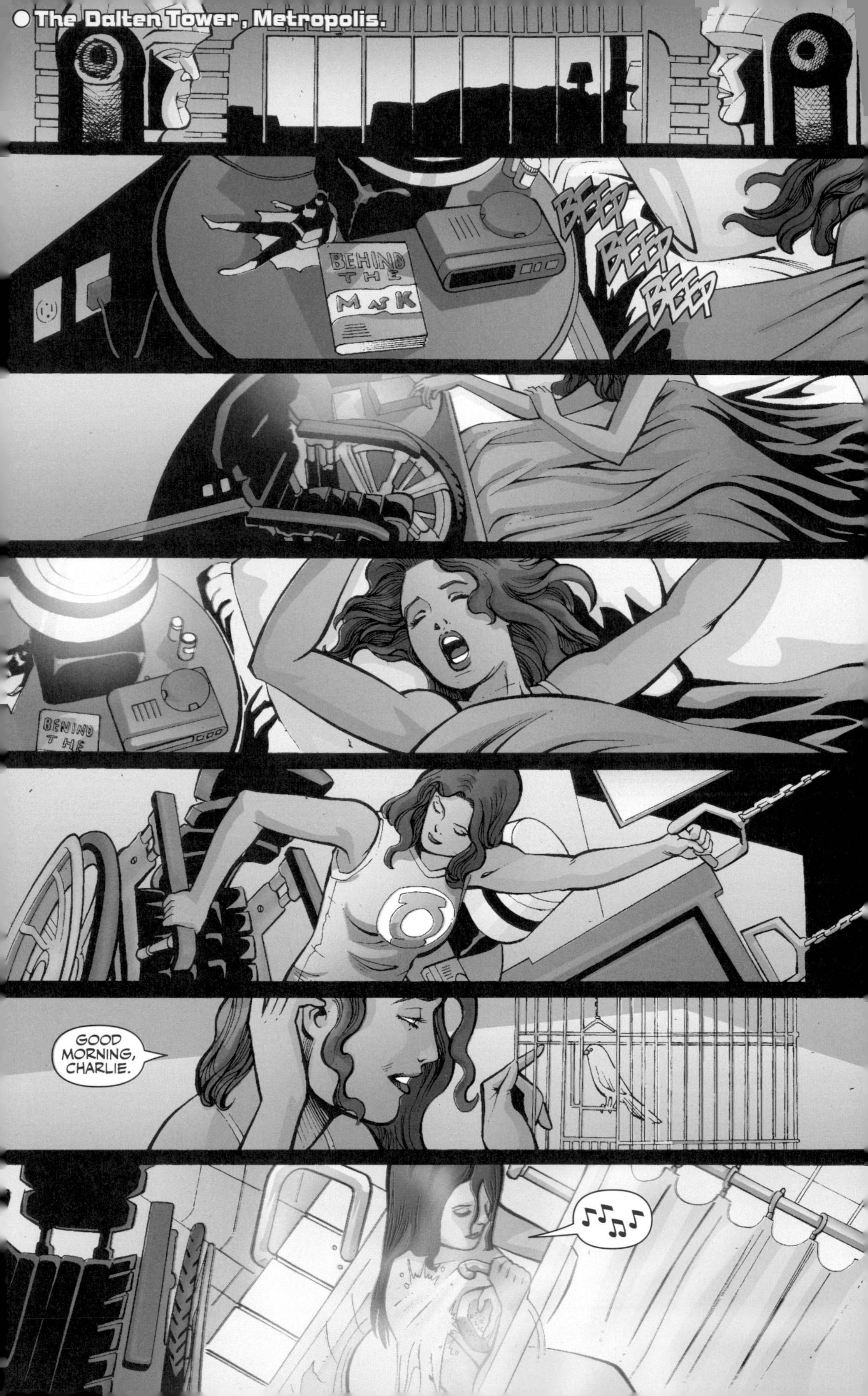
The Dalten Tower, Metropolis.
BEHIND THE MASK
BEEP BEEP BEEP
BEHIND THE
GOOD MORNING, CHARLIE.
♪♫♪

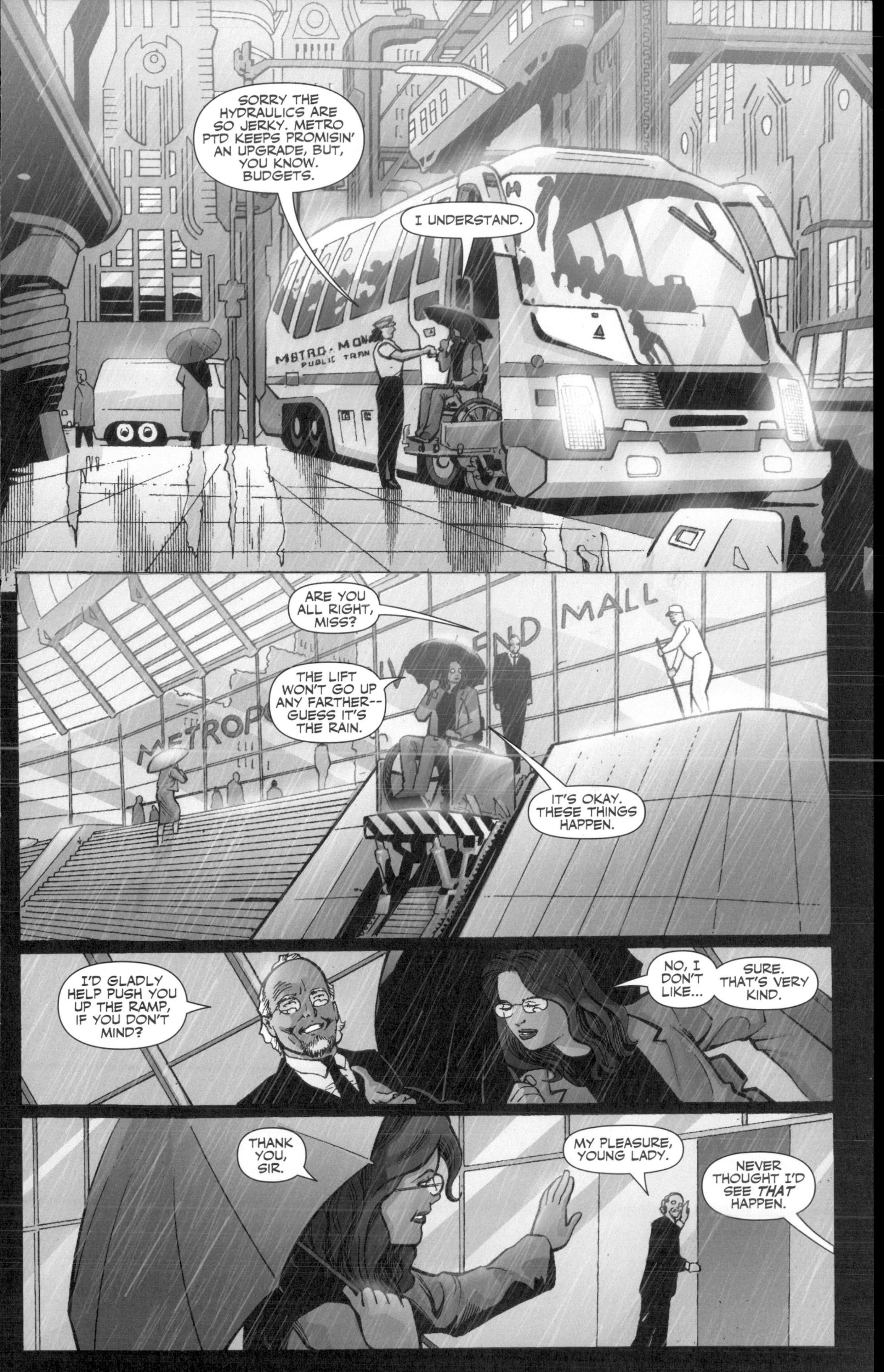
SORRY THE HYDRAULICS ARE SO JERKY. METRO PTD KEEPS PROMISIN' AN UPGRADE, BUT, YOU KNOW. BUDGETS.
I UNDERSTAND.
METRO-MON
PUBLIC TRAN
ARE YOU ALL RIGHT, MISS?
THE LIFT WON'T GO UP ANY FARTHER-- GUESS IT'S THE RAIN.
IT'S OKAY. THESE THINGS HAPPEN.
METROP
ND MALL
I'D GLADLY HELP PUSH YOU UP THE RAMP, IF YOU DON'T MIND?
NO, I DON'T LIKE...
SURE. THAT'S VERY KIND.
THANK YOU, SIR.
MY PLEASURE, YOUNG LADY.
NEVER THOUGHT I'D SEE *THAT* HAPPEN.

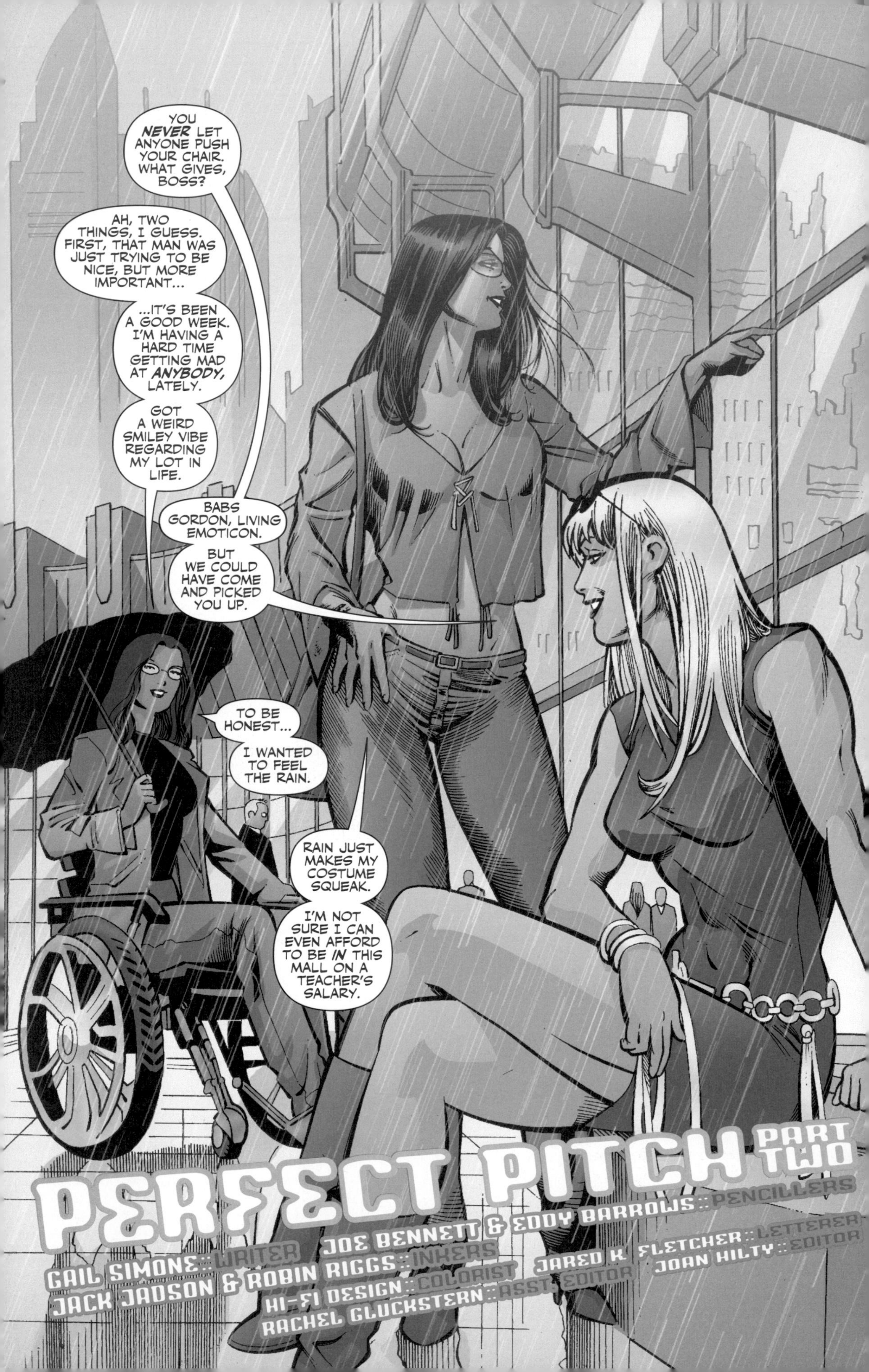
YOU NEVER LET ANYONE PUSH YOUR CHAIR. WHAT GIVES, BOSS?
AH, TWO THINGS, I GUESS. FIRST, THAT MAN WAS JUST TRYING TO BE NICE, BUT MORE IMPORTANT...
...IT'S BEEN A GOOD WEEK. I'M HAVING A HARD TIME GETTING MAD AT ANYBODY, LATELY.
GOT A WEIRD SMILEY VIBE REGARDING MY LOT IN LIFE.
BABS GORDON, LIVING EMOTICON.
BUT WE COULD HAVE COME AND PICKED YOU UP.
TO BE HONEST...
I WANTED TO FEEL THE RAIN.
RAIN JUST MAKES MY COSTUME SQUEAK.
I'M NOT SURE I CAN EVEN AFFORD TO BE IN THIS MALL ON A TEACHER'S SALARY.
PERFECT PITCH PART TWO
GAIL SIMONE::WRITER JOE BENNETT & EDDY BARROWS::PENCILLERS
JACK JADSON & ROBIN RIGGS::INKERS
HI-FI DESIGN::COLORIST JARED K. FLETCHER::LETTERER
RACHEL GLUCKSTERN::ASST. EDITOR JOAN HILTY::EDITOR

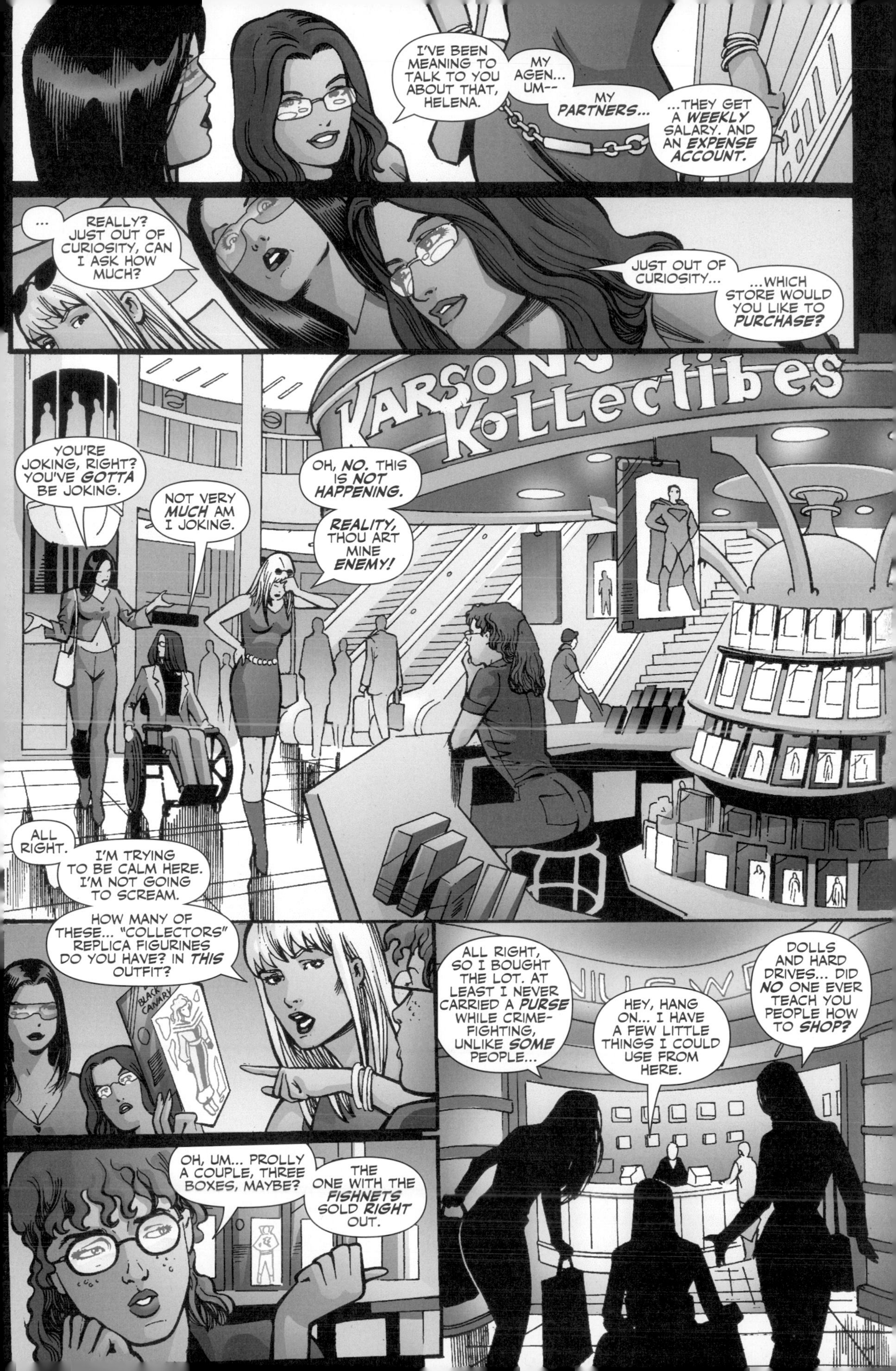

I'VE BEEN MEANING TO TALK TO YOU ABOUT THAT, HELENA.
MY AGEN... UM--
MY PARTNERS...
...THEY GET A WEEKLY SALARY. AND AN EXPENSE ACCOUNT.
...
REALLY? JUST OUT OF CURIOSITY, CAN I ASK HOW MUCH?
JUST OUT OF CURIOSITY...
...WHICH STORE WOULD YOU LIKE TO PURCHASE?
KARSON'S KOLLECTIBES
YOU'RE JOKING, RIGHT? YOU'VE GOTTA BE JOKING.
NOT VERY MUCH AM I JOKING.
OH, NO. THIS IS NOT HAPPENING.
REALITY, THOU ART MINE ENEMY!
ALL RIGHT.
I'M TRYING TO BE CALM HERE. I'M NOT GOING TO SCREAM.
HOW MANY OF THESE... "COLLECTORS" REPLICA FIGURINES DO YOU HAVE? IN THIS OUTFIT?
BLACK CANARY
OH, UM... PROLLY A COUPLE, THREE BOXES, MAYBE?
THE ONE WITH THE FISHNETS SOLD RIGHT OUT.
ALL RIGHT, SO I BOUGHT THE LOT. AT LEAST I NEVER CARRIED A PURSE WHILE CRIME-FIGHTING, UNLIKE SOME PEOPLE...
HEY, HANG ON... I HAVE A FEW LITTLE THINGS I COULD USE FROM HERE.
DOLLS AND HARD DRIVES... DID NO ONE EVER TEACH YOU PEOPLE HOW TO SHOP?

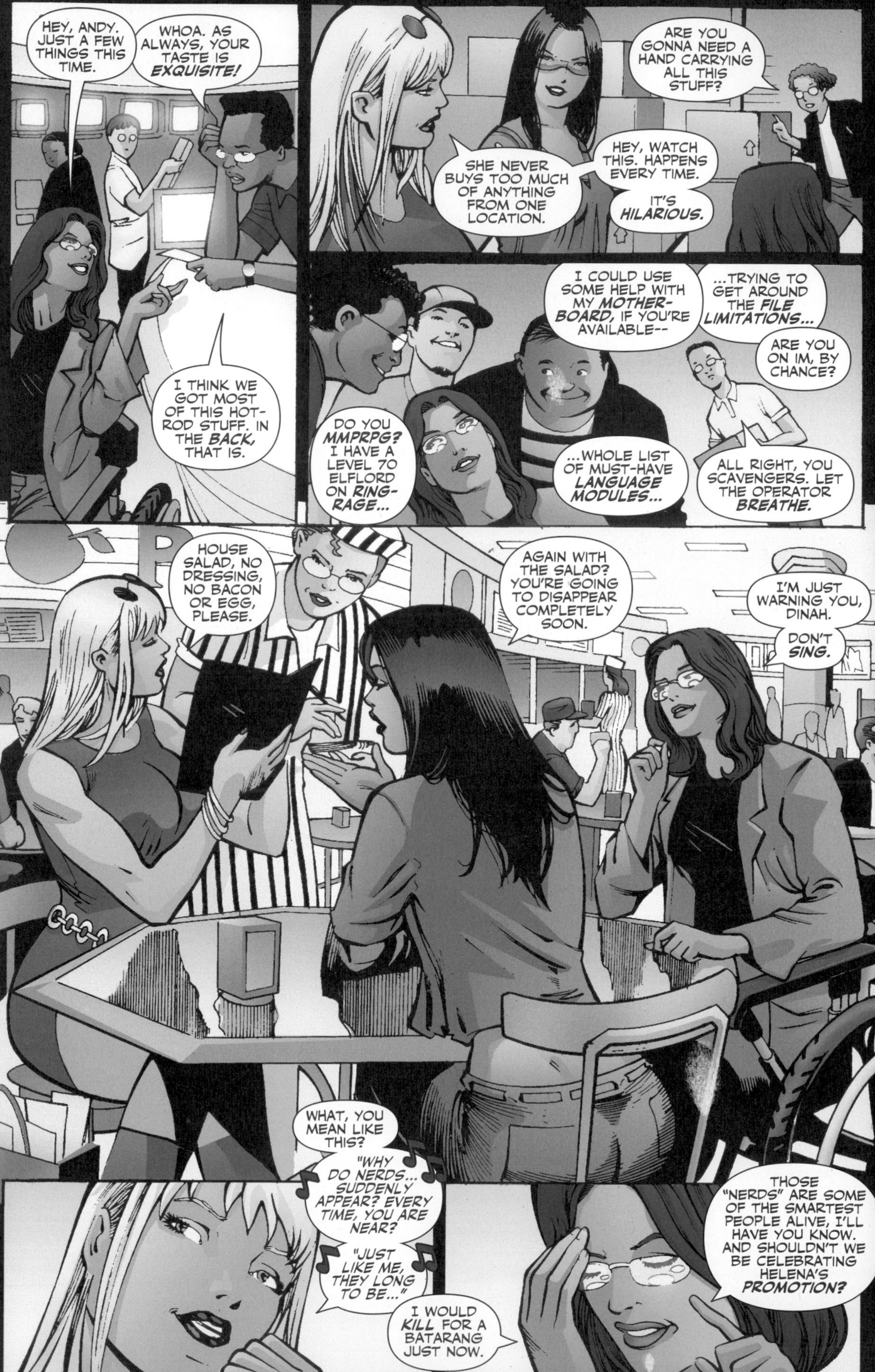
HEY, ANDY. JUST A FEW THINGS THIS TIME.
WHOA. AS ALWAYS, YOUR TASTE IS *EXQUISITE!*
I THINK WE GOT MOST OF THIS HOT-ROD STUFF. IN THE *BACK,* THAT IS.
ARE YOU GONNA NEED A HAND CARRYING ALL THIS STUFF?
SHE NEVER BUYS TOO MUCH OF ANYTHING FROM ONE LOCATION.
HEY, WATCH THIS. HAPPENS EVERY TIME.
IT'S *HILARIOUS.*
I COULD USE SOME HELP WITH MY *MOTHER-BOARD,* IF YOU'RE AVAILABLE--
...TRYING TO GET AROUND THE *FILE LIMITATIONS...*
ARE YOU ON IM, BY CHANCE?
DO YOU *MMPRPG?* I HAVE A LEVEL 70 ELFLORD ON *RING-RAGE...*
...WHOLE LIST OF MUST-HAVE *LANGUAGE MODULES...*
ALL RIGHT, YOU SCAVENGERS. LET THE OPERATOR *BREATHE.*
HOUSE SALAD, NO DRESSING, NO BACON OR EGG, PLEASE.
AGAIN WITH THE SALAD? YOU'RE GOING TO DISAPPEAR COMPLETELY SOON.
I'M JUST WARNING YOU, DINAH.
DON'T *SING.*
WHAT, YOU MEAN LIKE THIS?
"WHY DO NERDS... SUDDENLY APPEAR? EVERY TIME, YOU ARE NEAR?
"JUST LIKE ME, THEY LONG TO BE..."
I WOULD *KILL* FOR A BATARANG JUST NOW.
THOSE "NERDS" ARE SOME OF THE SMARTEST PEOPLE ALIVE, I'LL HAVE YOU KNOW. AND SHOULDN'T WE BE CELEBRATING HELENA'S *PROMOTION?*

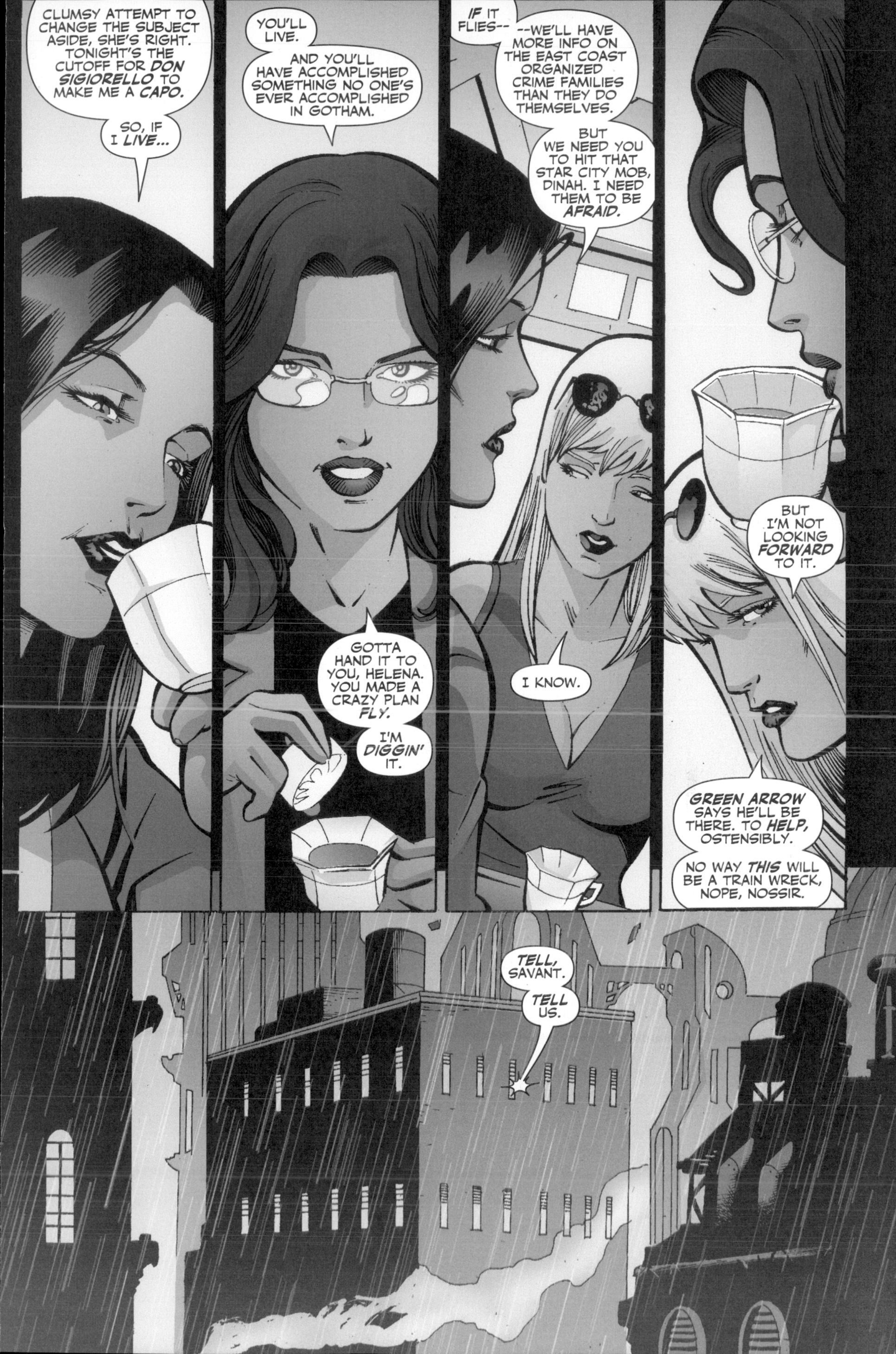

CLUMSY ATTEMPT TO CHANGE THE SUBJECT ASIDE, SHE'S RIGHT. TONIGHT'S THE CUTOFF FOR DON SIGIORELLO TO MAKE ME A CAPO.
SO, IF I LIVE...
YOU'LL LIVE.
AND YOU'LL HAVE ACCOMPLISHED SOMETHING NO ONE'S EVER ACCOMPLISHED IN GOTHAM.
GOTTA HAND IT TO YOU, HELENA. YOU MADE A CRAZY PLAN FLY.
I'M DIGGIN' IT.
IF IT FLIES--
--WE'LL HAVE MORE INFO ON THE EAST COAST ORGANIZED CRIME FAMILIES THAN THEY DO THEMSELVES.
BUT WE NEED YOU TO HIT THAT STAR CITY MOB, DINAH. I NEED THEM TO BE AFRAID.
I KNOW.
BUT I'M NOT LOOKING FORWARD TO IT.
GREEN ARROW SAYS HE'LL BE THERE. TO HELP, OSTENSIBLY.
NO WAY THIS WILL BE A TRAIN WRECK, NOPE, NOSSIR.
TELL, SAVANT.
TELL US.

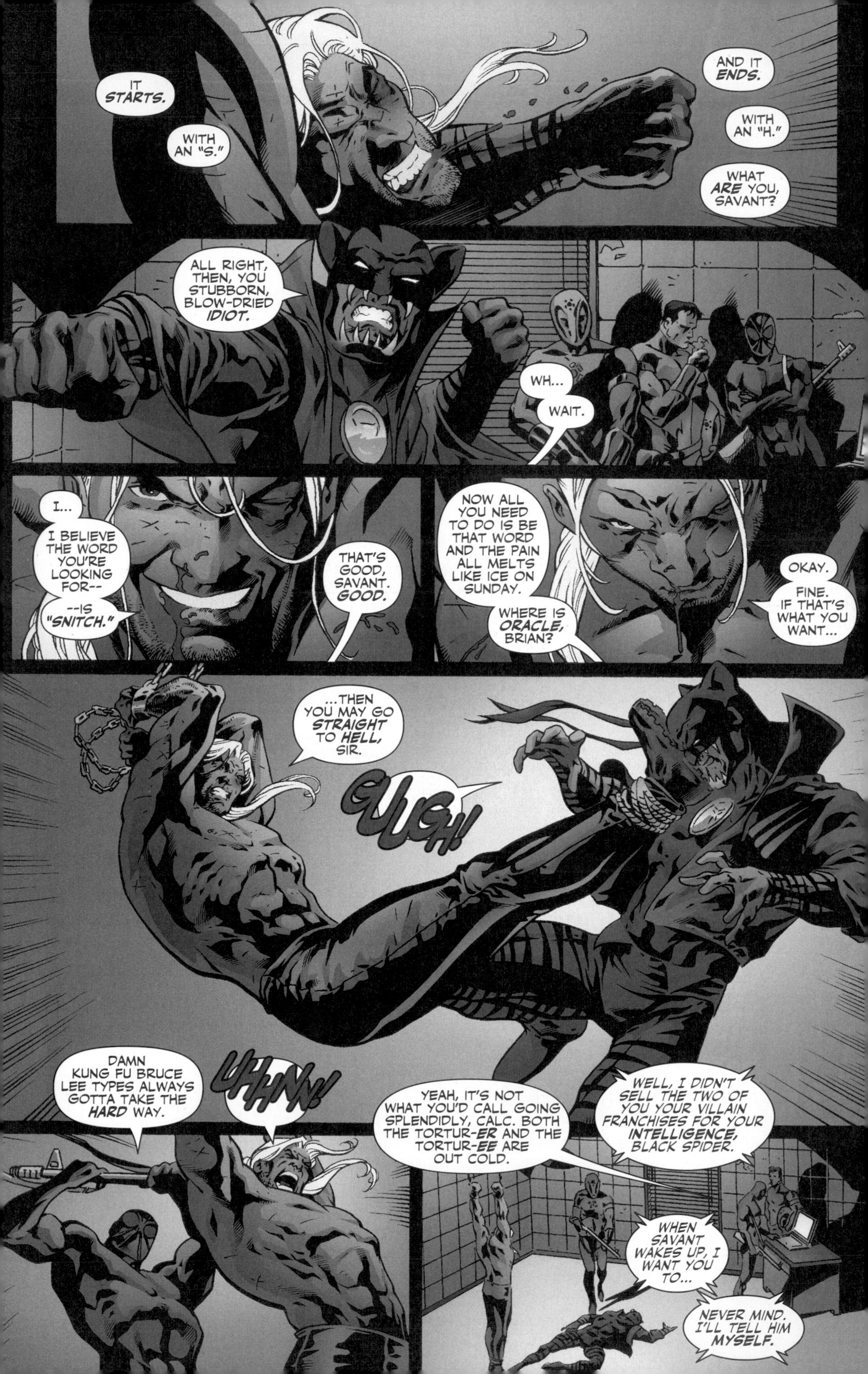
IT STARTS.
WITH AN "S."
AND IT ENDS.
WITH AN "H."
WHAT ARE YOU, SAVANT?
ALL RIGHT, THEN, YOU STUBBORN, BLOW-DRIED IDIOT.
WH...
WAIT.
I...
I BELIEVE THE WORD YOU'RE LOOKING FOR--
--IS "SNITCH."
THAT'S GOOD, SAVANT. GOOD.
NOW ALL YOU NEED TO DO IS BE THAT WORD AND THE PAIN ALL MELTS LIKE ICE ON SUNDAY.
WHERE IS ORACLE, BRIAN?
OKAY.
FINE. IF THAT'S WHAT YOU WANT...
...THEN YOU MAY GO STRAIGHT TO HELL, SIR.
GUUGH!
DAMN KUNG FU BRUCE LEE TYPES ALWAYS GOTTA TAKE THE HARD WAY.
UHHNN!
YEAH, IT'S NOT WHAT YOU'D CALL GOING SPLENDIDLY, CALC. BOTH THE TORTUR-ER AND THE TORTUR-EE ARE OUT COLD.
WELL, I DIDN'T SELL THE TWO OF YOU YOUR VILLAIN FRANCHISES FOR YOUR INTELLIGENCE, BLACK SPIDER.
WHEN SAVANT WAKES UP, I WANT YOU TO...
NEVER MIND. I'LL TELL HIM MYSELF.

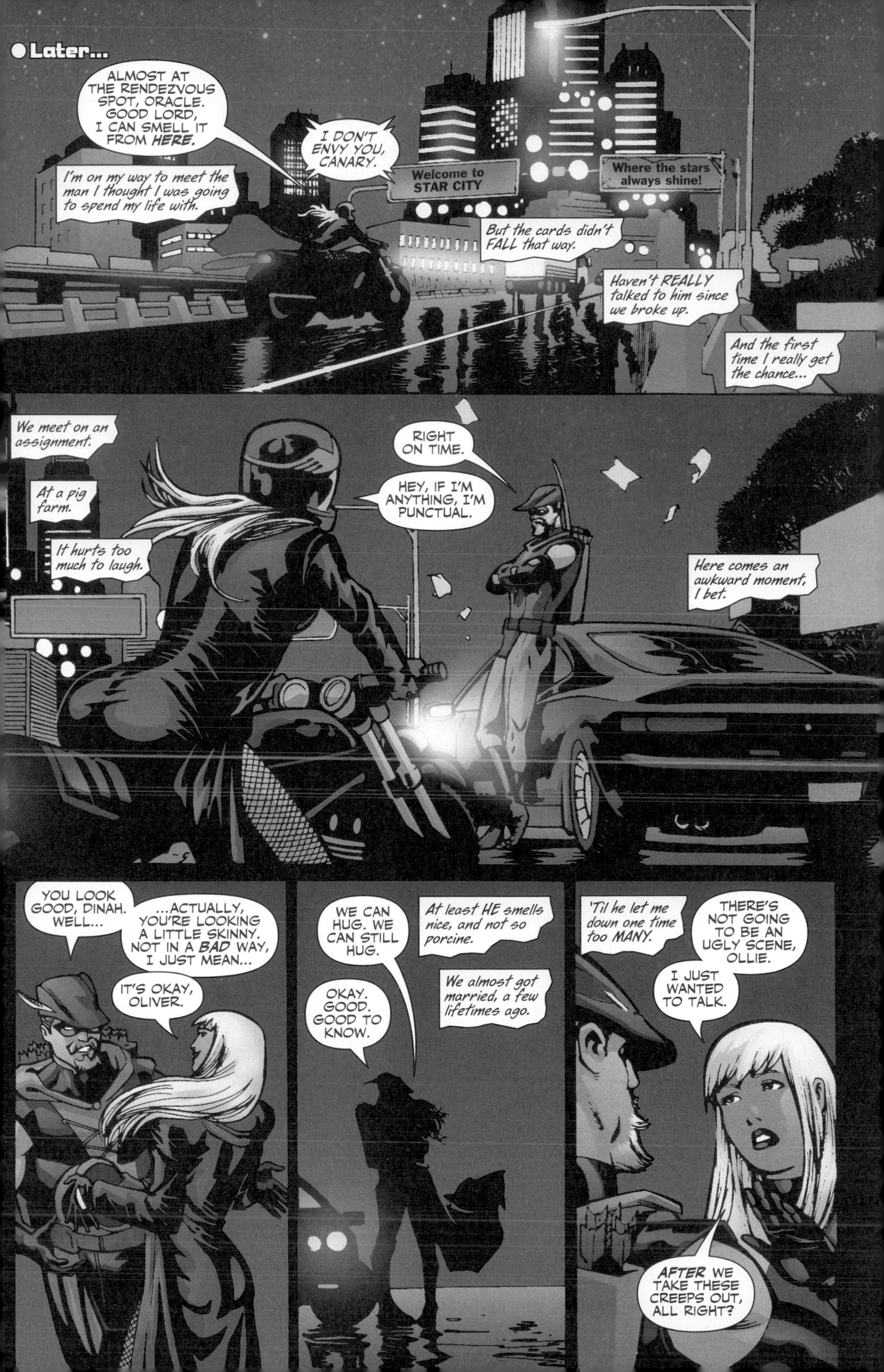
Later...
ALMOST AT THE RENDEZVOUS SPOT, ORACLE. GOOD LORD, I CAN SMELL IT FROM HERE.
I DON'T ENVY YOU, CANARY.
I'm on my way to meet the man I thought I was going to spend my life with.
Welcome to STAR CITY
Where the stars always shine!
But the cards didn't FALL that way.
Haven't REALLY talked to him since we broke up.
And the first time I really get the chance...
We meet on an assignment.
At a pig farm.
It hurts too much to laugh.
RIGHT ON TIME.
HEY, IF I'M ANYTHING, I'M PUNCTUAL.
Here comes an awkward moment, I bet.
YOU LOOK GOOD, DINAH. WELL...
...ACTUALLY, YOU'RE LOOKING A LITTLE SKINNY. NOT IN A BAD WAY, I JUST MEAN...
IT'S OKAY, OLIVER.
WE CAN HUG. WE CAN STILL HUG.
At least HE smells nice, and not so porcine.
We almost got married, a few lifetimes ago.
OKAY. GOOD. GOOD TO KNOW.
'Til he let me down one time too MANY.
THERE'S NOT GOING TO BE AN UGLY SCENE, OLLIE.
I JUST WANTED TO TALK.
AFTER WE TAKE THESE CREEPS OUT, ALL RIGHT?

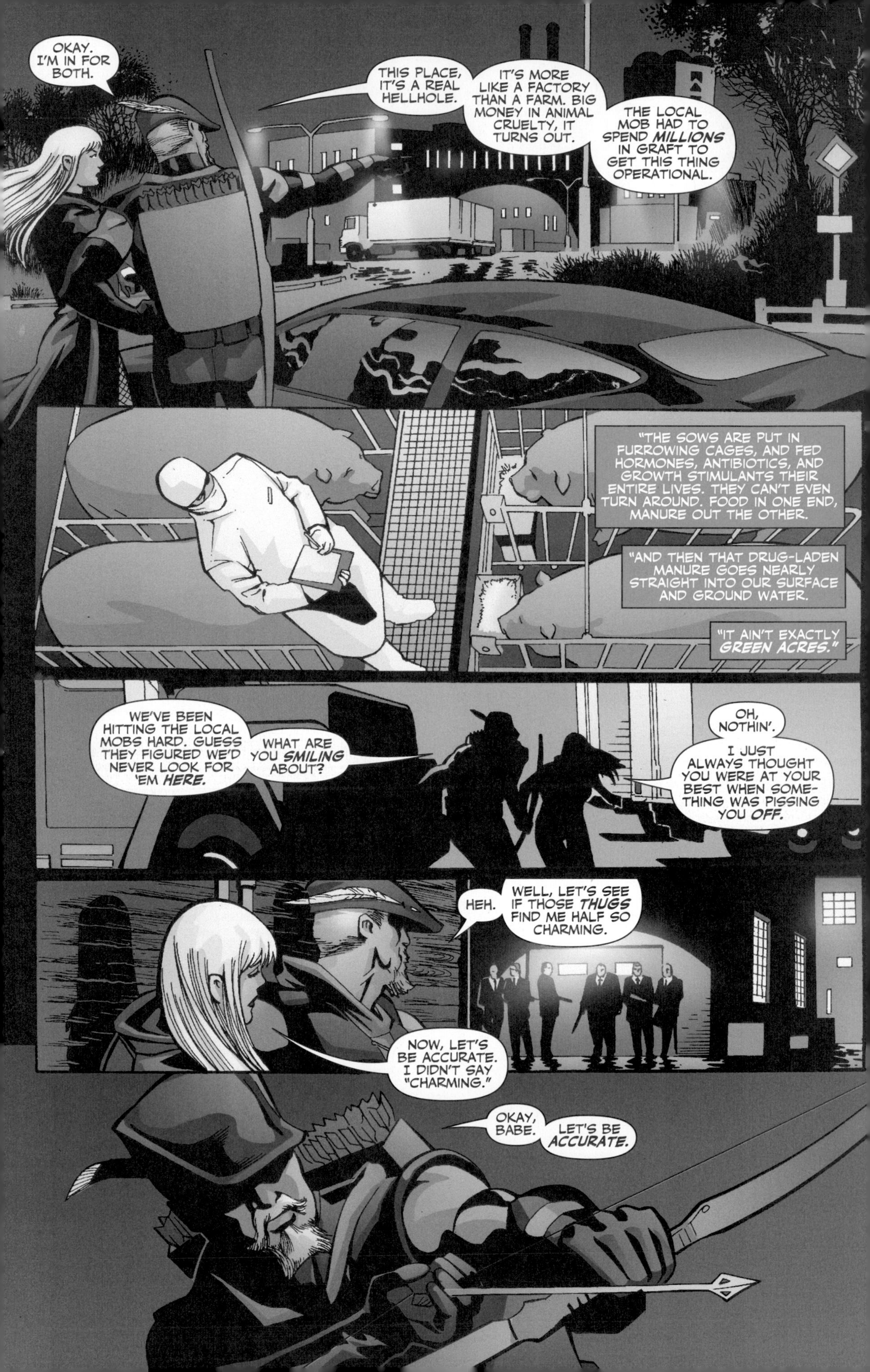
OKAY. I'M IN FOR BOTH.
THIS PLACE, IT'S A REAL HELLHOLE.
IT'S MORE LIKE A FACTORY THAN A FARM. BIG MONEY IN ANIMAL CRUELTY, IT TURNS OUT.
THE LOCAL MOB HAD TO SPEND MILLIONS IN GRAFT TO GET THIS THING OPERATIONAL.
"THE SOWS ARE PUT IN FURROWING CAGES, AND FED HORMONES, ANTIBIOTICS, AND GROWTH STIMULANTS THEIR ENTIRE LIVES. THEY CAN'T EVEN TURN AROUND. FOOD IN ONE END, MANURE OUT THE OTHER.
"AND THEN THAT DRUG-LADEN MANURE GOES NEARLY STRAIGHT INTO OUR SURFACE AND GROUND WATER.
"IT AIN'T EXACTLY GREEN ACRES."
WE'VE BEEN HITTING THE LOCAL MOBS HARD. GUESS THEY FIGURED WE'D NEVER LOOK FOR 'EM HERE.
WHAT ARE YOU SMILING ABOUT?
OH, NOTHIN'.
I JUST ALWAYS THOUGHT YOU WERE AT YOUR BEST WHEN SOME-THING WAS PISSING YOU OFF.
HEH.
WELL, LET'S SEE IF THOSE THUGS FIND ME HALF SO CHARMING.
NOW, LET'S BE ACCURATE. I DIDN'T SAY "CHARMING."
OKAY, BABE.
LET'S BE ACCURATE.

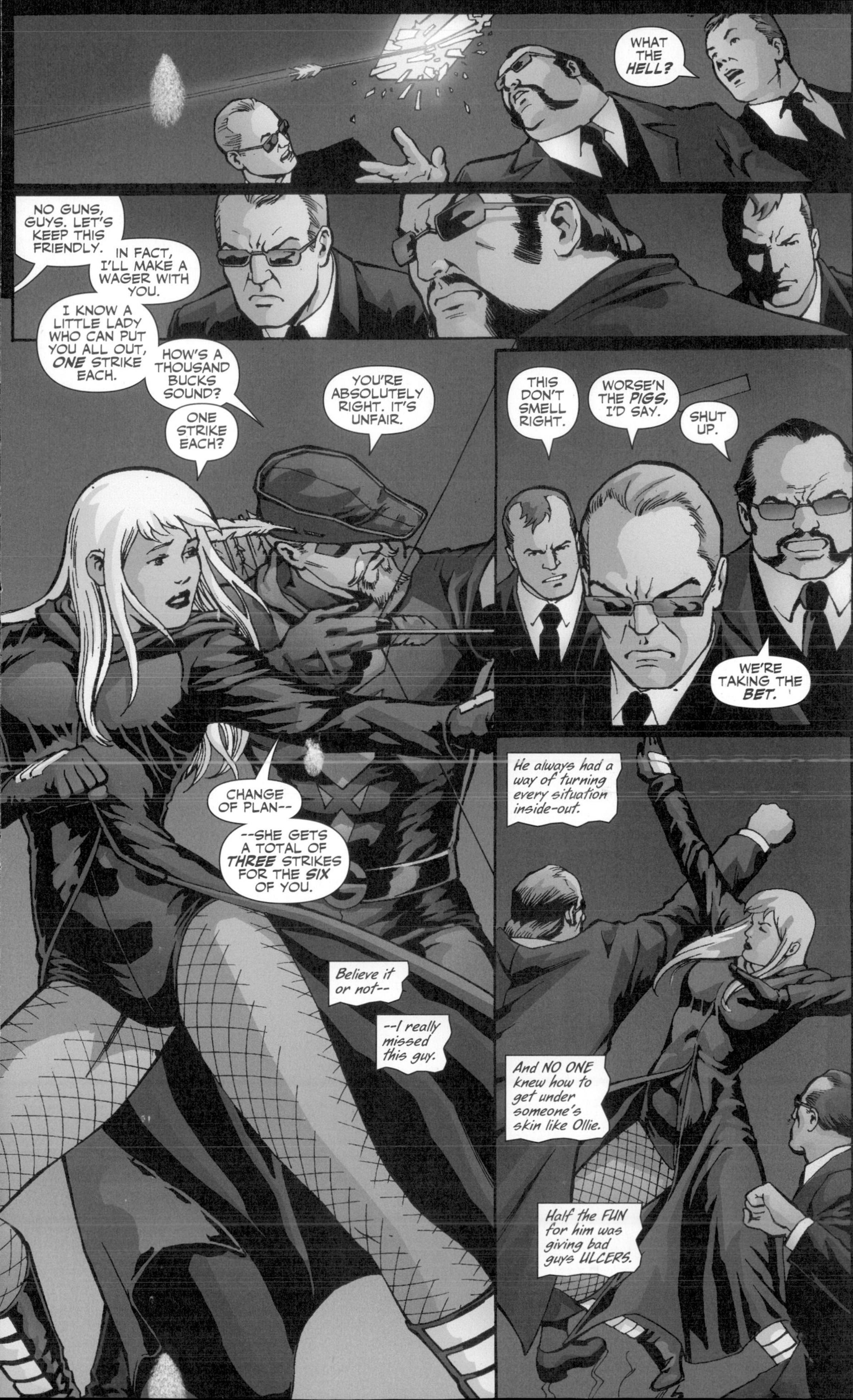
WHAT THE HELL?
NO GUNS, GUYS. LET'S KEEP THIS FRIENDLY.
IN FACT, I'LL MAKE A WAGER WITH YOU.
I KNOW A LITTLE LADY WHO CAN PUT YOU ALL OUT, ONE STRIKE EACH.
HOW'S A THOUSAND BUCKS SOUND?
ONE STRIKE EACH?
YOU'RE ABSOLUTELY RIGHT. IT'S UNFAIR.
THIS DON'T SMELL RIGHT.
WORSE'N THE PIGS, I'D SAY.
SHUT UP.
WE'RE TAKING THE BET.
CHANGE OF PLAN--
--SHE GETS A TOTAL OF THREE STRIKES FOR THE SIX OF YOU.
Believe it or not--
--I really missed this guy.
He always had a way of turning every situation inside-out.
And NO ONE knew how to get under someone's skin like Ollie.
Half the FUN for him was giving bad guys ULCERS.

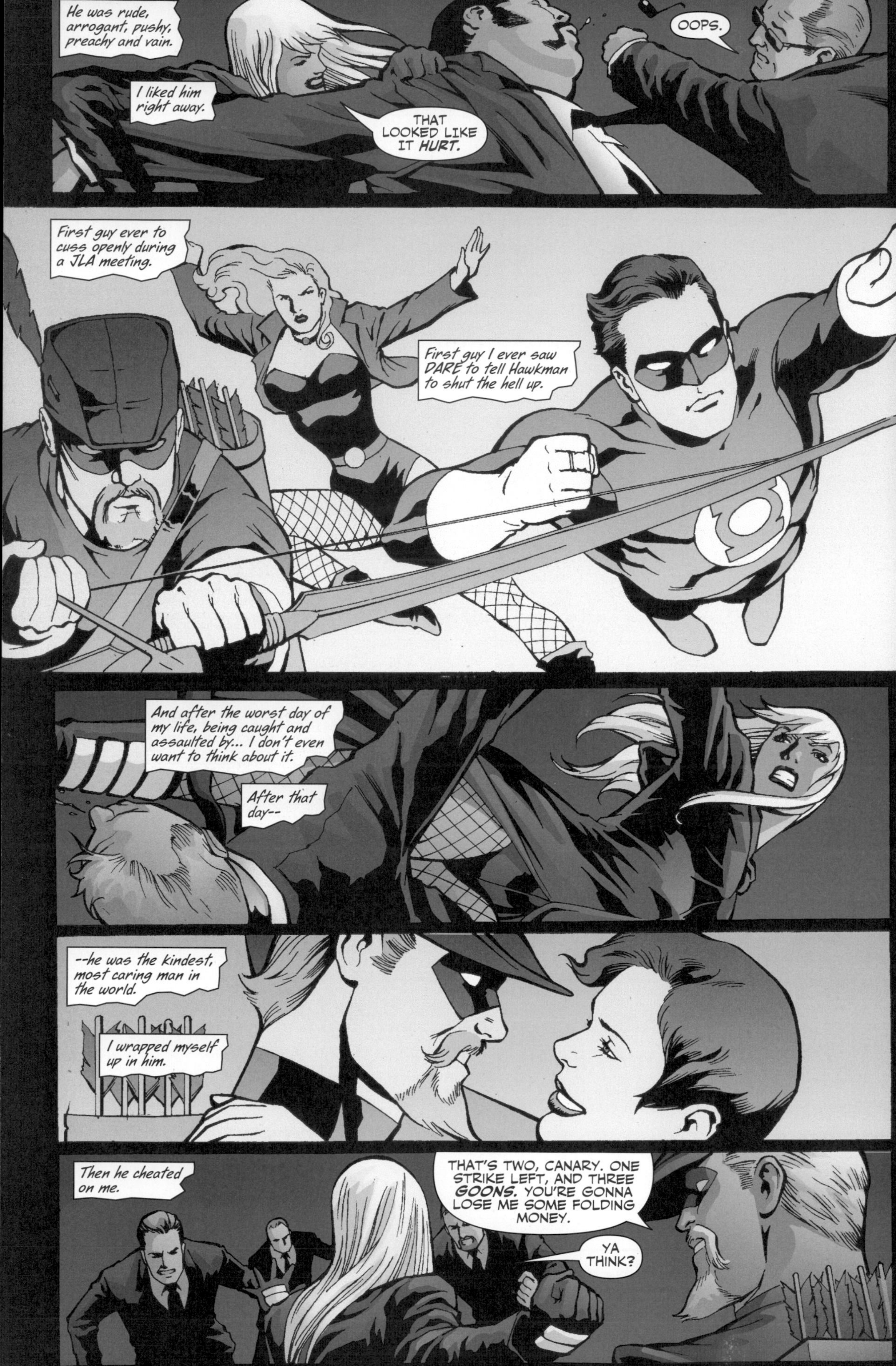
He was rude, arrogant, pushy, preachy and vain.
I liked him right away.
THAT LOOKED LIKE IT HURT.
OOPS.
First guy ever to cuss openly during a JLA meeting.
First guy I ever saw DARE to tell Hawkman to shut the hell up.
And after the worst day of my life, being caught and assaulted by... I don't even want to think about it.
After that day--
--he was the kindest, most caring man in the world.
I wrapped myself up in him.
Then he cheated on me.
THAT'S TWO, CANARY. ONE STRIKE LEFT, AND THREE GOONS. YOU'RE GONNA LOSE ME SOME FOLDING MONEY.
YA THINK?

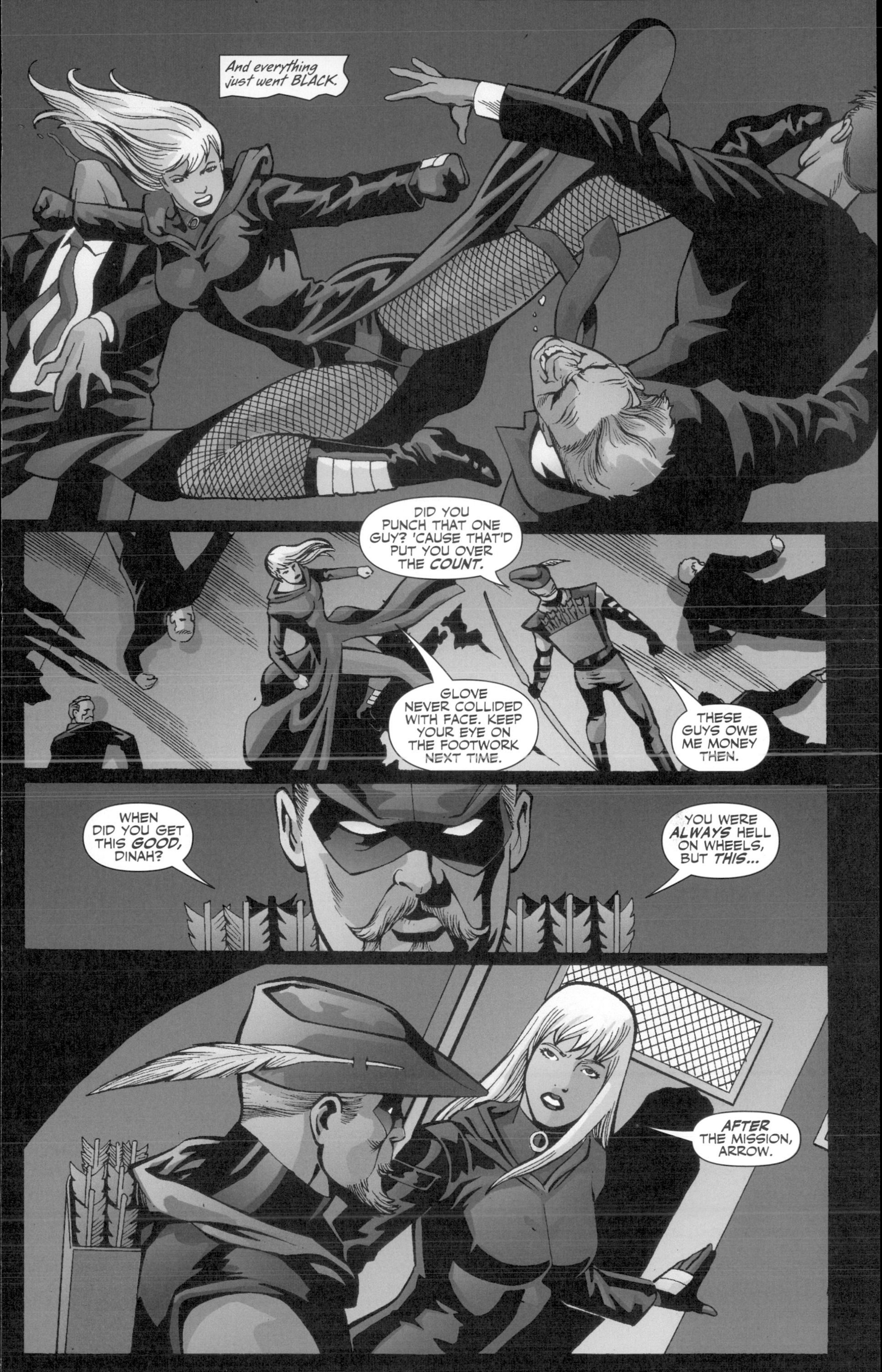

And everything just went BLACK.
DID YOU PUNCH THAT ONE GUY? 'CAUSE THAT'D PUT YOU OVER THE COUNT.
GLOVE NEVER COLLIDED WITH FACE. KEEP YOUR EYE ON THE FOOTWORK NEXT TIME.
THESE GUYS OWE ME MONEY THEN.
WHEN DID YOU GET THIS GOOD, DINAH?
YOU WERE ALWAYS HELL ON WHEELS, BUT THIS...
AFTER THE MISSION, ARROW.

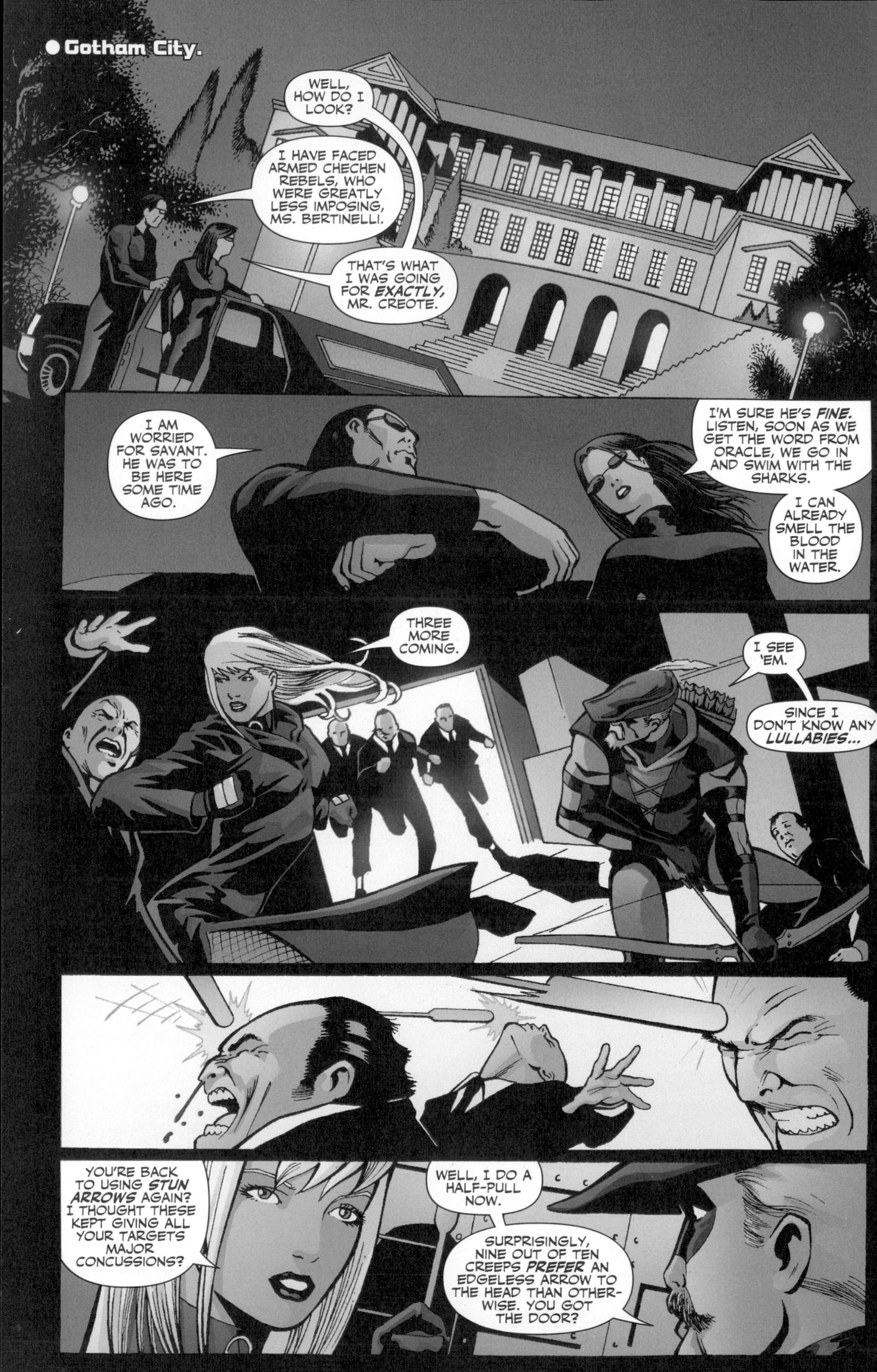
Gotham City.
WELL, HOW DO I LOOK?
I HAVE FACED ARMED CHECHEN REBELS, WHO WERE GREATLY LESS IMPOSING, MS. BERTINELLI.
THAT'S WHAT I WAS GOING FOR EXACTLY, MR. CREOTE.
I AM WORRIED FOR SAVANT. HE WAS TO BE HERE SOME TIME AGO.
I'M SURE HE'S FINE. LISTEN, SOON AS WE GET THE WORD FROM ORACLE, WE GO IN AND SWIM WITH THE SHARKS.
I CAN ALREADY SMELL THE BLOOD IN THE WATER.
THREE MORE COMING.
I SEE 'EM.
SINCE I DON'T KNOW ANY LULLABIES...
YOU'RE BACK TO USING STUN ARROWS AGAIN? I THOUGHT THESE KEPT GIVING ALL YOUR TARGETS MAJOR CONCUSSIONS?
WELL, I DO A HALF-PULL NOW.
SURPRISINGLY, NINE OUT OF TEN CREEPS PREFER AN EDGELESS ARROW TO THE HEAD THAN OTHER-WISE. YOU GOT THE DOOR?

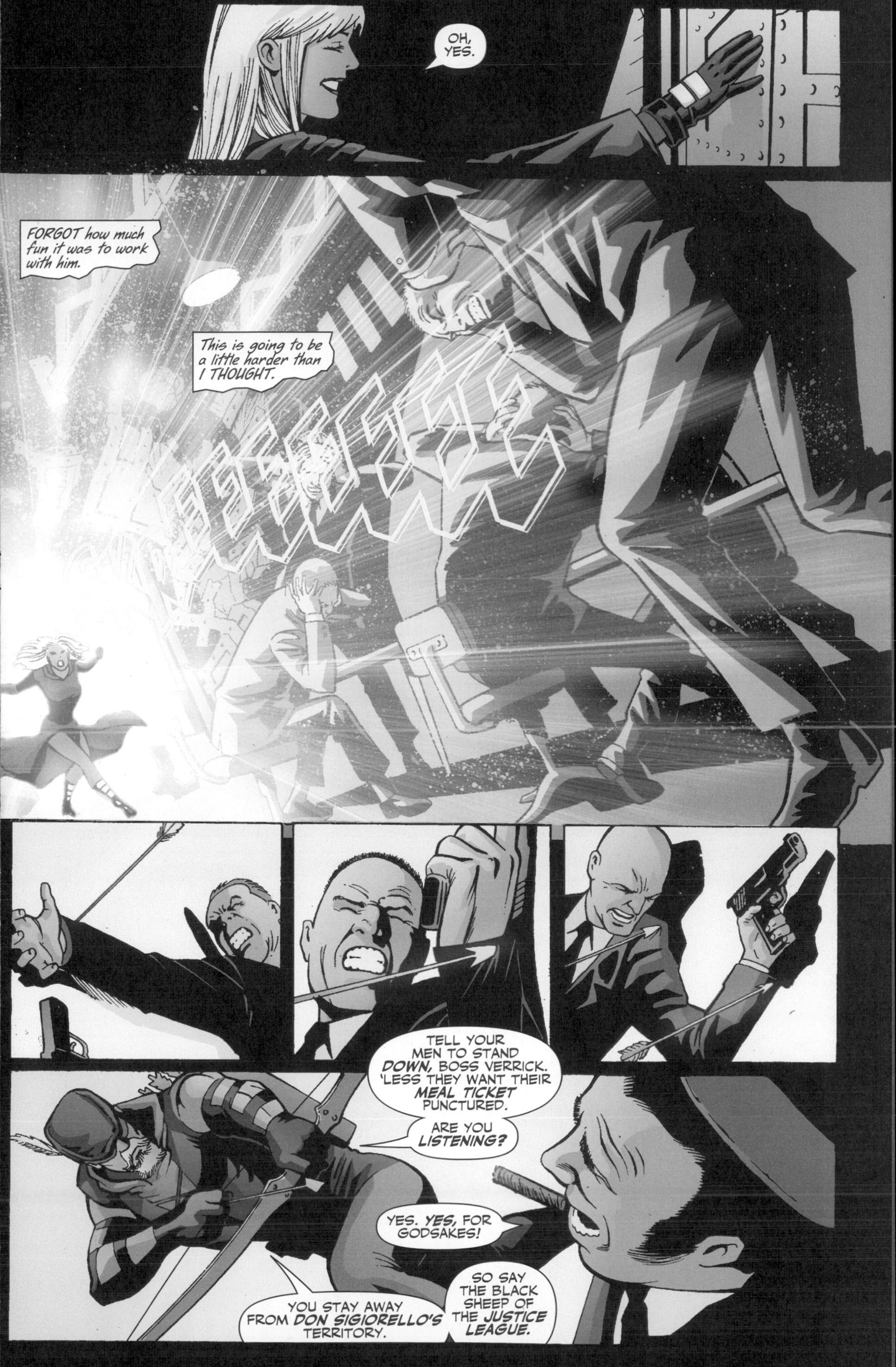
OH, YES.
FORGOT how much fun it was to work with him.
This is going to be a little harder than I THOUGHT.
TELL YOUR MEN TO STAND DOWN, BOSS VERRICK. 'LESS THEY WANT THEIR MEAL TICKET PUNCTURED.
ARE YOU LISTENING?
YES. YES, FOR GODSAKES!
YOU STAY AWAY FROM DON SIGIORELLO'S TERRITORY.
SO SAY THE BLACK SHEEP OF THE JUSTICE LEAGUE.

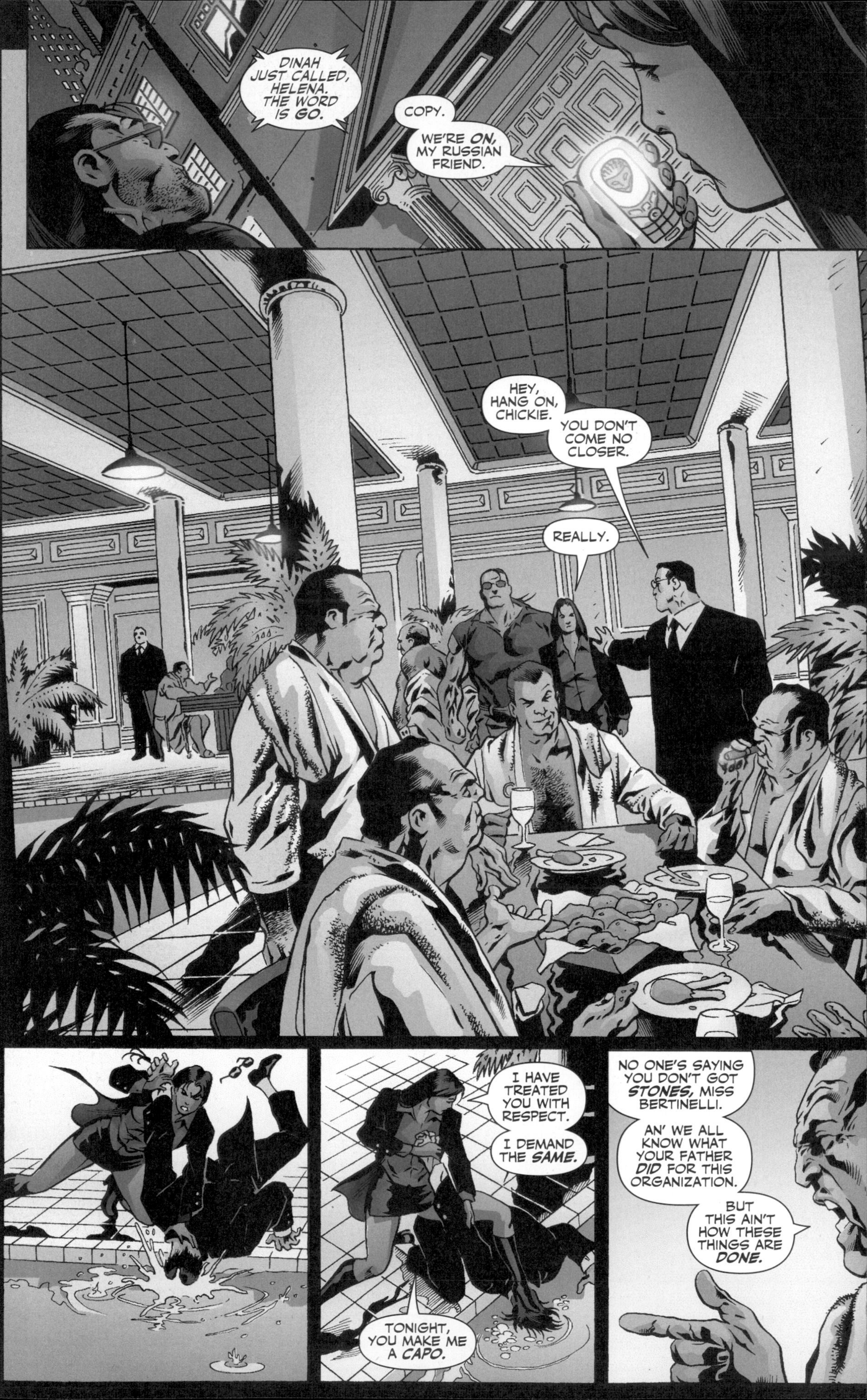
DINAH JUST CALLED, HELENA. THE WORD IS GO.
COPY.
WE'RE ON, MY RUSSIAN FRIEND.
HEY, HANG ON, CHICKIE.
YOU DON'T COME NO CLOSER.
REALLY.
I HAVE TREATED YOU WITH RESPECT.
I DEMAND THE SAME.
TONIGHT, YOU MAKE ME A CAPO.
NO ONE'S SAYING YOU DON'T GOT STONES, MISS BERTINELLI.
AN' WE ALL KNOW WHAT YOUR FATHER DID FOR THIS ORGANIZATION.
BUT THIS AIN'T HOW THESE THINGS ARE DONE.

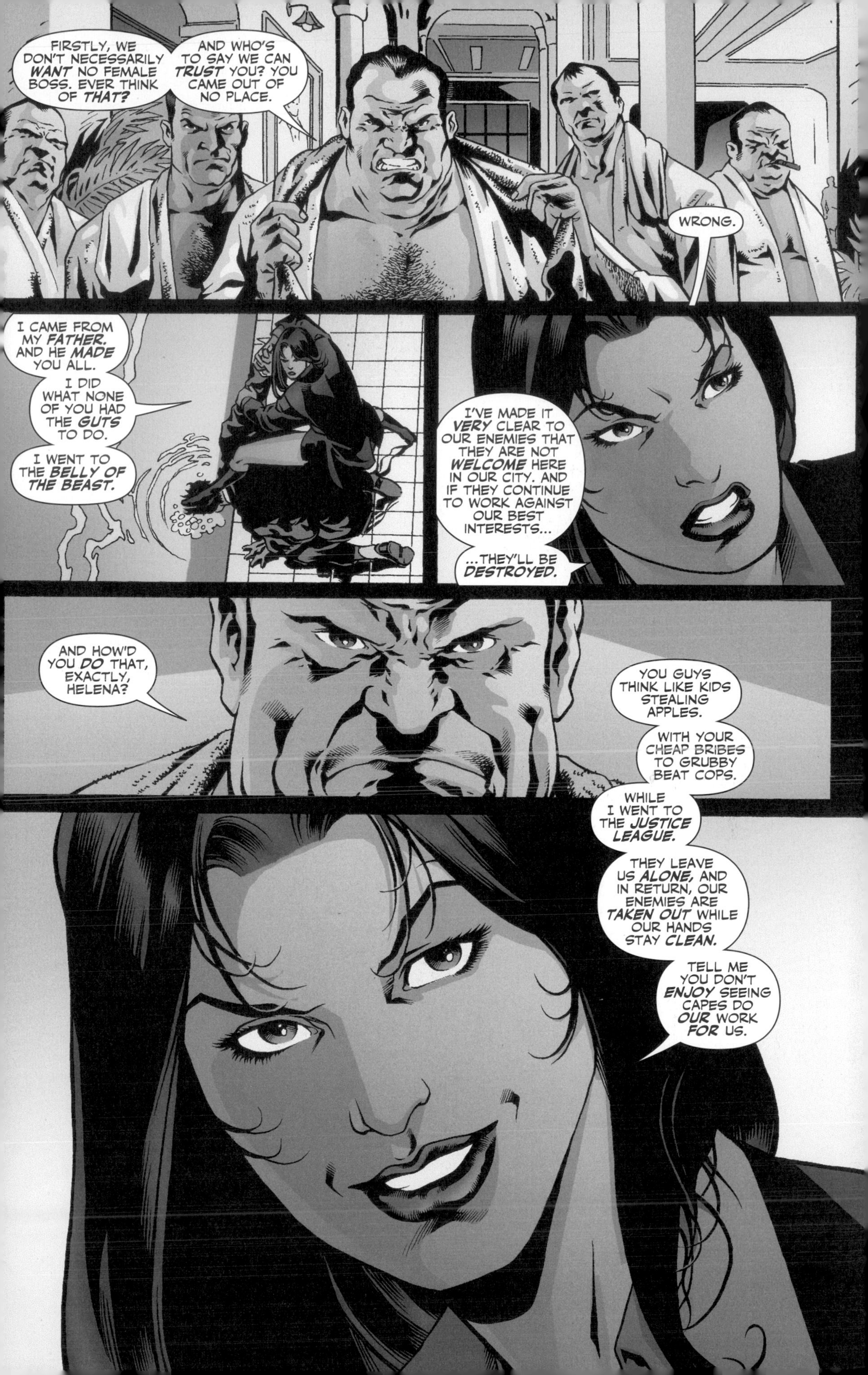
FIRSTLY, WE DON'T NECESSARILY WANT NO FEMALE BOSS. EVER THINK OF THAT?
AND WHO'S TO SAY WE CAN TRUST YOU? YOU CAME OUT OF NO PLACE.
WRONG.
I CAME FROM MY FATHER. AND HE MADE YOU ALL.
I DID WHAT NONE OF YOU HAD THE GUTS TO DO.
I WENT TO THE BELLY OF THE BEAST.
I'VE MADE IT VERY CLEAR TO OUR ENEMIES THAT THEY ARE NOT WELCOME HERE IN OUR CITY. AND IF THEY CONTINUE TO WORK AGAINST OUR BEST INTERESTS...
...THEY'LL BE DESTROYED.
AND HOW'D YOU DO THAT, EXACTLY, HELENA?
YOU GUYS THINK LIKE KIDS STEALING APPLES.
WITH YOUR CHEAP BRIBES TO GRUBBY BEAT COPS.
WHILE I WENT TO THE JUSTICE LEAGUE.
THEY LEAVE US ALONE, AND IN RETURN, OUR ENEMIES ARE TAKEN OUT WHILE OUR HANDS STAY CLEAN.
TELL ME YOU DON'T ENJOY SEEING CAPES DO OUR WORK FOR US.

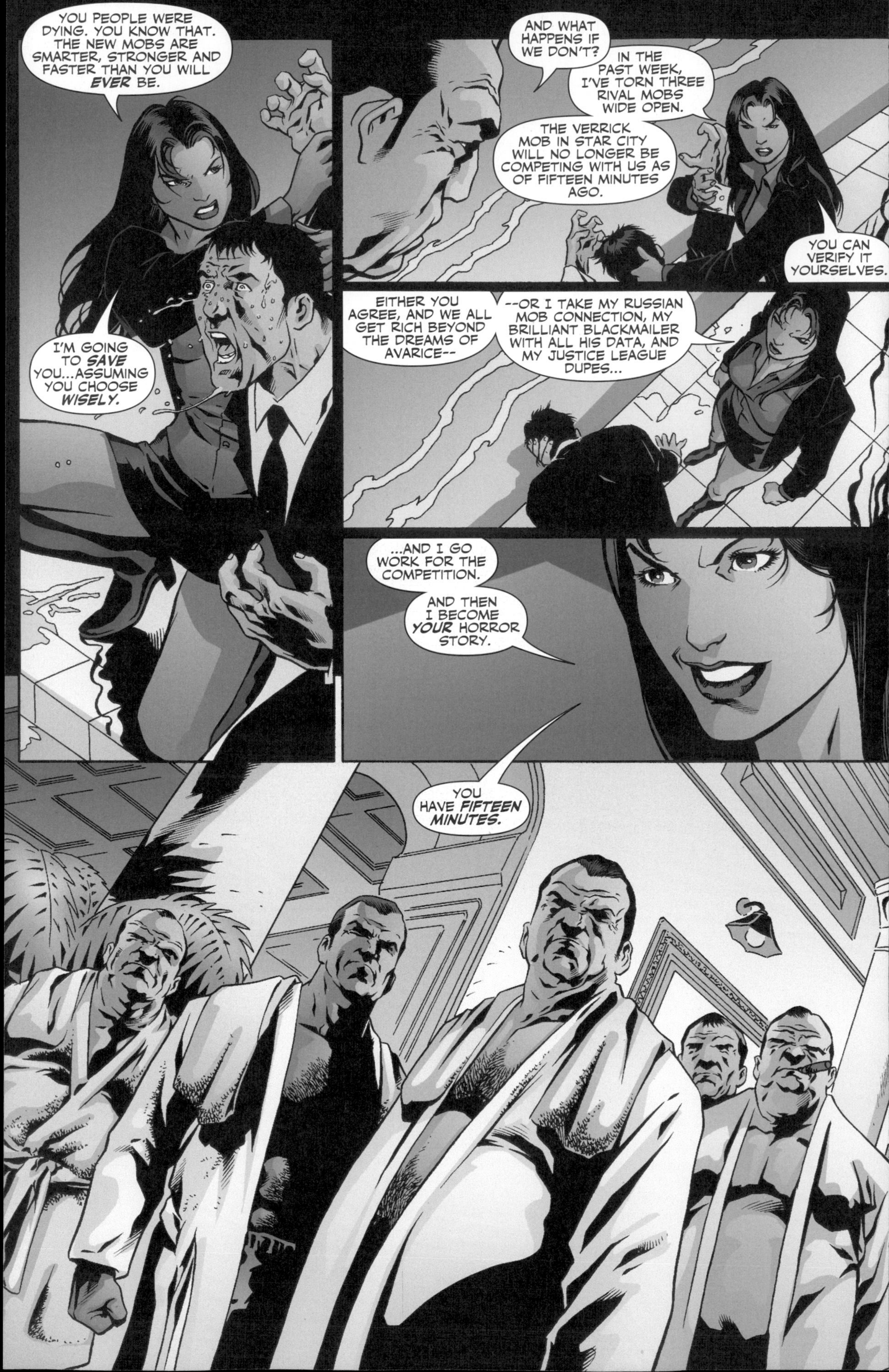
YOU PEOPLE WERE DYING. YOU KNOW THAT. THE NEW MOBS ARE SMARTER, STRONGER AND FASTER THAN YOU WILL EVER BE.
I'M GOING TO SAVE YOU...ASSUMING YOU CHOOSE WISELY.
AND WHAT HAPPENS IF WE DON'T?
IN THE PAST WEEK, I'VE TORN THREE RIVAL MOBS WIDE OPEN.
THE VERRICK MOB IN STAR CITY WILL NO LONGER BE COMPETING WITH US AS OF FIFTEEN MINUTES AGO.
YOU CAN VERIFY IT YOURSELVES.
EITHER YOU AGREE, AND WE ALL GET RICH BEYOND THE DREAMS OF AVARICE--
--OR I TAKE MY RUSSIAN MOB CONNECTION, MY BRILLIANT BLACKMAILER WITH ALL HIS DATA, AND MY JUSTICE LEAGUE DUPES...
...AND I GO WORK FOR THE COMPETITION.
AND THEN I BECOME YOUR HORROR STORY.
YOU HAVE FIFTEEN MINUTES.

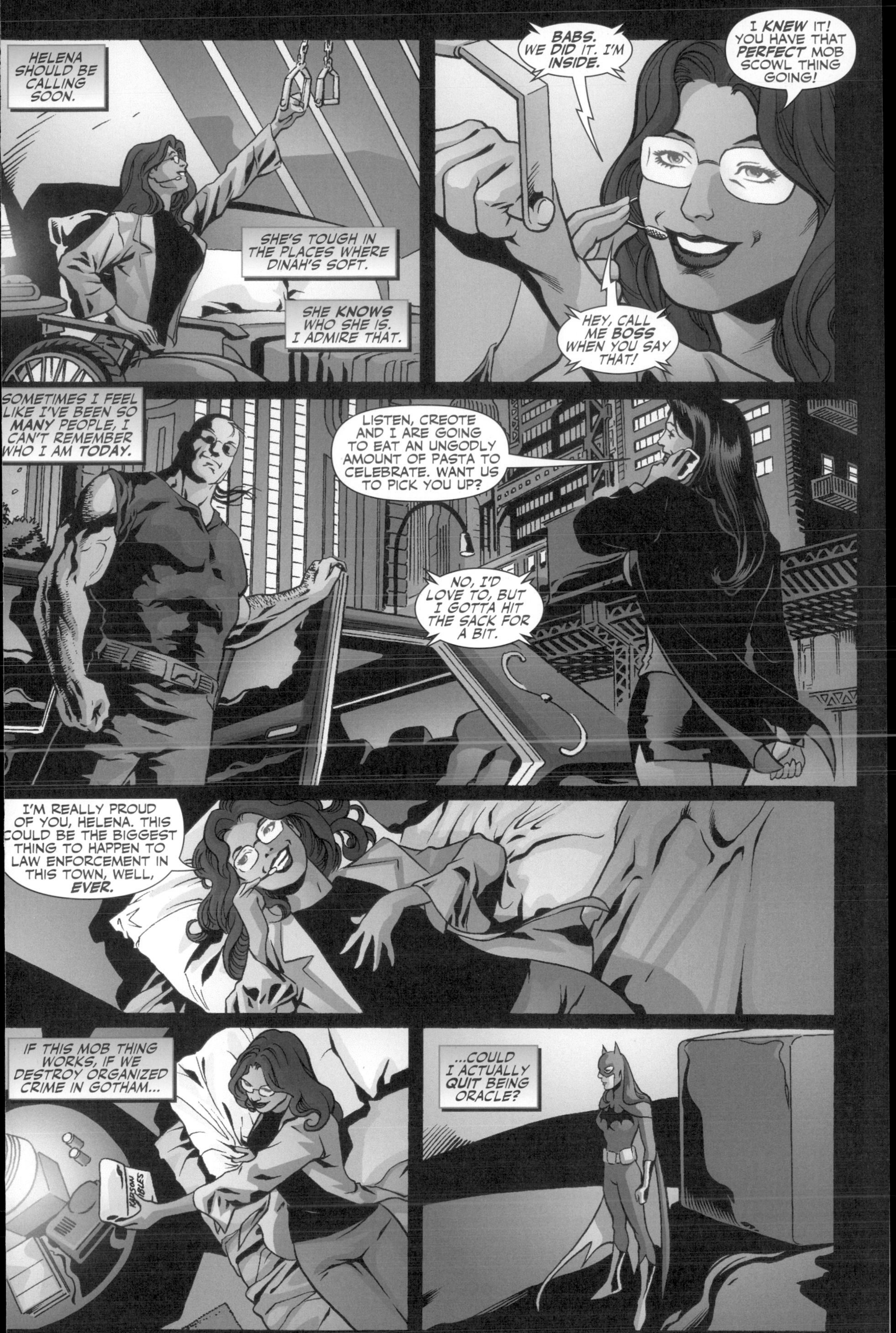
HELENA SHOULD BE CALLING SOON.
SHE'S TOUGH IN THE PLACES WHERE DINAH'S SOFT.
SHE KNOWS WHO SHE IS. I ADMIRE THAT.
BABS. WE DID IT. I'M INSIDE.
I KNEW IT! YOU HAVE THAT PERFECT MOB SCOWL THING GOING!
HEY, CALL ME BOSS WHEN YOU SAY THAT!
SOMETIMES I FEEL LIKE I'VE BEEN SO MANY PEOPLE, I CAN'T REMEMBER WHO I AM TODAY.
LISTEN, CREOTE AND I ARE GOING TO EAT AN UNGODLY AMOUNT OF PASTA TO CELEBRATE. WANT US TO PICK YOU UP?
NO, I'D LOVE TO, BUT I GOTTA HIT THE SACK FOR A BIT.
I'M REALLY PROUD OF YOU, HELENA. THIS COULD BE THE BIGGEST THING TO HAPPEN TO LAW ENFORCEMENT IN THIS TOWN, WELL, EVER.
IF THIS MOB THING WORKS, IF WE DESTROY ORGANIZED CRIME IN GOTHAM...
...COULD I ACTUALLY QUIT BEING ORACLE?

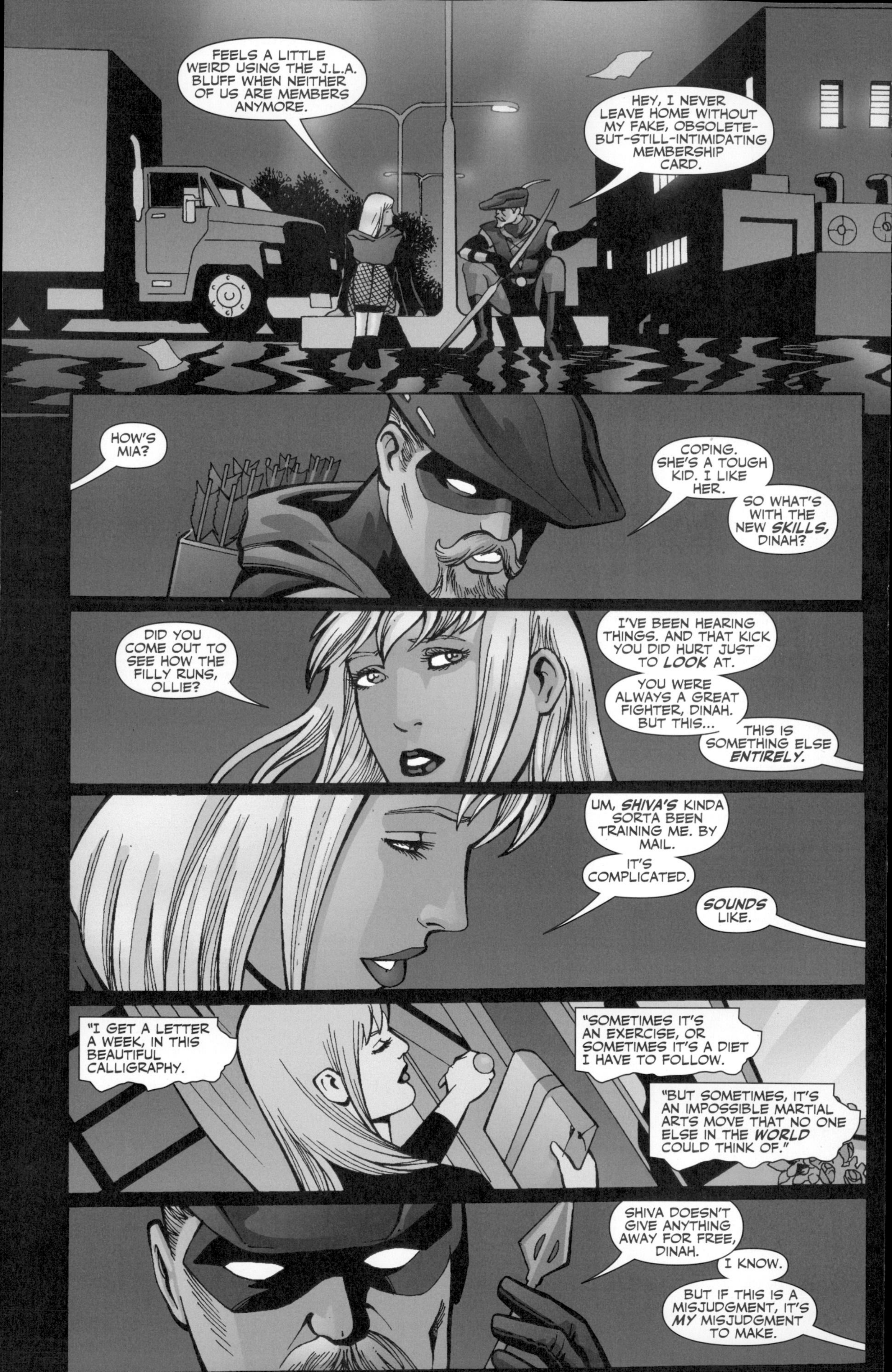
FEELS A LITTLE WEIRD USING THE J.L.A. BLUFF WHEN NEITHER OF US ARE MEMBERS ANYMORE.
HEY, I NEVER LEAVE HOME WITHOUT MY FAKE, OBSOLETE-BUT-STILL-INTIMIDATING MEMBERSHIP CARD.
HOW'S MIA?
COPING. SHE'S A TOUGH KID. I LIKE HER.
SO WHAT'S WITH THE NEW SKILLS, DINAH?
DID YOU COME OUT TO SEE HOW THE FILLY RUNS, OLLIE?
I'VE BEEN HEARING THINGS. AND THAT KICK YOU DID HURT JUST TO LOOK AT.
YOU WERE ALWAYS A GREAT FIGHTER, DINAH. BUT THIS...
THIS IS SOMETHING ELSE ENTIRELY.
UM, SHIVA'S KINDA SORTA BEEN TRAINING ME. BY MAIL.
IT'S COMPLICATED.
SOUNDS LIKE.
"I GET A LETTER A WEEK, IN THIS BEAUTIFUL CALLIGRAPHY.
"SOMETIMES IT'S AN EXERCISE, OR SOMETIMES IT'S A DIET I HAVE TO FOLLOW.
"BUT SOMETIMES, IT'S AN IMPOSSIBLE MARTIAL ARTS MOVE THAT NO ONE ELSE IN THE WORLD COULD THINK OF."
SHIVA DOESN'T GIVE ANYTHING AWAY FOR FREE, DINAH.
I KNOW.
BUT IF THIS IS A MISJUDGMENT, IT'S MY MISJUDGMENT TO MAKE.

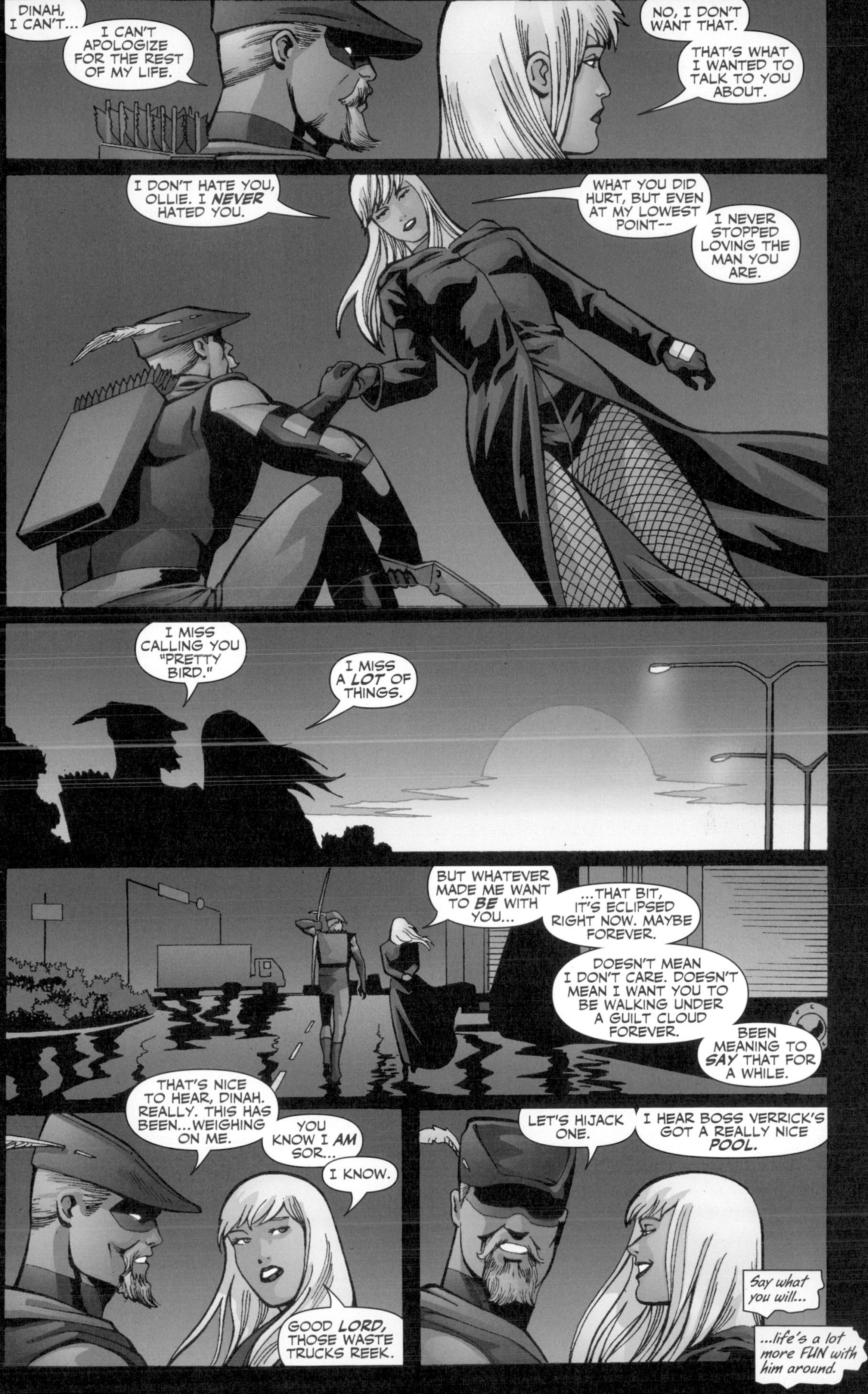
DINAH, I CAN'T...
I CAN'T APOLOGIZE FOR THE REST OF MY LIFE.
NO, I DON'T WANT THAT.
THAT'S WHAT I WANTED TO TALK TO YOU ABOUT.
I DON'T HATE YOU, OLLIE. I *NEVER* HATED YOU.
WHAT YOU DID HURT, BUT EVEN AT MY LOWEST POINT--
I NEVER STOPPED LOVING THE MAN YOU ARE.
I MISS CALLING YOU "PRETTY BIRD."
I MISS A *LOT* OF THINGS.
BUT WHATEVER MADE ME WANT TO *BE* WITH YOU...
...THAT BIT, IT'S ECLIPSED RIGHT NOW. MAYBE FOREVER.
DOESN'T MEAN I DON'T CARE. DOESN'T MEAN I WANT YOU TO BE WALKING UNDER A GUILT CLOUD FOREVER.
BEEN MEANING TO *SAY* THAT FOR A WHILE.
THAT'S NICE TO HEAR, DINAH. REALLY. THIS HAS BEEN...WEIGHING ON ME.
YOU KNOW I *AM* SOR...
I KNOW.
GOOD *LORD,* THOSE WASTE TRUCKS REEK.
LET'S HIJACK ONE.
I HEAR BOSS VERRICK'S GOT A REALLY NICE *POOL.*
Say what you will...
...life's a lot more FUN with him around.

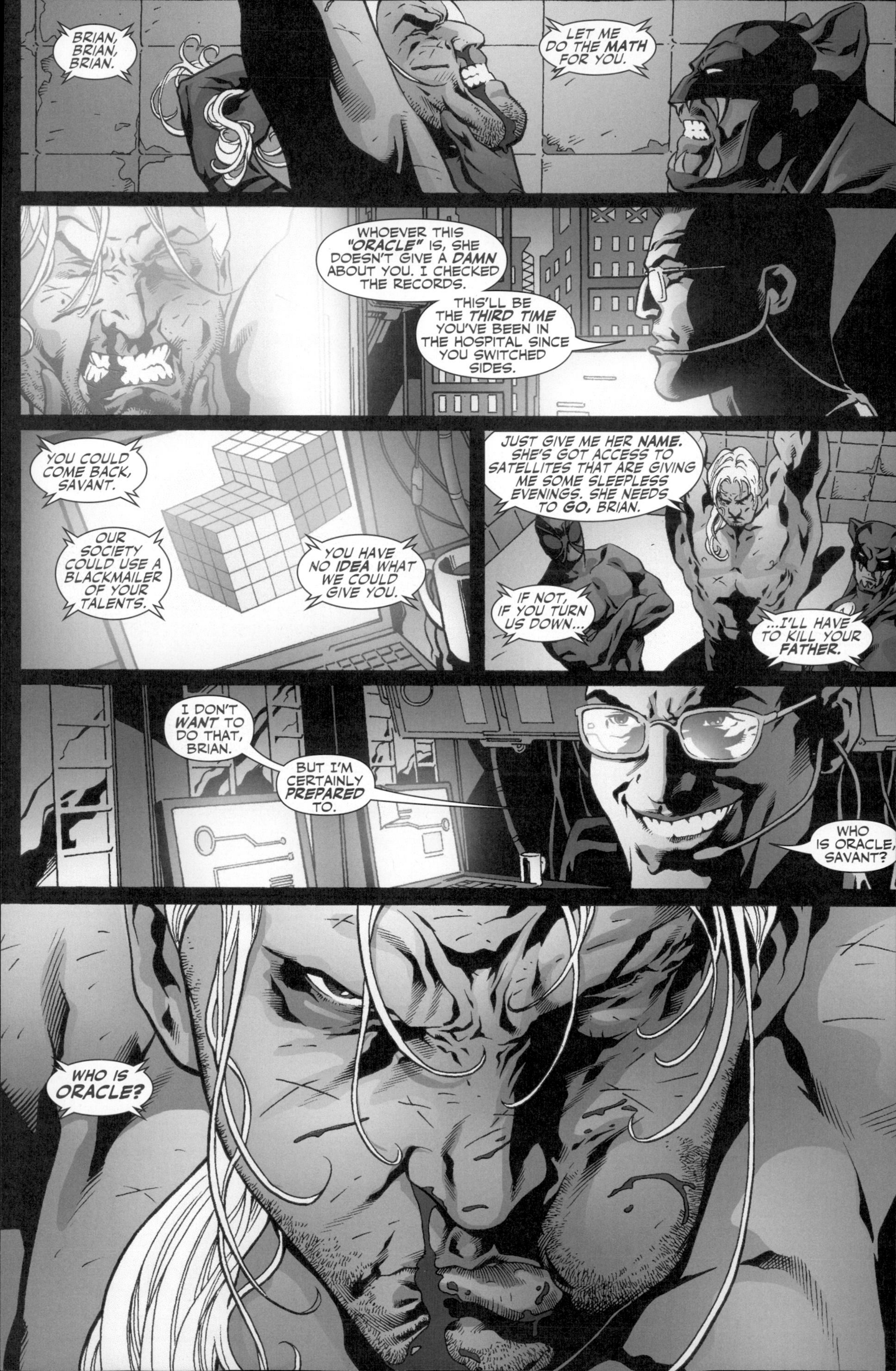
BRIAN, BRIAN, BRIAN.
LET ME DO THE MATH FOR YOU.
WHOEVER THIS "ORACLE" IS, SHE DOESN'T GIVE A DAMN ABOUT YOU. I CHECKED THE RECORDS.
THIS'LL BE THE THIRD TIME YOU'VE BEEN IN THE HOSPITAL SINCE YOU SWITCHED SIDES.
YOU COULD COME BACK, SAVANT.
OUR SOCIETY COULD USE A BLACKMAILER OF YOUR TALENTS.
YOU HAVE NO IDEA WHAT WE COULD GIVE YOU.
JUST GIVE ME HER NAME. SHE'S GOT ACCESS TO SATELLITES THAT ARE GIVING ME SOME SLEEPLESS EVENINGS. SHE NEEDS TO GO, BRIAN.
IF NOT, IF YOU TURN US DOWN...
...I'LL HAVE TO KILL YOUR FATHER.
I DON'T WANT TO DO THAT, BRIAN.
BUT I'M CERTAINLY PREPARED TO.
WHO IS ORACLE, SAVANT?
WHO IS ORACLE?

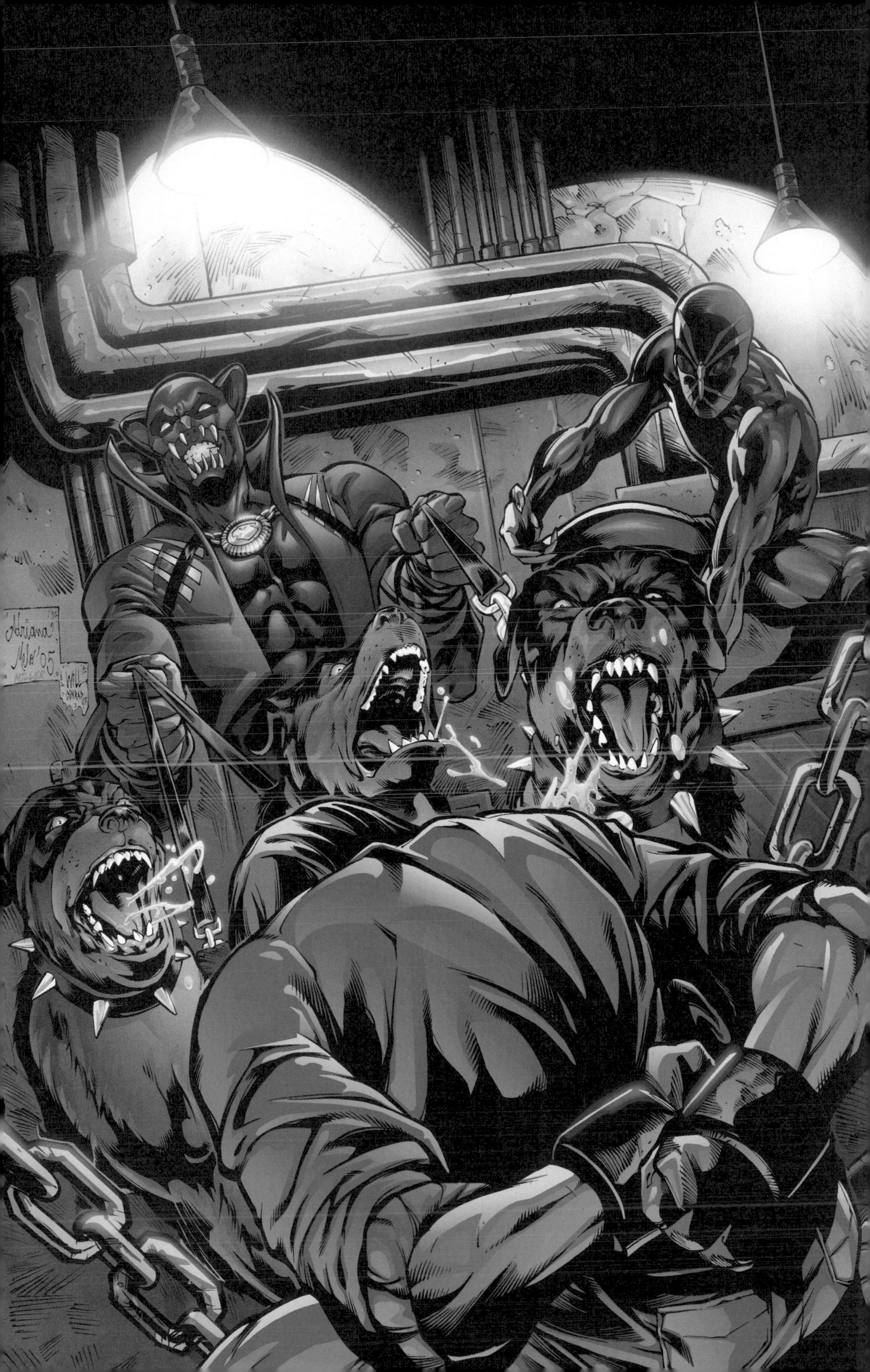
Adriana Melo '05
MILLER
WILL CONRAD 05

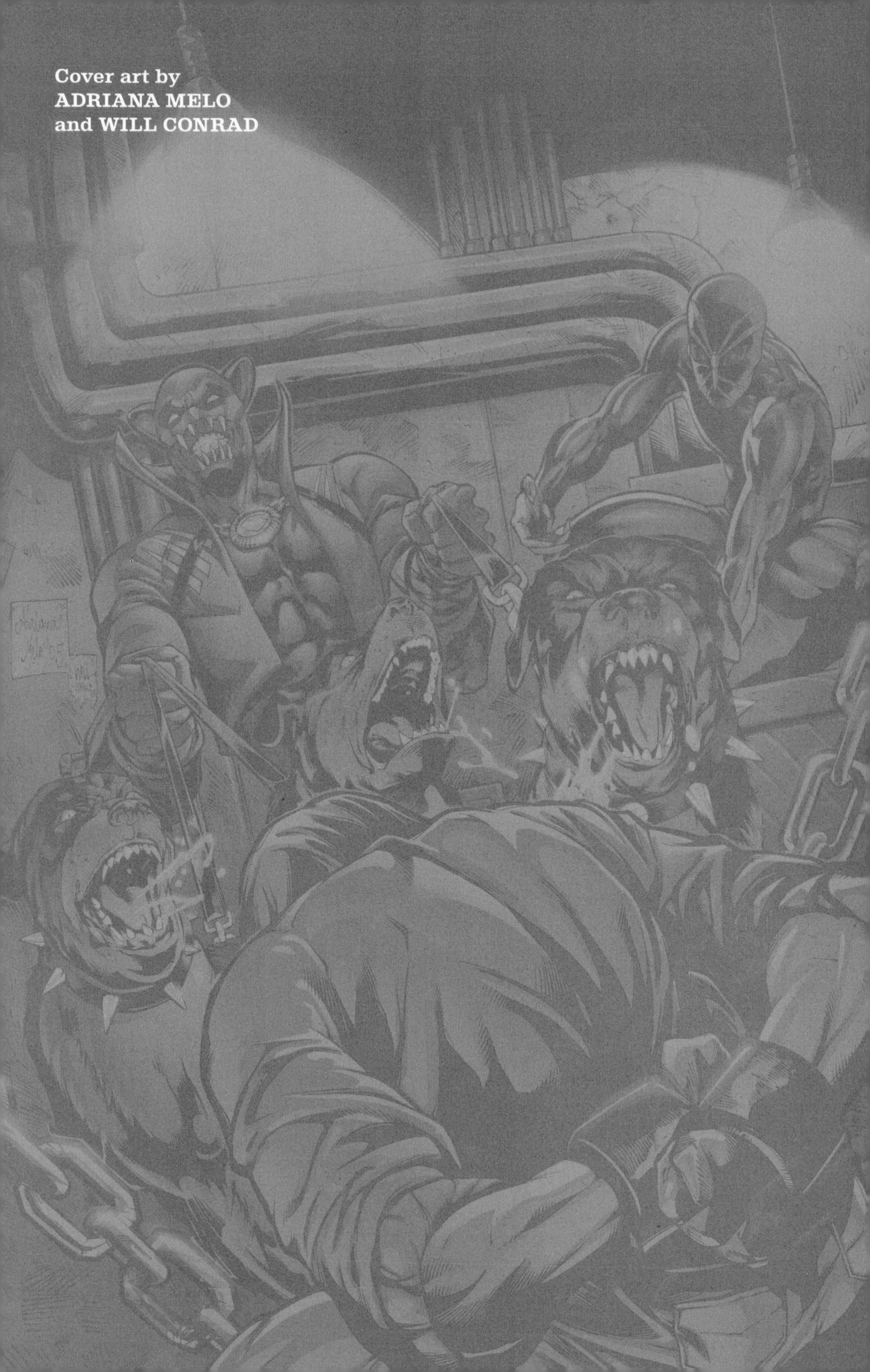

Cover art by
ADRIANA MELO
and WILL CONRAD

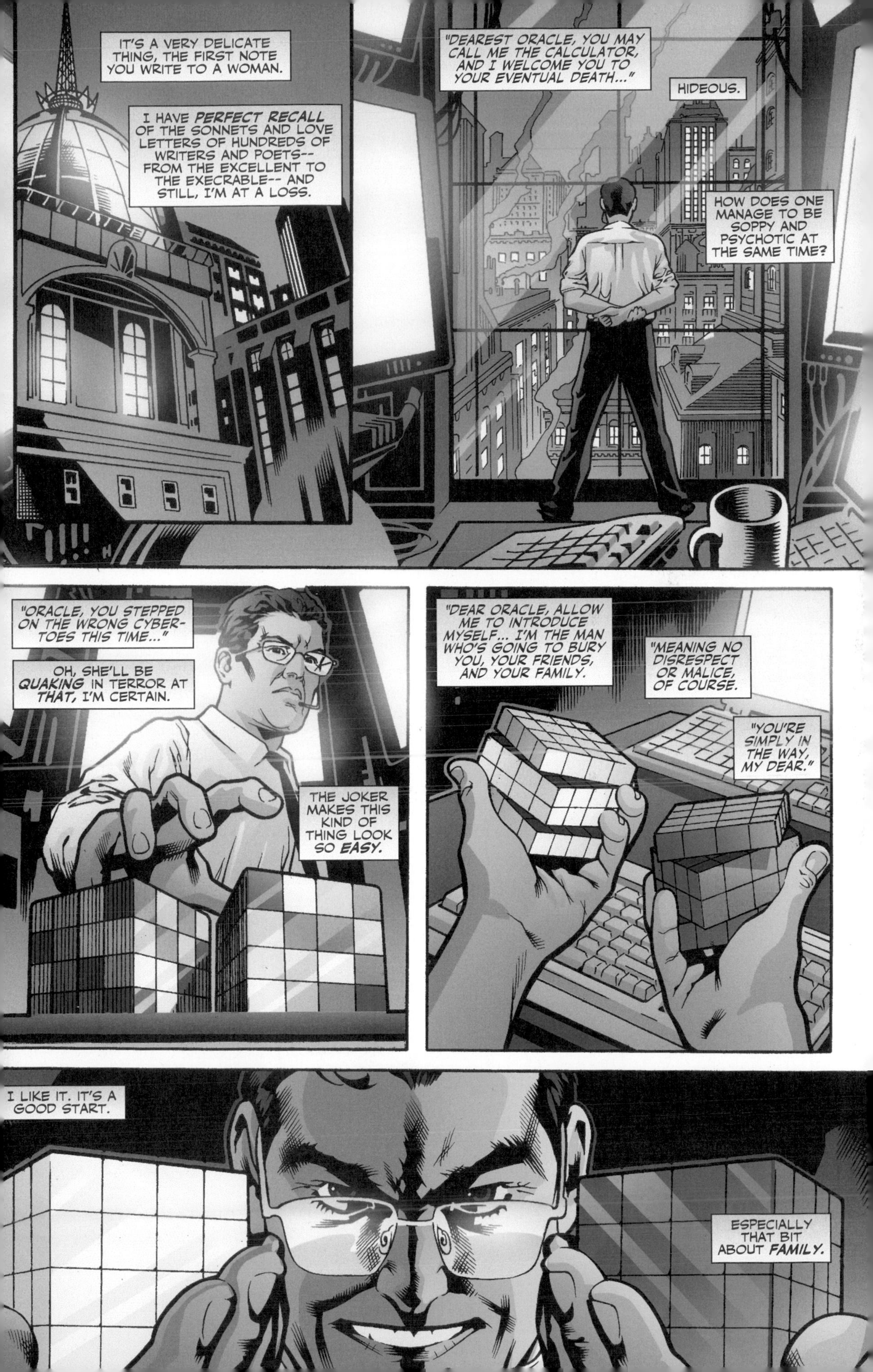
IT'S A VERY DELICATE THING, THE FIRST NOTE YOU WRITE TO A WOMAN.
I HAVE *PERFECT RECALL* OF THE SONNETS AND LOVE LETTERS OF HUNDREDS OF WRITERS AND POETS-- FROM THE EXCELLENT TO THE EXECRABLE-- AND STILL, I'M AT A LOSS.
"DEAREST ORACLE, YOU MAY CALL ME THE CALCULATOR, AND I WELCOME YOU TO YOUR EVENTUAL DEATH..."
HIDEOUS.
HOW DOES ONE MANAGE TO BE SOPPY AND PSYCHOTIC AT THE SAME TIME?
"ORACLE, YOU STEPPED ON THE WRONG CYBER-TOES THIS TIME..."
OH, SHE'LL BE *QUAKING* IN TERROR AT *THAT*, I'M CERTAIN.
THE JOKER MAKES THIS KIND OF THING LOOK SO *EASY*.
"DEAR ORACLE, ALLOW ME TO INTRODUCE MYSELF... I'M THE MAN WHO'S GOING TO BURY YOU, YOUR FRIENDS, AND YOUR FAMILY.
"MEANING NO DISRESPECT OR MALICE, OF COURSE.
"YOU'RE SIMPLY IN THE WAY, MY DEAR."
I LIKE IT. IT'S A GOOD START.
ESPECIALLY THAT BIT ABOUT *FAMILY*.

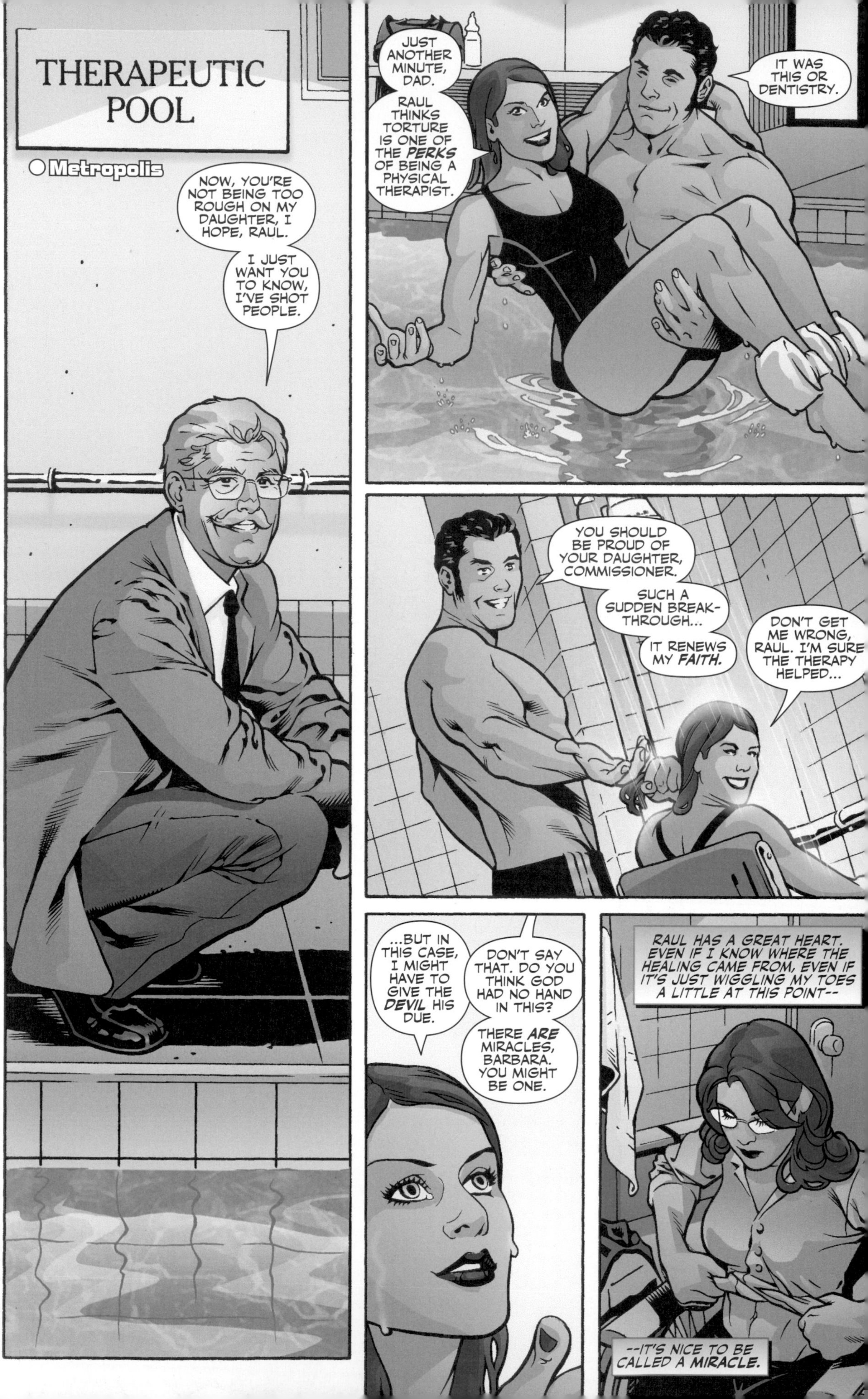
THERAPEUTIC POOL
Metropolis
NOW, YOU'RE NOT BEING TOO ROUGH ON MY DAUGHTER, I HOPE, RAUL.
I JUST WANT YOU TO KNOW, I'VE SHOT PEOPLE.
JUST ANOTHER MINUTE, DAD.
RAUL THINKS TORTURE IS ONE OF THE PERKS OF BEING A PHYSICAL THERAPIST.
IT WAS THIS OR DENTISTRY.
YOU SHOULD BE PROUD OF YOUR DAUGHTER, COMMISSIONER.
SUCH A SUDDEN BREAK-THROUGH...
IT RENEWS MY FAITH.
DON'T GET ME WRONG, RAUL. I'M SURE THE THERAPY HELPED...
...BUT IN THIS CASE, I MIGHT HAVE TO GIVE THE DEVIL HIS DUE.
DON'T SAY THAT. DO YOU THINK GOD HAD NO HAND IN THIS?
THERE ARE MIRACLES, BARBARA. YOU MIGHT BE ONE.
RAUL HAS A GREAT HEART. EVEN IF I KNOW WHERE THE HEALING CAME FROM, EVEN IF IT'S JUST WIGGLING MY TOES A LITTLE AT THIS POINT--
--IT'S NICE TO BE CALLED A MIRACLE.

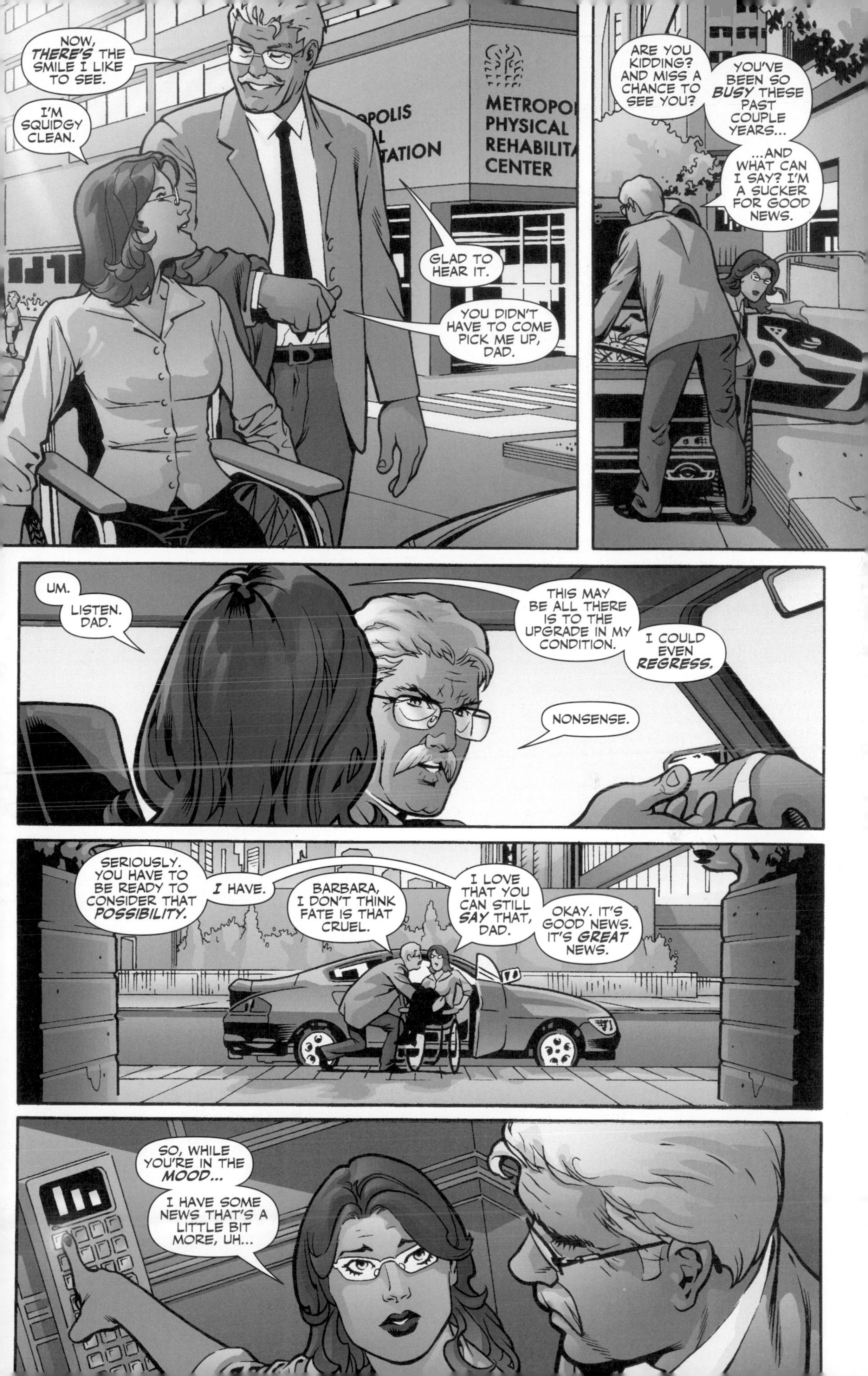
NOW, THERE'S THE SMILE I LIKE TO SEE.
I'M SQUIDGY CLEAN.
METROPOLIS PHYSICAL REHABILITATION CENTER
GLAD TO HEAR IT.
YOU DIDN'T HAVE TO COME PICK ME UP, DAD.
ARE YOU KIDDING? AND MISS A CHANCE TO SEE YOU?
YOU'VE BEEN SO BUSY THESE PAST COUPLE YEARS...
...AND WHAT CAN I SAY? I'M A SUCKER FOR GOOD NEWS.
UM.
LISTEN. DAD.
THIS MAY BE ALL THERE IS TO THE UPGRADE IN MY CONDITION.
I COULD EVEN REGRESS.
NONSENSE.
SERIOUSLY. YOU HAVE TO BE READY TO CONSIDER THAT POSSIBILITY.
I HAVE.
BARBARA, I DON'T THINK FATE IS THAT CRUEL.
I LOVE THAT YOU CAN STILL SAY THAT, DAD.
OKAY. IT'S GOOD NEWS. IT'S GREAT NEWS.
SO, WHILE YOU'RE IN THE MOOD...
I HAVE SOME NEWS THAT'S A LITTLE BIT MORE, UH...

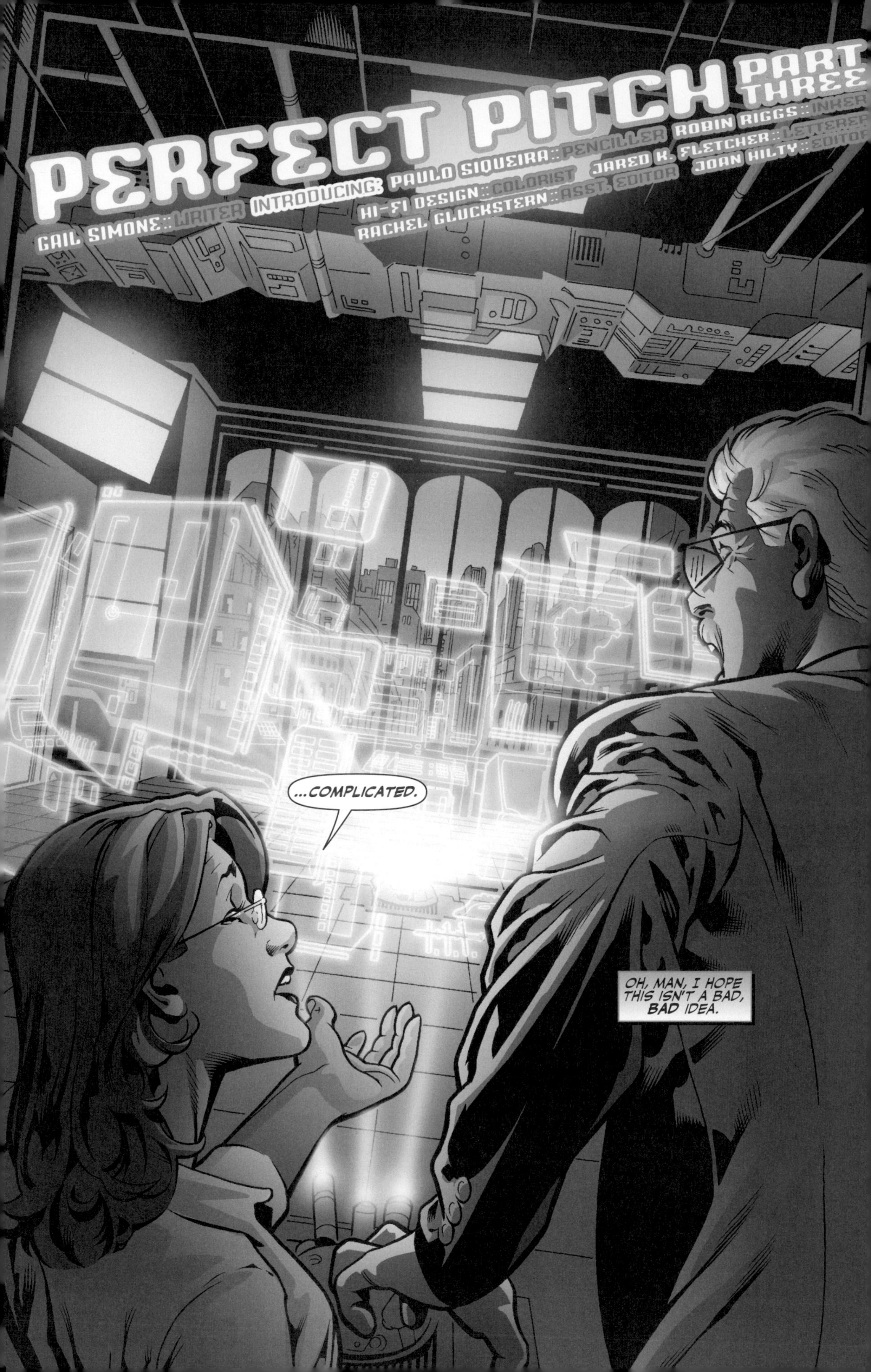
PERFECT PITCH PART THREE
GAIL SIMONE::WRITER INTRODUCING: PAULO SIQUEIRA::PENCILLER ROBIN RIGGS::INKER
HI-FI DESIGN::COLORIST JARED K. FLETCHER::LETTERER
RACHEL GLUCKSTERN::ASST. EDITOR JOAN HILTY::EDITOR
...COMPLICATED.
OH, MAN, I HOPE THIS ISN'T A BAD, BAD IDEA.

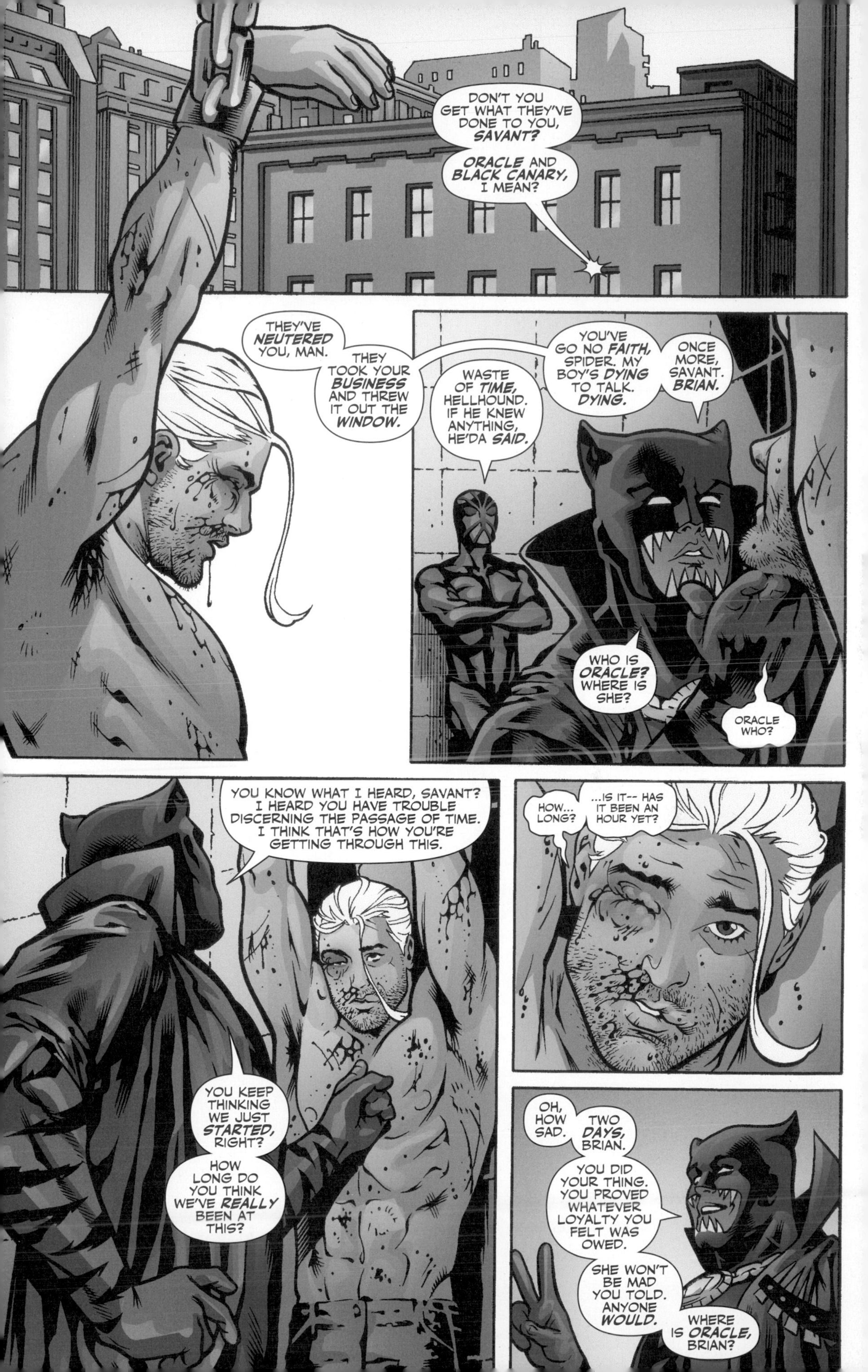
DON'T YOU GET WHAT THEY'VE DONE TO YOU, SAVANT?
ORACLE AND BLACK CANARY, I MEAN?
THEY'VE NEUTERED YOU, MAN.
THEY TOOK YOUR BUSINESS AND THREW IT OUT THE WINDOW.
WASTE OF TIME, HELLHOUND. IF HE KNEW ANYTHING, HE'DA SAID.
YOU'VE GO NO FAITH, SPIDER. MY BOY'S DYING TO TALK. DYING.
ONCE MORE, SAVANT. BRIAN.
WHO IS ORACLE? WHERE IS SHE?
ORACLE WHO?
YOU KNOW WHAT I HEARD, SAVANT? I HEARD YOU HAVE TROUBLE DISCERNING THE PASSAGE OF TIME. I THINK THAT'S HOW YOU'RE GETTING THROUGH THIS.
YOU KEEP THINKING WE JUST STARTED, RIGHT?
HOW LONG DO YOU THINK WE'VE REALLY BEEN AT THIS?
HOW... LONG?
...IS IT-- HAS IT BEEN AN HOUR YET?
OH, HOW SAD.
TWO DAYS, BRIAN.
YOU DID YOUR THING. YOU PROVED WHATEVER LOYALTY YOU FELT WAS OWED.
SHE WON'T BE MAD YOU TOLD. ANYONE WOULD.
WHERE IS ORACLE, BRIAN?

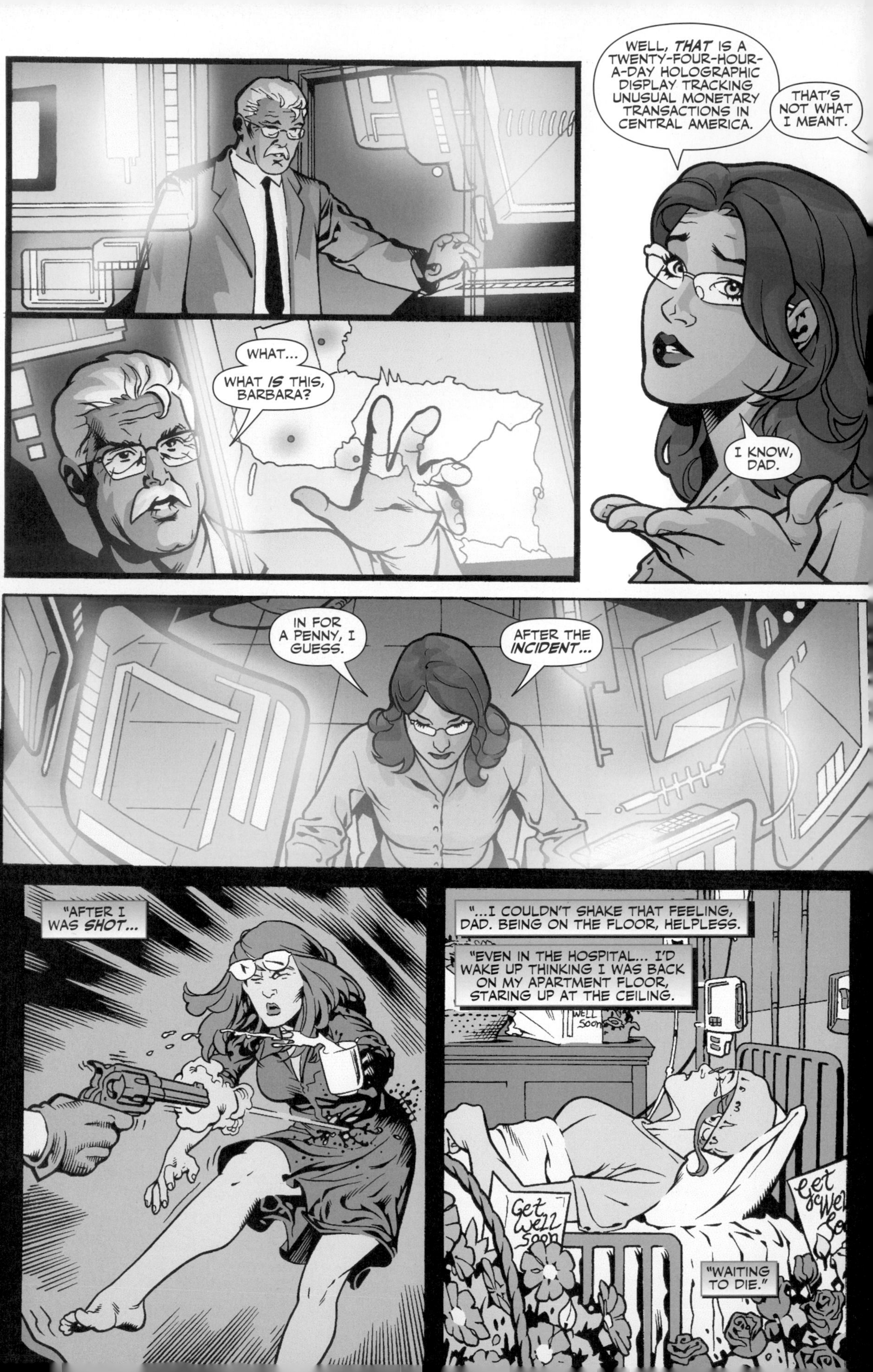

WELL, *THAT* IS A TWENTY-FOUR-HOUR-A-DAY HOLOGRAPHIC DISPLAY TRACKING UNUSUAL MONETARY TRANSACTIONS IN CENTRAL AMERICA.
THAT'S NOT WHAT I MEANT.
WHAT...
WHAT *IS* THIS, BARBARA?
I KNOW, DAD.
IN FOR A PENNY, I GUESS.
AFTER THE *INCIDENT*...
"AFTER I WAS *SHOT*...
"...I COULDN'T SHAKE THAT FEELING, DAD. BEING ON THE FLOOR, HELPLESS.
"EVEN IN THE HOSPITAL... I'D WAKE UP THINKING I WAS BACK ON MY APARTMENT FLOOR, STARING UP AT THE CEILING.
Get Well Soon
"WAITING TO DIE."

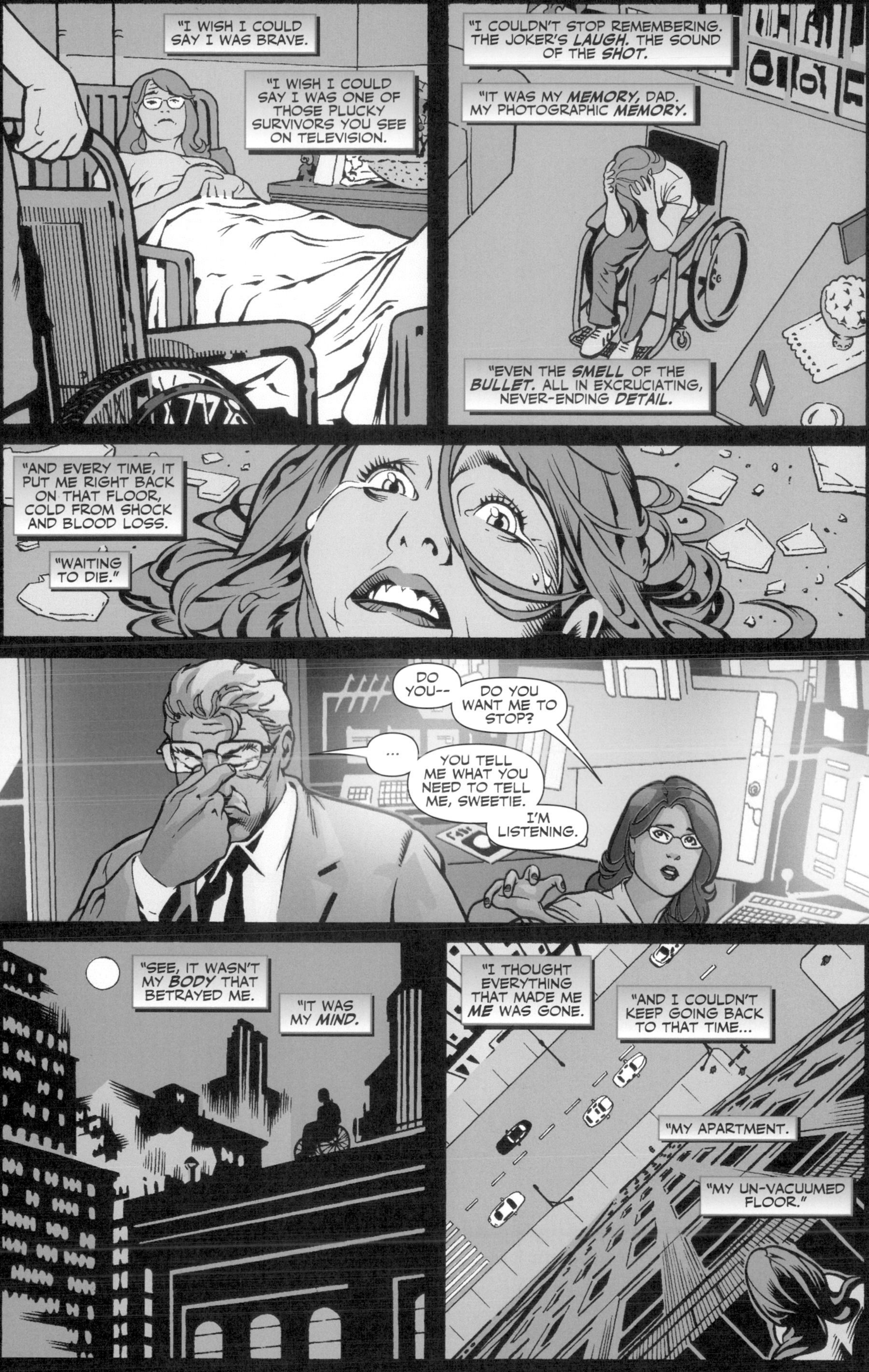
"I WISH I COULD SAY I WAS BRAVE.
"I WISH I COULD SAY I WAS ONE OF THOSE PLUCKY SURVIVORS YOU SEE ON TELEVISION.
"I COULDN'T STOP REMEMBERING. THE JOKER'S LAUGH. THE SOUND OF THE SHOT.
"IT WAS MY MEMORY, DAD. MY PHOTOGRAPHIC MEMORY.
"EVEN THE SMELL OF THE BULLET. ALL IN EXCRUCIATING, NEVER-ENDING DETAIL.
"AND EVERY TIME, IT PUT ME RIGHT BACK ON THAT FLOOR, COLD FROM SHOCK AND BLOOD LOSS.
"WAITING TO DIE."
DO YOU--
DO YOU WANT ME TO STOP?
...
YOU TELL ME WHAT YOU NEED TO TELL ME, SWEETIE.
I'M LISTENING.
"SEE, IT WASN'T MY BODY THAT BETRAYED ME.
"IT WAS MY MIND.
"I THOUGHT EVERYTHING THAT MADE ME ME WAS GONE.
"AND I COULDN'T KEEP GOING BACK TO THAT TIME...
"MY APARTMENT.
"MY UN-VACUUMED FLOOR."

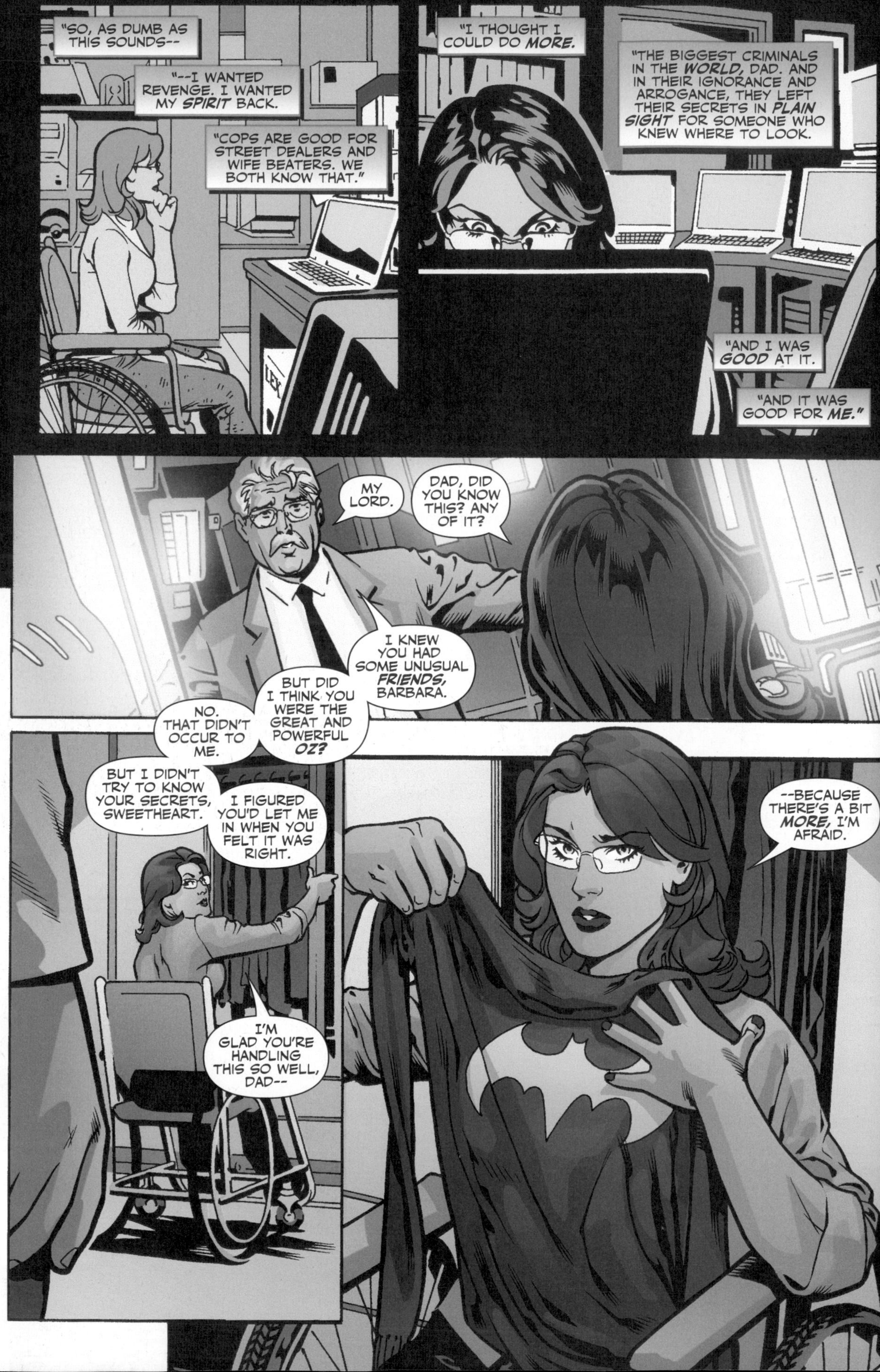
"SO, AS DUMB AS THIS SOUNDS--
"--I WANTED REVENGE. I WANTED MY SPIRIT BACK.
"COPS ARE GOOD FOR STREET DEALERS AND WIFE BEATERS. WE BOTH KNOW THAT."
"I THOUGHT I COULD DO MORE.
"THE BIGGEST CRIMINALS IN THE WORLD, DAD. AND IN THEIR IGNORANCE AND ARROGANCE, THEY LEFT THEIR SECRETS IN PLAIN SIGHT FOR SOMEONE WHO KNEW WHERE TO LOOK.
"AND I WAS GOOD AT IT.
"AND IT WAS GOOD FOR ME."
MY LORD.
DAD, DID YOU KNOW THIS? ANY OF IT?
I KNEW YOU HAD SOME UNUSUAL FRIENDS, BARBARA.
BUT DID I THINK YOU WERE THE GREAT AND POWERFUL OZ?
NO. THAT DIDN'T OCCUR TO ME.
BUT I DIDN'T TRY TO KNOW YOUR SECRETS, SWEETHEART.
I FIGURED YOU'D LET ME IN WHEN YOU FELT IT WAS RIGHT.
I'M GLAD YOU'RE HANDLING THIS SO WELL, DAD--
--BECAUSE THERE'S A BIT MORE, I'M AFRAID.

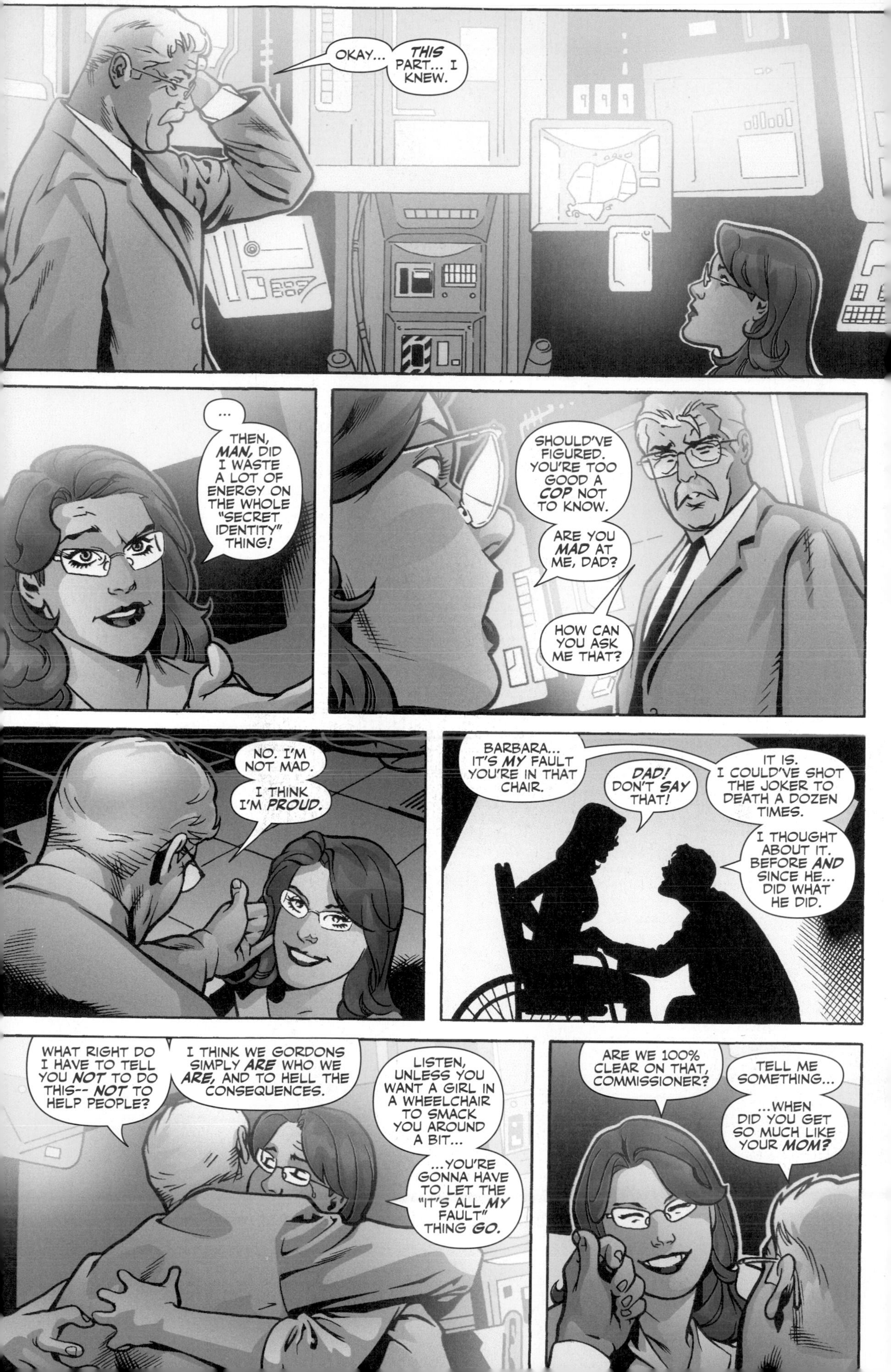
OKAY... *THIS* PART... I KNEW.
...
THEN, *MAN,* DID I WASTE A LOT OF ENERGY ON THE WHOLE "SECRET IDENTITY" THING!
SHOULD'VE FIGURED. YOU'RE TOO GOOD A *COP* NOT TO KNOW.
ARE YOU *MAD* AT ME, DAD?
HOW CAN YOU ASK ME THAT?
NO. I'M NOT MAD.
I THINK I'M *PROUD.*
BARBARA... IT'S *MY* FAULT YOU'RE IN THAT CHAIR.
DAD! DON'T *SAY* THAT!
IT IS. I COULD'VE SHOT THE JOKER TO DEATH A DOZEN TIMES.
I THOUGHT ABOUT IT. BEFORE *AND* SINCE HE... DID WHAT HE DID.
WHAT RIGHT DO I HAVE TO TELL YOU *NOT* TO DO THIS-- *NOT* TO HELP PEOPLE?
I THINK WE GORDONS SIMPLY *ARE* WHO WE *ARE,* AND TO HELL THE CONSEQUENCES.
LISTEN, UNLESS YOU WANT A GIRL IN A WHEELCHAIR TO SMACK YOU AROUND A BIT...
...YOU'RE GONNA HAVE TO LET THE "IT'S ALL *MY* FAULT" THING *GO.*
ARE WE 100% CLEAR ON THAT, COMMISSIONER?
TELL ME SOMETHING...
...WHEN DID YOU GET SO MUCH LIKE YOUR *MOM?*

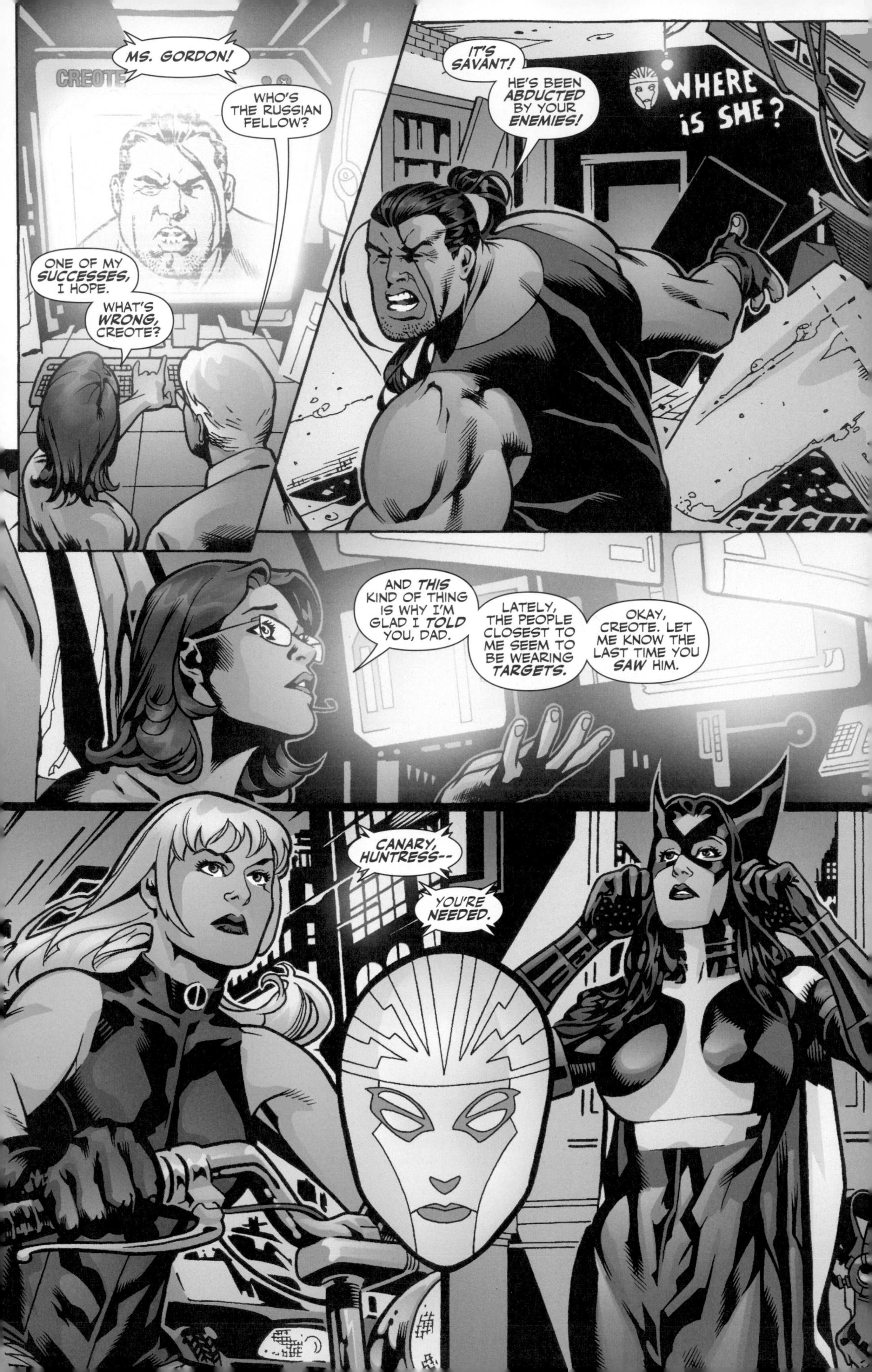
MS. GORDON!
CREOTE
WHO'S THE RUSSIAN FELLOW?
ONE OF MY SUCCESSES, I HOPE.
WHAT'S WRONG, CREOTE?
IT'S SAVANT!
HE'S BEEN ABDUCTED BY YOUR ENEMIES!
WHERE IS SHE?
AND THIS KIND OF THING IS WHY I'M GLAD I TOLD YOU, DAD.
LATELY, THE PEOPLE CLOSEST TO ME SEEM TO BE WEARING TARGETS.
OKAY, CREOTE. LET ME KNOW THE LAST TIME YOU SAW HIM.
CANARY, HUNTRESS--
YOU'RE NEEDED.

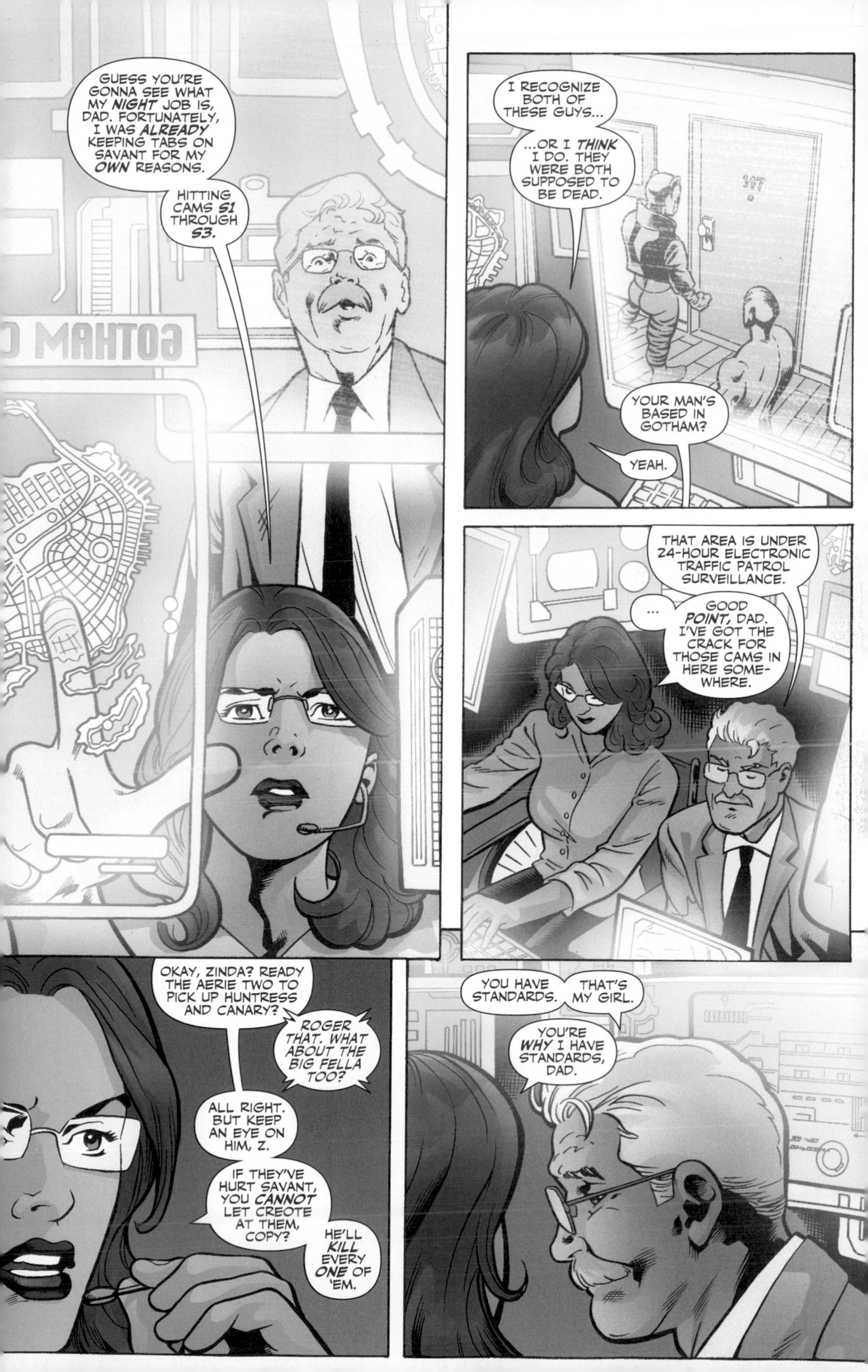
GUESS YOU'RE GONNA SEE WHAT MY NIGHT JOB IS, DAD. FORTUNATELY, I WAS ALREADY KEEPING TABS ON SAVANT FOR MY OWN REASONS.
HITTING CAMS S1 THROUGH S3.
GOTHAM
I RECOGNIZE BOTH OF THESE GUYS...
...OR I THINK I DO. THEY WERE BOTH SUPPOSED TO BE DEAD.
147
YOUR MAN'S BASED IN GOTHAM?
YEAH.
THAT AREA IS UNDER 24-HOUR ELECTRONIC TRAFFIC PATROL SURVEILLANCE.
...
GOOD POINT, DAD. I'VE GOT THE CRACK FOR THOSE CAMS IN HERE SOME-WHERE.
OKAY, ZINDA? READY THE AERIE TWO TO PICK UP HUNTRESS AND CANARY?
ROGER THAT. WHAT ABOUT THE BIG FELLA TOO?
ALL RIGHT. BUT KEEP AN EYE ON HIM, Z.
IF THEY'VE HURT SAVANT, YOU CANNOT LET CREOTE AT THEM, COPY?
HE'LL KILL EVERY ONE OF 'EM.
YOU HAVE STANDARDS.
THAT'S MY GIRL.
YOU'RE WHY I HAVE STANDARDS, DAD.

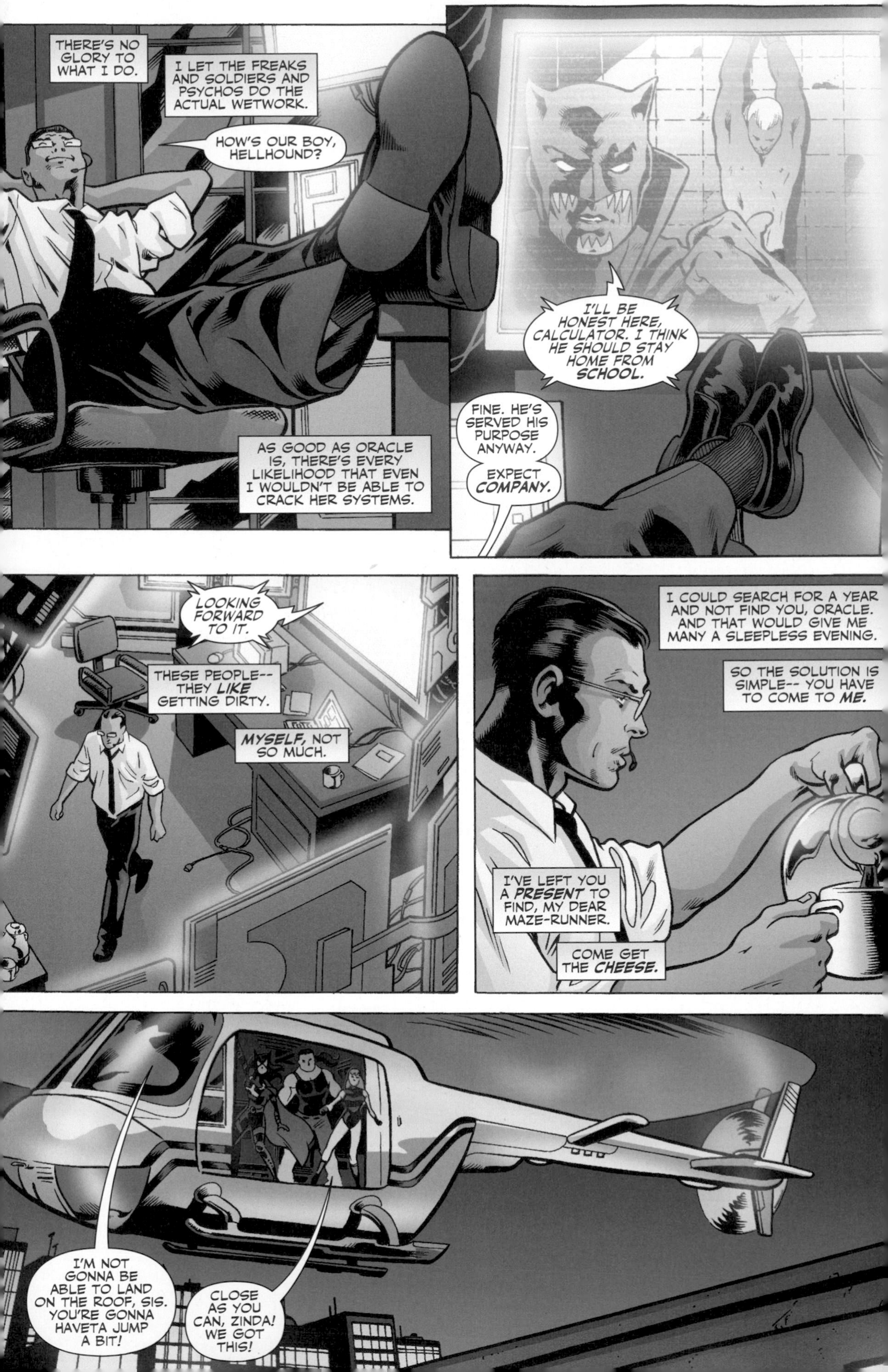
THERE'S NO GLORY TO WHAT I DO.
I LET THE FREAKS AND SOLDIERS AND PSYCHOS DO THE ACTUAL WETWORK.
HOW'S OUR BOY, HELLHOUND?
AS GOOD AS ORACLE IS, THERE'S EVERY LIKELIHOOD THAT EVEN I WOULDN'T BE ABLE TO CRACK HER SYSTEMS.
I'LL BE HONEST HERE, CALCULATOR. I THINK HE SHOULD STAY HOME FROM SCHOOL.
FINE. HE'S SERVED HIS PURPOSE ANYWAY.
EXPECT COMPANY.
LOOKING FORWARD TO IT.
THESE PEOPLE-- THEY LIKE GETTING DIRTY.
MYSELF, NOT SO MUCH.
I COULD SEARCH FOR A YEAR AND NOT FIND YOU, ORACLE. AND THAT WOULD GIVE ME MANY A SLEEPLESS EVENING.
SO THE SOLUTION IS SIMPLE-- YOU HAVE TO COME TO ME.
I'VE LEFT YOU A PRESENT TO FIND, MY DEAR MAZE-RUNNER.
COME GET THE CHEESE.
I'M NOT GONNA BE ABLE TO LAND ON THE ROOF, SIS. YOU'RE GONNA HAVETA JUMP A BIT!
CLOSE AS YOU CAN, ZINDA! WE GOT THIS!

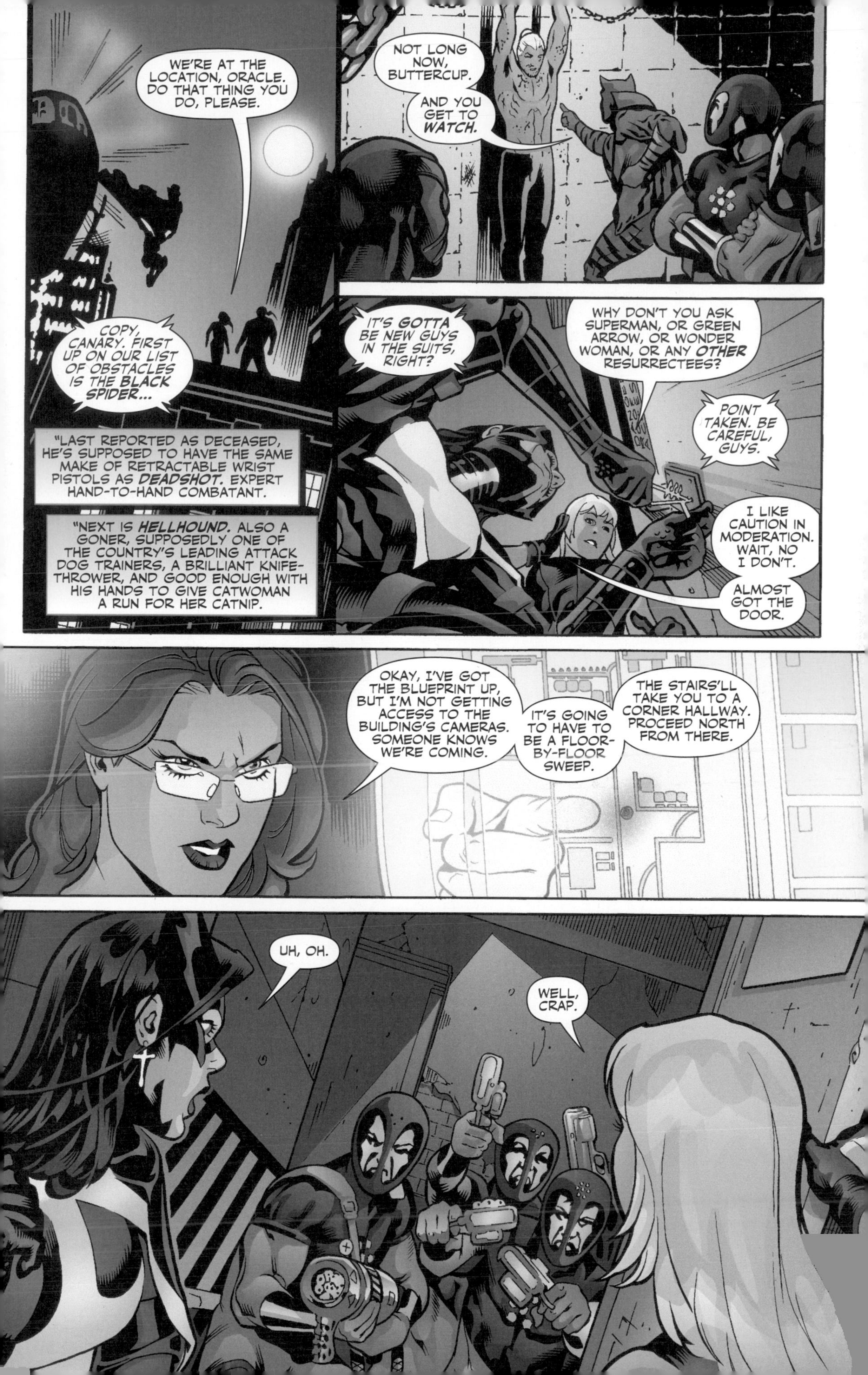
WE'RE AT THE LOCATION, ORACLE. DO THAT THING YOU DO, PLEASE.
COPY, CANARY. FIRST UP ON OUR LIST OF OBSTACLES IS THE BLACK SPIDER...
"LAST REPORTED AS DECEASED, HE'S SUPPOSED TO HAVE THE SAME MAKE OF RETRACTABLE WRIST PISTOLS AS DEADSHOT. EXPERT HAND-TO-HAND COMBATANT.
"NEXT IS HELLHOUND. ALSO A GONER, SUPPOSEDLY ONE OF THE COUNTRY'S LEADING ATTACK DOG TRAINERS, A BRILLIANT KNIFE-THROWER, AND GOOD ENOUGH WITH HIS HANDS TO GIVE CATWOMAN A RUN FOR HER CATNIP.
NOT LONG NOW, BUTTERCUP.
AND YOU GET TO WATCH.
IT'S GOTTA BE NEW GUYS IN THE SUITS, RIGHT?
WHY DON'T YOU ASK SUPERMAN, OR GREEN ARROW, OR WONDER WOMAN, OR ANY OTHER RESURRECTEES?
POINT TAKEN. BE CAREFUL, GUYS.
I LIKE CAUTION IN MODERATION. WAIT, NO I DON'T.
ALMOST GOT THE DOOR.
OKAY, I'VE GOT THE BLUEPRINT UP, BUT I'M NOT GETTING ACCESS TO THE BUILDING'S CAMERAS. SOMEONE KNOWS WE'RE COMING.
IT'S GOING TO HAVE TO BE A FLOOR-BY-FLOOR SWEEP.
THE STAIRS'LL TAKE YOU TO A CORNER HALLWAY. PROCEED NORTH FROM THERE.
UH, OH.
WELL, CRAP.

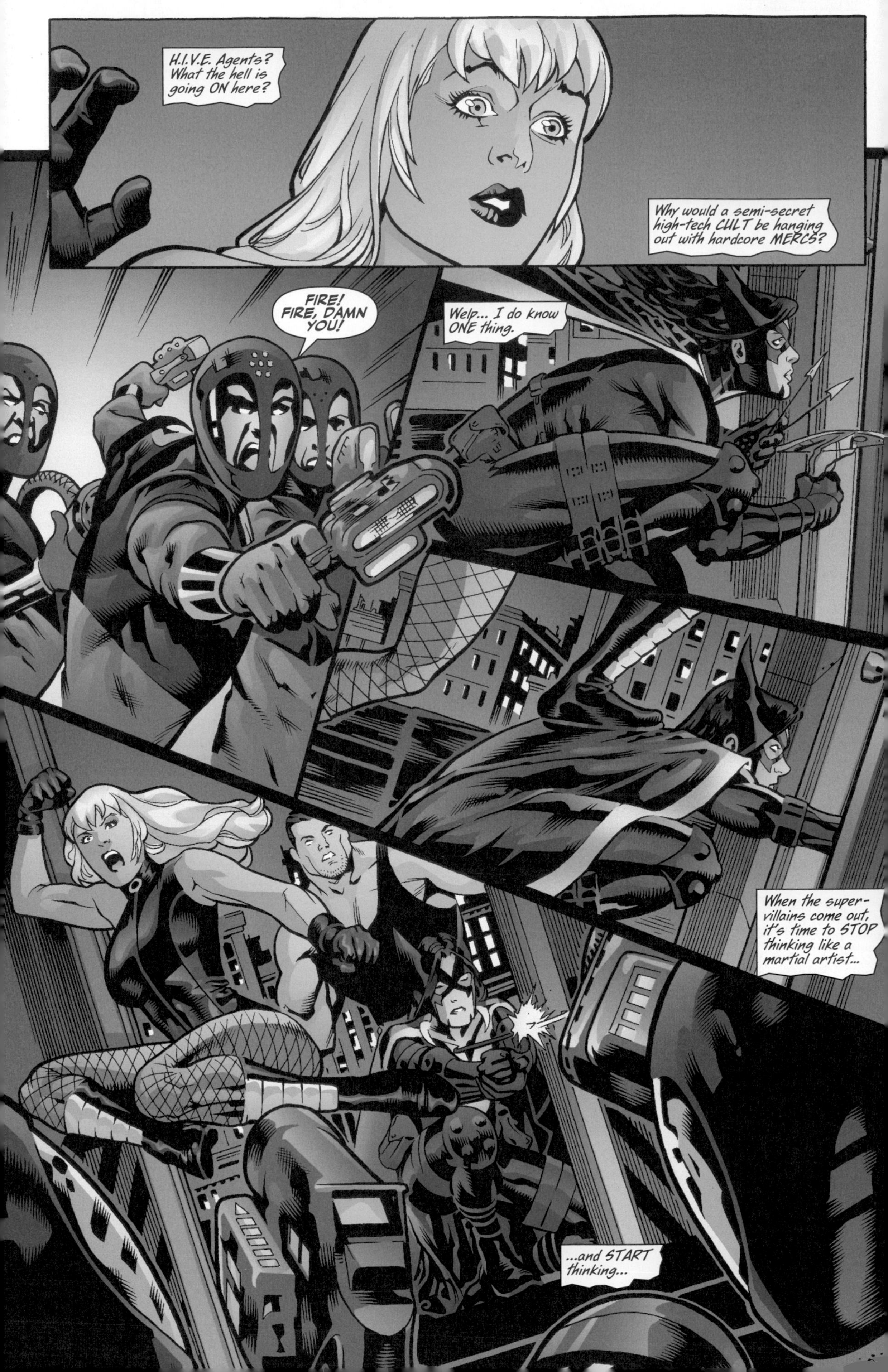
H.I.V.E. Agents? What the hell is going ON here?
Why would a semi-secret high-tech CULT be hanging out with hardcore MERCS?
FIRE! FIRE, DAMN YOU!
Welp... I do know ONE thing.
When the super-villains come out, it's time to STOP thinking like a martial artist...
...and START thinking...

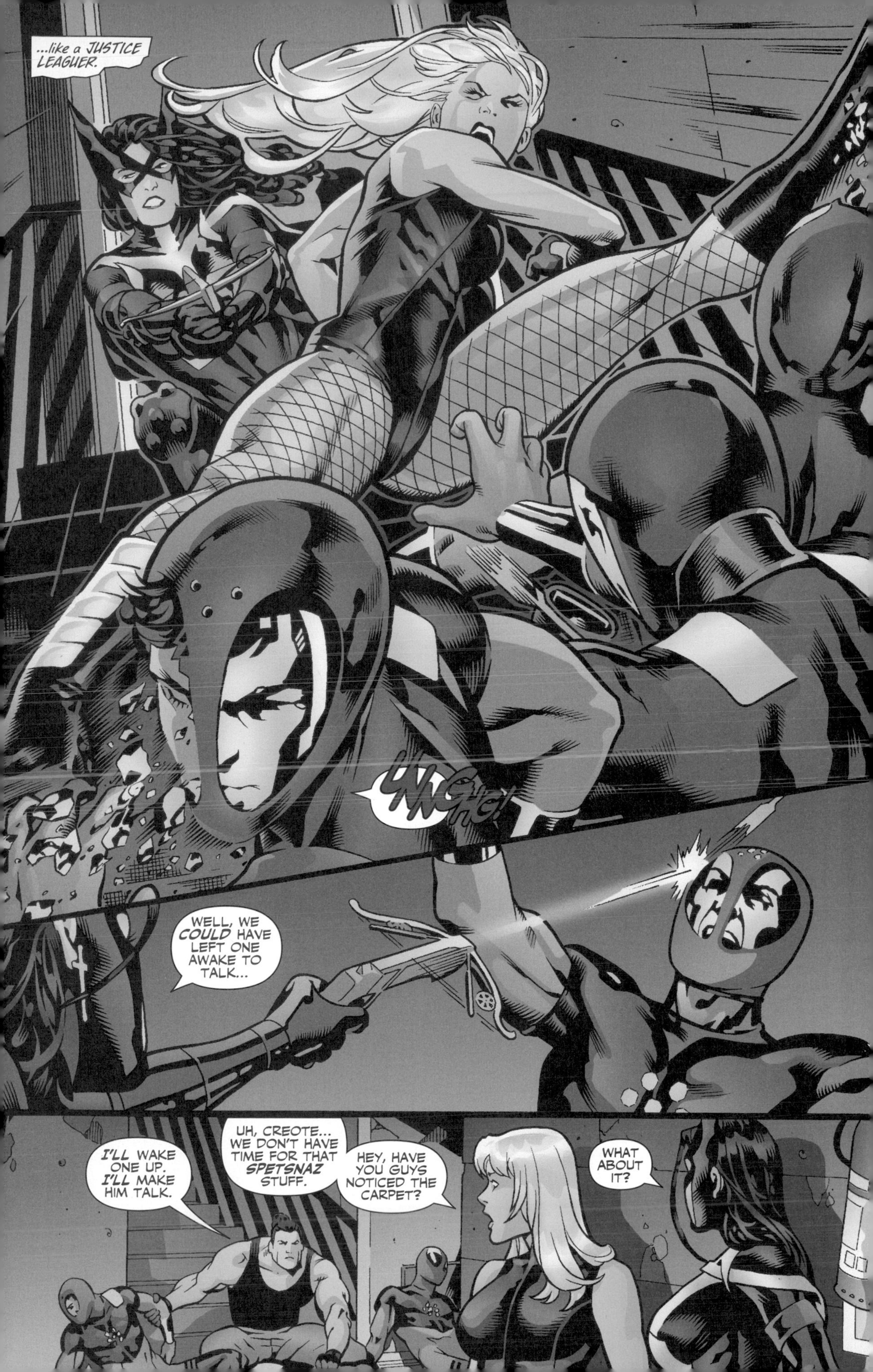
...like a JUSTICE LEAGUER.
UNNGH!
WELL, WE COULD HAVE LEFT ONE AWAKE TO TALK...
I'LL WAKE ONE UP. I'LL MAKE HIM TALK.
UH, CREOTE... WE DON'T HAVE TIME FOR THAT SPETSNAZ STUFF.
HEY, HAVE YOU GUYS NOTICED THE CARPET?
WHAT ABOUT IT?

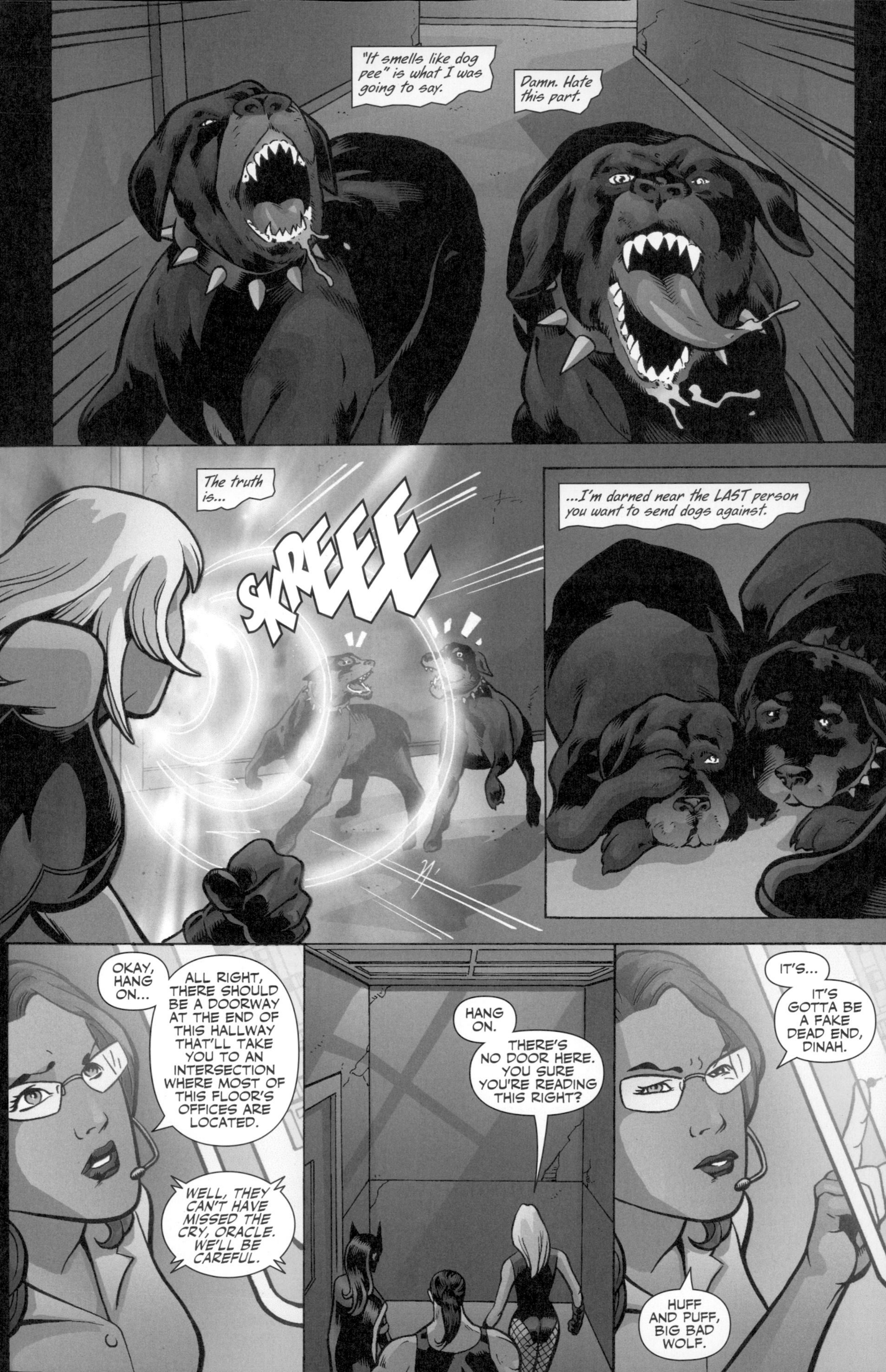
"It smells like dog pee" is what I was going to say.
Damn. Hate this part.
The truth is...
SKREEE
...I'm darned near the LAST person you want to send dogs against.
OKAY, HANG ON...
ALL RIGHT, THERE SHOULD BE A DOORWAY AT THE END OF THIS HALLWAY THAT'LL TAKE YOU TO AN INTERSECTION WHERE MOST OF THIS FLOOR'S OFFICES ARE LOCATED.
WELL, THEY CAN'T HAVE MISSED THE CRY, ORACLE. WE'LL BE CAREFUL.
HANG ON.
THERE'S NO DOOR HERE. YOU SURE YOU'RE READING THIS RIGHT?
IT'S...
IT'S GOTTA BE A FAKE DEAD END, DINAH.
HUFF AND PUFF, BIG BAD WOLF.

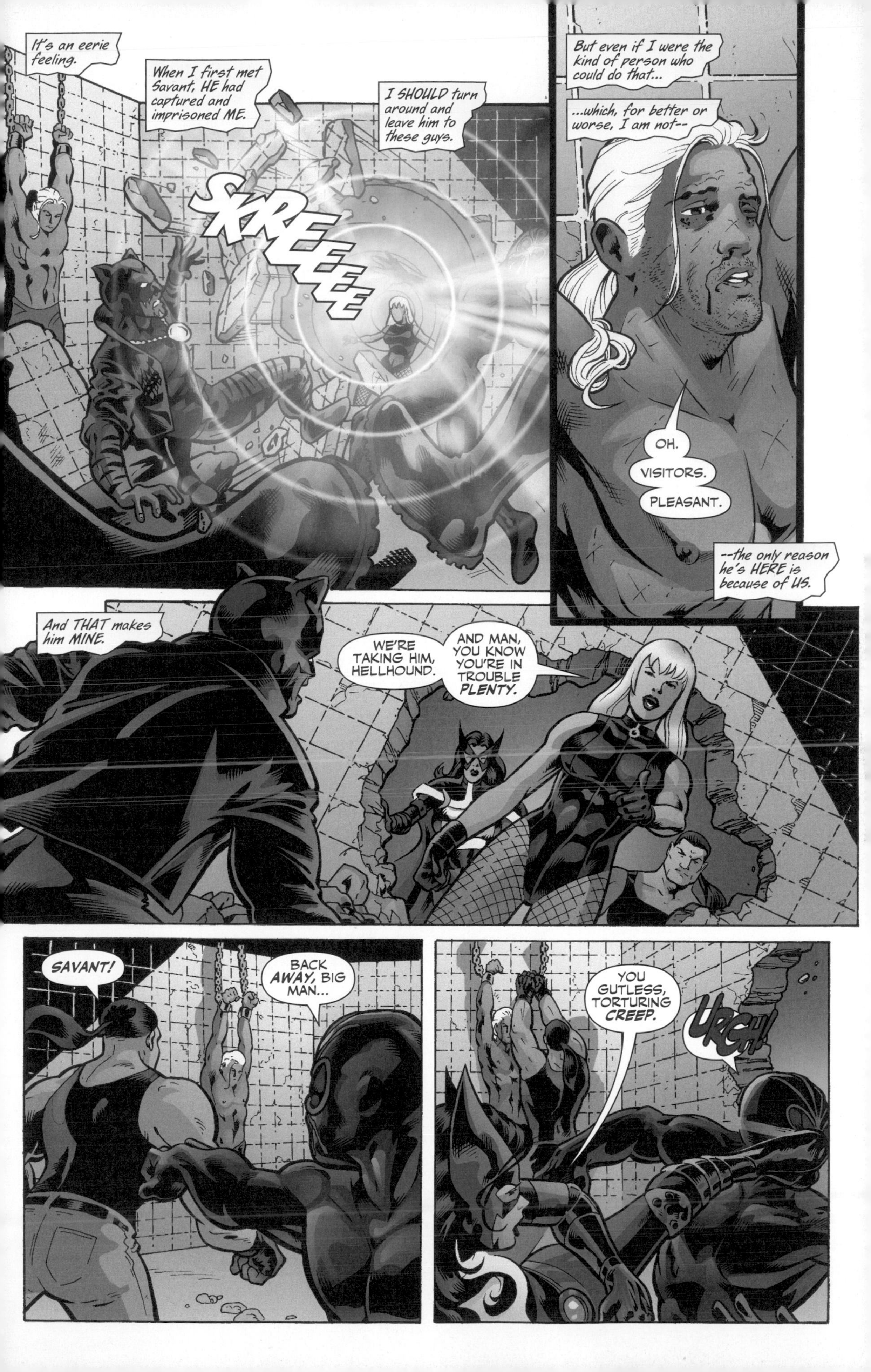
It's an eerie feeling.
When I first met Savant, HE had captured and imprisoned ME.
I SHOULD turn around and leave him to these guys.
SKREEEEE
But even if I were the kind of person who could do that...
...which, for better or worse, I am not--
OH.
VISITORS.
PLEASANT.
--the only reason he's HERE is because of US.
And THAT makes him MINE.
WE'RE TAKING HIM, HELLHOUND.
AND MAN, YOU KNOW YOU'RE IN TROUBLE PLENTY.
SAVANT!
BACK AWAY, BIG MAN...
YOU GUTLESS, TORTURING CREEP.
URGH!

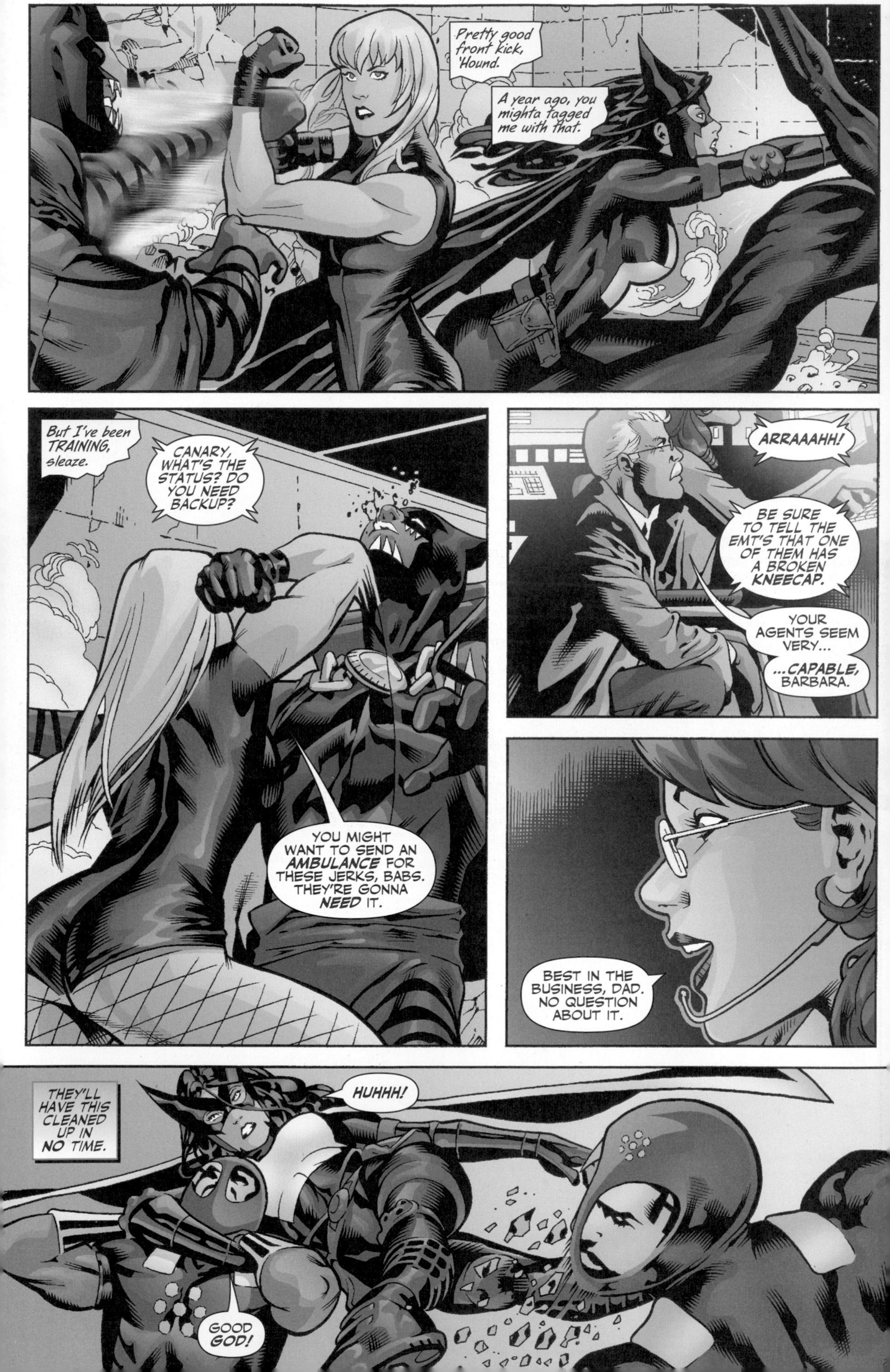
Pretty good front kick, 'Hound.
A year ago, you mighta tagged me with that.
But I've been TRAINING, sleaze.
CANARY, WHAT'S THE STATUS? DO YOU NEED BACKUP?
YOU MIGHT WANT TO SEND AN AMBULANCE FOR THESE JERKS, BABS. THEY'RE GONNA NEED IT.
ARRAAAHH!
BE SURE TO TELL THE EMT'S THAT ONE OF THEM HAS A BROKEN KNEECAP.
YOUR AGENTS SEEM VERY...
...CAPABLE, BARBARA.
BEST IN THE BUSINESS, DAD. NO QUESTION ABOUT IT.
THEY'LL HAVE THIS CLEANED UP IN NO TIME.
HUHHH!
GOOD GOD!

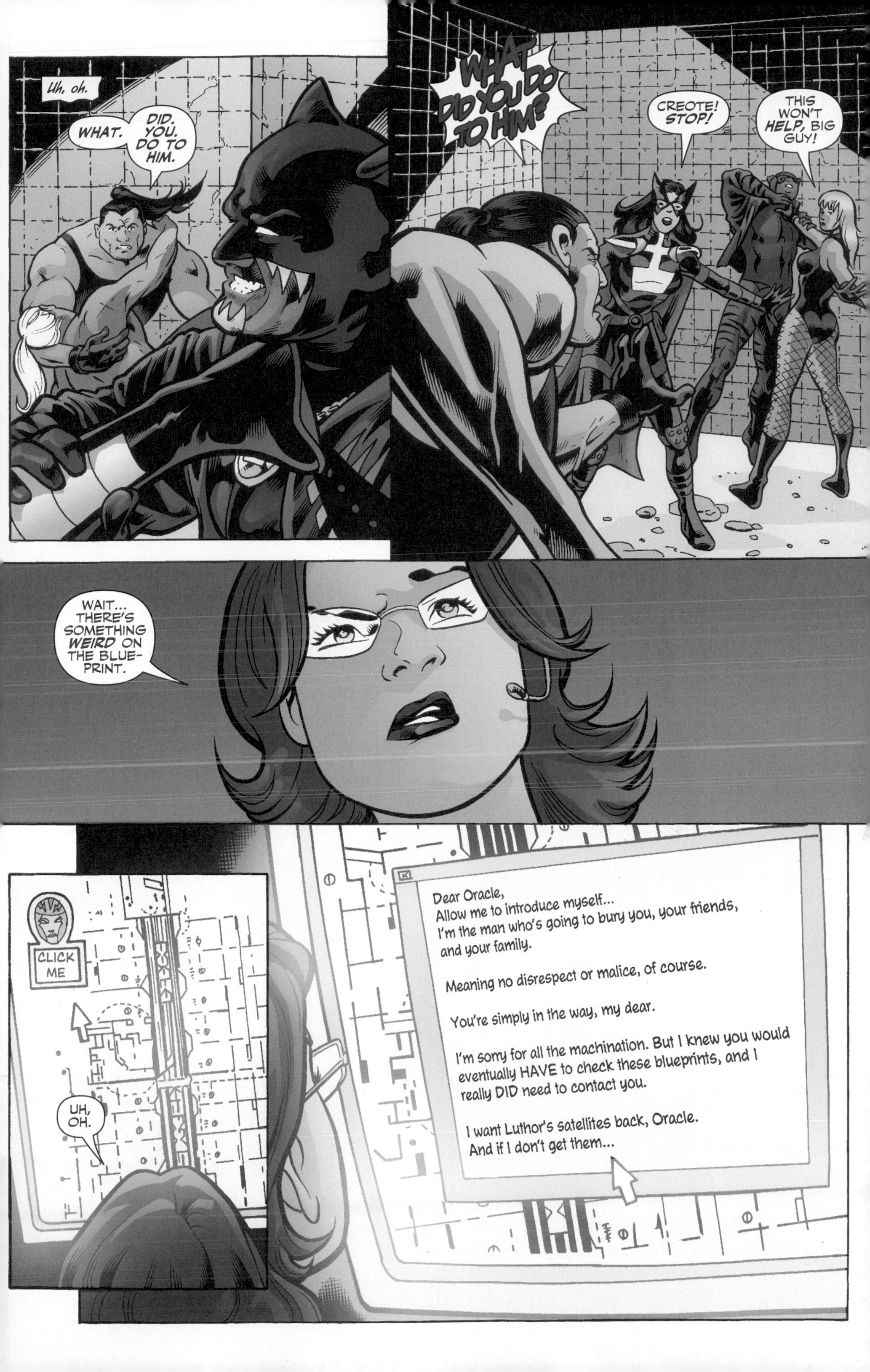
Uh, oh.
WHAT.
DID. YOU. DO TO HIM.
WHAT DID YOU DO TO HIM?
CREOTE! STOP!
THIS WON'T HELP, BIG GUY!
WAIT... THERE'S SOMETHING WEIRD ON THE BLUE-PRINT.
CLICK ME
UH, OH.
Dear Oracle,
Allow me to introduce myself...
I'm the man who's going to bury you, your friends, and your family.
Meaning no disrespect or malice, of course.
You're simply in the way, my dear.
I'm sorry for all the machination. But I knew you would eventually HAVE to check these blueprints, and I really DID need to contact you.
I want Luthor's satellites back, Oracle.
And if I don't get them...

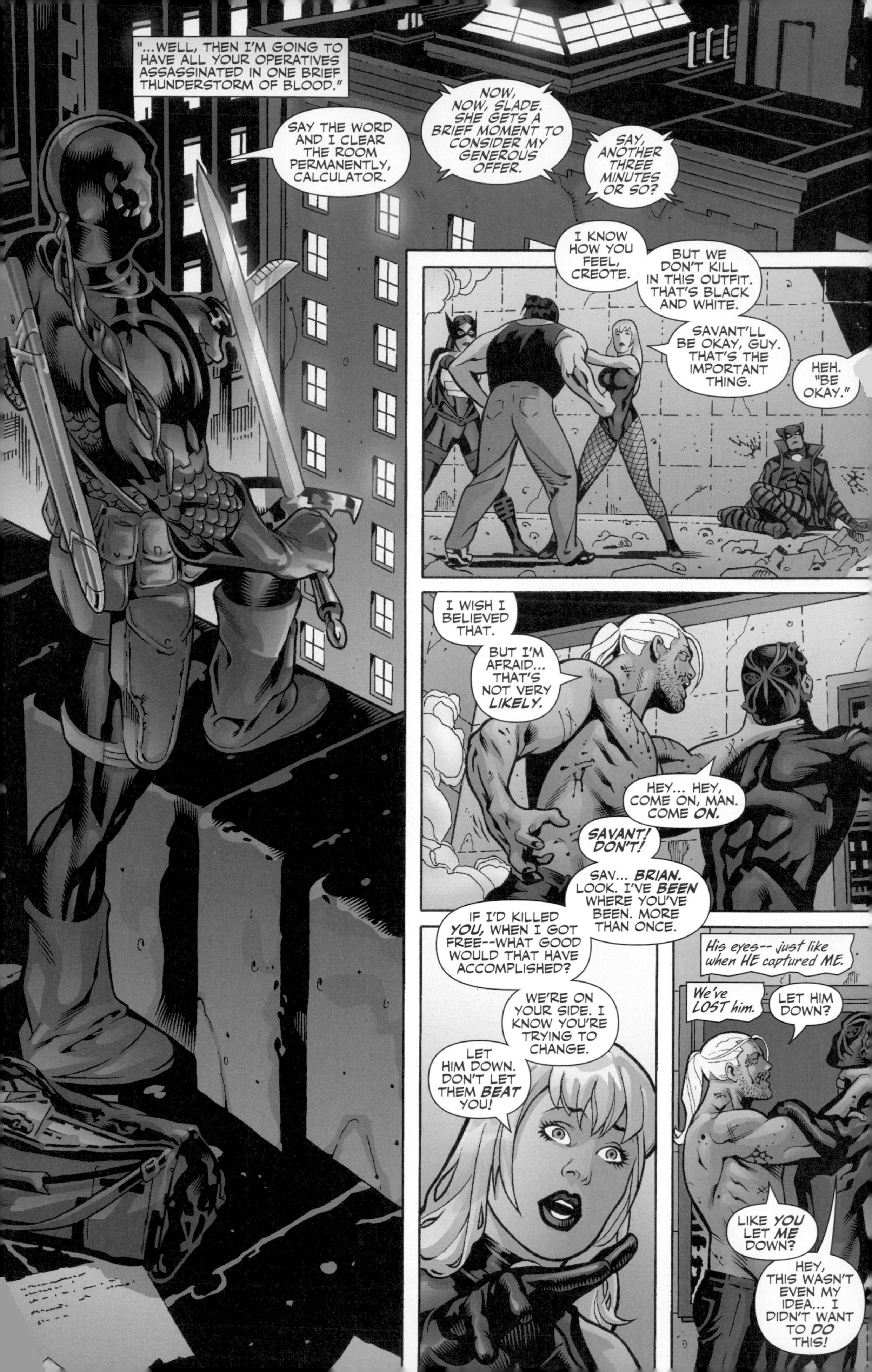
"...WELL, THEN I'M GOING TO HAVE ALL YOUR OPERATIVES ASSASSINATED IN ONE BRIEF THUNDERSTORM OF BLOOD."
SAY THE WORD AND I CLEAR THE ROOM PERMANENTLY, CALCULATOR.
NOW, NOW, SLADE. SHE GETS A BRIEF MOMENT TO CONSIDER MY GENEROUS OFFER.
SAY, ANOTHER THREE MINUTES OR SO?
I KNOW HOW YOU FEEL, CREOTE.
BUT WE DON'T KILL IN THIS OUTFIT. THAT'S BLACK AND WHITE.
SAVANT'LL BE OKAY, GUY. THAT'S THE IMPORTANT THING.
HEH. "BE OKAY."
I WISH I BELIEVED THAT.
BUT I'M AFRAID... THAT'S NOT VERY LIKELY.
HEY... HEY, COME ON, MAN. COME ON.
SAVANT! DON'T!
SAV... BRIAN. LOOK. I'VE BEEN WHERE YOU'VE BEEN. MORE THAN ONCE.
IF I'D KILLED YOU, WHEN I GOT FREE--WHAT GOOD WOULD THAT HAVE ACCOMPLISHED?
WE'RE ON YOUR SIDE. I KNOW YOU'RE TRYING TO CHANGE.
LET HIM DOWN. DON'T LET THEM BEAT YOU!
His eyes-- just like when HE captured ME.
We've LOST him.
LET HIM DOWN?
LIKE YOU LET ME DOWN?
HEY, THIS WASN'T EVEN MY IDEA... I DIDN'T WANT TO DO THIS!

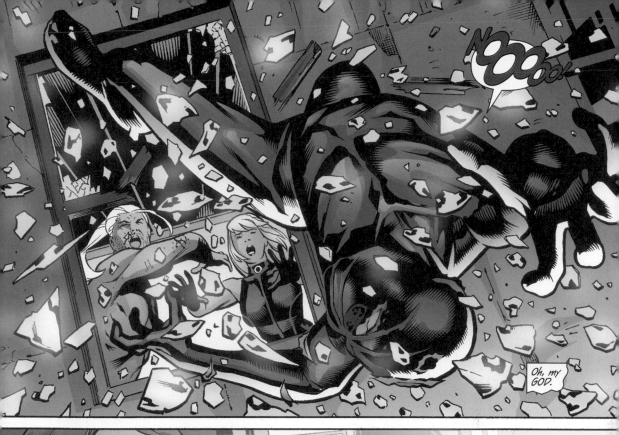

NOOOOO!

Oh, my GOD.

CANARY! DINAH! REPORT! WHAT JUST HAPPENED?

HE LOST IT, ORACLE! HE JUST THREW BLACK SPIDER OUT THE WINDOW--

HE'S NOT MOVING, ORACLE!

DID YOU HEAR ME? I THINK HE'S DEAD.

OH, NO.

DINAH... YOU HAVE TO HANDCUFF SAVANT.

WHAT? THEY TORTURED HIM, FOR TWO DAYS.

I KNOW, BUT...

...WE HAVE TO START PAYING FOR OUR MISTAKES.

WE HAVE TO... DO THINGS BY THE CODE.

OR THERE'S NO POINT TO ANY OF THIS.

I MIGHT HAVE SAVED YOU SOME TIME COMING TO THAT REALIZATION, BARBARA.

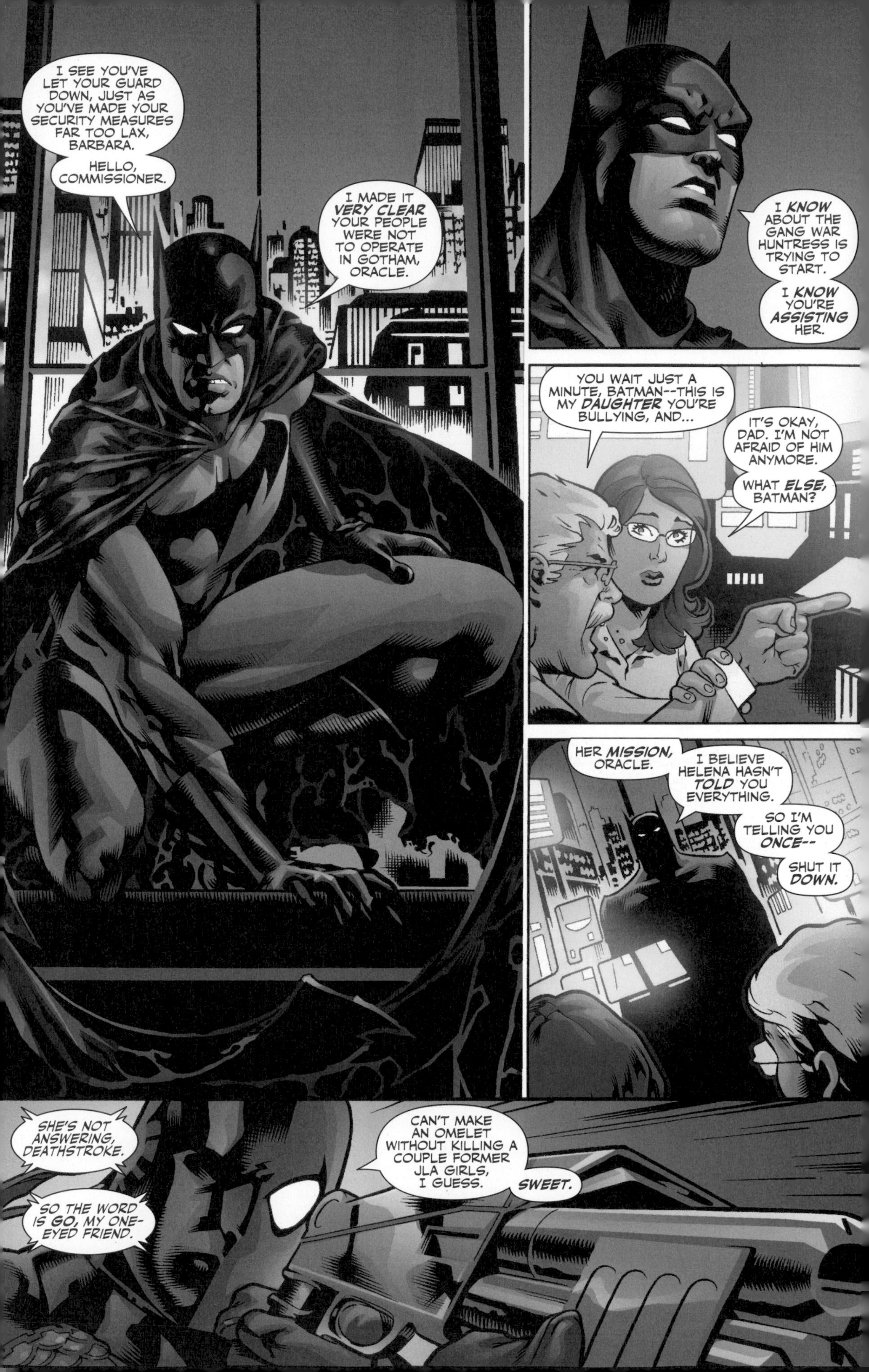
I SEE YOU'VE LET YOUR GUARD DOWN, JUST AS YOU'VE MADE YOUR SECURITY MEASURES FAR TOO LAX, BARBARA.
HELLO, COMMISSIONER.
I MADE IT VERY CLEAR YOUR PEOPLE WERE NOT TO OPERATE IN GOTHAM, ORACLE.
I KNOW ABOUT THE GANG WAR HUNTRESS IS TRYING TO START.
I KNOW YOU'RE ASSISTING HER.
YOU WAIT JUST A MINUTE, BATMAN--THIS IS MY DAUGHTER YOU'RE BULLYING, AND...
IT'S OKAY, DAD. I'M NOT AFRAID OF HIM ANYMORE.
WHAT ELSE, BATMAN?
HER MISSION, ORACLE.
I BELIEVE HELENA HASN'T TOLD YOU EVERYTHING.
SO I'M TELLING YOU ONCE--
SHUT IT DOWN.
SHE'S NOT ANSWERING, DEATHSTROKE.
SO THE WORD IS GO, MY ONE-EYED FRIEND.
CAN'T MAKE AN OMELET WITHOUT KILLING A COUPLE FORMER JLA GIRLS, I GUESS.
SWEET.

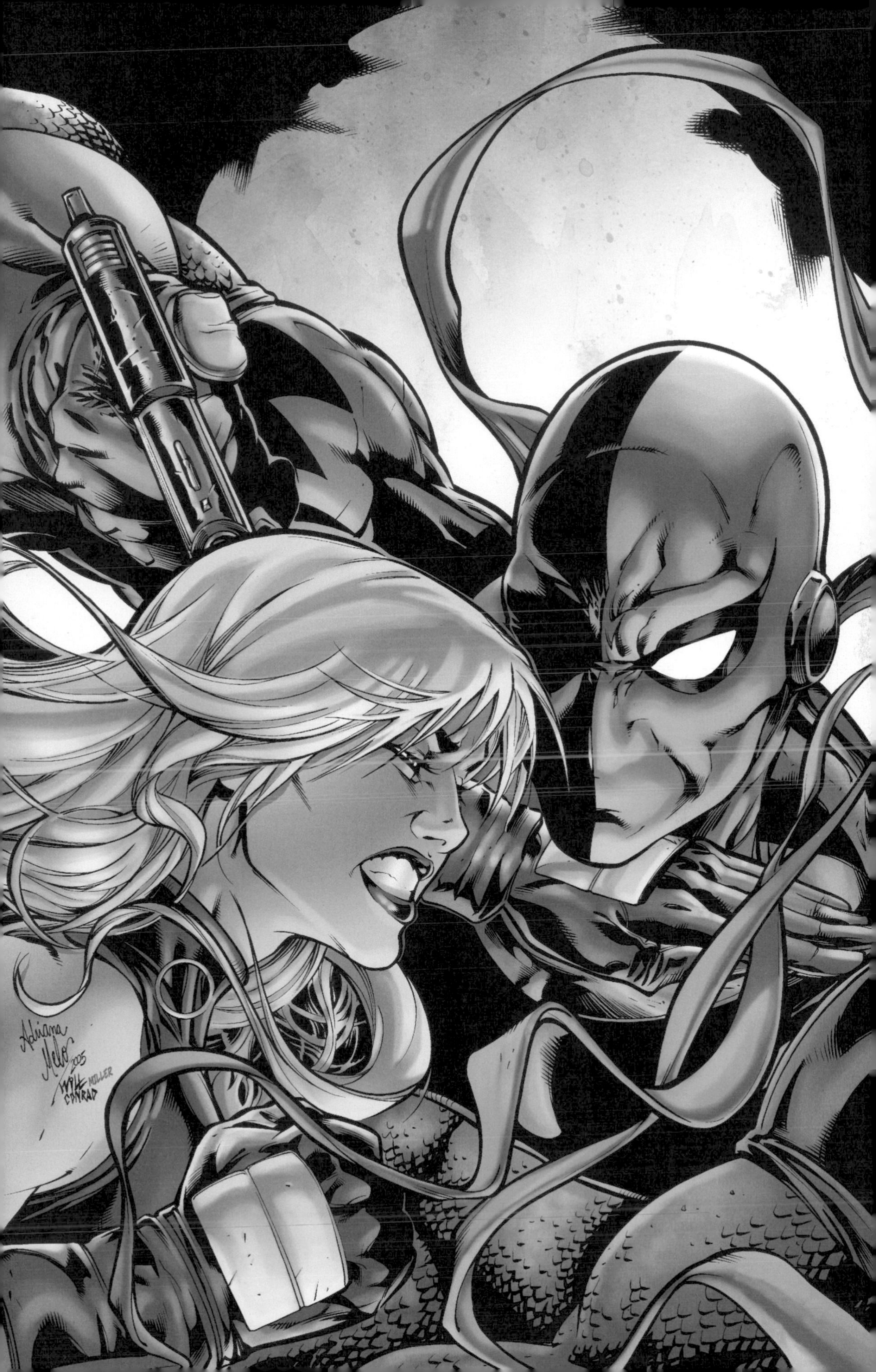
Adriana Melo 2005
Will Conrad
Miller

Cover art by
ADRIANA MELO
and WILL CONRAD

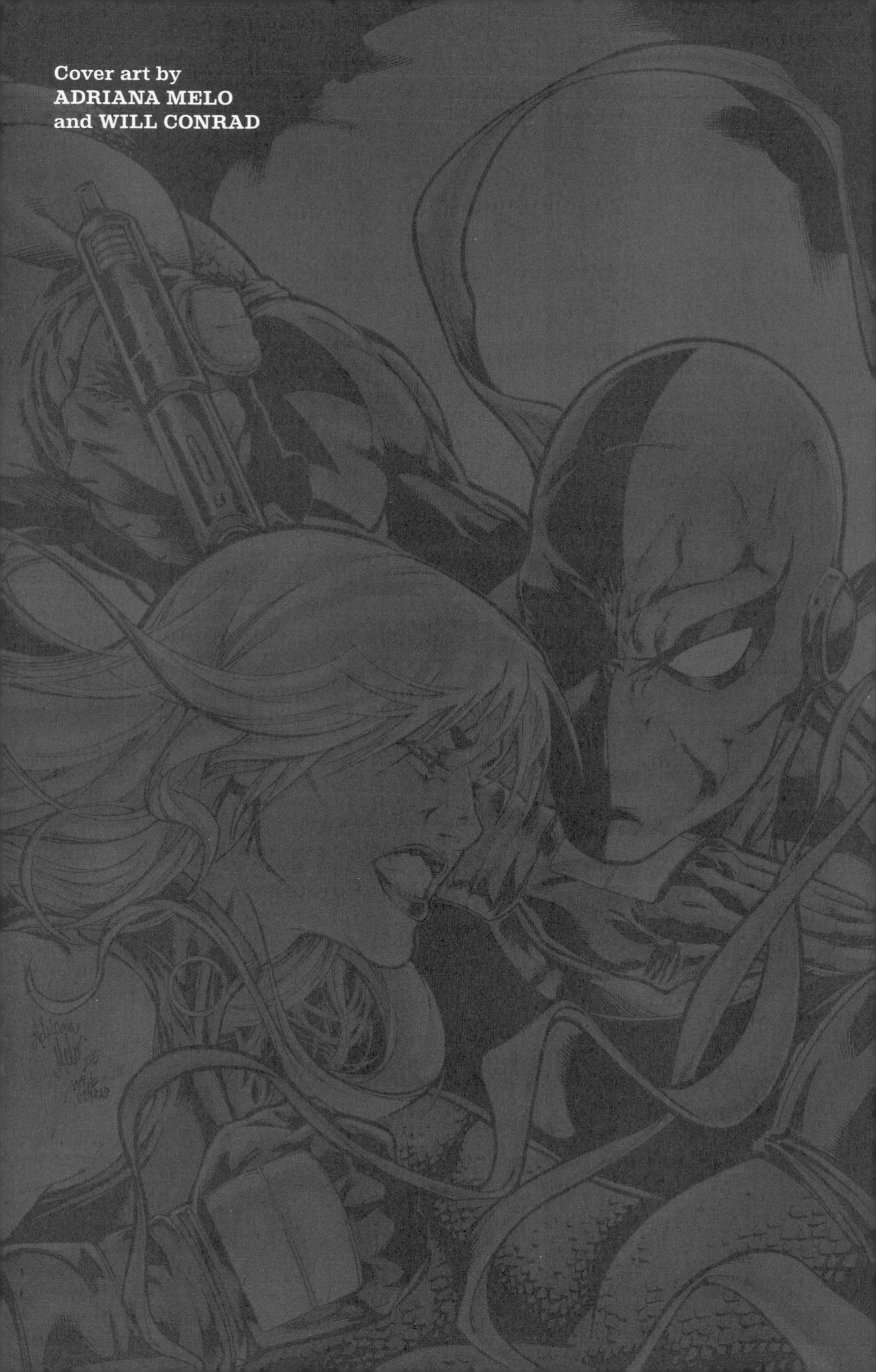

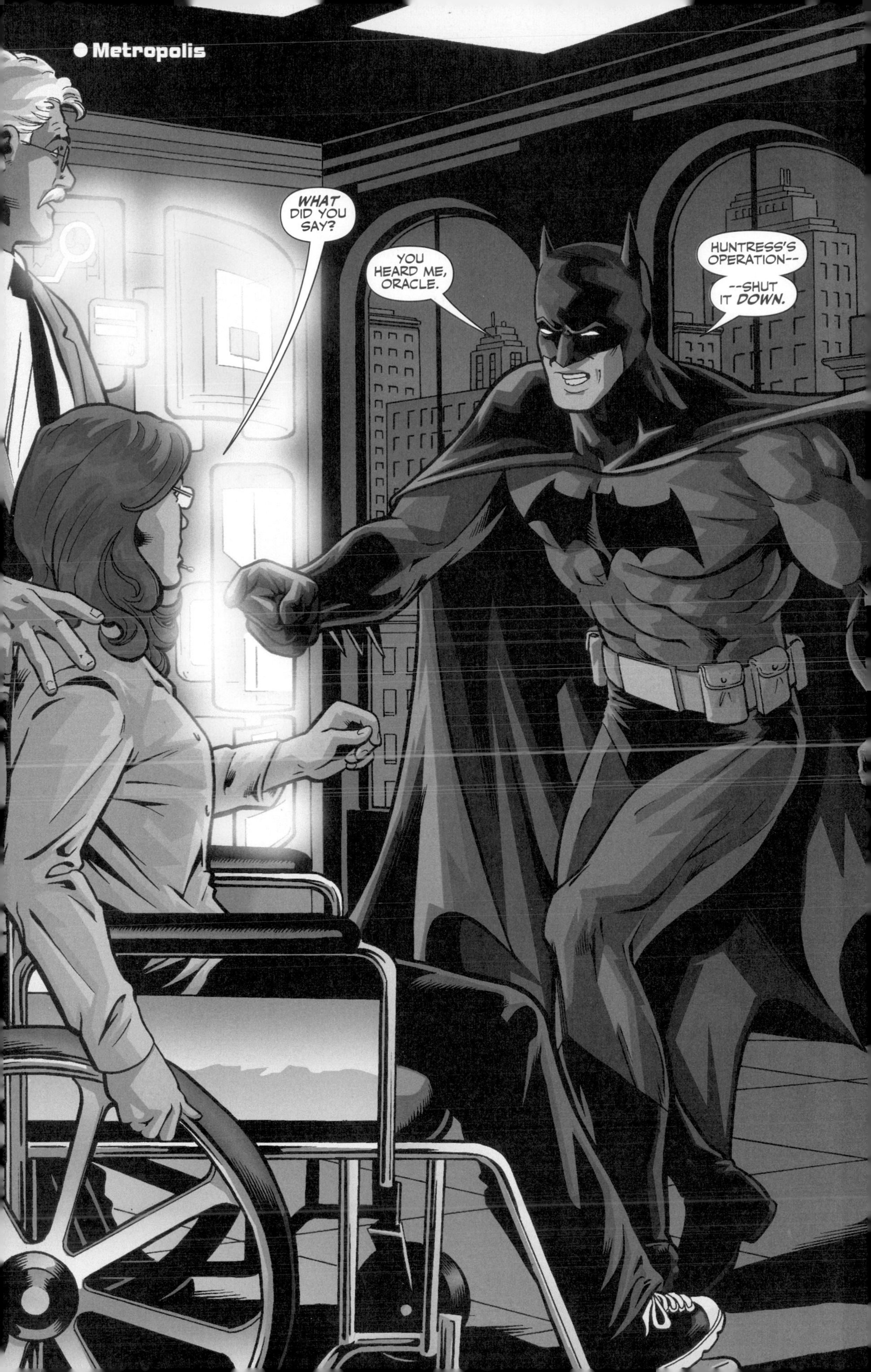
Metropolis
WHAT DID YOU SAY?
YOU HEARD ME, ORACLE.
HUNTRESS'S OPERATION--
--SHUT IT DOWN.

NOW YOU LISTEN, BATMAN. I DON'T KNOW WHAT'S GOING ON, BUT THIS IS MY *DAUGHTER* YOU'RE TALKING TO, AND I DO *NOT* APPRECIATE...

S'OKAY, DAD. THIS ISN'T NEW STUFF WITH HIM.

LET'S HEAR HIM OUT.

WHEN I SEE HIM, WITH THAT CONTROLLED RAGE OF HIS...

...I UNDERSTAND HOW HE CAN MAKE CROOKS BEG TO SIGN FULL CONFESSIONS JUST BY GLARING AT THEM.

IT WAS A *MISTAKE* TO LET THE COMMISSIONER IN HERE, BARBARA.

BUT I DON'T THINK I'M GOING TO SHOW HIM ANY FEAR. NOT TODAY.

MAYBE IT'S BECAUSE SOMEONE'S GOT MY *BACK* THIS TIME.

WAS IT?

AND I REMEMBER A TIME WHEN YOU CALLED ME *JIM*.

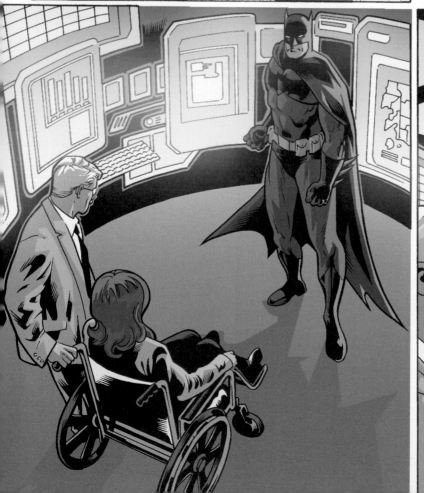

ALL RIGHT. I KNOW ABOUT *HUNTRESS* AND THE *SIGIORELLO* MOB.

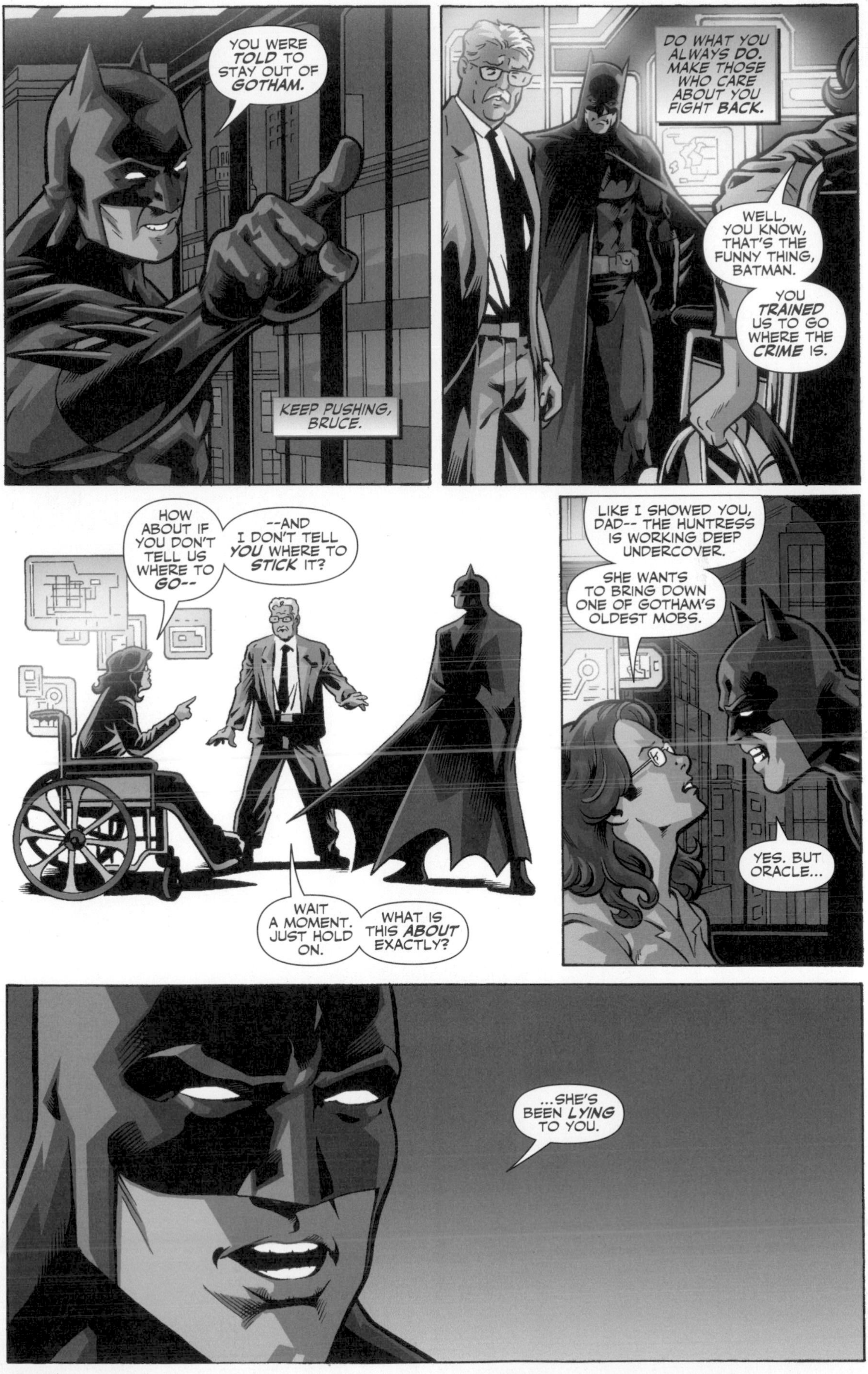
YOU WERE TOLD TO STAY OUT OF GOTHAM.
KEEP PUSHING, BRUCE.
DO WHAT YOU ALWAYS DO. MAKE THOSE WHO CARE ABOUT YOU FIGHT BACK.
WELL, YOU KNOW, THAT'S THE FUNNY THING, BATMAN.
YOU TRAINED US TO GO WHERE THE CRIME IS.
HOW ABOUT IF YOU DON'T TELL US WHERE TO GO--
--AND I DON'T TELL YOU WHERE TO STICK IT?
WAIT A MOMENT. JUST HOLD ON.
WHAT IS THIS ABOUT EXACTLY?
LIKE I SHOWED YOU, DAD-- THE HUNTRESS IS WORKING DEEP UNDERCOVER.
SHE WANTS TO BRING DOWN ONE OF GOTHAM'S OLDEST MOBS.
YES. BUT ORACLE...
...SHE'S BEEN LYING TO YOU.

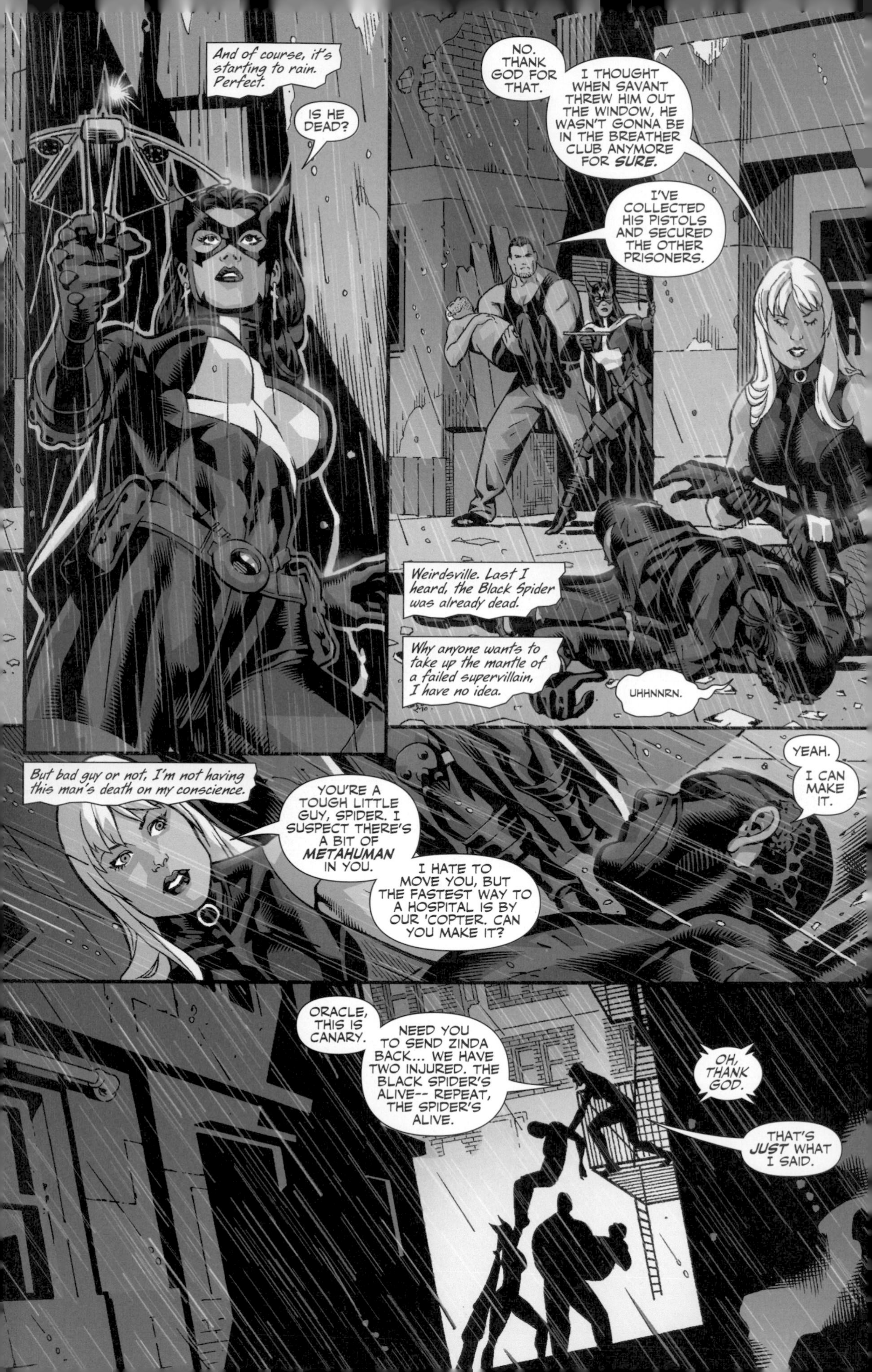
And of course, it's starting to rain. Perfect.
IS HE DEAD?
NO. THANK GOD FOR THAT.
I THOUGHT WHEN SAVANT THREW HIM OUT THE WINDOW, HE WASN'T GONNA BE IN THE BREATHER CLUB ANYMORE FOR SURE.
I'VE COLLECTED HIS PISTOLS AND SECURED THE OTHER PRISONERS.
Weirdsville. Last I heard, the Black Spider was already dead.
Why anyone wants to take up the mantle of a failed supervillain, I have no idea.
UHHNNRN.
But bad guy or not, I'm not having this man's death on my conscience.
YOU'RE A TOUGH LITTLE GUY, SPIDER. I SUSPECT THERE'S A BIT OF METAHUMAN IN YOU.
I HATE TO MOVE YOU, BUT THE FASTEST WAY TO A HOSPITAL IS BY OUR 'COPTER. CAN YOU MAKE IT?
YEAH.
I CAN MAKE IT.
ORACLE, THIS IS CANARY.
NEED YOU TO SEND ZINDA BACK... WE HAVE TWO INJURED. THE BLACK SPIDER'S ALIVE-- REPEAT, THE SPIDER'S ALIVE.
OH, THANK GOD.
THAT'S JUST WHAT I SAID.

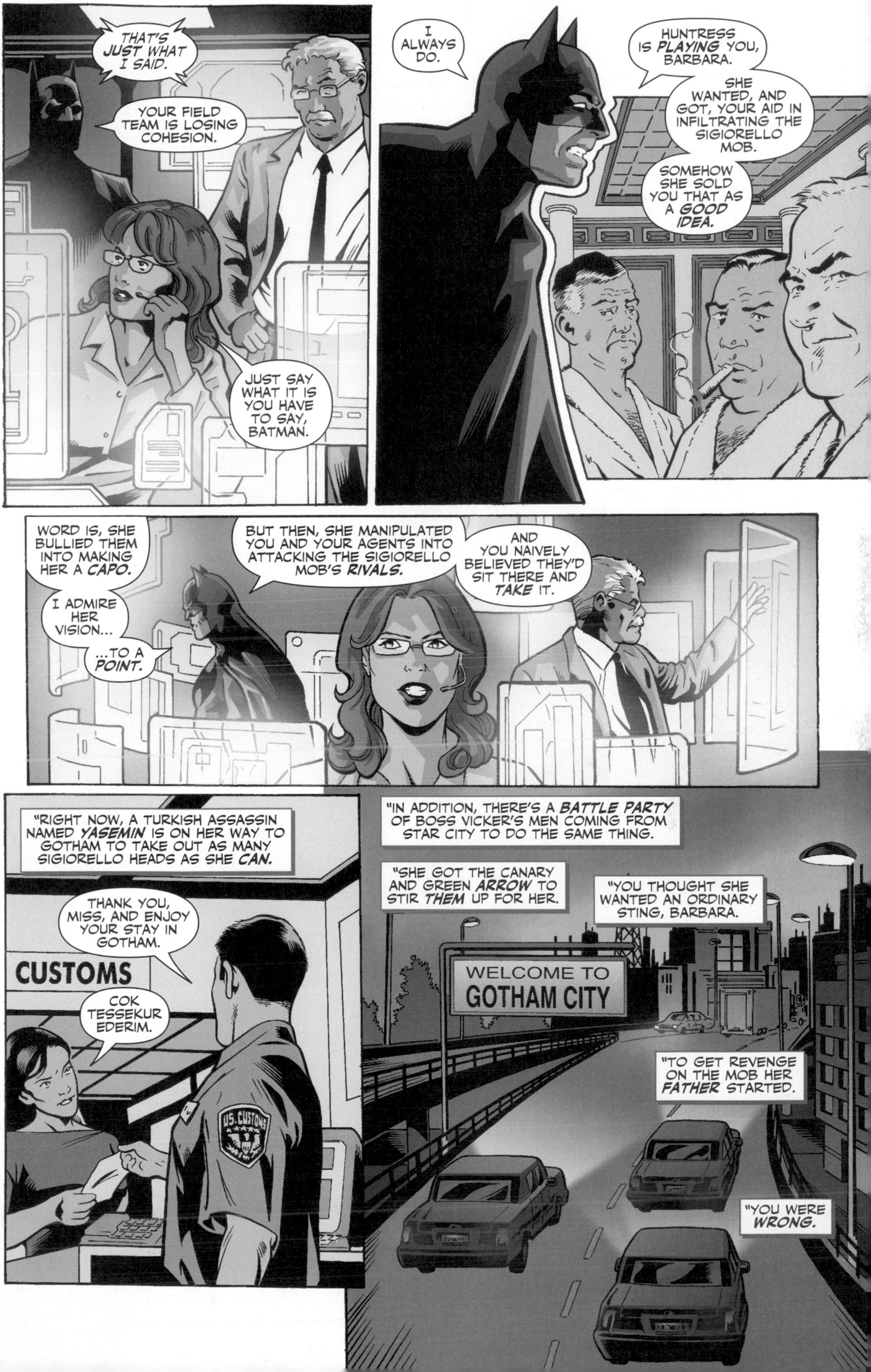
THAT'S JUST WHAT I SAID.
YOUR FIELD TEAM IS LOSING COHESION.
JUST SAY WHAT IT IS YOU HAVE TO SAY, BATMAN.
I ALWAYS DO.
HUNTRESS IS PLAYING YOU, BARBARA.
SHE WANTED, AND GOT, YOUR AID IN INFILTRATING THE SIGIORELLO MOB.
SOMEHOW SHE SOLD YOU THAT AS A GOOD IDEA.
WORD IS, SHE BULLIED THEM INTO MAKING HER A CAPO.
I ADMIRE HER VISION...
...TO A POINT.
BUT THEN, SHE MANIPULATED YOU AND YOUR AGENTS INTO ATTACKING THE SIGIORELLO MOB'S RIVALS.
AND YOU NAIVELY BELIEVED THEY'D SIT THERE AND TAKE IT.
"RIGHT NOW, A TURKISH ASSASSIN NAMED YASEMIN IS ON HER WAY TO GOTHAM TO TAKE OUT AS MANY SIGIORELLO HEADS AS SHE CAN.
THANK YOU, MISS, AND ENJOY YOUR STAY IN GOTHAM.
CUSTOMS
COK TESSEKUR EDERIM.
U.S. CUSTOMS
"IN ADDITION, THERE'S A BATTLE PARTY OF BOSS VICKER'S MEN COMING FROM STAR CITY TO DO THE SAME THING.
"SHE GOT THE CANARY AND GREEN ARROW TO STIR THEM UP FOR HER.
"YOU THOUGHT SHE WANTED AN ORDINARY STING, BARBARA.
WELCOME TO GOTHAM CITY
"TO GET REVENGE ON THE MOB HER FATHER STARTED.
"YOU WERE WRONG.

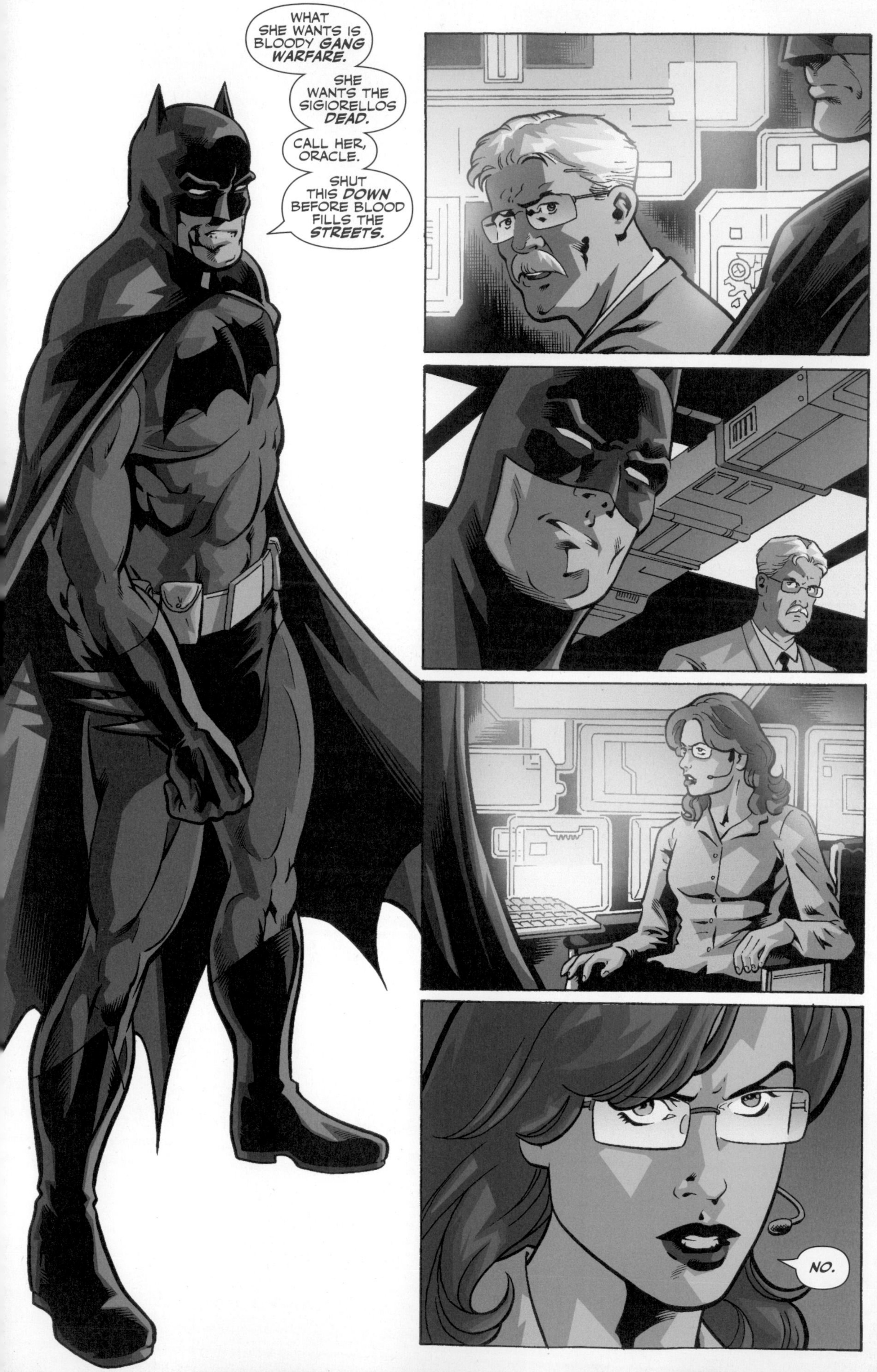
WHAT SHE WANTS IS BLOODY GANG WARFARE.
SHE WANTS THE SIGIORELLOS DEAD.
CALL HER, ORACLE.
SHUT THIS DOWN BEFORE BLOOD FILLS THE STREETS.
NO.

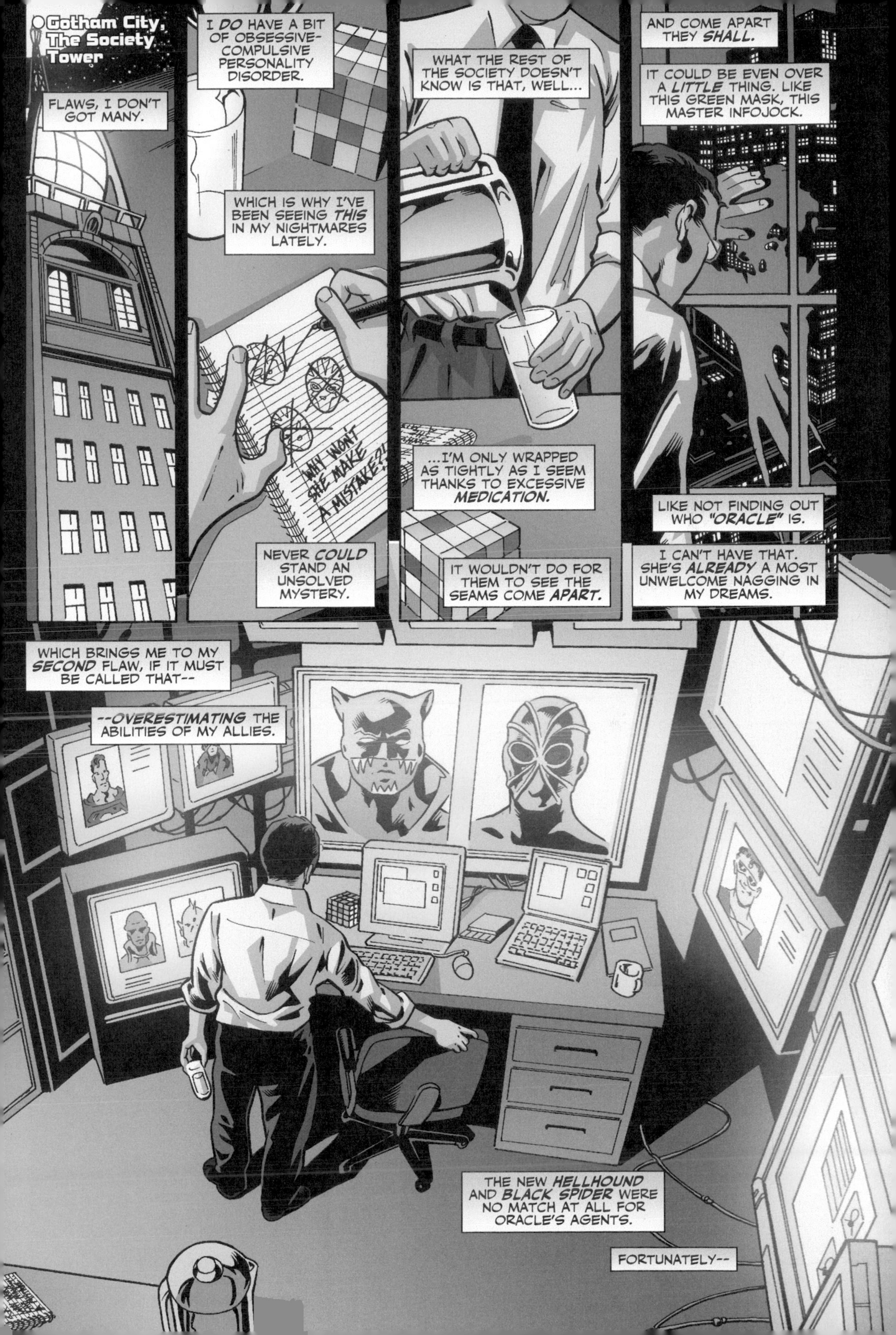
Gotham City, The Society Tower
FLAWS, I DON'T GOT MANY.
I DO HAVE A BIT OF OBSESSIVE-COMPULSIVE PERSONALITY DISORDER.
WHICH IS WHY I'VE BEEN SEEING THIS IN MY NIGHTMARES LATELY.
WHY WON'T SHE MAKE A MISTAKE?!
NEVER COULD STAND AN UNSOLVED MYSTERY.
WHAT THE REST OF THE SOCIETY DOESN'T KNOW IS THAT, WELL...
...I'M ONLY WRAPPED AS TIGHTLY AS I SEEM THANKS TO EXCESSIVE MEDICATION.
IT WOULDN'T DO FOR THEM TO SEE THE SEAMS COME APART.
AND COME APART THEY SHALL.
IT COULD BE EVEN OVER A LITTLE THING. LIKE THIS GREEN MASK, THIS MASTER INFOJOCK.
LIKE NOT FINDING OUT WHO "ORACLE" IS.
I CAN'T HAVE THAT. SHE'S ALREADY A MOST UNWELCOME NAGGING IN MY DREAMS.
WHICH BRINGS ME TO MY SECOND FLAW, IF IT MUST BE CALLED THAT--
--OVERESTIMATING THE ABILITIES OF MY ALLIES.
THE NEW HELLHOUND AND BLACK SPIDER WERE NO MATCH AT ALL FOR ORACLE'S AGENTS.
FORTUNATELY--

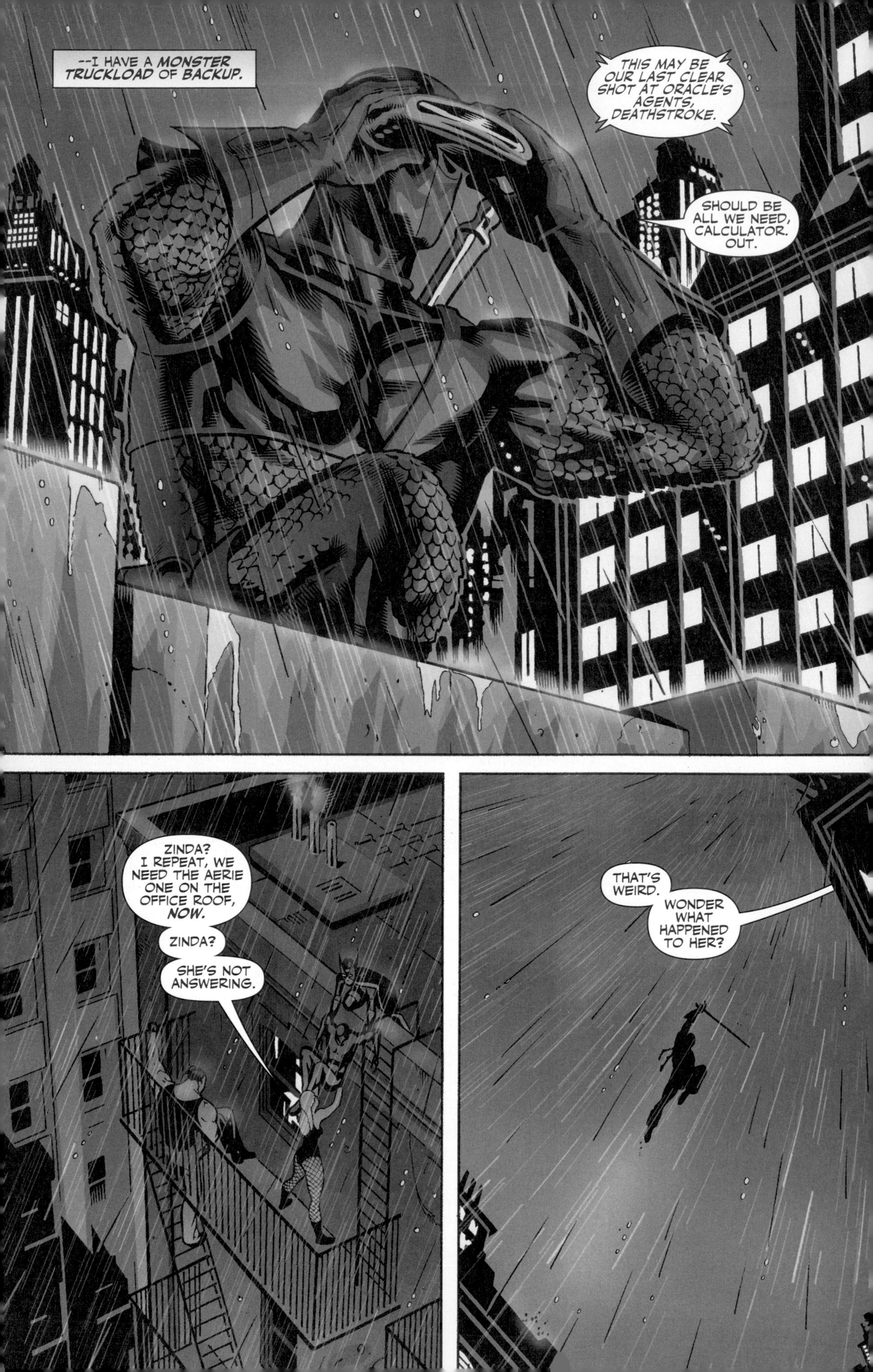
--I HAVE A *MONSTER TRUCKLOAD* OF *BACKUP.*
THIS MAY BE OUR LAST CLEAR SHOT AT ORACLE'S AGENTS, DEATHSTROKE.
SHOULD BE ALL WE NEED, CALCULATOR. OUT.
ZINDA? I REPEAT, WE NEED THE AERIE ONE ON THE OFFICE ROOF, *NOW.*
ZINDA?
SHE'S NOT ANSWERING.
THAT'S WEIRD.
WONDER WHAT HAPPENED TO HER?

I MADE THE MISTAKE OF MISJUDGING HUNTRESS MORE THAN ONCE, BATMAN.

NEVER AGAIN.

WE'RE STICKING WITH HER PLAN. MORE-OVER--

--YOU ARE *NOT* TO INTERFERE. BUT THANKS FOR STOPPING BY.

ORACLE. *BARBARA.*

YOU'RE LETTING FRIENDSHIP CLOUD YOUR *JUDGMENT.* I TRAINED YOU *BETTER* THAN THAT.

YES, YOU DID, BATMAN. YOU TRAINED ME TO BE *HARD.*

FORTUNATELY...

...SOMEONE *ELSE* TAUGHT ME TO BE *HUMAN.*

I BELIEVE THE LADY SAID YOU WERE LEAVING?

BARBARA, IF EVEN *ONE* OF THOSE MOBSTERS DIES TONIGHT, ON MY STREETS--

--I'LL SHUT YOU DOWN. FOR GOOD. DO YOU UNDER-STAND?

I'LL RETIRE *ALL* OF YOU.

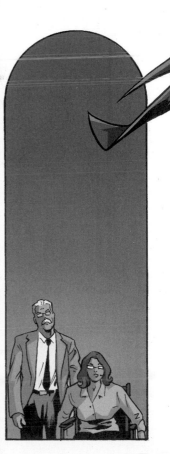

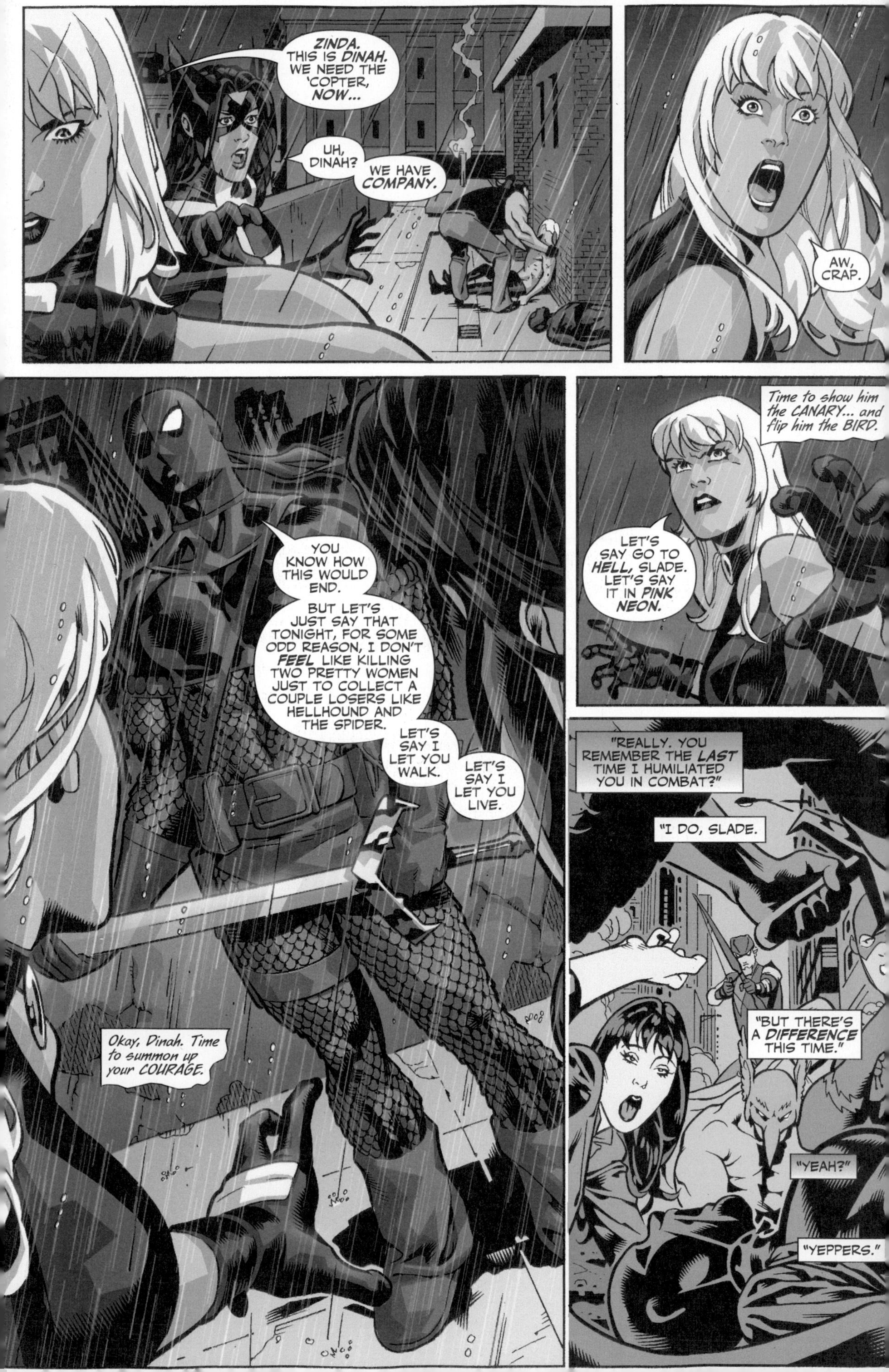
ZINDA. THIS IS DINAH. WE NEED THE 'COPTER, NOW...
UH, DINAH?
WE HAVE COMPANY.
AW, CRAP.
YOU KNOW HOW THIS WOULD END.
BUT LET'S JUST SAY THAT TONIGHT, FOR SOME ODD REASON, I DON'T FEEL LIKE KILLING TWO PRETTY WOMEN JUST TO COLLECT A COUPLE LOSERS LIKE HELLHOUND AND THE SPIDER.
LET'S SAY I LET YOU WALK.
LET'S SAY I LET YOU LIVE.
Okay, Dinah. Time to summon up your COURAGE.
Time to show him the CANARY... and flip him the BIRD.
LET'S SAY GO TO HELL, SLADE. LET'S SAY IT IN PINK NEON.
"REALLY. YOU REMEMBER THE LAST TIME I HUMILIATED YOU IN COMBAT?"
"I DO, SLADE.
"BUT THERE'S A DIFFERENCE THIS TIME."
"YEAH?"
"YEPPERS."

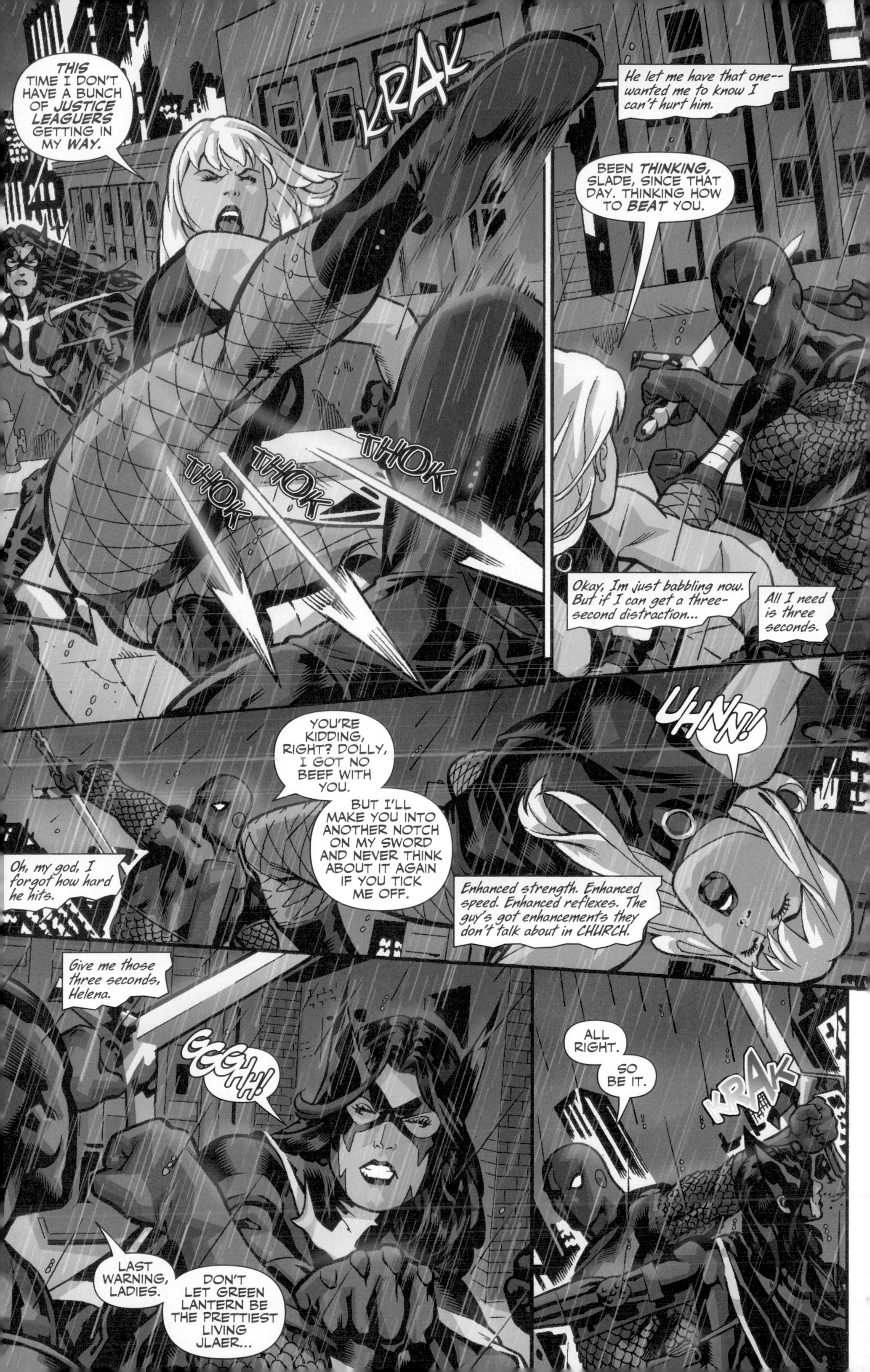
THIS TIME I DON'T HAVE A BUNCH OF JUSTICE LEAGUERS GETTING IN MY WAY.
KRAK
THOK
THOK
THOK
He let me have that one--wanted me to know I can't hurt him.
BEEN THINKING, SLADE, SINCE THAT DAY. THINKING HOW TO BEAT YOU.
Okay, Im just babbling now. But if I can get a three-second distraction...
All I need is three seconds.
UHNN!
YOU'RE KIDDING, RIGHT? DOLLY, I GOT NO BEEF WITH YOU.
BUT I'LL MAKE YOU INTO ANOTHER NOTCH ON MY SWORD AND NEVER THINK ABOUT IT AGAIN IF YOU TICK ME OFF.
Oh, my god, I forgot how hard he hits.
Enhanced strength. Enhanced speed. Enhanced reflexes. The guy's got enhancements they don't talk about in CHURCH.
Give me those three seconds, Helena.
GGGHH!
LAST WARNING, LADIES.
DON'T LET GREEN LANTERN BE THE PRETTIEST LIVING JLAER...
ALL RIGHT.
SO BE IT.
KRAK

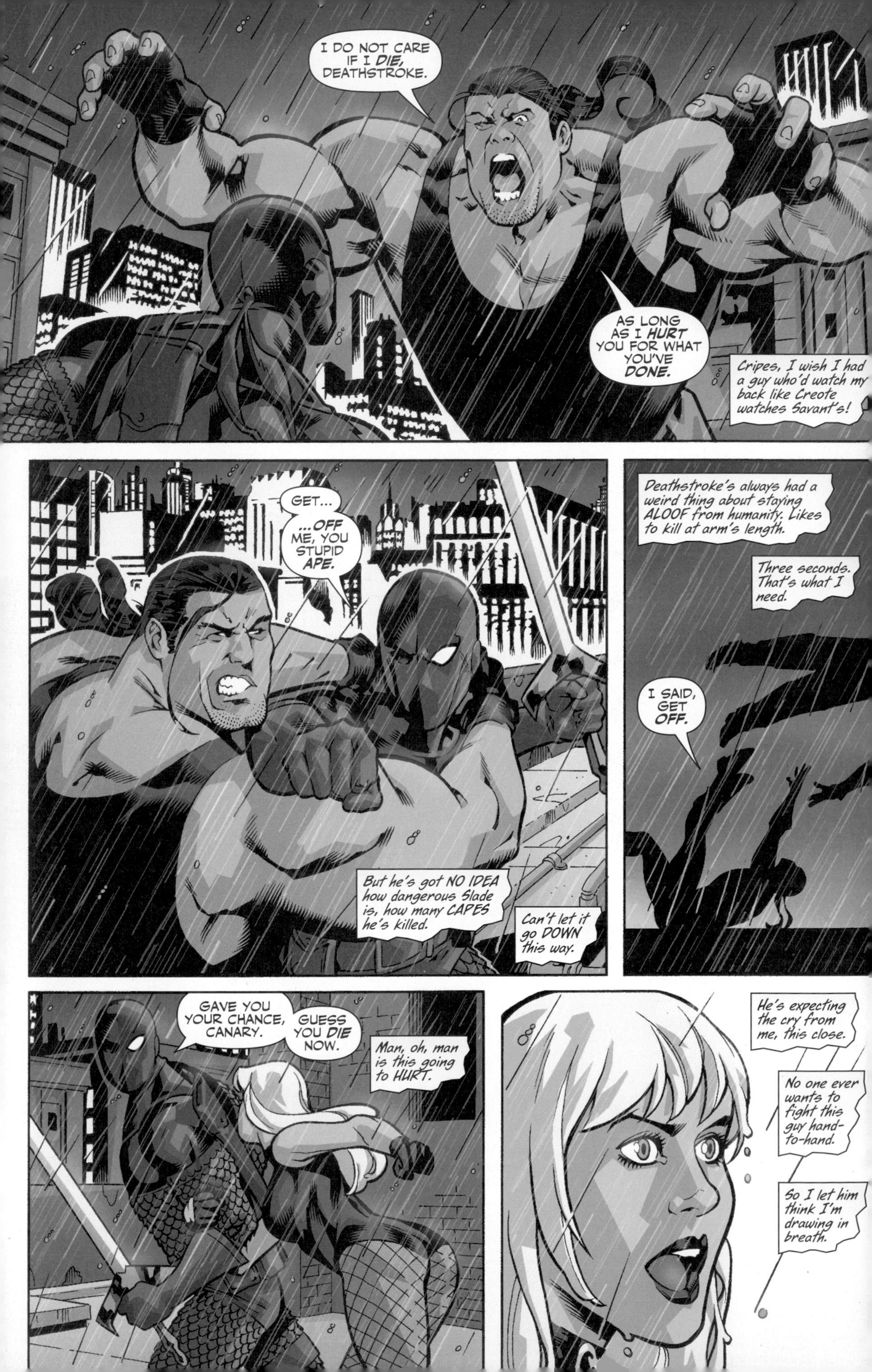

I DO NOT CARE IF I *DIE*, DEATHSTROKE.
AS LONG AS I *HURT* YOU FOR WHAT YOU'VE *DONE.*
Cripes, I wish I had a guy who'd watch my back like Creote watches Savant's!
GET...
...*OFF* ME, YOU STUPID *APE.*
But he's got NO IDEA how dangerous Slade is, how many CAPES he's killed.
Can't let it go DOWN this way.
Deathstroke's always had a weird thing about staying ALOOF from humanity. Likes to kill at arm's length.
Three seconds. That's what I need.
I SAID, GET *OFF.*
GAVE YOU YOUR CHANCE, CANARY.
GUESS YOU *DIE* NOW.
Man, oh, man is this going to HURT.
He's expecting the cry from me, this close.
No one ever wants to fight this guy hand-to-hand.
So I let him think I'm drawing in breath.

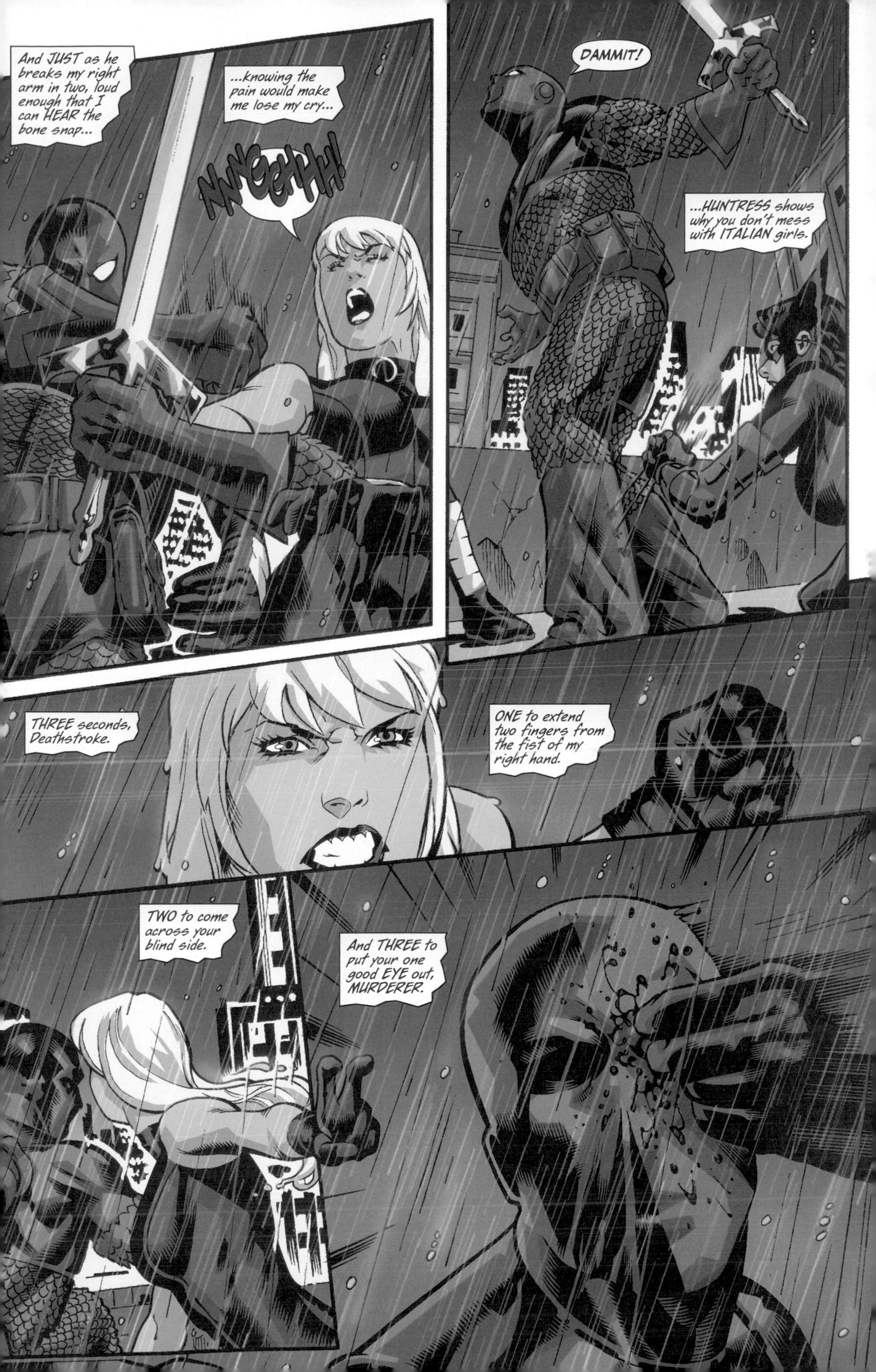

And JUST as he breaks my right arm in two, loud enough that I can HEAR the bone snap...
...knowing the pain would make me lose my cry...
NNNGGHHH!
DAMMIT!
...HUNTRESS shows why you don't mess with ITALIAN girls.
THREE seconds, Deathstroke.
ONE to extend two fingers from the fist of my right hand.
TWO to come across your blind side.
And THREE to put your one good EYE out, MURDERER.

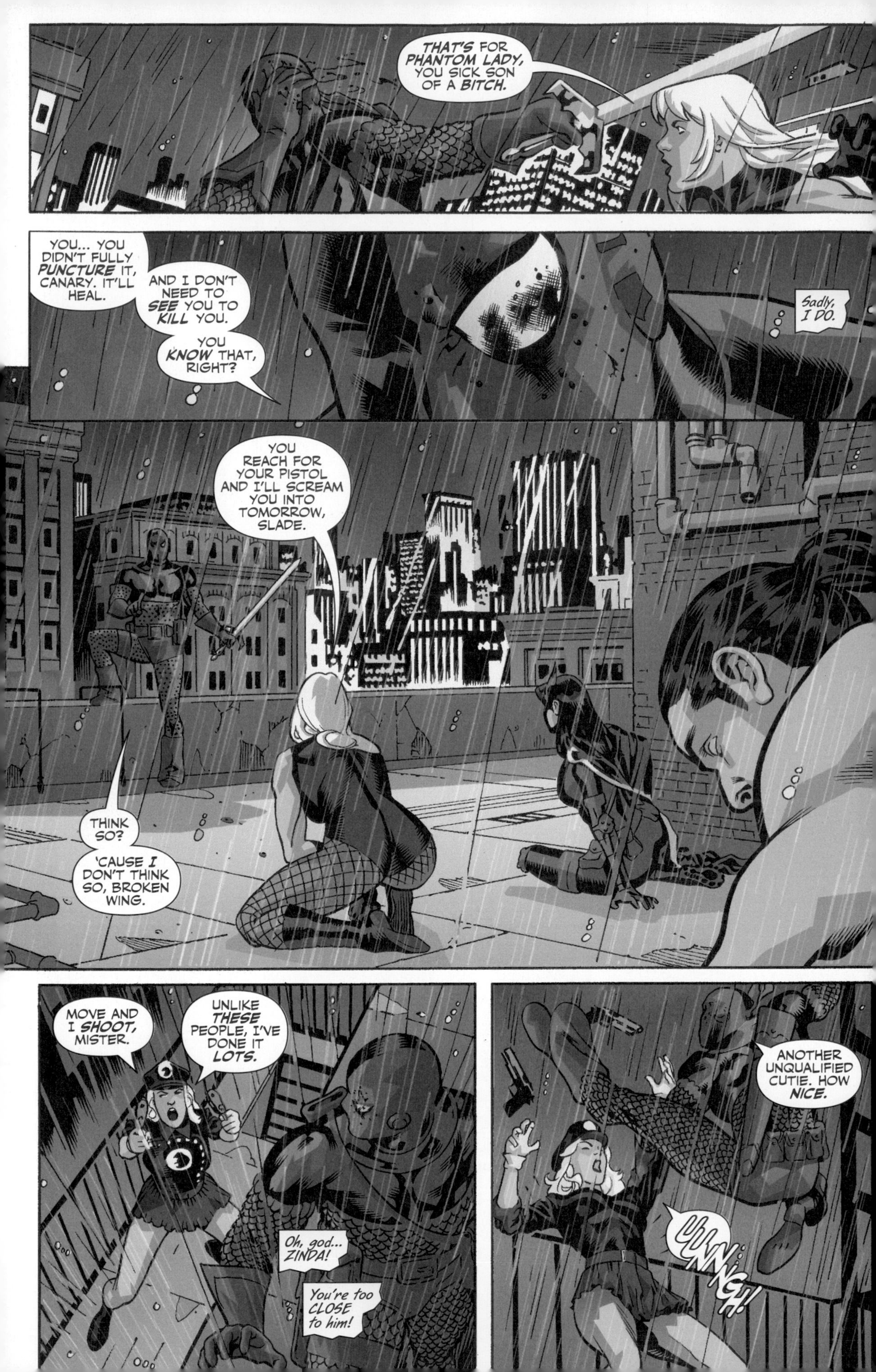
THAT'S FOR PHANTOM LADY, YOU SICK SON OF A BITCH.
YOU... YOU DIDN'T FULLY PUNCTURE IT, CANARY. IT'LL HEAL.
AND I DON'T NEED TO SEE YOU TO KILL YOU.
YOU KNOW THAT, RIGHT?
Sadly, I DO.
YOU REACH FOR YOUR PISTOL AND I'LL SCREAM YOU INTO TOMORROW, SLADE.
THINK SO?
'CAUSE I DON'T THINK SO, BROKEN WING.
MOVE AND I SHOOT, MISTER.
UNLIKE THESE PEOPLE, I'VE DONE IT LOTS.
Oh, god... ZINDA!
You're too CLOSE to him!
ANOTHER UNQUALIFIED CUTIE. HOW NICE.
UUNNNGH!

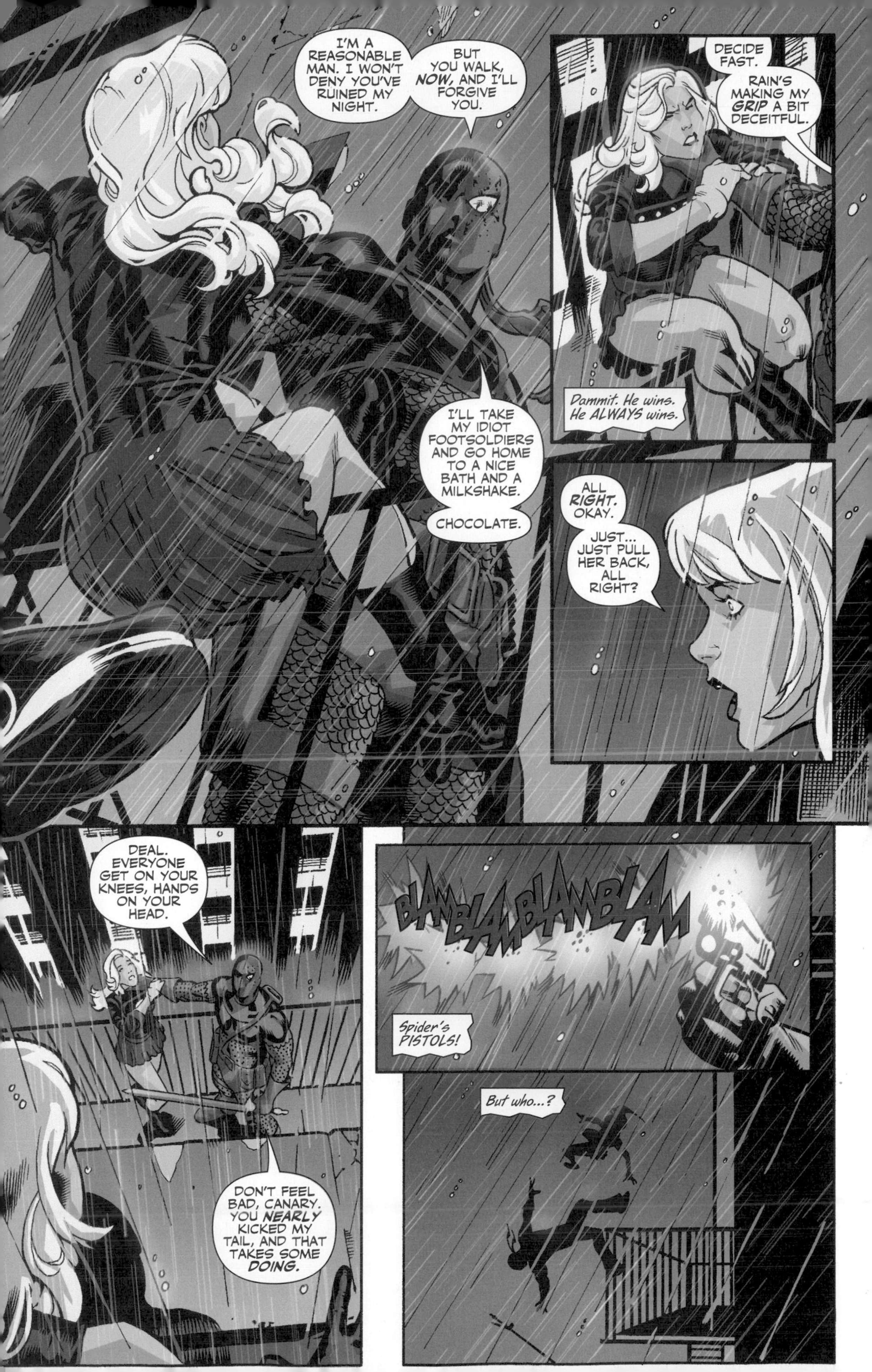
I'M A REASONABLE MAN. I WON'T DENY YOU'VE RUINED MY NIGHT.
BUT YOU WALK, NOW, AND I'LL FORGIVE YOU.
I'LL TAKE MY IDIOT FOOTSOLDIERS AND GO HOME TO A NICE BATH AND A MILKSHAKE.
CHOCOLATE.
DECIDE FAST.
RAIN'S MAKING MY GRIP A BIT DECEITFUL.
Dammit. He wins. He ALWAYS wins.
ALL RIGHT. OKAY.
JUST... JUST PULL HER BACK, ALL RIGHT?
DEAL. EVERYONE GET ON YOUR KNEES, HANDS ON YOUR HEAD.
DON'T FEEL BAD, CANARY. YOU NEARLY KICKED MY TAIL, AND THAT TAKES SOME DOING.
BLAMBLAMBLAMBLAM
Spider's PISTOLS!
But who...?

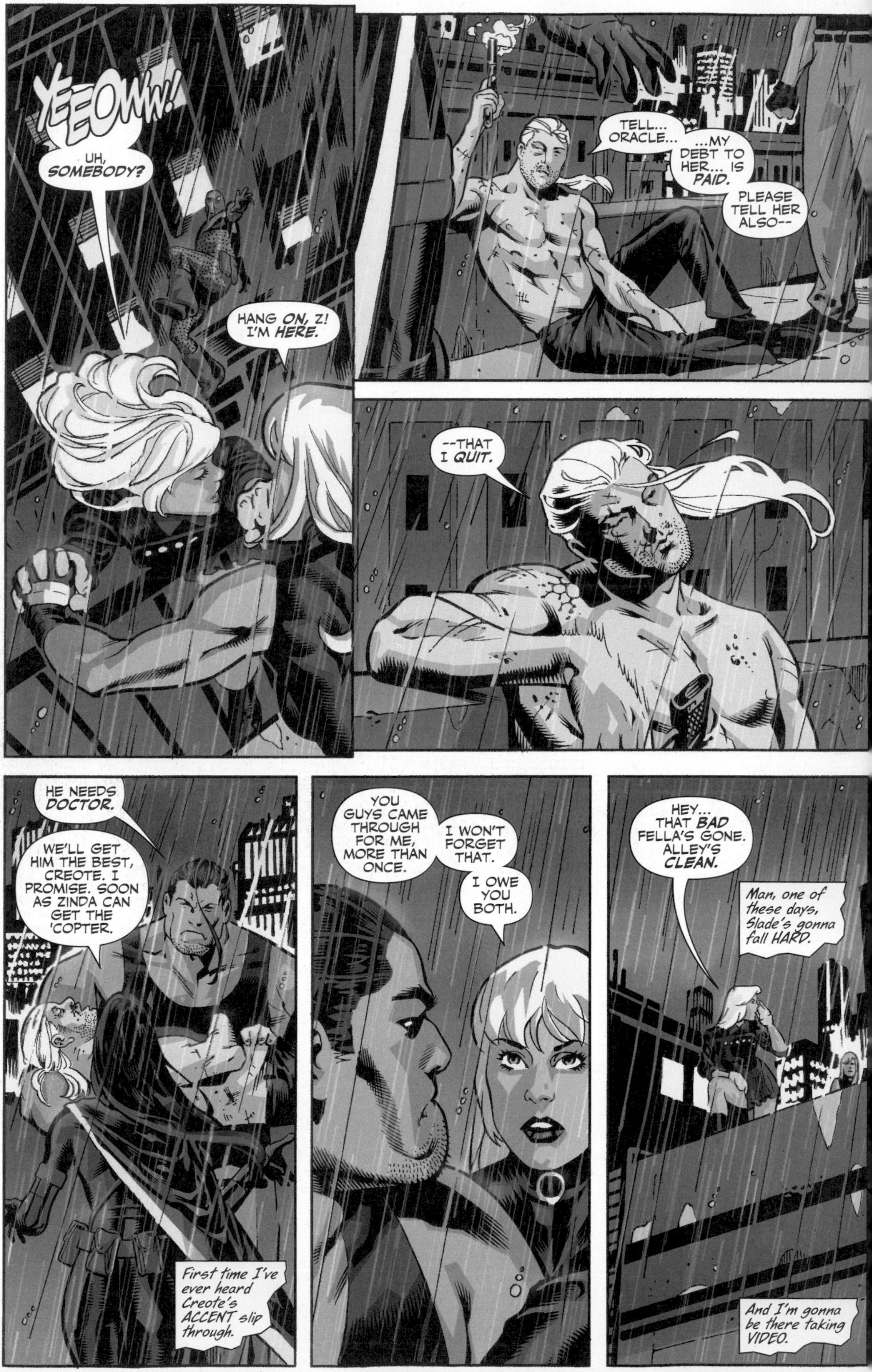
YEEOWW!
UH, SOMEBODY?
HANG ON, Z! I'M HERE.
TELL... ORACLE...
...MY DEBT TO HER... IS PAID.
PLEASE TELL HER ALSO--
--THAT I QUIT.
HE NEEDS DOCTOR.
WE'LL GET HIM THE BEST, CREOTE. I PROMISE. SOON AS ZINDA CAN GET THE 'COPTER.
First time I've ever heard Creote's ACCENT slip through.
YOU GUYS CAME THROUGH FOR ME, MORE THAN ONCE.
I WON'T FORGET THAT.
I OWE YOU BOTH.
HEY... THAT BAD FELLA'S GONE. ALLEY'S CLEAN.
Man, one of these days, Slade's gonna fall HARD.
And I'm gonna be there taking VIDEO.

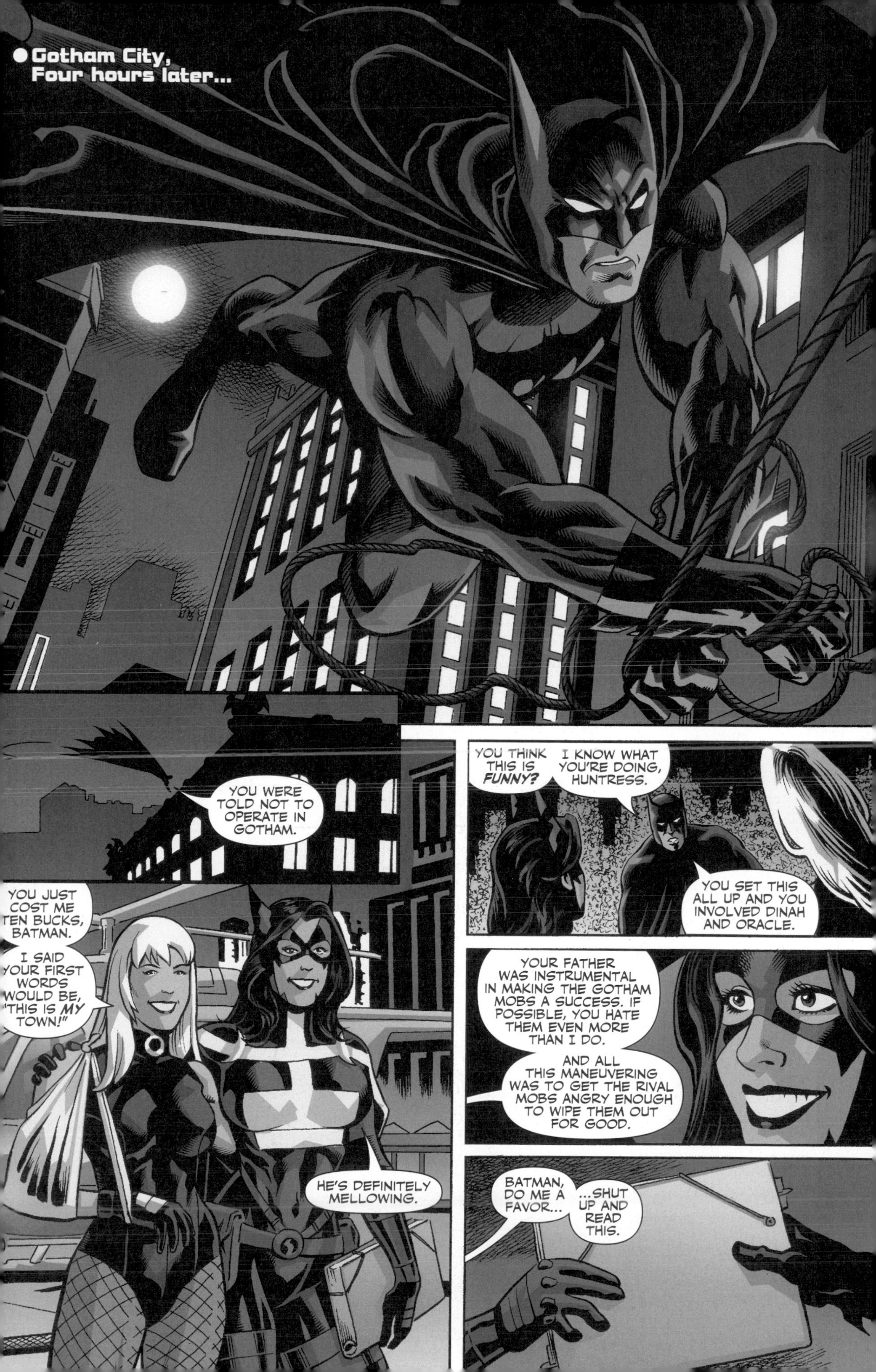
Gotham City,
Four hours later...
YOU WERE TOLD NOT TO OPERATE IN GOTHAM.
YOU JUST COST ME TEN BUCKS, BATMAN.
I SAID YOUR FIRST WORDS WOULD BE, "THIS IS *MY* TOWN!"
HE'S DEFINITELY MELLOWING.
YOU THINK THIS IS *FUNNY?*
I KNOW WHAT YOU'RE DOING, HUNTRESS.
YOU SET THIS ALL UP AND YOU INVOLVED DINAH AND ORACLE.
YOUR FATHER WAS INSTRUMENTAL IN MAKING THE GOTHAM MOBS A SUCCESS. IF POSSIBLE, YOU HATE THEM EVEN MORE THAN I DO.
AND ALL THIS MANEUVERING WAS TO GET THE RIVAL MOBS ANGRY ENOUGH TO WIPE THEM OUT FOR GOOD.
BATMAN, DO ME A FAVOR...
...SHUT UP AND READ THIS.

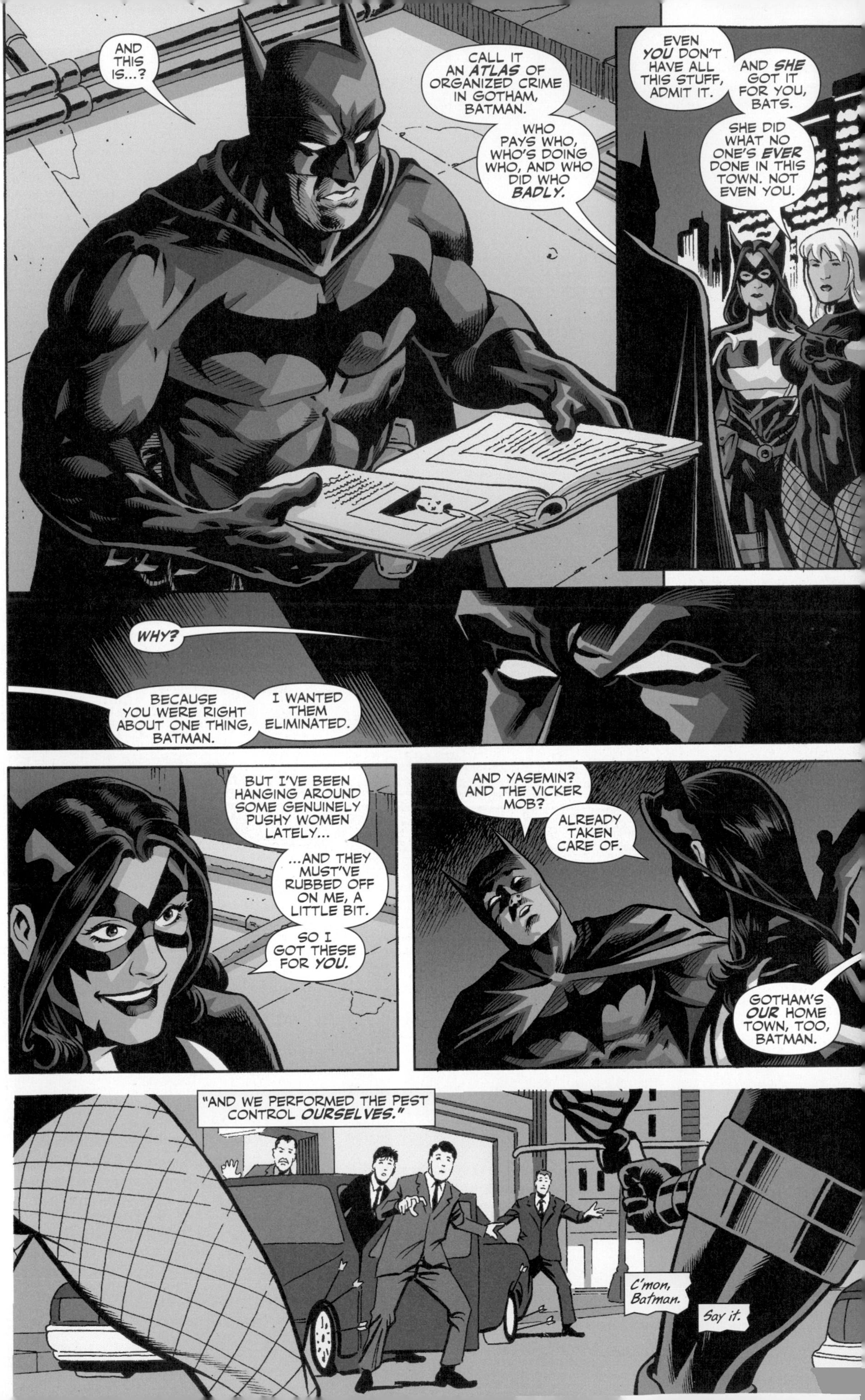

AND THIS IS...?
CALL IT AN ATLAS OF ORGANIZED CRIME IN GOTHAM, BATMAN.
WHO PAYS WHO, WHO'S DOING WHO, AND WHO DID WHO BADLY.
EVEN YOU DON'T HAVE ALL THIS STUFF, ADMIT IT.
AND SHE GOT IT FOR YOU, BATS.
SHE DID WHAT NO ONE'S EVER DONE IN THIS TOWN. NOT EVEN YOU.
WHY?
BECAUSE YOU WERE RIGHT ABOUT ONE THING, BATMAN.
I WANTED THEM ELIMINATED.
BUT I'VE BEEN HANGING AROUND SOME GENUINELY PUSHY WOMEN LATELY...
...AND THEY MUST'VE RUBBED OFF ON ME, A LITTLE BIT.
SO I GOT THESE FOR YOU.
AND YASEMIN? AND THE VICKER MOB?
ALREADY TAKEN CARE OF.
GOTHAM'S OUR HOME TOWN, TOO, BATMAN.
"AND WE PERFORMED THE PEST CONTROL OURSELVES."
C'mon, Batman.
Say it.

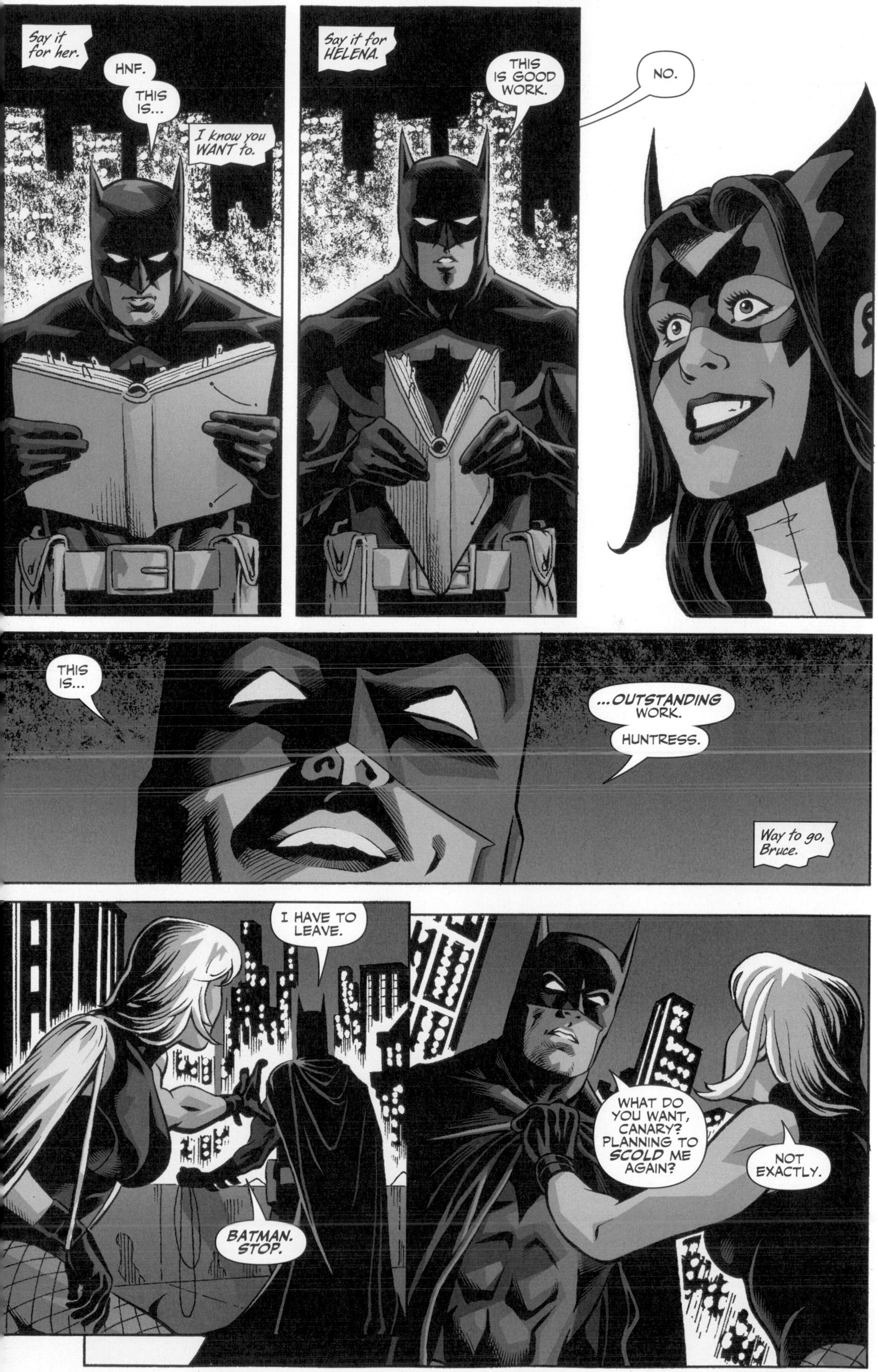
Say it for her.
HNF.
THIS IS...
I know you WANT to.
Say it for HELENA.
THIS IS GOOD WORK.
NO.
THIS IS...
...OUTSTANDING WORK.
HUNTRESS.
Way to go, Bruce.
I HAVE TO LEAVE.
BATMAN. STOP.
WHAT DO YOU WANT, CANARY? PLANNING TO SCOLD ME AGAIN?
NOT EXACTLY.

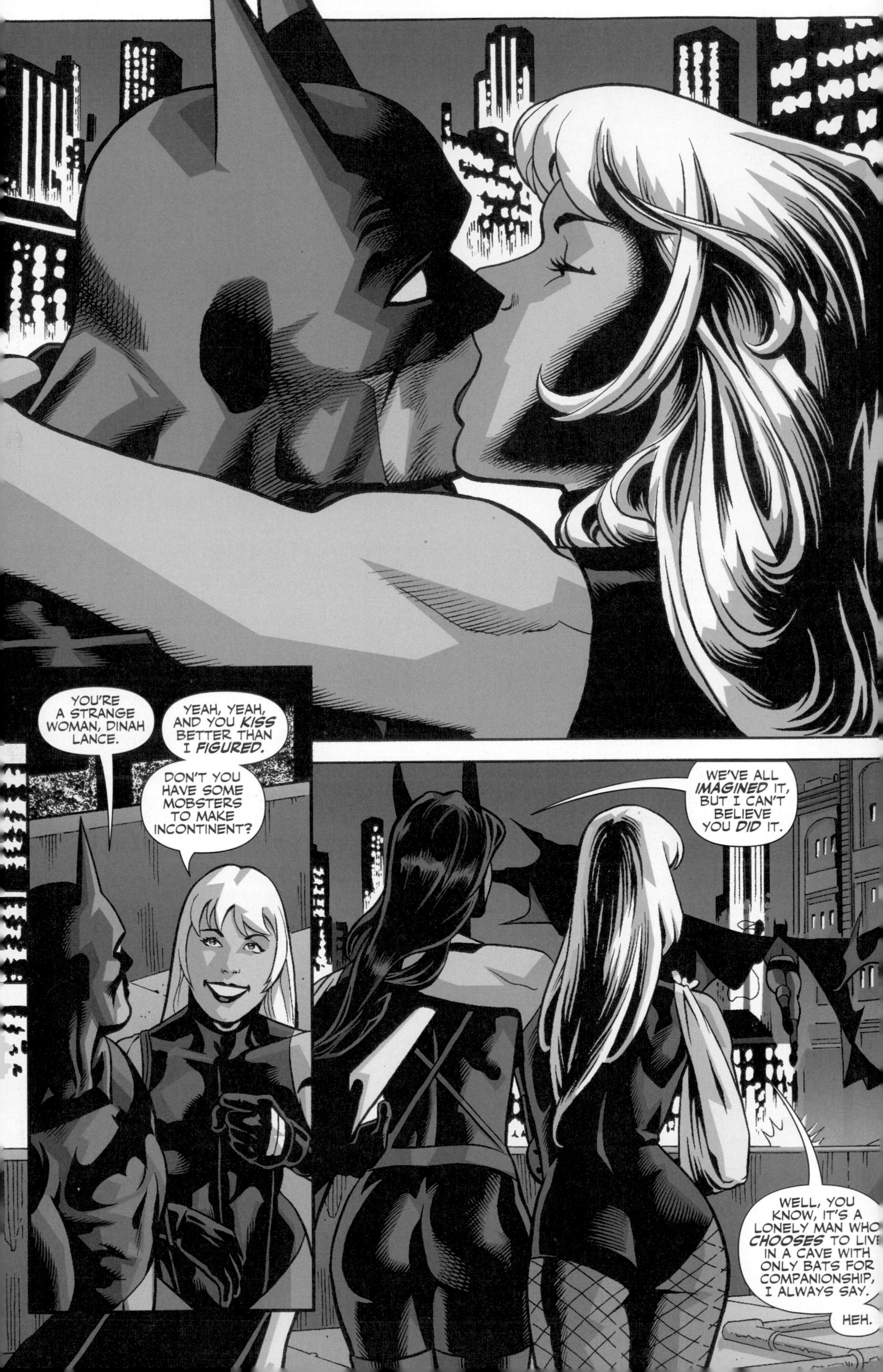
YOU'RE A STRANGE WOMAN, DINAH LANCE.
YEAH, YEAH, AND YOU KISS BETTER THAN I FIGURED.
DON'T YOU HAVE SOME MOBSTERS TO MAKE INCONTINENT?
WE'VE ALL IMAGINED IT, BUT I CAN'T BELIEVE YOU DID IT.
WELL, YOU KNOW, IT'S A LONELY MAN WHO CHOOSES TO LIVE IN A CAVE WITH ONLY BATS FOR COMPANIONSHIP, I ALWAYS SAY.
HEH.

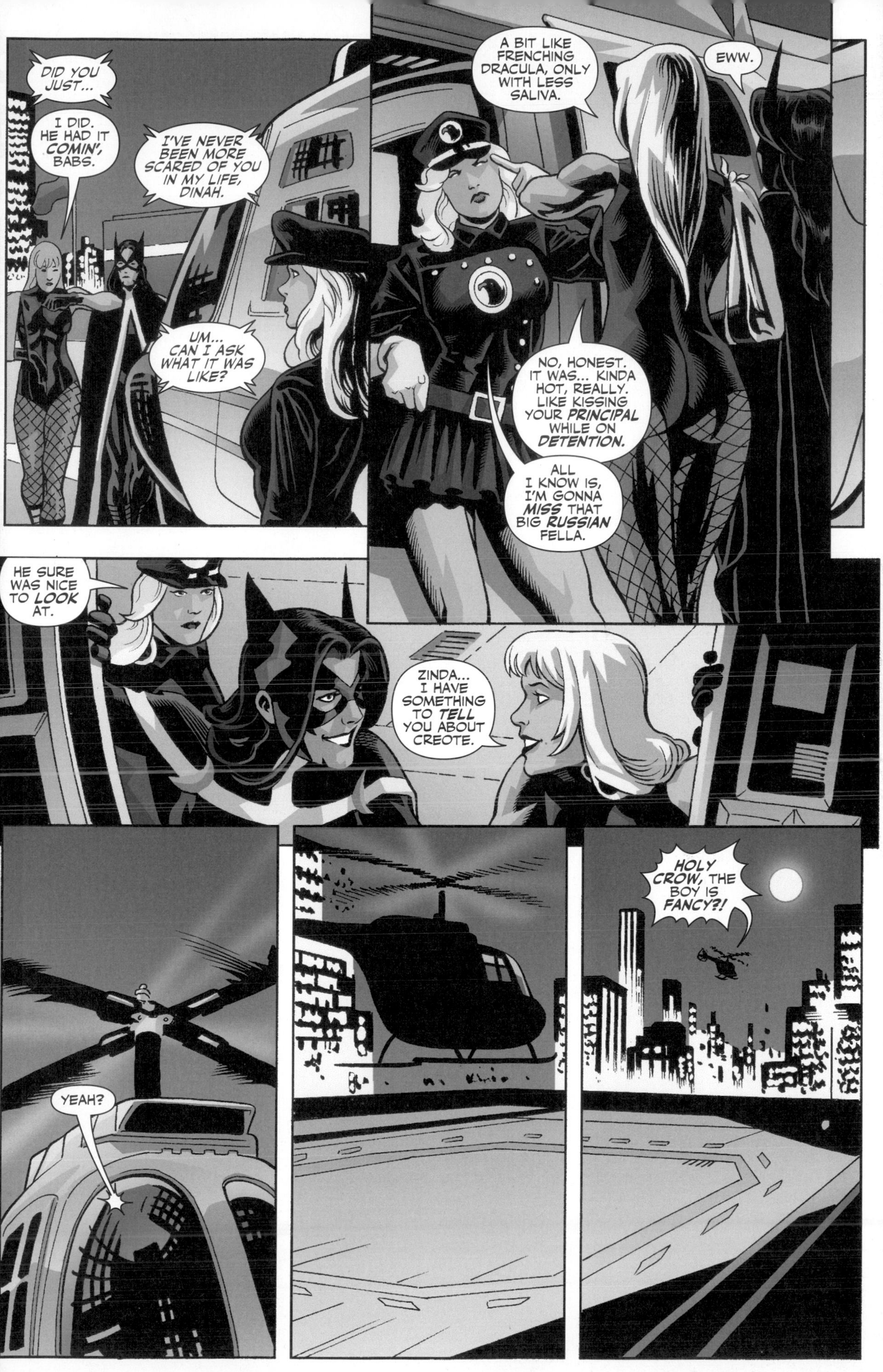
DID YOU JUST...
I DID. HE HAD IT COMIN', BABS.
I'VE NEVER BEEN MORE SCARED OF YOU IN MY LIFE, DINAH.
UM... CAN I ASK WHAT IT WAS LIKE?
A BIT LIKE FRENCHING DRACULA, ONLY WITH LESS SALIVA.
EWW.
NO, HONEST. IT WAS... KINDA HOT, REALLY. LIKE KISSING YOUR PRINCIPAL WHILE ON DETENTION.
ALL I KNOW IS, I'M GONNA MISS THAT BIG RUSSIAN FELLA.
HE SURE WAS NICE TO LOOK AT.
ZINDA... I HAVE SOMETHING TO TELL YOU ABOUT CREOTE.
YEAH?
HOLY CROW, THE BOY IS FANCY?!

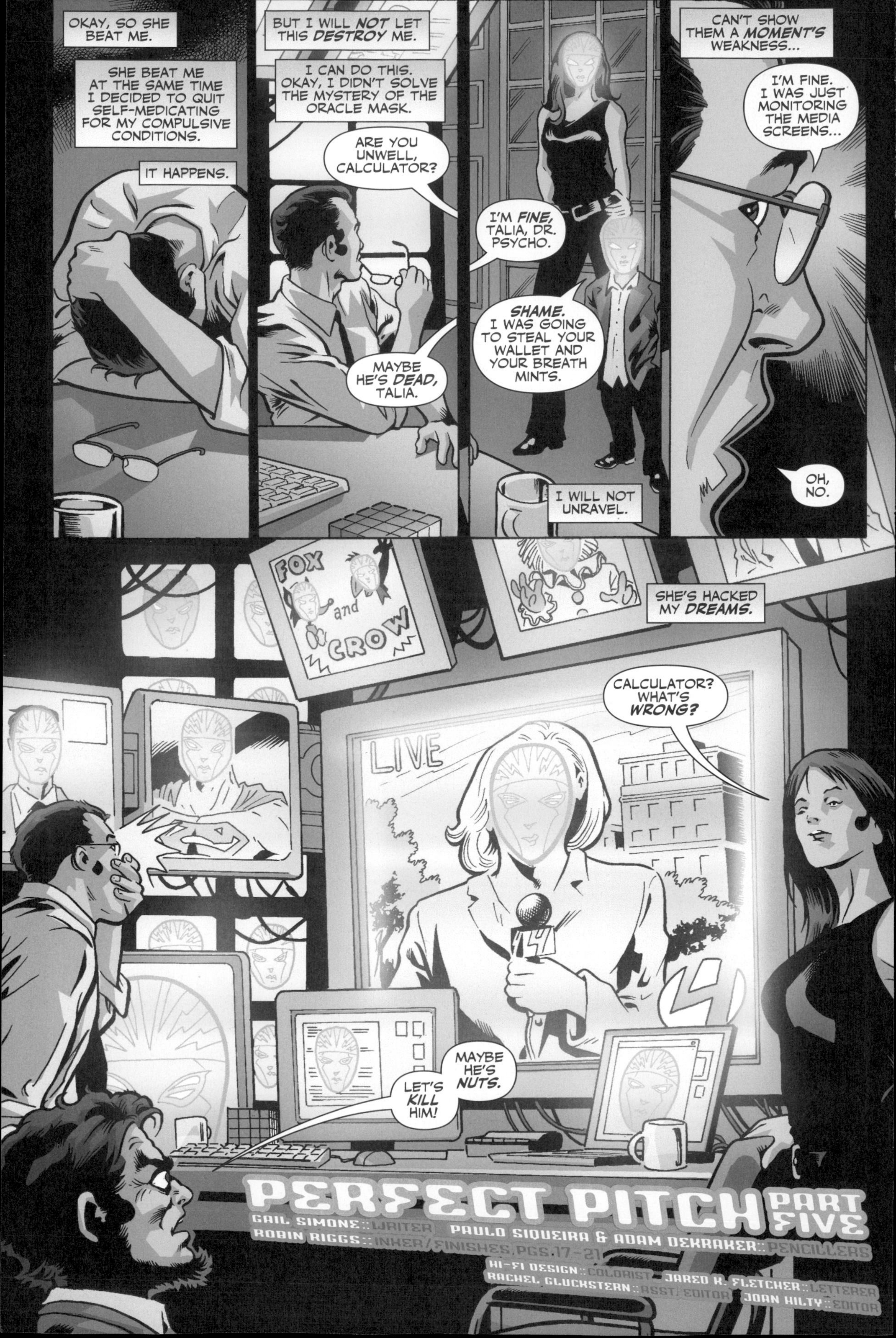
OKAY, SO SHE BEAT ME.
SHE BEAT ME AT THE SAME TIME I DECIDED TO QUIT SELF-MEDICATING FOR MY COMPULSIVE CONDITIONS.
IT HAPPENS.
BUT I WILL NOT LET THIS DESTROY ME.
I CAN DO THIS. OKAY, I DIDN'T SOLVE THE MYSTERY OF THE ORACLE MASK.
ARE YOU UNWELL, CALCULATOR?
MAYBE HE'S DEAD, TALIA.
I'M FINE, TALIA, DR. PSYCHO.
SHAME. I WAS GOING TO STEAL YOUR WALLET AND YOUR BREATH MINTS.
I WILL NOT UNRAVEL.
CAN'T SHOW THEM A MOMENT'S WEAKNESS...
I'M FINE. I WAS JUST MONITORING THE MEDIA SCREENS...
OH, NO.
FOX and CROW
SHE'S HACKED MY DREAMS.
CALCULATOR? WHAT'S WRONG?
LIVE
MAYBE HE'S NUTS.
LET'S KILL HIM!
PERFECT PITCH PART FIVE
GAIL SIMONE::WRITER PAULO SIQUEIRA & ADAM DEKRAKER::PENCILLERS
ROBIN RIGGS::INKER/FINISHES PGS.17-21
HI-FI DESIGN::COLORIST JARED K. FLETCHER::LETTERER
RACHEL GLUCKSTERN::ASST. EDITOR JOAN HILTY::EDITOR

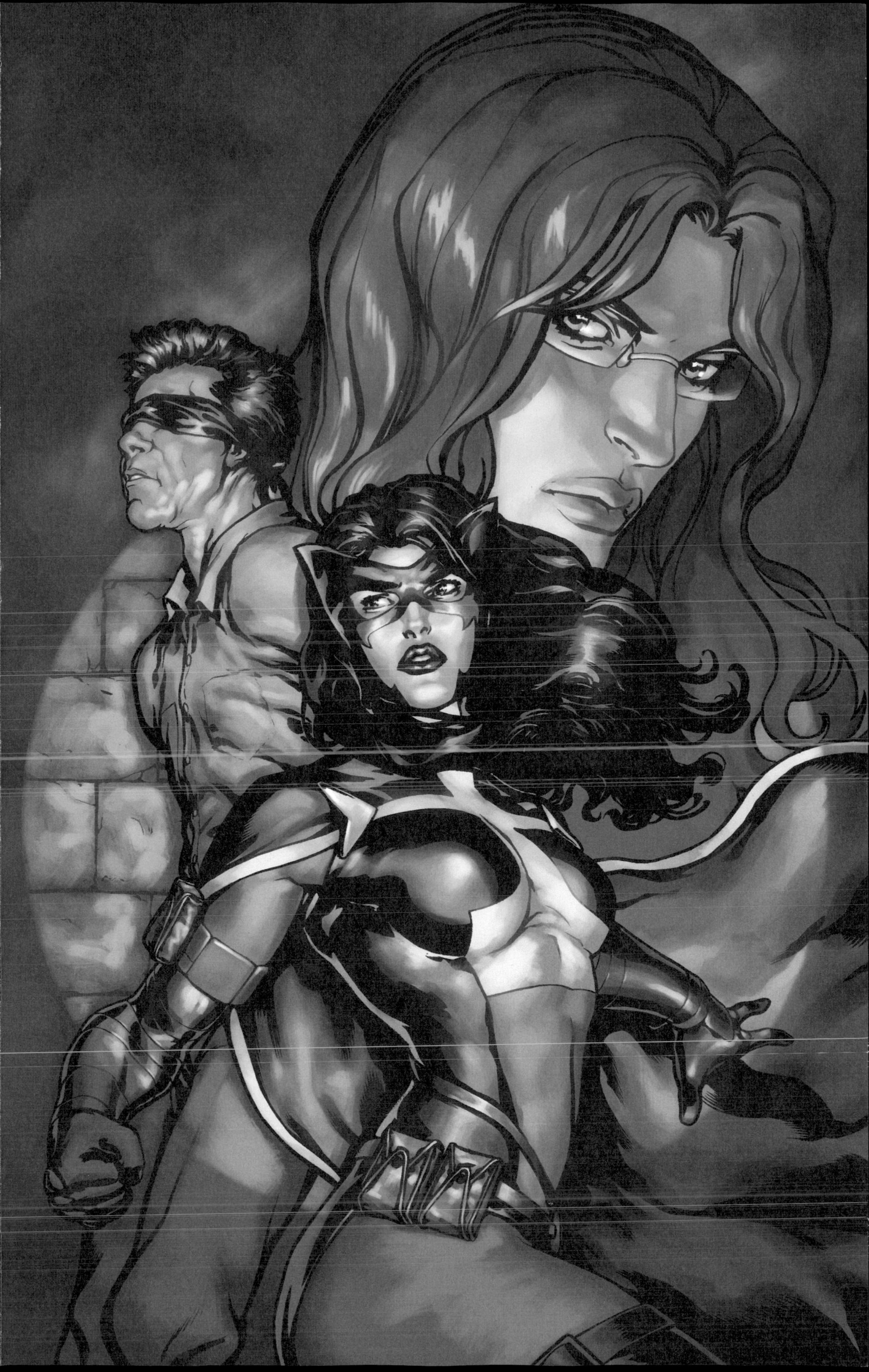

Cover art by
JESUS SAIZ

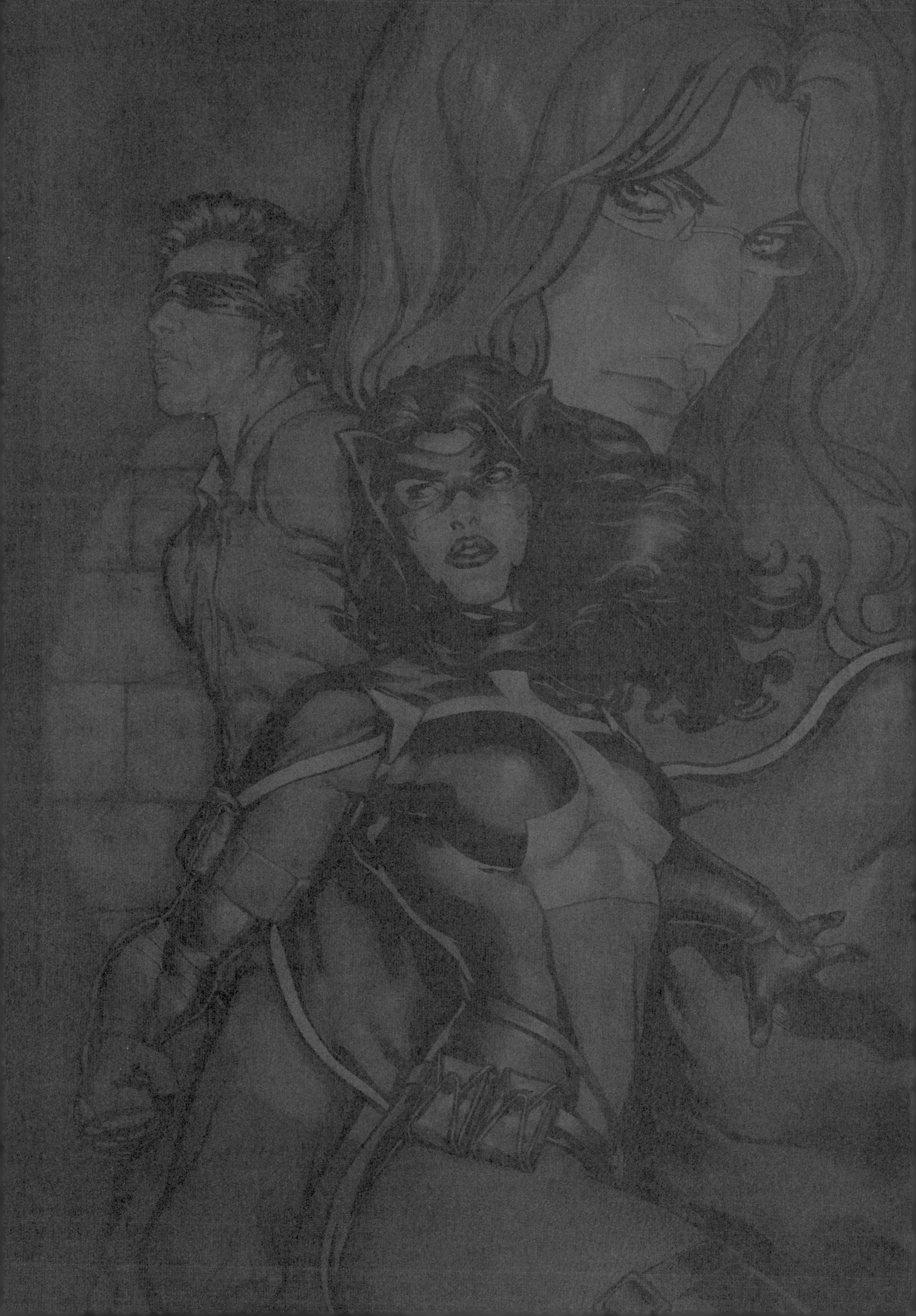

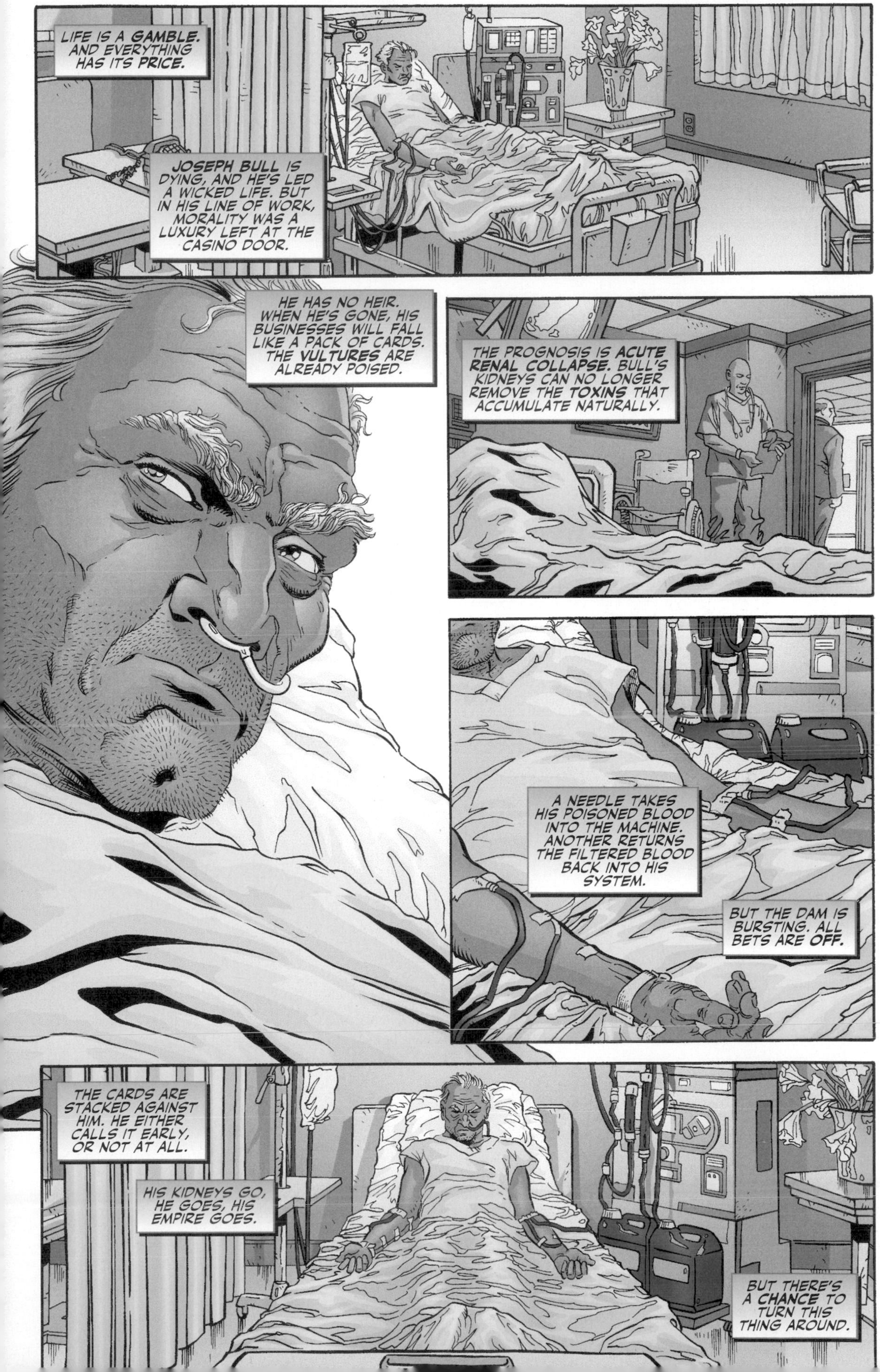
LIFE IS A GAMBLE. AND EVERYTHING HAS ITS PRICE.
JOSEPH BULL IS DYING, AND HE'S LED A WICKED LIFE. BUT IN HIS LINE OF WORK, MORALITY WAS A LUXURY LEFT AT THE CASINO DOOR.
HE HAS NO HEIR. WHEN HE'S GONE, HIS BUSINESSES WILL FALL LIKE A PACK OF CARDS. THE VULTURES ARE ALREADY POISED.
THE PROGNOSIS IS ACUTE RENAL COLLAPSE. BULL'S KIDNEYS CAN NO LONGER REMOVE THE TOXINS THAT ACCUMULATE NATURALLY.
A NEEDLE TAKES HIS POISONED BLOOD INTO THE MACHINE. ANOTHER RETURNS THE FILTERED BLOOD BACK INTO HIS SYSTEM.
BUT THE DAM IS BURSTING. ALL BETS ARE OFF.
THE CARDS ARE STACKED AGAINST HIM. HE EITHER CALLS IT EARLY, OR NOT AT ALL.
HIS KIDNEYS GO, HE GOES, HIS EMPIRE GOES.
BUT THERE'S A CHANCE TO TURN THIS THING AROUND.

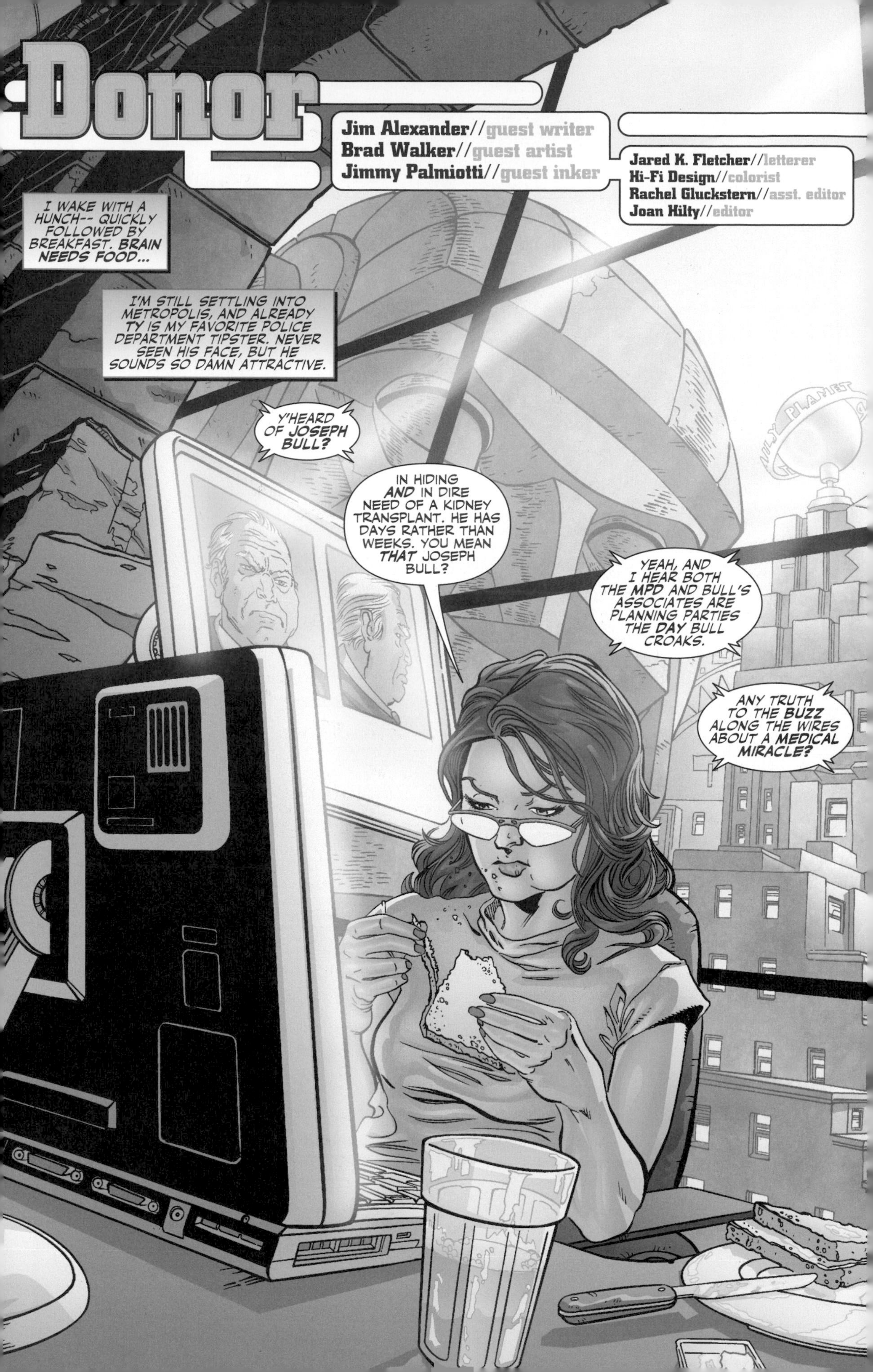
Donor
Jim Alexander//guest writer
Brad Walker//guest artist
Jimmy Palmiotti//guest inker
Jared K. Fletcher//letterer
Hi-Fi Design//colorist
Rachel Gluckstern//asst. editor
Joan Hilty//editor
I WAKE WITH A HUNCH-- QUICKLY FOLLOWED BY BREAKFAST. BRAIN NEEDS FOOD...
I'M STILL SETTLING INTO METROPOLIS, AND ALREADY TY IS MY FAVORITE POLICE DEPARTMENT TIPSTER. NEVER SEEN HIS FACE, BUT HE SOUNDS SO DAMN ATTRACTIVE.
Y'HEARD OF JOSEPH BULL?
IN HIDING AND IN DIRE NEED OF A KIDNEY TRANSPLANT. HE HAS DAYS RATHER THAN WEEKS. YOU MEAN THAT JOSEPH BULL?
YEAH, AND I HEAR BOTH THE MPD AND BULL'S ASSOCIATES ARE PLANNING PARTIES THE DAY BULL CROAKS.
ANY TRUTH TO THE BUZZ ALONG THE WIRES ABOUT A MEDICAL MIRACLE?

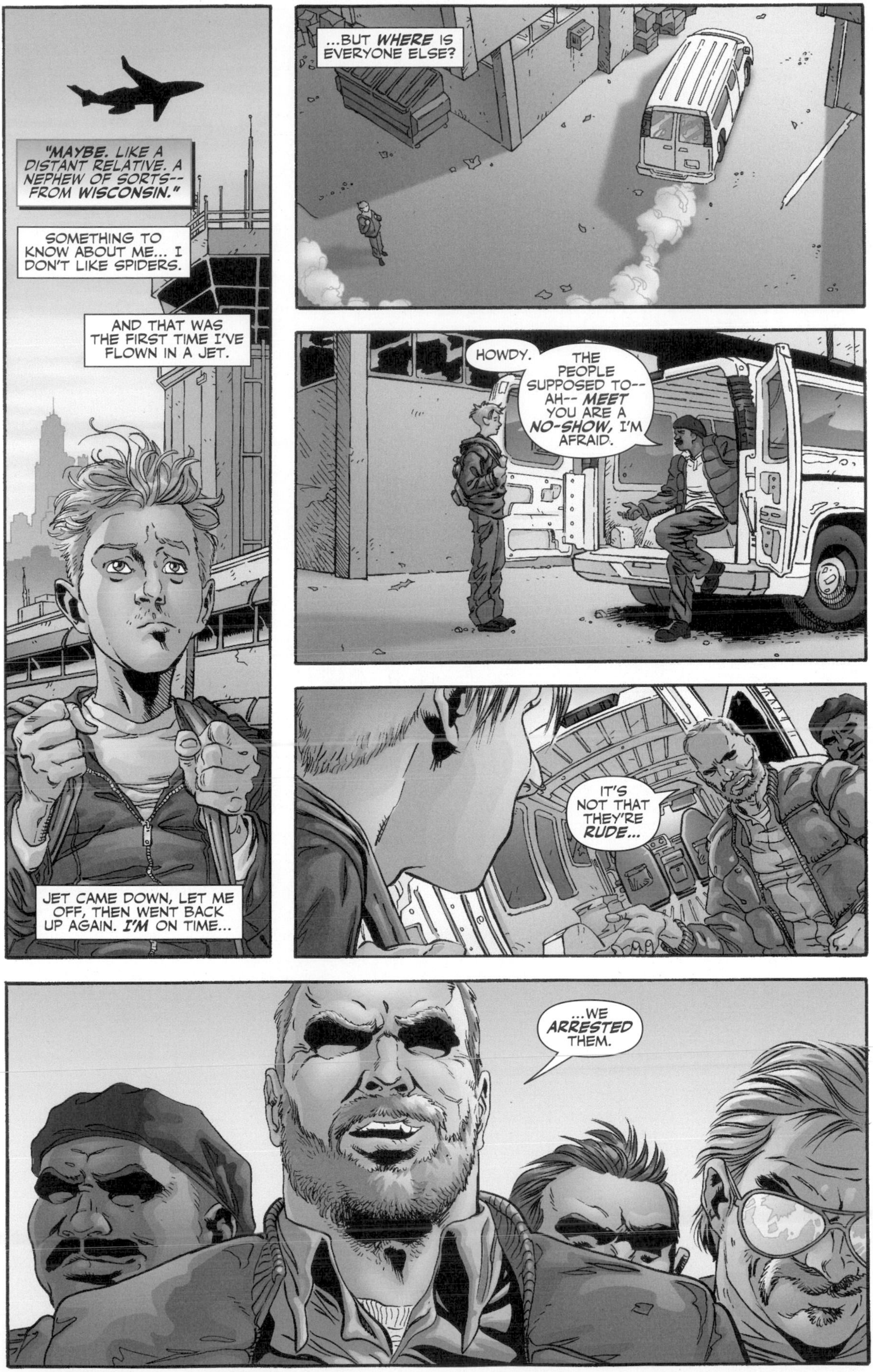
"MAYBE. LIKE A DISTANT RELATIVE. A NEPHEW OF SORTS-- FROM WISCONSIN."
SOMETHING TO KNOW ABOUT ME... I DON'T LIKE SPIDERS.
AND THAT WAS THE FIRST TIME I'VE FLOWN IN A JET.
JET CAME DOWN, LET ME OFF, THEN WENT BACK UP AGAIN. I'M ON TIME...
...BUT WHERE IS EVERYONE ELSE?
HOWDY.
THE PEOPLE SUPPOSED TO-- AH-- MEET YOU ARE A NO-SHOW, I'M AFRAID.
IT'S NOT THAT THEY'RE RUDE...
...WE ARRESTED THEM.

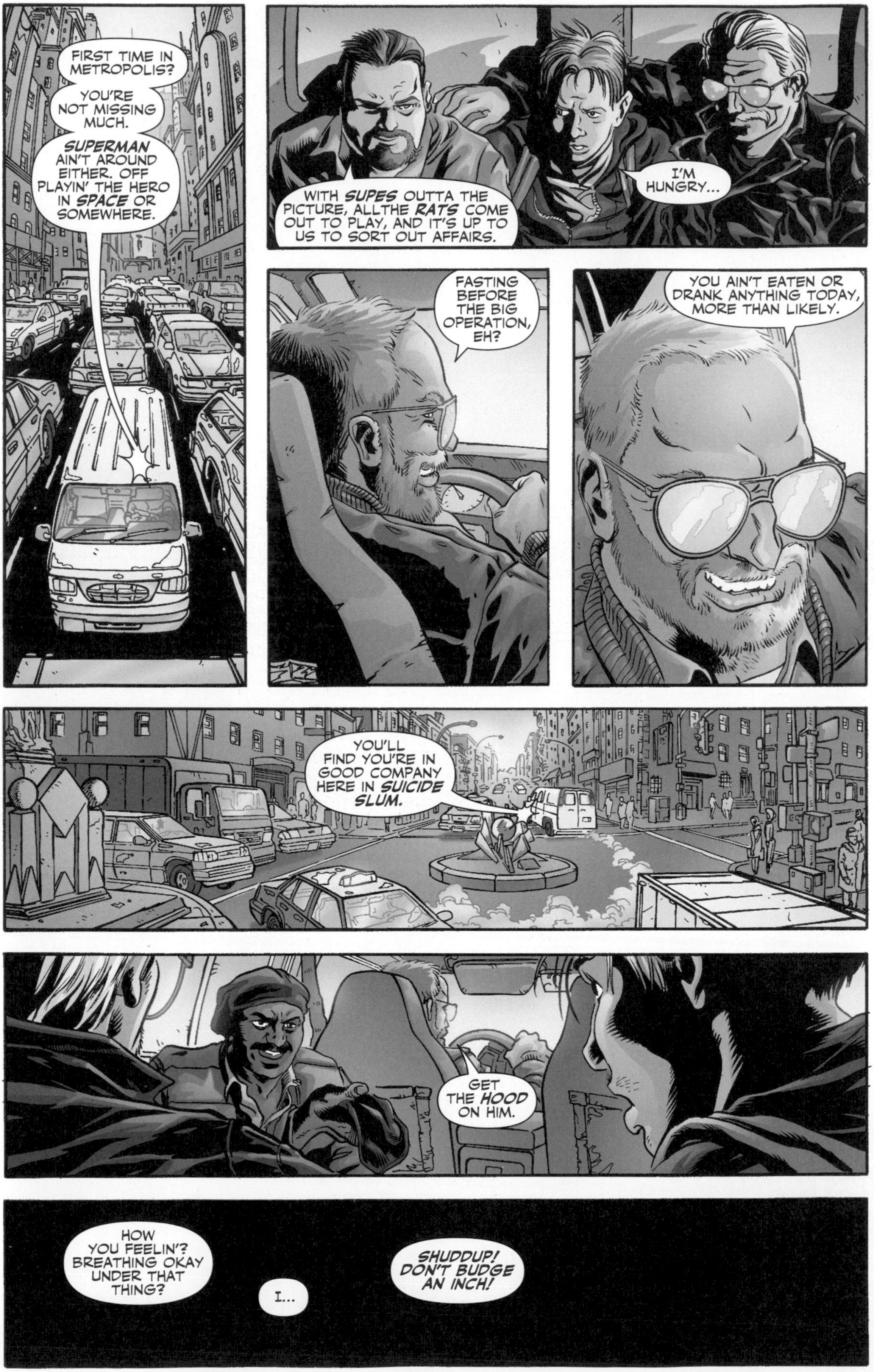
FIRST TIME IN METROPOLIS?
YOU'RE NOT MISSING MUCH.
SUPERMAN AIN'T AROUND EITHER. OFF PLAYIN' THE HERO IN SPACE OR SOMEWHERE.
WITH SUPES OUTTA THE PICTURE, ALLTHE RATS COME OUT TO PLAY, AND IT'S UP TO US TO SORT OUT AFFAIRS.
I'M HUNGRY...
FASTING BEFORE THE BIG OPERATION, EH?
YOU AIN'T EATEN OR DRANK ANYTHING TODAY, MORE THAN LIKELY.
YOU'LL FIND YOU'RE IN GOOD COMPANY HERE IN SUICIDE SLUM.
GET THE HOOD ON HIM.
HOW YOU FEELIN'? BREATHING OKAY UNDER THAT THING?
I...
SHUDDUP! DON'T BUDGE AN INCH!

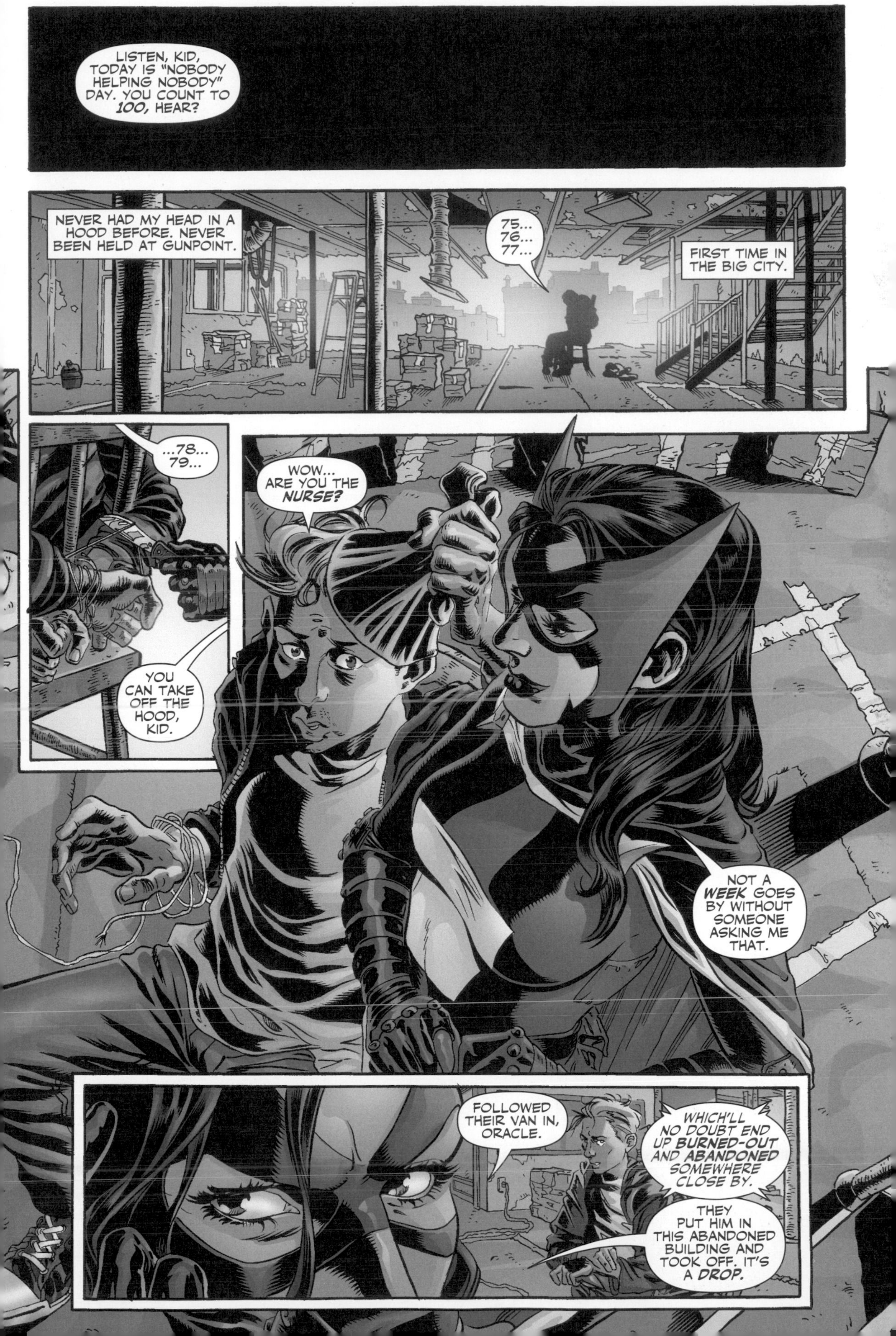
LISTEN, KID, TODAY IS "NOBODY HELPING NOBODY" DAY. YOU COUNT TO 100, HEAR?
NEVER HAD MY HEAD IN A HOOD BEFORE. NEVER BEEN HELD AT GUNPOINT.
75... 76... 77...
FIRST TIME IN THE BIG CITY.
...78... 79...
YOU CAN TAKE OFF THE HOOD, KID.
WOW... ARE YOU THE NURSE?
NOT A WEEK GOES BY WITHOUT SOMEONE ASKING ME THAT.
FOLLOWED THEIR VAN IN, ORACLE.
WHICH'LL NO DOUBT END UP BURNED-OUT AND ABANDONED SOMEWHERE CLOSE BY.
THEY PUT HIM IN THIS ABANDONED BUILDING AND TOOK OFF. IT'S A DROP.

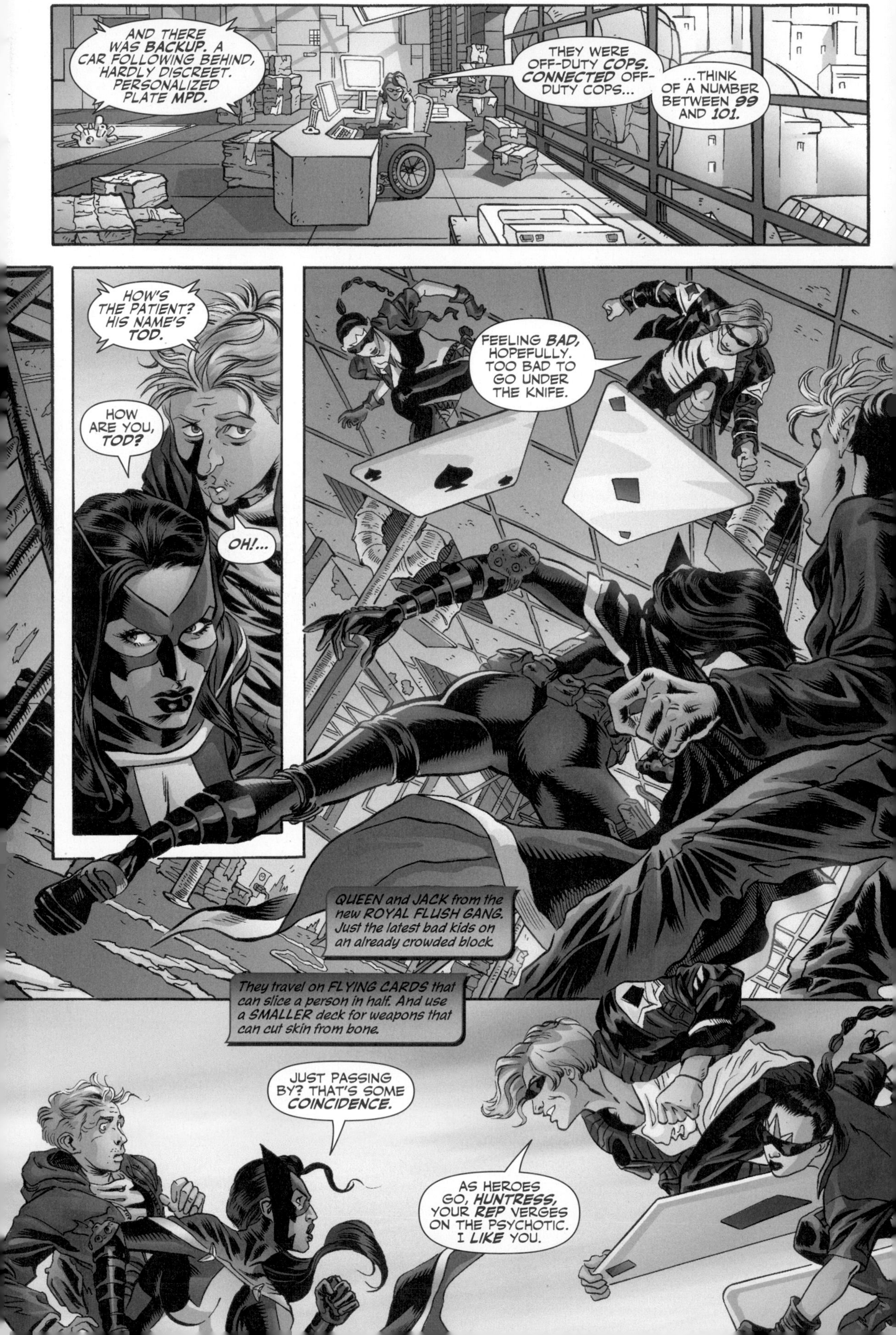
AND THERE WAS BACKUP. A CAR FOLLOWING BEHIND, HARDLY DISCREET. PERSONALIZED PLATE MPD.
THEY WERE OFF-DUTY COPS. CONNECTED OFF-DUTY COPS...
...THINK OF A NUMBER BETWEEN 99 AND 101.
HOW'S THE PATIENT? HIS NAME'S TOD.
HOW ARE YOU, TOD?
OH!...
FEELING BAD, HOPEFULLY. TOO BAD TO GO UNDER THE KNIFE.
QUEEN and JACK from the new ROYAL FLUSH GANG. Just the latest bad kids on an already crowded block.
They travel on FLYING CARDS that can slice a person in half. And use a SMALLER deck for weapons that can cut skin from bone.
JUST PASSING BY? THAT'S SOME COINCIDENCE.
AS HEROES GO, HUNTRESS, YOUR REP VERGES ON THE PSYCHOTIC. I LIKE YOU.

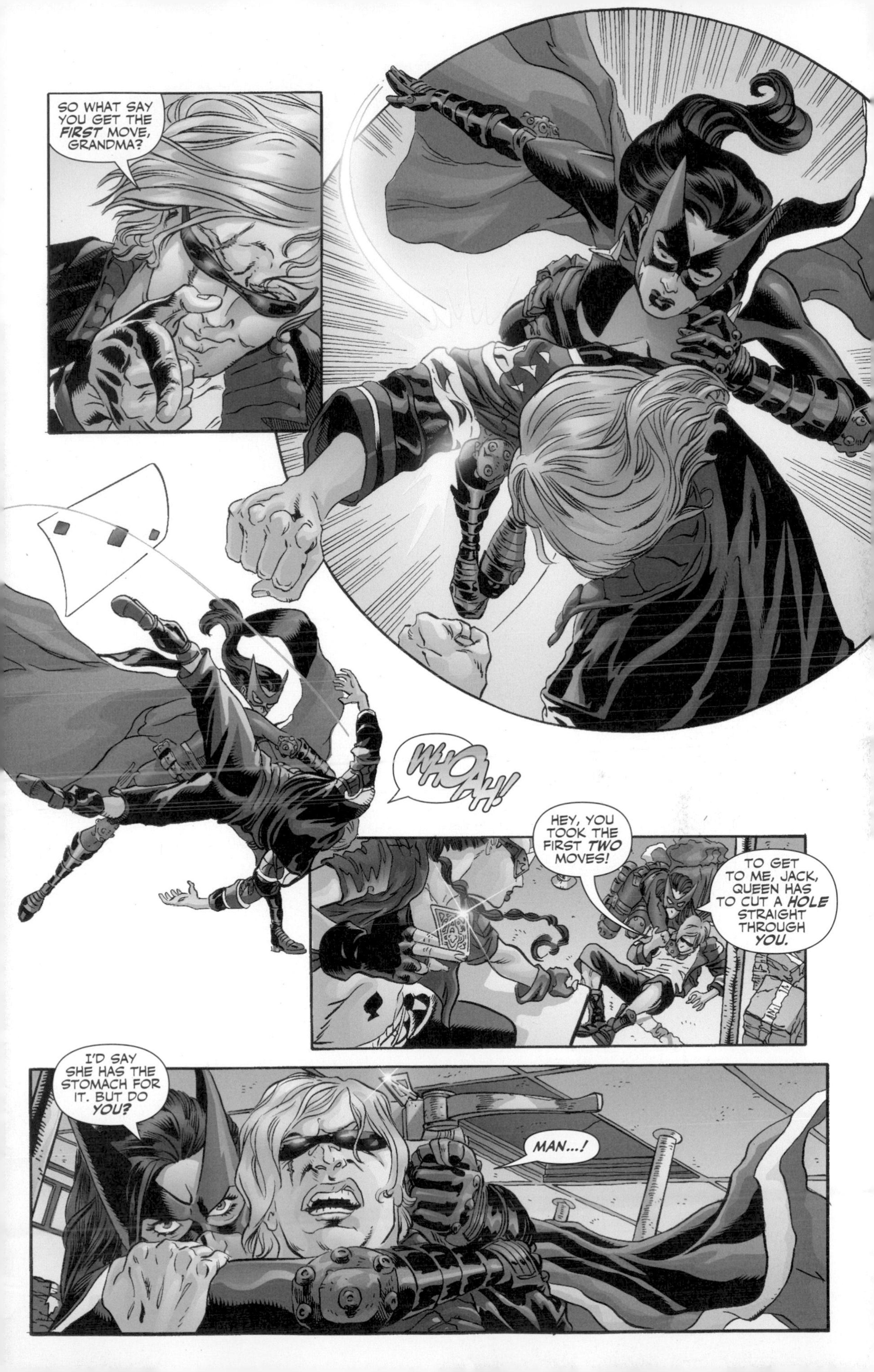
SO WHAT SAY YOU GET THE FIRST MOVE, GRANDMA?
WHOAH!
HEY, YOU TOOK THE FIRST TWO MOVES!
TO GET TO ME, JACK, QUEEN HAS TO CUT A HOLE STRAIGHT THROUGH YOU.
I'D SAY SHE HAS THE STOMACH FOR IT. BUT DO YOU?
MAN...!

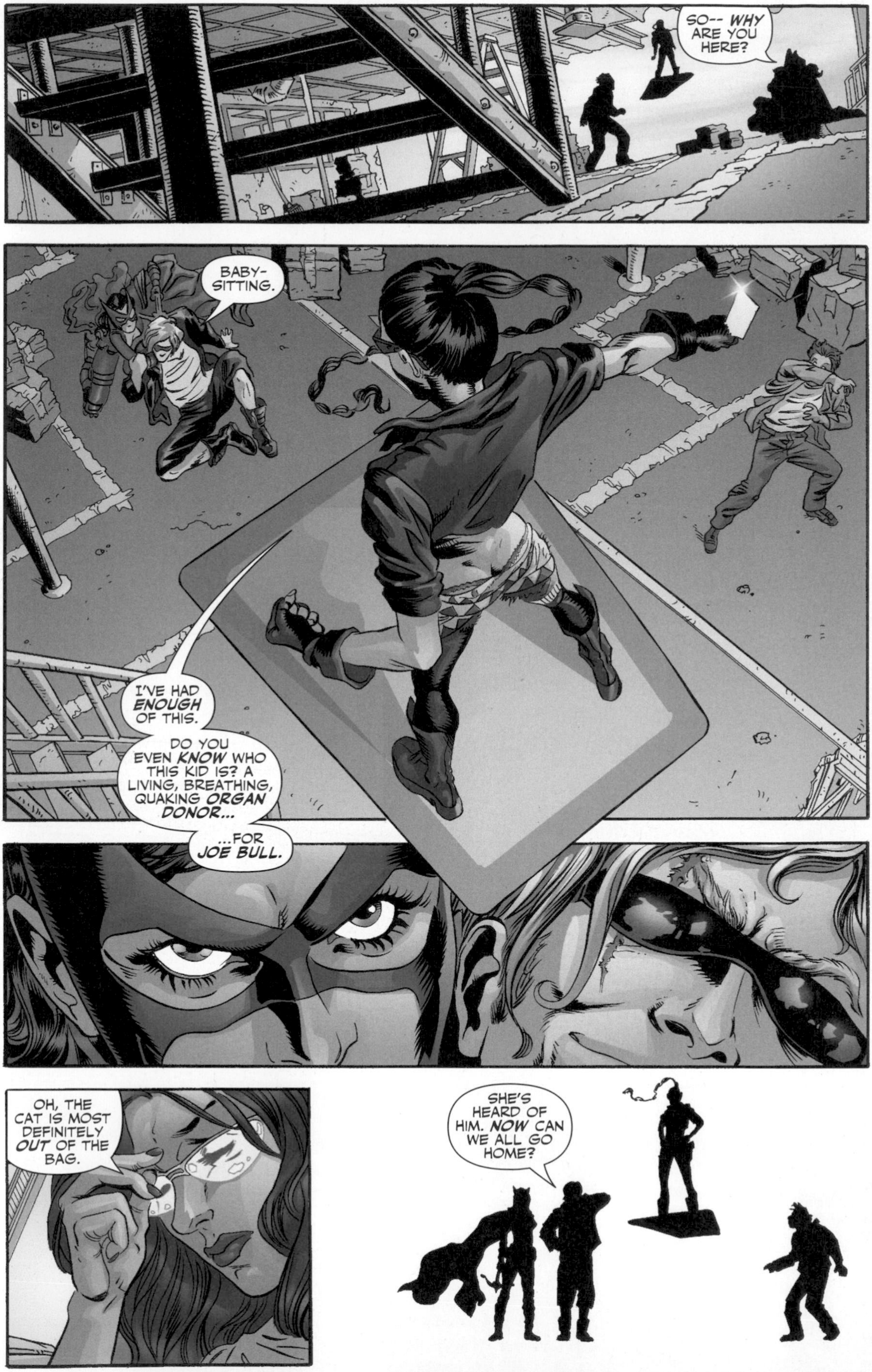
SO-- WHY ARE YOU HERE?
BABY-SITTING.
I'VE HAD ENOUGH OF THIS.
DO YOU EVEN KNOW WHO THIS KID IS? A LIVING, BREATHING, QUAKING ORGAN DONOR...
...FOR JOE BULL.
OH, THE CAT IS MOST DEFINITELY OUT OF THE BAG.
SHE'S HEARD OF HIM. NOW CAN WE ALL GO HOME?

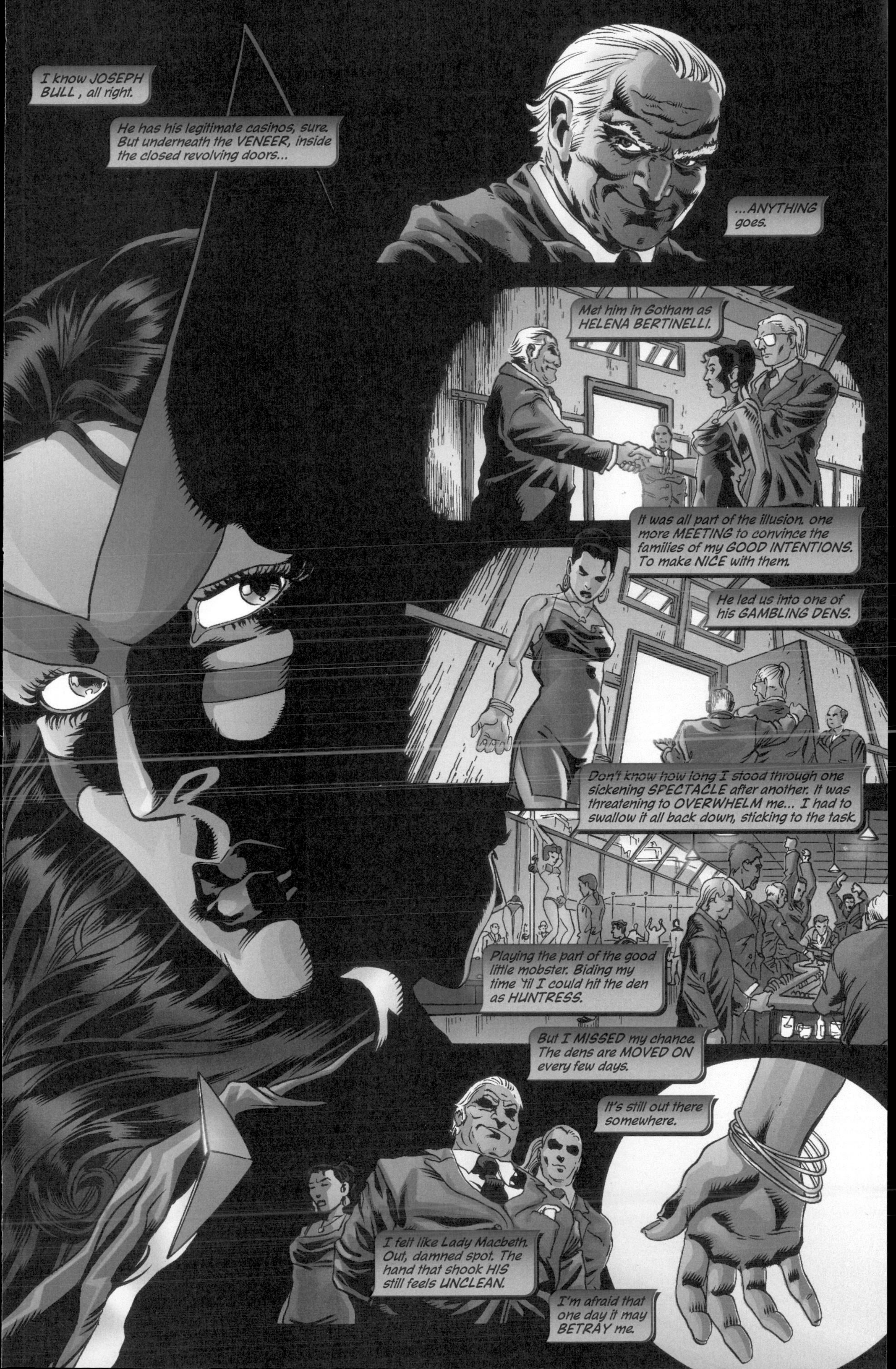

I know JOSEPH BULL, all right.
He has his legitimate casinos, sure. But underneath the VENEER, inside the closed revolving doors...
...ANYTHING goes.
Met him in Gotham as HELENA BERTINELLI.
It was all part of the illusion. one more MEETING to convince the families of my GOOD INTENTIONS. To make NICE with them.
He led us into one of his GAMBLING DENS.
Don't know how long I stood through one sickening SPECTACLE after another. It was threatening to OVERWHELM me... I had to swallow it all back down, sticking to the task.
Playing the part of the good little mobster. Biding my time 'til I could hit the den as HUNTRESS.
But I MISSED my chance. The dens are MOVED ON every few days.
It's still out there somewhere.
I felt like Lady Macbeth. Out, damned spot. The hand that shook HIS still feels UNCLEAN.
I'm afraid that one day it may BETRAY me.

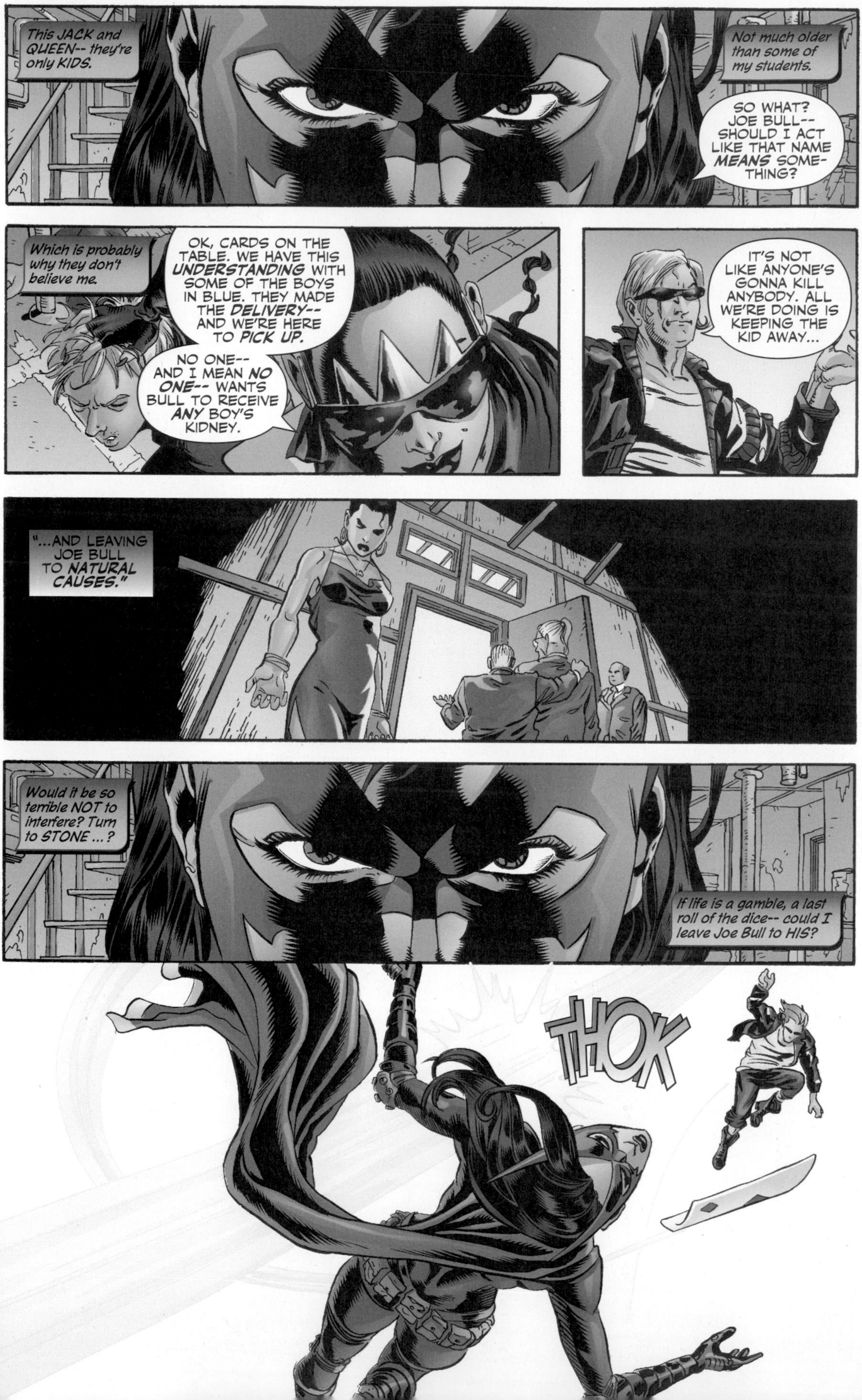

This JACK and QUEEN-- they're only KIDS.
Not much older than some of my students.
SO WHAT? JOE BULL-- SHOULD I ACT LIKE THAT NAME MEANS SOME-THING?
Which is probably why they don't believe me.
OK, CARDS ON THE TABLE. WE HAVE THIS UNDERSTANDING WITH SOME OF THE BOYS IN BLUE. THEY MADE THE DELIVERY-- AND WE'RE HERE TO PICK UP.
NO ONE-- AND I MEAN NO ONE-- WANTS BULL TO RECEIVE ANY BOY'S KIDNEY.
IT'S NOT LIKE ANYONE'S GONNA KILL ANYBODY. ALL WE'RE DOING IS KEEPING THE KID AWAY...
"...AND LEAVING JOE BULL TO NATURAL CAUSES."
Would it be so terrible NOT to interfere? Turn to STONE ...?
If life is a gamble, a last roll of the dice-- could I leave Joe Bull to HIS?
THOK

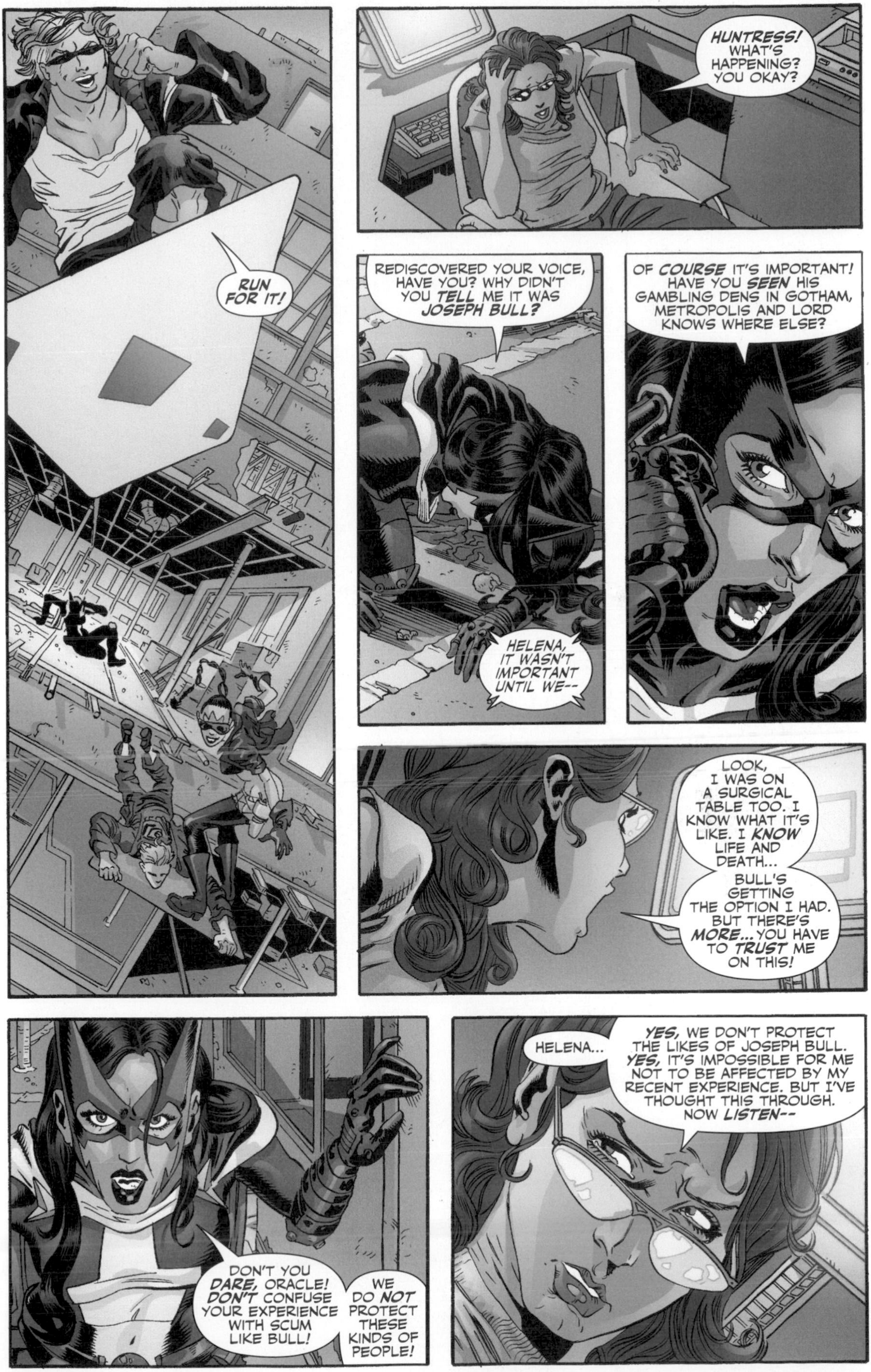

RUN FOR IT!
HUNTRESS! WHAT'S HAPPENING? YOU OKAY?
REDISCOVERED YOUR VOICE, HAVE YOU? WHY DIDN'T YOU TELL ME IT WAS JOSEPH BULL?
HELENA, IT WASN'T IMPORTANT UNTIL WE--
OF COURSE IT'S IMPORTANT! HAVE YOU SEEN HIS GAMBLING DENS IN GOTHAM, METROPOLIS AND LORD KNOWS WHERE ELSE?
LOOK, I WAS ON A SURGICAL TABLE TOO. I KNOW WHAT IT'S LIKE. I KNOW LIFE AND DEATH...
BULL'S GETTING THE OPTION I HAD. BUT THERE'S MORE... YOU HAVE TO TRUST ME ON THIS!
DON'T YOU DARE, ORACLE! DON'T CONFUSE YOUR EXPERIENCE WITH SCUM LIKE BULL!
WE DO NOT PROTECT THESE KINDS OF PEOPLE!
HELENA...
YES, WE DON'T PROTECT THE LIKES OF JOSEPH BULL. YES, IT'S IMPOSSIBLE FOR ME NOT TO BE AFFECTED BY MY RECENT EXPERIENCE. BUT I'VE THOUGHT THIS THROUGH. NOW LISTEN--

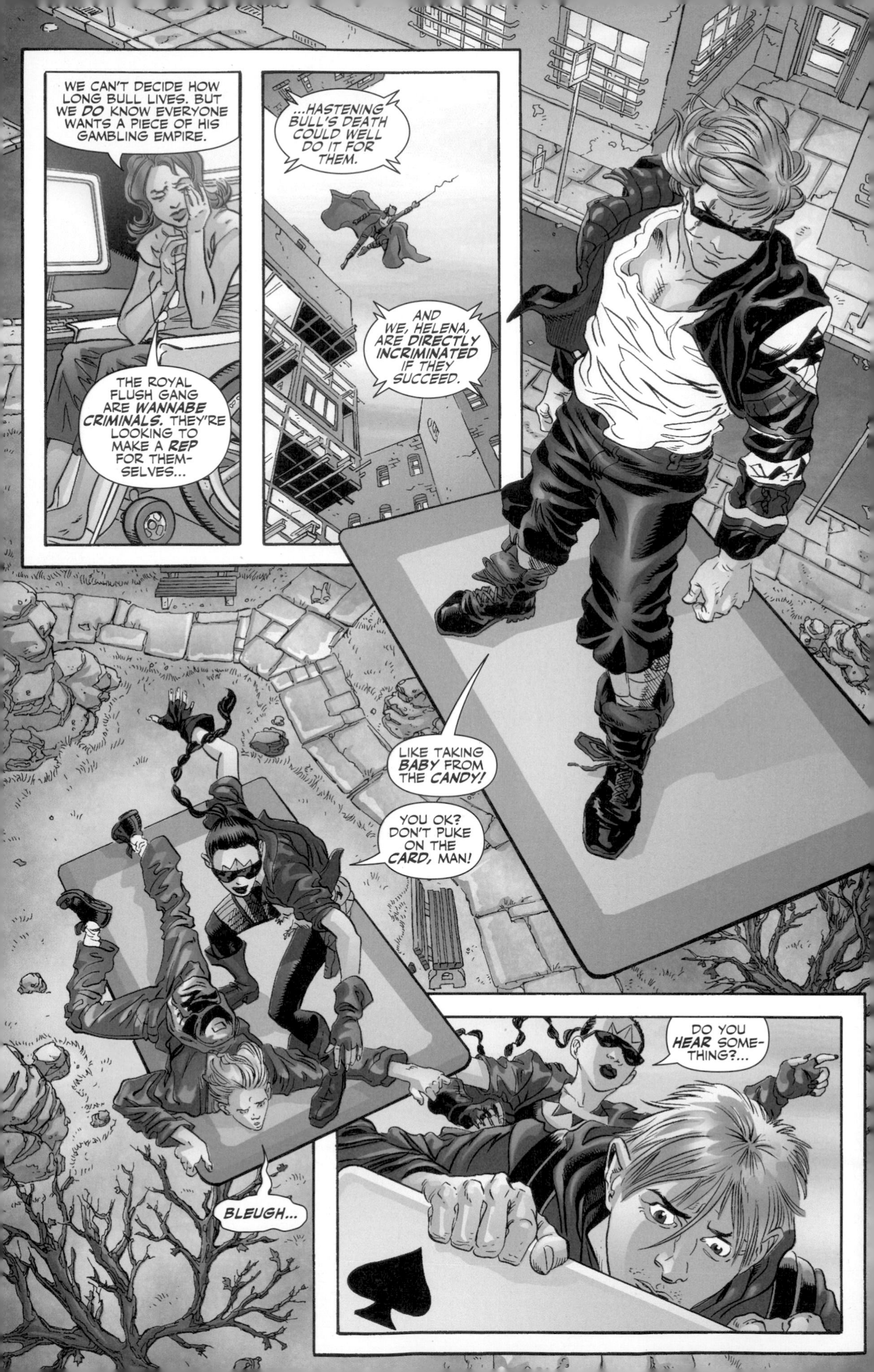
WE CAN'T DECIDE HOW LONG BULL LIVES. BUT WE DO KNOW EVERYONE WANTS A PIECE OF HIS GAMBLING EMPIRE.
THE ROYAL FLUSH GANG ARE WANNABE CRIMINALS. THEY'RE LOOKING TO MAKE A REP FOR THEM-SELVES...
...HASTENING BULL'S DEATH COULD WELL DO IT FOR THEM.
AND WE, HELENA, ARE DIRECTLY INCRIMINATED IF THEY SUCCEED.
LIKE TAKING BABY FROM THE CANDY!
YOU OK? DON'T PUKE ON THE CARD, MAN!
BLEUGH...
DO YOU HEAR SOME-THING?...

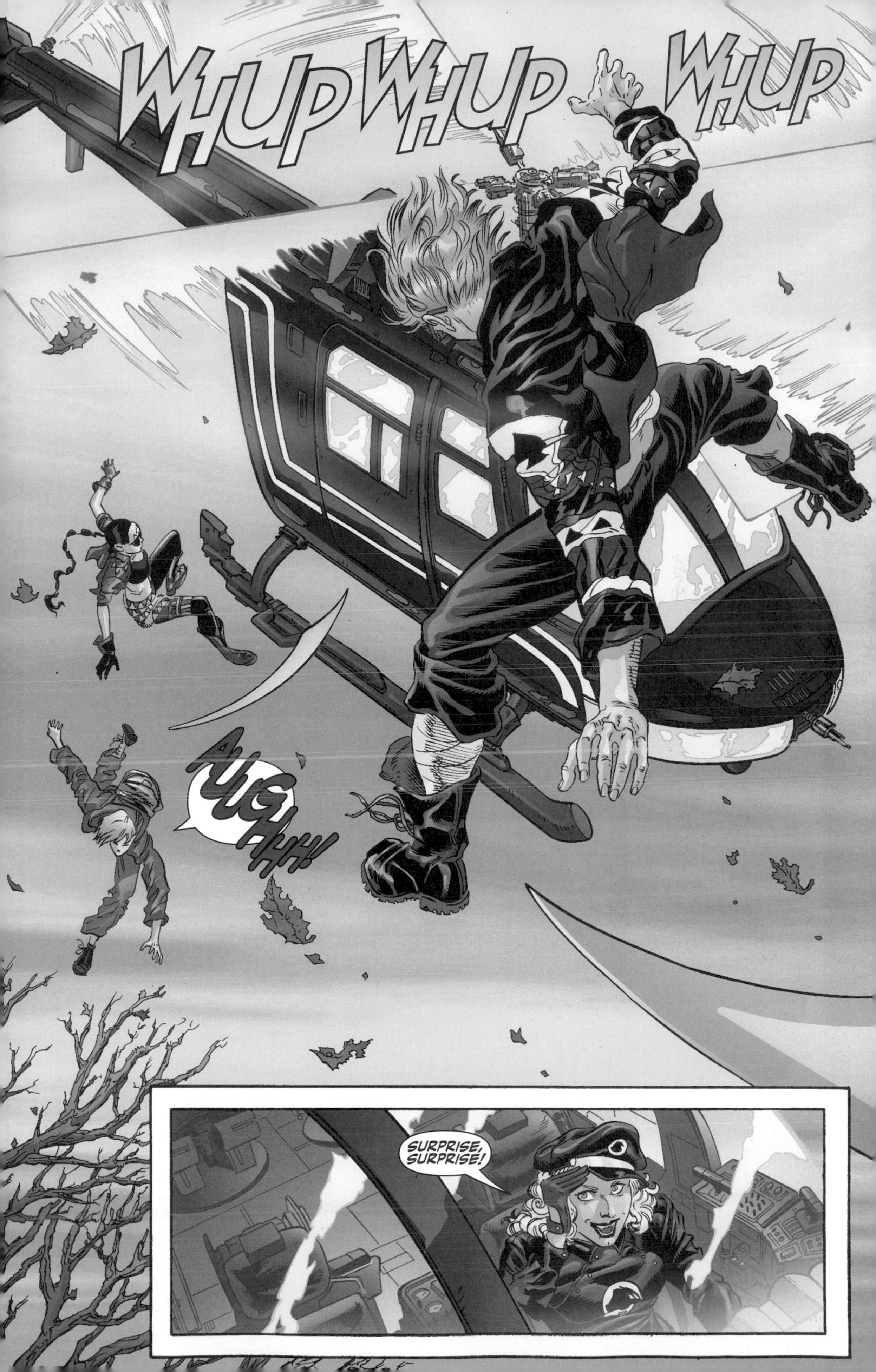
WHUP WHUP WHUP
AUGHHH!
SURPRISE, SURPRISE!

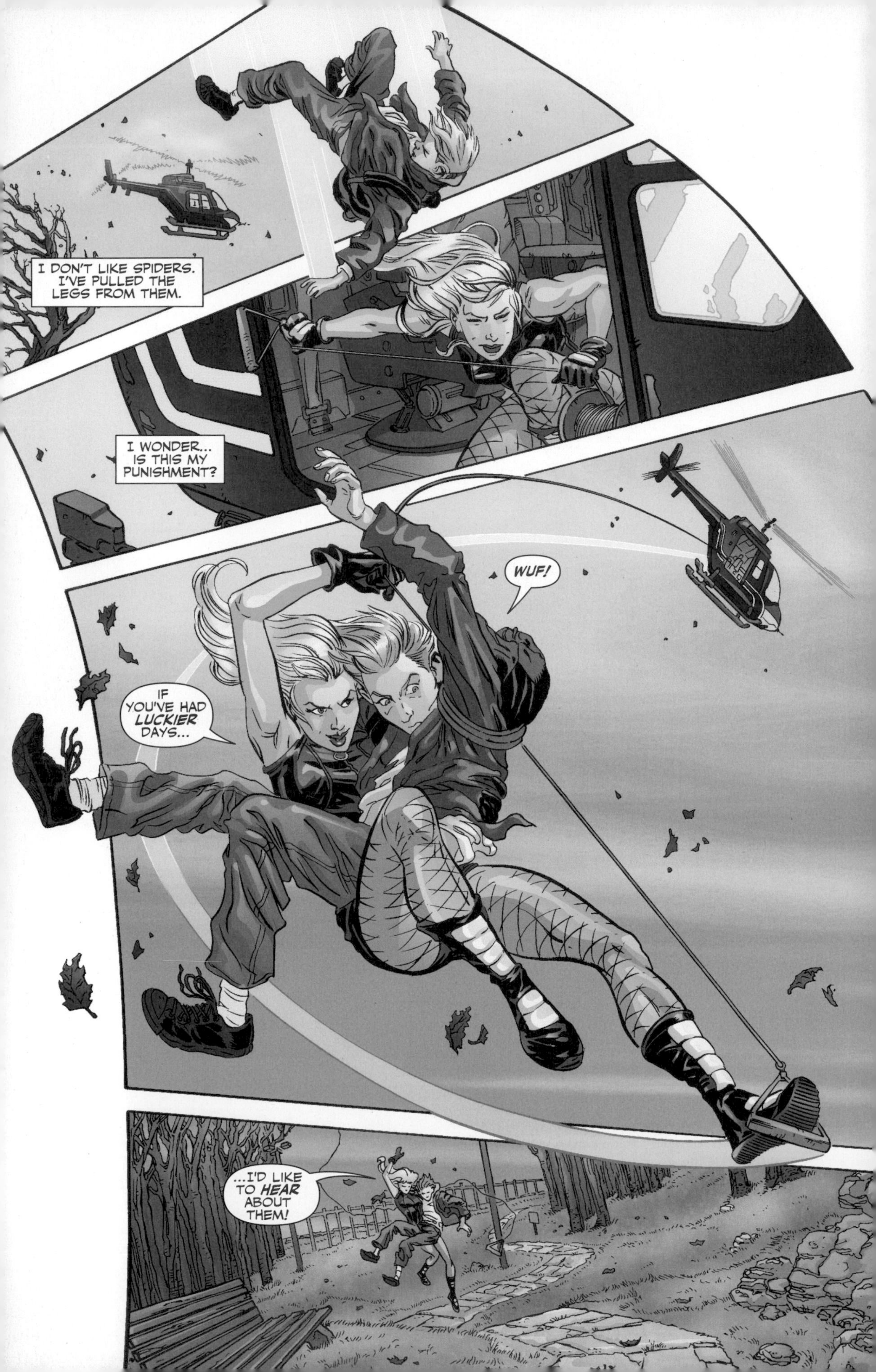
I DON'T LIKE SPIDERS. I'VE PULLED THE LEGS FROM THEM.
I WONDER... IS THIS MY PUNISHMENT?
WUF!
IF YOU'VE HAD *LUCKIER* DAYS...
...I'D LIKE TO *HEAR* ABOUT THEM!

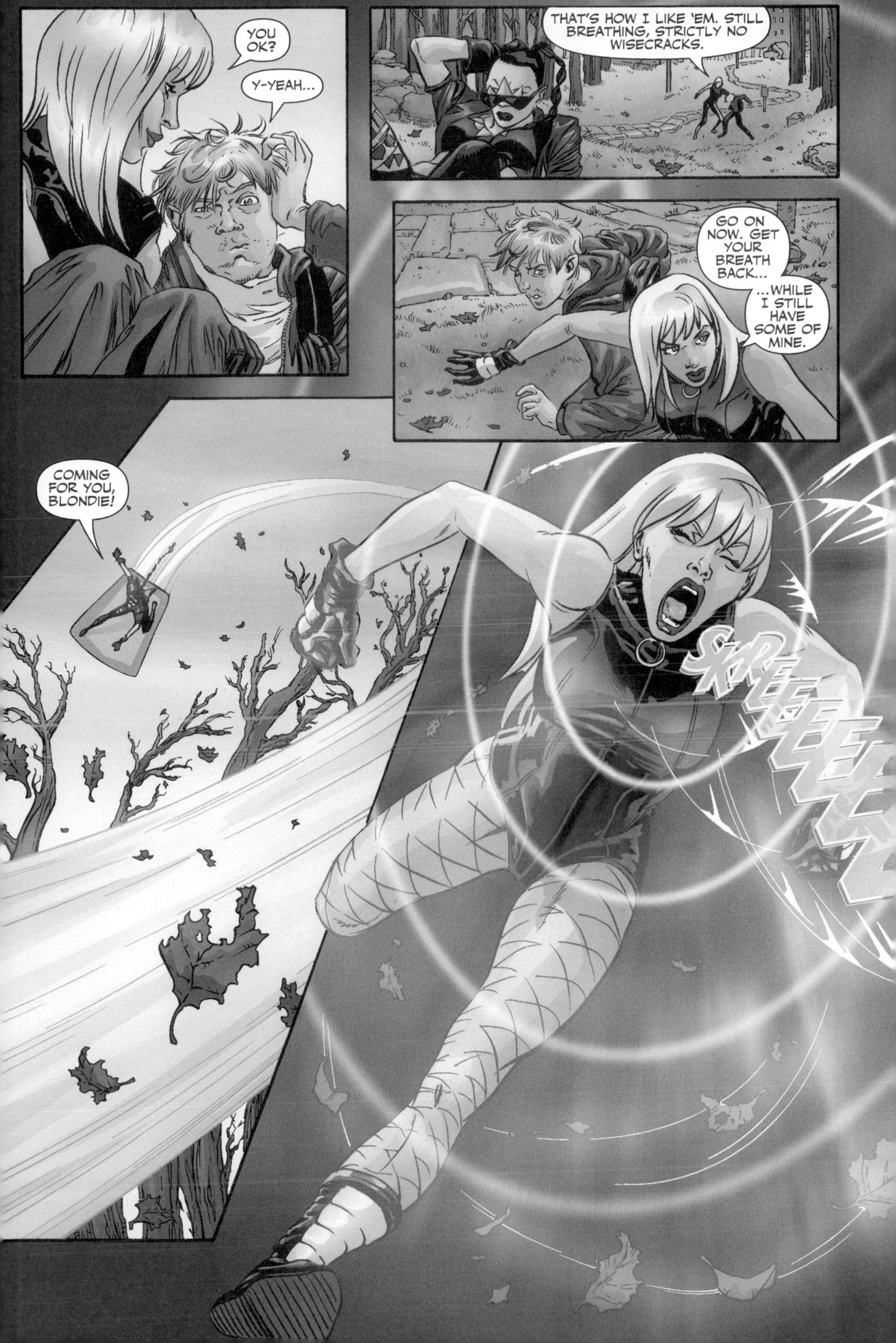
YOU OK?
Y-YEAH...
THAT'S HOW I LIKE 'EM. STILL BREATHING, STRICTLY NO WISECRACKS.
GO ON NOW. GET YOUR BREATH BACK...
...WHILE I STILL HAVE SOME OF MINE.
COMING FOR YOU, BLONDIE!

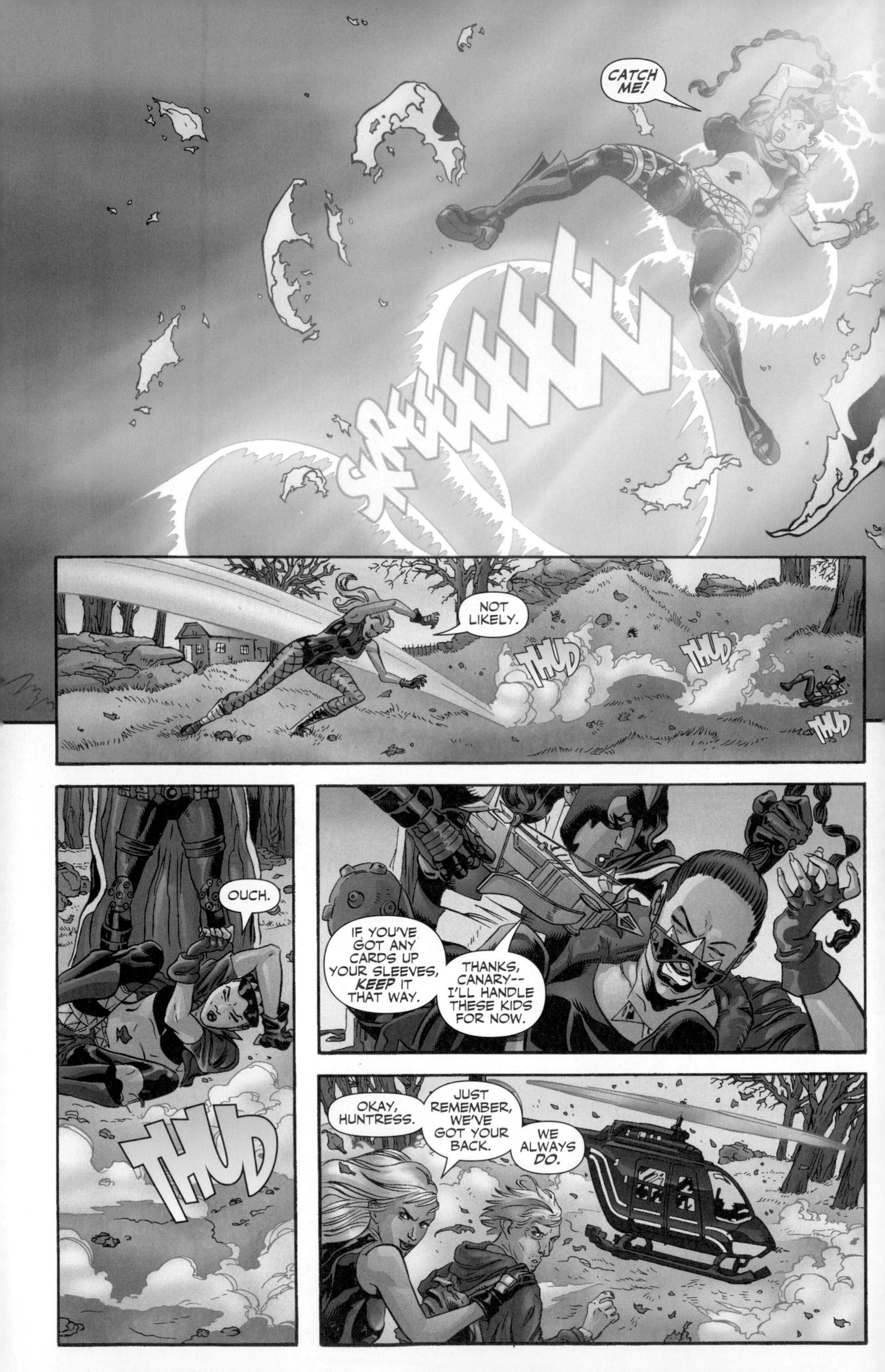

CATCH ME!
SKREEEEEEE
NOT LIKELY.
THUD
THUD
THUD
OUCH.
THUD
IF YOU'VE GOT ANY CARDS UP YOUR SLEEVES, *KEEP* IT THAT WAY.
THANKS, CANARY-- I'LL HANDLE THESE KIDS FOR NOW.
OKAY, HUNTRESS.
JUST REMEMBER, WE'VE GOT YOUR BACK.
WE ALWAYS *DO.*

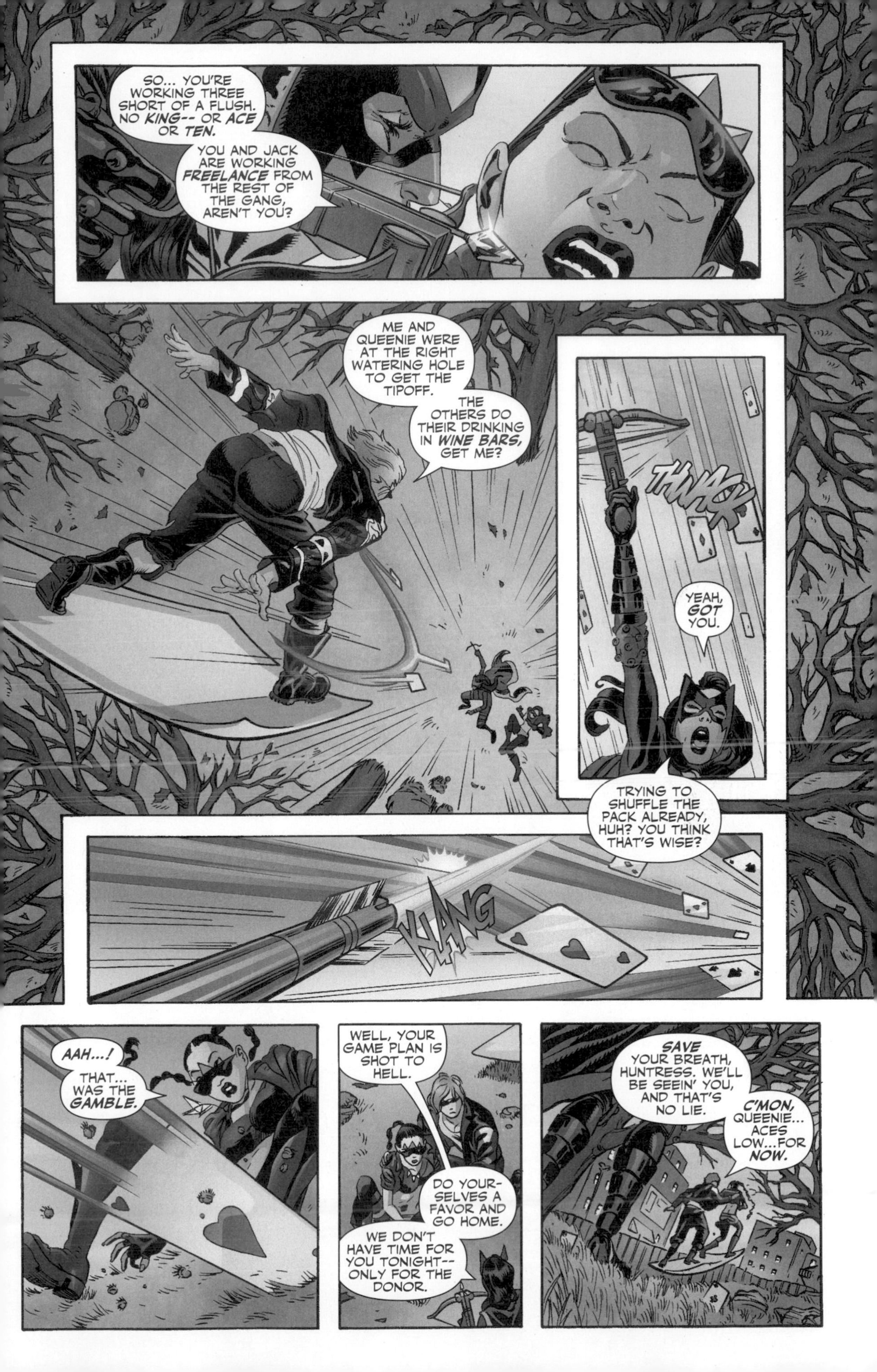
SO... YOU'RE WORKING THREE SHORT OF A FLUSH. NO *KING*-- OR *ACE* OR *TEN.*
YOU AND JACK ARE WORKING *FREELANCE* FROM THE REST OF THE GANG, AREN'T YOU?
ME AND QUEENIE WERE AT THE RIGHT WATERING HOLE TO GET THE TIPOFF.
THE OTHERS DO THEIR DRINKING IN *WINE BARS,* GET ME?
THWACK
YEAH, *GOT* YOU.
TRYING TO SHUFFLE THE PACK ALREADY, HUH? YOU THINK THAT'S WISE?
KLANG
AAH...!
THAT... WAS THE *GAMBLE.*
WELL, YOUR GAME PLAN IS SHOT TO HELL.
DO YOUR-SELVES A FAVOR AND GO HOME.
WE DON'T HAVE TIME FOR YOU TONIGHT-- ONLY FOR THE DONOR.
SAVE YOUR BREATH, HUNTRESS. WE'LL BE SEEIN' YOU, AND THAT'S NO LIE.
C'MON, QUEENIE... ACES LOW...FOR *NOW.*

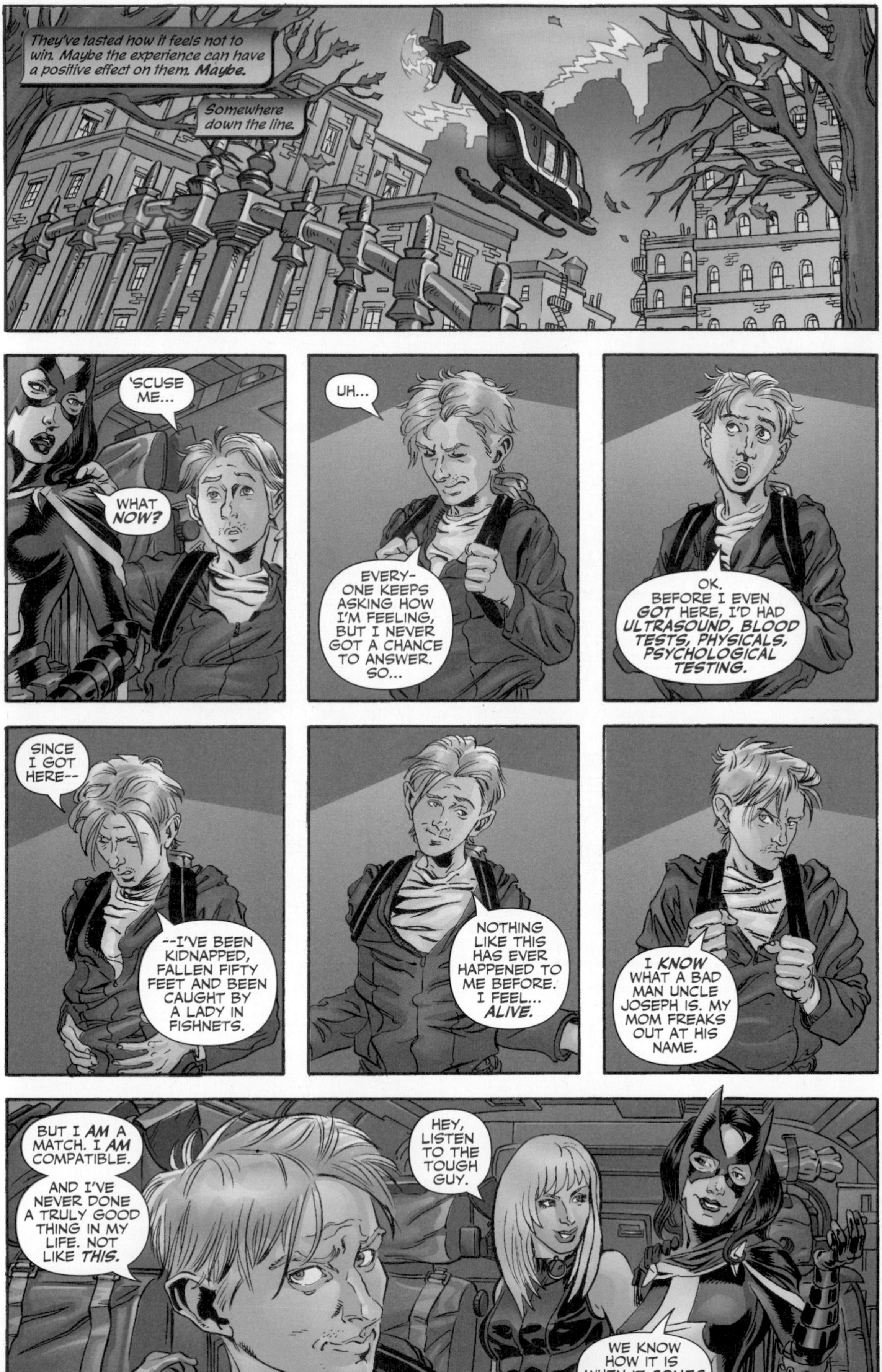
They've tasted how it feels not to win. Maybe the experience can have a positive effect on them. Maybe.
Somewhere down the line.
'SCUSE ME...
WHAT NOW?
UH...
EVERY-ONE KEEPS ASKING HOW I'M FEELING, BUT I NEVER GOT A CHANCE TO ANSWER. SO...
OK. BEFORE I EVEN GOT HERE, I'D HAD ULTRASOUND, BLOOD TESTS, PHYSICALS, PSYCHOLOGICAL TESTING.
SINCE I GOT HERE--
--I'VE BEEN KIDNAPPED, FALLEN FIFTY FEET AND BEEN CAUGHT BY A LADY IN FISHNETS.
NOTHING LIKE THIS HAS EVER HAPPENED TO ME BEFORE. I FEEL... ALIVE.
I KNOW WHAT A BAD MAN UNCLE JOSEPH IS. MY MOM FREAKS OUT AT HIS NAME.
BUT I AM A MATCH. I AM COMPATIBLE.
AND I'VE NEVER DONE A TRULY GOOD THING IN MY LIFE. NOT LIKE THIS.
HEY, LISTEN TO THE TOUGH GUY.
WE KNOW HOW IT IS WHEN IT COMES TO FAMILY, TOD.

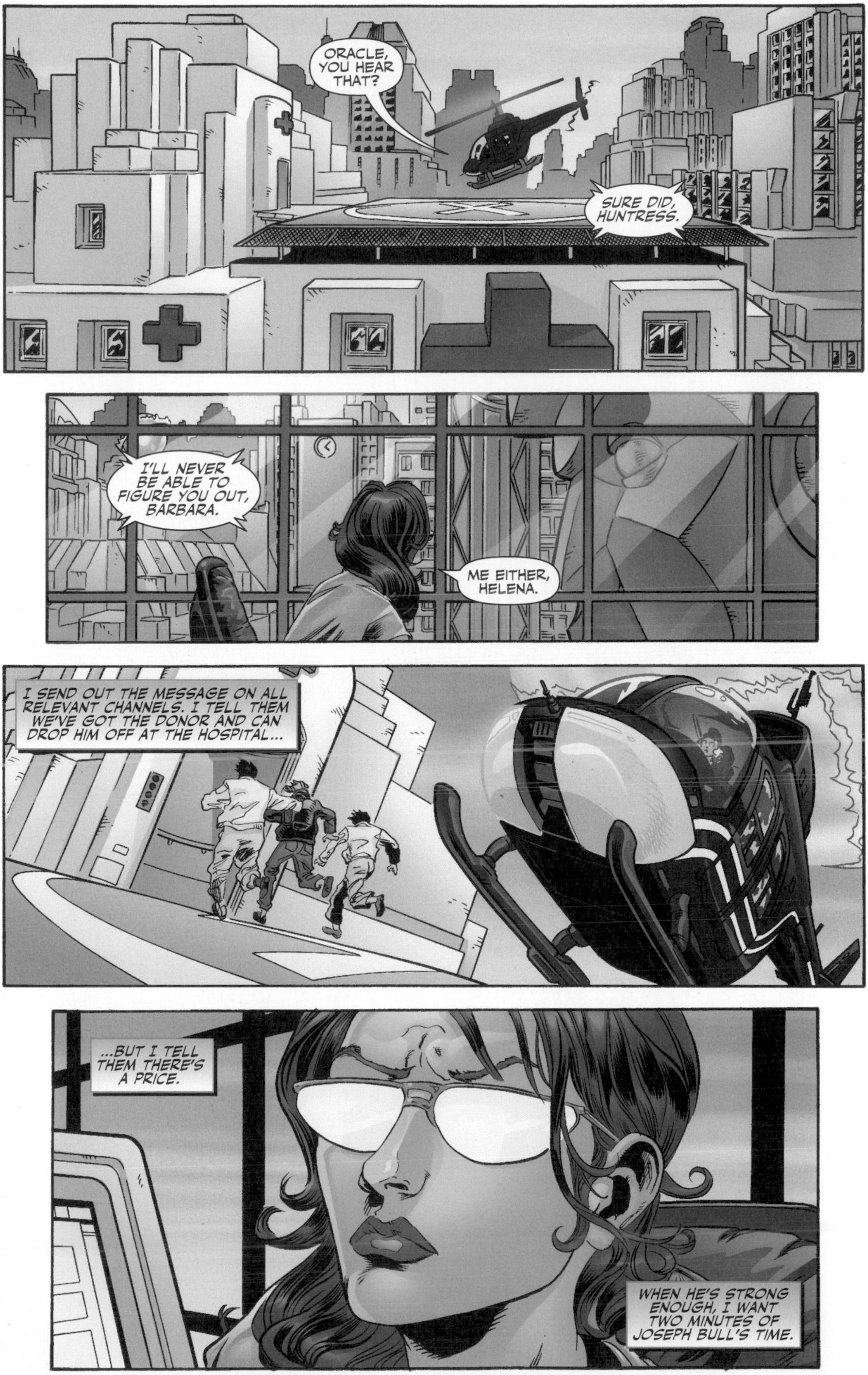
ORACLE, YOU HEAR THAT?
SURE DID, HUNTRESS.
I'LL NEVER BE ABLE TO FIGURE YOU OUT, BARBARA.
ME EITHER, HELENA.
I SEND OUT THE MESSAGE ON ALL RELEVANT CHANNELS. I TELL THEM WE'VE GOT THE DONOR AND CAN DROP HIM OFF AT THE HOSPITAL...
...BUT I TELL THEM THERE'S A PRICE.
WHEN HE'S STRONG ENOUGH, I WANT TWO MINUTES OF JOSEPH BULL'S TIME.

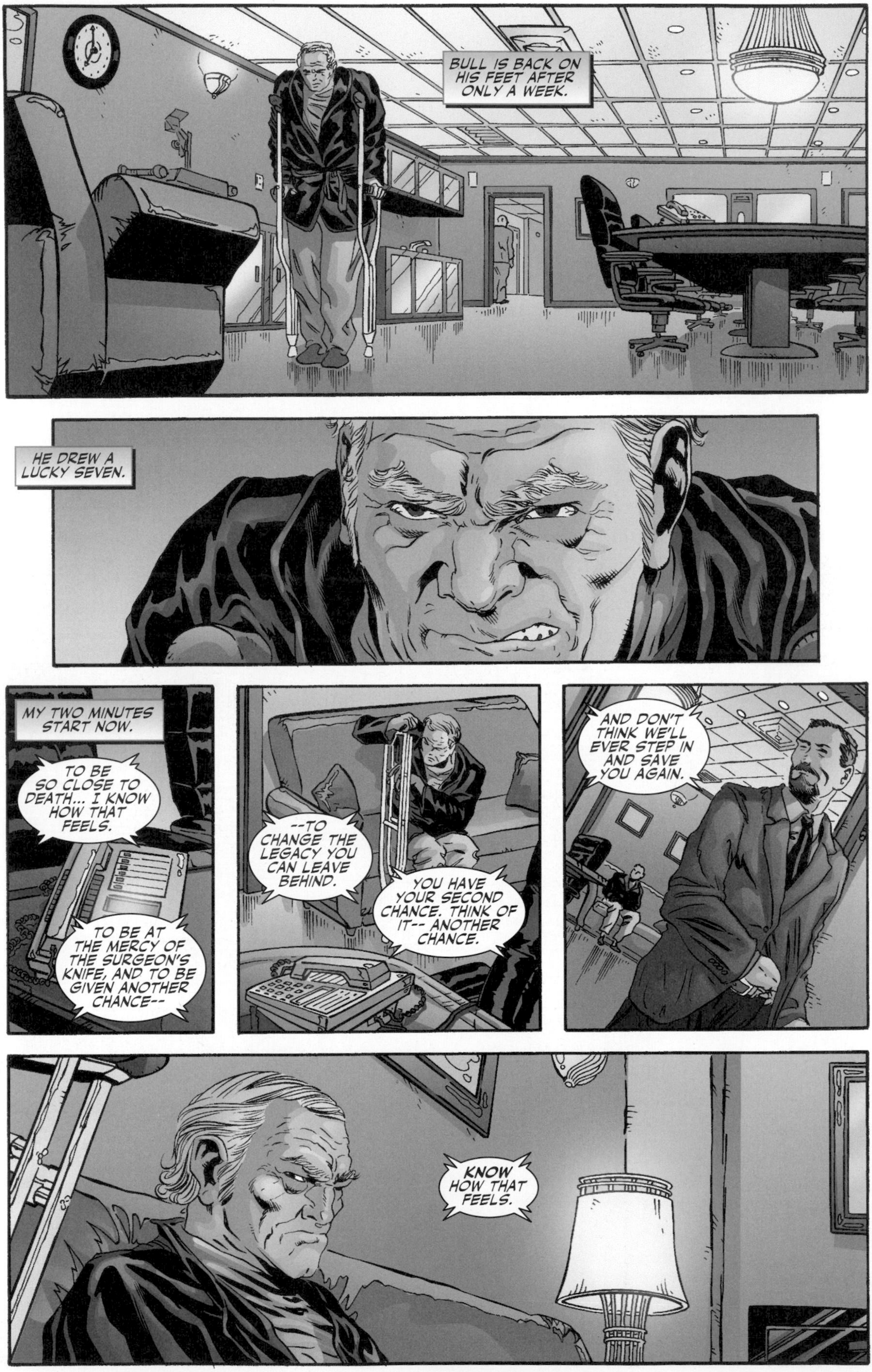
BULL IS BACK ON HIS FEET AFTER ONLY A WEEK.
HE DREW A LUCKY SEVEN.
MY TWO MINUTES START NOW.
TO BE SO CLOSE TO DEATH... I KNOW HOW THAT FEELS.
TO BE AT THE MERCY OF THE SURGEON'S KNIFE, AND TO BE GIVEN ANOTHER CHANCE--
--TO CHANGE THE LEGACY YOU CAN LEAVE BEHIND.
YOU HAVE YOUR SECOND CHANCE. THINK OF IT-- ANOTHER CHANCE.
AND DON'T THINK WE'LL EVER STEP IN AND SAVE YOU AGAIN.
KNOW HOW THAT FEELS.

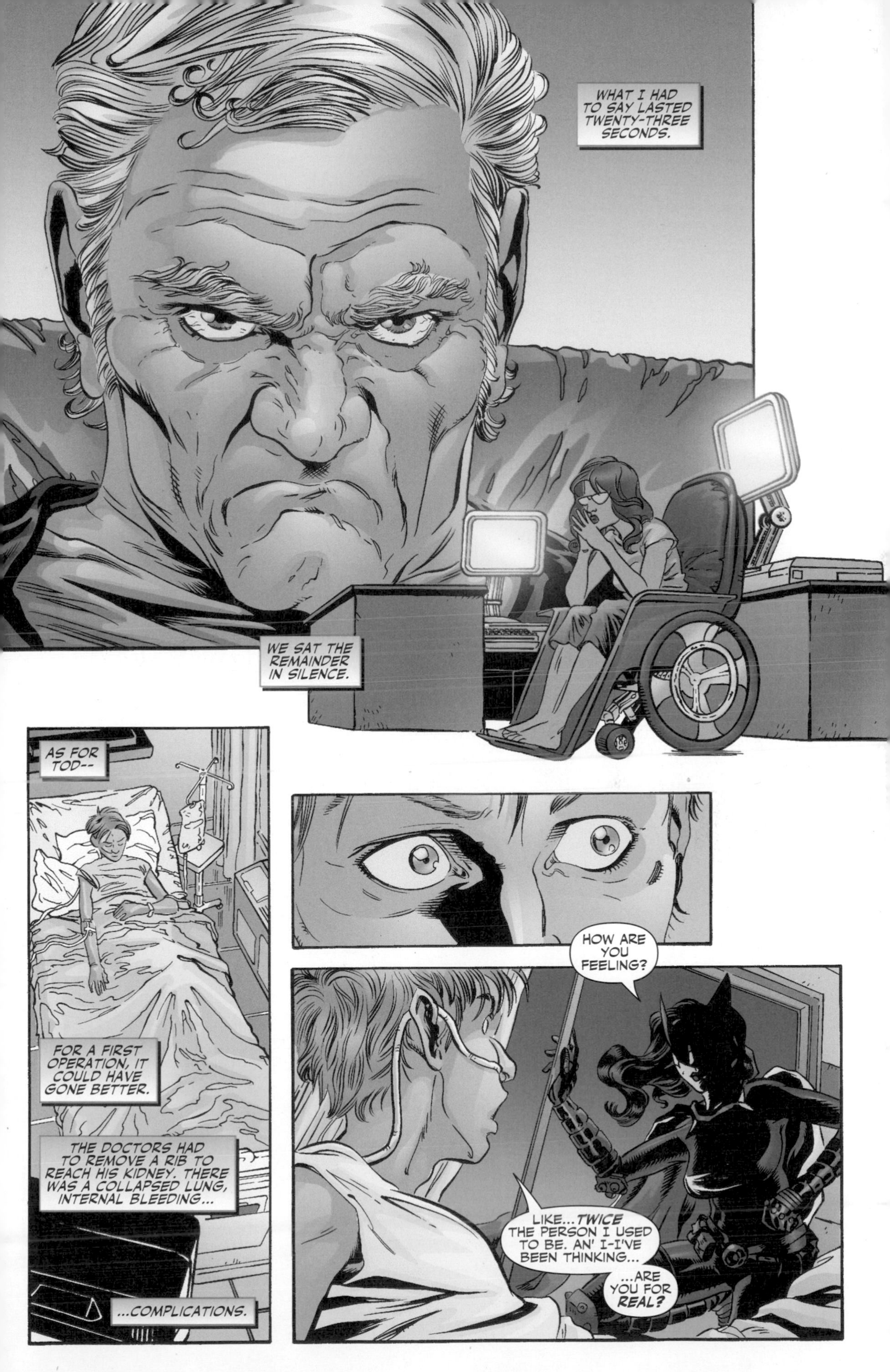
WHAT I HAD TO SAY LASTED TWENTY-THREE SECONDS.
WE SAT THE REMAINDER IN SILENCE.
AS FOR TOD--
FOR A FIRST OPERATION, IT COULD HAVE GONE BETTER.
THE DOCTORS HAD TO REMOVE A RIB TO REACH HIS KIDNEY. THERE WAS A COLLAPSED LUNG, INTERNAL BLEEDING...
...COMPLICATIONS.
HOW ARE YOU FEELING?
LIKE...*TWICE* THE PERSON I USED TO BE. AN' I-I'VE BEEN THINKING...
...ARE YOU FOR *REAL?*

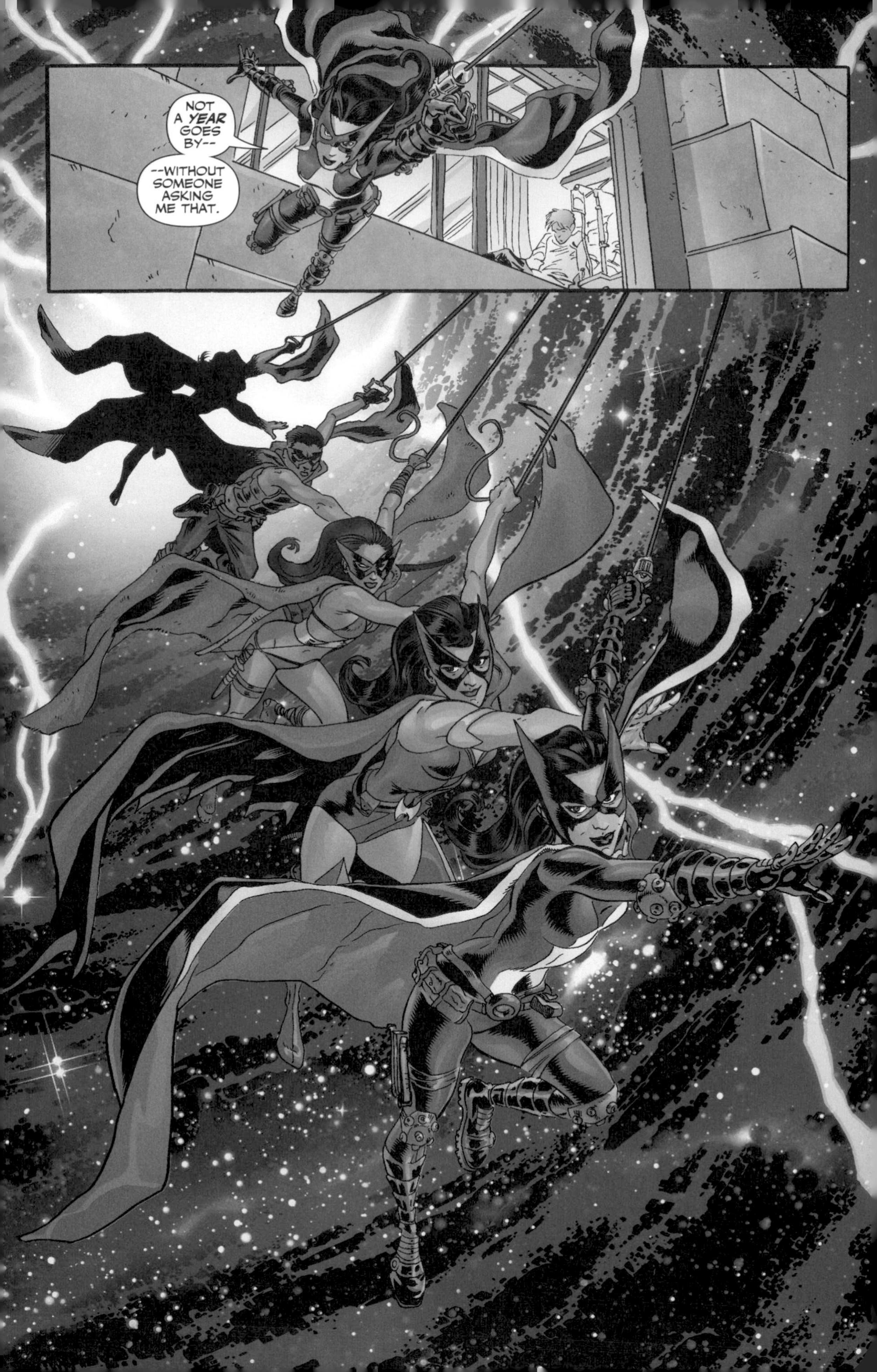
NOT A YEAR GOES BY--
--WITHOUT SOMEONE ASKING ME THAT.

BIRDS OF PREY
VOL. 1
CHUCK DIXON, GARY FRANK, GREG LAND, and MATT HALEY

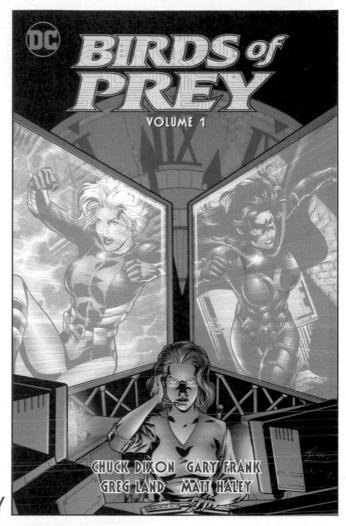

**BIRDS OF PREY
VOL. 2**

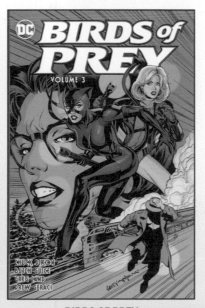

**BIRDS OF PREY
VOL. 3**

Celebrate the feature film **Birds of Prey (And the Fantabulous Emancipation of One Harley Quinn)** with these classic stories.

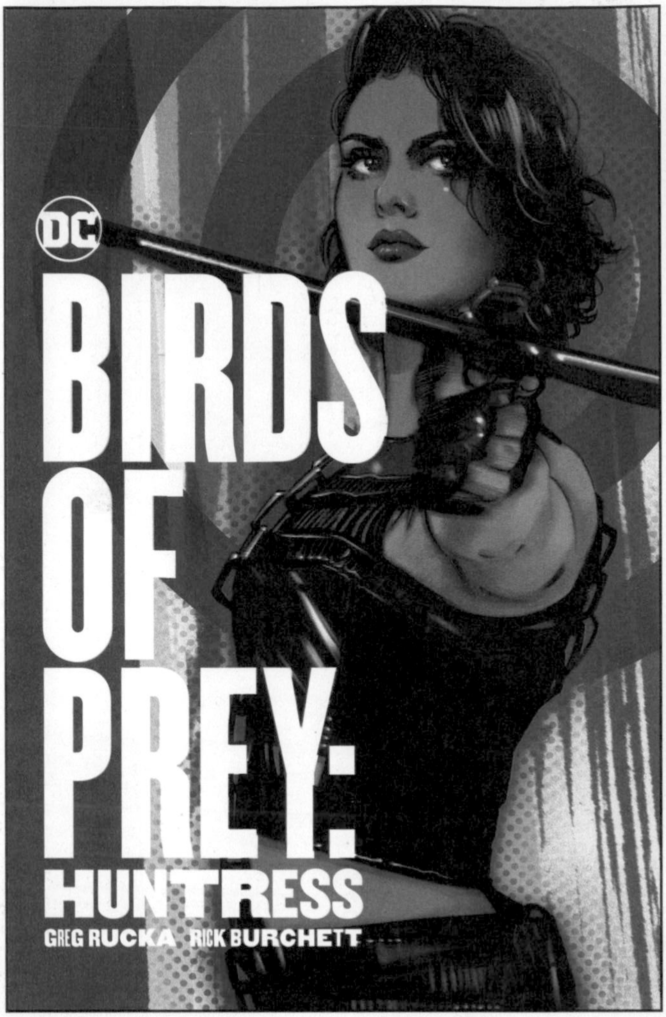
DC
BIRDS OF PREY:
HUNTRESS
GREG RUCKA RICK BURCHETT

BIRDS OF PREY:
HUNTRESS

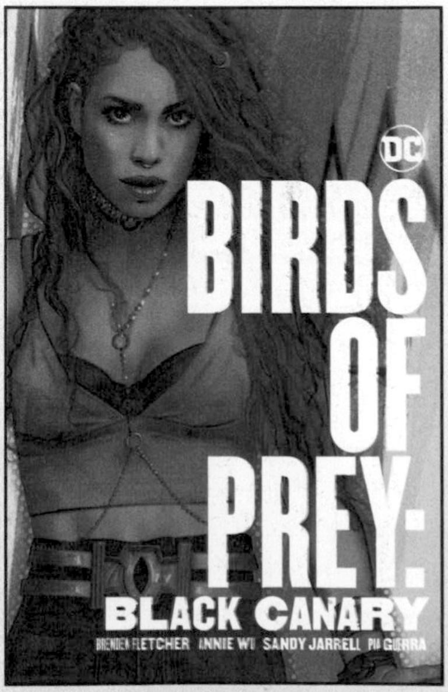
DC
BIRDS OF PREY:
BLACK CANARY

BIRDS OF PREY:
BLACK CANARY

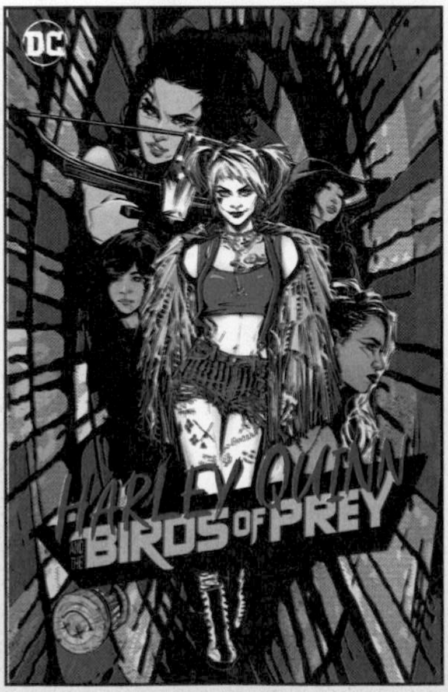
DC
HARLEY QUINN
AND THE BIRDS OF PREY

HARLEY QUINN
AND THE BIRDS OF PREY

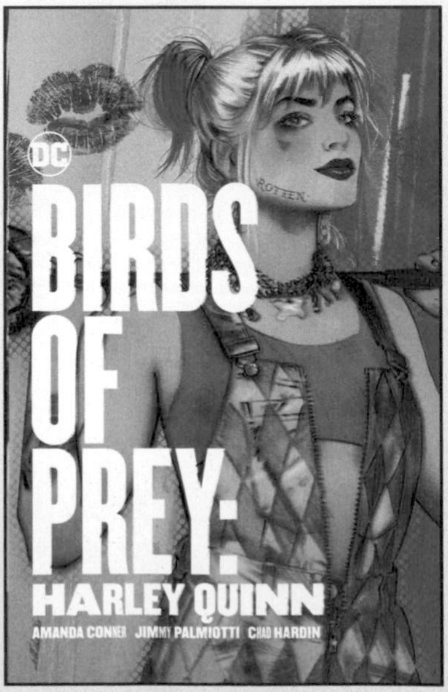
DC
BIRDS OF PREY:
HARLEY QUINN
AMANDA CONNER JIMMY PALMIOTTI CHAD HARDIN

BIRDS OF PREY:
HARLEY QUINN

Get more DC graphic novels wherever comics and books are sold!